Fodor's

ROME

8th Edition

Fodor's Travel Publications   New York, Toronto, London, Sydney, Auckland

www.fodors.com

Be a Fodor's Correspondent

Your opinion matters. It matters to us. It matters to your fellow Fodor's travelers, too. And we'd like to hear it. In fact, we *need* to hear it.

When you share your experiences and opinions, you become an active member of the Fodor's community. That means we'll not only use your feedback to make our books better, but we'll publish your names and comments whenever possible. Throughout our guides, look for "Word of Mouth," excerpts of your unvarnished feedback.

Here's how you can help improve Fodor's for all of us.

Tell us when we're right. We rely on local writers to give you an insider's perspective. But our writers and staff editors—who are the best in the business—depend on you. Your positive feedback is a vote to renew our recommendations for the next edition.

Tell us when we're wrong. We're proud that we update most of our guides every year. But we're not perfect. Things change. Hotels cut services. Museums change hours. Charming cafés lose charm. If our writer didn't quite capture the essence of a place, tell us how you'd do it differently. If any of our descriptions are inaccurate or inadequate, we'll incorporate your changes in the next edition and will correct factual errors at fodors.com *immediately.*

Tell us what to include. You probably have had fantastic travel experiences that aren't yet in Fodor's. Why not share them with a community of like-minded travelers? Maybe you chanced upon a beach or bistro or B&B that you don't want to keep to yourself. Tell us why we should include it. And share your discoveries and experiences with everyone directly at fodors.com. Your input may lead us to add a new listing or highlight a place we cover with a "Highly Recommended" star or with our highest rating, "Fodor's Choice."

Give us your opinion instantly at our feedback center at www.fodors.com/feedback. You may also e-mail editors@fodors.com with the subject line "Rome Editor." Or send your nominations, comments, and complaints by mail to Rome Editor, Fodor's, 1745 Broadway, New York, NY 10019.

You and travelers like you are the heart of the Fodor's community. Make our community richer by sharing your experiences. Be a Fodor's correspondent.

Buon viaggio!

Tim Jarrell, Publisher

FODOR'S ROME

Editors: Robert I. C. Fisher, *lead editor*; Carolyn Galgano, *restaurants and hotels editor*; Heidi Leigh Johansen

Editorial Contributors: Lynda Albertson, Nicole Arriaga, Martin Wilmot Bennett, Erica Firpo, Dana Klitzberg, Margaret Stenhouse

Production Editor: Carrie Parker
Maps & Illustrations: Mark Stroud, Moon Street Cartography; Henry Colomb; David Lindroth, Inc., *cartographers;* Bob Blake, Rebecca Baer, *map editors;* William Wu, *information graphics*
Design: Fabrizio La Rocca, *creative director*; Guido Caroti, Siobhan O'Hare, *art directors*; Tina Malaney, Chie Ushio, Ann McBride, Jessica Walsh, *designers*; Melanie Marin, *senior picture editor*
Cover Photo: Capitoline Museum: SIME s.a.s/eStock Photo
Production Manager: Angela L. McLean

8th Edition

ISBN 978–14000–0444–7

ISSN 0276–2560

SPECIAL SALES

This book is available at special discounts for bulk purchases for sales promotions or premiums. Special editions, including personalized covers, excerpts of existing books, and corporate imprints, can be created in large quantities for special needs. For more information, write to Special Markets/Premium Sales, 1745 Broadway, MD 6-2, New York, New York 10019, or e-mail specialmarkets@randomhouse.com.

AN IMPORTANT TIP & AN INVITATION

Although all prices, opening times, and other details in this book are based on information supplied to us at press time, changes occur all the time in the travel world, and Fodor's cannot accept responsibility for facts that become outdated or for inadvertent errors or omissions. So **always confirm information when it matters,** especially if you're making a detour to visit a specific place. Your experiences—positive and negative— matter to us. If we have missed or misstated something, **please write to us.** We follow up on all suggestions. Contact the Rome editor at editors@fodors.com or c/o Fodor's at 1745 Broadway, New York, NY 10019.

PRINTED IN SINGAPORE

10 9 8 7 6 5 4 3 2 1

CONTENTS

Fodor's Features

CONTENTS

ABOUT THIS BOOK

Sometimes you find terrific travel experiences and sometimes they just find you. But usually the burden is on you to select the right combination of experiences. That's where our ratings come in.

As travelers we've all discovered a place so wonderful that its worthiness is obvious. And sometimes that place is so unique that superlatives don't do it justice: you just have to be there to know. These sights, properties, and experiences get our highest rating, **Fodor's Choice**, indicated by orange stars throughout this book.

Black stars highlight sights and properties we deem **Highly Recommended**, places that our writers, editors, and readers praise again and again for consistency and excellence.

By default, there's another category: any place we include in this book is by definition worth your time, unless we say otherwise. And we will.

Disagree with any of our choices? Care to nominate a place or suggest that we rate one more highly? Visit our feedback center at www.fodors.com/feedback.

Budget Well

Hotel and restaurant price categories from ¢ to $$$$ are defined in the opening pages of each chapter. For attractions, we always give standard adult admission fees; reductions are usually available for children, students, and senior citizens. Want to pay with plastic? **AE, D, DC, MC, V** following restaurant and hotel listings indicate whether American Express, Discover, Diner's Club, MasterCard, and Visa are accepted.

Restaurants

Unless we state otherwise, restaurants are open for lunch and dinner daily. We mention dress only when there's a specific requirement and reservations only when they're essential or not accepted—it's always best to book ahead.

Hotels

Hotels have private bath, phone, TV, and air-conditioning and operate on the European Plan (aka EP, meaning without meals), unless we specify that they use the Continental Plan (CP, with a Continental breakfast) or Breakfast Plan (BP, with a full breakfast). We always list facilities but not whether you'll be charged an extra fee to use them, so when pricing accommodations, find out what's included.

Listings	
★	Fodor's Choice
★	Highly recommended
⊠	Physical address
⊕	Directions or Map coordinates
⊕	Mailing address
☎	Telephone
🖷	Fax
⊕	On the Web
✍	E-mail
☜	Admission fee
☉	Open/closed times
Ⓜ	Metro stations
⊟	Credit cards
Hotels & Restaurants	
☷	Hotel
⬎	Number of rooms
⚲	Facilities
⦿⊙	Meal plans
✕	Restaurant
☞	Reservations
⬀	Dress code
⤡	Smoking
☖	BYOB
Outdoors	
⚐	Golf
⛺	Camping
Other	
♨	Family-friendly
⇨	See also
⊠	Branch address
☞	Take note

Experience Rome

1

ROME TODAY

Coming off the Autostrada at Roma Nord or Roma Sud, you know by the convergence of heavily trafficked routes that you are entering a grand nexus: All roads lead to Rome. And then the interminable suburbs, the railroad crossings, the intersections—no wonder they call it the Eternal City.

As you enter the city proper, features that match your expectations begin to take shape: a bridge with heroic statues along its parapets; a towering cake of frothy marble decorated with allegorical figures in extravagant poses; a piazza and an obelisk under an umbrella of pine trees. Then you spot what looks like a multistory parking lot; with a gasp, you realize it's the Colosseum.

You have arrived. You're in the city's heart. You step down from your excursion bus onto the broad girdle of tarmac that encircles the great stone arena of the Roman emperors, and scurry out of the way of the passing Fiats—the motorists behind the wheels seem to display the panache of so many Ben-Hurs.

The excitement of arriving here jolts the senses and sharpens expectations. The timeless city to which all roads lead, Mamma Roma enthralls visitors today

as she has since time immemorial. More than Florence, more than Venice, this is Italy's treasure storehouse. Here, the ancient Romans made us heirs-in-law to what we call Western Civilization; where centuries later Michelangelo painted the Sistine Ceiling; where Gian Lorenzo Bernini's baroque nymphs and naiads still dance in their marble fountains; and where, at Cinecittà Studios, Fellini filmed *La Dolce Vita* and 8½. Today, the city remains a veritable Grand Canyon of culture: Ancient Rome rubs shoulders with the medieval, the modern runs into the Renaissance, and the result is like nothing so much as an open-air museum.

Little wonder Rome's enduring popularity feeds a gluttonous tourism industry that can feel more like *National Lampoon's European Vacation* than *Roman Holiday*. As tour buses belch black smoke and the line at the Vatican Museums stretches on into eternity, even the steeliest of sightseers have been known to wonder, why am I here?

The answer, with apologies to Dorothy, is: There's no place like Rome. Yesterday's Grand Tourists thronged the city for the same reason today's Expedians do. Majestic, complicated, enthralling, romantic,

. . . IS CREATING NEW "IT" NEIGHBORHOODS

The leader among Rome's "It" nabes is San Lorenzo, with Pigneto trailing just behind.

San Lorenzo is just a stone's throw away from the Termini train station. Rome's new "Left Bank" district is filled with students and a young bohemian crowd thanks to its

close proximity to La Sapienza University.

In fact, if you don't know what you're looking for, you could easily get lost in this maze of dark narrow streets, many now lined with underground caffè, bars, hip restaurants, and locales with live-music venues.

The leading scene-arenas include Formula 1 (Via degli Equi 13), for top pizzas; Da Franco ar Vicoletto (Via dei Falisci 1/b), just around the corner, for fish lovers; and Arancia Blu (Via dei Latini 55), which draws the green crowds thanks to its vegetarian menus.

chaotic, monumental Rome is one of the world's great cities—past, present, and, probably, future.

And today Rome is a future-forward city. In 2010, the Eternal City is outdazzling many of its Italian rivals with a newly unleashed vitality. Move over hip and chic Milan: Rome is moving up in the rankings ever higher to becoming the next posh metropolitan "It" city.

Romans are ready to show the world that its old-world ways—slow pace, antique-flair, and everything mini—are ancient history. Romans are changing gears and starting to live life in the fast lane.

Mega-shopping malls, tech-savvy sumptuousness, fusion food, and even gas-guzzling SUVs have made their way to the ancient home of the popes. Romans are more "connected" than ever before: even Pope Benedict XVI can't do without his Facebook.

Though resistance is bound to come with change, Romans seem to be embracing these tumultuous changes with open arms. Arriverderci, *Three Coins in the Fountain*—the Eternal City is busy leapfrogging into the 21st century.

TODAY'S ROME . . .

. . . is not the Roma your mother knew

Home to nearly 3 million residents and a gazillion tourists, Rome is virtually busting at the seams. For decades, the heart and soul of the city was concentrated in its *centro storico*, where a chunk of Rome's legendary museums, monuments, and ancient relics have stood for centuries. Replete with postcard landmarks, baroque palaces, and hyper-luxury hotels, the "Disneyfication" of the historic center is well under way.

As there was no room to grow upward, Rome has had to stretch outward. To relieve pressure in the City center, city officials have focused on building a "new" Rome beyond the historic quarter. In the process, old, economically weaker, satellite districts have been revitalized with the creation of cutting-edge palazzos and museums. Former working-class neighborhoods—San Lorenzo and Pigneto to the north, Ostiense and Testaccio to the south—are also on the fast track of unprecedented change and becoming trendy. This "other" Rome is shabby-chic, alternative, and full of flair.

The likes of bands such as the Cure, U2, and Pearl Jam have been known to play at I Giardini di Adone (Via dei Reti 38/A). Or throw down your best moves at Qube Disco (Viadi Portonaccio 212), where the vibe ranges from rock to house music and changes its scene and crowd from night to night.

Immortalized as the backdrop for Roberto Rossellini's magnificent Academy Award–nominated *Rome Open City* (Roma Città Aperta), Pigneto—set in the northwestern part of the city on the other side of the Porta Maggiore walls—has come a long way since the black-and-white days of the 1950s.

Sixty years ago, you couldn't find much more than old folks playing cards down the Via Fanfulla da Lodi and Via del Pigneto.

Fast forward to 2010 and this hot new *quartiere* has undergone a major transformation into a colorful hub for hipsters who tuck into the many wine bars, caffè, and bookshops

ROME TODAY

. . . is going multi-culti

Spend a day in Rome's Esquilino neighborhood and you'll see just how multicultural the Eternal City is becoming. Once famous for its spice market at Piazza Vittorio, the area neighborhood has fast become a multiethnic stomping ground.

In fact, finding a true Roman restaurant or a local shopkeeper is hard to come by in this area, now that Chinese, Indian African, and Middle Eastern restaurants have moved in (a typical example: The Syrian restaurant, *Zenobia,* perched on Piazza Dante, even includes a weekend belly-dancing show).

Homegrown and locally produced, the Orchestra di Piazza Vittorio is a perfect picture of the neighborhood's growing ethnic population. Made up of 16 musicians from Brazil, Senegal, Tunisia, Cuba, Argentina, Hungary, Ecuador, and Italy, the troupe was founded in 2002 and got its start in the ramshackle district just steps away from Rome's Termini train station.

. . . is breaking new ground

Eternal Rome is in the middle of a building boom, one kick-started by the Vatican's 2000 Jubilee celebrations and backed by Rome's former mayor, Walter Veltroni.

Voguish new landmarks, like the Parco della Musica, a set of three armadillolike music halls designed by modernist Renzo Piano, garnered magazine covers; the slaughterhouse-turned-contemporary art museum of MACRO al Mattatoio earned headlines; and minimalist masterpieces like Richard Meier's Jubilee Church may yet prove to be as enduring and image-defining as were Michelangelo's Palazzo Senatorio or Bernini's St. Peter's Square.

Even the five-story Città del Gusto (2005, in the Marconi district) made a splash onto the scene offering a culinary haven for the palates of afficionados and amateurs alike.

Part of the Gambero Rosso food and wine media group, this cooking complex not only has a wine bar and restaurant but even has its own culinary school and TV studios where Gambero Rosso's cooking channel is showcased.

When it comes to transforming an old working-class district into a scene-arena, "starchitects" and their new iconic buildings often lead the way.

Case in point: Rem Koolhaas won the competition to revamp Ostiense's Mercati Generali food market. Before long this

---

scattered in and around main drags like Fanfulla da Lodi and Via del Pigneto.

Definitely on the radar as one of Rome's up-and-coming districts, Pigneto is bohemian in all the good old ways.

Today, the area is now home to many artists, journalists, and designers.

And it has even become the backdrop for a slew of popular Italian TV shows.

Back in the day, Italian film legends Pier Paolo Pasolini and Luchino Visconti spent time here capturing the lives of Pigneto's working class families.

To channel those vibes, enjoy an *aperitivo* at the historic Bar Necci (Via Fanfulla da Lodi 68).

It was here at this neighborhood landmark that Pasolini filmed scenes for his award-winning 1961 *Accatone* (an unflinching look at how a pimp living in the slums of Rome attempts to go straight).

moldering landmark will be transformed into Rome's "Covent Garden."

Magliana is now the site of a new model residential complex rising up near Rome's airport and designed by Richard Rogers, architect of Paris's Beaubourg Centre and New York City's Hearst Tower.

Among the latest projects is the Casa della Ballo (House of Dance). After the successful openings of the Casa del Cinema (2004, Villa Borghese) and the Casa del Jazz (2005, EUR), city officials decided to back this €1,000,000 project, which will have a dance hall, library, and exhibition space spread out over 4,000 square meters in the Prenestina-Palmiro Togliatti area (Southeast Rome)-construction has begun recently and has a projected completion date of 2012.

. . . is becoming pricey

It is a good thing that Romans know how to pinch their euro-pennies. A recent report put out by the UBS Swiss Bank shows that Rome is the 17th-most-expensive city in the world. Not only is the Eternal City now more expensive than Milan, one of the fashion capitals of the world, but it has even surpassed London. It was a surprise to learn that the *Milanesi* get more bang for their buck at the grocery store than their fellow *Romani*. However, housing in Rome is still relatively cheaper than most European cities.

. . . is more commuter-friendly

Plans are underway to build Rome's third subway line, or "Line C." Slated for final completion in 2015, parts of the line will start running as early as 2011. The new line will cover key parts of the historic city center, including Piazza Venezia and Largo Argentina. City officials also approved construction of an extension of the B-line from the Metro's Piazza Bologna station, adding four more stops, with completion for 2011. And Romans probably wouldn't believe it if you told them, but talks are in progress for a "Line D," which will cover parts of northern Rome like Salario and Montesacro connecting them with neighborhoods to the south that are otherwise harder to reach, such as Trastevere, Marconi, and EUR. City officials say only after the Line B and Line C are successfully completed will it project a timeline for the ambitious Line D. Relief is also in store for commuters traveling aboveground: ATACw, Rome's public bus transportation company, has added GPS monitors to help track distances and waiting times.

To catch Pigneto's other celluloid moments of fame, check out Ciak si Mangia (Via Giovanni Brancaleone 72), a popular pizzeria with reasonable prices, where walls showcase photos from various movies shot in the neighborhood.

Want a later nightcap? Head to Fanfulla 101 (Via Fanfulla da Lodi 101) for some live music with bands ranging from rock to country.

Or, for those looking for something a little more laid back, VI(ci)NO (Via del Pigneto 25) is an *enoteca* that serves up a little art and jazz with a glass of wine.

A bit bohemian like its next-door neighbor San Lorenzo, Pigneto is definitely getting brighter these days on the traveler's radar screen.

WHAT'S WHERE

1 **Ancient Rome.** Today, no other archaeological park has so compact a nucleus of fabled history-laden sights. A walk through the Roman Forum—one-time playground for emperors Caesar and Augustus—leads you north to the Campidoglio, the Capitoline Hill, rebuilt by Michelangelo; to the west lies the Palatine Hill; to the east stand the Imperial Forums; and to the south looms the wonder that is the Colosseum.

2 **The Vatican.** A world in itself, residence of Pope Benedict XVI, and home base for the Catholic Church, the Vatican draws hundreds of thousands of pilgrims and art lovers to St. Peter's Basilica, the Vatican Museums, and the Sistine Chapel.

3 **Navona.** The *cuore*—heart—of the *centro storico* (historic quarter), this is Baroque Rome at its bravura best, thanks to Piazza Navona, graced with Bernini's most flamboyant fountain, and Caravaggio's paintings at San Luigi dei Francesi. Another showstopper: the ancient Pantheon.

4 **Campo.** A pop-up Renaissance painting, this nook of Rome is centered around the vibrant piazza of Campo de' Fiori, the 16th-century Via Giulia—"the most beautiful

street in Rome"—and the spectacular Farnese and Spada palaces.

5 **Corso.** Stretching from Piazza Venezia north to Piazza del Popolo, the Corso is Rome's "Broadway" and flaunts monuments of artistic opulence, ranging from Emperor Augustus's Ara Pacis Augustae to the 17th-century Palazzo Doria-Pamphilj and gilded church of Sant'Ignazio.

6 **Spagna.** Travel back to the days of the Grand Tour in this glamorous area enticingly wrapped around the Piazza de Spagna. After admiring the grandeur of the Spanish Steps, shop like a true VIP along Via dei Condotti, then be sure to throw a coin in the Trevi Fountain.

7 **Repubblica.** The Piazza del Repubblica is an example of how Rome's history is revealed in layers: The vast Baths of Diocletian here were transformed into a Renaissance church. Westward lie art treasures—like Bernini's *St. Theresa in Ecstasy* at Santa Maria della Vittoria—and Via Veneto, still basking in the afterglow of *La Dolce Vita*.

8 **Quirinale.** The Quirinale hill has long been crowned by the over-the-top Palazzo del Quirinale, home to Italy's president. Nearby, go for baroque at two great churches:

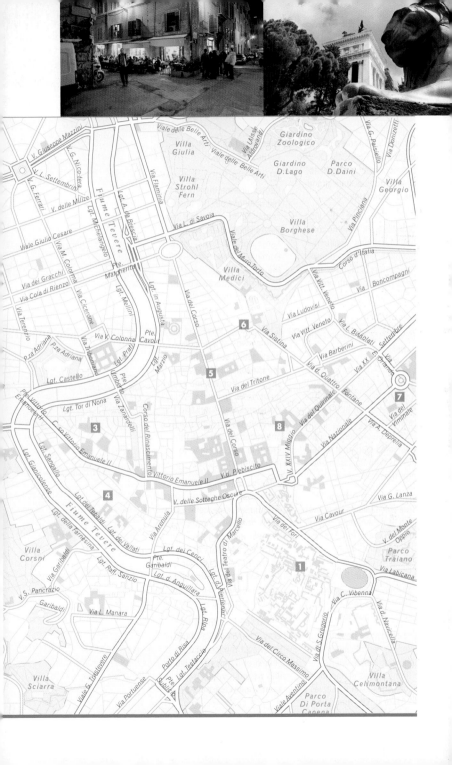

WHAT'S WHERE

Bernini's Sant'Andrea and Borromini's San Carlo alla Quattro Fontane. The two architects called a truce at their grand Palazzo Barberini.

9 Villa Borghese. The Villa Borghese park is home to an array of dazzling museums: Cardinal Scipione Borghese's 17th-century Galleria Borghese is loaded with great Bernini statues; Etruscan treasures fill the eye at Villa Giulia; while the gardens of the Villa Medici remain Edenic as ever.

10 Piazza del Popolo. After touring the Villa Borghese museums, give your less-than-bionic feet a rest at a caffè on the Piazza del Popolo, a prime watch-the-world-go-by spot. Here, Santa Maria del Popolo beckons with Raphaels and Caravaggios.

11 Trastevere. Rome's "Greenwich Village" has kept much of its authentic roots thanks to mom-and-pop *trattorie*, tiny winding alleyways, and the magnificent church of Santa Maria in Trastevere, stunningly lit at night (when hot new clubs take center stage in this quarter).

12 The Ghetto. Despite galloping gentrification, the Ghetto—once quarter to Rome's Jews during the Middle Ages—still preserves the flavor of Old Rome and

is centered on the ancient Portico d'Ottavia.

13 Aventino. An upscale residential district, the Aventine Hill is aloof from the bustle of central Rome. At its foot lies Piazza Bocca della Verità and Santa Maria in Cosmedin, a Romanesque masterpiece. To the south, working-class Testaccio draws trendy Romans working on their "nightclub tans."

14 Esquilino. While the multi-culti crowds of the Termini train station set the tone here, the Esqueline Hill has many "islands" of peace and calm: great basilicas (Santa Maria Maggiore), Early Christian wonders (Santa Pudenziana), and noted churches (San Pietro in Vincoli, home to Michelangelo's *Moses*).

15 Celio. Almost entirely given over to parks, churches, and ruins, the peaceful Celian Hill is home to time-travel marvels, including the Early Christian splendors of San Clemente, mystic Santo Stefano Rotondo al Celio, and medieval, magnificent Santi Quattro Coronati.

16 Catacombs and Appian Way. The Via Appia Antica leads past the landmark church of Domine Quo Vadis and walled gardens to the spirit-warm Catacombs.

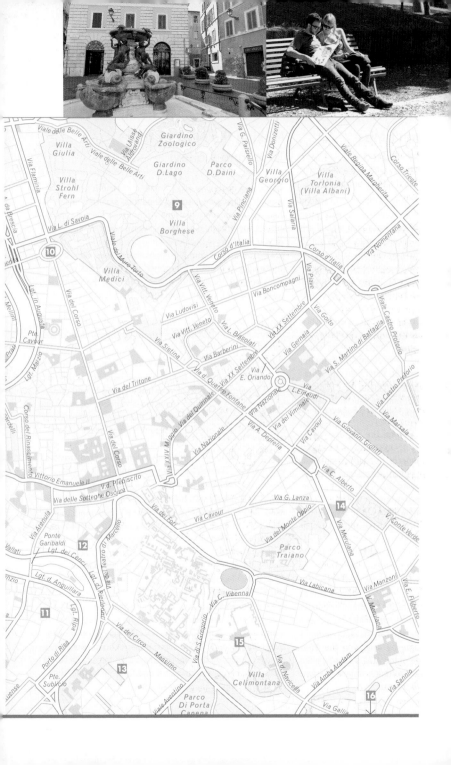

ROME PLANNER

Don't Miss the Metro

Fortunately for tourists, many of Rome's main attractions are concentrated in the *centro storico* (historic center) and can be covered on foot. But not to worry, wherever your feet won't take you, the Metro most probably will. Some sights nearer the border of this quarter can be reached via the Metro Line A, nicknamed the *linea turistica* (tourist line), and include: the Spanish Steps (Spagna stop), the Trevi Fountain (Barberini stop), St. Peter's Square (Ottaviano–San Pietro Musei Vaticani stop), and the Vatican Museums (Cipro stop), to name a few.

Tickets for the bus and metro can be purchased for €1 at any *tabacchi* (tobacco shop) and at most newsstands. These tickets are good for 75 minutes on buses and trams, or a single metro ride. Day passes can be purchased for €4, and weekly passes, which allow unlimited use of buses, trams, and the metro, for €16. For a better explanation of the metro routes, pick up a free map from one of the information booths around the city: Tech-savvy tourists can navigate around Rome by accessing the Web site of the ATAC (Rome's public transportation system) ⊕ *www. atac.roma.it.*

Making the Most of Your Time (and Money)

Roma, non basta una vita ("Rome, a lifetime is not enough"): this famous saying should be stamped on the passport of every first-time visitor to the Eternal City. Indeed, the ancient city certainly wasn't built in a day, so you shouldn't expect to see it in one either. Rome is so packed with sights that it is impossible to take them all in; it's easy to run yourself ragged trying to check off the items on your "To Do" list. At the same time, the saying is a celebration of the city's abundance. There's so much here, you're bound to make discoveries you hadn't anticipated. To conquer Rome, strike a balance between visits to major sights, leisurely neighborhood strolls (and a pit stop for some *gelato*, of course).

In the first category, the Vatican and the remains of ancient Rome loom the largest. Both require at least half a day; a good strategy is to devote your first morning to one and your second to the other. Leave the afternoons for exploring the neighborhoods that comprise "Baroque Rome" and the shopping district around the Spanish Steps and Via Condotti. Among the sights, Galleria Borghese and the church of San Clemente are particularly worthwhile, and Trastevere and the Ghetto make for great roaming.

Since there's a lot of ground to cover in Rome, it's wise to plan your sightseeing schedule with possible savings in mind, and purchasing the Roma Pass (⊕ *www.romapass.it*) allows you to do just that. The three-day pass costs €23 and is good for unlimited use of buses, trams, and the metro. It includes free admission to two of more than 40 participating museums or archaeological sites, including the Colosseum (and bumps you to the head of the long line there, to boot), the Musei Capitolini, and Galleria Borghese, plus discounted tickets to many other museums. The Roma & Più Pass costs €25 and has pretty much the same features but it also includes transportation on Cotral extra-urban coach buses and second-class seats on regional trains. Both passes can be purchased at tourist booths across the city, at Termini Station, or between Terminals B and C of the International Arrivals section of Fiumicino Airport.

Hop-On, Hop-Off

Rome has its own "hop-on, hop-off" sightseeing buses. The Trambus Open Roma 110 bus leaves with 10-minute frequencies from Piazza dei Cinquecento (at the main Termini station), with a two-hour loop including the Colosseum, Piazza Navona, St. Peter's, and the Trevi Fountain. Tickets are €15–€20, depending on whether you want to hop on and off or just stay on the whole time. There is also a Tram Open Bus by Night, only on Friday and Saturday and it leaves from Piazza Venezia at 10 PM and 10:30 PM (€12). A variant is the Archeobus (€13), which departs every 20 minutes from the Piazza dei Cinquecento and heads out to the Via Appia Antica, the Colosseum, and the Catacombs. Book online (⊕ www.trambusopen.com) for a 5% discount off the price.

Roman Hours

On Sunday, Rome virtually shuts down on its official day of rest. Meanwhile, museums, pastry shops, and most restaurants are closed Monday. Daily shop hours generally run from 10 AM to 1 PM, then 4 until 7:30 or 8 PM (but on Monday shops usually don't open until around 4 PM). Pharmacies tend to have the same hours as stores unless they advertise *orario notturno* (night hours). As for churches, most open at 8 or 9 in the morning, close from noon to 3 or 4, then reopen until 6:30 or 7. St. Peter's, however, has continuous hours from 7 AM to 7 PM (until 6 in the fall and winter) and the Vatican Museums are open on Monday but closed Sunday (except for the last one of month).

How's the Weather

Spring and fall are the best times to visit, with mild temperatures and many sunny days. Summers are often sweltering. In July and August, come if you like, but learn to do as the Romans do—get up and out early, seek refuge from the afternoon heat, resume activities in early evening, and stay up late to enjoy the nighttime breeze.

Come August, many shops and restaurants close as locals head out for vacation. Remember that air-conditioning is still a relatively rare phenomenon in this city. Roman winters are relatively mild, with persistent rainy spells.

Information Please

Rome's main APT (Azienda Per Turismo) Tourist Information Office is at Via Parigi 5–11 (✆ 06/488991 ⊕ www.roma-turismo.it), near the main Termini rail station.

In addition, green APT information kiosks with multilingual personnel are near the most important sights and squares, as well as at Termini Station and Leonardo da Vinci Airport. They provide information about cultural events, museums, opening hours, city transportation.

These kiosks, called Tourist Information Sites (Punti Informativi Turistici, or PIT) can be found at:

Castel S. Angelo, Lungotevere Vaticano; 9:30–7 PM

Cinque Lune, Piazza delle Cinque Lune (Piazza Navona); 9:30–7 PM

Fiumicino, Aeroporto Leonardo Da Vinci–Arrivi Internazionali Terminal C; 9–7:30 PM

Minghetti, Via Marco Minghetti (corner of Via del Corso); 9:30–7 PM

Nazionale, Via Nazionale (Palazzo delle Esposizioni); 9:30–7 PM

Santa Maria Maggiore, at Via dell'Olmata; 9:30–7 PM

Termini, Stazione Termini, at Via Giovanni Giolitti 34; 8–8

Trastevere, on Piazza Sidney Sonnino; 9:30–7 PM

TOP ROME ATTRACTIONS

The Pantheon

Constructed to honor all pagan gods, this best preserved temple of ancient Rome was rebuilt in the 2nd century AD by Emperor Hadrian, and to him much of the credit is due for the perfect dimensions: 141 feet high by 141 feet wide, with a vast dome that was the largest ever designed until the 20th century.

The Vatican

Though its population numbers only in the few hundreds, the Vatican—home base for the Catholic Church and the pope—makes up for them with the millions who visit each year. Embraced by the arms of the colonnades of St. Peter's Square, they attend Papal Mass, marvel at St. Peter's Basilica, and savor Michelangelo's Sistine Ceiling.

The Colosseum

(B) Legend has it that as long as the Colosseum stands, Rome will stand; and when Rome falls, so will the world. One of the seven wonders of the world, the mammoth amphitheater was begun by Emperor Vespasian and inaugurated by Titus in the year 80. For "the grandeur that was Rome," this obstinate oval can't be topped.

Piazza Navona

(D) You couldn't concoct a more Roman street scene: caffè and crowded tables at street level, coral- and rust-color houses above, most lined with wrought-iron balconies, street performers and artists and, at the center of this urban "living room," Bernini's spectacular Fountain of the Four Rivers and Borromini's super-theatrical Sant'Agnese.

Roman Forum

(A) This fabled labyrinth of ruins variously served as a political playground, a commerce mart, and a place where justice was dispensed during the days of the emperors (500 BC to 400 AD). Today, the Forum is

a silent ruin—*sic transit gloria mundi* (so passes away the glory of the world).

The Campidoglio

(C) Catch a bird's-eye view of the Roman Forum from Michelangelo's piazza, atop one of the highest spots in Rome, the Capitoline Hill. Here you'll find the Capitoline Museums and beloved Santa Maria in Aracoeli.

Trevi Fountain

(E) One of the few fountains in Rome that's actually more absorbing than the people crowding around it, the Fontana di Trevi was designed by Nicola Salvi in 1732. Immortalized in *Three Coins in the Fountain* and *La Dolce Vita*, this granddaddy of all fountains may be your ticket back to Rome—that is, if you throw a coin into it.

The Spanish Steps

(F) Byron, Shelley, and Keats all drew inspiration from this magnificent "Scalinata," constructed in 1723. Connecting the ritzy shops at the bottom with the ritzy hotels at the top, this is the place for prime people-watching. The steps face west, so sunsets offer great photo-ops.

Castel Sant'Angelo

(G) Originally constructed as a mausoleum for Roman emperor Hadrian, this cylindrical fortress, which towers over the city's skyline, has great views and opulent Renaissance-era salons.

Trastevere

Located just across the Tiber River, this time-stained, charming neighborhood is a maze of jumbled alleyways, traditional Roman *trattorie*, cobblestone streets, and medieval houses. The area also boasts the oldest church of Rome—Santa Maria in Trastevere.

TOP ROME MUSEUMS

FABIVS MAX

Musei Capitolini

(A) None other than the great Michelangelo would suffice to design the master plan for Rome's own collection of art and archaeological museums, which enticingly crown the Capitoline Hill. The museum is divided into two wings: Palazzo Nuovo, devoted to ancient sculpture; and the Palazzo dei Conservatori, with great Old Masters.

Palazzo Doria-Pamphilj

Waltzing through this 17th-century palace may be the closest you ever get to the aristocratic nobles. Fabled Old Master paintings line the walls, with pride of place going to Velàzquez's *Innocent X* (the family pope), perhaps the greatest portrait ever painted.

Palazzo Altemps

Catch a glimpse of exquisite taste in this 15th-century palace, once owned by Cardinal Altemps and today part of the Museo Nazionale Romano—on view are many legendary examples of classic Greek and Roman sculpture, including the "Ludovisi Throne."

Galleria Borghese

(D) Only the best could satisfy the aesthetic taste of Cardinal Scipione Borghese, whose holdings evoke the essence of Baroque Rome. Spectacularly frescoed ceilings and multihue marble walls frame great Bernini sculptures and paintings by Titian and Raphael.

Keats-Shelley House

During the 18th century, the Spanish Steps became a gathering place for Grand Tour artists and writers, so here in 1821 the English Romantic poet John Keats came to write—and ultimately die (of tuberculosis)—in the Casina Rossa, a dusty pink house at the base of the steps.

Museo Nazionale Romano

The city's own great collections of ancient Roman sculpture, paintings, and precious relics—salvaged from excavations completed over several centuries—is so vast that four separate museums at different locations are needed: Palazzo Altemps, Aula Ottagona, Terme di Diocleziano, and Palazzo Massimo alle Terme.

Villa Farnesina

Lifestyles of the Rich and Famous, Renaissance-era version, are on display at this extravagant villa, built around 1511 by banker Agostino Chigi, with loggias decorated by Raphael. After lavish dinners, Chigi would toss his gold plates into the Tiber and slyly retrieve them with a net in the water.

Vatican Museums

(C) The seemingly endless line waiting for entry here can be intimidating, but the reward—a vast collection of masterpieces, including the Raphael Rooms—make it worth it. The agony, not the ecstasy, of it all is summed up in Michelangelo's sublime *Last Judgment* and Sistine ceiling.

Palazzo Barberini

The three fathers of the baroque—Bernini, Borromini, and Pietro da Cortona—whipped up this imposing 17th-century palace for the Croesus-rich Barberini family. Built around 1625, with the Gran Salone, Rome's largest ballroom, the palazzo is now home to the city's collection of Old Master paintings.

Palazzo Spada

(B) A glorious 17th-century assemblage of stuccowork and statuary, together with the impressive trompe l'oeil "trick" of its courtyard colonnade, inspired by master designer Borromini, is what draws the crowds.

TOP ROME CHURCHES

St. Peter's Basilica

(B) Every year, millions of pilgrims flock to the world's most important Catholic church, as art lovers marvel at Michelangelo's cupola, Bernini's papal altar, and the vast nave. The burial site of its namesake, St. Peter's took such Italian masterminds as Raphael and Bramante more than a century to complete.

Santa Maria in Trastevere

(C) Even locals can't help being mesmerized by the splendors of this church's piazza, chief among them being the incandescent Byzantine mosaics on the basilica's facade and the elegant octagonal fountain. Inside, the vast nave stupefies with its gigantic Roman columns and glittering golden mosaics.

Sant'Ignazio

Studying the dome up high in this fantastically bejeweled 1626 Jesuit church, you may think your eyes are playing tricks on you. But it's not your eyes! That extraordinarily accurate replica of a baroque dome was painted in its place after plans for the cupola fell through.

Sant'Agnese in Agone

Prominently positioned in Piazza Navona, this church has some of Rome's most quintessential baroque architecture. Designed by Borromini (1652), a fervent rival of Bernini's, the church's facade is a stunning symphony of voluminous concave spaces and bell towers.

Santa Maria in Cosmedin

(A) Moody, medieval, and magnificent, this 12th-century Romanesque church draws throngs to its portico where the stone Bocca della Verità (Mouth of Truth) sits in judgment—dare you test the legend that its stone jaws clamp shut on the hands of the untruthful?

San Clemente

Uncover the layers of Medieval Rome here at this half-basilica, half archaeological site. Famed for its mosaics, this 12th-century church actually sits on top of another church that dates back to the 4th century *and* a 2nd-century BC temple to the pagan god, Mithras.

Santa Maria del Popolo

Few other churches in Rome reflect the richness of Renaissance art as does Santa Maria del Popolo, thanks to its nave enlarged by Bramante and the Chigi Chapel, a Raphael masterwork. But equally striking are baroque treasures like Caravaggio's Cerasi Chapel and Bernini's mosaic-covered dome.

Santa Maria sopra Minerva

Set on a piazza graced by Bernini's famed elephant obelisk, this Gothic-style church—best known for Michelangelo's *Risen Christ* and famed frescoes by Filippino Lippi—gives off a heavenly aura, thanks to arched blue ceilings ashimmer with gold stars.

Santa Maria in Aracoeli

On the Capitoline Hill and atop a towering, 137-step stairway (designed in 1348 to celebrate the passing of the Black Death), this Romanesque-Gothic landmark was begun in the 6th century and is home to the famed Santo Bambino, a carved-wood Baby Jesus figure.

San Giovanni in Laterno

It's hard to miss the 15 gargantuan marble statues (including Christ and the 12 Apostles) that tower over the facade of Rome's official cathedral and first church of the popes. The baroque interior was accomplished by Borromini, but many pilgrims head first to the legendary Scala Santa (Holy Steps).

ROME LIKE A LOCAL

"When in Rome, do as the Romans do." Undoubtedly, the catch phrase may sound a bit cliché, but locals themselves will even suggest this advice is not to be taken lightly. Romans certainly know how to live life to the fullest, indulging in the simplest pleasures and doing so with style. So put yourself in their shoes (Fendi preferably); try being Roman for a day and you'll learn how *la vita è bella!*

Il Mercato

There's no other place to take in a slice of real Roman life than at your local *mercato all'aperto*—or open-air market. Vendors take center stage turning the sale of some of the freshest fruits and vegetables (often at half-price), into a theatrical performance. The best mercato is the Campo de' Fiori (Piazza Campo de' Fiori), Rome's oldest food market, situated just south of Rome's Renaissance/Baroque quarter and the Piazza Farnese. Too wide to be called picturesque, the market is nevertheless a favorite photo-op, due to the *ombrelloni* (canvas umbrella) food stands. You have to look hard to find the interesting regional foodstuffs, such as Colle Romani strawberries or chestnuts. Other top food markets are the recently renovated Mercato Trionfale (on Via Tunisi in Prati, north of the Vatican) and Nuovo Mercato Esquilino (on Via Filippo Turati), which is strongly influenced by the multi-culti makeup of the district. Open-air markets typically run Monday through Saturday from 7 AM until 2 PM, with Saturday being the busiest shopping day.

For nonfoodies, there are plenty of other street markets scattered about Rome that specialize in clothing, fashion accessories, and every imaginable kind and variety of knickknack. The two largest are the one on Via Sannio in the San Giovanni district (Monday–Saturday), which deals mostly in new and used clothing and accessories, and the Porta Portese market in Trastevere (Sunday only), offering everything from antiques and bric-a-brac to clothing and souvenirs, including finds from your neighbor's trash or treasure. Make sure to ask for a *piccolo sconto*—a small discount.

La Piazza

For Italians young and old, *la piazza* serves as a *punto d'incontro*—a meeting place—for dinner plans, drinks, people-watching, catching up with friends, and, as Romans would say, exchanging *due chiacchere* (two words). Some of the most popular piazzas in Rome: Piazza di Spagna is not just a postcard-perfect moment for tourists, but is also a favored spot among adolescent Italian boys looking to meet American girls. By day, Piazza Campo de' Fiori is famous for its fresh food and flower market; by night, the piazza turns into a popular hangout for Romans and foreigners lured by its pubs, street caffè, and occasional street performers and magicians. Over the last few years, Campo de' Fiori has even been dubbed "the American college campus of Rome," as pubs in the area now cater to American students by advertising two-for-one drink specials and such. The main attractions of the Piazza Santa Maria in Trastevere are the grand bell tower and marvelous mosaics of its namesake church—a picture-perfect background for some pretty trattorias.

L'Aperitivo

Romans can't claim the fame to starting *l'aperitivo;* we have *i Milanesi* to thank for that. But *i Romani* can surely boast about making *aperitivo* time *molto moda* in the Ancient City. Similar to the concept of happy hour sans the two-for-one

IL GELATO

drinks, l'aperitivo is a time to meet up with friends and colleagues after work or on weekends—definitely an event at which to see and be seen. Aperitivo hours are usually 7–9 PM, with Sunday being the most popular day. Depending on where you go, the price of a drink often includes an all-you-can-eat appetizer buffet of finger foods, sandwiches, and pasta salads. Some aperitivo hot spots on the *trendissimo* list are Crudo (Via degli Specchi); Societè Lutece (Piazza Monte Vecchio); Gusto (Piazza Augusto Imperatore), and Salotto 42 (Piazza di Pietra) in the centro storico; and Friends Cafè (Piazza Trilussa) and Freni and Frizioni (Via del Politeama) in the Trastevere area.

Il Caffè

If there's something Romans certainly can't live without, it's their cup of Java. Caffeine, or *il caffè* (espresso), may be the most important part of their day, and there is no shortage of bars in the Eternal City to help satisfy that coffee craving. A breakfast caffè or cappuccino is typically enjoyed at the counter while debating last night's soccer game or some aspect of local politics. Another espresso or *caffè macchiato* (coffee with a dash of milk) is enjoyed after lunch, and again after dinner, especially when dining out. Thinking about ordering that *cappuccino*? Depends on what time it is. Italians consider it taboo to order one after 11 AM. During the summer months, Romans drink a *caffè shakerato* (freshly made espresso shaken briskly with sugar and ice, to form a froth when poured) or a *caffè freddo* (iced espresso). Rome's best coffee? Some say the Tazza D'Oro (Via degli Orfani), not far from the Pantheon; others, Il Caffè Sant'Eustachio (Piazza di Sant'Eustachio). If you like a dollop of chic along with your caffeine, head to Bar della Pace (Via della Pace 3),

set on one of the most fashionable piazzas in Rome (but don't forget that outdoor tables sometimes treble the price).

Il Gelato

A national obsession, this Italian version of ice cream is tastier, less creamy, and traditionally made with only the freshest ingredients. Though many bars and stands purvey it, the best gelatos are found only at *gelaterias*. Small cones cost anywhere from €1.20 to €2.50. Most places allow you up to three flavors (even on a small cone) and portions are usually quite generous. Typical flavors are *nocciola* (hazelnut), pistachio, chocolate, and anything fruity. Or hunt down the latest and greatest flavors, such as the sweet-with-a-kick *cioccolato con peperoncino* (chocolate with hot pepper) at Millenium (Piazza Santa Maria delle Grazie 2/a, near the Vatican Museums). Quality varies: A good sign is a long line at the counter, and two of the longest are at Old Bridge (Via Bastioni di Michelangelo 5, near St. Peter's Square), and Giolitti (Via degli Uffici del Vicario 40, by the Pantheon).

La Passeggiata

A favorite Roman pastime is the *passeggiata* (literally, the promenade). In the late afternoon and early evening, especially on weekends, couples, families, and packs of teenagers stroll Rome's main streets and piazzas. It's a ritual of exchanged news and gossip, window-shopping, flirting, and gelato-eating that adds up to a uniquely Italian experience. You may feel more like an observer than a participant, until you realize that observing is what la passeggiata is all about. Rome's top promenade is up or down the Corso, with a finale in the Piazza di Spagna shopping district.

ROME WITH KIDS

Whoever said Rome is a big playground just for grown-ups was mistaken. Don't let the ancient ruins and the baroque churches throw you off, because Rome abounds in child-oriented activities; you just have to know where to look. Here are some popular options, for both little and big kids alike.

Blast from the Past

Hurtle through 3,000 years of Roman history on the four-dimensional flight simulator ride at Time Elevator Roma (Via S.S. Apostoli 20, near Piazza Venezia). Through phenomenal special effects, the one-hour ride takes you on a tour of the city and its monuments as Caesar knew it.

Your start with a *Jeopardy!*-style quiz on Rome, then head into a movie theater with roller-coaster seats. Once the safety bar drops, lights dim and you're off to the founding of Rome with Romulus and Remus.

Chased by wolves, you dip into a time tunnel to the Ides of March to see Julius Caesar meet his untimely end before your eyes.

Then you hurtle on to the gladiator combats in the Colosseum, watch Michelangelo work in the Sistine Chapel, and dash on to Bernini's baroque fountains, and continue right up through Italy's modern history.

This ride is air-conditioned—a real plus in the summer—and the narration comes in English and other languages.

Say "Cheese," Spartacus

Taking a photo with one of those ersatz gladiators (who aren't Italian by the way) in front of the Colosseum will win some smiles—but maybe some frowns, too. Many of these costumed gladiators pounce on tourists who simply aim a camera at them and then proceed to shake them down for a "photo fee." Others have a craftier approach: before you know it, one may envelop your 8-year-old in his red cape and say "Formaggio."

Indeed, this may turn out to be the greatest souvenir back home in fourth-grade class, so if interested, step right up, shake hands, and exchange some euros.

But pick your Spartacus very carefully: some sloppy guys wear a helmet and cloak but have sweatsuits or sneakers on. Rumor has it that Rome's government is going to crack down on these "gladiators," but so far it is *caveat emptor.*

Playing with the Planets

After roamin' around Rome for a couple of days, your little ones may have had more than enough history than they can handle. If that's the case, you can always switch it up a bit by giving them a bit of science. Taking a trip through outer space is always an easy winner for kids, so head to the Planetarium of Rome (Piazza G. Agnelli 10). From martians to falling stars, the folks there always put on special programs for children on the weekends.

Talk to the Animals

For some wheel fun, think about renting bikes (Viale dell'Orologio on the Pincio hill or Piazzale M. Cervantes) before heading over to the city zoo or to Rome's Bioparco, both set in the massive Villa Borghese park. The Zoo (Piazzale del Giardino Zoologico 1), which is one of the oldest in Europe, is home to more than 1,000 animals.

At the zoo, kids get to participate in all sorts of cool educational activities and can even feed some of the animals.

For those uniquely Roman critters—*i gatti* (the street cats)—kids can go on a free guided tour of the ancient Largo di Torre Argentina, for it has been made into a sanctuary and home for hundreds of once-homeless Roman cats—Mom and Dad, meanwhile, can ooh-and-aah at the relics and remains of one of the oldest (300 BC) temples in Rome.

Truth or Dare

Long before the advent of lie-detector machines, and even before there were bibles to swear on, there was the Bocca della Verità—the Mouth of Truth, the famous gaping mouth that so successfully terrified Audrey Hepburn in *Roman Holiday*.

Long-ago legends have it that people suspected of telling lies would be marched up to the Bocca and have their hand put inside the mouth of this massive stone relief (originally an ancient street drain cover).

If the suspect told the truth, nothing to fear. But if lies were told, the grim unsmiling stone mouth would take its revenge. This is a great spot for kids to get the truth out of their brother or sister, so have your camera—and your probing questions!—ready.

Don't forget to take in the adjacent Santa Maria in Cosmedin church, one of Rome's most evocative and spooky churches.

Adventures in Learning

Kids love hands-on activities and Rome has one museum that encourages them to do just that.

The Explora Children's Museum (✉ *Via Flaminia 82* ☎ *06/3613776* ⊕ *www.mdbr. it*, near Piazza del Popolo) is a miniature realistic cityscape for children under 12 whose exhibits take them—and their bodies—through life in the big city.

Though the exhibits are mainly in Italian, the visuals, effects, and touchy-feely stuff seem to hold the children's attention whatever their language.

In the section called *Io* (Italian for "I"), everyone marvels at the giant, 5-foot version of a mouth.

Elsewhere, kids learn about the workings of a post office, a bank, and the ABCs of recycling. Other highlights: the TV weather forecast they get to star in, the Identikit section, and the life-size fire engine!

The World on Strings

Looming over Trastevere is the Janiculum Hill (Gianicolo), famed for its Cinerama view of the city below and for its colorful, open-air Teatro di Pulcinella puppet theater. Shows here run weekdays from 4 to 7 PM and from 10:30 AM to 1 PM on weekends. A small donation is expected.

Over on the Pincio hill in the Villa Borghese park (usually accessed via Piazza del Popolo) is the Teatro Stabile dei Burattini "San Carlino," which puts on live puppet shows on weekends (Viale dei Bambini Villa Borghese).

Don't forget to take a stroll through the pretty park over to the Cinema dei Piccoli, the smallest movie theater in the world—with all of 63 seats (Viale della Pineta 15)—and children's movies shown daily. Shows are in Italian, but most kids are amused by the images.

After these puppet shows, the perfect souvenir awaits at Bartolucci (Via de' Pastini 99, near the Pantheon), where you'll meet not one Pinocchio but hundreds, still or animated, from life- to pocket-size, all crafted by artisans.

GREAT ITINERARIES

As Romans would say, these one-day itineraries *basta e avanza* ("are more than enough") to get you started. For other great walks, see The Historic Heart, Across the Tiber, and Postcard Rome on the Rome On-the-Go Pullout Map in this edition plus those in our Roamin' Holiday chapter.

Rome 101

So you want to taste Rome, gaze at its beauty, and inhale its special flair, all in one breathtaking (literally) day? Think Rome 101, and get ready for a spectacular sunrise-to-sunset span.

Begin at 9 by exploring Rome's most beautiful neighborhood—"Vecchia Roma" (the area around Piazza Navona) by starting out on the Corso (the big avenue that runs into Piazza Venezia, the traffic hub of the historic center).

A block away from each other are two opulently over-the-top monuments that show off Rome at its baroque best: the church of Sant'Ignazio and the princely Palazzo Doria-Pamphilj, aglitter with great Old Master paintings. By 10:30, head west a few blocks to find the granddaddy of monuments, the fabled Pantheon, still looking like Emperor Hadrian might arrive. A few blocks north is San Luigi dei Francesi, home to the greatest Caravaggio paintings in the world.

At 11:30 saunter a block or so westward into beyond-beautiful Piazza Navona, studded with Bernini fountains. Then take Via Cucagna (at the piazza's south end) and continue several blocks toward Campo de' Fiori's open-air food market (for some lunch-on-the-run fixings).

Two more blocks toward the Tiber brings you to fashionable Via Giulia, laid out by Pope Julius II in the early 16th century. Walk past 10 blocks of Renaissance palaces and antiques shops to take a bus (from the stop near the Tiber) over to the Vatican.

Arrive around 1 to gape at St. Peter's Basilica, then hit the treasure-filled Vatican Museums (Sistine Chapel) around 1:45—during lunch, the crowds empty out! After two hours, head for the Ottaviano stop near the museum and Metro your way to the Colosseo stop.

Around 4, climb up into the Colosseum and picture it full of screaming toga-clad citizens enjoying the spectacle of gladiators in mortal combat. Striding past the massive Arch of Constantine, enter the back-entrance of the Roman Forum around 4:45. Photograph yourself giving a "Friends, Romans, Countrymen" oration (complete with upraised hand) on one of the marble fragments. At sunset, the Forum closes but the floodlights come on.

March down the forum's Via Sacra—people walked here centuries before Christ—and out into Via dei Fori Imperiali where you will head around "the wedding cake"—the looming Vittorio Emanuele Monument (Il Vittoriano)—over to the Campidoglio. Here, on the Capitoline Hill, tour the great ancient Roman art treasures of the Musei Capitolini (which is open most nights until 8), and snap the view from the terrace over the spotlit Forum.

After dinner, hail a cab—or take a long passeggiata walk down Dolce Vita memory lane—to the Trevi Fountain, a gorgeously lit sight at night. Needless to say, toss that coin in to insure your return trip back to the Mother of Us All.

Temples Through Time: Religious Rome

It's almost sinful to come to Rome and say you did not make your way to the Vatican Museums or St. Peter's Basilica. If you head out early enough (yes, 7 AM), you might get a jump on the line for the Vatican Museums, where one of the world's grandest and most comprehensive collections of artwork is stored. Once you've conquered both, take the Metro from Ottaviano to Piazza del Popolo (Metro stop: Flaminio) where Santa Maria del Popolo is not to be missed for its famous chapels decorated by Raphael and Caravaggio.

Head south along the Corso for about 10 blocks toward Sant'Ignazio, an eye-popping example of Baroque Rome, with its amazing trompe l'oeil fake dome. Take Via Sant' Ignazio to Via Piè di Marmo, which will lead you to Piazza della Minerva, where Bernini's elephant obelisk monument lies in wait. Take in the adjacent Gothic-style Santa Maria sopra Minerva, best known for Michelangelo's *Risen Christ*.

Then make your way south to Corso Vittorio Emanuele and the bus piazza at Largo Argentina where you'll take Tram No. 8 to picturesque Trastevere, one of Rome's quaintest quarters. Make your way through a series of winding tiny alleyways and piazzas toward the famed Piazza Santa Maria in Trastevere, where one of Rome's oldest churches—Santa Maria in Trastevere—stands. Dedicated to the Virgin Mary, the church has one of the finest displays of gilded mosaics, which cover the nave, perhaps Rome's most spectacular.

If evening has arrived, a stopover for dinner at any one of the numerous caffè located in this radiant piazza makes for fine dining and finer people-watching.

Retail Therapy: Shop-'Til-You-Drop Rome

All of the serious shopping takes place in Rome's centro storico. For those shoppers with bigger budgets, Rome's Via dei Condotti (Metro stop: Spagna) is *paradiso*.

VIPs can continue their shopping spree down streets Via del Babuino for fabled antique furniture and fine jewelry, and Via Frattina for exclusive boutiques.

Even if you're on a pinch, window shopping can be just as fun as you make your way down to the more affordable Via del Corso, where department-store-style shopping can be done at La Rinascente. Another popular shopping street is Via Cola di Rienzo in the Prati area (not far from St. Peter's Square).

If vintage is your thing, head toward Piazza Navona and down Via del Governo Vecchio, where there is an assortment of vintage consignment shops featuring high-end clothing, handbags, and accessories. Via Nazionale, heading toward Termini train station, also has a bunch of shops.

Now that you've blown your shopping budget, it's time for real bargain-shopping at Rome's famed street markets.

Rome's largest and most famous are markets on Via Sannio in San Giovanni (Monday–Saturday only) and the Porta Portese market (Sunday only) in Trastevere.

The market on Via Sannio specializes in new and used clothing, shoes, and accessories. The Porta Portese market sells everything but the kitchen sink: clothes, souvenirs, antiques, housewares, and knickknacks galore.

FREE AND ALMOST FREE

Though Rome is on the fast track to becoming one of the most expensive cities in Europe, fortunately the city also has an endless supply of free and inexpensive things to do and see without causing any serious damage to your wallet.

Budget Boosters: Art and Archaeological Sites

On Valentine's Day (February 14), the Italian Ministry for Culture hosts its annual *"Innamorati dell'Arte,"* or "In Love with Art," campaign where lovers or people in pairs can take advantage of two-for-one admission prices at all state-run museums and archaeological sites.

Also sponsored by the Ministry for Culture, during "Settimana della Cultura," or Cultural Week (typically held in April and May), many of the major archaeological sites and museums in and around Rome waive their entrance fees. Check out ⊕ *www.beniculturali.it* for exact dates and listings.

It usually costs €14 to visit the Vatican Museums, but on the last Sunday of nearly every month you can get in free. Make sure to bring comfy shoes, as the wait in line can be a bit overwhelming!

Wallet-Watchers: Movies

If you're up for seeing a flick, head over to the Casa del Cinema (Largo Marcello Mastroianni 1, near Villa Borghese). The movie theater, sponsored by the City of Rome, has free showings daily. See ⊕ *www.casadelcinema.it* for listings.

Coincidentally, the Casa del Cinema also does up a nice brunch spread on Sunday.

Looking for a cheap movie night? The Metropolitan (Via del Corso 7, near Piazza del Popolo) and Warner Village (Piazza della Repubblica, 45/46) often show new releases in English during the first week of the month; on Wednesday night, ticket prices are reduced.

Econo-Tips: Music and Performances

Every year on May 1, Italy's Labor Day, hundreds of thousands of people gather for the free concert held in Piazza San Giovanni in Laterano.

Headliners are usually Italian rock bands, but occasionally folk troupes perform as well.

During the summer (mid-June through August), one of Rome's loveliest parks, Villa Ada, hosts its annual Roma Incontro il Mondo–"Rome Meets the World"—concert series.

Concerts are held nightly, with ticket prices ranging €5 to €13. Check ⊕ *www.villaada.org* for details.

Euro-Stretchers: Eats

The aperitivo hour allows you to dine out, sort of, in some of Rome's trendiest and finest establishments without breaking the bank.

Here's how: for the price of a drink (usually €5 to €8), you can feast on an all-you-can-eat buffet.

Politicians head for the Riccioli Caffè, near the Italian Senate (Via delle Coppelle 13), for its sushi, oysters, and cold pastas.

A posh scene can be found at Crudo (Via degli Specchi 6) and Gusto (Piazza Augusto Imperatore, 9), where the spread includes veggies, pastas, and finger food.

The Piazza Bologna district's Momart attracts a young college crowd (Viale XXI Aprile 19) with its wood-oven pizza.

BEATING THE EURO

It's easy to avoid the scam artists and pickpockets, but finding good value is a little trickier.

We asked travelers on Fodor's Travel Talk Forums (⊕ *www.fodors.com*) to reveal some of their insider know-how.

Their response?

When in Rome, spend like a Roman!

Fodorites know that if you live like a local, you'll save like a local as well, and perhaps have a richer traveling experience to boot.

1. "If you aren't hungry and don't want pasta, skip to secondo—the "second course." Rarely do Italians eat a primo e secondo when they go out." —glittergirl

2. "Bars always have two different prices: If you have your coffee at the counter it's cheaper than when a waiter serves it at a table (servizio al tavolo)." —quokka

3. "For the art lover on a budget: Most of the art I saw in Rome is free. Where else can you see countless Caravaggios, two Michelangelos, and even more Berninis for the cost of the wear and tear on the soles of your shoes?" —amyb

4. "Instead of taking the Leonardo Express from Fiumicino to Termini, take the FR1 to whichever station is most convenient for you. The FR1 departs every 15 minutes (instead of every 30 minutes for the Express), costs only €5 (instead of €9.50 for the Express), and avoids the hullabaloo of Termini." —Therese

5. "The boat trips down the Tiber, from the bridge by Castel Sant'Angelo to Isola Tiberina is only €1 (a great way to get from St. Peter's to Trastevere or the Forum)." —annhig

6. "One way to save on the expense of guided tours is to register online at Sound Guides (⊕ *www.sound-guides.com/*) and download the various free self-guided tours to your iPod or MP3 player." —monicapileggi

7. "I eat at working folks places, like the 'Goose,' near the Vatican. Dinner (three courses) runs €20 with wine; if you leave hungry it's your own fault." —JoanneH

8. "Visit wine fill-up shops in Italy; get table wine from the cask for €2–€3 a liter. In Rome we would get them filled at the Testaccio market. I will usually ask at the local bar where I go for my coffee." —susanna

9. "Go off-season—March or November have better air prices and also accommodations, particularly if you stay in apartments, which you can rent for much less off-season (and plan some meals in-house—make the noon meal your biggest of the day, then have a small dinner in the apartment)." —bobthenavigator

10. "Invest in the bus schedule/map—at any place they sell tickets. Cost is €4. It gives you all the routes, how long between buses, hours they run, where you hop on/off to transfer, etc." —JoanneH

11. "The smaller restaurants in Trastevere also offer better value for money than, say, the ones in the alleys near the Spanish Steps or any of the other "tourist" areas in central Rome. "—friendindelhi

12. "Order your coffee or drinks from the bar before you sit down. Take your coffee, whatever, with you to the table, then return the cup or glass afterwards. That way you'll be charged the much cheaper *al banco* price that the locals pay." —WiseOwl

ROMANTIC ROME

Whether you're looking for love or hoping to rekindle the romance, there's no better place to do so than the Eternal City. Ah yes, it certainly seems that love lurks behind every street corner, park bench, and monument. And if you don't find the abundance of public displays of affection off-putting, you'll be sure to find scores of places to steal both that first and ultimo *bacio*.

The hopeless romantics should start their rendezvous through Rome with a horse-drawn carriage ride that begins at the Spanish Steps (Piazza di Spagna) and continues through the streets of the *centro storico*. Make a stop for some aphrodisiacal treats, such as the decadent, mouthwatering chocolates made by Moriondo e Gariglio (Via Piè di Marmo 21), off the central Corso near Palazzo Doria Pamphilj.

When you're through, ask the driver to drop you off at the famous Villa Borghese park. Whether it's a picnic in the park, a cruise on the lake, or just a hand-in-hand stroll up to the Pincio—the park's terrace that boasts the city's most breathtaking views—you will find *amore* everywhere.

If the hopelessly romantic can spare the time, a trip up to Tivoli's Villa D'Este (a half hour outside Rome via bus) is definitely worth it. Its seductive garden and endless array of fountains (about 500 of them) is the perfect setting to put you in the mood for love and it won't be long before you hear Frank Sinatra warble "Three Coins in the Fountain" in your head. For extra brownie points, during the summer months, take her or him to the Villa D'Este at night for a spectacular candle-lit setting.

That's your cue to return to Rome and make a beeline for the luminous Trevi Fountain, even more enchanting at night than in the daytime. Make sure you and that special someone throw a coin into the fountain, for good luck. For your wish to come true, you must toss the coin over your shoulder with your back to the fountain, left hand over right shoulder (or vice versa). Legend has it that those who do so are guaranteed a return trip back to Rome.

A great way to lift the curtain on a night of romance is a serenaded dinner cruise along the Tiber, where dessert includes views of some of Rome's jewels by night: Castel Sant'Angelo, St. Peter's, and the Janiculum (Gianicolo) hill. See ⊕ *www. battellidiroma.it* for more details.

If you prefer to stay on terra firma, at sundown head to the Hotel Hassler and its rooftop garden-restaurant, Imàgo, perched just over the Spanish Steps, for unforgettable views of the city's greatest landmarks, best viewed through a glass of prosecco. Dinner here will set you back a pretty euro-cent, but you may get to rub shoulders with celebs and VIPs at this exclusive locale, whose past visitors included Princess Diana and Hollywood diva Audrey Hepburn.

For an after-dinner stroll, head to north Rome and wander over to the illuminated Ponte Milvio bridge, known as "Lovers Lane" in Roman circles. Inspired by a scene in the recent hit Italian movie, *Ho Voglia Di Te* (*I Really Want You*), prove your eternal love to your *inammorata* by padlocking him or her to one of the bridge's chains—the city specifically erected 24 columns with chains here so that lovers can do just that. Remember that part of the charm is throwing the key into the river!

2

Roamin' Holiday

THREE STEP-BY-STEP WALKS: BAROQUE ROME, TRASTEVERE, AND THE ROMAN FORUM

WORD OF MOUTH

"I love walking Rome. Keep in mind, though, that estimated times do not include stops for cappuccini, gelati, shopping and/or all those moments where you want to just take all of this amazing city in."

—LucieV

By Martin Wilmot Bennett

With more masterpieces per square foot than any other city in the world, Rome presents a particular challenge for visitors: just as they are beginning to feel hopelessly smitten by the spell of the city, they realize they don't have the time—let alone the stamina—to see more than a fraction of its treasures. Rome may not have been built in a day, but neither can it be seen in one day, or even two or three. As the Italian author Silvio Negro once put it: *"Roma, non basta una vita"* (Rome, a lifetime is not enough).

It's wise to start out knowing this, and to have a focused itinerary. To provide just that, here are three strolls that introduce you to especially evocative stretches of the city: Vecchia Roma, where Rome's bravura baroque style sets the city's tone; Trastevere—Rome's Greenwich Village—and the picturesque Tiber Island; and the Roman Forum, where the glory that was (and is) Rome is best captured.

Along the way, terra-cotta-hued palaces, baroque squares, and time-stained ruins will present an unfolding panorama of color upon color—an endlessly varied palette that makes Rome into one of Europe's most enjoyable cities for walking. Forget about deadly earnest treks through marble miles of museum corridors and get ready to immerse yourself in some of Italy's best "street theater."

In addition, these three tours of clustered sightseeing capture quintessential Rome while allowing roamers to make minidiscoveries of their own. Use these itineraries as suggestions to keep you on track as you explore both the famous sights and those off the beaten path. Remember that people who stop for a caffè get more out of these breaks than those who breathlessly try to make every second count. So be Neroesque in your rambles and fiddle while you roam.

ENJOYING THE GILT: A STROLL THROUGH THE BAROQUE QUARTER

The most important clue to the Romans is their baroque art—not its artistic technicalities, but its spirit. When you understand that, you'll no longer be a stranger in Rome. Flagrantly emotional, heavily expressive, and sensuously visual, the 17th-century artistic movement known as the baroque was born in Rome, the creation of four geniuses, Gian Lorenzo Bernini, Francesco Borromini, Annibale Caracci, and Caravaggio. Ranging from the austere drama found in Caravaggio's painted altarpieces to the jewel-encrusted, gold-on-gold decoration of 17th-century Roman palace decoration, the baroque sought to both shock and delight by upsetting the placid, "correct" rules of the Renaissance masters. By appealing to the emotions, it became a powerful weapon in the hands of the Counter-Reformation. Although this walk passes such sights as the Pantheon—ancient Rome's most perfectly preserved building—it's mainly an excursion into the 16th and 17th centuries, when baroque art triumphed in Rome. ⇨ *For a handy introduction to this spectacular style, see the photo-feature, "Baroque and Desperate: The Tragic Rivalry between Bernini & Borromini" in Chapter 7.*

We wend our way through one of Rome's most beautiful districts—Vecchia Roma (Old Rome), a romantic nickname given to the areas around Piazza Navona and the Campo de' Fiori. Thick with narrow streets with curious names, airy baroque piazzas, and picturesque courtyards, and occupying the horn of land that pushes the Tiber westward toward the Vatican, this has been an integral part of the city since ancient times. For centuries, artisans and shopkeepers toiled in the shadow of the huge palaces built to consolidate the power and prestige of the leading figures in the papal court who lived and worked here. The greatest artists flocked here to get commissions. Today, artisans still live hereabouts but their numbers are diminishing as the district has become one of Rome's ritziest.

FROM EARTHLY
TO HEAVENLY
GLORY

We begin just off the main thoroughfare of Rome, the Via del Corso, about four blocks northwest of Piazza Venezia's traffic hub. Heading up the Corso, make a left turn down tiny Via Montecatini to emerge into the delightful proportions of the ocher and stone **Piazza di Sant'Ignazio.** Any lack in size of this square is made up for in theatricality. Indeed, a Rococo theater set was exactly what its architect, Filippo Raguzzini, had in mind when he designed it in 1727. The exits and entrances these days, however, are by carabinieri, not actors, the main building "backstage" being a police station. With perfectly matching concave facades, two other buildings make up "the wings." A rare example of the barochetto—that is, the "cute" baroque—a term that demonstrates how Italian art critics have a name for everything.

At one time the chapel of the gigantic Collegio Romano, the church of **Sant'Ignazio**—on your left—was Rome's largest Jesuit church. Honoring the order's founding saint, it is famous for its over-the-top baroque spectacle—few churches are as gilt-encrusted, jewel-studded, or stupen-

Why Go?:	Rome gave birth to the baroque—the lavish, eye-popping style that revolutionized Europe in the 17th century—and this walk shows off Rome's baroque at its best.
Good in the 'Hood:	Marveling at Bernini fountains, time-traveling back to the 17th century, watching the world pass by on Piazza Navona, and Rome's best cup of coffee.
Highlights:	Caravaggio paintings at San Luigi dei Francesci, Sant'Ignazio, Via Giulia, Palazzo Farnese, Piazza Navona.
Where to Start:	Piazza di Sant'Ignazio, a few blocks north of Piazza Venezia (turn left off the Corso on Via Montecatina to access the piazza); take Bus 40 or 64 to Piazza Venezia or Bus No. 122 down the Corso to get here.
Where to Stop:	Sant'Andrea della Valle, on the Corso Vittorio Emanuele, a few blocks west of Piazza Venezia.
Time:	Four to six hours, depending on your pace.
Best Time to Go:	Get an early start, around 9 AM, and you'll be able to visit most of the churches before they close for their midday siesta at noon.
Worst Time to Go:	If the weather is inclement or gray, wait for a sunnier day.

dously stuccoed. This is the 17th-century Counter-Reformation pulling out all the stops: religion as supreme theater.

Walk down the vast nave and position yourself on the yellow marble disc on the floor and prepare to be transported heavenward. Soaring above you, courtesy of painter-priest Fra Andrea Pozzo, is a frescoed *Allegory of the Missionary Work of the Jesuits* (1691–94). While an angel holding the Jesuit battle motto HIS (*In Hoc Signo*)—"In this sign we conquer"—just below, upward, ever upward, soars Saint Ignatius in triumph, trailed by a cast of thousands. A masterly use of perspective opens giddying vistas where clouds and humans interact until the forces of gravity seem to flounder. *"Diavolerie"*—fiendish tricks—a commentator of the time called such wonders. To rephrase a hopefully not too sacrilegious modern essay: Not until *Superman* comics does anything get close.

Looking back toward the entrance door, notice how the painted columns—continuations more or less of their real marble equivalents below—seem to rise straight into heaven. Now walk 20 yards back toward the door, and gaze again. And experience an optical earthquake: Those straight columns have tilted 60 degrees. Believe it or not, the whole towering edifice of classic arches, columns, and cornices from the windows upward is entirely flat.

Time to walk down the nave and admire the massive dome—although it is anything but. Dome, windows, the golden light, they're all illusion—all that majestic space is in reality flat as the top of a drum, mere paint masterfully applied across a round canvas 17 meters in diameter in trompe l'oeil fashion. Funds for a real dome ran out, so Pozzo created the less costly but arguably no less marvelous "flat" version here. Another disc set in the marble floor marks the spot where his deception takes maximum effect.

GOD'S LITTLE MASCOT   Head out of the church, turning left to find Via S. Ignazio, then left again to Via Pie' di Marmo, which leads into Piazza Santa Caterina di Siena and the Piazza della Minerva, site of Santa Maria sopra Minerva, the only major church in Rome built in Gothic style, and famous as the home of Michelangelo's *Risen Christ*. But the object of our delight is right on the piazza: the **Obelisk of Santa Maria sopra Minerva,** an astounding conceit of an obelisk astride an elephant, masterfully designed by Gian Lorenzo Bernini. Romans pet-name it "Il Porcino," or little pig. The obelisk is a soaring emblem for theology and the vertiginous weight of knowledge, the beast beneath embodying that which is needed to support it—a mind that is both humble and robust, and never, thank heaven, beyond a jest, even when at its own expense.

Straight ahead is the curving, brick-bound mass of the **Pantheon,** the most complete building surviving from antiquity, and a great influence on baroque architects. Follow Via della Minerva to Piazza della Rotonda and go to the north end of the square to get an overall view of the temple's columned portico: it once bore two baroque bell towers of Bernini's design but, after being ridiculed for their similarity to "donkey's ears," they were demolished. Enjoy the piazza and side streets, where you will find a busy caffè and shopping scene.

Returning to the Piazza della Rotunda, continue northward on Via della Maddalena and proceed into Piazza della Maddelena. In the corner is the excellent Gelateria Pasqualetti. Meanwhile, in front is the Rococo facade of the church of **S. Maria Maddelena**, its curly and concave stone appearing as malleable as the ice cream that you may have just eaten, a gelato for the eyes. Inside the church observe how the late-17th-century baroque twists and meanders into the 18th-

> ### COUNTING NOSES
>
> For some merriment around the Piazza della Rotonda, head to Via de' Pastini 99, where you'll meet not one Pinocchio but several hundreds, still or animated, from life- to pocket-size. The artisans responsible are the Bartolucci, and this family keeps Pinocchio not just alive and well, but multiplying to a dizzying degree.

century Rococo style. Marble work was seldom given such ornate or sumptuous treatment, and here is often gilded as well, as is the magnificent organ loft.

Head to Via Pozzo delle Cornacchia, directly opposite the church facade, and take it one block to the looming church across the square, **San Luigi dei Francesi,** the church of Rome's French community. In the left-side chapel closest to the altar are the masterpieces painted by Caravaggio on the life and martyrdom of Saint Matthew—these three gigantic paintings had the same effect on 17th-century art that Picasso's *Demoiselles d'Avignon* had on 20th-century artists. Illuminated in Caravaggio's landmark chiaroscuro (light and shadow) style, these are works unrivaled for emotional spectacle. The artist's warts-and-all drama was a deeply original response to the Counter-Reformation writings by St. Carlo Borromeo and the result is baroque at its sublime best.

THE STING OF WISDOM

Continue south on Via della Dogana Vecchia to Piazza di Sant'Eustachio. As culture-vulture exhaustion may be setting in, it's time for a coffee. There's no better place than Il Caffè, which, a true Roman will tell you, serves the best coffee in Rome, if not the universe. Inside the bar a cup costs only €1; outside, the price triples, but then, up on your left, the best available view of S. Ivo's dome is thrown in. **Sant'Ivo alla Sapienza** is considered by many to be Francesco Borromini's most astounding building. To get another look at the bizarre pinnacle crowning its dome (the church's rear entrance is on Piazza Sant'Eustachio), head down Via del Salvatore and turn left on Corso del Rinascimento to Number 40. Here a grand courtyard view of the church reveals Borromini—Bernini's great rival—at the dizzying top of his form.

Admire the church's concave facade and follow your gaze upward to see how Borromini mixes concave and convex shapes like a conjurer in stone. This performance is topped first with the many-niched lantern, and then the spiraling, so-called *"puntiglione,"* or giant stinger. Some suggest Borromini was inspired by that ziggurat of ziggurats—the Tower of Babel, featured in many paintings of the time. A more popular theory cites the sting of a bee, and indeed the nickname means just that. This would also square with the building having been begun under Pope Urban VIII of the Barberini family, whose three-bee'd crest is much in evidence all over Rome. Neatly enough, the bee is also a symbol of wisdom and this palace of "Sapienza" was once the hoary home of the University of Rome.

Leaving the courtyard, follow all the crowds one block to reach that showstopper of baroque Rome, **Piazza Navona**. The crown jewel of the *centro storico,* this showcases Bernini's extravagant Fontana dei Quattro Fiumi, whose statues represent the four corners of the earth and, in turn, the world's great rivers. Emperor Domitian's stadium once stood on this site, hence the piazza's unusual oval shape. Before someone figured out that the piazza's church of **Sant'Agnese in Agone** was designed prior to the fountain, common belief held that Bernini's fountain-figures were poised as if looking in horror at the inferior creation of Borromini, Bernini's rival. For lunch, grab a ringside caffè seat and take in the piazza spectacle—this is some of the most delicious scenery on view in Europe.

After lunch, escape the madding crowds by exiting the piazza on the little vicolo (alleyway) to the right of the church complex, Via di Tor Millina, to turn right on Via di S. Maria dell'Anima. Continue to the soaring bell tower of the church of S. Maria dell'Anima, then make a sharp left up a narrow alley to emerge on pretty Piazza della Pace. The centerpiece of one of the city's cutest streetscapes is the church of **Santa Maria della Pace**, commissioned by the great Chigi-family art patron, Pope Alexander VII. Although there are two great Renaissance treasures inside—Raphael's *Sibyls* and Bramante's cloister—the baroque masterstroke here is the church facade, designed in 1657 by Pietro da Cortona to fit into the tiny *piazzina,* created to accommodate the 18th-century carriages of fashionable parishioners.

Take the street leading to the church, Via della Pace (past the always chic Antico Caffè delle Pace) and continue a few blocks south down to the big avenue, Corso Vittorio Emmanuele II. Turn right for one or two blocks to reach the Chiesa Nuova, another of Rome's great Counter-Reformation churches (with magnificent Rubens paintings inside) and, directly to the left, Borromini's Oratorio dei Filippini. Head across the Corso another two blocks toward the Tiber along Via D. Cartari and turn left on Via Giulia, often called Rome's most beautiful street. While laid out—as a ruler-straight processional to St. Peter's—by Michelangelo's patron, Pope Julius II, it is lined with numerous baroque palaces (Palazzo Sachetti, at No. 66, is still home to one of Rome's princeliest families). At No. 1 is **Palazzo Falconieri**, probably Borromini's most regal palace and now home to the Hungarian academy—note the architect's rooftop belvedere adorned with the family "falcons."

Looming over everything else is the massive **Palazzo Farnese**, a Renaissance masterpiece topped off by Michelangelo himself. You can tour the palace (today the French Embassy) on Monday and Thursday at 3, 4, and 5 PM (though not from July 24 to September 7; see write-up of palace in Navona section for details). Inside is the fabled Galleria, with frescoes painted by Annibale Carracci. These florid depictions of gods and goddesses were among the first painted in the baroque style and were staggeringly influential.

No need to pack bottled Pellegrino on your walks—just savor the refreshing water from city fountains along the way, just as Romans have done for centuries.

If you can't get into the Farnese, no problem. Just a block to the south is the grand **Palazzo Spada**. The rich exterior trim of painted frescoes on the top story hint at the splendors within: grand salons nearly wall-papered with Old Master paintings capture the opulent, 17th-century version of *Lifestyles of the Rich and Famous.*

But don't miss the *colonnato prospettico* in the small courtyard between the library and the palace cortile. While the colonnaded tunnel, with a mythological figure in marble at the far end, seems to extend for 50 feet, it is actually only one-third that length.

Due to anamorphic deformation used as a trick by the designer, once thought to be Borromini himself (now seen as the work of Giovanni Maria da Bitono), the columns at the far end are only two feet high!

PUCCINI'S CHOICE For the finale, head four blocks northward along Via Biscione back to the Corso Vittorio Emmanuele. Landmarking the famous baroque church of **Sant'Andrea della Valle** is the highest dome in Rome (after St. Peter's).

Designed by Carlo Maderno, the nave is adorned with 17th-century frescoes by Lanfranco, making this one of the earliest ceilings in full baroque fig.

Richly marbled chapels flank the nave, the setting Puccini chose for Act I of his opera *Tosca.* The arias sung by Floria Tosca and her lover Cavaradossi (load it on your iPod) strike exactly the right note to conclude this tour of Rome.

TRASTEVERE: THE VILLAGE WITHIN THE CITY

Charming, cobblestoned Trastevere might be nicknamed the world's third-smallest nation (after the Vatican, No. 2). Staunchly resisting the tides of change for centuries, the off-the-beaten-path district was known—until the millionaires and chichi real estate agents arrived a decade ago—as "the real Rome." Heavily populated by *romani di Roma*—those born and bred in the Eternal City for at least three generations—these locals called themselves the only true Romans. To brook no arguments, they named their charming July fete the Festa de Noantri: the "Festival of We Others," as the people of Trastevere pugnaciously labeled themselves so as to be distinguished from "Voiantri," the "you others" of the rest of Rome or anywhere else.

In fact, the Trasteverini have always been proud and combative, a breed apart. Dating back to Republican times when it hosted both Jewish and Syriac communities as well as assorted slaves and sailors, the area was only incorporated into the "Urbs" (or city proper) by Emperor Augustus in 7 BC. By the Middle Ages, Trastevere still wasn't considered truly part of Rome, and the "foreigners" who populated its maze of alleys and piazzas fought bitterly to obtain recognition for the neighborhood as a *rione,* or official district of the city. In the 14th century the Trasteverini won out and became full-fledged Romans, continuing, however, to stoutly maintain their separate identity, however.

It's been the case ever since. Trastevere has always attracted "outsiders," and those have included celebrated artists and artisans. Raphael's model and mistress, the dark-eyed Fornarina (literally, "the baker's daughter"), is believed to have been a Trasteverina. The artist reportedly took time off from painting the *Galatea* in the nearby Villa Farnesina to woo the winsome girl at the tavern now occupied by the district's most toothsome restaurant, Romolo's. Long cocooned from "the strange disease of modern life," the district these days has been colonized with trendy boutiques and discos. Today, the district is newly hip with actors and alternative thinkers. No matter: tourists still love the place, with good reason. Long considered Rome's "Greenwich Village," Trastevere remains a delight for dialecticians, biscuit-eaters, winebibbers, and book-browsers alike.

TIBER'S ISLAND The best gateway to Trastevere turns out to be one of Rome's most picturesque: the Ponte Fabrizio over the **Isola Tiberina**, the island wedged between Trastevere and the Campo area. As you stride over Rome's

A MIDSUMMER NIGHT'S DREAM

Rome's most charming festival begins on the first Saturday after July 16, when a statue of the Madonna is dressed in precious clothes and jewels and transported from the church of Sant'Agata to the church of San Crisogono. The eight days it remains there signal a local holiday: Trastevere streets are hung with colored lights and lanterns and everyone joins in festive merriment, complete with open-air singing contests, *cocomero* (watermelon) vendors, public dances, and *stornellatori* (quip-makers) passing from table to table.

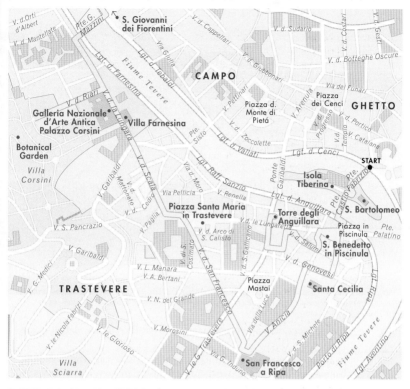

Why Go?:	Frozen-in-amber, this enchanting little nook of Rome has the city's best neighborhood vibe.
Good in the 'Hood:	Chilling out in Piazza Santa Maria in Trastevere, walking in Raphael's footsteps, "Middle-Age"-d alleyways, lunching on Romolo's gorgeous terrace.
Highlights:	Mosaic splendor at Santa Maria in Trastevere, tiny Piazza in Piscinula, picturesque Isola Tiberina, Bernini's Blessed Ludovica Albertoni.
Where to Start:	Isola Tiberina (Tiber Island), accessed via bus from Largo Torre Argentina—get off near the Ghetto area, a few blocks from the Isola.
Where to Stop:	Via della Lungara heads north to the Principe Amadeo bridge, which leads to buses, including No. 64, back to city center.
Time:	Three to five hours, depending on your pace.
Best Time to Go:	The afternoon light here is best, but some churches close for a midday siesta at noon.
Worst Time to Go:	As the sun sets, hipster crowds arrive—Trastevere has a completely different vibe at night.

The Ponte Cestio (above) connects the Isola Tiberina with Trastevere; the Ponte Fabricio (opposite)—Rome's oldest (62 AD)—links the island with the Ghetto.

oldest bridge, let's not forget that Trastevere, literally translated, means "across the Tiber."

In Rome every stone worth its weight has a story attached. The one behind the Tiber Island, writes ancient historian Livy, is that Etruscan leader Tarquin, on his banishment, left behind a crop of grain in the Campo Marzio. For various superstitious reasons this was uprooted, put in baskets, and thrown into the Tiber for good riddance. Mud and sediment did the rest. The resulting island was eventually walled in the shape of a ship, ready to take on board another myth: Allegedly this is where Aesculapius, god of Medicine, landed from Greece (or his serpent double did). Whatever, the medical tradition continues to this day in the Hospital of Fratebenefratelli, the large building to your right. For one of Rome's most unique ancient survivals, head (in the opposite direction) down the embankment to the island's southern tip to the **ancient "stone prow"** carved with Medicine's serpent. Take in the 18th-century facade of the church of **San Bartolomeo**, built above Aesculapius's Temple. Off to the right is what some call the world's most beautiful movie theater, the open-air Cinema d'Isola di Tiberina (which operates during the summer festival of Estate Romana). Cross the bridge—the Ponte Cestio (dated 26 BC)—to get to Trastevere proper.

MEDIEVAL NOOKS AND CRANNIES You're now on the Lungotevere riverside road but continue for another block into the district to hit **Piazza in Piscinula** (from *piscina*, pool), one of Rome's most time-stained squares, home to **S. Benedetto in Piscinula**, a 17th-century church with a much earlier campanile, one of the smallest and cutest in Rome. Here St. Benedict, the founder of Western monasticism, once had a cell. The church has recently been restored by the

Brazilian "Heralds of the Gospel" who, in resplendent uniform, are there on Sunday to greet visitors and worshippers alike. The multicolor 12th-century floor is a wonder in itself. On the opposite flank of the square is the 14th-century **Casa dei Mattei**, replete with cross-mullioned windows and loggias.

History nestles quietly in every nook and cranny off the square, but opt for the charming incline at the northern end, the **Via dell'Arco dei Tolomei**, graced with a medieval house built over an arch. One block north, let history take a rest in Via della Luce at a bakeshop par excellence—just look for the sign Biscotti. Several blocks farther north, the "Middle-Aged" want to detour up to Piazza Belli, where they'll find one of the largest medieval structures in Trastevere, the **Torre degli Anguillara**, a much-restored mini-fortress whose main tower dates from the 13th century.

Back under the Tolomei arch, this street leads into the Via dei Salumi and one block leftward brings you to **Via dell'Atleta**, with a number of picturesque medieval houses. Via dell'Atleta runs into **Via dei Genovesi**, which commemorates the Genovese sailors who thronged Trastevere when it was the papal harbor in the 15th century: these gents roomed in the vicinity of the 15th-century church of San Giovanni dei Genovesi, which has an extraordinary 15th-century cloister. Whether Christopher Columbus ever stayed here is not recorded, but the dates would fit. Meanwhile, at a ring of the bell (at No. 12 Via Anicia), the cloister is still visitable every afternoon 3–6.

SAINTLY
PORTRAITS
IN STONE
Via dei Genovesi leads directly to one of the district's majestic medieval landmarks, the church of **Santa Cecilia,** which was built above the Roman house of this martyr and patron saint of music. In 1599 her sarcophagus was found, her body inside being miraculously intact. Sculptor Stefano Maderno was summoned to attest in stone to what he saw, and sketched before decomposition set in. In a robe-turned-shroud the saint lies on her side, head turned away and a deep gash across her neck, that she's supposed to have survived for three days after suffocation in a steam bath had left her not only unscathed but singing (all this sent Marquis de Sade into rather dubious raptures). With its almost mystically white marble, the work has a haunting quality that few statues can match. But the greatest treasure can be seen only if you exit and ring the bell on the left: for €3 a nun will show you to an elevator that ascends to a *Christ in Judgment* by Pietro Cavallini, who art historians believe was Giotto's master. Painted in 1293, the frescoes are remarkably intact.

> **TIME-TESTED
> TASTE TREAT**
>
> On the right of Ponte Cestio you will see the beloved kiosk of "La Gratachecca del 1915." Using recipes going back to ancient Roman times, its variety of ice-crushes are famous enough locally to cause lines 100 feet long.

Leaving the church, turn left and walk down Via Anicia several blocks to Piazza S. Francesco d'Assisi and **San Francesco a Ripa.** The fourth chapel on the left features Bernini's eye-knocking statue of the *Blessed Ludovica Albertoni,* a Franciscan nun whose body is buried beneath the altar. It has been remarked that the baroque, at its most effective, served not just to educate, but to sweep you off your feet. Here's an example. Marble pillow, folds, and drapery in abundance, all set off the deathbed agony and ecstasy of the nun—her provocative gesture of clutching at her breast is actually an allusion to the "milk of charity."

MAJESTIC
SANTA MARIA
We now set off for the walk's northern half by heading upward Via San Francesco a Ripa, one of Trastevere's main shopping strips. But this dreary stretch actually enhances the delight at finding, at the end of the street, **Santa Maria in Trastevere,** famously set on one of Rome's dreamiest piazzas. Noted for its fountain and caffè, it is the photogenic heart of the *rione. Fellini evidently thought the same, making it a supporting star of his film Roma.*

Staring down at you from the 12th-century church facade are the famed medieval frescoes of the Wise and Foolish Virgins. Dramatically spotlit at night, these young ladies refer to the "miraculous" discovery of oil here in 39 BC. In the mosaic, the Virgin is set between the wise virgins and two foolish ones—the latters' crownless heads bowed with shame at having left their lamps empty, the flame extinguished. In the church's presbytery the *fons olii* marks the spot from whence the oil originally flowed.

Thanks to its gilded ceiling, shimmering mosaics, and vast dimensions, the church nave echoes the spectacle of an ancient Roman basilica— the columns are said to have come from the Baths of Caracalla. The church's main wonder, however, must be the golden mosaics behind the altar. The famous mosaics of Pietro Cavallini depict episodes in the life of the Virgin so often revisited during the Renaissance. With its use of perspective, the work—completed in 1291—is seen as something of a watershed between the old, static Byzantine style and the more modern techniques soon to be taken up by Giotto. This is the very dawn of Western art.

The piazza outside is the very heart of the Trastevere *rione* (district). With its elegant raised fountain and sidewalk caffè, this is one of Rome's most beloved outdoor "living rooms," open to all comers. Through innumerable generations, this piazza has seen the comings and goings of tourists and travelers, intellectuals and artists, who lounge on the steps of the fountain or eat lunch at Sabatini's, whose food has seen much better days but whose real estate, with its tables set up directly in front of the fountain, among Rome's most coveted. Here the paths of Trastevere's residents intersect repeatedly during the day; they pause, gathering in clusters to talk animatedly in the broad accent of Rome or in a score of foreign languages. At night, it's the center of Trastevere's action, with street festivals, musicians, and gamboling dogs vying for attention from the throngs of people taking the evening air.

WHEREFORE ART THOU, ROMOLO?

No visit to Trastevere is complete without a visit to its landmark restaurant, Romolo (Via di Porta Settimiana 8), not far from the Villa Farnesina. Haunted by the spirit of Raphael—who wooed his Fornarina here—it has Rome's prettiest garden terrace, menus embellished by Miró, and scumptious specialties, like the chef's famous artichoke sauce.

RAPHAEL WAS HERE Directly north of the church is Piazza di S. Egidio (the small but piquant Museo di Trastevere is here) and then you enter Via della Lungara, where, several blocks along on the right, the **Villa Farnesina** stands (hours are 9–1 daily, except Sunday). Originally built by papal banker and high-roller Agostino "Il Magnifico" Chigi, this is Rome at its High Renaissance best.

Enter the Loggia di Galatea to find, across the ceiling, Peruzzi's 1511 horoscope of the papal banker, presumably not foretelling the family's eventual bankruptcy and the selling off of the same property (and horoscope) to the wealthy Farnese family. Off left, next to the wall, sits Sebastiano di Piombo's depiction of one-eyed giant *Polyphemus* with staff and giant panpipes; this is what, just next door, Raphael's *Galatea* is listening to in her shell-chassis, paddle-wheeled chariot. With the counter-movement of its iconic putti, nymphs, sea-gods, and dolphins, this legendary image became a hallmark of Renaissance harmony.

In the next room, also—or at least mostly—decorated by Raphael is the *Marriage of Cupid and Psyche*. After provoking the jealousy of Venus, Psyche has to overcome a number of trials before being deemed fit to drink the cup of immortality and marry Cupid. Here, of course is an alter-ego for Agostino Chigi. The paintings are made still more wonderful by Giovanni da Udine's depictions of flower and fruit separating one from the other as if it were a giant *pergolato* (or arbor)—gods float

At night, Piazza di Santa Maria in Trastevere—the beloved heart of Trastevere—is a spot-lit spectacular.

at every angle while ornithologists will delight in spotting Raphael's repertoire of bird species. Climbing upstairs one passes through Peruzzi's Hall of Perspectives to Chigi's private rooms. Here, in Il Sodoma's *Alexander's Wedding*, Roxanna is being lovingly undressed by a bevy of cupids. Note the one who is so overexcited he attempts a somersault like a footballer after a winning goal.

QUEEN CHRIS-
TINA AT HOME Directly across the street from the Villa Farnesina is the **Galleria Corsini** (open Tuesday through Sunday, 8:30–1:30), entered via a gigantic stone staircase right out of a Piranesi print. This was formerly the palazzo of pipe-smoking Christina of Sweden, immortalized by Greta Garbo on the silver screen and to whom history, that old gossip, attaches the label, "Queen without a Realm, Christian without a Faith, and a woman without shame." Her artistic taste is indisputable.

The second room alone contains a magnificent Rubens, Van Dyck's *Madonna of the Straw,* an Andrea del Sarto, and then, courtesy of Hans Hoffman, surely the hare of all hares. Worth the price of admission alone is Caravaggio's *John the Baptist.* In other rooms, for aficionados of high-class gore, there's Salvator Rosa's *Prometheus*, the vulture *in flagrante* and on Prometheus's face a scream to rival Munch. A visit to the **Botanical Gardens** that stretch behind the Galleria is well worth a visit, if just to restore a sense of calm after all that baroque bloodletting.

To get back to central Rome, continue on up Via della Lungara (past the church of Giacomo Apostolo, which has a fine Bernini inside) and cross over the Ponte Principe Amadeo. Taking advantage of one of the bus stops by the Tiber, you can take any number of buses, including the famous No. 64, back to *il centro.*

ROME OF THE EMPERORS: A ROMAN FORUM WALK

Taking in the famous vista of the Roman Forum from the terraces of the Capitoline Hill, you have probably already cast your eyes down and across two millennia of history in a single glance. Here, in one fabled panorama, are the world's most striking and significant concentrations of historic remains. From this hilltop aerie, however, the erstwhile heart of ancient Rome looks like one gigantic jigsaw puzzle, the last piece being the Colosseum, looming in the distance. Historians soon realized that the Forum's big chunks of weathered marble were the very seeds of our civilization and early-20th-century archaeologists moved in to weed it and reap: in the process, they uncovered the very heart of the ancient Roman Empire. While it is fine to just let your mind contemplate the scattered pieces of the once-impressive whole, it is even better to go exploring to decipher the significance of the Forum's noble fragments. This walk does precisely that.

WORLD'S
MIGHTEST
HEIRLOOM

To kick things off, we start just south of the Forum at ancient Rome's hallmark monument, the **Colosseum** (with its handy Colosseo metro stop). Convincingly austere, the Colosseum is the Eternal City's yardstick of eternity. Weighing in at 100,000 tons, it must be the world's mightiest heirloom. A special road having been built to transport the Travertine stone from nearby Tivoli—these quarries are still there to this day—the building was begun under the emperor Titus Flavius Vespasianus (aka Vespasian) and named the Flavian Amphitheater after his family. His son Titus, according to his father's will, inherited the task of finishing it in AD 80 while his other son, Domitian, built the gladiatorial schools on the adjacent Colle Oppio.

One rationale for the building was that Rome's only previous amphitheater, the Theater of Taurus, had been destroyed in the great fire of AD 64. Another was that the new version would erase memories of wicked Nero, who had privatized a vast swath of land near the public Forum for his private palace, the so-called Domus Aurea. In fact, the Colosseum was positioned directly over a former lake in Nero's gardens, and nearby would have towered the 110-foot-high, colossal statue of Nero himself. In one of History's ironic twists, the term "Flavian amphitheater" never caught on. Even in its name, the Colosseum serves to publicize the very emperor whose memory it was meant to bury.

A typical day at the Colosseum? The card would usually begin with a wild-beast hunt, then a pause for lunch, during which the sparse crowd was entertained with tamer displays by jugglers, magicians, and acrobats, along with third-tier fights involving "lesser" combatants, such as the Christians. Then, much gorier, would come the main event: the gladiators. The death rates among them have been much debated—30,000 is one estimate.

The building could evidently be filled in as little as 10 minutes, thanks to the 80 entrance archways. Nowadays, you can take one of the elevators upstairs to level one (the uppermost levels are closed for excavation) to

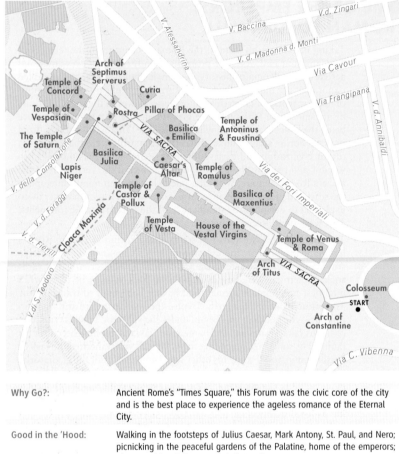

Why Go?:	Ancient Rome's "Times Square," this Forum was the civic core of the city and is the best place to experience the ageless romance of the Eternal City.
Good in the 'Hood:	Walking in the footsteps of Julius Caesar, Mark Antony, St. Paul, and Nero; picnicking in the peaceful gardens of the Palatine, home of the emperors; photographing Colosseum "gladiators."
Highlights:	Arches of Septimus Severus, Titus, and Constantine; the Colosseum; the Via Sacra; the Roman Forum.
Where to Start:	Piazza del Colosseo, with its handy Colosseo metro stop.
Where to Stop:	Northern edge of the Roman Forum, near the Temple of Vespasian and the exit to Via di San Teodoro, leading to the Capitoline Hill.
Time:	Two to five hours, depending on your pace.
Best Time to Go:	Around 9 AM, when you can get a jump on the Colosseum crowds.
Worst Time to Go:	Midday, when the sun is high and merciless—remember, there are no roofs and few trees to shelter under at these archaeological sites.

spy the extensive subterranean passageways that used to funnel all the unlucky animals and gladiators into the arena.

ANCIENT
ARCHES TELL
THE TALE

Leaving the Colosseum behind, admire the **Arch of Constantine,** standing just to the north of the arena. The largest and best preserved of Rome's triumphal arches, it was erected in AD 315 to celebrate the victory of the emperor Constantine (280–337) over Maxentius—it was shortly after this battle that Constantine converted Rome to Christianity. Something of an amalgam historically, it features carved depictions of the triumphs of emperors Trajan, Marcus Aurelius, and Hadrian as well, a cost-cutting recycling that indicates the empire was no longer quite what it once was. Now proceed back westward along the black basalt stones leading to the Via Sacra and into the Forum. Albeit minus the traditional four-horse chariot and Jovian costume, you are treading the same route used by the emperors returning in triumph.

Up there on the mighty pedestal of its hillock stretches the **Temple of Venus and Roma.** In part it was proudly designed by would-be architect Hadrian—at least until the true professional Apollodurus pointed out that with Hadrian's measurements the goddess risked bumping her head on the apse, a piece of advice for which he was repaid with banishment. Off to your left, on the spur of hillside jutting from the Palatine Hill, stands the famed **Arch of Titus.** Completed by his brother, and successor, Domitian in 81 AD, the arch in one frieze shows the Roman soldiery carrying away booty—Moses's candelabra, silver trumpets, an altar table—from the destruction of the Temple in Jerusalem 10 years earlier. On the other side there is Titus on the same Via Sacra, in this case being charioted toward the Capitol after the campaign in Palestine begun by his father Vespasian. Through the Arch, photograph the great vista of the entire Forum as it stretches toward the distant Capitoline Hill.

MASSIVE
MAXENTIUS

After carrying on for some hundred yards down the Via Sacra, take a small detour, doubling back to take in the massive **Basilica of Maxentius,** or the third of it left standing. Heavily damaged during Alaric's sack of Rome in 410, it had been founded by Maxentius in 306–310, then completed by Constantine the Great, Maxentius's archenemy at the battle of the Milvian Bridge. The three remaining side vaults give an idea of the building's scale; also to how, through their use of brick and barrel vaulting, the Romans had freed themselves from the tyranny of gravity. Here once stood—or sat rather—the surrealistically large head and other body fragments of Constantine (now in the outside courtyard of the Palazzo dei Conservatori), the first Christian emperor. Rome's first Christian basilica, San Giovanni in Laterano, originated many of the features used in the basilica here. Not surprisingly this most majestic of ruins was much admired and studied by the great Renaissance architects and painters alike—in Raphael's *School of Athens* the background edifice is surely a depiction of what you are seeing here. Today, the Basilica is the site of wonderful concerts in summer and the occasional dramatized trial of this or that emperor (i.e., Nero and Tiberius).

TEMPLES STILL
STANDING
TALL

Resuming your walk back toward the Capitoline Hill, the next building is the **Temple of Romulus.** The Romulus here is not Rome's founder but the son of Emperor Maxentius. Apart from the Pantheon, this is the only Roman temple to remain entirely intact—so intact even the lock in the original bronze doors is said to still function. This is due to its having subsequently been used, at least until the late 19th century, as the atrium of a Christian church above. The stone work across the lintel is as perfect as when it was made, as are the two porphyry pillars. For an inside view of the same temple and, until a century ago, the attached church atrium, enter the Church of Cosma and Damiano from the Via dei Fori Inperiali side and peer through the glass at the end of the main chapel.

Proof of how deeply buried the Forum was throughout Medieval times can be seen in the wonderful pillars of the next building down, the **Temple of Antoninus and Faustina,** his wife. Those stains reaching halfway up are in fact centuries-old soil marks. Further evidence of the sinking Forum are the doors of the 13th-century church above—note how they seem to hang almost in midair. Now a full 30 feet above the temple's rebuilt steps, originally they would, of course, have been at ground level. Here we see an example of the Christian world not so much supplanting the pagan world as growing out of it. Meanwhile, there against the blue, read the words "Divo Antonino" and "Diva Faustina," proclaiming the couple's self-ordained "divination."

A CAESAR AMONG CAESARS Continue your walk toward the Capitoline Hill by strolling by the largely vanished **Basilica Emilia.** To the left, however, is the Temple of Caesar, sometimes referred to as **Caesar's Altar,** where, after his assassination from 23 knife wounds, Caesar's body was brought hotfoot for cremation. Peep behind the low wall and now in Caesar's honor there are flowers instead of flames. Now look up and head over, just across the road known as the Vicus Tuscus, to the three wonderfully white pillars of the **Temple of Castor and Pollux.** This was reconstructed by Augustus to pay homage to the twin sons of Jupiter and Leda who helped the Roman army to victory back in the 5th century BC. The emperor Caligula, says Suetonius, "had part of the temple incorporated into his palace as his own vestibule. Often he would stand between the divine brothers displaying himself for worship by those visiting the temple."

To this temple's right sits the **Basilica Julia.** After the death of Julius Caesar, all chaos broke loose in Rome, but a prelude to another long bout of civil war. This ended with the victory of Augustus who, ever the dutiful stepson, had this massive basilica completed in his father's honor. Pitted with column marks, the rectangular piece of ground remains. As with other Roman basilicas, the place was more judicial in nature, swarming, according to Pliny, with 180 judges and a plague of lawyers. Look carefully at the flooring and you might still spy a chessboard carved into the marble, perhaps by a bored litigant.

HAUNT OF THE VESTAL VIRGINS Backtrack a bit along the Via Sacra past the Temple of Castor and Pollux to the circular **Temple of Vesta.** In a tradition going back to an age when fire was a precious commodity, the famous Vestal Virgins kept the fire of Rome burning here. Of the original 20 columns only three remain, behind which stretch the vast remains of the **House of the Vestal Virgins.** Privileged in many ways—they had front-row seats in the Colosseum and rights of deciding life and death for poor gladiators,

See you later, gladiator: the Colosseum hosted gladiatorial combats for centuries and up to 30,000 may have tragically perished in its arena.

for example—they were also under a 30-year-long vow of chastity. As everyone knows, the notorious punishment for breaking their vow was being buried alive. But it is time to turn back and press on with our walk. Crossing the central square and walking back toward the towering Capitoline Hill, you are now entering the mid-section of the open area of the Forum proper; you can see to your left the **Pillar of Phocas.** The last monument to be built on the by now largely abandoned Forum was this column, erected by an otherwise forgotten Byzantine emperor. In 1813, on the orders of Pope Pius VII, the area was excavated, with the assumption that the column belonged to the Temple of Jove Custode. Then, at the base, surfaced the inscription, describing how it had been erected in 608 to the Christian emperor from the east on his bequeathing the Pantheon to the Roman Church.

A BURIAL TOO SOON The long stone platform presiding over this area is the famous **Rostra.** "Forum" coming from an old Latin word "to meet," from here Rome's political elite would address the people. Indeed, this is where, with some help from Shakespeare, Mark Antony would have pronounced his rabble-rousing "I come to bury Caesar, not to praise him." The name Rostra dates to the custom of adorning the platform with prows of captured ships following an early naval victory off Antium/Anzio in 338 BC.

Going back even farther is, on the other side of the Via Sacra, the so-called **Lapis Niger,** or Black Stone, which marks the site of a Temple to Romulus. The small sanctuary underneath goes back to the 6th century BC as does a strange column with the oldest Latin inscription yet known, cursing all those who profaned the place—irreverent archaeologists take note!

Altogether mightier in scale is the **Curia**—the Senate house of ancient Rome—nearby. Not the building of the earlier Republican period, this is a version rebuilt by Diocletian and in turn rebuilt in 1937. Here sat the 300 members of Senate, then rendered largely powerless by Diocletian. Originally decorating the nearby rostra, the two friezes show the much earlier emperor Trajan. Meanwhile the porphyry statue without a head has been attributed to Trajan also. But there is a neater theory: With the turnover in emperors reaching to as many as six per year and porphyry being almost priceless, the head was replaceable by whatever emperor happened to be in power.

HEADS AND TALES

Continue back down the Via Sacra, where towers one of the Forum's extant spectaculars, the **Arch of Septimus Severus.** Built by his sons, it celebrates Septimus's campaign against the Parthians and the ensuing influx into Rome of booty and slaves. A number of these, their hands tied behind them, are depicted. Also on view is the murderous Caracalla, son number two, though the head of his elder brother Gaeta has, Stalin-fashion, been erased. Sadly, many other heads have also had a Caracalla done on them by the erosive fumes of Roman traffic.

Continuing left and up the Via Sacra, you reach the base of the celebrated **Temple of Saturn.** Now the name of a planet, Saturn was then as close to the earth as you can get, the word originating from "sero"—to sow. Saturn was originally a corn god, first worshipped in Magna Grecia, then allowed, so goest the patriotic myth, to settle in Rome by the city's presiding deity, Janus. That Saturn was the God of Plenty in more than an agricultural sense is also attested to by the fact that beneath the floor was kept the wealth of the Roman treasury.

Position yourself below the easternmost two of the eight columns of Egyptian marble and peer upward as they reach higher than a rocket at Cape Kennedy and are every bit as majestic.

HAIL AND FAREWELL

Meanwhile, up ahead ascends the last stretch of the Via Sacra—the so-called Clivus Capitolinus. On the left is the **Temple of Vespasian.**

Bowing to the powerful nature of time, now only three splendid columns remain. Next door once stood the **Temple of Concord.**

Built back in Republican times, it celebrated the peace between the often warring patricians and plebs, the two cardinal elements in the winning formula of SPQR—in other words the patrician Senate (S) and the people (PQ). A few stones mark the spot—and the last piece in the Forum's monumental jigsaw.

For a better sense of the whole—a sort of archaeological gestalt—take the steps alongside to ascend to the Campidoglio, the Capitoline Hill, where vistas from the piazza balconies will put your two or three past hours of walking into panoramic context.

You cannot help but ponder on the truth of "sic transit Gloria"—a similar view by moonlight inspired Edward Gibbon to embark on his epic *Decline and Fall of the Roman Empire.*

Ancient Rome

CAMPIDOGLIO, ROMAN FORUM, IMPERIAL FORA, COLOSSEUM

WORD OF MOUTH

"Buy tickets at the Forum or Palatine and you can then walk straight to the bag-check area when you get to the Colosseum." —Cathies

"I walked to the Colosseum's center, stretched out my arms and yelled, 'Are you not entertained?' There was a small rumble of laughter and a few people chanted 'Maximus! Maximus!' "
—Edward2000

GETTING ORIENTED

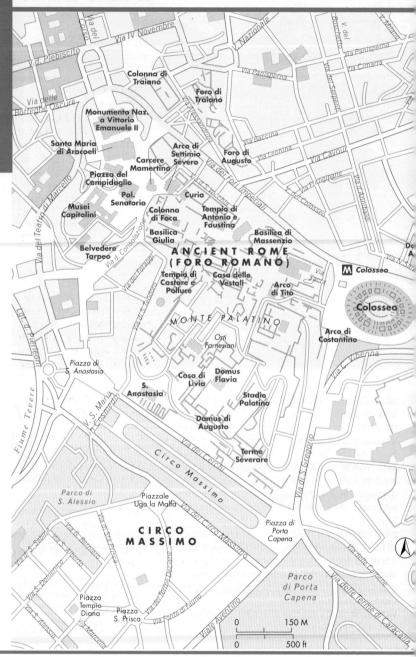

TOP 5 REASONS TO GO

The Colosseum: Clamber up the stands to the emperor's box, and imagine the gory games as Trajan saw them.

The Roman Forum: Walk through the crumbling, romantic ruins, a trip back through 2,000 years of history.

Sunset: Watch the sun go down over Ancient Rome from the back of the Campidoglio, the best view in town.

Capitoline Museums: Look eye-to-eye with the ancients—the busts of emperors and philosophers are more real than ideal.

Caffè Capitolino: Sip prosecco on the terrace of the Palazzo Caffarelli—part of the Musei Capitolini complex—while you take in a Cinerama scene of Roman rooftops.

O.K., WHERE DO I START?

On the congested Via di Teatro di Marcello, on the spot where emperors once halted their triumphal processions—and Fiats now honk in unison—climb Michelangelo's sloping cordonata walkway up the famed Capitoline Hill. Take in the views over the entire Foro Romano from the piazza terrace, then tour the celebrated museum complex—use the linking terrace to visit Santa Maria in Aracoeli. Use the church's staircase back down to the street (or backtrack to the cordonata to avoid the hundred-plus steps!) and walk past the "eighth hill of Rome"—the Monument to Victor Emmanuel—to find the entrance to the Roman Forum on the Via dei Fori Imperiali. From the Forum buy tickets to the Palatine Hill complex—these will allow you to jump the lines at the Colosseum. As all these sites are almost entirely outdoors, good weather is a must; the beaten-earth paths of the Foro Romano become muddy. In summer, get an early start on touring, as most sites are open to the sun, or consider an evening tour; the Capitoline museums are open until 8 PM, and the spotlit Victor Emmanuel II Monument and the Roman Forum are spectacularly striking at night.

GETTING HERE

The Colosseo metro station is right across from the Colosseum proper and a short walk from both the Roman and Trajan forums, as well as the Palatine Hill. Hoofing from the historic center will take about 20 minutes, much of it along the wide and busy Via dei Fori Imperiali. The little electric Bus No. 117 from the center or No. 175 from Termini will also deliver you to the Colosseum's doorstep. Any of the following buses will take you to or near the Roman Forum: Nos. 60, 75, 85, 95, and 175.

BEST TIME-OUTS

High-back leather couches, lounge music, and a hipster crowd make **Maud** (✉ *Via Capo d'Africa 6* ☎ *06/77590809*) the coolest watering hole in the Colosseum area. Reservations are a must for dining.

Who says ice cream has to make you fat? For generous scoops of delicious gelato—many of them soy-based, sugar-free, or fruit only—head from the Forum across Via dei Fori Imperiali to **Il Gelatone** (✉ *Via dei Serpenti 28* ☎ *06/4820187*).

About half a block east of the Colosseum is **Pasqualino** (✉ *Via dei Santi Quattro 66* ☎ *06/7004576*), a trattoria with sidewalk tables.

For an afternoon beer and a board-game break, stop by **La Pace per il Cervello 2** (✉ *Via Santi Quattro 63* ☎ *06/7005173*).

If you ever wanted to feel like the Caesars—with all of ancient Rome (literally) at your feet—simply head to Michelangelo's famed Piazza del Campidoglio. There, make a beeline for the terrace flanking the side of the center building, the Palazzo Senatorio, Rome's ceremonial city hall. From this balcony atop the Capitoline Hill you can take in a panorama that seems like a remnant of some forgotten Cecil B. DeMille movie spectacular.

For looming before you is the entire Roman Forum, the *"caput mundi"*—the center of the known world for centuries, where much of the history of the past 2,500 years happened. Here, all Rome shouted as one, "Caesar has been murdered," and crowded to hear Mark Antony's eulogy for the fallen leader. Here, legend has it that St. Paul traversed the Forum en route to his audience with Nero. Here, Roman law and powerful armies were created, keeping the barbarian world at bay for a millennium. And here the Roman emperors staged the biggest blowout extravaganzas ever mounted for the entire population of a city, outdoing even Elizabeth Taylor's Forum entry in *Cleopatra*.

But after a more than 27-century-long parade of pageantry you'll find that much has changed in this area, known to many locals as the Campitelli (or "Fields"). The rubble-scape of marble fragments scattered over the Forum area makes all but students of archaeology ask: Is this the grandeur that was Rome? After viewing the same, it's not surprising that Shelley and Gibbon once reflected on the sense of *sic transit gloria mundi*—"thus pass the glories of the world." Yet spectacular monuments—the Arch of Septimius Severus, the Palatine Hill, and the Colosseum (looming in the background), among them—remind us that this was indeed the birthplace of much of Western civilization.

Before the Christian era, before the emperors, before the powerful Republic that ruled the ancient seas, Rome was founded on seven hills, and two of them—the Capitoline and the Palatine—surround the Roman Forum, where the Romans of the later Republic and Imperial ages worshipped deities, debated politics, and wheeled and dealed. It's all history now (except on the fringes, this area has no residents besides lazy lizards and complacent cats) but this remains one of the world's most striking and significant concentrations of ancient remains—an emphatic reminder of the genius and power that made Rome the fountainhead of the Western world.

THE CAMPIDOGLIO

3

Your first taste of ancient Rome should start from a point that embodies some of Rome's earliest and greatest moments: the Campidoglio. Here, on the Capitoline Hill (which towers over the traffic hub of Piazza Venezia), a meditative Edward Gibbon was inspired to write his 1764 classic, *The History of the Decline and Fall of the Roman Empire,* for here is where it all began. Of Rome's famous seven hills, the Capitoline is the smallest and most sacred—it has always been the seat of Rome's government and its Latin name is echoed in the designation of the national and state capitol buildings of every country in the world.

TOP ATTRACTIONS

Fodor's Choice
★
Musei Capitolini. Surpassed in sheer size and richness only by the Musei Vaticani, this immense collection was the first public museum in the world. A greatest-hits collection of Roman art through the ages, from the ancients to the baroque, it is housed in the twin Museo Capitolino and Palazzo dei Conservatori that bookend Michelangelo's famous piazza. Here, you'll find some of antiquity's most famous sculptures, such as the poignant *Dying Gaul,* the regal *Capitoline Venus,* the *Esquiline Venus* (identified as another Mediterranean beauty, Cleopatra herself), and the *Lupa Capitolina,* the very symbol of Rome itself. Although some pieces in the collection—first assembled by Sixtus IV (1414–84), one of the earliest of the Renaissance popes—may excite only archaeologists and art historians, others are unforgettable, including the original bronze statue of Marcus Aurelius whose copy sits in the piazza.

Buy your ticket and enter the museums on the right of the piazza (as you face the center Palazzo Senatorio), into the building known as the Palazzo dei Conservatori. Before picking up a useful free map from the cloakroom, you cannot miss some of the biggest body parts ever: that giant head, foot, elbow, and imperially raised finger across the courtyard are what remains of the fabled seated statue of Constantine, which once filled the Basilica of Maxentius, his defeated rival (and the other body parts were of wood, lest the figure collapse under its own weight). Constantine the Great believed that Rome's future lay with Christianity and such immense effigies were much in vogue in the latter days of the Roman Empire. Take the stairs up past a series of intricately detailed ancient marble reliefs to the resplendent Salone dei Orazi e Curiazi (Salon of Horatii and Curatii) on the first floor. The ceremonial hall is decorated with a magnificent gilt ceiling, carved wooden doors, and 16th-century frescoes depicting the history of ancient Rome. At both ends of the hall are statues of the baroque era's most charismatic popes: a marble Urban VIII (1568–1644) by Gian Lorenzo Bernini (1598–1680) and a bronze Innocent X (1574–1655) by Bernini's rival, Algardi (1595–1654).

THE CAMPIDOGLIO

✉ *Piazza dei Campidoglio, incorporating the Palazzo Senatorio and the 2 Capitoline Museums, the Palazzo Nuovo, and the Palazzo dei Conservatori.*

TIPS

■ The piazza centerpiece is the legendary equestrian statue of Emperor Marcus Aurelius but, as of 1999, a copy took up residence here when the actual 2nd-century ad statue moved to a new wing in the surrounding Musei Capitolini: the Sala Marco Aurelio and its glass room also protect a gold-plated Hercules along with more massive body parts, this time bronze, of what might be Constantine or that of his son Constans II (archaeologists are still undecided).

■ While there are great views to be had of the Roman Forum from the terrace balconies on either side of the Palazzo Senatorio, remember the best view may be from the Tabularium, the arcade balcony below the Senatorio building and accessed with admission to the Musei Capitolini—the museum also has the Terrazza Cafarelli, featuring a restaurant with a magical view looking toward Trastevere and St. Peter's.

Spectacularly transformed by Michelangelo's late-Renaissance designs, the Campidoglio was once the epicenter of the Roman empire, the place where the city's first shrines stood, including its most sacred, the Temple of Jupiter.

Originally, the Capitoline Hill consisted of two peaks: the Capitolium and the Arx (where Santa Maria in Aracoeli now stands). The hollow between them was known as the Asylum: here, prospective settlers once came to seek the protection of Romulus, legendary first king of Rome—hence the term "asylum." Later, during the Republic, in 78 BC, the Tabularium, or Hall of Records, was erected here.

By the Middle Ages, however, the Capitoline had become an unkempt hill strewn with ancient rubble.

In preparation for the impending visit of Charles V in 1536, triumphant after the empire's victory over the Moors, his host, Pope Paul III Farnese, decided that the Holy Roman Emperor should follow the route of the emperors, climaxing at the Campidoglio.

But the pope was embarrassed by the decrepit goat pasture the hill had become and commanded Michelangelo to restore the site to glory; he added a third palace along with Renaissance-style facades and a grand paved piazza.

Newly excavated ancient sculptures, designed to impress the visiting emperor, were installed in the palaces, and the piazza was ornamented with the giant stone figures of the Discouri and the ancient Roman equestrian statue of Emperor Marcus Aurelius (original now in Musei Capitolini)—the latter a visual reference to the corresponding glory of Charles V and the ancient emperor.

Proceeding to the collection of ancient sculpture, the first room contains the exquisite "Spinario": proving that the most everyday action can be as poetic as any imperial bust, a small boy in the act removing a thorn becomes unwittingly immortalized. Nearby is the rather eery glass-eyed bust of Junius Brutus, first Roman Consul. Farther along is a separate room devoted to the renowned symbol of Rome, the Capitoline Wolf, a 5th-century BC Etruscan bronze, the Romulus and Remus below being late additions by Antonio Pollaiolo (15th century). Donated by Sixtus IV, the work came to symbolize Roman unity.

MARCUS
AURELIUS
STATUE

The heart of the museum, however, is the Exedra of Marcus Aurelius (Sala Marco Aurelio), a large, airy room with skylights and high windows, which showcases the spectacular original bronze statue of the Roman emperor whose copy sits in the piazza below. Created in the 2nd century AD, the statue should have been melted down like so many other bronze statues of emperors after the decline of Rome, but this one is thought to have survived because it was mistaken for the Christian emperor Constantine. To the right the room segues into the area of the Temple of Jupiter, with its original ruins rising organically into the museum space. A reconstruction of the temple and Capitol Hill from the Bronze Age to present day make for a fascinating glance through the ages. Some of the pottery and bones on display were dug up from as early as the 12th century BC, recasting Romulus and Remus as Johnny-come-latelies.

Off left are rooms dedicated to statuary from the so-called Horti, or gardens of Ancient Rome's great and mega-rich. From the Horti Lamiani is the Venere Esquilina doing her hair. (Look for the fingers at the back, at the end of the missing arms.) Believe or not, you might be gazing at the young Cleopatra invited to Rome by Julius Caesar. So, anyway, say some experts—a further clue is the asp. In the same room is an extraordinary bust of the Emperor Commodus, seen here as Hercules and unearthed in the late 1800s during building work for the new capital. On the top floor is the museum's pinacoteca, or painting gallery, which has some noted baroque masterpieces, including Caravaggio's *The Fortune Teller* (1595) and *St. John the Baptist* (1602; albeit, given the ram, some critics see here a representation of Isaac, the pose this time influenced by Michelangelo's "Ignudi"), Peter Paul Rubens's (1577–1640) *Romulus and Remus* (1614), and Pietro da Cortona's (1627) sumptuous portrait of Pope Urban VIII. Adjacent to the Palazzo dei Conservatori is **Palazzo Caffarelli,** where temporary exhibitions are mounted. Here, set on the Piazzale Caffarelli, the new Caffè Capitolino offers a spectacular vista over Rome (looking toward St. Peter's)—it is open daily (except Monday) 9 to 8.

To reach the Palazzo Nuovo section of the museum (the palace on the left-hand side of the Campidoglio), take the stairs or elevator to the basement of the Palazzo dei Conservatori, where a an underground corridor called the Galleria Congiunzione holds a poignant collection of ancient gravestones. But before going up into Palazzo Nuovo, be sure to take the detour to the right to the Tabularium Gallery with its unparalleled view over the Forum.

A treasure of the Musei Capitolini, this highly ornate ancient Roman sarcophagus proclaimed the wealthy status of the owner, even in death.

ROOM OF THE EMPERORS Inside the Palazzo Nuovo on the stairs you find yourself immediately dwarfed by Mars in full military rig and lion-topped sandals. Upstairs is the noted Sala degli Imperatori, lined with busts of Roman emperors, along with the Sala dei Filosofi, where busts of philosophers sit in judgment—a fascinating who's who of the ancient world, and a must-see of the museum. Although many ancient Roman treasures were merely copies of Greek originals, portraiture was one area in which the Romans took precedence. Within these serried ranks are 48 Roman emperors, ranging from Augustus to Theodosius (AD 346–395). On one console, you'll see the handsomely austere Augustus, who "found Rome a city of brick and left it one of marble." On another rests Claudius "the stutterer," an indefatigable builder brought vividly to life in the history-based novel *I, Claudius*, by Robert Graves. Also in this company is Nero, one of the most notorious emperors who built for himself the fabled Domus Aurea. And, of course, there are the standout baddies: cruel Caligula (AD 12–41) and Caracalla (AD 186–217), and the dissolute, eerily modern boy-emperor, Heliogabalus (AD 203–222). In the adjacent Great Hall, be sure to take in the 16 resplendently restored marble statues. Nearby are rooms filled with masterpieces, including the legendary *Dying Gaul*, *The Red Faun* from Hadrian's Villa, and a *Cupid and Psyche*—each worth almost a museum to itself. Downstairs near the exit is the gigantic, reclining figure of Oceanus, found in the Roman Forum and later dubbed Marforio, one of Rome's famous "talking statues" to which citizens from the 1500s to the 1900s affixed anonymous satirical verses and notes of political protest. ⊠ *Piazza del Campidoglio, Campidoglio* ☎ *06/39967800, reservations 06/82059127* ⊕ *www.museicapitolini.org*

3

€6.50, €6 *with Romacard; audio guide €5* ⊙ *Tues.–Sun. 9–8* Ⓜ *Bus 44, 63, 170, 175, 186, 571.*

Santa Maria di Aracoeli. Sitting atop its 124 steps—"the grandest loafing place of mankind," as Henry James put it, and the spot on which Gibbon was inspired to write his great history of the decline and fall of the Roman empire—Santa Maria di Aracoeli perches on the north slope of the Capitoline Hill (where you can also access the church using a less challenging staircase from Michelangelo's piazza). The church rests on the site of the temple of Juno Moneta (Admonishing Juno), which also housed the Roman mint (hence the origin of the word "money"). According to legend, it was here that the Sibyl (a prophetess) predicted to Augustus the coming of a Redeemer. The emperor supposedly responded by erecting an altar, the Ara Coeli (Altar of Heaven). This was eventually replaced by a Benedictine monastery then church, which passed in 1250 to the Franciscans, who restored and enlarged it in Romanesque-Gothic style. Today, the Aracoeli is best known for the **Santa Bambino,** a much-revered olive-wood figure of the Christ Child (today a copy of the 15th-century original stolen in 1994 and as yet unfound). At Christmas, everyone pays homage to the Bambi Gesù as children recite poems from a miniature pulpit. In true Roman style, the church interior is a historical hodgepodge—classical columns and large marble fragments from pagan buildings, as well as a 13th-century Cosmatesque pavement. The richly gilded Renaissance ceiling commemorates the naval victory at Lepanto in 1571 over the Turks. The first chapel on the right is noteworthy for Pinturicchio's frescoes of San Bernardino of Siena (1486). ✉ *Via del Teatro di Marcello, on top of steep stairway, Campidoglio* ☎ *06/6798155* ⊙ *9–12:30, 3–6:30* Ⓜ *Bus 44, 160, 170, 175, 186.*

THAT FACE, THAT FACE!

Unlike the Greeks, whose portraits were idealized, the Romans preferred the "warts and all" school of representation. Many of the busts that have come down to us, notably that of Commodus (AD 161–192), the emperor-gladiator, are almost brutally realistic. Movie-lovers will want to search out this bust of the man who added nothing to the Roman way of life except new ways of dying—this was the original of the amazing man portrayed by Christopher Plummer in *The Fall of the Roman Empire* and by Joaquin Phoenix in *Gladiator.*

WORTH NOTING

Belvedere Tarpeo. This was the infamous Tarpeian Rock from which traitors were hurled to the ground in Roman times. In the 18th and 19th centuries, it became a popular stop for people making the Grand Tour, because of the view it gave of the Palatine Hill. Today, the Belvedere viewing point has actually been long shuttered for restoration, but you can proceed a short walk down to Via di Monte Tarpeio where the view is spectacular enough. It was on this Rock that, in the 7th century BC, Tarpeia betrayed the Roman citadel to the early Romans' sworn enemies, the Sabines, only asking in return to be given the heavy gold bracelets the Sabines wore on their left arm. The scornful Sabines did indeed shower her with their gold, then added the crushing weight of

An Emperor Cheat Sheet

CLOSE UP

OCTAVIAN, later known as Caesar Augustus, was Rome's first emperor (27 BC– AD 14), and his rule began a 200-year peace known as the Pax Romana.

The name of **NERO** (AD 54–68) lives in infamy as a violent persecutor of Christians, and as the murderer of his wife, his mother, and countless others. Although it's not certain whether he actually fiddled as Rome burned in AD 64, he was well known as an actor.

DOMITIAN (AD 81–96) declared himself "Dominus et Deus," Lord and God. He stripped away power from the Senate, and as a result after his death he suffered "Damnatio Memoriae"— the Senate had his name and image erased from all public records.

TRAJAN (AD 98–117), the first Roman emperor to be born outside Italy (in southern Spain), enlarged the empire's boundaries to include modern-day Romania, Armenia, and Upper Mesopotamia.

HADRIAN (AD 117–138) is best known for designing and rebuilding the Pantheon, constructing a majestic villa at Tivoli, and initiating myriad other constructions, including the famed wall across Britain.

MARCUS AURELIUS (AD 161–180) is remembered as a humanitarian emperor, a Stoic philosopher whose *Meditations* are still read today. Nonetheless, he was devoted to expansion and an aggressive leader of the empire.

CONSTANTINE I (AD 306–337) made his mark by legalizing Christianity, an act that changed the course of history, legitimizing the once-banned religion and paving the way for the papacy in Rome.

their heavy shields, also carried on their left arm. ⊠ *Via del Tempio di Giove, Campidoglio.*

Carcere Mamertino *(Mamertine Prison)*. The Mamertino consists of two subterranean cells where Rome's enemies, most famously the Goth, Jugurtha, and the indomitable Gaul, Vercingetorix, were imprisoned and died, of either starvation or strangulation. In the lower cell, St. Peter himself is believed to have been held prisoner and to have miraculously brought forth a spring of water, from which to baptize his jailers. A church, San Giuseppe dei Falegnami, now stands over the prison. ⊠ *Via del Tulliano, Campidoglio Venezia* ▨ *Donations requested* ☉ *Closed for restoration with possible reopening in 2010.*

Palazzo Senatorio. During the Middle Ages this city hall looked like the medieval town halls you can see in Tuscan hill towns, part fortress and part assembly hall. The building was entirely rebuilt in the 1500s as part of Michelangelo's revamping of the Campidoglio for Pope Paul III; the master's design was adapted by later architects, who wisely left the front staircase as the focus of the facade. The ancient statue of Minerva at the center was renamed the Goddess Rome, and the river gods (the River Tigris remodeled to symbolize the Tiber, to the right, and the Nile, to the left) were hauled over from the Terme di Costantino on the Quirinal Hill. Today, it is the regional seat of Rome's Comune administration and is not open to the public. ⊠ *Piazza del Campidoglio, Campidoglio.*

THE ROMAN FORUM

From the main entrance on Via dei Fori Imperali, descend into the extraordinary archaeologial complex that is the Foro Romano. This was once the heart of Republican Rome, the austere enclave that preceded the hedonistic society of the emperors and the pleasure-crazed citizens of imperial Rome from the 1st to the 4th century AD. It began life as a marshy valley between the Capitoline and Palatine hills—a

valley crossed by a mud track and used as a cemetery by Iron Age settlers. Over the years a market center and some huts were established here, and after the land was drained in the 6th century BC, the site eventually became a political, religious, and commercial center—namely, the Forum.

Hundreds of years of plunder reduced the Forum to its current desolate state. It's difficult to imagine that this enormous area was once Rome's pulsating heart, filled with stately and extravagant temples, palaces, and shops, and crowded with people from all corners of the empire. Adding to the confusion is the fact that the Forum developed over many centuries; what you see today are not the ruins from just one period but from a span of almost 900 years, from about 500 BC to AD 400. Nonetheless, the enduring romance of the place, with its lonely columns and great broken fragments of sculpted marble and stone, makes for a quintessential Roman experience. ⊠ *Entrances at Via dei Fori Imperiali and Piazza del Colosseo, Roman Forum* ☎ *06/39967700* ⊕ *www.pierreci.it* ⬚ *€12 (combined ticket with the Colosseum, Palatine Hill, and Imperial Forums, if used within 2 days), €4.50 Roman* Forum *and Palatine Hill only; guided tour €4.50, audio guide €4* ⊗ *Daily 8:30–7:15 (6:15 last entrance)* Ⓜ *Colosseo.*

TOP ATTRACTIONS

Fodor'sChoice ★ **Arco di Settimio Severo** *(Arch of Septimius Severus).* One of the grandest arches of triumph erected by a Roman emperor, this richly decorated monument was built in AD 203 to celebrate Severus's victory over the Parthians. It was once topped by a bronze statuary group of a chariot drawn by four or perhaps as many as six life-size horses. Masterpieces of Roman statuary, the stone reliefs on the arch were probably based on huge painted panels depicting the event, a kind of visual report on his foreign campaigns that would have been displayed during the emperor's triumphal parade in Rome to impress his subjects (and, like all statuary back then, were painted in florid, lifelike colors). ⊠ *West end of Foro Romano, Roman Forum.*

★ **Arco di Tito** *(Arch of Titus).* Standing at a slightly elevated position at the northern approach to the Palatine Hill on the Via Sacra, this triumphal arch was erected in AD 81 to celebrate the sack of Jerusalem 10 years earlier, after the great Jewish revolt. The view of the Colosseum from the arch is superb, and reminds us that it was the emperor Titus who helped finish the vast amphitheater, begun earlier by his father, Vespasian. Under the arch are the two great sculpted reliefs, both showing scenes from Titus's triumphal parade along this very Via Sacra, including the spoils of war plundered from Herod's Temple—a gigantic seven-branched candelabrum (menorah) and silver trumpets. During his sacking of Jerusalem, Titus killed or deported most of the Jewish population, thus initiating the Jewish diaspora, an event that would have historical consequences for millennia. ⊠ *East end of Via Sacra, Roman Forum.*

Basilica di Massenzio *(Basilica of Maxentius).* What remains of this gigantic basilica—or meeting hall—is only about one-third of the original, so you can imagine what a wonder this building was when erected. Today, the great arched vaults of this structure still dominate the north side of the Via Sacra. Begun under the emperor Maxentius about AD 306, the edifice was a center of judicial and commercial activity, the last of its kind to be built in Rome. Over the centuries, like so many Roman monuments, it was exploited as a quarry for building materials and was stripped of its sumptuous marble and stucco decorations. Its coffered vaults, like the coffering inside the Pantheon's dome, were later copied by many Renaissance artists and architects. ⊠ *Via Sacra, Roman Forum.*

Comitium. The open space in front of the Curia was the political hub of ancient Rome. Julius Caesar had rearranged the Comitium, moving the Curia to its current site and transferring the imperial **Rostra**, the podium from which orators spoke to the people (decorated originally with the prows of captured ships, or *rostra*, the source for the term "rostrum"), to a spot just south of the Arch of Septimius Severus. It was from this location that Mark Antony delivered his funeral address in Caesar's honor. On the left of the Rostra stands what remains of the **Tempio di Saturno,** which served as ancient Rome's state treasury. ⊠ *West end of Foro Romano, Roman Forum.*

Curia. The best-preserved building of the Forum, this large brick building next to the Arch of Septimius Severus was built during the era of Diocletian in the late 3rd century AD. By that time the Senate, which met here, had lost practically all of the power and prestige that it had possessed during the Republican era, becoming a mere echo chamber for the decisions reached in other centers of power. Still, this gives one a haunting

THE RISE AND FALL OF ANCIENT ROME

ca. 800 BC	Rise of Etruscan city-states.
510	Foundation of the Roman republic; expulsion of Etruscans from Roman territory.
343	Roman conquest of Greek colonies in Campania.
264–241	First Punic War (with Carthage): increased naval power helps Rome gain control of southern Italy and then Sicily.
218–200	Second Punic War: Hannibal's attempted conquest of Italy, using elephants, is eventually crushed.
150 BC	Roman Forum begins to take shape as the principal civic center in Italy.

image of Roman life back when. ✉ *Via Sacra, northwest corner of Foro Romano, Roman Forum.*

★ **Tempio di Castore e Polluce.** One of the most evocative images of ancient Roman architecture, the sole three remaining Corinthian columns of this temple beautifully conjure up the former elegant grandeur of the Forum. This temple was dedicated in 484 BC to Castor and Pollux, the twin brothers of Helen of Troy who carried to Rome the news of victory at Lake Regillus, southeast of Rome—the definitive defeat of the deposed Tarquin dynasty. The twins flew on their fabulous white steeds over the 20 km (12 mi) distance between the lake and the city to bring the news to the people before mortal messengers could

AIN'T MISBEHAVIN'

Whoever said that bad girls have all the fun? In ancient Rome, the six physically perfect Vestal Virgins, chosen when they were prepubescent, lived a life of luxury in the sumptuous Casa dell Vestali. As protectors of the Empire, the Virgins had to keep the sacred fire of Vesta lit (if it went out, the Empire would fall). In return, the fortunate femmes were given the best seats in the Colosseum, rode around in special chariots, knew all the imperial gossip, and acted as judges. The catch: if they broke their 30-year vow of chastity, they were buried alive.

arrive. Rebuilt over the centuries before Christ, the temple suffered a major fire and was reconstructed by Emperor Tiberius in 12 BC, the date of the three standing columns. ✉ *West of House of the Vestals, Roman Forum.*

★ **Tempio di Vesta.** While just a fragment of the original building, the remnant of this temple is evidence of the sophisticated elegance that architecture achieved under the later Empire. Set off by florid Corinthian columns, the circular tholos was rebuilt by Emperor Septimius Severus when he restored this temple around AD 205. Dedicated to Vesta—the goddess of the hearth—the highly privileged vestal virgins kept the sacred vestal flame alive. Next to the temple, the ruins of the **Casa delle Vestali** give no hint of the splendor in which the women lived out their 30-year vows of chastity. Inside was the garden courtyard of their palace, surrounded by lofty colonnades, behind which extended at least 50 rooms. Chosen when they were between 6 and 10 years old, the

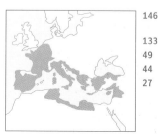

146	Third Punic War: Rome razes city of Carthage and emerges as the dominant Mediterranean force.
133	Rome rules entire Mediterranean Basin except Egypt.
49	Julius Caesar conquers Gaul.
44	Julius Caesar is assassinated.
27	Rome's Imperial Age begins; Octavian (now named Augustus) becomes the first emperor and is later deified. The Augustan Age is celebrated in the works of Virgil (70 BC–AD 19), Ovid (43 BC–AD 17), Livy (59 BC–AD 17), and Horace (65–8 BC).

six vestal virgins dedicated the next 30 years of their lives to keeping the sacred fire, a tradition that dated back to the very earliest days of Rome, when guarding the community's precious fire was essential to its well-being. Their standing in Rome was considerable; indeed, among women, they were second in rank only to the empress. Their intercession could save a condemned man, and they did, in fact, rescue Julius Caesar from the lethal vengeance of his enemy Sulla. The virgins were handsomely maintained by the state, but if they allowed the sacred fire to go out, they were scourged by the high priest, and if they broke their vows of celibacy, they were buried alive. The vestal virgins were one of the last of ancient Rome's institutions to die out, enduring as late as the end of the 4th century AD, even after Rome's emperors had become Christian. ⊠ *South side of Via Sacra, Roman Forum.*

Via Sacra. The celebrated basalt-paved road that loops through the Roman Forum, lined with temples and shrines, was also the traditional route of religious and triumphal processions. It's now little more than a dirt track, but there are occasional patches of the paving stones—stones once trod by Caesars and plebs—rutted with the ironclad wheels of Roman wagons. If you ever wanted to walk where Mark Antony did, this is your chance. ⊠ *Roman Forum.*

WORTH NOTING

Basilica Emilia. Once a great colonnaded hall, this served as a meeting place for merchants and a kind of community center of the 2nd century BC; it was later rebuilt in the 1st century AD by Augustus. The term "basilica" refers not strictly to the purpose of a church, but to a particular architectural form developed by the Romans. A rectangular hall flanked by colonnades, it could serve as a court of law or a center for business and commerce. Some Roman basilicas were later converted into churches, and the early models proved remarkably durable in the design of later Roman churches; there are 13th-century churches in the city that are fundamentally no different from many built during the 5th and 6th centuries AD. ⊠ *On right as you descend into Roman Forum from Via dei Fori Imperiali entrance, Roman Forum.*

Basilica Giulia. The Basilica Giulia owes its name to Julius Caesar, who ordered its construction, and was later completed by his adopted heir Augustus. One of several such basilicas in the center of Rome, it was

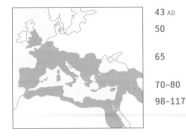

43 AD	Rome invades Britain.
50	Rome is the largest city in the world, with a population of a million.
65	Emperor Nero begins the persecution of Christians in the Empire; Saints Peter and Paul are executed.
70–80	Vespasian builds the Colosseum.
98–117	Trajan's military successes are celebrated with his Baths (98), Forum (110), and Column (113); the Roman Empire reaches its apogee.

where the Centumviri, the hundred-or-so judges forming the civil court, met to hear cases. The open space between the Basilica Emilia and this basilica was the heart of the Forum proper, prototype of Italy's famous piazzas, and the center of civic and social activity in ancient Rome. ⊠ *Via Sacra, Roman Forum.*

Colonna di Foca *(Pillar of Phocas).* The last monument to be added to the Forum was erected in AD 608 in honor of a Byzantine emperor who had donated the Pantheon to Pope Boniface IV. It stands 44 feet high and remains in good condition. ⊠ *West end of Foro Romano, Roman Forum.*

3

Santa Francesca Romana. This church, a 10th-century edifice with a Renaissance facade, is dedicated to the patron saint of motorists; on her feast day, March 9, cars and taxis crowd the Via dei Fori Imperiali below for a special blessing—a cardinal and carabinieri on hand plus special siren to start off the ceremony. The incomparable setting continues to be a favorite for weddings. ⊠ *Piazza di Santa Francesca Romana, next to Colosseum Roman Forum.*

Santa Maria Antiqua. The earliest Christian site in the Forum was originally part of an imperial temple, before it was converted into a church some time in the 5th or 6th century. Within are some exceptional but faded 7th- and 8th-century frescoes of the early church fathers, saints, and popes; the styles vary from typically classical to Oriental, reflecting the empire's expansion eastward. Largely destroyed in a 9th-century earthquake, the church was abandoned only to be rebuilt in 1617, then knocked down again in 1900 following excavation work on the Forum. Its latest incarnation is still off-limits to visitors, along with restored frescoes you can read about but still not see. ⊠ *South of Tempio di Castore and Polluce, at foot of Palatine Hill, Roman Forum.*

Tempio di Antonino e Faustina. Erected by the Senate in honor of Faustina, deified wife of emperor Antoninus Pius (AD 138–161), Hadrian's successor, this temple was rededicated to the emperor himself upon his death. Because it was transformed into a church, it's one of the best-preserved ancient structures in the Forum. ⊠ *North of Via Sacra, Roman Forum.*

Tempio di Cesare. Built by Augustus, Caesar's successor, the temple stands over the spot where Julius Caesar's body was cremated. A pyre was

238 AD	The first wave of Germanic invasions penetrates Italy.
293	Diocletian reorganizes the Empire into West and East.
330	Constantine founds a new Imperial capital (Constantinople) in the East.
410	Rome is sacked by Visigoths.
476	The last Roman emperor, Romulus Augustus, is deposed. The Roman Empire falls.

improvised by grief-crazed citizens who kept the flames going with their own possessions. ⊠ *Between 2 forks of Via Sacra, Roman Forum.*

Tempio di Venere e Roma. The now-truncated columns of this temple (once Rome's largest), dedicated to Venus and Rome, begun by Hadrian in AD 121, frame a view of the Colosseum. ⊠ *East of Arco di Tito, Roman Forum.*

Tempio di Vespasiano. All that remains of Vespasian's temple are three graceful Corinthian columns. They marked the site of the Forum through the centuries while the rest was hidden beneath overgrown rubble. Nearby is the ruined platform that was the **Tempio di Concordia.** ⊠ *West end of Foro Romano, Roman Forum.*

THE PALATINE HILL

Just beyond the Arch of Titus lies the Clivus Palatinus, which rises up a slight incline to the heights of the **Colle Palatino** (Palatine Hill), the oldest inhabited site in Rome. Despite its location overlooking the Forum's traffic and attendant noise, the Palatine was the most coveted address for ancient Rome's rich and famous. More than a few of the Twelve Caesars called the Palatine home, including Caligula, who was murdered in the still-standing and unnerving (even today) tunnel, the Cryptoporticus. The palace of Tiberius was the first to be built here; others followed, notably the gigantic extravaganza constructed for Emperor Domitian. But perhaps the most famous lodging goes back to Rome's very beginning. Once upon a time, skeptics thought Romulus was a myth. Then about a century ago, Rome's greatest archaeologist, Rodolfo Lanciani, excavated a site on the hill and uncovered the remains of an Iron Age settlement dating back to the 9th century BC, supporting the belief that Romulus, founder of Rome, lived here. Then in the fall of 2007, archaeologists unearthed a sacred sanctuary dedicated to Romulus and Remus set beneath the House of Augustus near the Palatine Hill; this sanctuary is now being renovated but it will undoubtedly take many years for this project to be completed.

During the Republican era the Palatino became the "Beverly Hills" of ancient Rome. Hortensius, Cicero, Catiline, Crassus, and Agrippa all had homes here. Augustus was born on the hill; the House of Livia, reserved for Augustus's wife, is today the best-preserved structure. To visit the ruins of the Palatine (some scholars think this name gave rise to our term "palace") in a roughly chronological order, start from the southeast area facing the Aventine. ⊠ *Entrances at Piazza del Colosseo and Via di San Gregorio 30, Roman Forum* ☎ *06/39967700 (guided visits 06/520726)* ⊕ *www.pierreci.it* ✎ *€12 (combined ticket with the Colosseum, Roman Forum, and Imperial Forums, if used within 2 days), €4.50 Roman Forum and Palatine Hill only* ⊙ *Daily 8:30 –7:15 (6:15 last entrance)* Ⓜ *Colosseo.*

TOP ATTRACTIONS

★ **Casa di Augustus** *(House of Augustus).* First discovered in the 1970s and only opened in 2006, this was the residence of the great Emperor Augustus (27 BC–14 AD)—before he became great (or at least one side

The "Bel Air" of ancient Rome, the Palatine Hill was the address of choice of Cicero, Agrippa, and the emperors Tiberius, Caligula, and Domitian.

of his residence, archaeologists having recently discovered, in the style of Rome's ancient Greek kings, two courtyards rather than one). The house here dates to the time when Augustus was known merely as Octavio, before he was adopted by his great uncle Julius Caesar as next in line to rule. Four rooms have exquisite examples of Roman wall decorative frescoes (so precious that only five people at a time are admitted). Startlingly vivid and detailed are the depictions of a narrow stage with side doors and some striking comic theater masks. ⊠ *Northwest crest of Palatino* ☎ *06/39967700* ⊕ *www.pierreci.it* ⊙ *July–Sept., Mon. 10:30–1:30, Wed., Thurs., weekends 8:30–1:30.*

★ **Casa di Livia** *(House of Livia).* First excavated in 1839, this house was identifiable from the name inscribed on a lead pipe, Iulia Augusta. In other words, the notorious Livia that made a career of dispatching half of the Roman imperial family—if Robert Graves's *I, Claudius* can be believed. She was the wife of perhaps the greatest emperor of them all, Augustus. Once he defeated Antony and Cleopatra, he inaugurated the Imperial Age, when Roman civilization exploded across the world. Back at home, Livia was busy dispatching successors to the royal line, to ensure that her son Tiberius, product of an earlier marriage, would take the throne. Here, atop the Palatine, she hatched her plots in this Casa—this was her private retreat and living quarters, not part of her state apartments. The delicate, delightful frescoes reflect the sophisticated taste of wealthy Romans, whose love of beauty and theatrical conception of nature were revived by their descendants in the Renaissance Age. ⊠ *Northwest crest of Palatino* ☎ *06/39967450* ⊕ *www.pierreci.it* ⊙ *Tues.–Thurs. 9–1.*

Continued on page 86

ROME WAS NOT
BUILT IN A DAY

by Robert I. C. Fisher

RE-CREATING THE ANCIENT CITY

"All roads lead to Rome" but leave many visitors confused, disoriented, and befuddled. Travelers arrive at the Roman Forum hoping to discover Caesar's World, only to find a picturesque pile of rubble. Could this actually be where Nero once fiddled? Where Mark Antony buried Caesar? To dish the dirt—archaeologically speaking—this guide skillfully interweaves gobs of ancient landmarks to help re-create the ancient city, connecting the dots through time and space. Part atlas, part rendering, part historical tip-sheet, it unfolds like a cloak-and-trowel thriller.

Although it has been the capital of the Republic of Italy only since 1946, Rome has been the capital of *something* for more than 2,500 years, and it shows. The magnificent ruins of the Palatine Hill, the ancient complexity of the Forum, the Renaissance harmony of the Campidoglio—all are part of Rome's identity as one of the world's most enduring seats of government.

This is not to say that it's been an easy 2½ millennia. The Vandal hordes of the 3rd century, the Goth sacks of the Middle Ages, the excavations of a modern-day Mussolini, and today's "army"—the motorized Barbarians—all played a part in transforming Rome into a city of fragments. Semi-preserved ruins of ancient forums, basilicas, stadiums, baths, and temples are strewn across the city like remnants of some Cecil B. DeMille movie-set. Even if you walk into the Termini McDonalds, you'll find three chunks of the 4th century BC Servian Wall. No wonder first-time visitors feel the only thing more intimidating than crossing a Roman intersection at rush hour is trying to make sense of the layout of ancient Rome.

Now, to your aid, comes this "ancient atlas." Overlapping the new Rome with the old, it is crammed with details of all the city's ageless walls and ancient sites, even though some of them now lie hidden underneath the earth. Written in these rocks is the story of the emperors, the city's greatest builders. Thanks in large part to their dreams of glory—combined with their architectural megalomania—Imperial Rome became the fountainhead of Western civilization.

Colosseum; (top) Head of Emperor Constantine, Musei Capitolini

3

IN FOCUS ROME WAS NOT BUILT IN A DAY

THE WAY ROME WAS

Circus Maximus: Atop the Palatine Hill, the emperor's royal box looked down on the races and games of this vast stadium—most Early Christians met their untimely end here, not in the Colosseum.

Capitoline Hill (Campidoglio): Most important of Rome's original seven hills, and home to the Temple of Jupiter, the "capital" hill was strategically located high above the Tiber and became the hub of the Roman Republic.

Palatine Hill (Palatino): The birthplace of Rome, settled by Romulus and Remus, the Palatine ultimately became Rome's

Theater of Pompey

Circus of Domitian

Pantheon

CAMPUS MARTIUS

Isola Tiberina

Theater of Marcellus

Temple of Jupiter

CAMPIDOGLIO

Campus Borum

TRASTEVERE

House of Augustus

PALATINO

AVENTINO

Circus Maximus

Rome in the Year 300 AD

"Beverly Hills" for it was home to Cicero, Julius Caesar, and a dozen Emperors.

Roman Forum: Downtown ancient Rome, this was the political heart of the Republic and Empire—the place for processions, tribunals, law courts, and orations, it was here that Mark Antony buried Caesar and Cleopatra made her triumphant entry.

Colosseum: Gladiators fought for the chance to live another day on the floor before 50,000 spectators in this giant arena, built in a mere eight years and inaugurated in AD 80.

Domus Aurea: Nero's "Golden House," a sprawling example of the excesses of Imperial Rome, once comprised 150 rooms, some shimmering with gold.

THEY CAME, THEY SAW, THEY BUILT

Remember the triumphal scene in the 2000 film *Gladiator*? Awesome expanses of pristine marble, a cast of thousands in gold-lavished costumes, and close-ups of Joaquin Phoenix (playing Emperor Commodus) on his way to the Colosseum: Rome à la Hollywood. But behind all the marble splendor seen in the film lies an eight-centuries-long trail that extends back from Imperial Rome to a tiny village of mud-huts along the Tiber river.

Museo della Civiltà Romana's model of Imperial Rome

ROMULUS GOES TO TOWN

Legend has it that Rome was founded by Romulus and Remus, twin sons of the god Mars. Upon being abandoned in infancy by a wicked uncle, they were taken up and suckled by a she-wolf living on a bank of the Tiber. (Ancient gossip says the wolf was actually a woman nicknamed Lupa for her multiple infidelities to her shepherd husband.)

As young men, Romulus and Remus returned in 753 BC to the hallowed spot to found a city but came to blows during its building, ending in the death of Remus—which is how the city became Roma, not Rema.

Where myth ends, archaeology takes over. In 2007, Roman excavators uncovered a cavernous sanctuary dedicated to the brothers situated in the valley between the Palatine and Capitoline (Campidoglio) hills in central Rome. Often transformed into "islands" when the Tiber river overflowed, these two hills soon famously expanded to include seven hills, including the Esquiline, Viminale, Celian, Quirinale, and Aventine.

SIMPLY MARBLE-LOUS

Up to 510 BC, the style of the fledging city had been set by the fun-loving, sophisticated Etruscans—Rome was to adopt their vestal virgins, household gods, and gladiatorial games. Later, when the Republic took over the city (509 BC—27 BC), the austere values promulgated by its democratic Senate eventually fell to the power-mad triumvirate of Crassus, Pompey, and Julius Caesar, who waved away any detractors—including Rome's main power-players, the patrician Senators and the populist Tribunes—by invoking the godlike sovereignty of emperorship.

Republican Rome's city was badly planned, in fact not planned at all, and the great contribution of the Emperor Augustus—who took over when his stepfather Caesar was assassinated in 43 BC—was to commence serious town planning, with results far surpassing even his own claim that he "found Rome brick and left it marble." Which was only fitting, as floridly colored marbles began to flow into Rome from all of the Mediterranean provinces he had conquered (including obelisks transported from Egypt to flaunt his victory over Cleopatra).

Via Sacra in the Roman Forum with the Temple of Saturn in the foreground and the Basilica Julia on the right.

A FUNNY THING HAPPENED ON THE WAY TO THE ROMAN FORUM

It was during Augustus' 40-year-long peaceful reign that Rome began its transition from glorified provincial capital into great city. While excavations have shown that the area of the Roman Forum was in use as a burial ground as far back as the 10th century BC, the importance of the Forum area as the political, commercial, and social center of Rome and, by extension, of the whole ancient world, grew immeasurably during Imperial times. The majestic ruins still extant are remnants of the massive complex of markets, civic buildings, and temples that dominated the city center in its heyday.

After Rome gained "empire" status, however, the original Forum was inadequate to handle the burden of the many trials and meetings required to run Western civilization, so Julius Cae-sar built a new forum. This apparently started a trend, as over the next 200-plus years (43 BC—AD 180), four different emperors—Augustus, Domitian, Vespasian, and Trajan—did the same. Oddly enough, the Roman Forum became four different Forums. They grew, in part, thanks to the Great Fire of AD 64, which Nero did not set but for which he took credit for laying waste to shabbier districts to build new ones.

For half a millennium, the Roman Forum area became the heart and soul of a worldwide empire, which eventually extended from Britain to Constantinople. Unfortunately, another thousand years of looting, sacking, and decay means you have to use your vivid imagination to see the glory that once was.

■TIP➜ For a step-by-step tour of the Roman Forum, see the "Roamin' Holiday" chapter.

WHERE ALL ROADS LEAD

Even if you don't dig ruins, a visit to
the Centro Archeologico—the area
in and around the Roman Forum—is
a must. Rome's foundation as a world
capital and crossroads of culture are
to be found here, literally. Over-
lapped with Rome's current streets,
this planimetric map shows the main
monuments of the Foro Romano
(in tan) as they originally stood.

Via IV Novembre

Via C. Battisti

Trajan's Column

TRAJAN'S FORUM

V. Alessandrina

Palazzo Senatorio

Tabularium

CAMPIDOGLIO

Carcere Mamertino

Arch of Septimus Severus

Curia

Via del Teatro di Marcello

Umbilcus Urbis Romae

The Rostra

TEMPLE OF JUPITER

Temple of Vespasian

Roman Forum

V. L. Petroselli

Basilica Julia

Tarpeian Rock

Temple of Saturn

Temple of Castor and Pollux

V. della Consolazione

V. d. Faraggi

V. di S. Teodoro

V. C. Jugario

Basilica Julia

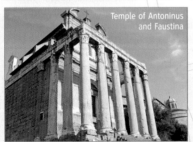
Temple of Antoninus and Faustina

Cloaca Maxima

V. d. Freni

TIBERIAN PALACE

MONTE

House of Livia

V. del Velabro

Temple of Castor and Pollux

Domitian's Palace

Circus Maximus

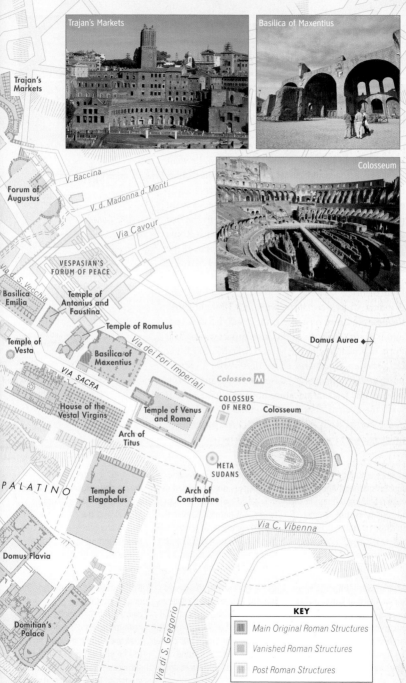

Trajan's Markets

Basilica of Maxentius

3

Colosseum

Trajan's Markets

V. Baccina

V. d. Madonna d. Monti

Forum of Augustus

Via Cavour

VESPASIAN'S FORUM OF PEACE

Via d. S. Vecchia

Basilica Emilia

Temple of Antonius and Faustina

Temple of Romulus

Via dei Fori Imperiali

Domus Aurea ◆→

Temple of Vesta

Basilica of Maxentius

VIA SACRA

Colosseo Ⓜ

House of the Vestal Virgins

Temple of Venus and Roma

COLOSSUS OF NERO

Colosseum

Arch of Titus

PALATINO

Temple of Elagabalus

META SUDANS

Arch of Constantine

Via C. Vibenna

Domus Flavia

Domitian's Palace

Via di S. Gregorio

KEY

Main Original Roman Structures

Vanished Roman Structures

Post Roman Structures

URBIS ROMÆ: THE EXPANDING CITY

Pantheon

Today's Campitelli district—the historic area comprising the Forums and the Colosseum—was, in fact, a relatively small part of the ancient city. From the center around the Forum, the old city dramatically grew outwards and in AD 7, the emperor Augustus organized ancient Rome into 14 *regiones*, administrative divisions that were the forerunners of today's historic *rioni* (districts). Rome's first city walls went up in the 6th century BC when King Servius Tullius built an eight-mile ring. As the city's borders greatly expanded, however, the outlaying areas needed extra protection. This became a dire necessity in the 3rd century when Germanic tribes arrived to sack Rome while Emperor Aurelian was fighting wars on the southern border of the empire. Fueled by fear, the emperor commissioned an 11-mile bulwark to be built of brick between 271 and 275. Studding the Aurelian Walls were 380 towers and 18 main gates, the best preserved of which is the Porta di San Sebastiano, at the entrance to the Via Appia Antica. The Porta is now home to the Museo delle Mura (✉ *Via di Porta San Sebastiano 18* ☎ *06/060608* ⊕ *www. museodellemuraroma.it* ✉ *Open Tues.-Sun., 9–2*), a small but fascinating museum that allows you to walk the ancient ramparts today; take Bus No. 118 to the Porta. From the walls' lofty perch you can see great vistas of the timeless Appian Way.

KEY

Archeological area of Rome

Hills

Mausoleum of Hadrian (Castel S. Angelo)

CAMPUS MARTIUS

Circus of Domitian (Piazza Navona)

Fiume Tevere

Theater of Pompey (Campo de' Fiori)

TRASTEVERE

Pantheon: Built in 27 BC by Augustus's general Agrippa and totally rebuilt by Hadrian in the 2nd century AD, this temple, dedicated to all the pagan gods, was topped by the largest dome ever built (until the 20th century).

Isola Tiberina: The Temple of Aesculapius once presided over this island—which was shaped by ancient Romans to resemble a ship, complete with obelisk mast and (still visible) marble ship prow—and was Rome's shrine to medicine.

Campus Borum: Today's Piazza della Bocca della Verità was ancient Rome's cattle market and the site of two beautifully preserved 2nd-century BC temples, one dedicated to Fortuna Virilis, the other to Hercules.

Baths of Caracalla: These gigantic thermal baths, a stunning example of ancient Roman architecture, were more than just a place to bathe—they functioned somewhat like today's swank athletic clubs.

Circus of Domitian: Rome's present Piazza Navona follows the shape of this ancient oval stadium built in 96 AD—houses now stand on top of the *cavea*, the original stone seating, which held 30,000 spectators.

Porta di San Sebastiano: The largest extant gate of the 3rd-century Aurelian Walls, located near the ancient aqueduct that once brought water to the nearby Baths of Caracalla, showcases the most beautiful stretch of Rome's ancient walls.

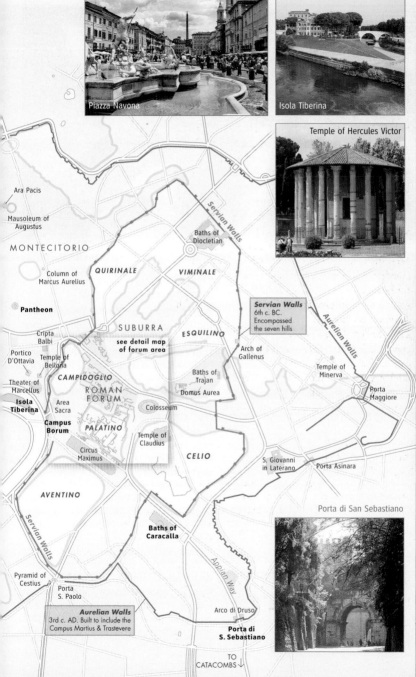

Piazza Navona

Isola Tiberina

Temple of Hercules Victor

Ara Pacis

Mausoleum of Augustus

MONTECITORIO

Column of Marcus Aurelius

QUIRINALE

VIMINALE

Baths of Diocletian

Servian Walls

Pantheon

SUBURRA

see detail map of forum area

ESQUILINO

Servian Walls
6th c. BC.
Encompassed the seven hills

Aurelian Walls

Cripta Balbi

Portico D'Ottavia

Temple of Bellona

CAMPIDOGLIO

Theater of Marcellus

Isola Tiberina

ROMAN FORUM

Area Sacra

Arch of Gallenus

Baths of Trajan

Domus Aurea

Temple of Minerva

Porta Maggiore

Campus Borum

PALATINO

Colosseum

Circus Maximus

Temple of Claudius

CELIO

S. Giovanni in Laterano

Porta Asinara

AVENTINO

Porta di San Sebastiano

Servian Walls

Baths of Caracalla

Appian Way

Pyramid of Cestius

Porta S. Paolo

Aurelian Walls
3rd c. AD. Built to include the Campus Martius & Trastevere

Arco di Druso

Porta di S. Sebastiano

TO CATACOMBS ↓

BUILDING BLOCKS OF THE EMPERORS

Vespasian's Colosseum

The oft quoted remark of Augustus, that he found Rome brick and left it marble, omits a vital ingredient of Roman building: concrete. The sheer size and spectacle of ancient Rome's most famous buildings owe everything to this humble building block. Its use was one of the Romans' greatest contributions to the history of architecture, for it ennabled them not only to create vast arches, domes, and vaults—undreamed of before—but also to build at a scale and size never before attempted. The fall of the Roman empire ultimately arrived, but great architectural monuments remain to remind us of its glory.

THE ARCH
VESPASIAN'S COLOSSEUM

Born in Riete, Titus Flavius Vespasian was the first of the new, military emperors. A down-to-earth countryman, with a realistic sense of humor, his dying words "I think I am in the process of becoming a god" have lived on. Along with generally restoring the city, which had burned down under Nero, he started the Colosseum, (his son, Titus, finished it, in AD 80). Erected upon the swampy marsh that once held the *stagnum*, or lake, of Nero's Golden House, the Colosseum was vast; its dimensions underscored how much Romans had come to value audacious size. The main architectural motif was the arch—hundreds of them in four ascending birthday tiers, each tier adorned with a different style of column: Doric, Ionic, Corinthian, Corinthian pilaster. Inside each arch was a statue (all of which have disappeared). Under these arches, called *fornices*, ancient Romans were fond of looking for bedfellows (so famously said the great poet Ovid), so much so that these arches gave a new word to the English language.

Domus Aurea

Hadrian's Pantheon

THE VAULT
NERO'S DOMUS AUREA

Most notorious of the emperors, but by no means the worst, Nero had domestic and foreign policies that were popular at first. However, his increasing megalomania was apparent in the size of his Domus Aurea, the "Golden House," so huge that the cry went up "All Rome has become a villa." Taking advantage of the Great Fire of AD 64, Nero wanted to re-create his seaside villa at Baia (outside Naples) right in the middle of Rome, building a vast palace of polychrome marble with a dining room with perforated ivory ceilings so that diners could be showered with flowers and perfume (designed by Fabullus, Nero's decorator). But the masterstrokes were the gigantic vaulted rooms—the Room of the Owls and the octagonal-shaped center room—designed by Nero's architects, Severus and Celer. Greek post-and-lintel architecture was banished for these highly dramatic spaces created by soaring vaults. You can still tour the ruins of Nero's "villa" but his 120-foot-high colossal bronze statue gave way to make room for the Colosseum.

THE DOME
HADRIAN'S PANTHEON

The concrete Roman dome at its most impressive can be seen in the Pantheon (around 125 AD), a massive construction 141 feet across. It is a fascinating feat of both design and engineering, for it is modeled on a sphere, the height of the supporting walls being equal to the radius of the dome. Larger than Saint Peter's, this dome of domes was constructed by the greatest Imperial builder of them all, the Emperor Hadrian. Poised on top of the dome's mighty concrete ring, the five levels of trapezoid-shaped coffers represent the course of the five then-known planets and their concentric spheres. Then, ruling over them, comes the sun, represented symbolically and literally by the so-called oculus—the giant "eye" open to the sky at the top. The heavenly symmetry is further paralleled by the coffers themselves: 28 to each row, the number of lunar cycles. In the center of each would have shone a small bronze star. All of the dome's famous gilt trim was stripped away by the Barberini popes in the 17th century, who melted it down to decorate the Vatican.

Circo Massimo *(Circus Maximus).* From the palace belvedere of the Domus Flavia, you can see the Circus Maximus, the giant arena where more than 300,000 spectators watched chariot races while the emperor looked on from this very spot. Ancient Rome's oldest and largest racetrack lies in a natural hollow between two hills. The oval course stretches about 650 yards from end to end; on certain occasions, there were as many as 24 chariot races a day and competitions could last for 15 days. The charioteers could amass fortunes rather like the sports stars of today (the Portuguese Diocles—one of many such "miliari"—is said to have totted up winnings of 35 million sesterci). The noise and the excitement of the crowd must have reached astonishing levels as the charioteers competed in teams, each with its own colors—the Reds, the Blues, etc. Betting also provided Rome's majority of unemployed with a potentially lucrative occupation. The central ridge was the site of two Egyptian obelisks (now in Piazza del Popolo and Piazza San Giovanni in Laterano). Picture the great chariot race scene from MGM's *Ben-Hur* and you have an inkling of what this all looked like. ⊠ *Valley between Palatine and Aventine hills* Ⓜ *Circo Massimo.*

Domus Augustana. In the Palazzi Imperiali complex, this palace named for the "August" emperor, consisted of private apartments for Emperor Domitian and his family. Here Domitian—Master and God as he liked to be called—would retire to dismember flies (at least according to Suetonius). ⊠ *Southern crest of Palatino.*

Domus Flavia. This palace in the Palazzi Imperiali complex was used by Domitian for official functions and ceremonies. Also called Palazzo dei Flavi, it included a basilica where the emperor could hold judiciary hearings. There were also a large audience hall, a peristyle (a columned courtyard), and the imperial triclinium (dining room), the latter set in a sunken declivity overlooking the Circus Maximus—some of its mosaic floors and stone banquettes are still in place. Domitian had the walls and courtyards of this and the adjoining Domus Augustana covered with the shiniest marble, these to act as mirrors to alert him to any knife in the back. They failed in their purpose. He died in a palace plot, engineered, some say, by his wife Domitia. ⊠ *Southern crest of Palatino.*

WORTH NOTING

Museo Palatino. The Palatine Museum charts the history of the hill from Archaic times with quaint models of early villages (ground floor) through to Roman times (ground and upper floors). On display in Room V are painted terra-cotta moldings and sculptural decorations from various temples (notably the Temple of Apollo Actiacus, whose name derives from the god to whom Octavian attributed his victory at Actium; the severed heads of the Medusa in the terra-cotta panels symbolize the defeated Queen of Egypt). Upon request, museum staff will accompany visitors to see the 16th-century frescoes of the Loggia Mattei. Portions of the paintings have been returned here from the Metropolitan Museum of Art in New York City. In the same building are frescoes detached from the Aula Isaica, one of the chambers belonging to the House of Augustus. ⊠ *Northwest crest of Palatino* 🎟 *€12 (combined ticket with the Colosseum, Roman Forum, and Imperial Forums, if used within 2 days), €4.50 Roman Forum and Palatine Hill only (admission to museum is* *included with Palatine Hill ticket)* ☉ *Daily 8:30–4* Ⓜ *Colosseo.*

Orti Farnesiani. Alessandro Farnese, a nephew of Pope Paul III, commissioned the 16th-century architect Vignola to lay out this archetypal Italian garden over the ruins of the Palace of Tiberius, up just a few steps from the House of Livia. This was yet another example of the Renaissance renewing an ancient Roman tradition. To paraphrase the poet Martial, the statue-studded gardens of the Flavian Palace were such as to make even an Egyptian potentate turn green with envy. ✉ *Monte Palatino.*

Stadio Palatino. Domitian created this vast open space immediately adjoining his palace. It may have been his private hippodrome, or it may simply have been an immense sunken garden. It could also have been used to stage games and other amusements for the benefit of the emperor. ✉ *Southeast crest of Palatino.*

> **IN ROME, EAT LIKE THE ROMANS DID**
>
> There are few more atmospheric places in Rome to wander about in than the Palatine Hill, with its hidden corners and shady lanes. Though picnicking is frowned on, some die-hard visitors to the Domus Flavia area insist on enjoying a circumspect snack while sitting on the very stone banquettes in the sunken Triclinium where emperors once feasted on truffled peacock (the room is by the cliff overlooking the Circus Maximus). In all events, don't forget to bring some fixings for the famous stray cats of the Forum.

THE IMPERIAL FORUMS

A complex of five grandly conceived squares flanked with colonnades and temples, the **Fori Imperiali** (Imperial Fora) formed the magnificent monumental core of ancient Rome, together with the original Roman Forum. Excavations at the start of the 21st century have revealed more of the Imperial Fora than has been seen in nearly a thousand years.

From Piazza del Colosseo, head northwest on Via dei Fori Imperiali toward Piazza Venezia. On the walls to your left, maps in marble and bronze put up by Benito Mussolini show the extent of the Roman Republic and Empire. The dictator's own dreams of empire led him to construct this avenue, cutting brutally through the Imperial Fora area, so that he would have a suitable venue for parades celebrating his expected military triumphs. Among the Fori Imperiali along the avenue you can see the Foro di Cesare (Forum of Caesar) and the Foro di Augusto (Forum of Augustus). The grandest of all the Imperial Fora was the Foro di Traiano (Forum of Trajan), with its huge semicircular Mercati Traianei and the Colonna di Traiano (Trajan's Column). The fora are illuminated at night and on rare occasions are open for evening visits, when guided tours in English may also be offered (check with the tourist office). ✉ *Via dei Fori Imperiali, Roman Forum* ☎ *06/820771* ⊕ *www.pierreci.it* 🎫 *€12 (combined ticket with the Colosseum, Roman Forum, and Palatine Hill, if used within 2 days)* ☉ *Tues.–Sun. 9–6* Ⓜ *Colosseo.*

TOP ATTRACTIONS

★ **Colonna di Traiano** *(Trajan's Column).* The remarkable series of reliefs spiraling up this column celebrate the emperor's victories over the Dacians in what is today Romania. It has stood in this spot since AD 113. The scenes on the column are an important primary source for information on the Roman army and its tactics. An inscription on the base declares that the column was erected in Trajan's honor and that its height corresponds to the height of the hill that was razed to create a level area for the grandiose Foro di Traiano. The emperor's ashes, no longer here, were kept in a golden urn in a chamber at the column's base, and his statue stood atop the column until 1587, when the pope had it replaced with a statue of St. Peter. ⊠ *Via del Foro di Traiano.*

★ **Foro di Traiano** *(Forum of Trajan).* Of all the Imperial Fora complexes, Trajan's was the grandest and most imposing, a veritable city unto itself. Designed by architect Apollodorus of Damascus, it comprised a vast basilica (at the time of writing closed for restoration), two libraries, and a colonnade laid out around the square, all once covered with rich marble ornamentation. Adjoining the forum were the **Mercati Traianei** (Trajan's markets), a huge, multilevel brick complex of shops, walkways, and terraces that was essentially an ancient shopping mall. Opened in 2008 is the new **Museo dei Fori Imperiali** (Imperial Forums Museum), which takes advantage of the soaring vaulted spaces of the forum to showcase archaeological fragments and sculptures while presenting a video re-creation of the original complex. In addition, the series of terraced rooms offers an impressive overview of the entire forum.

To build a complex of this magnitude, Apollodorus and his patron clearly had to have great confidence, not to mention almost unlimited means, and cheap labor at their disposal, this readily provided by captives from Trajans' Dacian wars. Formerly thought to be the Roman equivalent of a multipurpose commercial center, with shops, taverns, and depots, the site is now believed to be more of an administrative complex for storing and regulating Rome's enormous food supplies. They also contained two semicircular lecture halls, one at either end, which were likely associated with the libraries in Trajan's Forum. The markets' architectural centerpiece is the enormous curved wall, or *hexedra,* that shores up the side of the Quirinal Hill exposed by Apollodorus's gangs of laborers. Covered galleries and streets were constructed at various levels, following the hexedra's curves and giving the complex a strikingly modern appearance.

As you enter the markets, a large, vaulted hall stands in front of you. Two stories of shops or offices rise up on either side. It's thought that they were an administrative center for food handouts to the city's poor. Head for the flight of steps at the far end that leads down to Via Biberatica. (*Bibere* is Latin for "to drink," and the shops that open onto the street are believed to have been taverns.) Then head back to the three tiers of shops/offices that line the upper levels of the great hexedra and look out over the remains of the forum. Though empty and bare today, the cubicles were once ancient Rome's busiest market stalls. Though it seems to be part of the market, the **Torre delle Milizie** (Tower of the Militia), the tall brick tower, which is a prominent feature of Rome's skyline, was built in the early 1200s. ⊠ *Entrance: Via IV Novembre 94* ☎ *06/820771* ⊕ *www.mercatiditraiano.it* 🎫 *€6.50* ⊙ *Tues.–Sun. 9–7 (ticket office closes at 6)* Ⓜ *Bus 85, 175, 186, 810, 850, H 64, 70.*

Santi Cosma e Damiano. Home to one of the most striking Early Christian mosaics in the world, this church was adapted in the 6th century from two ancient buildings: the library in Vespasian's Forum of Peace and a hall of the Temple of Romulus (dedicated to the son of Maxentius and at Christmas the setting for a Christmas crib). In the apse is the famous 6th-century mosaic (circa 530) of Christ in Glory. It reveals how popes at the time strove to re-create the splendor of impe-

A CLASSY LOOKOUT

The exit of the Palatino leads to the Arch of Titus, where you turn east toward the Colosseum and the Arco di Costantino. Cross Piazza del Colosseo and stroll through the park on the Colle Oppio (Oppian Hill) to get to Nero's fabulous palace, the Domus Aurea (Golden House), which is hidden under the remains of the monumental baths that were built over it. The park here has some great views over the Colosseum; one of the best vantage points is from Via Nicola Salvi, which climbs uphill from the Colosseum.

rial audience halls into Christian churches, for Christ wears a gold, Roman-style toga, and his pose recalls that of an emperor addressing his subjects. He floats on a blue sky streaked with a flaming sunset—a miracle of tesserae mosaic-work. To his side are the figures of Sts. Peter and Paul, who present Cosmas and Damian, two Syrian benefactors whose charity was such they were branded Christians and condemned to death. Beneath this awe-inspiring work is an enchanting mosaic frieze of holy lambs. ⊠ *Off Via Sacra, opposite Tempio di Antonino e Faustina* ☎ *06/6920441* ⊙ *Daily 8–1 and 3–7* Ⓜ *Bus 85, 850.*

WORTH NOTING

Foro di Augusto *(Forum of Augustus).* These ruins, along with those of the **Foro di Nerva,** on the northeast side of Via dei Fori Imperiali, give only a hint of what must have been impressive edifices. ⊠ *Via dei Fori Imperiali* Ⓜ *Colosseo.*

Foro di Cesare *(Forum of Caesar).* Julius Caesar was the first to attempt to rival the original Roman Forum, when he had this forum built in the middle of the 1st century BC. Each year without fail, on the Ides of March, an unknown hand lays a bouquet at the foot of Caesar's statue. Call several days in advance to arrange a visit. ⊠ *Via dei Fori Imperiali* ☎ *06/69780532.*

THE COLOSSEUM AND ENVIRONS

Legend has it that as long as the Colosseum stands, Rome will stand; and when Rome falls, so will the world. No visit to Rome is complete without a trip to the obstinate oval that has been the iconic symbol of the city for centuries. Looming over a group of the Roman Empire's most magnificent monuments to imperial wealth and power, the Colosseo was the gigantic sports arena built by Vespasian and Titus.

THE COLOSSEUM

✉ *Piazza del Colosseo*
☎ *06/39967700* ⊕ *www.
pierreci.it* 💰 *€12 (combined
ticket with the Roman Forum,
Palatine Hill, and Imperial
Forums, if used within 2 days)*
🕒 *Daily 8:30–1 hr before sunset* Ⓜ *Colosseo; Bus 117, 87,
186, 85, 850.*

TIPS

■ Are there ways to beat the
big ticket lines at the Colosseum? Yes and no. First off, if
you go to the Roman Forum—
a couple of hundred yards
down Via dei Fori Imperiali
on your left—and purchase a
ticket there for €12, this also
includes admission to the
Colosseum and, even better,
lets you jump to the head of
the *loooooong* line. Another
way is to buy the Romapass
(⊕ *www.romapass.it*) ticket—
the Colosseo is covered and
you get booted to the front
of the line. Still another way
is to book a ticket in advance
through ⊕ *www.pierreci.it*
(small surcharge)—the main
ticket reservation service for
many Italian cultural sights.
Private tours usually have
advance bookings. Now for
the bad news: Even people
who jump to the front of the
line still have to wait on the
security line.

■ Guided tours in English are
available. The small exhibition space at the arena often
features fascinating temporary
exhibitions (for an additional
admission charge of €3). A
bookshop is also on-site.

The most spectacular extant edifice of ancient Rome,
the Colosseo, has a history that is half-gore, half-glory.
Here, before 50,000 spectators, gladiators would salute
the emperor and cry *Ave, imperator, morituri te salutant*
("Hail, emperor, men soon to die salute thee"); it is said
that when one day they heard the emperor Claudius
respond, "or maybe not," they became so offended that
they called a strike.

Scene of countless Hollywood spectacles—Deborah
Kerr besieged by lions in *Quo Vadis*, Victor Mature
laying down his arms in *Demetrius and the Gladiators*,
and Russell Crowe fighting an emperor in a computer-
generated stadium in *Gladiator*, to name just a few—the
Colosseum still awes onlookers today with its power
and might.

Designed by order of the Flavian emperor Vespasian in
AD 72, the Colosseum was inaugurated by Titus eight
years later with a program of games lasting 100 days.

Such shows were a quick way to political popularity—
or to put it another way, a people that yawns is ripe
for revolt.

The arena has a circumference of 573 yards and was
faced with stone from nearby Tivoli. Its construction
was a remarkable feat of engineering, for it stands on
marshy terrain reclaimed by draining an artificial lake
on the grounds of Nero's Domus Aurea.

Originally known as the Flavian amphitheater, it came
to be called the Colosseo because it stood on the site
of the Colossus of Nero, a 115-foot-tall gilded bronze
statue of the emperor that once towered here.

Inside, senators sat on the marble seating arrangements
up front, along with the Vestal Virgins taking the ringside position while the plebs sat in wooden tiers at the
back, then the masses above on the top tier. Over all

was the amazing velarium, an ingenious system of sail-like awnings rigged on ropes and maneuvered by sailors from the imperial fleet, who would unfurl them to protect the arena's occupants from sun or rain.

Once inside, you can take the wooden walkway across the arena floor for a gladiator's-eye view, then explore the upper level to study a scale model of the Colosseum as it was (sheathed with marble, with statues ornamenting arcades of arches decorated with Doric, Ionic, and Corinthian pillars; one arch near the Metro station still has traces of stucco decoration). From the upper tier study the so-called ipogei, the subterranean passageways that were the architectural engine rooms that made the slaughter above proceed like clockwork. In a scene prefiguring something from Dante's Inferno, hundreds of beasts would wait to be eventually launched via a series of slave-powered hoists and lifts into the bloodthirsty sand of the arena above.

Legend has it that as long as the Colosseum stands, Rome will stand; and when Rome falls, so will the world. This prophecy didn't deter Renaissance princes from using the Colosseum as a quarry or the Nazis from riddling it with bullets. In the 19th century, poets came to view the arena by moonlight; today, mellow golden spotlights make the arena a spectacular sight.

Thumbs Down Although the Colosseum had 80 entrances, it only had one exit named after the Roman goddess of death—the Porta Libitinaria—which was how dead gladiators were trundled out of the arena. Historians state that most of these warriors did survive to fight another day. If the die was cast, however, the rule was a victorious gladiator was the person to decide to take his opponent's life. He was often spurred on by the audience and the emperor—*pollice verso* meant the downturned thumb. Gladiatorial combat, or *munera*, is now traced back to the funeral rites of the early Etruscans when prisoners of war would sometimes be sacrificed to placate the spirits of the underworld. Rome's City Council, in conjunction with Amnesty International, tries to make amends for these horrors by floodlighting the Colosseum by night every time a death sentence is commuted or a country votes to abolish capital punishment.

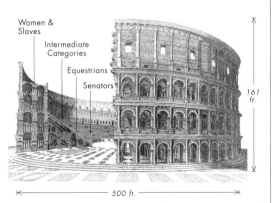

Women & Slaves

Intermediate Categories

Equestrians

Senators

161 ft.

500 ft.

To its west is the Arch of Constantine, a majestic, ornate triumphal arch, built solely as a tribute to the emperor Constantine; victorious armies purportedly marched under it on their return from war. On the eastern side of the Colosseum, hidden under the Colle Oppio, is Nero's opulent Domus Aurea, a palace that stands as testimony to the lavish lifestyles of the emperors.

TOP ATTRACTIONS

Arco di Costantino *(Arch of Constantine)*. This majestic arch was erected in AD 315 to commemorate Constantine's victory over Maxentius at the Milvian Bridge. It was just before this battle, in AD 312, that Constantine—the emperor who converted Rome to Christianity—had a vision of a cross in the heavens and heard the words "In this sign thou shalt conquer." The economy-minded Senate ordered that many of the rich marble decorations for the arch be scavenged from earlier monuments. It is easy to picture ranks of Roman legionnaires marching under the great barrel vault. ⊠ *Piazza del Colosseo* Ⓜ *Colosseo.*

WORTH NOTING

★ **Domus Aurea** *(Golden House of Nero)*. Legend has it that Nero famously fiddled while Rome burned. Fancying himself a great actor and poet, he played, as it turns out, his harp to accompany his recital of "The Destruction of Troy" while gazing at the flames of Rome's catastrophic fire of AD 64. Anti-Neronian historians propagandized that Nero, in fact, had set the Great Fire to clear out a vast tract of the city center to build his new palace. Today's historians discount this as historical folderol (going so far as to point to the fact that there was a full moon on the evening of July 19, hardly the propitious occasion to commit arson). But legend or not, Nero did get to build his new palace, the extravagant Domus Aurea (Golden House)—a vast "suburban villa" that was inspired by the emperor's pleasure palace at Baia on the Bay of Naples. His new digs were huge and sumptuous, with a facade of pure gold, seawater piped into the baths, decorations of mother-of-pearl, fretted ivory, and other precious materials, and vast gardens. It was said that after completing this gigantic house Nero exclaimed "Now I can live like a human being!" Unfortunately, following damage due to flooding in December 2008 the Domus is closed for restorations once again. But if you call (days in advance) you may snag an advance reservation ticket—keep in mind that the temperature underground is about 50°F year-round. Unfortunately, all of the fabulous decors designed by Fabullus have vanished but you can still be awed by the famous Octagon Room, topped by an oculus, where Nero once displayed famous Greek statues like the *Dying Gaul* (now on view at Rome's Musei Capitolini). ⊠ *Via della Domus Aurea* ☎ *06/39967700 reservations* ⊕ *www. domusaurea.info/ita* 🎟 *€4.50* Ⓜ *Colosseo.*

4

The Vatican

ST. PETER'S BASILICA, SISTINE CHAPEL, VATICAN MUSEUMS, CASTEL SANT'ANGELO

WORD OF MOUTH

"Like the Vatican Museums, the Sistine Chapel was packed, but you know, you look up and since people still don't fly (yet) the crowd didn't bother me."   — Chevre

"Bring a good pair of small binoculars to really see the work on the Sistine ceiling—and enjoy it all from the bench seats along the sides of the chapel. . . ."   — Rescue

GETTING ORIENTED

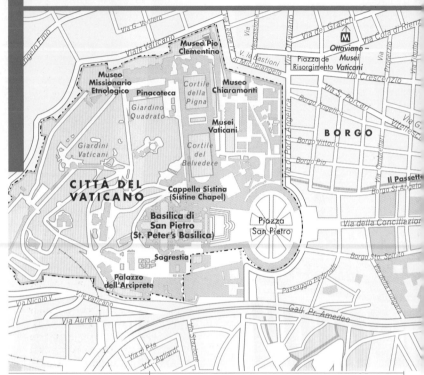

GETTING HERE

From Termini station, hop on the No. 40 Express or the famously crowded (watch out for pickpockets) No. 64 to deliver you to Piazza San Pietro.

Both routes swing past Piazza Venezia, where you can also get the J4. Metro stops Cipro or Ottaviano (Musei Vaticani) will get you within about a 10-minute walk of the entrance to the Vatican Museums.

A leisurely meander from the historic center across the exquisite Ponte Sant'Angelo footbridge will take about a half hour.

HOW TO BEAT THOSE LONG LINES

Home to the Sistine Chapel and the Raphael Stanze, the Vatican Museums are among the most congested of all Rome's attractions.

For years, people thought the best way to get a jump on the crowds was to be at the front entrance when it opened at 8:30 AM, particularly on the last Sunday of the month when entrance is free (other Sundays the museums are closed).

The problem was that everyone else had the same idea. Result: Rome's version of the Calgary Stampede.

Instead, the best way to avoid long lines is to arrive between noon and 2, when lines will be very short or even nonexistent, except Sundays when admissions close at 12:30.

Even better is to schedule your visit during the Wednesday Papal Mass, normally held in Aula Paolo Sesto. This is usually 10:30 AM—to see the pope's calendar, log on to: ⊕ www.vatican.va/news.

TOP 5 REASONS TO GO

Michelangelo's Sistine Ceiling: The most sublime example of artistry in the world, this 10,000-square-foot fresco took the artist four long, neck-craning years to finish.

St. Peter's Dome: Climb the claustrophobic and twisting Renaissance stairs to the very top, for a view that you will really feel you've earned (or take the elevator on the right of the main church portico).

Papal Blessing: Join the singing, flag-waving throngs from around the world at the Wednesday general audience on St. Peter's Square (October–June only).

Vatican Museums: Savor one of the Western world's best art collections—from the *Apollo Belvedere* to Raphael's *Transfiguration*, this is pure Masterpiece Theaters. Taken all together, culture here approaches critical mass.

St. Peter's Basilica: Stand in awe of the seat of world Catholicism and a masterwork of the Renaissance, and pay homage to millennia of popes, including John Paul II, in its crypt.

All this with the proviso that, traditionally, in July the pope is away on holiday in Val d'Aosta, then in August to mid-September moves to Castel Gandolfo, papal masses being held there instead.

Hours for the Vatican Museums now run 9–4 (last entrance) and exit by 6 (including Saturdays)—for the last Sunday of the month, 9–2 (sometimes this closure is stretched to 4) when entrance is free.

The Museums close the first three Sundays of every month; other dates of closures include January 1 and 6, February 11, May 1 and 21, June 11 and 29, August 15, and December 8, 25, and 26.

Another way to leapfrog over long lines is to reserve one of the guided tours offered by the Vatican Museums—this guarantees you an entrance time.

These tours (which can only be booked by fax) cost about €25, which is not much more than the main entrance ticket plus an audio-guide rental.

Sightseeing
★★★★★
Nightlife
★★
Dining
★★★
Lodging
★★★
Shopping
★★

Climbing the steps to St. Peter's Basilica feels monumental, like a journey that has reached its climactic end. Harlequin-costumed Swiss Guards stand at attention, curly spears at their sides, dreaming fiercely of their God and His country as you pass through the gates. Suddenly, all is cool, and dark, and you are dwarfed by a gargantuan hall and its magnificence.

Like jewels for giants, colored stones stud the floor and walls; above is a ceiling so high it must lead to heaven itself. Great, shining marble figures of saints frozen mid-whirl loom from niches and corners. And at the end, a throne, for an unseen king whose greatness (it is implied) must mirror the greatness of his palace. For this Basilica is a palace, the dazzling center of power for a king and a place of supplication for his subjects. Whether his kingdom is earthly or otherwise, is perhaps in the eye of the beholder.

For good Catholics and sinners alike, the Vatican is an exercise in spirituality, requiring patience but delivering joy. This is a retreat where some people go to savor a heavenly Michelangelo fresco—others come to find their soul. In between these two extremes lies an awe-inspiring landscape that offers a famous sight for every taste. Rooms decorated by Raphael, antique sculptures like the Apollo Belvedere, walls daubed by Fra Angelico, famous paintings by Giotto and Bellini, and chief among revered ne plus ultras, the Sistine Chapel: For the lover of beauty, few places are as historically important as this epitome of faith and grandeur.

What gave all this impetus while the emperors of ancient Rome presided over their declining empire was the emergence of a new force: namely, Christianity; the seat of the popes was established over the tomb of St. Peter, thereby making the Vatican the spiritual core of the Roman Catholic Church. But the massive walls surrounding Vatican City strongly underscore the fact that this is also a temporal power—an independent, sovereign state, established by the Lateran Treaty of

1929 between the Holy See and the Mussolini government. Vatican City covers 108 acres on a hill west of the Tiber and is separated from the city on all sides, except at Piazza di San Pietro, by high walls. Within the walls, about 1,000 people are permanent residents. The Vatican has its own daily newspaper (*L'Osservatore Romano*), issues its own stamps, mints its own coins, and runs its own postal system. Within its territory are administrative and foreign offices, a pharmacy, banks, an astronomical observatory, a print shop, a mosaic school and art restoration institute, a tiny train station, a supermarket, a small department store, and several gas stations. The sovereign of this little state is the pope, Benedict XVI (elected April 2005). His main role is as spiritual leader to the world's Catholic community.

Today, there are two principal reasons for sightseeing at the Vatican. One is to visit the Basilica di San Pietro, the most overwhelming architectural achievement of the Renaissance; the other is to visit the Vatican Museums, which contain collections of staggering richness and diversity. Here at the Vatican great artists are honored almost as much as any holy power: the paintings, frescoes, sculptures, and buildings here are as much monuments to their genius as to the Catholic church.

Inside the Basilica—breathtaking both for its sheer size and for its extravagant interior—are artistic masterpieces including Michelangelo's *Pietà* and Bernini's great bronze baldacchino canopy over the main altar. A robust outdoor walk from the piazza is the entrance to the Vatican Museums; the blisters will be worth it as the endless collections here contain many of the greatest works of Western art, period. The *Laocoön*, Leonardo's *St. Jerome*, and Raphael's *Transfiguration* are just the smallest sample. The Sistine Chapel, accessible through the Museums, is Michelangelo's magnificent artistic legacy and his ceiling is the High Renaissance in excelsis, in more ways than one. Between the Vatican and the once-moated bulk of Castel Sant'Angelo—erstwhile mausoleum of Emperor Hadrian and now an imposing relic of medieval Rome—the pope's covered passageway flanks an enclave of workers and craftspeople, the old Borgo neighborhood, whose workaday charm has begun to succumb to gentrification.

TOP ATTRACTIONS

★ **Basilica di San Pietro.** The largest church in the world, built over the tomb of St. Peter, is the most imposing and breathtaking architectural achievement of the Renaissance (although much of the lavish interior dates to the baroque). The physical statistics are impressive: it covers 18,000 square yards, runs 212 yards in length, and is surmounted by a dome that rises 435 feet and measures 138 feet across its base. Its history is equally impressive: No less than five of Italy's greatest artists—Bramante, Raphael, Peruzzi, Antonio Sangallo the Younger, and Michelangelo—died while striving to erect this new St. Peter's.

The history of the original St. Peter's goes back to AD 349, when the emperor Constantine completed a basilica over the site of the tomb of St. Peter, the Church's first pope. The original church stood for more than 1,000 years, undergoing a number of restorations and alterations, until, toward the middle of the 15th century, it was verging on collapse.

The Vatican

Via Seb

Via V. Pisani

V.le Vaticano

to

V

Via Angelo Emo

Via R. Fiore

V. Marcantonio Bragadin

Via Melona

Museo
Missionario
Etnologico

V.le

Serre

Via F. Sivori

Via D. Millelire

Sta. Maria
Mediatrice

V.le Benedetto

V.le Centrale del Bosco

Giardini
Vaticani

V.le dei Giardini Quadrato

Via Angelo Emo

Madonna
della Guardia

Fontana
dell'Aquilone

Radio Vaticano
(Direzione)

Clivo delle Mura Vaticane

V.le Vaticano

Entrance to
the Gardens

Grotta di
Lourdes

V.le dell'Osservatorio

Sto.
Marta

Via

Via di Utu

Collegio
Etiopico

Via del Seminario Etiopico

Mura di
Leone IV

Radio
Vaticana

Via Vaticano

Sto.
Stefano

Scuola
d'Arte Mosaica

Pala
di Giu

Via del Mosaico

V.le Vaticano

Via Pio XII

V.le Vaticano

Via Aurelia

N

0   200 feet

0   200 m

Via Aurelia

Via Nicolò V

V. St. Antonino

Via Benedetto XIV

Via Aurelia

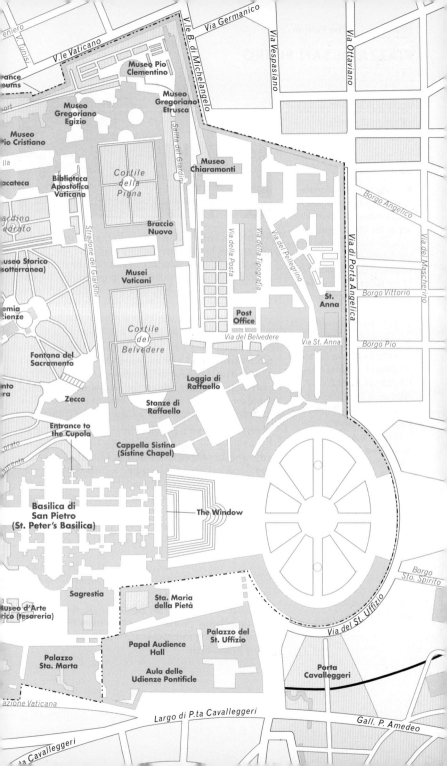

Museo Pio Clementino

Museo Gregoriano Etrusca

Museo Gregoriano Egizio

Museo Pio Cristiano

Biblioteca Apostolica Vaticana

Cortile della Pigna

Museo Chiaramonti

Braccio Nuovo

Musei Vaticani

Museo Storico (sotterranea)

Cortile del Belvedere

Fontana del Sacramento

Zecca

Entrance to the Cupola

Loggia di Raffaello

Stanze di Raffaello

Cappella Sistina (Sistine Chapel)

Basilica di San Pietro (St. Peter's Basilica)

The Window

Sagrestia

Museo d'Arte rico (tesoreria)

Sta. Maria della Pietà

Palazzo del St. Uffizio

Papal Audience Hall

Aula delle Udienze Pontificle

Palazzo Sta. Marta

Porta Cavalleggeri

Post Office

St. Anna

V.le Vaticano

V.le Vaticano

V.le B. di Michelangelo

Via Germanico

Via Vespasiano

Via Ottaviano

Salita del Giardini

Stradone dei Giardini

Via della Posta

Via della Tipografia

Via del Pellegrino

Via di Porta Angelica

Borgo Angelico

Borgo Vittorio

Via del Mascherino

Via del Belvedere

Via St. Anna

Borgo Pio

Via del St. Uffizio

Borgo Sto. Spirito

Largo di P.ta Cavalleggeri

Gall. P. Amedeo

ta Cavalleggeri

azione Vaticana

PIAZZA DI SAN PIETRO

✉ *West end of Via della Con-*
ciliazione, Vatican 🕒 *Mon.–*
Sat. 8–6:45 ☎ *06/69881662*
✉ *upt@vaticanstate.va*
Ⓜ *Cipro-Musei Vaticani.*

TIPS

■ Officially called Informazi-
oni per turisti e pellegrini, the
Main Information Office is just
left of the Basilica entrance,
a couple of doors down from
the Braccio di Carlo Magno
bookshop. On the south side
of the Piazza Pio XII square
you'll find the main Vatican
Bookshop, the shop also containing Libreria Benedetto XVI.

■ As for the famous Vatican
post offices (known for fast
handling of outgoing mail),
they can be found on both
sides of St. Peter's Square and
inside the Vatican Museums
complex. You can also buy
Vatican stamps and coins
at the shop annexed to the
information office. Although
postage rates are the same at
the Vatican as elsewhere in
Italy, the stamps are not interchangeable, so any material
stamped with Vatican stamps
must be placed into a blue or
yellow Posta Vaticana box.

■ Public toilets are near the
Information Office, under the
colonnade and outside the
exit of the crypt.

Mostly enclosed within high walls that recall the papacy's stormy history, the Vatican opens the spectacular
arms of Bernini's Colonnade to embrace the world only
at St. Peter's Square, scene of the pope's public appearances. Actually an oval, and one of Bernini's most
spectacular masterpieces, Piazza di San Pietro was completed in 1667 after only 11 years' work and is capable
of holding 400,000 people.

Surrounded by a pair of quadruple colonnades, it is
gloriously studded with more than 140 statues of saints
and martyrs. Look for the two disks set into the piazza's
pavement on either side of the central obelisk. If you
stand on either disk, a trick of perspective makes the colonnades seem to consist of a single row of columns.

Bernini had an even grander visual effect in mind when
he designed the square. By opening up this immense,
airy, and luminous space in a neighborhood of narrow, shadowy streets, he created a contrast that would
surprise and impress anyone who emerged from the
darkness into the light, in a characteristically baroque
metaphor.

At the piazza center, the 85-foot-high Egyptian obelisk
was brought to Rome by Caligula in AD 38, moved here
in 1586 by Pope Sixtus V. The emblem at the top of the
obelisk is the Chigi star, in honor of Pope Alexander
VII, a member of the powerful Chigi family, who commissioned the piazza.

Alexander demanded that Bernini make the pope visible to as many people as possible from the Benediction Loggia and to provide a covered passageway for
papal processions.

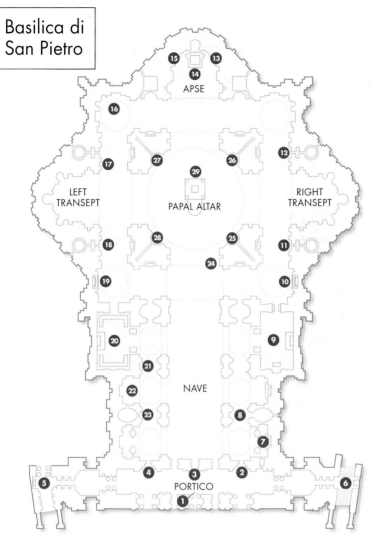

Basilica di San Pietro

In 1452 a reconstruction job began but was quickly abandoned for lack of money. In 1503 Pope Julius II instructed the architect Bramante to raze all the existing buildings and to build a new basilica, one that would surpass even Constantine's for grandeur. It wasn't until 1626 that the basilica was completed and consecrated.

IT'S ALWAYS WHO YOU KNOW

Bernini's Barberini patron, Pope Urban VIII, had no qualms about stripping the bronze from the Pantheon to provide Bernini with the material to create the gigantic bronze *baldacchino* canopy over St. Peter's main altar. The Romans reacted with the famous quip *"Quod non fecerunt barbari, fecerunt Barberini"* ("What the barbarians didn't do, the Barberini did").

St. Peter's Crossing and Dome. Though Bramante made little progress in rebuilding St. Peter's, he succeeded nonetheless in outlining a basic plan for the church, plus, and this was a crucial step, he built the piers of the crossings—the massive pillars supporting the dome. After Bramante's death in 1514, Raphael, the Sangallos, and Peruzzi all proposed, at one time or another, variations on the original plan. In 1546, however, Pope Paul III turned to Michelangelo and forced the aging artist to complete the building. He returned to Bramante's first idea of having a centralized Greek-cross plan—that is, with the "arms" of the church all the same length—and completed most of the exterior architecture except for the dome and the facade. His design for the dome, however, was modified after his death by Giacomo della Porta (his dome was much taller in proportion). Pope Paul V wanted a Latin-cross church (a church with one "arm" longer than the rest), so Carlo Maderno lengthened one of the arms to create a longer central nave.

Works by Giotto and Filarete. As you climb the shallow steps up to the great church, flanked by the statues of Sts. Peter and Paul, you'll see the **Loggia delle Benedizioni** (Benediction Loggia) over the central portal. This is the balcony where newly elected popes are proclaimed, and where they stand to give their apostolic blessing on solemn feast days. The vault of the vestibule is encrusted with rich stuccowork, and the mosaic above the central entrance to the portico is a much-restored work by the 14th-century painter Giotto that was in the original basilica. The bronze doors of the main entrance also were salvaged from the old basilica. The sculptor Filarete worked on them for 12 years; they show scenes from the martyrdom of St. Peter and St. Paul, and the life of Pope Eugene IV (1431–47), Filarete's patron.

Pause a moment to appraise the size of the great building. The people near the main altar seem dwarfed by the incredible dimensions of this immense temple. The statues, the pillars, and the holy-water stoups borne by colossal cherubs are all imposing—walk over to where the cherub clings to a pier and place your arm across the sole of the cherub's foot; you will discover that it's as long as the distance from your fingers to your elbow. It's because the proportions of this giant building are in such perfect harmony that its vastness may escape you at first. Brass inscriptions in the marble pavement down the center of the nave indicate the approximate lengths of the world's other principal

Christian churches, all of which fall far short of the 186-meter span of St. Peter's Basilica. In its megascale—inspired by the spatial volumes of ancient Roman ruins—the church reflects Roman *grandiosità* in all its majesty.

As you enter the great nave, immediately to your right, behind a protective glass partition, is Michelangelo's *Pietà*, sculpted when the artist was only 25. The work was of such genius, some rivals spread rumors it was by someone else, prompting the artist to inscribe his name—very unusually for him—across Mary's sash. Further down, with its heavyweight crown barely denting its marble cushion, is Carlo Fontana's monument to Catholic convert and abdicated Queen Christina of Sweden (who is buried in the Grotte Vaticane below). Exquisite bronze grilles and doors by Borromini open into the third chapel in the right aisle, the **Cappella del Santissimo Sacramento** (Chapel of the Most Holy Sacrament, closed off after 11:30 AM), with a baroque fresco of the Trinity by Pietro da Cortona. The lovely carved angels are by Bernini. At the last pillar on the right (the pier with Bernini's statue of St. Longinus) is a bronze statue of St. Peter, whose right foot is ritually touched by lines of pilgrims. In the right transept, over the door to the **Cappella di San Michele** (Chapel of St. Michael), usually closed, Canova created a brooding Neoclassical monument to Pope Clement XIII.

Bernini's Baldacchino. In the central crossing, Bernini's great bronze *baldacchino*—a huge, spiral-columned canopy—rises high over the *altare papale* (papal altar). Bernini's Barberini patron, Pope Urban VIII, had no qualms about stripping the bronze from the Pantheon to provide Bernini with the material to create this curious structure. The Romans reacted with the famous quip *"Quod non fecerunt barbari, fecerunt Barberini"* ("What the barbarians didn't do, the Barberini did"). The splendid gilt-bronze **Cattedra di San Pietro** (throne of St. Peter) in the apse above the main altar was designed by Bernini to contain a wooden and ivory chair that St. Peter himself is said to have used, though in fact it doesn't date from farther back than medieval times. (You can see a copy of the chair in the treasury.) Above it, Bernini placed a window of thin alabaster sheets that diffuses a golden light around the dove, symbol of the Holy Spirit, in the center.

Two of the major papal funeral monuments in St. Peter's Basilica are on either side of the apse and unfortunately are usually only dimly lighted. To the right is the **tomb of Pope Urban VIII**; to the left is the **tomb of Pope Paul III**. Paul's tomb is of an earlier date, designed between 1551 and 1575 by Giacomo della Porta, the architect who completed the dome of St. Peter's Basilica after Michelangelo's death. The nude figure of Justice was widely believed to be a portrait of the pope's beautiful sister, Giulia. The charms of this alluring figure were such that in the 19th century, it was thought that she should no longer be allowed to distract worshippers from their prayers, and she was thenceforth clad in marble drapery. It was in emulation of this splendid late-Renaissance work that Urban VIII ordered Bernini to design his tomb. The real star here, however, is *la Bella Morte* ("Beautiful Death") who, all bone and elbows, dispatches the deceased pope above to a register of blue-black marble. The **tomb of Pope Alexander VII**, also designed by Bernini,

CLOSE UP

Meet the Pope

Piazza San Pietro is the scene of large **papal audiences** as well as special commemorations, masses, and beatification ceremonies. When he's in Rome, the pope makes an appearance every Sunday around 11 AM (call the Vatican Information office to find out if the pope is in town and the exact time) at the window of the Vatican Palace. He addresses the crowd and blesses all present. The pope holds mass audiences on Wednesday morning about 10 (at 9 in the hotter months). Whether they are held in the square depends on the weather. There's an indoor audience hall adjacent to the basilica (Aula Paolo Sesto). During summer, while the pope is vacationing at Castel Gandolfo in the Castelli Romani hills outside Rome, he gives a talk and blessing from a balcony of the papal palace there. For admission

to an audience (✒ *Prefettura della Casa Pontefice, 00120 Vatican City* ☎ *06/69883273* 🖷 *06/69885863*), apply for free tickets by mail or fax in advance, indicating the date you prefer, the language you speak, and the hotel in which you will stay. Or apply for tickets on the Monday or Tuesday before the Wednesday audience at the Prefettura della Casa Pontifice, open on weekdays 9–1, which you reach through the Portone di Bronzo (Bronze Door) at the end of the right-hand colonnade. You can also arrange to pick up free tickets on Tuesday from 5 to 6:45 at the Santa Susanna American Church (✉ *Via XX Settembre 15, near Termini* ☎ *06/42014554*); call first. For a fee, travel agencies make arrangements that include transportation. Arrive early, as security is tight and the best places fill up fast.

stands to the left of the altar as you look up the nave, behind the farthest pier of the crossing. This may be the most haunting memorial in the basilica, thanks to another frightening skeletonized figure of Death, holding an hourglass in its upraised hand to tell the pope his time is up. Pope Alexander, however, was well prepared, having kept a coffin (also designed by Bernini) in his bedroom and made a habit of dining off plates embossed with skulls.

Subsidiary Attractions. With advance notice you can take a 1¼-hour guided tour in English of the **Vatican Necropolis** (☎ *06/69885318* 🖷 *06/69873017* 💶 *€10* 🕐 *Ufficio Scavi Mon.–Sat. 9–5, visits 9–3:30*), under the basilica, which gives a rare glimpse of Early Christian Roman burial customs. Apply by fax or e-mail (✉ *scavi@fsp.va*) at least 10 days in advance, specifying the number of people in the group (all must be age 15 or older), preferred language, preferred time, available dates, and your contact information in Rome. Under the Pope Pius V monument, the entrance to the sacristy also leads to the **Museo Storico-Artistico e Tesoro** (*Historical-Artistic Museum and Treasury* ☎ *06/69881840* 💶 *€6* 🕐 *Apr. 1–Sept. 30, daily 8–7; Oct. 1–Mar. 31, daily 8–6:30*), a small collection of Vatican treasures. They range from the massive and beautifully sculptured 15th-century tomb of Pope Sixtus IV by Pollaiuolo, which you can view from above, to a jeweled cross dating from the 6th century and a marble tabernacle by Donatello. Continue on down the left nave past Algardi's **tomb of St. Leo.** The handsome bronze grilles in the **Capella del Coro** (Chapel of the Choir) were designed by Borromini to complement those opposite in the Cappella del Santissimo Sacramento. The next pillar holds a rearrangement of the Pollaiuolo brothers' monument to Pope Innocent VIII, the only major tomb to have been transferred from the old basilica. Lacking in bulk compared to many of its baroque counterparts, it more than makes up in Renaissance elegance. The next

> **ART AND FAITH**
>
> Presiding over the great nave of St. Peter's is Michelangelo's legendary *Pietà*. Could you question whether this moving work, sculpted when the artist was only 22, owes more to man's art than to a man's faith? Perhaps as we contemplate this masterpiece we are able to understand a little better that art and faith sometimes partake of the same impulse.

4

chapel contains the handsome bronze monument to Pope John XXIII by contemporary sculptor Emilio Greco. On the last pier in this nave stands a monument by the late-18th-century Venetian sculptor Canova to the ill-fated Stuarts—the 18th-century Roman Catholic claimants to the British throne, who were long exiled in Rome and some of whom are buried in the crypt below.

Above, the vast sweep of the basilica's dome is the cynosure of all eyes. To reach it proceed to the right side of the Basilica's vestibule; from here you can either take the elevator or climb the long flight of shallow stairs to the **roof of the church** (☎ *06/69883462 ☜Elevator €7, stairs €5 ⊙ Daily Apr.–Sept., 8–6; Oct.–Mar., 8–5; on a Papal Audience Wed., 11:30–5, closed during ceremonies in piazza*). From here you'll see a surreal landscape of vast sloping terraces punctuated by cupolas that serve as skylights over the various chapels. The roof affords unusual perspectives on the dome above and the piazza below. The terrace is equipped with the inevitable souvenir shop and restrooms. A short flight of stairs leads to the entrance of the *tamburo* (drum)—the base of the dome—where, appropriately enough, there's a bust of Michelangelo, the dome's principal designer. Within the drum, another short ramp and staircase give access to the **gallery** encircling the base of the dome. From here you have a dove's-eye view of the interior of the church. It's well worth the slight effort to make your way up here—unless you suffer from vertigo.

Only if you're of stout heart and strong lungs should you then make the taxing climb from the drum of the dome up to the *lanterna* (lantern) at the very apex of the dome. A narrow, seemingly interminable staircase follows the curve of the dome between inner and outer shells, finally releasing you into the cramped space of the lantern balcony for an absolutely gorgeous panorama of Rome and the countryside on a clear day. There's also a nearly complete view of the palaces, courtyards, and gardens of the Vatican. Be aware, however, that it's a tiring, slightly claustrophobic climb. There's one stairway for going up and a different one for coming down, so you can't change your mind halfway and turn back.

For St. Peter's, Michelangelo originally designed a dome much higher than the one ultimately built and designed by his follower Giacomo della Porta.

The entrance to the **Grotte Vaticane** (*Vatican Grottoes* ✉ *Free* ⊘ *Apr.–Sept., daily 7–6; Oct.–Mar., daily 7–5*) is right of the main entrance to the Basilica. The crypt is lined with marble-face chapels and tombs occupying the area of Constantine's basilica and standing over what is believed to be the tomb of St. Peter himself, flanked by two angels and visible through glass. Among the most beautiful tombs leading up to it are that of Borgia pope Calixtus III with its carving of the Risen Christ, and then the tomb of Paul II featuring angels carved by Renaissance great Mino da Fiesole. Also, on the right, is the simple grave of Pope John Paul II. ✉ *Piazza di San Pietro, Vatican* ⊘ *Daily 8–6* Ⓜ *Cipro-Musei Vaticani.*

NEED A
BREAK?

Insalata Ricca (✉ *Piazza Risorgimento 6, Vatican* ☎ 06/39730387), about halfway between the Vatican Museums and St. Peter's Basilica, offers no-nonsense light meals: pasta, salads, and pizza. While unremarkable, keep it in mind on a hot day—its air-conditioning is the best in the neighborhood.

Fodor's Choice
★

Cappella Sistina *(Sistine Chapel).* In 1508, the redoubtable Pope Julius II commissioned Michelangelo to fresco the more than 10,000 square feet of the Sistine Chapel's ceiling. (*Sistine,* by the way, is simply the adjective from *Sixtus,* in reference to Pope Sixtus IV, who commissioned the chapel itself.) The task took four years, and it's said that for many years afterward Michelangelo couldn't read anything without holding it up over his head. The result, however, was the greatest artwork of the Renaissance. A pair of binoculars helps greatly, as does a small mirror—hold the mirror facing the ceiling and look down to study the reflection.

Before the chapel was consecrated in 1483, its lower walls had been decorated by a group of artists including Botticelli, Ghirlandaio, Perugino, Signorelli, and Pinturicchio. They had painted scenes from the life of Moses on one wall and episodes from the life of Christ on the other. Later, Julius II, dissatisfied with the simple vault decoration—it consisted of no more than stars painted on the ceiling—decided to call in Michelangelo. At the time, Michelangelo was carving Julius II's resplendent tomb—a project that never came near completion. He had no desire to give the project up to paint a ceiling, considering the task unworthy of him. Julius was not, however, a man to be trifled with, and Michelangelo reluctantly began work. The project proceeded in fits and starts until Michelangelo decided to dedicate himself wholeheartedly to it. See our special photo feature, "Agony and Ecstasy: The Sistine Ceiling," for the complete back story.

4

More than 20 years later, Michelangelo was called on again, this time by the Farnese pope Paul III, to add to the chapel's decoration by painting the *Last Judgment* on the wall over the altar. The subject was well suited to the aging and embittered artist, who had been deeply moved by the horrendous Sack of Rome in 1527 and the confusions and disturbances of the Reformation. The painting stirred up controversy even before it was unveiled in 1541, shocking many Vatican officials, especially one Biagio di Cesena, who criticized its "indecent" nudes. Michelangelo retaliated by painting Biagio's face on the figure with donkey's ears in Hades, in the lower right-hand corner of the work. Biagio pleaded with Pope Paul to have Michelangelo erase his portrait, but the pontiff replied that he could intercede for those in purgatory but had no power over hell. As if to sign this, his late great fresco, Michelangelo painted his own face on the wrinkled human skin in the hand of St. Bartholomew. ⊠ *Vatican Palace; entry only through Musei Vaticani.*

Castel Sant'Angelo. Standing between the Tiber and the Vatican, this circular and medieval "castle" has long been one of Rome's most distinctive landmarks. Opera-lovers know it well as the setting for the final scene of Puccini's *Tosca;* on the upper terrace is the rampart from which the tempestuous diva throws herself to end the opera. In fact, the structure began life many centuries before as a mausoleum for the emperor Hadrian. The structure dates from AD 135, with the work being completed by the emperor's successor, Antoninus Pius, about five years later. It initially consisted of a great square base topped by a marble-clad cylinder on which was planted a ring of cypress trees. Above them towered a gigantic statue of Hadrian. From the mid-6th century the building became a fortress, the military key to Rome for almost 1,000 years and the place of refuge for numerous popes during wars and sieges. Its name dates from 590, when Pope Gregory the Great, during a procession to plead for the end of a plague, saw an angel standing on the summit of the castle in the act of sheathing its sword. Taking this as a heavenly sign that the plague was at an end, the pope built a small chapel at the top, placing a statue next to it to celebrate his vision, thus the name, Castel Sant'Angelo.

Continued on page 118

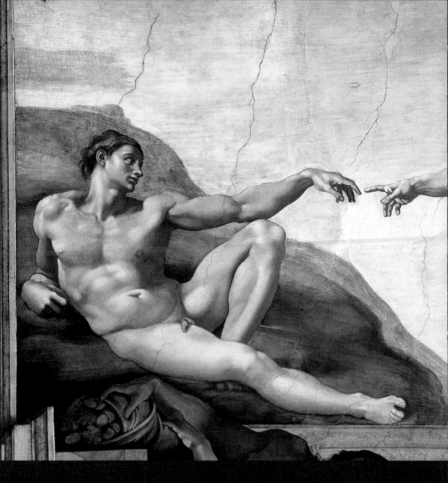

AGONY AND ECSTASY:
THE SISTINE CEILING

Forming lines that are probably longer than those waiting to pass through the Pearly Gates, hordes of visitors arrive at the Sistine Chapel daily to view what may be the world's most sublime example of artistry:

4

Michelangelo: *The Creation of Adam*, Sistine Chapel, The Vatican, circa 1511.

Michelangelo's Sistine Ceiling. To paint this 12,000-square-foot barrel vault, it took four years, 343 frescoed figures, and a titanic battle of wits between the artist and Pope Julius II. While in its typical fashion, Hollywood focused on the element of agony, not ecstasy, involved in the saga of creation, a recently completed restoration of the ceiling has revolutionized our appreciation of the masterpiece of masterpieces.

By Martin Wilmot Bennett

View of the Cappella Sistina

MICHELANGELO'S
MISSION IMPOSSIBLE

Designed to match the proportions of Solomon's Temple described in the Old Testament, the Sistine Chapel is named after Pope Sixtus VI, who commissioned it as a place of worship for himself and as the venue where new popes could be elected. Before Michelangelo, the barrel-vaulted ceiling was an expanse of azure fretted with golden stars. Then, in 1504, an ugly crack appeared. Bramante, the architect, managed do some patchwork using iron rods, but when signs of a fissure remained, the new Pope Julius II summoned Michelangelo to cover it with a fresco 135 feet long and 44 feet wide.

Taking in the entire span of the ceiling, the theme connecting the various participants in this painted universe could be said to be mankind's anguished waiting. The majestic panel depicting the Creation of Adam leads, through the stages of the Fall and the expulsion from Eden, to the tragedy of Noah found naked and mocked by his own sons; throughout all runs the underlying need for man's redemption. Witnessing all from the side and end walls, a chorus of ancient Prophets and Sibyls peer anxiously forward, awaiting the Redeemer who will come to save both the Jews and the Gentiles.

APOCALYPSE NOW

The sweetness and pathos of his Pietà, carved by Michelangelo only ten years earlier, have been left behind. The new work foretells an apocalypse, its congregation of doomed sinners facing the wrath of heaven through hanging, beheading, crucifixion, flood, and plague. Michelangelo, by nature a misanthrope, was already filled with visions of doom thanks to the fiery orations of Savonarola, whose thunderous preachments he had heard before leaving his hometown of Florence. Vasari, the 16th-century art historian, coined the word "terribilità" to describe Michelangelo's tension-ridden style, a rare case of a single word being worth a thousand pictures.

Michelangelo wound up using a *Reader's Digest* condensed version of the stories from Genesis, with the dramatis personae overseen by a punitive and terrifying God. In real life, poor Michelangelo answered to a flesh-and-blood taskmaster who was almost as vengeful: Pope Julius II. Less vicar of Christ than latter-day Caesar, he was intent on uniting Italy under the power of the Vatican, and was eager to do so by any means, including riding into pitched battle. Yet this "warrior pope" considered his most formidable adversary to be Michelangelo. Applying a form of blackmail, Julius threatened to wage war on Michelangelo's Florence, to which the artist had fled after Julius canceled a commission for a grand papal tomb unless Michelangelo agreed to return to Rome and take up the task of painting the Sistine Chapel ceiling.

MICHELANGELO, SCULPTOR

A sculptor first and foremost, however, Michelangelo considered painting an inferior genre—"for rascals and sissies" as he put it. Second, there was the sheer scope of the task, leading Michelangelo to suspect he'd been set up by a rival, Bramante, chief architect of the new St. Peter's Basilica. As Michelangelo was also a master architect, he regarded this fresco commission as a Renaissance mission-impossible. Pope Julius's powerful will prevailed—and six years later the work of the Sistine Ceiling was complete. Irving Stone's famous novel *The Agony and the Ecstasy*—and the granitic 1965 film that followed—chart this epic battle between artist and pope.

THINGS ARE LOOKING UP

To enhance your viewing of the ceiling, bring along opera-glasses, binoculars, or just a mirror (to prevent your neck from becoming bent like Michelangelo's). Note that no photos are permitted. Insiders know the only time to get the chapel to yourself is during the papal blessings and public audiences held in St. Peter's Square. Failing that, get there during lunch hour. Admission and entry to the Sistine Chapel is only through the Musei Vaticani (Vatican Museums).

SCHEMATIC OF THE SISTINE CEILING

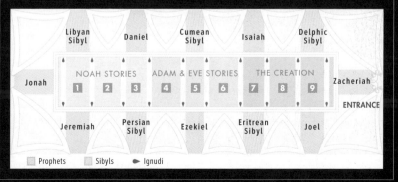

Libyan Sibyl   Daniel   Cumean Sibyl   Isaiah   Delphic Sibyl

Jonah

NOAH STORIES · 1 2 3 · ADAM & EVE STORIES · 4 5 6 · THE CREATION · 7 8 9

Zacheriah

ENTRANCE

Jeremiah   Persian Sibyl   Ezekiel   Eritrean Sibyl   Joel

Prophets   Sibyls   Ignudi

HEAVEN'S ABOVE

The ceiling's biblical symbols were ideated by three Vatican theologians, Cardinal Alidosi, Egidio da Viterbo, and Giovanni Rafanelli, along with Michelangelo. As for the ceiling's painted "framework," this *quadratura* alludes to Roman triumphal arches because Pope Julius II was fond of mounting "triumphal entries" into his conquered cities (in imitation of Christ's procession into Jerusalem on Palm Sunday).

THE CENTER PANELS

Prophet turned art-critic or, perhaps doubling as ourselves, the ideal viewer, Jonah the prophet (painted at the altar end) gazes up at the

Creation, or Michelangelo's version of it.

1 The first of three scenes taken from the Book of Genesis: God separates Light from Darkness.

2 God creates the sun and a craterless pre-Galilean moon

while the panel's other half offers an unprecedented rear view of the Almighty creating the vegetable world.

3 In the panel showing God separating the Waters from the Heavens, the Creator

tumbles towards us as in a self-made whirlwind.

4 Pausing for breath, next admire probably Western Art's most famous image— God giving life to Adam.

Adam's rib leads to the sixth panel.

6 In a sort of diptych divided by the trunk of the Tree of Knowledge of Good and Evil, Michelangelo retells the Temptation and the Fall.

Illustrating Man's fallen nature, the last three panels narrate, in un-chronological order, the Flood. In the first Noah offers a pre-Flood sacrifice of thanks.

8 Damaged by an explosion in 1794, next comes Michel-

angelo's version of Flood itself.

9 Finally, above the monumental Jonah, you can just make out the small, wretched figure of Noah, lying drunk— in pose, the shrunken anti- type of the majestic Adam five panels down the wall.

THE CREATION OF ADAM

Michelangelo's Adam was partly inspired by the Creation scenes Michelangelo had studied in the sculpted doors of Jacopo della Quercia in Bologna and Lorenzo Ghiberti's Doors of Paradise in Florence. Yet in Michelangelo's version Adam's hand hangs limp, waiting God's touch to impart the spark of life. Facing his Creation, the Creator—looking a bit like the pagan god Jupiter—is for the first time ever depicted as horizontal, mirroring the Biblical "in his own likeness." Decades after its completion, a crack began to appear, amputating Adam's fingertips. Believe it or not, the most famous fingers in Western art are the handiwork, at least in part, of one Domenico Carnevale.

Ezekiel

Jeremiah

Ignudi

Cumaean Sibyl

Libyan Sibyl

Ignudi

PROPHETS & SIBYLS

Uniting the pagan and pre-Christian worlds of antiquity, below the central painted panels sit seven Prophets and five of their Classical equivalents, the Sibyls, while the lunettes feature Christ's ancestors as listed in Matthew's Gospel.

Ezekiel & the Cumaean Sibyl

Illustrating Hebrew and pagan worlds are Ezekiel, his body and beard straining sideways, full of prophetic tension, and the Cumaean Sibyl, as impressive for her majestic ugliness as the other four sibyls are for their beauty. Look closely at the angels attending the scary prophetess to see how one of them, in Italian-fashion, is "giving the thumb"—then, as today, considered an obcene gesture.

Jeremiah & the Libyan Sibyl

The doomy-faced Jeremiah is taken to be a self portrait of the long-suffering Michelangelo himself while opposite, showing the artist's range, is the almost playful Libyan Sibyl, about on the point of tripping over as her tunic catches on the plinth while she reaches to put her book of prophecy back on its shelf.

THOSE SCANDALOUS "IGNUDI"

The immediate function of the ceiling's naked giants, the "ignudi"—Michelangelo's own coinage—is to carry the shields celebrating famous Israelite victories and so, indi-rectly, those of bellicose Pope Julius. Some refer to them as angels without wings, yet the passion in their faces seem all too human, fear and anxiety of a pagan world awaiting its overthrow in its very redemption. Historians note that the famed ancient sculpture of *Laocoon and His Sons*—a writhing nude grouping—was excavated in Rome recently. The iconographic tradition of the "ascetic athlete"—a figure of virtue—was also known at this time. Other critics see them as an excuse for Michelangelo to paint his favorite male models, discreetly filtered through the homo-erotic optic of Platonic Love, a current trend taken up by Florentine philosophers like Poliziano.

THE SISTINE CEILING REBORN

In 2003, a twenty-year restoration of Michelangelo's frescoes was finally completed. After more than 500 time-stained years of candle-smoke, applied varnishes, and salt mold were removed, the world acclaimed a revolutionary "new" Michelangelo. Gone were the dark shadows and gloomy hues considered so "Michelangelesque." In their place were an array of pink raspberries, sherbet greens, and *changeant* tangerines—a palette even the Impressionist painters might have considered gaudy. Or, as one critic put it, "Michelangelo on Prozac." Some felt there was a gain in definition, but a loss in shadows and underpainting. For the most part, art historians hailed the new look,

proclaiming it the long-lost antecedent for the acidic Mannerist colors that emerged in Italian art in the 1520s. Artists, however, remain scandalized, finding the evocative subtlety of the Renaissance master replaced by a paint-by-numbers version.

But with much of Michelangelo's overpainting removed, it is easier to track his changing artistic style. Halfway through, Michelangelo decided his earlier panels were too busy and, beginning with the *Creation of Adam*, he painted much larger figures and simpler compositions. Another factor was, undoubtedly, the sheer physical difficulty of the execution. Michelangelo left a sonnet describing with stoical humor

the contortions to which his body was subjected daily: for almost four years, he had to stand with aching, bending back just under the ceiling, paint dripping in his face, a worse position in many ways than the false Hollywood image of Michelangelo on his back. Compared to the first executed of the main panels, *The Flood* (which took forty days to paint, just as the biblical flood did), the last of the center panels, *God separating Light from Darkness*, was almost miraculously the work of a single day. Michelangelo's brush had come to obey the same time frame as the Creator himself, a proof of how far the so-called "sculptor" had mastered his technique.

CLOSE UP

Don't Forget

To enter the Musei Vaticani, the Sistine Chapel, and the Basilica di San Pietro you must comply with the Vatican's dress code, or you will be turned away by the implacable custodians stationed at the doors. (Also no penknives, which will show up under the metal detector.) For both men and women, shorts and tank tops are taboo, as are miniskirts and other revealing clothing. Wear a jacket or shawl over sleeveless tops, and avoid T-shirts with writing or pictures that could risk giving offense. If you opt to start at the Musei Vaticani (Vatican Museums), note that the entrance on Viale Vaticano (there's a separate exit on the same street) can be reached by Bus No. 49 from Piazza Cavour, which stops right in front; or on foot from Piazza del Risorgimento (Bus 81 or Tram 19) or a brief walk from the Via Cipro–Musei Vaticani stop on Metro line A. The collections of the museums are immense, covering about 7 km (4½ mi) of displays.

You can rent a taped commentary in English explaining the Sistine Chapel and the Raphael Rooms. You're free to photograph what you like, barring use of flash, tripod, or other special equipment, for which permission must be obtained. To economize on time and effort, once you've seen the frescoes in the Raphael rooms, you can skip much of modern religious art in good conscience, and get on with your tour. With more than 4.5 million visitors in 2008 alone, recession notwithstanding, lines at the entrance to the Capella Sistina (Sistine Chapel) can move slowly, as custodians block further entrance when the room becomes crowded. Keep in mind that sometimes it's possible to exit the museums from the Sistine Chapel into St. Peter's, saving further legwork. A sign at the entrance to the museums indicates whether the "For Tour Groups" exit is open, which you can use if you just follow an exiting tour group.

Enter the building from the former moat, and through the original Roman door of Hadrian's tomb. From here you pass through a courtyard that was enclosed in the base of the classical monument. You enter a vaulted brick corridor that hints at grim punishments in dank cells. On the right, a spiral ramp leads up to the chamber in which Hadrian's ashes were kept. Where the ramp ends, the Borgia pope Alexander VI's staircase begins. Part of it consisted of a wooden drawbridge, which could isolate the upper part of the castle completely. The staircase ends at the Cortile dell'Angelo, a courtyard that has become the resting place of neatly piled stone cannonballs as well as the marble angel that stood above the castle. (It was replaced by a bronze sculpture in 1753.) In the rooms off the Cortile dell'Angelo, look for the **Cappella di Papa Leone X** (Chapel of Pope Leo X), with a facade by Michelangelo.

In the courtyard named for Pope Alexander VI, a wellhead bears the Borgia coat of arms. The courtyard is surrounded by gloomy cells and huge storerooms that could hold great quantities of oil and grain in case of siege. Benvenuto Cellini, the rowdy 16th-century Florentine goldsmith, sculptor, and boastful autobiographer, spent some time in Castel Sant'Angelo's foul prisons; so did Giordano Bruno, a heretical monk who was later burned at the stake in Campo de' Fiori, and Beatrice Cenci, accused of patricide and incest and executed just across Ponte Sant'Angelo.

Take the stairs at the far end of the courtyard to the open terrace for a view of the Passetto, the fortified corridor connecting Castel Sant'Angelo with the Vatican and recently featured in the book and film *Angels and Demons* (also occasionally visitable at an extra charge of €3). Pope Clement VII used the Passetto to make his way safely to the castle during the Sack of Rome in 1527. Near here is a caffè for refreshments. Continue your walk along the perimeter of the tower and climb the few stairs to the *appartamento papale* (papal apartment). As if times of crisis were no object, the Sala Paolina (Pauline Room), the first you enter, was decorated in the 16th century by Pierino del Vaga and assistants with lavish frescoes of scenes from the Old Testament and the lives of St. Paul and Alexander the Great. Look for the trompe l'oeil door with a figure climbing the stairs. From another false door, a black-clad figure peers into the room. This is believed to be a portrait of an illegitimate son of the powerful Orsini family. Out on to the upper terrace, at the feet of the bronze angel, take in a magnificent view of the city below.

Every July and August there are the so-called Notti Animate di Castel Sant'Angelo ("Animated Nights") when the terraces are lined with restaurants, bars, and gelaterie; along with live shows and performances, the prisons and Passetto are visitable during evening hours. ✉ *Lungotevere Castello 50, Vatican* ☎ *06/6819111* ⊕ *www.castelsantangelo.com* 💶 *€5* ⊙ *Tues.–Sun. 8:30– 7:30* Ⓜ *Ottaviano.*

NEED A BREAK?   **A tiny take-out pastry shop, Le Delizie del Borgo** (✉ *Borgo Pio 142, Vatican* ☎ *0668801338*) **offers Neapolitan and Sicilian cakes, confections of fresh fruit, and so-called** *artigianale* **(artisanal) ice cream, which will give you a boost after a day of pounding the pavement. Walk down Borgo Pio from Via Porta Angelica; you will find it on the left.**

Fodor's Choice ★   **Musei Vaticani** *(The Vatican Museums).* Other than the pope and his papal court, the occupants of the Vatican are some of the most famous artworks in the world. The museums that contain them are part of the **Vatican Palace,** residence of the popes since 1377. The palace consists of a number of individual buildings containing an estimated 1,400 rooms, chapels, and galleries. The pope and his household occupy only a small part of the palace, most of the rest of which is given over to the Vatican Library and Museums. Beyond the glories of the Sistine Chapel, the collection is so extraordinarily rich you may just wish to skim the surface, but few will want to miss out on the great antique sculptures, the Raphael Stanze, and Old Master paintings, such as Leonardo da Vinci's *St. Jerome.*

Subsidiary Museums. Among the collections on the way to the chapel, the **Egyptian Museum** (in which Room II reproduces an underground chamber tomb of the Valley of Kings) is well worth a stop. The **Chiaramonti Museum** was organized by the Neoclassical sculptor Canova and contains almost 1,000 copies of classical sculpture. The gems of the Vatican's sculpture collection are in the **Pio-Clementino Museum,** however. Just off the hall in Room X, you can find the *Apoxyomenos* (Scraper), a beautiful 1st-century AD copy of a bronze statue of an athlete. There are other even more famous pieces in the **Octagonal Courtyard,** where Pope Julius II installed the pick of his private collection: on the left stands the celebrated *Apollo Belvedere.* In the far corner, on the same side of the courtyard, is the *Laocoön* group, found on Rome's Esquiline Hill in 1506, held to be possibly the single most important antique sculpture group in terms of its influence on Renaissance artists.

> ### SOMETHING IN PAPAL PURPLE?
>
> If you've come to the Eternal City looking for ecclesiastical garb or religious memorabilia, you'll hit gold in the shops near the Vatican on Via Porta Angelica. A celestial array of pope portraits, postcards, figurines, and even snow globes can be had for low prices. The pious can have their purchases blessed at a papal audience; blasphemers can put pope stickers on their cars. Lay shoppers may want to stick to the windows.

In the **Hall of the Muses,** the *Belvedere Torso* occupies center stage: this is a fragment of a 1st-century BC statue, probably of Hercules, all rippling muscles and classical dignity, much admired by Michelangelo. The lovely neoclassical room of the **Rotonda** has an ancient mosaic pavement and a huge porphyry basin from Nero's palace.

The room on the Greek-cross plan contains two fine porphyry sarcophagi (great marble burial caskets), one of St. Constantia and one of St. Helena, mother of the emperor Constantine.

Upstairs is an **Etruscan Museum,** an **Antiquarium,** with Roman originals; and the domed **Sala della Biga,** with an ancient chariot. In addition, there are the **Candelabra Gallery** and the **Tapestry Gallery,** including some designed by Raphael. Perhaps used more as a grand passageway, the incredibly long **Gallery of Maps** is frescoed with 40 maps of Italy and the papal territories, commissioned by Pope Gregory XIII in 1580. Nearby is the **Apartment of Pius V.**

The Raphael Stanze. Rivaling the Sistine Chapel for artistic interest are the **Stanze di Raffaello** (Raphael Rooms), which are directly over the Borgia apartments and can be very crowded with people. Pope Julius II moved into this suite of rooms in 1507, four years after his election. Reluctant to continue living in the Borgia apartments with their memories of his ill-famed predecessor, Alexander VI, he called in Raphael to decorate his new quarters. When people talk about the Italian High Renaissance—thought to be the very pinnacle of Western art—it's Raphael's frescoes they're probably thinking about. The theme of the **Segnatura Room,** the first to be frescoed, was painted almost entirely by Raphael himself (as opposed to the other rooms, which were painted in large part by his assistants). The theme of the room—which may broadly be said to be "enlightenment"—reflects the fact that this was Julius's private library.

Theology triumphs in the fresco known as the *Disputa,* or *Debate on the Holy Sacrament,* on the wall behind you as you enter. Opposite, the

School of Athens glorifies philosophy in its greatest exponents. Plato (perhaps a portrait of Leonardo da Vinci), in the center, is debating a point with Aristotle. The pensive figure on the stairs is thought to be modeled after Michelangelo, who was painting the Sistine ceiling at the same time Raphael was working here. Michelangelo does not appear in preparatory drawings, so Raphael may have added his fellow artist's portrait after admiring his work. In the foreground on the right are Euclid and the architect Bramante, and, on the far right, the handsome youth just behind the white-clad older man is Raphael himself. Over the window on the left are Parnassus, who represents

VATICAN MUSEUMS' TOP 10
Michelangelo's Sistine Ceiling
Raphael's Stanze
Apollo Belvedere
Leonardo's *St. Jerome*
Laocoön
Caravaggio's *Deposition*
Raphael's *Transfiguration*
Aldobrandini Marriage
The Good Shepherd
Belvedere Torso

poetry, and Apollo, the Muses, and famous poets, many of whom are likenesses of Raphael's contemporaries. In the lunette over the window opposite, Raphael painted figures representing and alluding to the Cardinal and Theological Virtues, and subjects showing the establishment of written codes of law. Beautiful personifications of the four subject areas, Theology, Poetry, Philosophy, and Jurisprudence, are painted in circular pictures on the ceiling above.

The first in the series is the **Incendio Room**; it was the last to be painted in Raphael's lifetime, and was executed mainly by Giulio Romano, who worked from Raphael's drawings for the new pope, Leo X. It served as the pope's dining room. The frescoes depict stories of previous popes called Leo, the best of them showing the great fire in the Borgo (the neighborhood between the Vatican and Castel Sant'Angelo), which threatened to destroy the original St. Peter's Basilica in AD 847; miraculously, Pope Leo IV extinguished it with the sign of the cross. The other frescoes show the coronation of Charlemagne by Leo III in St. Peter's Basilica, the *Oath of Leo III,* and a naval battle with the Saracens at Ostia in AD 849, after which Pope Leo IV showed clemency to the defeated.

The **Eliodoro Room** is a private antechamber. Working on the theme of Divine Providence's miraculous intervention in defense of endangered faith, Raphael depicted Leo the Great's encounter with Attila; it's on the wall to your left as you enter. The *Expulsion of Heliodorus from the Temple of Jerusalem,* opposite the entrance, refers to Pope Julius II's insistence on the Church's right to worldy possessions. He appears on the left, watching the scene. On the left window wall, the *Liberation of St. Peter* is one of Raphael's best-known and most effective works.

Adjacent to the Raphael Rooms, the **Hall of Constantine** was decorated by Giulio Romano and other assistants of Raphael after the master's untimely death in 1520. The frescoes represent various scenes from

Tips on Touring the Vatican Museums

Remember that the Vatican's museum complex is humongous—only after walking through what seems miles of galleries do you see the entrance to the Sistine Chapel (which, note should be made, cannot be entered from St. Peter's Basilica directly). Check out the Sistine location vis-à-vis the main church on their Web site ⊕ *www. stpetersbasilica.org/*. Most people—especially those who rent an audio guide, who must return it to the main desk—tour the complex, see the Sistine, then trudge back to the main museum entrance, itself a 15-minute walk from St. Peter's Square.

However, there is an "insider" way to exit directly from the Sistine Chapel to St. Peter's Basilica: Look for the "tour groups only" door on the right as you face the rear of the chapel—when a group exits, go with the flow and follow them. This will deposit you in St. Peter's Basilica and you won't have to take that 15-minute hike back to St. Peter's Square, nor run the gauntlet of the basilica's security line (note: the X-ray machines can prove

hazardous to your camera film). Note that if you run to the Sistine Chapel, then do the "short-cut" exit into the basilica, you will have missed all the rest of the Vatican Museum collection. This means you should probably plan on touring the complete complex, including the ancient statues and the Pinacoteca painting collection, before you get to the Sistine.

Plans are afoot to broaden the sidewalk leading to the museum, to install electronic information panels, and also to build a streamlined roof to protect queuers from sun or rain (until then umbrellas are recommended). With as many as 70,000 visitors daily, the wait can be a long one. Another possibility in the future might be to visit in the evening. This experiment began in July 2009, and the Vatican hopes to open the museum every Friday evening from 7 to 11, though reservations are essential (and possible over the Internet at ⊕ *www.vatican. va*). To date, however, no definite timetable has been fixed.

the life of the emperor Constantine, including the epic-sized action-packed *Battle of the Milvian Bridge.* Guided by three low-flying angels, Constantine charges to victory as his rival Maxentius drowns in the river below. Don't miss the tiny **Chapel of Nicholas V,** aglow with Fra Angelico (1395–1455) frescoes of episodes from the life of St. Stephen (*above*) and St. Lawrence (*below*), one of the greatest gems of Renaissance art. If it weren't under the same roof as Raphael's and Michelangelo's works, it would undoubtedly draw greater attention.

Returning downstairs, you enter the **Borgia apartments,** where some intriguing historic figures are depicted in the elaborately painted ceilings, designed but only partially executed by Pinturicchio at the end of the 15th century, and greatly retouched in later centuries. It's generally believed that Cesare Borgia murdered his sister Lucrezia's husband, Alphonse of Aragon, in the Room of the Sibyl. In the Room of the Saints, Pinturicchio painted his self-portrait in the figure to the left of the possible portrait of the architect Antonio da Sangallo. (His profession is made clear by the fact that he holds a T-square.) The lovely picture of

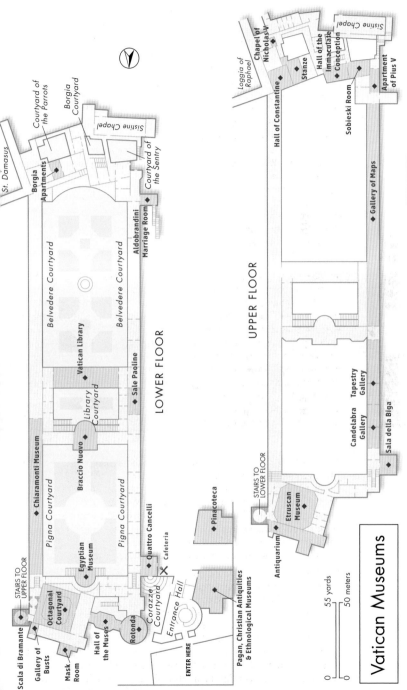

Vatican Museums

LOWER FLOOR

UPPER FLOOR

St. Damasus

Courtyard of the Parrots

Borgia Courtyard

Borgia Apartments

Sistine Chapel

Courtyard of the Sentry

Aldobrandini Marriage Room

Belvedere Courtyard

Belvedere Courtyard

Vatican Library

Sale Paoline

Library Courtyard

Chiaramonti Museum

Braccio Nuovo

Pigna Courtyard

Pigna Courtyard

Egyptian Museum

STAIRS TO UPPER FLOOR

Scala di Bramante

Gallery of Busts

Octagonal Courtyard

Mask Room

Hall of the Muses

Rotonda

Corazze Courtyard

Quattro Cancelli

Cafeteria

Entrance Hall

ENTER HERE

Pinacoteca

Pagan, Christian Antiquities & Ethnological Museums

Loggia of Raphael

Chapel of Nicholas V

Stanze

Hall of the Immaculate Conception

Sistine Chapel

Hall of Constantine

Sobieski Room

Apartment of Pius V

Gallery of Maps

STAIRS TO LOWER FLOOR

Antiquarium

Etruscan Museum

Candelabra Gallery

Tapestry Gallery

Sala della Biga

55 yards

50 meters

0

0

4

St. Catherine of Alexandria is said to be a representation of Lucrezia Borgia herself.

In the frescoed exhibition halls that are part of the Vatican Museums, the **Vatican Library** displays precious illuminated manuscripts and documents from its vast collections. The **Aldobrandini Marriage Room** contains beautiful ancient frescoes of a Roman nuptial rite, named for their subsequent owner, Cardinal Aldobrandini. The **Braccio Nuovo** (New Wing) holds an additional collection of ancient Greek and Roman statues, the most famous of which is the *Augustus of Prima Porta*, in the fourth niche from the end on the left. It's considered a faithful likeness of the emperor Augustus, who was 40 years old at the time. Note the workmanship in the reliefs on his armor.

LAW AND ORDER, 16TH-CENTURY STYLE

Raphael's Stanze frescoes represent all the revolutionary characteristics of High Renaissance art: naturalism (Raphael's figures lack the awkwardness that pictures painted only a few years earlier still contained); humanism (the idea that man is the most noble and admirable of God's creatures); and a profound interest in the ancient world, the result of the 15th-century rediscovery of archaeology and classical antiquity. The frescoes in this room virtually dared its occupants to aspire to the highest ideas of law and learning—an amazing feat for an artist not yet 30.

The Vatican Pinacoteca. Much more celebrated are the works on view in the **Pinacoteca** (Picture Gallery). These often world-famous paintings are almost exclusively of religious subjects and are arranged in chronological order, beginning with works of the 11th and 12th centuries. Room II has a marvelous Giotto triptych, painted on both sides, which formerly stood on the high altar in the old St. Peter's. In Room III you'll see Madonnas by the Florentine 15th-century painters Fra Angelico and Filippo Lippi. The Raphael Room contains some of the master's greatest creations, including the exceptional *Transfiguration*, the *Coronation of the Virgin*, and the *Foligno Madonna* as well as the tapestries that Raphael designed to hang in the Sistine Chapel. The next room contains Leonardo's beautiful (though unfinished) *St. Jerome* and a Bellini *Pietà*. A highlight for many is Caravaggio's gigantic *Deposition*. In the courtyard outside the Pinacoteca you can admire the reliefs from the base of the Colonna di Marco Aurelio, the column in Piazza Colonna. A fitting finale to your Vatican visit can be found in the **Museo Pio Cristiano** (Museum of Christian Antiquities), where the most famous piece is the 3rd-century AD statue called the *Good Shepherd*, much reproduced as a devotional image.

For those interested in guided visits to the Vatican Museums, head to the Office of Guided Visits to Vatican Museums located on the Piazza San Pietro. Most tours run €19.50–€25.50 and need to be booked at least a day in advance by phone (☎ 06/69884676) or fax (🖷 06/69885100) or Internet (⊕ *www.vatican.va*). Note that most of these tours are offered between 8 and 10 AM only. Tentative at this writing were the new evening hours—the Notte Vaticane ("Vatican Nights")—which allow visitors to the museums during Friday evenings; call to confirm. ☎ *06/69883332, 06/69883860 for group tours and visits to gardens, 06/69884667 for private tours of museum only, 06/69884947 for tours for the disabled (some wheelchairs are available at entrance, 06/69881589)* ⊕ *www. vatican.va* 💳*€14* ☉ *Mon.–Sat. 9–6 (last entrance at 4); closed Sun., except for last Sun. of month (9–12:30), when admission is free; other dates of closure include Jan. 1 and 6; Feb. 11; May 1 and 21; June 11 and 29; Aug. 15; Dec. 25 and 26* ☞ *Note: Ushers at entrance of St. Peter's and Vatican Museums will bar entry to people with bare knees or bare shoulders* Ⓜ *Cipro-Musei Vaticani. Bus 64, 40.*

NEED A BREAK?

About five minutes from the Vatican Museums exit are two good neighborhood trattorias that are far less touristy than those directly opposite the museums. At **Hostaria Dino e Toni** (✉ *Via Leone IV 60, Vatican* ☎ *06/39733284*) you can dine on typical Roman fare, fresh from the nearby outdoor market on Via Andrea Doria, and pizza. Closed Sunday. **La Caravella** (✉ *Via degli Scipioni 32, at Via Vespasiano, three blocks down from Piazza Risorgimento, Vatican* ☎ *06/39726161*) serves classic Roman food and pizza.

4

WORTH NOTING

Giardini Vaticani *(Vatican Gardens).* Extending over the hill behind St. Peter's Basilica is Vatican City's enclave of neatly trimmed lawns and flower beds, which are dotted with some interesting constructions and other, duller ones that serve as office buildings. The Vatican Gardens occupy almost 40 acres of land on the Vatican hill, behind St. Peter's Basilica. The mandatory tour begins in front of the Centro Servizi on Piazza San Pietro. It takes about two hours and includes a visit to the little-used Vatican railroad station, which now houses a museum of coins and stamps made in the Vatican, and the Torre di San Giovanni (Tower of St. John), restored by Pope John XXIII as a place where he could retreat to work in peace, and now used as a residence for distinguished guests. The tower is at the top of the hill, which you explore on foot. The plantings include a formal Italian garden, a flowering French garden, a romantic English landscape, and a small forest. Wear good walking shoes and observe the Vatican dress code. Call for a reservation (which is required) two or three days in advance. ✉ *Centro Servizi, south side of Piazza San Pietro, Vatican* ☎ *06/69884676* ⊕ *www.vatican.va* 💳*€12* ☉ *Mar.–Oct., Tues., Thurs., and Sat. 11* AM; *Nov.–Feb., Sat. 11* AM, *office Mon.–Sat. 8:30–7* Ⓜ *Cipro-Musei Vaticani.*

Ponte Sant'Angelo. One of the most beautiful of central Rome's 20 or so bridges is lined with angels designed by Bernini, baroque Rome's most prolific architect and sculptor. Bernini himself carved only two of the angels (those with the scroll and the crown of thorns), both of which were moved to the church of Sant'Andrea delle Fratte shortly afterward due to the wishes of the Bernini family. Though copies, the angels on the bridge today convey forcefully the grace and characteristic sense of movement—a key element of baroque sculpture—of Bernini's best work. Originally built in 133–134, the Ponte Elio, as it was originally called, was a bridge over the Tiber to the Hadrian's Mausoleum. The bridge changed its name in memory of Pope Gregory's vision of an angel sheathing its sword to signal the ending of the Plague of 590. In Medieval times, continuing its sacral function, the bridge became an important element in funneling pilgrims toward St. Peter's and, as such, in 1667 Pope Clement IX commissioned Bernini to design 10 angels bearing the symbols of the Passion, turning the bridge into a sort of Via Crucis. ⊠ *Between Lungotevere Castello and Lungotevere Altoviti, San Pietro* Ⓜ *Ottaviano.*

Navona and Campo

PIAZZA NAVONA, PANTHEON, CAMPO DE' FIORI, VIA GIULIA

WORD OF MOUTH

"The Campo de' Fiori square has a different personality at 9 AM than it does at 9 PM, which is different yet than that at 11 PM. I just love that Rome's piazzas are used just as much today as 500 years ago. (Minus the public executions, of course.)"

—Missypie

GETTING ORIENTED

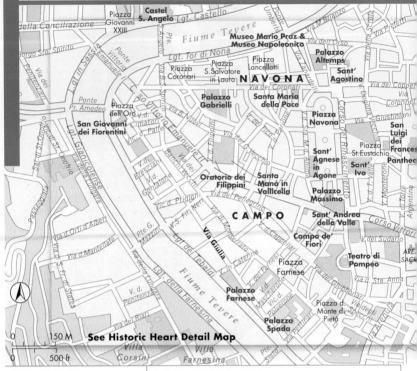

See Historic Heart Detail Map

GETTING HERE	O.K., WHERE DO I START?
This neighborhood is the heart of "Vecchia Roma," an easy walk across the river from the Vatican or Trastevere and a half-hour amble from the Spanish Steps neighborhood.	Two blocks west of Piazza Venezia—the square that is Rome's central transportation hub—sits the grandmother of all Rome's 17th-century churches, Il Gesù, whose splendor makes it a fitting overture to this sumptuously baroque quarter. After this curtain-raiser, cross Corso Vittorio Emanuele and take Via del Gesù, turning left onto Via Piè di Marmo to enter Piazza della Minerva. On the right is Santa Maria sopra Minerva, whose piazza contains Rome's most delightful baroque conceit, the 17th-century elephant obelisk memorial sculpted by Bernini. Straight ahead is one of the wonders of the world—the ancient Pantheon—with that postcard icon, Piazza Navona, just a few blocks to the north. As cornucopic with art treasures as any in Rome, this district would take about five hours to explore, not counting breaks—but taking breaks is what this area is all about. Chill out at Campo de' Fiori, a Monday–Saturday morning market that becomes a nighttime scene-arena, or hit the Piazza Navona in late afternoon, the ideal time for an aperitivo.
Bussing it from Termini or the Vatican, take the No. 40 Express or the No. 64 and get off at Largo Torre Argentina, a 10-minute stroll to either Campo dei Fiori or Piazza Navona.	
Another option is the little electric No. 116 that winds its way from Via Veneto past the Spanish Steps to Campo de' Fiori and Via Giulia.	

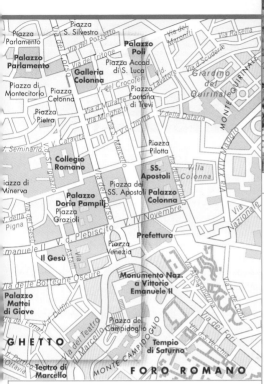

TOP 5 REASONS TO GO

Piazza Navona: Take yourself for the ultimate Roman passeggiata (promenade) in the city's most glorious piazza, which embodies the exuberant spirit of the baroque age better than any other. Crowds devouring gelati savor how Bernini's fantastic fountain is set off by the curves and steeples of Borromini's church of Sant'Agnese.

Caravaggio: Feel the power of 17th-century Rome's rebel artist in three of his finest paintings, at the church of San Luigi dei Francesi, dazzling with his masterful use of light and shadow (chiaroscuro).

The Pantheon: Gaze up to the heavens, through the dome of Rome's best-preserved ancient temple—could this be the world's only architecturally perfect building?

Campo de' Fiori: Stroll through the morning market, basket in hand, for a taste of the sweet life.

Via Giulia: Lined with regal palaces—still home to some of Rome's *princeliest* families—this is a Renaissance-era diorama you can walk through.

BEST TIME-OUTS

The first of its kind in the world, **Obikà Mozzarella Bar** (✉ *Via dei Prefetti 26* ☎ *06/6832630*) takes the sushi bar concept and instead offers a mouthwatering range of buffalo mozzarella from Naples. The decor is blond-wood and white-wall minimalism, the clientele chic, and the weekend brunch to die for. You can also grab a coffee or a salad to go.

An Italian-style "tapas bar" just steps from Piazza Navona, **Cul de Sac** (✉ *Piazza Pasquino 73* ☎ *06/68801094*) offers delightful samplings of everything from escargot to Italian regional favorites. The wine cellar is also well worth dipping into.

The Pantheon area is ice-cream heaven, with some of Rome's best gelaterias within a few steps of each other. Romans consider **Giolitti** (✉ *Via Uffizi del Vicario 40* ☎ *06/6991243*) superlative; the scene at the counter often looks like the storming of the Bastille. Remember to pay the cashier first, and hand the stub to the counter-person when you order your cone. Giolitti also has a good snack counter.

Sightseeing
★★★★★
Nightlife
★★★★
Dining
★★★
Lodging
★★★★★
Shopping
★★★★

If the Navona quarter doesn't enchant you, nothing in Rome will. Flowered balconies, brilliantly colored palazzi, Bernini's best fountain, friendly sidewalk caffé, priceless Caravaggio altarpieces, and the city's most baroque squares all make Navona into the crown jewel of the city's historic center. This is not where Roma began (that's the Capitoline Hill), but it's where all the centuries come together most beautifully. As you wander from the ethereal interior of the ancient Pantheon to explore the Raphaels at Santa Maria della Pace and then discover the gold-on-gold splendor of Il Gesu, you'll quickly learn that this part of Rome supersaturates the senses.

Today, the district's tiny streets brim over with parliamentarians doing deals over plates of *saltimbocca*, fashionistas shopping for shoes, and tourists from every part of the world. Everywhere, caffè, restaurants, and artisan shops line the twisted streets and the lopsided *piazze*, even as elegant ladies living in apartments upstairs lean out French windows for a breath of air. It's crowded here, and often noisy, but every moment in the *centro* is a slice of Roman life, and you'd be perfectly justified in just strolling the streets and taking it all in.

But it would be a crime to miss out on the cultural treasures this neighborhood holds. The baroque, Rome's finest artistic moment, was born and raised here, in Bernini's marvelous statuary, in Caravaggio's almost unbearably realistic paintings, in the frippery and froth of its best and most beautiful churches. Piazza Navona is the most theatrical piazza in town, its pedestrian-only oval focused on three of Bernini's fountains, including the sensational Fontana dei Quattro Fiumi (Fountain of the Four Rivers). It's flanked by some of the city's most elegant buildings, first among them Borromini's church of Sant'Agnese in Agone, a masterpiece of the baroque. Just one street over, the church of San Luigi dei Francesi showcases three of Caravaggio's greatest paintings. The churches of Il Gesu', Sant'Ivo alla Sapienza, and Santa Maria della Pace are each treasures in their own way: Il Gesu' grand and imposing, Sant'Ivo eccentric and whimsical, and Santa Maria jewel-like and theatrical.

GILT TRIP

For a full guided itinerary walk through this magical quarter, be sure to see our "Roamin' Holiday" chapter and its step-by-step tour, "Enjoying the Gilt: A Stroll Through the Baroque Quarter."

In Piazza Navona the baroque rules. However, just across the road is the Pantheon, ancient Rome's best-preserved temple, which escaped destruction due to its consecration in 608 AD as a Christian church, which it still is today. Its dome was until the last century the largest ever built, anywhere; its architectural balance and harmony are at least partly responsible for inspiring and informing the Renaissance. But not all the area's treasures are of the artistic nature: Campo de' Fiori, the famous market piazza, is a must-see in the morning, when farm and fish stalls bring the square to life with shouting, shopping, and smells. In the evening until past midnight, outdoor bars and restaurants transform this humble square into a hot spot. For Romans Navona is their downtown—a largely residential area that stretches eastward of the Tiber over to the main Corso avenue. While this district is referred to by the locals by a number of names—most notably Campo Marzio, Parione, and Regola—we choose the most popular moniker to refer to the northern half of the district set around Piazza Navona. The southern half is called Campo, referring to its charming hub, the Campo de' Fiori. Occupying the horn of land that pushes the Tiber westward toward the Vatican, the entire area has been an integral part of the city since ancient times. Rome's first emperor and prime scenographer Augustus got things started by transforming the Campo Marzio's military exercise ground into an alternative city-center to the Forum. During the Renaissance the area's proximity to both the Vatican and Lateran palaces drew many of Rome's richest people to settle here and greatest artists to work here. Today, when a busker sings a melancholy song about his *bella città*, chances are he's moved to music by the winding alleys and gentle light of Vecchia Roma—a nickname meaning "Old Rome" bestowed by residents on this achingly beautiful district.

NAVONA

In terms of sheer sensual enjoyment—from a mouthwatering range of restaurants and caffè to the ornate baroque settings—it's tough to top this area of Rome. Just a few blocks—and some 1,200 years—separate the two main showstoppers: the Piazza Navona and the ancient Pantheon. The first is the most beautiful baroque piazza in the world, which serves as the open-air salon for this quarter of Rome. As if this is not grandeur enough, across Corso di Rinascimento—and a millennia again in time—stands the Pantheon, the grandest extant building still standing from ancient Rome. Until Saint Peter's surpassed it, this was the world's largest dome. Near the same massive hub Bernini's delightful Elephant Obelisk in the nearby square shows small can also be beautiful. And

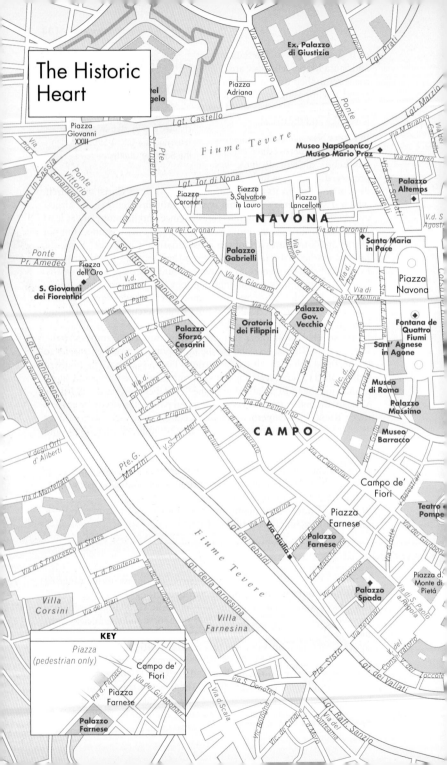

The Historic
Heart

KEY

Piazza
(pedestrian only)

Campo de'
Fiori

Piazza
Farnese

**Palazzo
Farnese**

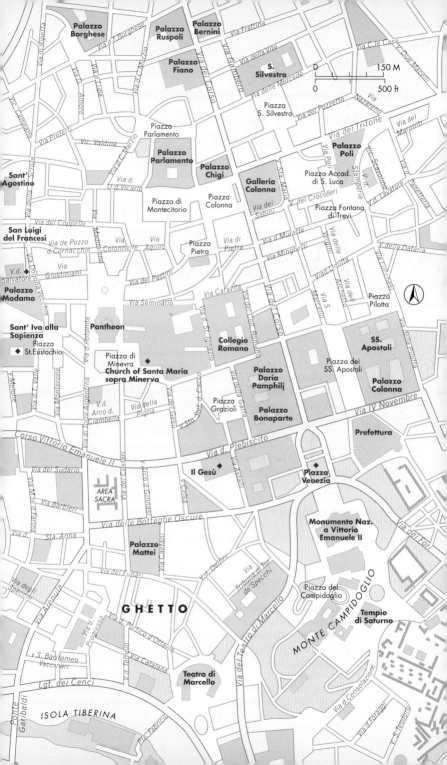

beautiful is the word to describe this entire area, one that is packed with baroque wonders, charming stores, and very happy sightseers.

TOP ATTRACTIONS

Biblioteca Angelica. If you've watched the film *Angels and Demons,* you'll have seen this library before, albeit under the false name of "Biblioteca Vaticana," the real Vatican library having refused permission due to the book/film's dodgy theology and even more improbable plot. Founded by Augustinian Cardinal Angelo Rocca in 1604, this bibliophile's paradise now contains 180,000 books (a preliminary letter attesting genuine research interest is needed). The ground floor stages temporary exhibitions from time to time. ⊠ *Piazza S. Agostino 8, Navona* ☎ *06/6840801* ⊕ *www.biblioangelica.it* ⊑ *Free* ⊙ *Mon. 8:30–1:30, Tues.–Thurs. 8:30–6:30.*

Fodor's Choice
★

Palazzo Altemps. Containing some of the finest ancient Roman statues in the world, this collection formerly formed the core of the Museo Nazionale Romano. As of 1995, it was moved to these new, suitably grander digs. The palace's sober exterior belies a magnificence that appears as soon as you walk into the majestic courtyard, studded with statues and covered in part by a retractable awning. The restored interior hints at the Roman lifestyle of the 16th through 18th centuries while showcasing the most illustrious pieces from the Museo Nazionale, including the Ludovisi family collection. In the frescoed salons you can see the *Galata,* a poignant work portraying a barbarian warrior who chooses death for himself and his wife rather than humiliation by the enemy. Another highlight is the large Ludovisi sarcophagus, magnificently carved from marble. In a place of honor is the Ludovisi Throne, which shows a goddess emerging from the sea and being helped by her acolytes. For centuries this was heralded as one of the most sublime statues of Greek sculpture but, today, at least one authoritative art historian considers it a colossally overrated fake. Look for the framed explanations of the exhibits that detail (in English) how and exactly where Renaissance sculptors, Bernini among them, added missing pieces to the classical works. In the lavishly frescoed Loggia stand busts of the Caesars. In the wing once occupied by early-20th-century poet Gabriele D'Annunzio (who married into the Altemps family), three rooms newly opened in 2009 now host the museum's Egyptian collection. ⊠ *Piazza Sant'Apollinare 46, Navona* ☎ *06/39967700* ⊕ *www.pierreci.it* ⊑ *€7, 3-day pass including other 3 venues of Museo Nazionale Romano (Crypta Balbi/Palazzo Massimo/ Museo Diocleziano)* ⊙ *Tues.–Sun. 9–6:45.*

Fodor's Choice
★

Pantheon. One of the wonders of the ancient world, this onetime pagan temple, a marvel of architectural harmony and proportion, is the best-preserved monument of imperial Rome. It was entirely rebuilt by the emperor Hadrian around AD 120 on the site of an earlier pantheon (from the Greek *pan,* all, and *theon,* gods) erected in 27 BC by Augustus's general Agrippa. The majestic circular building was actually designed *by* Hadrian, as were many of the temples, palaces, and lakes of his enormous villa outside the city at Tivoli. Hadrian nonetheless retained the inscription over the entrance from the original building that named Agrippa as the builder, in the process causing enormous confu-

PIAZZA NAVONA

✉ *Junction of Via della Cuccagna, Corsia Agonale, Via di Sant'Agnese, and Via Agonale.*

TIPS

■ On the eve of Epiphany (January 5–6), Piazza Navona's toy fair explodes in joyful conclusion, with much noise and rowdiness to encourage Befana, an old woman who brings toys to good children and pieces of coal (represented by similar-looking candy) to the naughty. Dealers also set up before Christmas to sell trinkets and presepio (crèche) figures while the toy stores of Al Sogno (at No. 53) and Berté (at No. 3) enchant year-round.

■ Some say the perfect Roman afternoon is spent caffè-sitting on the Piazza Navona. The sidewalk tables of the Tre Scalini (Piazza Navona 30; 06/6879148) caffè offer a grandstand view of all the action. This is the place that invented the tartufo, a luscious chocolate ice-cream specialty. The restaurant-pizzeria annex has the same view. Rome's most popular place to meet, have ice cream and coffee, take the children and dogs for a walk, and watch the passing parade, Piazza Navona is lined with caffè, so you can pick and choose.

Here everything that makes Rome unique is compressed into one beautiful baroque piazza. Always camera-ready, Piazza Navona has Bernini sculptures, three gorgeous fountains, a magnificently baroque church (Sant'Agnese in Agone), and, above all, the excitement of people out to enjoy themselves-strolling, caffè-loafing, seeing, and being seen.

The piazza has been an entertainment venue for Romans ever since being built over Domitian's circus (pieces of the arena are still visible near adjacent Piazza Sant'Apollinare).

The square still has the carefree air of the days when it was the scene of medieval jousts and 17th-century carnivals—even now it's the site of a lively Christmas "Befana" fair.

The piazza still looks much as it did during the 17th century, after the Pamphili pope Innocent X decided to make it over into a monument to his family to rival the Barberini's palace at the Quattro Fontane.

At center-stage is the Fontana dei Quattro Fiumi, created for Innocent X by Bernini in 1651. Bernini's powerful figures of the four rivers represent the four corners of the world: the Nile; the Ganges; the Danube; and the Plata, with its hand raised.

One story has it that the figure of the Nile—the figure closest to Sant' Agnese in Agone—is hiding its head because it can't bear to look upon the church's "inferior" facade designed by Francesco Borromini.

In fact, the facade was built after the fountain, and the statue hides its head because it represents a river whose source was then unknown (for more on Bernini and Borromini, see our special photo feature in Chapter 7).

5

sion among historians until, in 1892, a French architect discovered that all the bricks used in the Pantheon dated from Hadrian's time.

The most striking thing about the Pantheon is not its size, immense though it is (until 1960 the dome was the largest ever built), nor even the phenomenal technical difficulties posed by so vast a construction; rather, it's the remarkable unity of the building. You don't have to look far to find the reason for this harmony: the diameter described by the dome is exactly equal to its height. It's the use of such simple mathematical balance that gives classical architecture its characteristic sense of proportion and its nobility and why some call it the world's only architecturally perfect building. The great opening at the apex of the dome, the oculus, is nearly 30 feet in diameter and was the temple's only source of light. It was intended to symbolize the "all-seeing eye of heaven."

To do the interior justice defied even Byron. He piles up adjectives, but none seems to fit: "Simple, erect, severe, austere, sublime." Not surprising, perhaps, when describing a dome 43 meters high and the same across and built to mirror the universe itself, albeit in Roman times a geocentric one. Poised on top of a mighty concrete ring, the five levels of trapezoidal coffers represent the course of the five then-known planets and their concentric spheres. Then, ruling over them, comes the sun represented symbolically and literally by the 9-meter-wide eye at the top. The heavenly symmetry is further paralleled by the coffers themselves: 28 to each row, the number of lunar cycles. Note how each coffer takes five planetary steps toward the wall. Then in the center of each would have shone a small bronze star. Down below the seven large niches were occupied, not by saints, but statues of Mars, Venus, the deified Caesar, and the other "astral deities," including the moon and sun, the "sol invictus." And in their midst, to quote one historian, would sit the emperor, his authority bolstered by the system above "while in the role of universal legislator he set in motion new laws and presided over the Supreme Court."

The Pantheon is by far the best preserved of the major monuments of imperial Rome, a condition that is the result of it being consecrated as a church in AD 608. No building, church or not, escaped some degree of plundering through the turbulent centuries of Rome's history after the fall of the empire. In 655, for example, the gilded bronze covering the dome was stripped. Similarly, in the early 17th century, Pope Urban VIII removed the bronze beams of the portico, using the metal to produce the *baldacchino* (canopy) that covers the high altar at St. Peter's Basilica. Most of its interior marble facing has also been stripped and replaced over the centuries. Nonetheless, the Pantheon suffered less than many other structures from ancient Rome.

The Pantheon serves as one of the city's important burial places. Its most famous tomb is that of Raphael (between the second and third chapels on the left as you enter). The inscription reads "Here lies Raphael; while he lived, mother Nature feared to be outdone; and when he died, she feared to die with him." Two of Italy's 19th-century kings are buried here, too: Vittorio Emanuele II and Umberto I. The tomb of the former was partly made from bronze that had been taken from the

Pantheon by Urban VIII to cast as cannon. Thankfully, the temple's original bronze doors have remained intact for more than 1,800 years. Be sure to ponder them as you leave. ⊠ *Piazza della Rotonda, Navona* ☎ *06/68300230* ◻ *Free* ☉ *Mon.–Sat. 8:30–7:30, Sun. 9–6.*

NEED A BREAK? On Via degli Orfani (No. 86), on the east corner of Piazza del Pantheon, the Tazza d'Oro coffee bar (no tables, no frills) is the place for serious coffee drinkers, who also indulge in *granita di caffè con panna* (coffee ice with whipped cream). For a classy but economically priced meal try snazzily named Il Desiderio preso per la Coda ("Desire taken by the Tail"), just a corner away from Palazzo Altemps (off tiny Via de' Gigli d'Oro or Via del Orso). The restaurant's title comes from a play written by Picasso, although its address is Vicolo della Palomba 23.

Fodor'sChoice ★ **San Luigi dei Francesi.** A pilgrimage spot for art lovers everywhere, San Luigi is home to the Cerasi Chapel, adorned with three stunningly dramatic works by Caravaggio (1571–1610), the baroque master of the heightened approach to light and dark. Set in the Chapel of St. Matthew (at the altar end of the left nave), they were commissioned for San Luigi, the official church of Rome's French colony (San Luigi is St. Louis, patron of France). The inevitable coin machine will light up his *Calling of St. Matthew, Matthew and the Angel,* and *Matthew's Martyrdom,* seen from left to right, and Caravaggio's mastery of light takes it from there. When painted, they caused considerable consternation to the clergy of San Luigi, who thought the artist's dramatically realistic approach was scandalously disrespectful. A first version of the altarpiece was rejected; the priests were not particularly happy with the other two, either. Time has fully vindicated Caravaggio's patron, Cardinal Francesco del Monte, who secured the commission for these works and stoutly defended them. They're now recognized to be among the world's greatest paintings. ⊠ *Piazza San Luigi dei Francesi, Navona* ☎ *06/688271* ☉ *Weekdays 10–12:30 and 4–7 (closed Thurs. afternoon).*

★ **Sant'Agnese in Agone.** The absolute quintessence of baroque architecture, this church has a facade that remains a wonderfully rich mélange of bell towers, concave spaces, and dovetailed stone and marble, the creation of Francesco Borromini (1599–1667), a contemporary and rival of Bernini. Next to his new Pamphilj family palace, Pope Innocent X had the adjacent chapel expanded into this full-fledged church. The work was first assigned to the architect Rainaldi. However, Donna Olimpia, the pope's famously domineering sister, became increasingly impatient with how the work was going so in was brought Borromini, whose wonderful concave entrance has the magical effect of making the dome appear much larger than it actually is. The name of this church comes from *agona,* the source of the word *navona* and a corruption of the Latin *agonalis,* describing the type of games held there in Roman times. The saint associated with the church is Agnes, who was martyred here in the piazza's forerunner, the Stadium of Domitian. As she was stripped nude before the crowd, hair miraculously grew to maintain her modesty before she was killed. The interior is a marvel of modular baroque space and is ornamented by giant marble reliefs sculpted by Raggi and Ferrata. ✉ *Piazza Navona, Navona* ☎ *06/68192134* ⊙ *Mon.–Sat. 9–noon and 4–7, Sun. 10–1 and 4–8.*

★ **Santa Maria della Pace.** In 1656, Pietro da Cortona (1596–1669) was commissioned by Pope Alexander VII to enlarge the tiny Piazza della Pace in front of the 15th-century church of Santa Maria (to accommodate the carriages of its wealthy parishioners). His architectural solution was to design a new church facade complete with semicircular portico, demolish a few buildings here and there to create a more spacious approach to the church, add arches to give architectural unity to the piazza, and then complete it with a series of bijou-size palaces. The result was one of Rome's most delightful little architectural stage sets. Within are two great Renaissance treasures: Raphael's fresco above the first altar on your right depicts the *Four Sibyls*, almost exact, if more relaxed, replicas of Michelangelo's. The fine decorations of the Cesi Chapel, second on the right, were designed in the mid-16th century by Sangallo. Opposite is Peruzzi's wonderful fresco of the *Madonna and Child*. Meanwhile, the octagon below the dome is also something of an art gallery in itself with works by Cavalliere Arpino, Orazio Gentileschi, and others as Cozzo's *Eternity* fills the lantern above. Behind the church proper is its cloister, designed by Bramante (architect of St. Peter's) as the very first expression of High Renaissance style in Rome. At times, the cloister is the venue for modern art shows and, thanks to the Caffè alla Pace, the little piazza has become the core of a trendy caffè scene. ✉ *Via Arco della Pace 5, Navona* ☎ *06/6861156* ⊙ *Mon., Wed., and Sat. 9–noon.*

Santa Maria sopra Minerva. The name of the church reveals that it was built *sopra* (over) the ruins of a temple of Minerva, ancient goddess of wisdom. Erected in 1280 by the Dominicans on severe Italian Gothic lines, it has undergone a number of more or less happy restorations to the interior. Certainly, as the city's major Gothic church, it provides a refreshing contrast to baroque flamboyance. Have some coins handy to illuminate the **Cappella Carafa** in the right transept, where Filippino Lippi's (1457–1504) glowing frescoes are well worth the small investment, opening up the deepest azure expanse of sky where musical angels hover around the Virgin. Under the main altar is the tomb of St. Catherine of Siena, one of Italy's patron saints. Left of the altar you'll find Michelangelo's *Risen Christ* and the tomb of the gentle artist Fra Angelico, behind a modern sculptured bronze screen. Bernini's unusual and little-known monument to the Blessed Maria Raggi is on the fifth pier from the door on the left as you leave the church. In front of the church, the little obelisk-bearing elephant carved by Bernini is perhaps the city's most charming sculpture. An inscription on the base of **Bernini's Elephant Obelisk** makes reference to the church's ancient patroness, reading something to the effect that it takes a strong mind to sustain solid wisdom. ✉ *Piazza della Minerva, Navona* ☎ *06/6793926* ⊙ *Mon.–Sun. 9–7.*

Sant'Ivo alla Sapienza. The main facade of this eccentric baroque church, probably Borromini's best, is on the stately courtyard of an austere building that once housed Rome's university. Sant'Ivo has what must surely be one of the most delightful domes in all of Rome—a golden spiral said to have been inspired by a bee's stinger *(for more information on Borromini, see our special photo feature, "Baroque and Desperate: The*

Tragic Rivalry of Bernini and Borromini" in Chapter 6). The bee symbol is a reminder that Borromini built the church on commission from the Barberini pope Urban VIII (a swarm of bees figure on the Barberini family crest). The interior, open only for two hours on Sunday, is worth a look, especially if you share Borromini's taste for complex mathematical architectural idiosyncrasies. "I didn't take up architecture solely to be a copyist," Borromini once said. Sant'Ivo is certainly the proof. ⊠ *Corso Rinascimento 40, Navona* ☎ *06/6864987* ⊙ *Sun. 9–noon.*

WORTH NOTING

Sant'Agostino. Caravaggio's celebrated *Madonna of the Pilgrims*—which scandalized all of Rome because a kneeling pilgrim is pictured, all too realistically for the taste of the time, with dirt on the soles of his feet, and the Madonna stands in a less than majestic pose in a dilapidated doorway—is in the first chapel on the left. Third column down the nave, admire Raphael's blue-robed *Isaiah*, said to be inspired by Michelangelo's prophets on the Sistine ceiling (Raphael, with the help of Bramante, had taken the odd peek at the master's original against strict orders of secrecy). Directly below is Sansovino's Leonardo-influenced sculpture, *St. Anne and the Madonna with Child.* As you leave, in a niche just inside the door, is the sculpted *Madonna and Child,* known to the Romans as the "Madonna del Parto" (of Childbirth) and piled high with ex-votos. The artist is Jacopo Tatti, also sometimes confusingly known as Sansovino after his master. ⊠ *Piazza Sant'Agostino, Navona* ☎ *06/68801962* ⊙ *Daily 7:45–12:30 and 4–7:30.*

Museo Mario Praz. On the top floor of the Palazzo Primoli—the same building (separate entrance) that houses the Museo Napoleonico—is one of Rome's most unusual museums. As if in amber, the apartment in which the famous Italian essayist Mario Praz lived is preserved intact, decorated with a lifetime's accumulation of delightful baroque and Neoclassical art and antiques arranged and rearranged to create symmetries that take the visitor by surprise like the best trompe d'oeil. As author of *The Romantic Sensibility* and *A History of Interior Decoration,* Praz was fabled for his taste for the arcane and the bizarre; here his reputation for the same lives on. The apartment, prettily done up in Empire style, can only be seen on group tours. ⊠ *Via Zanardelli 1, Navona* ☎ *06/6861089* ⊕ *www.museopraz.beniculturali.it* 🎟 *Free* ⊙ *Guided visits in groups of 10 max: Mon. 2:30, 3:30, 4:30, 5:30, and 6:30, Tues.–Sun. 9, 10, 11, noon, 2:30, 3:30, 4:30, 5:30, and 6:30.*

Museo Napoleonico. Housed in an opulent collection of velvet-and-crystal salons that hauntingly capture the fragile charm of early-19th-century Rome, this small museum in the Palazzo Primoli contains a specialized and rich collection of Napoléon memorabilia, including a bust by Canova of the general's sister, Pauline Borghese (as well as a plaster cast of her left bust). You may well ask why this outpost of Napoléon is in Rome, but in 1809 the French emperor had made a grab for Rome, kidnapping Pope Pius VII in 1809 and proclaiming his young son the King of Rome. All came to naught a few years later, when the emperor was routed off his French throne. Upstairs is the Museo Mario Praz. ⊠ *Museo Napoleonico: Palazzo Primoli, Piazza di Ponte Umberto I, Navona* ☎ *06/4288888* ⊕ *www.museonapoleonico.it* 🎟 *€3* ⊙ *Tues.–Sat. 9–7.*

Oratorio dei Filippini. Housed in a baroque masterwork by Borromini, this former religious residence is named for Saint Philip Neri, founder in 1551 of the Congregation of the Oratorians, now contains Rome's Archivio Storico. Only the courtyard is visitable, and that also is still subject to restoration. Like the Jesuits, the Oratorians—or Filippini, as they were commonly known—were one of the new religious orders established in the mid-16th century as part of the Counter-Reformation. Neri, a man of rare charm and wit, insisted that the members of the order—most of them young noblemen whom he had recruited personally—not only renounce their worldly goods, but also work as common laborers in the building of Neri's great church of Santa Maria in Vallicella. The Oratory itself, once headquarters of the order, was built by Borromini between 1637 and 1662. Its gently curving facade is typical of Borromini's insistence on introducing movement into everything he designed. The inspiration here is that of arms extended in welcome to the poor (but perhaps also to gulls and pigeons who, with infallible architectural taste, line the parapets in the cooler months). ⊠ *Piazza della Chiesa Nuova (Corso Vittorio Emanuele), Navona* ☎ *06/6892537* ☉ *Under extensive restoration at this writing time (courtyard may be visitable).*

Palazzo Massimo alle Colonne. Following the shape of Emperor Domitian's Odeon arena, a curving, columned portico identifies this otherwise inconspicuous palace on a traffic-swept bend of Corso Vittorio Emanuele. In the 1530s Renaissance architect Baldassare Peruzzi built this new palace for the Massimo family, after their previous dwelling had been destroyed during the Sack of Rome. (High in the papal aristocracy, they boasted an ancestor who had been responsible for the defeat of Hannibal.) If you're here on March 16, you'll be able to go upstairs to take part (on an individual basis but not in groups) in commemorations of a miracle performed here in 1583 by Philip Neri, who is said to have recalled a young member of the family, one Paolo Massimo, from the dead. The palazzo's name comes from the sole surviving column from Domitian's *Odeon,* which still stands in the square at the back of the palazzo. ⊠ *Corso Vittorio Emanuele II 141, Navona.*

Piazza di Pasquino. This remaining part of an old Roman statue depicting Menelaus underwent a name change in the 16th century when a certain Pasquino, a cobbler or barber and part-time satirist, started writing comments around the base. The habit caught on and soon everyone was doing it. The most loquacious of Rome's "talking statues," its lack of arms or face is more than made up for in commentary of any topic of the day. ⊠ *Piazza di Pasquino, Navona.*

Santa Maria in Vallicella/Chiesa Nuova. This church, also known as Chiesa Nuova (New Church), was built toward the end of the 16th century at the urging of Philip Neri, and like Il Gesù is a product of the fervor of the Counter-Reformation. It has a sturdy baroque interior, all white and gold, with ceiling frescoes by Pietro da Cortona depicting a miracle reputed to have occurred during the church's construction: the Virgin and strong-armed angels hold up the broken roof to prevent it crashing down onto the congregation below. The Church is most famed for its three magnificent altarpieces by Rubens. ⊠ *Piazza della Chiesa*

Nuova, Corso Vittorio Emanuele II, Navona ☎ 06/6875289 ⊘ Daily
7:30–noon and 4:30–7:30.

CAMPO

Picture a district as the most charming theatre, a cast of gods and god-
lings, saints and sibyls, tritons and cherubs, with the odd ice-cream
seller, acrobat, or clown wandering in-between. Add a backdrop to
please an emperor or pope, lowlier caffè-owners and restaurateurs
charging for a stageside view. Such is Campo, which anchors the southern sector of the "Vecchia Roma" quarter. The heart of the area is the
Campo de' Fiori, barely changed from the days of the Renaissance. The
area is also studded with other 16th-century treasures like the Palazzo
Farnese—Michelangelo helped design this palace—the Palazzo Spada,
and Via Giulia, the ruler-straight street laid out by Pope Julius II and
long considered Rome's most coveted address.

TOP ATTRACTIONS

Il Gesù. The mother church of the Jesuits in Rome is the prototype of
all Counter-Reformation churches. Considered the first fully baroque
church, its spectacular decor tells a lot about an ea of religious triumph
and turmoil. Its architecture (the overall design was by Vignola, the
facade by della Porta) influenced ecclesiastical building in Rome for
more than a century and was exported by the Jesuits throughout the
rest of Europe. Though consecrated as early as 1584, the interior of the
church wasn't decorated for another 100 years. It had been originally
intended that the interior be left plain to the point of austerity—but,
when it was finally embellished, no expense was spared. Its interior
drips with gold and lapis lazuli, gold and precious marbles, gold and
more gold, all covered by a fantastically painted ceiling by Baciccia.
Unfortunately, the church is also one of Rome's most crepuscular, so its
visual magnificence is considerably dulled by lack of light.

The architectural significance of Il Gesù extends far beyond the splendid
interior. The first of the great Counter-Reformation churches, it was put
up after the Council of Trent (1545–63) had signaled the determina-
tion of the Roman Catholic Church to fight back against the Reformed
Protestant heretics of northern Europe. The church decided to do so
through the use of overwhelming pomp and majesty, in its effort to woo
believers. As a harbinger of ecclesiastical spectacle, Il Gesù spawned
imitations throughout Italy and the other Catholic countries of Europe
as well as the Americas.

The most striking element is the ceiling, which is covered with frescoes
that swirl down from on high to merge with painted stucco figures at
the base, the illusion of space in the two-dimensional painting becoming
the reality of three dimensions in the sculpted figures. Baciccia, their
painter, achieved extraordinary effects in these frescoes, especially in
the *Triumph of the Holy Name of Jesus,* over the nave. Here, the figures
representing evil cast out of heaven seem to be hurtling down onto the
observer. For details, the spectacle is best viewed through a specially
tilted mirror in the nave.

Continued on page 150

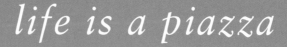

life is a piazza

A small square with two personalities as
different as day and night, the Campo
de' Fiori is Rome's mecca for people
with a picky purpose—whether it is
picking out food or picking out that
night's amorous avventura.

You can explore the Colosseum until your ears ring with roars of wild beasts, and make the rounds of churches until visions of putti dance in your head. But you won't know Rome until you have paused to appreciate the loveliness and vibrancy of the cityscape, perhaps from a table on one of Rome's beautiful squares. The Campo de' Fiori is particularly well endowed with such ringside seats, for here you can enjoy the show 24/7.

The Campo is heavily foot-trafficked at any given hour, whether for its sunlit market stalls or its moon-shadowed cobblestones. If you only have 24 hours in Rome (and especially if the past 20 have been dedicated to sightseeing), take a breather here and inhale a truly Roman social scene, no matter what time of day or night.

In the daytime, the piazza is a buzzing produce market where ancient vendors shout out the day's specialties and caffè-goers gossip behind newspapers while enjoying the morning's cappuccino. In the late afternoon, Campo transforms into the ultimate hangout with overflowing bars, caffès, and restaurants filled with locals and tourists all vying for the perfect '*posto*' to check out passersby.

Campo life is decidedly without pause. The only moment of repose happens in the very wee hours of the morning when the remaining stragglers start the stumble home and just before the produce-filled mini-trucks begin their magnificent march in to the square. At any given hour, you will always find something going on in Campo, the "living room" of today's Rome.

By Erica Firpo

5

IN FOCUS LIFE IS A PIAZZA

24 HOURS IN THE CAMPO DE' FIORI

5-6 am The Flight of the Bumble-Bees: *Ape* ("bee" in Italian) trucks file into Campo to unload the day's goods. These mini-trucks are very cute, no? *Ao! Claudia che sta a fa?!* ("Hey, Claudia how ya doin'"), Daniele yells across to Claudia as market guys and gals joke around. Good lessons in Roman slang.

7-8 am The Calm before the Storm: The only time Campo seems a bit sluggish, as stands have just opened, shoppers have yet to arrive, and everyone is just waking up. Market locals gather before heading off to work and school.

9-10 am The Herd: Tourists arrive, whether on their own or bearing colorful (and matching) t-shirts and hats. The locals take their "Pausa" coffee break while shops and late-opening caffès set up.

11-12 am The Eye of the Storm: Everyone is taking photos—photos of food, market goers, vendors, models, caffè-goers, anything.

1-2 pm Pranzo: Lunchtime in Campo. Everyone is hawking for an outdoor table. Top spots: **1** Magnolia, **2** Obika, **3** Aristo Campo, **4** Roscioli (indoors). Vendors start to pack up.

3-4 pm The Denoument: Campo is officially shutting down, marked by the notable odor of Campo refuse and the loud din of the cleaning trucks. Perhaps the absolute worst time to be in Campo. When the trucks depart, they leave the square to parents and toddlers.

5-6 pm Gelato Time: Shoppers and strollers replace replace marketgoers. The first of Campo's many musicians begin warming up

for the evening's concert. Favorites always include: "Guantanamera," "My Way," and "Volare."

7-8 pm Happy Hours: The pre-*aperitivi* people enjoy the cocktail before the cocktails. Always good for the punctual. By 6 aperitivi have been served. Are you "in" or "out"? Outside means picking any of the umbrella *tavoli* that line the piazza—**5** Baccanale, **2** Okika, **6** Nolano. If you prefer to be on the sly, try an indoor *enoteca*—

7 Camponeschi, **8** Angolo Divino, **4** Roscioli (three of Rome's best wine bars). Late-comers arrive for a last sip of wine before deciding where to dine.

9-10 pm Dining Hour: Dining in Rome is an all-evening experience. It's common custom to argue for a half-hour about the perfect restaurant. To make it easy:

9 La Carbonara (on the piazza, Roman cuisine); **10** Taverna del Lucifero (side street, fresh pastas and fondue); **11** Baffetto 2 (in a side piazza, best pizza); **4** Roscioli—an inside, cave-like spot for the gourmand.

11 pm-12 am After-dinner Drinks: Everyone moves back to the Campo for a drink (or many). Drunkenness can include catcalls, stiletto falls, volleyed soccer balls, and the cops (polizia or carabinieri, take your pick).

1-2 am Time to Go Home: Bars begin to shut down, with lingering kisses and hugs ("Dude, I love you!"). Clean-up crews come back. The din returns, this time as trucks clean up broken bottles and plastic cups.

3-4 am Some stragglers are still hanging around. For the first time Campo de' Fiori is silent, to the delight of the residents around it. They have to hurry...because the Ape (see 5 am) are pressing to get back in.

Piazza
Campo de' Fiori

10 ↗
9
← 7
2
Via del Baullari
11 ↘
3
7
6
1
8
5
To Via del Giubbonari
4

TE CAMPO DE FIORI

THE COGNOSCENTI'S CAMPO

WHERE THE POPE BUYS HIS ASPARAGUS

No longer a simple flower market, from Monday through Saturday mornings, Campo is Rome's most famous produce market, with prices that seemingly only the pope can afford. Shopping here is a worthy guilty pleasure as all produce is organic and homegrown, coming directly from the surrounding Lazio countryside and as far away as Sicily. It's here that you find standard Italian favorites (like Pacchino tomatoes, peppers, and eggplant), as well as seasonal delicacies such as *puntarelle* (variety of chicory) and *carciofi romani* (artichokes). For more exotic fruits, visit the stand on the southeast corner—Claudio is reputed to be the pope's *frutti vendolo*

(fruit man), thanks to such specialties as star fruit and white asparagus.

Campo's vendors also sell meats (of all beasts), regional cheeses, international spices, and homegrown honeys. On Tuesdays and Fridays, the *penscivendoli* (fish vendors) show off the morning's catch. A recent addition to the market are the several *bancarelle* (tchotchke stands) selling t-shirts, purses, bangles, and cookware. Though less charming than the fruit and flower stands, these bancarelle are great places to find off-beat *ricordi di Roma* (souvenirs) like Bialetti mokas (stovetop espresso-makers) and *"Ciao Roma"* t-shirts.

DRESS TO IMPRESS—OR DIGRESS?

Campo de' Fiori is one of Rome's best people-watching piazzas. Fashion-sense is either right on the money for marketgoers and late-night boozers (fanny packs and heavy metal t-shirts respectively), or else it is short-changed where style makes absolutely no sense. Combining both ends of the spectrum, *nonne* (grandmothers) catwalk in orthopedic shoes, accessorized with training-wheeled, plaid shopping bags, on the very cusp of trendy. If you come to Campo to shop for the perfect tomato, follow their lead—wear sensible shoes and bring a sturdy bag to hold all the day's goodies.

Rather sit stylishly at a caffè? Do like the Romans do: big sunglasses, shot of espresso, and a newspaper. Add a slight twist for the afternoon aperitivo by replacing the coffee and newspaper with a glass of prosecco or wine. Now this is what you came to Italy for!

Fashion Must Have: Umbrella:

Fashion No-No: Ladies, leave the stilettos at home—there's nothing quite like watching a tube-topped, twenty-something twist her ankle in the *sampietrini*. Save those heels for the *discoteca*!

HERALD TRIBUNE TO HAUTE COUTURE

Missing some down-home gossip? Campo de' Fiori and the adjacent Piazza Farnese boast two of Rome's best newspaper kiosks that cater to the international set with publications from *Vogue* (French to Russian) to the *Herald Tribune*. On the streets adjacent to the Campo can be found boutiques to delight serious shoppers:

Via dei Giubbonari: standard shops

Via del Pellegrino: stylish boutiques

Via dei Cappellari: artisan craftwork (i.e. furniture restorers, frame makers, art galleries)

Piazza del Paradiso: high-style stores (Nuvoricca has the season's *alta moda* couture favorites)

Dining Al Fresco in the Campo de' Fiori

THE SUN ALSO RISES

Bars and caffès in Campo may look different but all have approximately the same menu, which makes choosing a bar very easy. Mornings mean coffee and pastries while evenings offer wine, beer, and mixed drinks. There is only one requirement for the ideal repast: sunshine. Romans stay away from the shadows. Rule of thumb: Sit on the sunny side of the piazza. FYI: For those who must work while at play, the majority of Campo's bars have Wi-Fi.

Caffè Farnese: a quiet morning cappuccino and newspaper

Obika: mozzarella-centric antipasti

Nolana: known for its inexpensive wine list

Sloppy Sam's and/or The Drunken Ship: if you are homesick for America

Further grandeur is represented in the altar in the Chapel of St. Ignatius in the left-hand transept. This is surely the most sumptuous baroque altar in Rome; as is typical, the enormous globe of lapis lazuli that crowns it is really only a shell of lapis over a stucco base—after all, baroque decoration prides itself on achieving stunning effects and illusions. The heavy bronze altar rail by architect Carlo Fontana is in keeping with the surrounding opulence. ⊠ *Piazza del Gesù, off Via del Plebiscito, Campo* ☎ *06/3613717* ☉ *Daily 6:45–12:30 and 4–7:30.*

Campo de' Fiori. A bustling marketplace in the morning (Mon.–Sat. 8 AM–1 PM) and trendy meeting place the rest of the day (and night), this piazza has plenty of earthy charm. By sunset, all the fish, fruit, and flower vendors disappear and this so-called *piazza trasformista* takes on another identity, bar-life bulging out into the street, one person's carousal another's insomnia (for the full scoop, see our special photo feature, "Life is a Piazza"). Brooding over the piazza is a hooded statue of the philosopher Giordano Bruno, who was burned at the stake here in 1600 for heresy. His was the first of the executions that drew Roman crowds to Campo de' Fiori in the 17th century. ⊠ *Junction of Via dei Baullari, Via Giubbonari, Via del Pellegrino, and Piazza della Cancelleria, Campo.*

FodorśChoice ★ **Palazzo Farnese.** The most beautiful Renaissance palace in Rome, the Palazzo Farnese is fabled for the Galleria Carracci, whose ceiling is to the baroque Age what the Sistine ceiling is to the Renaissance. The Farnese family rose to great power and wealth during the Renaissance, in part because of the favor Pope Alexander VI showed to the beautiful Giulia Farnese. The massive palace was begun when, with Alexander's aid, Giulia's brother became cardinal; it was further enlarged on his election as Pope Paul III in 1534. The uppermost frieze decorations and main window overlooking the piazza are the work of Michelangelo, who also designed part of the courtyard, as well as the graceful arch over Via Giulia at the back. The facade on Piazza Farnese has recently been cleaned, further revealing geometrical brick configurations that have long been thought to hold some occult meaning. When looking up at the palace, try to catch a glimpse of the splendid frescoed ceilings, including the **Galleria Carracci** vault painted by Annibale Carracci between 1597 and 1604. The Carracci gallery depicts the loves of the gods, a supremely pagan theme that the artist painted in a swirling style that announced the birth of the baroque. Other opulent salons are among the largest in Rome, including the Salon of Hercules, which has an overpowering replica of the ancient *Farnese Hercules* front and center. Due to demand, the embassy now offers free tours (in French and Italian only) of their palace's historic rooms four times a week. You'll need to send a letter or e-mail to reserve tickets, one to four months in advance (depending on peak season visit or not), specifying the number in your party, when you wish to visit, and a local phone number, for confirmation a few days before the visit. ⊠ *French Embassy, Servizio Culturale, Piazza Farnese 67, Campo* ☎ *06/686011* ✎ *visite-farnese@france-italia.it* ▨ *Free* ☉ *Tours by appointment only on Mon. and Thurs. at 3, 4, and 5 PM. Closed July 24 to Sept. 7.*

★ **Palazzo Spada.** In this neighborhood of huge, austere palaces, Palazzo Spada strikes an almost frivolous note, with its upper stories covered with stuccos and statues and its pretty ornament-encrusted courtyard. While the palazzo houses an impressive collection of Old Master paintings, it is most famous for its trompe l'oeil garden gallery, a delightful example of the sort of architectural games rich Romans of the 17th century found irresistible. Even if you don't go into the gallery, step into the courtyard and look through the glass window of the library to the colonnaded corridor in the adjacent courtyard. See—or seem to see—Borromini's 8-meters-long gallery quadrupled in depth, a sort of optical telescope taking the Renaissance's art of perspective to another level, as it stretches out for a great distance with a large statue at the end. In fact the distance is an illusion: the corridor grows progressively narrower and the columns progressively smaller as they near the statue, which is just 2 feet tall. As if reality only existed to be surpassed, the baroque prided itself on special effects, and this is rightly one of the most famous. It was long thought that Borromini was responsible for this ruse; in fact it's now known that it was designed by an Augustinian priest, Giovanni Maria da Bitonto. Upstairs is a seignorial picture gallery, housed in period rooms. Outstanding works include Brueghel's *Landscape with Windmills,* Titian's *Musician,* and Andrea del Sarto's *Visitation.* Better still, these salons come with help-notes scattered freely around the baroque chairs furnishing each room. ⊠ *Piazza Capo di Ferro 13, Campo* ☎ 06/6832409, 06/22582493 *guided tours* ⊕ *www. galleriaborghese.it* ⏵ €5 ⏰ *Tues.–Sun. 8:30–7:30.*

Sant'Andrea della Valle. Topped by the highest dome in Rome (designed by Maderno) after St. Peter's, this huge and imposing 17th-century church is remarkably balanced in design. Note the early-17th-century frescoes in the choir vault by Domenichino and those by Lanfranco in the dome, one of the earliest ceilings in full baroque style, its upward vortex influenced by Correggio's dome in Parma of which Lanfranco was also a citizen. The three massive paintings of Saint Andrew's martyrdom are by Maria Preti (1650–51). Richly marbled and decorated chapels flank the nave, and in such a space, Puccini set the first act of *Tosca.* ⊠ *Piazza Vidoni 6, Corso Vittorio Emanuele II, Campo* ☎ 06/6861339 ⏰ *Daily 7–noon and 4–7:45.*

Fodor'sChoice
★ **Via Giulia.** Still a Renaissance-era diorama and one of Rome's most exclusive addresses, Via Giulia was the first street in Rome since ancient times to be laid out in a straight line. Named for Pope Julius II (of Sistine Chapel fame) who commissioned it in the early 1500s as part of a scheme to open up a grandiose approach to St. Peter's Basilica (using funds from the taxation of prostitutes), it became flanked with elegant churches and palaces. Though the pope's plans to change the face of the city were only partially completed, Via Giulia became an important thoroughfare in Renaissance Rome. Today, after more than four centuries, it remains the "salon of Rome," address of choice for Roman aristocrats. A stroll will reveal elegant palaces and old churches (one, **San Eligio,** at No. 18, reputedly designed by Raphael himself). The area around Via Giulia is a wonderful section to wander through and get the feel of daily life as carried on in a centuries-old setting. Among

the buildings that merit your attention are **Palazzo Sacchetti** (⊠ *Via Giulia 66*), with an imposing stone portal (inside are some of Rome's grandest state rooms, still, after 300 years, the private quarters of the Marchesi Sacchetti), and the forbidding brick building that housed the **Carceri Nuove** (*New Prison* ⊠ *Via Giulia 52*), Rome's prison for more than two centuries and now the offices of Direzione Nazionale Antimafia. Near the bridge that arches over the southern end of Via Giulia is the church of **Santa**

> **TOSCA'S ROME**
>
> Puccini lovers have been known to hire a horse-drawn carriage at night for an evocative journey that traces the course of the opera: from Sant'Andrea della Valle (on Corso Vittorio Emanuele II), then south on Via Biscione to head up Via Giulia past Palazzo Farnese—Scarpia's headquarters—to the locale of the opera's climax, Castel Sant'Angelo.

Maria dell'Orazione e Morte (Holy Mary of Prayer and Death), with stone skulls on its door. These are a symbol of a confraternity that was charged with burying the bodies of the unidentified dead found in the city streets. Home since 1927 to the Hungarian Academy, the **Palazzo Falconieri** (⊠ *Via Giulia 1* ☎ *06/6889671*) was designed by Borromini—note the architect's roof-top belvedere adorned with statues of the family "falcons," best viewed from around the block along the Tiber embankment. Now, with prior booking and a €3 fee it is possible to visit the Borromini-designed salons. Remnant of a master plan by Michelangelo, the arch over the street was meant to link massive Palazzo Farnese, on the east side of Via Giulia, with the building across the street and a bridge to the Villa Farnesina, directly across the river. Finally, on the right and rather green with age, dribbles that star of many a postcard, the Fontana del Mascherone. ⊠ *Between Piazza dell'Oro and Piazza San Vincenzo Pallotti, Campo.*

WORTH NOTING

★ **San Giovanni dei Fiorentini.** Imbued with the supreme grace of the Florentine Renaissance, this often overlooked church dedicated to Florence's patron saint, John the Baptist, stands in what was the heart of the Florentine colony in Old Rome. Many of these Florentines were goldsmiths, bankers, and money changers who contributed to the building of the church. Talented goldsmith and sculptor Benvenuto Cellini of Florence, known for his vindictive nature as much as for his genius, lived nearby. While the church was designed by Sansovino, Raphael (yes, he was also an architect) was among those who competed for this commission. Today, the church interior makes you feel you have wandered inside a perfect Renaissance space, one so harmonious it seems to be a Raphael pop-up 3-D painting. Borromini executed a splendid altar for the Falconieri family chapel in the choir. He's buried under the dome, despite the fact that those who committed suicide normally were refused a Christian burial. The late animal-loving pastor allowed well-behaved pets to keep their owners company at services, a tradition that lives on with his successor. ⊠ *Via Accaioli 2 (Piazza dell'Oro), Campo* ☎ *06/68892059* ⊗ *Daily 7–2:30 and 4–7.*

Corso and Spagna

WORD OF MOUTH

"Lurking around the Trevi fountain, several Fodorites were acting mysteriously: what were they up to?," PalenQ "They wanted to reenact the famous scene from *La Dolce Vita*?," Kismetchimera "A modern dance interpretation of *Swan Lake*?," mcnyc "Trying to figure out if they could get the marble horses in their carry-ons?," MelJ "Trying to swap Euro coins for U.S.?," cfc "Clifton Webb's body is buried within the Trevi Fountain,"

—George W

GETTING ORIENTED

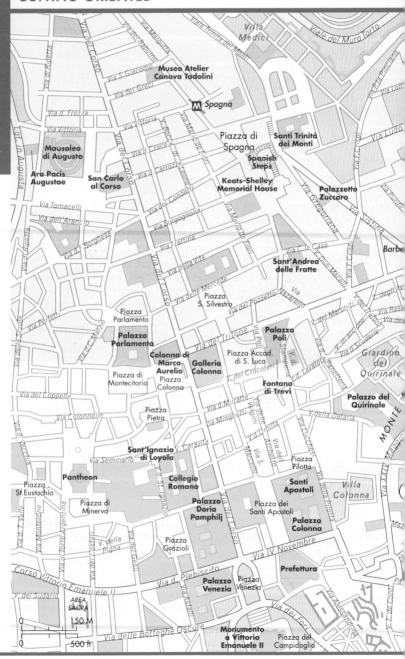

Villa Medici

Viale Trinità dei Monti

Viale del Muro Torto

Via d. Ripetta

Via d. Babuino

Via del Corso

Via S. Giacomo

Museo Atelier Canova Tadolini

Via dei Greci

M *Spagna*

Via d. Frezza

Via Vittoria

Via Vittoria

Via Mario de' Fiori

Via Margutta

Mausoleo di Augusto

Via d. Croce

Via d. Carrozze

Piazza di Spagna

Santi Trinità dei Monti

Spanish Steps

Ara Pacis Augustae

San Carlo al Corso

Via dei Condotti

Keats–Shelley Memorial House

Palazzetto Zuccaro

Via Sistina

Via Tomacelli

Via Borgognona

Via Gregoriana

Via dell'Arancio

Via d. Borghese

Via Frattina

Via d. Ripetta

Via d. Fontanella Borghese

Via d. Croce

Via della Vite

Via C.le Case

Barbe

Via F. Crispi

Via d. Due Macelli

Sant'Andrea delle Fratte

Via delle Mercede

Piazza S. Silvestro

Via del Pozzetto

Via Nazareno

degli A

Via del Tritone

V. d. Maroniti

V. del Traforo

Via Rase

Via d. Scuderie

Piazza Parlamento

Palazzo Parlamento

Via del Corso

Via Poli

Palazzo Poli

Piazza Accad. di S. Luca

V. d. Stamperia

V. d. Lavatore

Via d. Panetteria

Giardino del Quirinale

Piazza di Montecitorio

Colonna di Marco Aurelio

Galleria Colonna

Piazza Colonna

V. del Crociferi

Fontana di Trevi

Palazzo del Quirinale

Via del Coppelle

Piazza Pietra

Via d. Muratte

Via Minghetti

Via delle Vergini

Via d. Pilotta

Via dell'Archetto

V. della Dataria

MONTE

Via Colonnelle

Via dei Prefetti

Sant'Ignazio di Loyola

V. Caravita

Via Seminario

V. di S. Marcello

Piazza della Chiesa Nuova

Piazza Pilotta

Via XXIV Maggio

Piazza St. Eustachio

Pantheon

Collegio Romano

V. di S. Ignazio

Santi Apostoli

Villa Colonna

Via Monterone

Via di Torre Argentina

Piazza di Minerva

Palazzo Doria Pamphilj

Via del Corso

Via S. Marcello

Piazza dei Santi Apostoli

Palazzo Colonna

Piazza Grazioli

V. della Pigna

V. del Gesù

Via del Plebiscito

Piazza Venezia

V. IV Novembre

Prefettura

Corso Vittorio Emanuele II

V. del Sudario

AREA SACRA

150 M

500 ft

Via d. Astalli

Palazzo Venezia

Piazza Venezia

Via dei Fori

Via delle Botteghe Oscure

Monumento a Vittorio Emanuele II

Piazza del Campidoglio

TOP 5 REASONS TO GO

Trevi Fountain: In the pantheon of waterworks, this is Elvis—overblown, flashy, and reliably thronged by its legions of fans.

The Spanish Steps: Sprawl seductively on the world's most celebrated stairway—everyone's doing it. If you're able to make it to the top, a Cinerama view awaits you.

See Heaven: Stand beneath the stupendous ceiling of San Ignazio—Rome's most splendiferous baroque church—and, courtesy of painter-priest Fra Andrea Pozzo, prepare to be transported heavenward.

Lifestyles of the Rich and Famous: Take a peek through the keyhole of two of Rome's grandest palaces—the Palazzo Doria-Pamphilj and the Palazzo Colonna—for an intimate look at the homes of Rome's 17th-century grandees.

Luxe Shopping on Via Condotti: You can get from Bulgari to Gucci to Valentino to Ferragamo with no effort at all, except perhaps that of navigating (and ogling) the crowds of shoppers.

O.K., WHERE DO I START?

Begin at Piazza Venezia, the square in front of the gigantic Monumento a Vittorio Emanuele II. Head north on Via del Corso—Rome's main drag (or, a must if it is Saturday morning, head west one block to the gilded Palazzo Colonna art collection) for a block or so to dazzling Palazzo Doria Pamphilj, loaded with priceless Old Master paintings and one resident prince. Farther up the Corso, Via di Sant'Ignazio leads leftward to the 18th-century stage-set of Piazza di Sant'Ignazio, home to Sant' Ignazio, where the famous ceiling frescoes hold a surprise or two. A few blocks farther up the Corso, turn right and you'll soon hear the enchanting Fontana di Trevi. Continuing northwest you'll hit that postcard icon, the Spanish Steps, surrounded by Rome's most glamorous shops.

BEST TIME-OUTS

Recafè (✉ *Piazza Augusto Imperatore 36* ☎ *06/68134730*), located on the other side of Piazza Augusto Imperatore from the newly sheltered Ara Pacis monument, is all southern-Italian trendy. There's an affordable lunch menu, but for a quick snack, check out the caffè at the back where the rich Neapolitan espresso and assortment of pastries will keep you going for hours.

Just off the Corso in the jewel of a piazza, San Lorenzo in Lucina, sits **Caffè Ciampini** (✉ *Piazza San Lorenzo in Lucina 29* ☎ *06/6876606*), a turn-of-the-century tearoom-gelateria-caffè. Stand at the elegant bar for a quick espresso or sit outdoors under a big umbrella and linger over an aperitivo and a plateful of yummy hors d'oeuvres that come with it.

GETTING HERE

A short walking distance of Piazza del Popolo, Villa Borghese, the Pantheon, and the Trevi Fountain, the Spanish Steps and the Corso avenue are nearly impossible to miss. One of Rome's handiest subway stations, the Spagna metro station is tucked just left of the Spanish Steps, complete with elevator to spare the climb to the top if need be. Electric buses No. 117 and No. 119 hum through the neighborhood (the latter tootles up Via del Balbuino, famed for its shops); the No. 117 from Via Veneto and the No. 119 from Piazza del Popolo.

6

Sightseeing
★★★★★
Nightlife
★
Dining
★★★★★
Lodging
★★★★★
Shopping
★★★★★

In spirit, and in fact, this section of Rome is its most grandiose. The overblown Vittoriano monument, the labyrinthine treasure-chest palaces of Rome's surviving aristocracy, even the diamond-draped denizens of Via Condotti: all embody the exuberant ego of a city at the center of its own universe. Here's where you'll see ladies in furs, gobbling pastries at caffè tables, and walk through a thousand snapshots as you climb the famous Spanish Steps, admired by generations from Byron to Versace. As if to keep up with the area's gilded palaces, the local monuments seem aware that they, too, are expected to put on a show.

Right at the top of everyone's sightseeing list is the great Rococo confection of the Trevi Fountain: the Elton John of hydrants tinkling tirelessly for its droves of fans. Legend has it that a coin in the water guarantees, courtesy Fortune Airways, a cut-price return—even the most rational of us may find it hard to resist throwing one in, just in case. The Trevi is Rome's most celebrated waterwork, and you can rest assured, you are not the only one who knows it. Once you've chucked your change, follow the crowds and get ready to take some very serious time to explore this neighborhood, which extends along the Corso, the ruler-straight avenue that divides central Rome neatly in half.

If Rome has a Main Street, it's Via del Corso, which is often jammed with swarms of Roman teenagers, in from the city's outlying districts for a ritual stroll that resembles a strutting migration of lemmings in blue jeans. The Corso begins at noisy, chaotic Piazza Venezia, the imperial-size hub of all this ostentation, presided over by the Vittoriano, also known as the Altare della Patria (Altar of the Nation), or, less piously, as the "typewriter," the "wedding cake," or the Eighth Hill of Rome. Sitting grandly off the avenue are the Palazzo Doria-Pamphilj and the

Palazzo Colonna—two of the city's great art collections housed in magnificent family palaces.

Extending just east of Via del Corso, but miles away in style, Piazza di Spagna and its surrounding streets are where the elite meet. Back when, 19th-century artists used to troll the area around the Spanish Steps for models; today, it remains a magnet all day and well into the night for smooching Romans and camera-toting tourists. The density of high-fashion boutiques and trendy little shops leaves little room for residents—the closest thing to locals are the ladies loaded down with bags from Prada and tottering on Gucci stilettos. Lest you think the neighborhood is all Johnny-come-lately frivolity, stop into the Antico Caffè Greco, the one-time haunt of Franz Lizst, Mark Twain, and Hans Christian Andersen. It's been operating since 1760, making it one of the oldest caffè in the world. Prepare to linger.

AROUND VIA DEL CORSO

Because of the 20th-century grime, traffic-ridden Via del Corso appears to be nothing more than a major thoroughfare connecting Piazza Venezia and Piazza del Popolo. In fact, between dodging Vespas, it's easy to forget that the gray and stolid atmosphere comes partially from the enormous palaces lining both sides of the street. Most of them were built over the past 300 years by princely families who wanted to secure front-row seats for the frantic antics of Carnivale. But once you step past entrances here, you'll discover some of Rome's grandest 17th- and 18th- century treasures, including baroque ballrooms, glittering churches, and great Old Master paintings. And, oh, yes, the god-sized and thundering Trevi Fountain. For that, be sure to have your camera—and coins—ready.

TOP ATTRACTIONS

★ **Ara Pacis Augustae** (*Altar of Augustan Peace*). This vibrant monument of the imperial age has been housed in one of Rome's newest architectural landmarks: a gleaming, rectangular glass-and-travertine structure designed by American architect Richard Meier. Overlooking the Tiber on one side and the ruins of the marble-clad **Mausoleo di Augusto** (Mausoleum of Augustus), on the other, the result is a serene, luminous oasis right in the center of Rome. Opened in 2006, after a decade of bitter controversy over the monument's relocation, the altar itself dates back to 13 BC to celebrate the Pax Romana, the era of peace ushered in by Augustus's military victories. It is covered with spectacular and moving relief sculptures showing the procession of the Roman imperial family. Notice the poignant presence of several forlorn children; historians now believe they attest to the ambition of Augustus's notorious wife, the Empress Livia, who gained the throne for her son, Tiberius, by dispatching his family rivals with poison, leaving a slew of orphans in her wake. ⊠ *Lungotevere in Augusta, around Via del Corso* ☎ *06/32111605* ⊕ *www.arapacis.it* 🎫 *€6.50 (€8.50 if special exhibition is on view)* ⊗ *Tues.–Sun. 9–7 (last admission 1 hr before closing)* Ⓜ *Flaminio (Piazza del Popolo)*.

6

Monumento a Vittorio Emanuele II, or Altare della Patria *(Victor Emmanuel Monument, or Altar of the Nation)*. The huge white mass of the "Vittoriano" is an inescapable landmark—Romans say you can avoid its image only if you're actually standing on it. Some have likened it to a huge wedding cake; others, to an immense typewriter. Though not held in the highest esteem by present-day citizens, it was the source of great civic pride at the time of its construction, at the turn of the 20th century. To create this elaborate marble monster and the vast piazza on which it stands, architects blithely destroyed many ancient and medieval buildings and altered the slope of the Capitoline Hill, which abuts it. Built to honor the unification of Italy and the nation's first king, Victor Emmanuel II, it also shelters the eternal flame at the tomb of Italy's Unknown Soldier killed during World War I. The flame is guarded day and night by sentinels, while inside the building there is the (rather dry) Institute of the History of the Risorgimento. You can't avoid the Monumento, so enjoy neo-imperial grandiosity at its most bombastic.

The views from the top are some of Rome's most panoramic. The only way up is by elevator (located to the right as you face the monument); stop at the museum entrances (to the left and right of the structure) to get a pamphlet identifying the sculpture groups on the monument itself and the landmarks you will be able to see once at the top. Opposite the monument, note the enclosed olive-green wooden veranda fronting the palace on the corner of Via del Plebiscito and Via Corso. For the many years that she lived in Rome, Napoléon's mother had a fine view from this spot of the local goings-on. ⊠ *Entrance at Piazza Ara Coeli, next to Piazza Venezia, a round Via del Corso* ☏ *06/6991718* ⊕ *www. ambienterm.arti.beniculturali.it/vittoriano/index.html* ⌨ *Monument free, museum free, elevator €7* ◷ *Mon.–Thurs. 9:30–6:30, Fri.–Sun. 9:30–7:30.*

Fodor's Choice   **Palazzo Colonna.** Rome's grandest family built itself Rome's grandest
★   palazzo in the 18th century—it's so immense, it faces Piazza Santi Apostoli on one side and the Quirinal Hill on the other (a little bridge over Via della Pilotta links the palace with the gardens on the hill). While still home to some Colonna patricians, the palace also holds the family picture gallery, open to the public one day a week. The galleria is itself a setting of aristocratic grandeur; you'll recognize the **Sala Grande** as the site where Audrey Hepburn meets the press in *Roman Holiday*. At one end looms the ancient red marble column (*colonna* in Italian), which is the family's emblem; above the vast room is the spectacular ceiling fresco of the Battle of Lepanto painted by Giovanni Coli and Filippo Gherardi in 1675—the center scene almost puts the computer-generated special effects of Hollywood to shame. Adding redundant luster to the opulently stuccoed and frescoed salons are works by Poussin, Tintoretto, and Veronese, and a number of portraits of illustrious members of the family such as Vittoria Colonna—Michelangelo's muse and long-time friend—and Marcantonio Colonna, who led the papal forces in the great naval victory at Lepanto in 1577. Lost in the array of madonnas, saints, goddesses, popes, and cardinals is, spoon at the ready, with mouth missing some front teeth, Annibale Carracci's lonely *Bean-eater*. As W.H. Auden put it, "Grub first, art later." ⊠ *Via della Pilotta 17,*

Three Coins and a Triton

Who hasn't wanted to emulate Dorothy McGuire, Jean Peters, and Maggie McNamara in *Three Coins in the Fountain*—your Roman fountain fantasy will cost no more than the change in your pocket, and who knows? Your wish might come true.

Anyone who's thrown a coin backward over his or her shoulder into the Fontana di Trevi to ensure a return to Rome appreciates the magic of the city's fountains.

From the magnificence of the Fontana dei Quattro Fiumi in Piazza Navona to the graceful caprice of the Fontana delle Tartarughe in the Ghetto, the water-spouting sculptures seem as essential to the piazzas they inhabit as the cobblestones and ocher buildings that surround them.

Rome's original fountains date back to ancient times, when they were part of the city's remarkable aqueduct system, but from AD 537 to 1562 the waterworks were in disrepair and the city's fountains lay dry and crumbling— Romans were left to draw their water from the Tiber and from wells.

During the Renaissance, the popes brought running water back to the city as a means of currying political favor.

To mark the restoration of the Virgin Aqueduct, architect Giacomo della Porta designed 18 unassuming, functional fountains, each consisting of a large basin with two or three levels of smaller basins in the center, which were built and placed throughout the city at points along the water line.

Although nearly all of della Porta's fountains remain, their spare Renaissance design is virtually unrecognizable, because most were elaborately redecorated with dolphins, obelisks, and sea monsters, in the flamboyant style of the baroque.

Of this next generation of baroque fountaineers, the most famous is Gian Lorenzo Bernini.

Bernini's writhing, muscular creatures of myth adorn most of Rome's most visible fountains, including the Fontana di Trevi (so named for the three streets—*tre vie*—that converge at its piazza); the Fontana del Nettuno, with its tritons, in Piazza Barberini; and, in Piazza Navona, the Fontana dei Quattro Fiumi, whose hulking figures represent the four great rivers of the known world: the Nile, the Ganges, the Danube, and the Rio de la Plata.

The most common type of fountain in Rome is a kind rarely noted by visitors: the small, inconspicuous drinking fountains that burble away from side-street walls, old stone niches, and fire hydrant–like installations on street corners.

You can drink this water—many of these *fontanelle* even have pipes fitted with a little hole from which water shoots up when you hold your hand under the main spout.

To combine the glorious Roman fountain with a drink of water, head to Piazza di Spagna, where the Barcaccia fountain is outfitted with spouts from which you can wet your whistle.

6

around Via del Corso ☎ *06/6784350* ⊕ *www.galleriacolonna.it* 📷 *€7* ☉ *Sept.–July, Sat. 9–1.*

Fodor'sChoice **Palazzo Doria Pamphilj.** Along with the Palazzo Colonna and the Gal-
★ leria Borghese, this spectacular family palace provides the best glimpse
of aristocratic Rome. Here, the main attractions are the legendary Old
Master paintings, including treasures by Velázquez and Caravaggio,
the splendor of the main galleries, and a unique suite of private family apartments. The beauty of the graceful 18th-century facade of this
patrician palace may escape you unless you take time to step to the
opposite side of the street for a good view; it was designed by Gabriele
Valvassori in 1730. The foundations of the immense complex of buildings probably date from classical times. The current building dates from
the 15th century, with the exception of the facade. It passed through
several hands before it became the property of the famous seafaring
Doria family of Genoa, who had married into the Roman Pamphilj (also
spelled Pamphili) clan. As in most of Rome's older patrician residences,
the family still lives in part of the palace.

Housed in four *braccia* (wings) that line the palace's courtyard, the
picture gallery contains 550 paintings, including three pictures by
Caravaggio—a young *St. John the Baptist, Mary Magdalene*, and the
breathtaking *Rest on the Flight to Egypt*. Off the eyepopping **Galleria
degli Specchi** (Gallery of Mirrors)—a smaller version of the one at
Versailles—are the famous Velázquez *Pope Innocent X*, considered by
some historians to be the greatest portrait ever painted, and the Bernini bust of the same Pamphilj pope. Elsewhere you'll find a Titian, a
double portrait by Raphael, and some noted 17th-century landscapes
by Claude Lorrain and Gaspar Dughet. The audio guide by Prince
Jonathan Doria Pamphilj, the current heir (born in England, he was
adopted by the late Principessa Orietta), provides an intimate family
history well worth listening to. ✉ *Via del Corso 305, around Via del
Corso* ☎ *06/6797323* ⊕ *www.doriapamphilj.it* 📷 *€9* ☉ *Daily 10–5.*

Fodor'sChoice **Sant'Ignazio.** Rome's largest Jesuit church, this 17th-century landmark
★ harbors some of the most magnificent illusions typical of the baroque
style. To get the full effect of the marvelous illusionistic ceiling by priest-
artist Andrea Pozzo, stand on the small disk set into the floor of the
nave. The heavenly vision above you, seemingly extending upward
almost indefinitely, represents the *Allegory of the Missionary Work of
the Jesuits* and is part of Pozzo's cycle of works in this church exalting
the early history of the Jesuit Order, whose founder was the reformer
Ignatius of Loyola. The saint soars heavenward, supported by a cast
of thousands; not far behind is Saint Francis Xavier, apostle of the
Indies, leading a crowd of Eastern converts; a bare-breasted, spear-
wielding America in American Indian headdress rides a jaguar; Europe
with crown and scepter sits serene on a heftily rumped horse; while a
splendid Africa with gold tiara perches on a lucky crocodile. The artist
repeated this illusionist technique, so popular in the late 17th century,
in the false dome, which is actually a flat canvas—a trompe l'oeil trick
used when the budget was drained dry. The overall effect of the frescoes
is dazzling (be sure to have coins handy for the machine that switches
on the lights) and was fully intended to rival that produced by Baciccia

TREVI FOUNTAIN

✉ *Piazza di Trevi, accessed by Via Tritone, Via Poli, Via delle Muratte, Via del Lavatore, and Via di San Vincenzo.*

TIPS

■ Everyone knows the famous legend that if you throw a coin into the Trevi Fountain you will ensure a return trip to the Eternal City. But not everyone knows you have to do the ritual the right way: Toss a coin with your right hand over your left shoulder (or left hand over your right shoulder), with your back to the fountain. Others point out that to better your chances, toss two: one to guarantee that return trip, the other to make the wish come true. The fountain grosses about €120,000 a year, most of it donated to charity.

■ Even though you might like to reenact Anita Ekberg and Marcello Mastroianni's famous Trevi dip in La Dolce Vita, be forewarned: police guard the fountain 24 hours a day to keep out movie buffs and lovebirds alike, and transgressors risk a fine of up to €500.

■ Set on the Piazza di Trevi, the Gelateria San Crispino (Via della Panetteria 42; 06/6793924) is for discerning palettes, with unusual taste combinations and natural ingredients.

Alive with rushing waters commanded by an imperious Oceanus, the Fontana di Trevi (Trevi Fountain) earned full-fledged iconic status in 1954 when it starred in 20th-Century Fox's *Three Coins in the Fountain*. As the first color film in Cinemascope to be produced on location, it caused practically half of America to pack their bags for the Eternal City.

From the very start, however, the Trevi has been all about theatrical effects. An aquatic marvel in a city filled with them, the fountain's unique drama is largely due to the site: its vast basin is squeezed into the tight meeting of three little streets (the "tre via," which gives the fountain its name) with cascades emerging as if from the back wall of Palazzo Poli.

The conceit of a fountain emerging full-force from a palace was first envisioned by Bernini and Pietro da Cortona for Pope Urban VIII's plan to rebuild the fountain (which marked the end-point of the ancient Acqua Vergine aqueduct, created in 18 BC by Agrippa).

Only three popes later, under Pope Clement XIII, did Nicolo Salvi finally break ground with his winning design.

Salvi had his cake and ate it, too, for while he dazzles the eye with Rococo pyrotechnics—the sculpted seashells, the roaring seabeasts, the divalike mermaids—he has slyly incorporated them a stately triumphal arch (in fact, Clement was then restoring Rome's Arch of Constantine).

Salvi, unfortunately, did not live to see his masterpiece completed in 1762: working in the culverts of the aqueduct 11 years earlier, he caught his death of cold and died.

6

in the nearby mother church of Il Gesù. Scattered around the nave are several awe-inspiring altars—gigantic jewels, their soaring columns, gold-on-gold decoration, and gilded statues make these the last word in splendor. The church is often host to concerts of sacred music performed by choirs from all over the world; look for posters at the church doors for more information. ⊠ *Piazza Sant'Ignazio, around Via del Corso* ☎ *06/6794560* ⊙ *Daily 7:30–12:15 and 3–7:15.*

WORTH NOTING

Colonna di Marco Aurelio. Inspired by Trajan's Column, this 2nd-century AD column is composed of 27 blocks of marble covered with a series of reliefs recording Marcus Aurelius's victory over the Germans. At the top is a bronze statue of St. Paul, which replaced the effigy of Marcus Aurelius in the 16th century. The column is the centerpiece of Piazza Colonna. ⊠ *Piazza Colonna, alongside Via del Corso.*

Palazzo Venezia. Centerpiece of Palazzo Venezia, this palace was originally built for Venetian cardinal Pietro Barbo, who became Pope Paul II. It was also the backdrop used by Mussolini to harangue crowds with dreams of empire from the balcony over the main portal. Lights were also left on through the night during his reign to suggest that the Fascist leader worked without pause. The palace shows a mixture of Renaissance grace and heavy medieval lines, and today houses an eclectic collection of decorative objects, paintings, sculptures, and ceramics in handsome salons. Important temporary exhibitions are also often held here. The caffè on the loggia has a pleasant view over the garden courtyard. ⊠ *Via del Plebiscito 118, around Via del Corso* ☎ *06/699941* ⊠ *€4* ⊙ *Tues.–Sun. 8:30–7:30.*

Piazza Venezia. The geographic heart of Rome, this is the spot from which all distances from Rome are calculated, and the principal crossroads of city traffic. Piazza Venezia stands at what was the beginning of Via Flaminia, the ancient Roman road that leads east across Italy to Fano on the Adriatic Sea. Via Flaminia was, and still is, a vital artery. The initial tract of Via Flaminia, from Piazza Venezia to Piazza del Popolo, is now known as the Corso (Via del Corso, one of the busiest shopping streets in the city), after the horse races (*corse*) that were run here during the wild Roman carnival celebrations of the 17th and 18th centuries. The massive female bust, a fragment of the statue of Isis near the church of San Marco in the corner of the piazza, is known to the Romans as Madama Lucrezia. In another era this was one of the "talking statues" on which anonymous poets hung verses pungent with political satire, a practice that has not entirely disappeared. ⊠ *Junction of Via del Corso, Via Plebiscito, and Via Cesare Battisti, around Via del Corso.*

SPAGNA

Piazza di Spagna may be the soul of tourist Rome, but forget the "meet you at the Spanish Steps" thing—it can take hours to find familiar faces in the dense throng. Conversely, heavy crowds mean prime people-watching: Besides the riot of artists and panhandlers, there's an army of travelers fashion snobs drawn by Rome's most elegant shops, and plenty of young Italians. This entire area has eternally hosted the grandest of Grand Tourists: Goethe, Lord Byron, the Brownings, and Buffalo Bill frequented the Antico Caffè Greco on Via Condotti—why not take a time-out here just as those hallowed names once did? Piazza di Spagna's main draw remains the 18th-century Spanish Steps, which connect ritzy shops at the bottom of the hill with ritzy hotels at the top. The reward for climbing the *scalinatella* is a dizzying view of central Rome. Because the steps face west, the views are especially good around sunset.

TOP ATTRACTIONS

Keats-Shelley Memorial House. Sent to Rome in a last-ditch attempt to treat his consumption, the English Romantic poet John Keats lived—and died—here, in the "Casina Rossa" (the name refers to the blush-pink facade) at the foot of the Spanish Steps. At that point, this was the heart of the colorful bohemian quarter of Rome that was especially favored by the English. Keats had become celebrated through such poems as "Ode to a Nightingale" and "She Walks in Beauty," but his trip to Rome was fruitless, as he breathed his last here on February 23, 1821, aged only 25, forevermore the epitome of the doomed poet. In this "Casina di Keats," you can visit his rooms, although all his furnishings were burned after his death as a sanitary measure by the local authorities. You'll find a rather quaint collection of memorabilia of English literary figures of the period—Lord Byron, Percy Bysshe Shelley, Joseph Severn, and Leigh Hunt as well as Keats—and an exhaustive library of works on the Romantics. ✉ *Piazza di Spagna 26, Spagna* ☎ *06/6784235* ⊕ *www.keats-shelley-house.org* ▨ *€4* ☉ *Weekdays 10–1 and 2–6, Sat. 11–2 and 3–6* Ⓜ *Spagna.*

Museo-Atelier Canova Tadolini. A gorgeous remnant of Rome's 19th-century artistic milieu, this is the former atelier of Antonio Canova, Europe's greatest Neoclassic sculptor. Fabled for his frostily perfect statues of antique goddesses and fashionable princesses (sometimes in the same work, as in the Galleria Borghese's nearly naked *Principessa Pauline Borghese* posing as a "Victorious Venus"), he was given commissions by the poshest people. Today, his studio—atmospherically crammed to the gills with *modelli*, study sketches, and tools of the trade—has become a caffè and restaurant, so you can only ogle Canova's domain for the price of a very expensive meal. ✉ *Via del Babuino 150 A/B, Spagna* ☎ *06/32110702* ☉ *Closed Sun.* Ⓜ *Spagna.*

Fodor's Choice ★ **Palazzetto Zuccaro.** The most amusing house in all of Italy, this folly was designed in 1591 by noted painter Federico Zuccaro to form a monster's face. Typical of the outré Mannerist style of the period, the eyes are the house's windows; the entrance portal is through the monster's mouth. Zuccaro (1540–1609)—whose frescoes adorn many Roman churches, including Trinità del Monti just up the block—sank all of his money into his new home, dying in debt before his curious memorial, as it turned out to be, was completed. Today, it is the property of the Biblioteca Hertziana, Rome's prestigious fine-arts library; at press time, it has been sheathed for a long-term renovation project. Leading up to the quaint Piazza Trinità del Monti, Via Gregoriana is a real charmer and has long been one of Rome's most elegant addresses, home to such residents as French 19th-century painter Ingres and famed couturier Valentino's

6

first couture salon. ⊠ *Via Gregoriana 30, Spagna* Ⓜ *Spagna*.

🕐 ★ Fodor'sChoice **The Spanish Steps.** That icon of postcard Rome, the Spanish Steps—called the Scalinatella di Spagna in Italian—and the Piazza di Spagna from which they ascend both get their names from the Spanish Embassy to the Vatican on the piazza—in spite of the fact that the staircase was built with French funds in 1723. In honor of a diplomatic visit by the king of Spain, the hillside was transformed by architect Francesco de Sanctis to link the church of Trinità dei Monti at the top with the Via dei Condotti below. In an allusion to the church, the staircase is divided by three landings (beautifully banked with azaleas from mid-April to mid-May). For centuries, the Scalinatella ("staircase") has always welcomed tourists, dukes, and writers in search of inspiration—among them Stendhal, Honoré de Balzac, William Makepeace Thackeray, and Byron, along with today's enthusiastic hordes. Bookending the bottom of the steps are two monuments to the 18th-century days when the English colonized the area: to the right, the Keats-Shelley House, to the left, Babington's Tea Rooms, both beautifully redolent of the Grand Tour era. For weary sightseers, there is an elevator at Vicolo del Bottino 8 (next to the adjacent Metro entrance). ⊠ *Junction of Via Condotti, Via del Babuino, and Via Due Macelli, Spagna* Ⓜ *Spagna*.

A LITTLE CORNER OF ENGLAND

On the left foot of the Spanish Steps is **Babington's Tea Rooms** (⊠ *Piazza di Spagna 23* ☎ *06/6786027* ⊕ *www.babingtons.net* 🕐 *Daily 9–8:15*), which has ritzily catered to the refined cravings of Anglo-Saxon travelers since opening in 1896. The "Inglesi" had long been a mainstay of Grand Tour visitors to Rome so Anna Maria Babington found her "corner of England" a great success from the start. Inside, it is *molto* charming and you half expect to see Miss Lavish buttering a scone for Lucy Honeychurch, but it's not a budgeteer's cup of tea.

NEED A BREAK?

You may prefer to limit your shopping on Via Condotti to the window variety, but there's one thing here that everybody can afford—a stand-up coffee at the bar at the **Antico Caffè Greco** (⊠ *Via Condotti 86, Piazza di Spagna* ☎ *06/6791700*), set just off the Piazza di Spagna and the Fontana della Barcaccia. With its tiny marble-top tables and velour settees, this 200-year-old institution has long been the haunt of artists and literati; it's closed Sunday. Johann Wolfgang van Goethe, Byron, and Franz Liszt were habitués. Buffalo Bill stopped in when his road show hit Rome. The caffè is still a haven for writers and artists, along with plenty of Gucci-clad ladies. The tab picks up considerably if you decide to sit down to enjoy table service.

For that view of views from atop the Spanish Steps, with a highly priced price, which actually seems worth it, take the Steps elevator (at Vicolo del Bottino 8) to the bar called **Il Palazzetto** (⊠ *Vicolo del Bottino 8* ☎ *06/699934100*).

Sant'Andrea delle Fratte. On either side of the choir in this floridly baroque church are the two original angels that Bernini himself carved for the Ponte Sant'Angelo, where copies now stand. The door in the right aisle leads into one of Rome's hidden gardens, where orange trees bloom in the cloister. Borromini's fantastic contributions—the dome and a curious bell tower with its droop-winged angels looking out over the city—are best seen from Via Capo le Case, across Via Due Macelli, where there is also a fine and reasonably priced caffè. ⊠ *Via Sant'Andrea delle Fratte 1 (Via della Mercede), Spagna* ☎ *06/6793191* ⊙ *Daily 6:30 –12:30 and 4–7* Ⓜ *Spagna.*

WORTH NOTING

Gagosian Gallery. One of the most prestigious modern art galleries opened this Rome branch in 2007. In a former bank, temporary exhibitions include many mega-stars, including Cy Twombly, Damien Hirst, and Jeff Koons. ⊠ *Via Francesco Crispi 16, Spagna* ☎ *06/42086498* ⊕ *www.gagosian.com* Ⓜ *Spagna.*

Fontana della Barcaccia *(Leaky Boat Fountain).* At the center of Piazza di Spagna and at the bottom of the Spanish Steps, this curious, half-sunken boat gently spills out water rather than cascading it dramatically into the air; it may have been designed that way to make the most of the area's low water pressure. It was thanks to the Barberini pope Urban VIII, who commissioned the fountain, that there was any water at all in this area, which was becoming increasingly built up during the 17th century. He restored one of the ancient Roman aqueducts that once channeled water here. The bees and suns on the boat constitute the Barberini motif. Some insist that the Berninis (Pietro and his more famous son Gian Lorenzo) intended the fountain to be a reminder that this part of town was often flooded by the Tiber; others that it represents the Ship of the Church; and still others that it marks the presumed site of the emperor Domitian's water stadium in which sea battles were reenacted in the glory days of the Roman Empire. ⊠ *Piazza del Spagna* Ⓜ *Spagna.*

Trinità dei Monti. Standing high above the Spanish Steps, this church is beautiful not so much in itself but for its dramatic location and magnificent views. ⊠ *Piazza Trinità dei Monti, Spagna* ☎ *06/6794179* ⊙ *Daily 8–8* Ⓜ *Spagna.*

Repubblica and Quirinale

PALAZZO DEL QUIRINALE, QUATTRO FONTANE,
PIAZZA DELLA REPUBBLICA, BATHS OF DIOCLETIAN

WORD OF MOUTH

"We were on our way to Santa Maria della Vittoria and another Bernini masterpiece (man, did this guy ever get to sleep?), the *Ecstasy of St. Theresa*. Although 'churched-out,' we still had some of the biggies left to see before departing Rome, so there would be no losing my religion today."

— maitaitom

GETTING ORIENTED

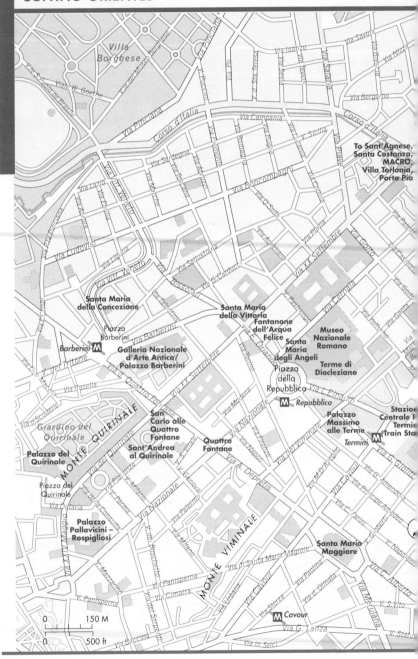

GETTING HERE

Between Termini station and the Spanish Steps, this area is about a 15-minute walk from either. Bus No. 40 will get you from Termini to the Quirinale in two stops; from the Vatican take Bus No. 64. The very busy and convenient Repubblica Metro stop is on the piazza of the same name.

O.K., WHERE DO I START?

Coming up from the Metro stop at Piazza della Repubblica, beyond the circular Fountain of the Naiads, you can see the church of Santa Maria degli Angeli, once part of the Roman baths. Some of the best art of ancient Rome is found at the Palazzo Massimo alle Terme at the corner of nearby Piazza Cinquecento, while off another side of the same square stretches its sister museum, Museo di Terme di Diocleziano. To the northwest of Piazza Repubblica, Via Vittorio Emanuele Orlando leads to Piazza San Bernardo where Santa Maria della Vittoria is home to Bernini's famed *Ecstasy of St. Theresa*. Follow Via XX Settembre to Borromini's noted church of San Carlo alle Quattro Fontane—or alternatively take Via di Quattro Fontane down the hill to magnificent Palazzo Barberini. Back on Via XX Settembre, beyond Bernini's church of Sant'Andrea, Via del Quirinale leads to Palazzo del Quirinale and the grand view from its piazza.

BEST TIME-OUT

With a wide enough assortment of creamy Sicilian pastries and ice-cream flavors to satisfy a mouthful of sweet tooths, the historic **Cremeria Bar Dagnino** (✉ *Via Vittorio Emanuele Orlando 75* ☎ *06/4818660*) in the Esedra Galleria on Piazza della Repubblica is the place to go. Enjoy the 1950s feel and the solid selection of dishes for lunch.

Along Via degli Avignonesi and Via Rasella (opposite Palazzo Barberini) there are an array of good, moderately priced trattorias, with **Gioia Mia** (✉ *Via degli Avignonesi 34, Via Veneto* ☎ *06/4882784*) among the best; it's closed Wednesday.

TOP 5 REASONS TO GO

Bernini's *Ecstasy of St. Theresa*: Admire, or just blush at, the worldly realism of Theresa's allegedly spiritual rapture. Star of the Cappella Cornaro, this sculpture climaxes one of Bernini's most audacious fusions of architecture, painting, and sculpture.

Palazzo Barberini: Take in five centuries of art at one of Rome's greatest family palaces, where you can gape at Rome's biggest 18th-century ballroom and Raphael's La Fornarina.

Changing of the Guard: Snap photos of stony-faced guards as they march in formation at the Quirinale presidential palace, which perches atop the highest of ancient Rome's seven hills.

Santa Maria della Concezione: Contemplate eternity in a creepy, creative, and (hopefully) unique crypt "decorated" with the skeletons of 4,000 monks, replete with fluted arches made of collarbones and arabesques of shoulder blades.

On a Clear Day You Can See Forever: Crowning the Quirinale Hill—the loftiest of Rome's seven hills—is the Piazza del Quirinale, offering a spectacular view over the city, with the horizon marked by "Il Cupolino," the dome of St. Peter's. Framing the vista are the enormous ancient statues of Castor and Pollux—the "Discouri" (or Horse-Tamers)—which still give the Quirinale its nickname of Monte Cavallo ("Horse Hill").

7

Sightseeing
★★★★
Nightlife
★★
Dining
★★★★
Lodging
★★★★★
Shopping
★★★

Just west of Rome's modern Termini train station, this area offers an extraordinary Roman blend of old and new. Although ancient artworks, great Bernini sculptures, and baroque landmarks lure the traveler, this was, for the most part, the "new" Rome of the 19th century—the area owes its broad avenues and dignified palazzi to the city's transformation after 1870, when it became the capital of a newly unified Italy. Toward Via Veneto, the influx of ministries set off a frenzied building boom and distinguished turn-of-the-20th-century architecture became the neighborhood's hallmark. As a gateway, Piazza della Repubblica was laid out to serve as a monumental foyer between the rail station and the rest of the city. And as this square proves, time in Rome comes layered like nowhere else on earth.

Flanking the train station's plate-glass entrance is an elephantine-colored mass of masonry that dates back millennia—a stretch, no less, of the so-called Servian Walls, the city boundary built when Rome was still a Republic way back in the 6th century BC. Fast forward about three centuries to find the piazza's main landmark: the vast ruin of the Baths of Diocletian—the Terme di Diocleziano—which were subsequently transformed into a Renaissance monastery and, designed by Michelangelo himself, the church of Santa Maria degli Angeli. Following the layout of the ancient baths and the concave entrance to the church (with the nearby 1890s buildings curving likewise as if in tribute), the piazza is a square only in name. At its center lies the turn-of-the-20th-century Fountain of the Naiads, which works wonders with the Roman sunlight. Its busty nymphs and buffed sea tritons announce that beauty awaits at many of the sights in this district.

Off right or west from Via Nazionale lies the Quirinale, a hill set with various jewels of the baroque era, including masterpieces by Bernini and Borromini. Nearby is Palazzo Barberini, a grand and gorgeous 16th-century palace holding five centuries of masterworks. For ancient art treasures, head for Palazzo Massimo, famed for the fabulously frescoed rooms of the Empress Livia's summer villa, colorful and vibrant with birds.

Mercifully situated away from traffic is the lofty Quirinale hill, set with various jewels of the baroque

FULL FRONTAL FASHION

Outside the gates of the Palazzo del Quirinale, you can see the changing of the military guard at 4 PM daily, and occasionally you can glimpse the *corazzieri* (presidential guard). All extra-tall, they are a stirring sight in their magnificent crimson-and-blue uniforms, gleaming knee-high boots, and embossed steel helmets adorned with flowing manes.

era. Crowning the piazza is the enormous Palazzo del Quirinale, built in the 16th century as a summer residence for the popes. It became the presidential palace in 1946—you can tour its reception rooms, which are as splendid as you might imagine. The changing of the guard (daily at 4), outside on the piazza with its oversize stairway, is an old-fashioned exercise in pomp and circumstance.

While Bernini's work feels omnipresent in much of the city center, the Renaissance-man range of his work is particularly notable here. The artist as architect considered the church of Sant'Andrea al Quirinale one of his best; Bernini the urban designer and waterworker is responsible for the muscle-bound sea gods who wrestle so provocatively in the fountain at the center of whirling Piazza Barberini. And Bernini the master gives religious passion a joltingly corporeal treatment in what is perhaps his greatest work, the *Ecstasy of St. Theresa,* in the church of Santa Maria della Vittoria. Along with Bernini, this area has big boulevards, big buildings, and big delights.

REPUBBLICA

Climbing the stairs out of the Metro at Piazza della Repubblica is something like stepping into a tornado. The clanging of sirens and car horns, the squeal of brakes, and the roar of mopeds, not to mention the smell of the fast-food joints, may make you want to duck back down underground and get out at another stop. But to do so would be to miss out on a district featuring an array of fascinating attractions. The streets here may not be conducive to wandering but the ancient treasures at Palazzo Massimo, Bernini's spectacular Cornaro Chapel, and the modern MACRO museum will always be vying for your attention.

TOP ATTRACTIONS

Museo delle Terme di Diocleziano *(Baths of Diocletian).* Though part of the ancient structure is now the church of Santa Maria degli Angeli, and other parts were transformed into a Carthusian monastery or razed to make room for later urban development, a visit gives you an idea of the scale and grandeur of this ancient bathing establishment. Upon entering the church you see the major structures of the baths, partly covered by 16th- and 17th-century overlay, some of which is by Michelangelo. The monastery cloister is filled with the lapidary collection of the Museo Nazionale Romano while other rooms have archaeological works, along with a virtual representation of Livia's villa, which you can tour with the help of a joystick. ⊠ *Viale E. De Nicola 79, Repubblica* ☎ *06/39967700* 🖃 *€5* ⊘ *Tues.–Sun. 9–7:30* Ⓜ *Repubblica.*

★ **Palazzo Massimo alle Terme.** The enormous collections of the Roman National Museum—which range from striking classical Roman sculptures and paintings to marble bric-a-brac and fragments picked up in excavations over the centuries—have been organized in four locations: Palazzo Massimo alle Terme, Palazzo Altemps, Crypta Balbi, and the Museo delle Terme di Diocleziano. The vast structure of the Palazzo Massimo holds the great ancient treasures of the archaeological collection and also the coin collection. Highlights include the *Niobid*, the famous bronze *Boxer* and the *Discobolus Lancelloti*. Pride of place goes, however, to the great ancient frescoes on view. These include decorative stuccos and wall paintings found in the area of the Villa della Farnesina (in Trastevere) and the legendary frescoes from Empress Livia's villa at Prima Porta, delightful depictions of a garden in bloom and an orchard alive with birds. Their colors are remarkably well preserved. These delicate decorations covered the walls of cool, sunken rooms in Livia's summer house outside the city. ⊠ *Largo Villa Peretti 1, Repubblica* ☎ *06/3996770* ⊕ *www.pierreci.it* 🖃 *€9* ⊘ *Tues.–Sun. 9–7:30* Ⓜ *Repubblica.*

Piazza della Repubblica. Often the first view that spells "Rome" to weary travelers walking from the Stazione Termini, this broad square was laid out in the late 1800s and includes the exuberant **Fontana delle Naiadi** (Fountain of the Naiads). This pièce de résistance is draped with voluptuous bronze ladies wrestling happily with marine monsters. The nudes weren't there when the pope unveiled the fountain in 1870, sparing him any embarrassment. But when the figures were added in 1901, they caused a scandal, for it's said that the sculptor, Rutelli, modeled them on the ample figures of two musical comedy stars of the day. The piazza owes its curved lines to the structures of the Terme di Diocleziano; the curving, colonnaded neoclassic buildings on the southwest side trace the underlying form of the ancient baths. Today, one of them is occupied by the superdeluxe Hotel Exedra—which shows you how much the fortunes of the formerly tatterdemalion part of the city have changed. ⊠ *Junction of Via Nazionale, Via Vittorio Emanuele Orlando, and Via delle Terme di Diocleziano, Repubblica* Ⓜ *Repubblica.*

Fodor's Choice   **Santa Maria della Vittoria.** Like the church of Santa Susanna across Piazza
★   San Bernardo, this church was designed by Carlo Maderno, but this one is best known for Bernini's sumptuous baroque decoration of the **Cappella Cornaro** (Cornaro Chapel), on the left as you face the altar, where you'll find his interpretation of heavenly ecstasy in his statue of the *Ecstasy of St. Theresa* (⇨ *For more on Bernini, see our special photo feature, "Baroque and Desperate: The Tragic Rivalry of Bernini and Borromini" in this chapter*). Your eye is drawn effortlessly from

the frescoes on the ceiling down to the marble figures of the angel and the swooning saint, to the earthly figures of the Cornaro family (who commissioned the chapel), to the two inlays of marble skeletons in the pavement, representing the hope and despair of souls in purgatory.

As evidenced in other works of the period, the theatricality of the chapel is the result of Bernini's masterly fusion of elements. This is one of the key examples of the mature Roman High Baroque. Bernini's audacious conceit was to model the chapel as a theater: Members of the Cornaro family—sculpted in colored marbles—watch from theater boxes as, center stage, the great moment of divine love is played out

> ### AURORA'S HOUSE
>
> Set just off the Piazza del Quirinale is the **Palazzo Pallavinici-Rospigliosi** (⌧ Via XXIV Maggio 43 ☎ 06/4744019 ⌨ Free). Originally built for Cardinal Scipione Borghese, it is, unfortunately, closed to the public. However, on the first day of every month, 10–noon and 3–5, you are allowed in to see the palace's summer pavilion, which is graced with a legendary ceiling fresco of Aurora painted by baroque artist Guido Reni—this painting was once thought to be the last word in 17th-century style.

before them. The swooning saint's robes appear to be on fire, quivering with life, and the white marble group seems suspended in the heavens as golden rays illuminate the scene. An angel assists at the mystical moment of Theresa's vision as the saint abandons herself to the joys of heavenly love. Bernini represented this mystical experience in what, to modern eyes, may seem very earthly terms. Or, as the visiting dignitary President de Brosses put it in the 19th century, "If this is divine love, I know what it is." No matter what your reaction, you'll have to admit it's great theater. ⌧ *Via XX Settembre 17, Largo Santa Susanna, Repubblica* ☎ *06/42740571* ⊙ *Mon.–Sat. 8:30–noon and 3:30–6, Sun. 3:30–6* Ⓜ *Repubblica.*

☾ ★ **Villa Torlonia.** Built for aristocrats-come-lately, the Torlonia family—the Italian Rockefellers of the 19th century—this villa became Mussolini's residence as prime minister under Italy's king and is now a public park. Long neglected, the park's vegetation and buildings are gradually being refurbished. Newly restored is the **Casina Nobile,** the main palace designed by the great architect Giuseppe Valadier. A grand, Neoclassical edifice, it comes replete with a gigantic ballroom, frescoed salons, and soaring templelike facade. While denuded of nearly all their furnishings and art treasures, some salons have important remnants of decor, including the reliefs once fashioned by the father of Italian Neoclassical sculpture, Antonio Canova. In the park, a complete contrast is offered by the **Casina delle Civette** (Little House of Owls), a hypercharming example of the Stil Liberty (Art Nouveau) of the early 1900s: the gabled, fairy-tale-like cottage-palace now displays majolica and stained-glass decorations, including windows with owl motifs, and is a stunning, overlooked find for lovers of 19th-century decorative arts. Temporary exhibits are held in the small and elegant **Il Casino dei Principi** (**The House of Princes**), designed in part by Valadier. ⌧ *Villa Torlonia, Via Nomentana 70* ☎ *06/44235455* ⊕ *www.museivillatorlonia.it* ⌨ *Casino*

Nobile €4.50, Casina delle Civette €3; combined ticket for Musei di Villa Torlonia €6.50 ⊘ Nov.–Feb., Tues.–Sun. 9–4:30; Mar.–Oct., Tues.–Sun. 9–5:30; Apr.–Sept., Tues.–Sun. 9–7.

WORTH NOTING

Fontanone dell'Acqua Felice *(Fountain of Happy Water)*. When Pope Sixtus V completed the restoration of the Acqua Felice aqueduct toward the end of the 16th century, Domenico Fontana was commissioned to design this commemorative fountain. As the story goes, a sculptor named Prospero da Brescia had the unhappy task of executing the central figure, which was to represent Moses (Sixtus liked to think of himself as, like Moses, having provided water for his thirsting population). The comparison with Michelangelo's magnificent *Moses* in the church of San Pietro in Vincoli was inevitable, and the largely disparaging criticism of Prospero's work is said to have driven him to his grave. Perhaps the most charming aspects of the fountain are the smug little lions spewing water in the foreground. ⊠ *Piazza San Bernardo, Repubblica* Ⓜ *Repubblica.*

MACRO. Formerly known as Rome's Modern and Contemporary Art Gallery, and before that formerly known as the Peroni beer factory, this redesigned industrial space has brought new life to the gallery and museum scene of a city formerly known for its then, not its now. The collection here covers Italian contemporary artists from the 1960s through today. Its sister museum, **MACRO al Mattatoio** (⊠ *Piazza O. Giustiniani*) is housed in a renovated slaughterhouse in Testaccio district, Rome's "Left Bank," and features temporary exhibits and installations by current artists, open until midnight, with free admission. The goal of both spaces is to bring current art to the public in innovative spaces, and, not incidentally, to give support and recognition to Rome's contemporary art scene, which labors in the shadow of the city's artistic heritage. After a few days—or millennia—of dusty marble, it's a breath of fresh air. The No. 90 and 60 buses get you here. ⊠ *Via Reggio Emilia 54, Repubblica* ☎ *06/671070400* ⊕ *www.macro.roma.museum* ✉ *Free* ⊘ *Tues.–Sun. 9–7* Ⓜ *Repubblica.*

Santa Maria degli Angeli. The curving brick facade on the northeast side of Piazza della Repubblica is one small remaining part of the colossal Terme di Diocleziano, the largest and most impressive of the baths of ancient Rome. A gift to the city from Emperor Diocletian, it was erected about AD 300 with forced labor of 40,000 Christians. In 1561 Michelangelo was commissioned to·convert the vast *tepidarium,* the central hall of the baths, into a church. His work was altered by Vanvitelli in the 18th century, but the huge transept, which formed the nave in Michelangelo's plan, has remained as he adapted it. The eight enormous monolithic columns of red granite that support the great beams are the original columns of the tepidarium, 45 feet high and more than 5 feet in diameter. The great hall is 92 feet high. ⊠ *Via Cernaia 9, Repubblica* ☎ *064880812* ⊕ *www.santamariadegliangeliroma.it* ⊘ *Mon.–Sat. 7–6:30, Sun. 7* AM*–7:30* PM Ⓜ *Repubblica.*

7

QUIRINALE

Rome's highest, the Quirinale Hill has hosted, in their turn, ancient Roman senators, Renaissance popes (it was breezier here than at the Vatican) and, with the end of papal rule, Italy's kings. The latter took up residence in the palace that still diadems the hill, looking down the slope to where lordly families (the Colonna, for one) built palaces to be near all that power. In this district, the triumvirate of Rome's baroque—Bernini, Borromini, and Pietro di Cortona—vie, even after four centuries, to amaze the visitor. As if Bernini and Borromini could not get away from each other, some of their greatest works are within blocks of each other.

TOP ATTRACTIONS

★ **Palazzo del Quirinale.** For centuries used as home of the popes, now official residence of the president of Italy, this spectacular palace was begun in 1574 by Pope Gregory XIII, who planned to use it as a summer residence, choosing the hilltop site mainly for its superb views. However, as early as 1592 Pope Clement VIII decided to make the palace, safely elevated above the malarial miasmas shrouding the low-lying location of the Vatican, the permanent residence of the papacy. It remained the official papal residence until 1870, in the process undergoing a series of enlargements and alterations by a succession of architects. When Italian troops under Garibaldi stormed Rome in 1870, making it the capital of the newly united Italy, the popes moved back to the Vatican and the Quirinale became the official residence of the kings of Italy. When the Italian people voted out the monarchy in 1946, the Quirinal Palace passed to the presidency of the Italian Republic. Visitable only on Sundays with sometimes a concert included, the state reception rooms are some of Italy's most majestic. You already get a fair idea of the palace's splendor from the size of the building, especially the interminable flank of the palace on Via del Quirinale. Behind this wall are the palace gardens, which, like the gardens of Villa d'Este in Tivoli, were laid out by Cardinal Ippolito d'Este when he summered here. Unfortunately, they are open to the public only once a year on Republic Day (June 2). ✉ *Piazza del Quirinale, Quirinale* ☎ *06/46991* ⊕ *www.quirinale.it* 🎟 *€5* ⊙ *Sept.–June, Sun. 8:30–noon* Ⓜ *Barberini.*

Piazza del Quirinale. This strategic location atop the Quirinal Hill has long been of great importance. It served as home of the Sabines in the 7th century BC, then deadly enemies of the Romans, who lived on the Capitoline and Palatine Hills (all of 1 km [½ mi] away). Today it's the foreground for the presidential residence, Palazzo del Quirinale, and home to **Palazzo della Consulta,** where Italy's Constitutional Court sits. The open side of the piazza has an impressive vista of the rooftops and domes of central Rome and St. Peter's in the distance. The **Fontana di Montecavallo** or Fontana dei Dioscuri, is composed of a huge Roman statuary group and an obelisk from the tomb of the emperor Augustus. The group of the Dioscuri trying to tame two massive marble steeds was found in the Baths of Constantine, which occupied part of the summit of the Quirinal Hill. Unlike just about every other ancient statue in Rome, this group survived the Dark Ages intact and accordingly

Continued on page 185

BAROQUE & DESPERATE

By Martin
Wilmot Bennett

THE TRAGIC RIVALRY OF BERNINI AND BORROMINI

Consider the famous feuding duos of Lennon vs. McCartney, Mozart vs. Salieri, Michelangelo vs. Raphael. None of them match the rivalry of Gian Lorenzo Bernini vs. Francesco Borromini. In a pitched battle of anything-you-can-do-I-can-do-better, these two great geniuses of the Baroque style transformed 17th-century Rome into a city of spectacle, the "theater of the entire world." While it was Bernini who triumphed and Borromini who wound up taking his own life, the real winner was Rome itself—a banquet for the eyes cooked up by these two Baroque masters.

Borromini's dome in San Carlo alle Quattro Fontane

United in genius, the two could not have been more different in fortune and character. Born within a year of each other at the turn of the 1600s, they spent decades laying out majestic squares, building precedent-shattering churches, all the while outdoing each other in Baroque bravado.

AN ARTISTIC THROWDOWN

Compared and contrasted, the pair form the ultimate odd couple: Bernini, perhaps the greatest master showman of all time, exulted in Technicolor-hued theatricality; Borromini, the purist and reclusive genius, pursued the pure light of geometry, although with an artisan's hankering after detail. Bernini grew into the famed lover and solid family man; Borromini seems not to have had any love life at all. Bernini became a smooth mingler with society's great and worthy ranks; Borromini remained the quirky outsider. Bernini triumphed as the all-rounder, he of the so-called *"bel composto,"* as in the Cornaro Chapel where his talents as sculptor/architect/dramatist come stunningly together. Borromini was an architect, pure and simple. Throughout their lives, they had tried to turn the tables—psychologically as well as architecturally—on each other, a struggle that ended with Borromini's tragic suicide.

OPERATION AMAZEMENT

Both, however, fervently believed in the Baroque style and its mission to amaze, as well as edify. Thanks to the Counter-Reformation, the Catholic church discovered, and exploited, the effects on its congregants of such overtly Baroque tricks-of-the-trade as *chiaroscuro* (light-and-dark) and *trompe l'oeil* (fool-the-eye) techniques. Using emotion and motion, Bernini and Borromini learned how to give stone wing. In Bernini's famed *Pluto and Persephone,* the solid stone seems transmuted into living flesh—sculpted effects previously thought possible only in paint. Together transforming the city into a "giant theater," the rivals thus became the principal dramaturges and stage managers of Baroque Rome.

7

IN FOCUS BAROQUE AND DESPERATE

BERNINI (1598 – 1680): THE POPE'S FAVORITE

Born: December 7, 1598, in Naples, southern Italy.

Greatest Works: St. Peter's Square, *Ecstasy of St. Theresa*, Piazza Navona's *Fountain of Four Rivers*, *Apollo and Daphne*, Sant'Andrea al Quirinale.

Personality Profile: Extrovert and fully aware of his genius or, to quote his own mother, "He acts as if he were master of the world."

Scandal: Just imagine the headlines: "Brother Attacked with Crowbar/Costanza Slashed with Razor by Jealous Genius." Bernini went ballistic on learning his wife, Costanza Nonarelli, was having an affair with his brother Luigi. Protected by Pope Urban VIII, Bernini was let off with a fine of 3,000 scudi.

Career Low: Largely on Borromini's expert insistence, the two crack-ridden bell-towers Bernini designed for St. Peter's were subsequently pulled down.

"La Bella Morte": Death in Bernini becomes star performer. His tomb for Urban VIII has a skeleton writing the pope's name in a marble registry of death, while his tomb for Alexander VII has a golden skeleton riffling marble drapery (this pope kept a Bernini-designed coffin in his bedroom).

"An ignorant Goth who has corrupted architecture. . . ."

Bernini on Borromini

Considered the "father of the Baroque," Bernini enjoyed almost too many career highs to count, starting from a drawing done as a youth, for which Pope Paul V awarded him a handful of gold ducats, to his being dubbed with the honorarium of "cavaliere" at age 23 (Borromini only received the same honor when he was past fifty). Born "under a happy star," as he himself put it, Bernini had patrons lining up, starting with church potentate and eventual pope, Maffeo Barberini, and Pope Paul's nephew, cardinal and art-dealer, Scipio Borghese, who claimed a bevy of Bernini's sculptures for his new Roman palace.

Bernini was a genius of self-promotion.

Bernini's David

Cupola, Sant'Andrea al Quirinale

Trick No. 1: In an early bust of Cardinal Borghese, there was an unsightly crack across the forehead; as cardinal turns away in disappointment, Bernini whips out a perfect copy, no more crack. Trick No. 2: On inaugurating Piazza Navona's River Fountain, Innocent X is distressed upon realizing that the water isn't running; Bernini explains technical hitch; pope steps away; abracadabra, Bernini switches water on. Bravo, Bernini!?

BORROMINI (1599—1667): THE ICONOCLAST

Born: September 27, 1599 in Bissone near Lake Lugano in Italy's far north, but with the name Castelli, the name-change coming later, partly to honor San Carlo Borromeo, whose San Carlo church will be Borromini's first major commission.

Greatest Works: San Carlo alle Quattro Fontane, Sant' Ivo della Sapienza, Sant'Agnese in Piazza Navona, Palazzo Falconieri.

Personality Profile: If Bernini is the "instant hit," Borromini is the "struggling genius," the introspective loner, and the complex, often misunderstood perfectionist.

Scandal: A young man, caught filching marble, was beaten and left for dead in San Giovanni in Lanterno, evidently on Borromini's orders. He avoids murder charges thanks to Pope Innocent's intervention.

Scale: Arguably his greatest work, San Carlo could be fitted into one of the four giant crossing-piers of the dome in St Peter's (in one of which towers Bernini's statue of St. Longinus).

"La Brutta Morte": His messy suicide was anything but "bella," as his brave note written in the hours it took him to expire after he fell on his sword attests.

> *"What I mind is not that the money goes to Bernini but that he should enjoy the honor of my labors."*
>
> Borromini on Bernini

Usually dressed in Spanish black, Borromini evidently had few attachments beyond his art. He not only had great artistic vision but an astounding command of geometry, an impeccable hankering after detail, and an artisan's willingness to get his hands dirty. The main influences on him range from Hiram, the builder of Solomon's temple in Jerusalem (who also died by falling on his sword) to Milan's Gothic cathedral, whose influence has been traced to S. Ivo's spiraled dome. On Urban VIII's death, Borromini's star began to ascend. The new pope, Innocent X, makes him papal architect, responsible for restructuring the S. Giovanni basilica and turning the S. Agnese church into a papal chapel. Bernini, however, is again waiting in the wings, readying himself for a startling come back.

While he had a long run of patrons, Borromini was often overshadowed by Bernini's showmanship. He is done out of designing the *Four Rivers* fountain after Bernini submits a silver model of his own design to the new pope. After Innocent's death, commissions become scarce and depression followed. His suicide note is famously calm: "I've been wounded like this since half past eight this morning and I will tell you how it happened. . . ." Once forgotten and derided, Francesco Borromini is now considered "the architect's architect."

Church of Sant' Agnese

7

IN FOCUS BAROQUE AND DESPERATE

BERNINI & BORROMINI TOP 20 MASTERPIECES

Bernini

1. Apollo and Daphne, Galleria Borghese

2. The Baldacchino, Basilica di San Pietro

3. Ecstasy of Saint Theresa, Santa Maria della Vittoria

4. David, Galleria Borghese

5. Pluto and Persephone, Galleria Borghese

6. Tomb of Pope Urban VIII, Basilica di San Pietro

7. Fountain of the Four Rivers, Piazza Navona

8. Two Angels, Ponte Sant'Angelo

9. Elephant and Obelisk, Piazza Sta Maria sopra Minerva

10. Ludovica Albertoni, San Francesco a Ripa

11. Fontana della Barcaccia, Piazza di Spagna

12. Fontana del Tritone, Piazza Barberini

Borromini

13. San Carlo alla Quattro Fontane, Quirinale

14. Sant' Agnese, Piazza Navona

15. Sant' Ivo alla Sapienza, Piazza Navona

16. Oratory of Saint Phillip Neri, Piazza Chiesa Nuova

17. Palazzo Spada, Piazza Capo di Ferro

18. Palazzo Barberini, Via Barberini

19. Sant'Andrea delle Fratte, Via dell Mercede

20. Palazzo Falconieri, Via Giulia

BERNINI VS. BORROMINI: A MINI-WALK

In Rome, you may become lost looking for the work of one rival, then suddenly find yourself gazing at the work of the other. As though an eerily twinned path was destined for the two giants, several of their greatest works are just a few blocks from each other.

A short street away (Via Orlando) from mammoth Piazza Repubblica stands **Santa Maria della Vittoria**, famed for Bernini's **Cornaro Chapel.** Out of favor with new anti-Barberini Pope Innocent X, Bernini was rescued by a commission from Cardinal Cornaro to build a chapel for his family. Here, as if in a "theater," sculpted figures of family members look down from two marble balconies on the so-called "transverberation" of Carmelite Saint Theresa of Avila being pierced by the arrow of the Angel of Divine Love, eyes shut in agony, mouth open in rapture. Spiritual ecstasy has become shockingly real—to quote the famed comment by President de Brosses, "If this is divine love, I know what it is."

Leave the church and head down Via Barberini to Piazza Barberini where perch three of the largest bees you'll ever see. The **Fountain of the Bees** is Bernini's tribute to his arch-patron from the Barberini family, Pope Urban VIII. The bees were family emblems. Another Bernini masterstroke is the **Triton Fountain** in the center of Piazza Barberini. Turn left up Via delle Quattro Fontane. On your left is spectacular **Palazzo Barberini**, where Bernini and Borromini worked together in an

uneasy partnership. The wonderful winding staircase off to the right is the work of Borromini, while the other more conventionally angled staircase on the left is by Bernini, who also has a self-portrait hanging in the art gallery upstairs.

Borromini's prospects soon took a turn for the better thanks to the Barefoot Spanish Trinitarians, who commissioned him to design **San Carlo alla Quatto Fontane**, set at the crossroads up the road.

One of the marvels of architecture, its dome—not much bigger than a down-turned bathtub—is packed immaculately throughout with hexagons, octagons, and crosses. Like jigsaw pieces they diminish upwards until the tiny roof seems anything but: to a space that in another architect might turned out claustrophobic Borromini is able to bring a touch of infinity. In the adjoining cloister, revel in Borromini's rearrangement of columns, which transform what would be a conventional rectangle into an energetic oc-

tagon. Don't forget to stop and admire the church's *movementé* facade.

On the same Via del Quirinale stands a famous Bernini landmark, the Jesuits' **Sant' Andrea al Quirinale**. With steps flowing out into the street, it could be viewed as Bernini's response to his rival's

nearby masterpiece. Ironically, the commission for the Jesuit church was originally earmarked for Borromini (but transferred when Pope Alexander VII took over). Note how the hexagons in Bernini's dome diminish upwards to create an illusion of space—in Borrominiesque fashion.

PALAZZO BARBERINI

✉ *Via Barberini 18, Quiri-nale* ☎ *06/32810* 🌐 *www. galleriaborghese.it* 💶 *€6* 🕐 *Tues.–Sun. 8:30–7:30* Ⓜ *Barberini, Buses 52, 56, 60, 95, 116, 175, 492*

TIPS

■ Part of the family of museums that includes the Galleria Borghese, Palazzo Spada, Palazzo Venezia, and Palazzo Corsini, the Palazzo Barberini has gone into marketing in a big way—visit the shop here for some distinctive gifts for Aunt Ethel back home, including tote bags bearing the beloved visage of Raphael's La Fornarina, bookmarks with Caravaggio's Judith slicing off Holofernes's head, and coffee mugs bearing the famous Barberini heraldic bees.

■ Look for the hidden treasure of the Palazzo Barberini palace in the palace's attic: the charming suite created in 1728 for the marriage of a Barberini heiress—the boudoir bedroom of Principessa Cornelia Costanza Barberini and her Colonna prince is nearly unchanged from the wedding night. The low-hanging rooms are festooned in silk hangings, Japanese porcelains, and an antique baby carriage.

One of Rome's most splendid 17th-century palaces, the Palazzo Barberini is a landmark of the Roman baroque style. Pope Urban VIII had acquired the property and given it to a nephew, who was determined to build an edifice worthy of his generous uncle and the ever-more-powerful Barberini clan. The result was, architecturally, a precedent-shattering affair: a "villa suburbana" set right in the heart of the urban city and designed to be strikingly open to the outdoors. Note how Carlo Maderno's grand facade seems almost entirely composed of window tiers rising up in proto-20th-century fashion.

Ascend Bernini's staircase to the Galleria Nazionale d'Arte Antica, hung with famed paintings including Raphael's *La Fornarina*, a luminous portrait of the artist's lover (a resident of Trastevere, she was reputedly a baker's daughter)—study the bracelet on her upper arm bearing Raphael's name. Also noteworthy are Guido Reni's portrait of the doomed *Beatrice Cenci* (beheaded in Rome for parricide in 1599)—Hawthorne called it "the saddest picture ever painted" in his Rome-based novel, *The Marble Faun*—and Caravaggio's *Judith and Holofernes*.

But the showstopper here is the palace's Gran Salone, a vast ballroom with a ceiling painted in 1630 by the third (and too-often neglected) master of the Roman baroque, Pietro da Cortona. It depicts the *Glorification of Urban VIII's Reign* and has the spectacular conceit of glorifying Urban VIII as the agent of Divine Providence and escorted by a "bomber squadron" (to quote art historian Sir Michael Levey) of some huge, mutantlike Barberini bees, the heraldic symbol of the family. You may find the sound of humming disturbing but don't worry—it is only the fluorescent lights in adjacent hallways. At this writing, some rooms were closed for renovation.

became one of the city's great sights, especially during the Middle Ages. Next to the figures, the ancient obelisk from the Mausoleo di Augusto (Tomb of Augustus) was put here by Pope Pius VI at the end of the 18th century. ⊠ *Junction of Via del Quirinale and Via XXIV Aprile, Quirinale* Ⓜ *Barberini.*

Quattro Fontane *(Four Fountains)*. The intersection takes its name from its four baroque fountains, representing the Tiber (on the San Carlo corner), the Arno, Juno, and Diana. Sadly, the fumes from constant heavy traffic have managed to deface them to the point where they're unrecognizable. Despite the traffic, it's worthwhile taking in the views from this point in all four directions: to the southwest as far as the obelisk in Piazza del Quirinale; to the northeast along Via XX Settembre to the Porta Pia; to the northwest across Piazza Barberini to the obelisk of Trinità dei Monti; and to the southeast as far as the obelisk and apse of Santa Maria Maggiore. The prospect is a highlight of Pope Sixtus V's campaign of urban beautification and an example of the baroque influence on city planning. ⊠ *At intersection of Via Quattro Fontane, Via XX Settembre, and Via del Quirinale* Ⓜ *Barberini.*

★ **San Carlo alle Quattro Fontane.** San Carlo (sometimes identified by the diminutive San Carlino because of its tiny size) is one of Borromini's masterpieces. In a space no larger than the base of one of the piers of St. Peter's Basilica, he created a church that is an intricate exercise in geometric perfection, with a coffered dome that seems to float above the curves of the walls. Borromini's work is often bizarre, definitely intellectual, and intensely concerned with pure form. In San Carlo, he invented an original treatment of space that creates an effect of rippling movement, especially evident in the double-S curves of the facade. Characteristically, the interior decoration is subdued, in white stucco with no more than a few touches of gilding, so as not to distract from the form. Don't miss the **cloister,** a tiny, understated baroque jewel, with a graceful portico and loggia above, echoing the lines of the church. ⇨ *For more on Borromini and this church, see our special photo feature, "Baroque and Desperate: The Tragic Rivalry of Bernini and Borromini" in this chapter.* ⊠ *Via del Quirinale 23, Quirinale* ☎ *06/4883261* ⊕ *www.sancarlino-borromini.it* ⊙ *Weekdays 10–noon and 1–3, Sat. 10–1, Sun. noon–1* Ⓜ *Barberini.*

★ **Santa Maria della Concezione.** Although not for the easily spooked, the crypt under the main Capuchin church holds the bones of some 4,000 dead Capuchin monks. Arranged in odd decorative designs around the shriveled and decayed skeletons of their kinsmen, a macabre reminder of the impermanence of earthly life, the crypt is actually touching and oddly beautiful. Signs declare, "What you are, we once were. What we are, you someday will be." Upstairs in the church, the first chapel on the right contains Guido Reni's mid-17th-century *St. Michael Trampling the Devil.* The painting caused great scandal after an astute contemporary observer remarked that the face of the devil bore a surprising resemblance to the Pamphili Pope Innocent X, arch-enemy of Reni's Barberini patrons. Compare the devil with the bust of the pope that you saw in the Palazzo Doria Pamphilj and judge for yourself. ⊠ *Via Veneto 27, Quirinale* ☎ *06/4871185* ⊕ *www.capucciniviaveneto.it* ✉ *Donation* *expected of at least €1 for crypt* ⊙ *Daily 9–noon and 3–6 Cripta dei Cappuccini* Ⓜ *Barberini.*

★ **Sant'Andrea al Quirinale.** Designed by Bernini, this is an architectural gem of the baroque. His son wrote that Bernini considered it one of his best works and that he used to come here occasionally just to sit and enjoy it. Bernini's simple oval plan, a classic of baroque architecture, is given drama and movement by the church's decoration, which carries the story of St. Andrew's martyrdom and ascension into heaven, starting with the painting over the high altar, up past the figure of the saint over the chancel door, to the angels at the base of the lantern and the dove of the Holy Spirit that awaits on high. Unfortunately, various cracks appeared as a collateral effect of the April 2009 Aquila earthquake; at this writing, the church was closed to the public and awaiting restoration work. ✉ *Via del Quirinale 29, Quirinale* ☎ *06/4740807* ⊙ *Mon.–Sat., 8:30–noon and 3:30–7; Sun., 9–noon and 4–7* Ⓜ *Barberini.*

WORTH NOTING

Fontana delle Api *(Fountain of the Bees).* Decorated with the famous heraldic bees of the Barberini family, the upper shell and the inscription are from a fountain that Bernini designed for Pope Urban VIII; the rest was lost when the fountain had to be moved to make way for a new street. This inscription was the cause of a considerable scandal when the fountain was first put up in 1644. It said that the fountain had been erected in the 22nd year of the pontiff's reign, although in fact the 21st anniversary of Urban's election to the papacy was still some weeks away. The last numeral was hurriedly erased, but to no avail—Urban died eight days before the beginning of his 22nd year as pope. The superstitious Romans, who had immediately recognized the inscription as a foolhardy tempting of fate, were vindicated. ✉ *Via Veneto at Piazza Barberini, Quirinale* Ⓜ *Barberini.*

NEED A BREAK?

Along Via degli Avignonesi and Via Rasella (both narrow streets off Via delle Quattro Fontane, opposite Palazzo Barberini), there are some good, moderately priced trattorias. One of the most popular with Romans is **Gioia Mia** (✉ *Via degli Avignonesi 34, Via Veneto* ☎ *06/4882784*); it's closed Wednesday.

Scuderie del Quirinale. Directly opposite the main entrance of the Palazzo del Quirinale sits the Scuderie Papale (the Quirinal Stables), a grand 18th-century stable strikingly remodeled in the late 1990s by architect Gae Aulenti and now host to big temporary art shows. ✉ *Via XXIV Maggio 16, Quirinale* ☎ *06/39967500* ⊕ *www.scuderiequirinale.it* 🎟 *€10* ⊙ *Sun.–Thurs. 10–8, Fri. and Sat. 10–10:30* Ⓜ *Barberini. Buses 16, 36, 60, 62, 136, 175.*

Villa Borghese and Piazza del Popolo

MUSEO BORGHESE, THE PINCIO

WORD OF MOUTH

"We found the Electric Bus No. 119 and rode it to the Galleria Borghese. I loved riding around on this little bus—better than any tour bus could have been. But when I checked on-line at home there were plenty of open spots for the museum, so I didn't reserve. Big mistake: we couldn't get in."

—nancythenice

GETTING ORIENTED

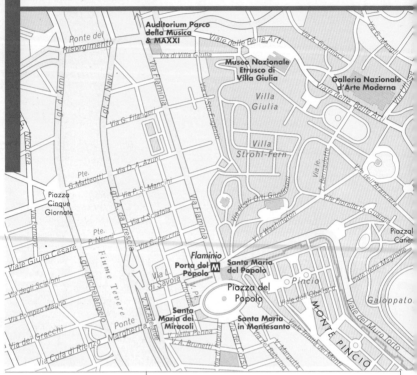

GETTING HERE	TOP 5 REASONS TO GO
Electric Bus No. 119 does a loop that connects Piazza del Popolo to Piazza Venezia. If you're coming from the Colosseum or San Giovanni, take the No. 117. The No. 116, starting at the Villa Borghese museum, is the only bus that motors through the park, plus stops throughout the historic center. The metro stop for Piazza del Popolo is Flaminio on Line A. The Villa Giulia, the Galleria Nazionale d'Arte Moderna, and Villa Borghese's Biopark are easily accessible from Via Flaminia, 1 km (½ mi) from Piazza del Popolo. Trams Nos. 3 and 19 stops at each.	**Piazza del Popolo:** At the end of three of the centro istorico's most important streets—Via del Babuino, Via del Corso, and Via di Ripetta—the People's Square, as the name translates, offers a ringside seat for some of Rome's best people-watching. **Villa Borghese:** Drink in the oxygen in Rome's largest park—stretches of green and plenty of leafy pathways encourage wandering, biking, or just chilling out. **The Pincio:** 19th-century fashion plates, aristocrats, and even strolling popes once made these formal gardens the place to see and be seen. **Santa Maria del Popolo:** Marvel at the incredible realism of Caravaggio's gritty paintings in the Cerasi Chapel, then savor Raphael's Chigi Chapel. **Museo e Galleria Borghese:** Wink at Canova's sexy statue of Pauline Borghese in one of Rome's most spectacularly opulent museums.

BEST TIME-OUTS

The luxurious **Stravinskij Bar** (✉ *Hotel de la Russie, Via del Babuino 9* ☎ *06/328881*) may not be cheap, but it offers a leafy courtyard refuge from the cacophony of Rome. This is where visiting Hollywood stars sip their martinis and international political movers and shakers clinch their deals. Definitely worth the splurge for a vicarious thrill.

Fellini's old haunt and honored as such with a small exhibition of his sketches and some photographs, the freshly renovated historic caffè **Canova** (✉ *Piazza del Popolo 16* ☎ *06/3612227*) is a hot spot to sip your cappuccino or eat a light lunch and watch the fashionplates float past.

The **Caffè delle Arti** (✉ *Via Gramsci 73, Villa Borghese* ☎ *06/32651236*), attached to the Galleria d'Arte Moderna, has a pretty terrace and is a favorite all-day rendezvous for Romans and visitors to Villa Borghese park and its museums. This is the place to break up your walk with a gelato or lunch.

O.K., WHERE DO I START?

At the head of famed Via Veneto, the Porta Pinciana is one of the historic city gates in the Aurelian walls, built by Emperor Aurelianus late in the 3rd century AD. Take care—the traffic comes hurtling in here from all directions. Once inside the verdant Villa Borghese park, head north on Viale del Museo Borghese to reach the art-filled Museo e Galleria Borghese, probably Rome's most stupendous palace.

Come back to earth with a park stroll along Viale dell'Uccelliera to Rome's once-forlorn zoo, now a "biopark" or alternatively turn left (south) on Viale dei Pupazzi to Piazza dei Cavalli Marini's sea-horse fountain. Continue on Viale dei Pupazzi to Piazza di Siena, then turn left onto Viale Canonica and you'll come to the Giardino del Lago (Lake Garden)—the prettiest set-piece of the park, replete with lake and a faux "Grecian" temple. Continue south to the famed Pincio gardens, which overlook Rome's vast Piazza del Popolo, home to treasure-filled Santa Maria del Popolo and some great caffès.

Sightseeing
★★★★
Nightlife
★
Dining
★★
Lodging
★★
Shopping
★

If beautiful masterpieces are as common as bricks in Rome, parks are far rarer. Happily, although you'll find few ilex and poplars dotting piazzi and streets, a verdant hoard can be found to the north of central Rome's cobblestoned chaos. Here breathes the city's giant green lung: the Villa Borghese park, where residents love to escape for some serious R&R. But don't think you can completely prevent gallery gout: Three of Rome's most important museums are inside the park, and Piazza del Popolo (which has some art-crammed churches) is close by.

The city's second-largest park started life as a "pleasure garden" for Cardinal Scipione Borghese in the 17th century, but it now serves the democratic pleasure of Rome and its hot and weary visitors. Stretch out under umbrella pines and watch horses trot their riders past, or take in the view from the Pincio, a quiet and shady overlook that's been enchanting visitors since Lucullus hosted his fabulous banquets here back in the days of the Caesars. The heart-shaped park encompasses 19 acres of landscaped plains and formal gardens, adorned with the noseless busts of famous Italians lining paths at the park's southern end. But encircling the park are Renaissance and baroque palaces, many of which are now museums. Rome's most sumptuous palace, the Museo Borghese has long been home to the great Borghese art treasures, with a seemingly endless array of Bernini statuary and paintings by Raphael and Caravaggio to rival the Vatican Museums. (Although one work that belongs squarely in the secular world is Canova's seductive sculptural portrait of Napoléon's sister, the undraped Principessa Pauline Borghese.) A pleasant and green 20-minute walk away on the opposite side of the park, the Museo Etrusco at Villa Giulia offers the world's most comprehensive collection of Etruscan art and artifacts, and next door, the Galleria Nazionale d'Arte Moderna provides a welcome link to the "modern" Italian art of the 19th and 20th centuries.

The formal garden terraces of the Pincio, on the southwestern side of Villa Borghese, gives way to a stone staircase down to Piazza del Popolo, a mercifully traffic-free piazza that is one of Rome's best people-watching spots. The caffè and restaurant tables on the southern end of the square are prime real estate, but the entertainment value is well worth the rent of an over-priced coffee—sip slowly. More

improving amusement is to be found in the church of Santa Maria del Popolo, on the north side of the square, whose chapels decorated by Raphael and Caravaggio are justly celebrated.

To the southeast of the park is the famed Via Veneto, which, after its 1950s and early '60s heyday as the focus of dolce vita excitement, fell out of fashion as the in-crowd headed elsewhere. Basically unchanging, the Via Veneto neighborhood has preserved its solid, bourgeois palaces—many of them now elegant hotels—and enormous ministries. And it keeps trying to woo back the mainstream of Roman sidewalk caffè society from the lively scenes at Piazza del Pantheon and Piazza Navona—as yet to no avail.

VILLA BORGHESE

Rome's largest open space is filled with playful fountains, sculptured gardens, and picturesque forests of shady pine trees. But that's not the point, for on the parkland perimeter lie three of Rome's most important museums: the Galleria Borghese, for the very best of Renaissance and baroque art; the Villa Giulia, for the world's ultimate collection of Etruscan remains; and the Galleria d'Arte Moderna, a reminder that the Italians had their version of the Impressionists, too. For theatergoers, there are summer performances of Shakespeare in a replica of London's Globe. All in all, there's enough here to satisfy the most avid culture vulture. For real vultures, and an excellent day out with the children, head for the new Biopark, Rome's former Zoo recently given an ecologically friendly makeover.

TOP ATTRACTIONS

Fodor'sChoice
★
Museo e Galleria Borghese. It's a real toss-up which is more magnificent—the villa built for Cardinal Scipione Borghese in 1615 or the collection of 17th- and 18th-century art that lies within. The luxury-loving cardinal built Rome's most splendiferous palace as a showcase for his fabulous antiquities collection. The Casino Borghese, as the building is known, was constructed also to provide an elegant venue for summer parties and musical evenings. Today, it's a monument to Roman 17th-century interior decoration at its most extravagant: room after room opulently adorned with porphyry and alabaster and topped with vast ceiling frescoes make for an eye-popping spectacle unequaled in Rome. With the passage of time, the building has become less celebrated than

the collections housed within it, including one of the finest collections of baroque sculpture to be found anywhere.

Like the gardens, the casino and its collections have undergone many changes since the 17th century. Camillo Borghese, the husband of Napoléon's sister Pauline, was responsible for most of them. He sold off a substantial number of the paintings to Napoléon and swapped 200 of the classical sculptures for an estate in Piedmont, in northern Italy, also courtesy of Napoléon. All of those paintings and sculptures are in the Louvre in Paris. At the end of the 19th century, a later member of the family, Francesco Borghese, replaced some of the gaps in the collections with new acquisitions, and also transferred to the casino the remaining works of art then housed in Palazzo Borghese. In 1902 the casino, its contents, and the park were sold to the Italian government.

The most famous work in the collection is Canova's Neoclassical sculpture of Pauline Borghese. It is technically known as *Venus Victrix*, but there has never been any doubt as to the identity of its real subject. Pauline reclines on a Roman sofa, bare-bosomed, her hips swathed in classical drapery, the very model of haughty detachment and sly come-hither.

The next two rooms hold two key early baroque sculptures: Bernini's *David* and *Apollo and Daphne*. Both illustrate Bernini's extraordinary technical facility. Both also demonstrate the baroque desire to invest sculpture with a living quality, to imbue inert marble with a sense of live flesh. Whereas Renaissance sculptors wanted to capture the idealized beauty of the human form that they had admired in ancient Greek and Roman sculptures, baroque sculptors such as Bernini wanted movement and drama as well, capturing not an essence but an instant, infused with theatricality and emotion. The *Apollo and Daphne* shows the moment when, to escape the pursuing Apollo, Daphne is turned into a laurel tree. Leaves and twigs sprout from her fingertips as she stretches agonizingly away from Apollo, who instinctively recoils in terror and amazement. This is the stuff that makes the baroque exciting. There are other Berninis on view in the collection, notably a very uncharacteristic work, a large unfinished figure called *Verità*, or Truth. Bernini had started work on this brooding figure after the death of his principal patron, Pope Urban VIII. It was meant to form part of a work titled *Truth Revealed by Time*. The next pope, Innocent X, had little love for the ebullient Urban, and, as was the way in Rome—as also the world at large—this meant that Bernini, too, would be excluded from the new pope's favors. However, Bernini's towering genius was such that the new pope came around with his patronage with almost indecent haste.

The Caravaggio Room holds works by this hotheaded genius, who died of malaria at age 37. The disquieting *Sick Bacchus* and charming *Boy with a Basket of Fruit* are naturalistic early works, bright and fresh compared with a dark *Madonna* and the *David and Goliath*, in which Goliath is believed to be a self-portrait. In the Pinacoteca (Picture Gallery) on the second floor of the casino, three Raphaels (including his moving *Deposition*), a Botticelli, and a Pinturicchio are only a few of the paintings that the cardinal chose for his collection. Probably the most famous painting in the gallery is Titian's allegorical *Sacred and Profane Love*, with a nude figure representing sacred love.

Admission to the Museo is by reserved ticket. Visitors are admitted in two-hour shifts 9 AM to 5 PM. Prime-time slots can sell out days in advance, so in high season reserve by phone or through www.ticket-eria.it. You need to collect your reserved ticket at the museum ticket office a half hour before your entrance. However, when it's not busy you can purchase your ticket at the museum for the next entrance appointment. ⊠ *Piazza Scipione Borghese 5, off Via Pinciana, Villa Borghese* ☎ *06/8413979 information, 06/32810 reservations* ⊕ *www. galleriaborghese.it* ⌨ *€10.50, including €2 reservation fee; audio guide or English tour €6* ☉ *Tues.–Sun. 9–7, with sessions on hr every 2 hrs (9, 11, 1, 3, 5). Bus 910 from Piazza della Repubblica or Tram 19 or 3 from Policlinico.*

☾ **Pincio.** Redolent of the yesteryears of Henry James and Edith Wharton, the Pincio gardens have always been a favorite spot for strolling. Grand Tour-ists, and even a pope or two, would head here to see and be seen among the beau monde of Rome. Today, the Pincio terrace remains a favorite spot to cool off overheated locals. The rather formal, early-19th-century style contrasts with the far more elaborate terraced gardens of Lucullus, the Roman gourmand who held legendary banquets here. The pathways are lined these days with off-white marble busts of Italian heroes and artists. Along with similar busts on the Gianicolo (Janiculum Hill), their noses have been victims of vandalism. One theory to explain such nose-bashing is the fear of ghosts. A belief going back to ancient times held that the nose was the source of breath and therefore life itself, even after death. By depriving a bust of the same organ, its accompanying spirit would be deprived the oxygen, which evidently spirits need to walk the night.

The Pincio is separated from the southwest corner of Villa Borghese by a stretch of ancient walls. From the balustraded Pincio terrace you can look down at Piazza del Popolo and beyond, surveying much of Rome. Southeast of the Pincio terrace is the **Casina Valadier,** a magnificently decorated templelike Neoclassic building that was reopened to the public in 2007 after a decade-long renovation—it remains one of Rome's most historic restaurants. ⊠ *Piazzale Napoleone I and Viale dell'Obelisco, Villa Borghese* Ⓜ *Flaminio (Piazza del Popolo).*

★ **Villa Medici.** Purchased by Napoléon to create an academy where artists could hone their knowledge of Italian art and so put it to the (French) national good, the villa originally belonged to Cardinal Ferdinando Medici who also laid out the immaculate Renaissance garden to set off his sculpture collection. Garden tours are offered, allowing you to walk in the footsteps of Velázquez, Fragonard, and Ingres, who all worked here (which is now officially called the French Academy in Rome). As in their day all the explanations are strictly in French (or Italian), but the €8 guided tour is also the only way you can see the incredibly picturesque garden facade, which is studded with Mannerist and Rococo sculpted reliefs and overlooks a loggia with a beautiful fountain devoted to Mercury. ⊠ *Viale Trinità dei Monti, 1 Villa Borghese* ☎ *06/67611*

8

Sister of Napoléon, Principessa Pauline Borghese scandalized all Europe by posing as a half-naked Venus for Canova; the statue is on view at Museo Borghese.

⊕ *www.villamedici.it* ⊙ *Open daily for tours of at least 10 people (at 9:45, 11, 12, 3, 4, 5:30)* Ⓜ *Spagna.*

Ⓒ **Villa Borghese.** Rome's "Central Park," the Villa Borghese was originally part of the pleasure gardens laid out in the early 17th century by Cardinal Scipione Borghese, a worldly and cultivated cleric and nephew of Pope Paul V. The word "villa" was used to mean suburban estate, of the type developed by the ancient Romans and adopted by Renaissance nobles. Today's gardens bear little resemblance to the originals. Not only do they cover a much smaller area—by 1630, the perimeter wall was almost 5 km (3 mi) long—but they have also been almost entirely remodeled. This occurred at the end of the 18th century, when a Scottish painter, Jacob More, was employed to transform them into the style of the "cunningly natural" park so popular in 18th-century England. Until that time, the park was probably the finest example of an Italian-style garden in the entire country.

In addition to the gloriously restored Galleria Borghese museum, the highlights of the park are Piazza di Siena, a graceful amphitheater; and the botanical garden on Via Canonica, where there is a pretty little lake, a Neoclassical faux–Temple of Aesculapius (a favorite photo-op), the newly designed Zoo/Biopark, Rome's own replica of London's Globe Theatre, and the Villa Giulia museum.

The also recently opened Carlo Bilotti museum is particularly visitable for De Chirico fans, although there is more modern art in nearby Galleria Nazionale d'Arte Moderna. The park is dotted with bike, in-line skating, and electric scooter rental concessions and has a children's movie theater (showing films for adults in the evening), as well as a cinema center, Casa del Cinema, where film buffs can view DVDs for free from its collection of 5,000 films or sit at the slick, cherry red, indoor-outdoor caffè. See the park's Web site for a handy list of places to rent bikes and other facilities. ✉ *Main entrances at Porta Pinciana, the Pincio, Piazzale Flaminio (Piazza del Popolo), Viale delle Belle Arti, and Via Mercadante Villa Borghese* ⊕ *en.villaborghese. it* Ⓜ *Flaminio (Piazza del Popolo).*

WORTH NOTING

Biopark. Especially good for a day out with the children, this zoo has been remodeled under eco-friendly lines—more space for the animals, most brought from other zoos or born from animals already in captivity rather than snatched from the wild. A special ecological chamber of horrors section outlines the evils

of poaching as well as including a drawing room with the most bio-unfriendly decor. Other features are the Biopark train (€1), the Reptilarium (€2.25), a picnic area next to the flamingos, and a farm where children can help feed the domestic animals. No rhino, no koalas, no panda, no polar bears, but there are local bears from Abruzzo. To round off the day outside it's possible to hire a rickshaw to tour the outlying park. The Tram or Bus 3 from Trastevere or the Colosseum stops at Biopark. ✉ *Piazzale del Giardino Zoologico 1, Villa Borghese* ☎ *06/3608211* ⊗ *Mar. 28–Oct. 25, weekdays 9:30–5; Oct. 26–Dec. 31, weekdays 9:30–4; Apr. 4–Sept. 27, weekends 9:30–6* ⊠ *€10 (€ 8 for children)* ⊕ *www.bioparco.it.*

Galleria Nazionale d'Arte Moderna *(National Gallery of Modern Art).* This massive white Beaux Arts building looks anything but modern, yet it contains one of Italy's leading collections of 19th- and 20th-century works. It's primarily dedicated to the history of Italian modernism, examining the movement's development over the last two centuries, but crowd-pleasers Degas, Monet, Courbet, Van Gogh, and Cézanne put in appearances along with an outstanding Dadaist collection. ✉ *Via delle Belle Arti 131, Villa Borghese* ☎ *06/322981 (guided tours in English: 06/39967051)* ⊕ *www.gnam.beniculturali.it* ⊠ *€10* ⊗ *Tues.–Sun. 8:30–7:30. Tram or Bus 3 or 19, Bus 88, 95, 490, 495.*

Globe Theater. Directed by prolific Roman actor Gigi Proietti, this theater replicates the London original inaugurated in 1576. Rome's homage to Shakespeare is built entirely of wood, seats 1,250 with standing room for 420 groundlings (following Elizabethan custom). Performances are from July to September, generally in Italian. Set in the Villa Borghese park, it is roughly between the Biopark and the

8

Carlo Bilotti museum. ⊠ *Silvani Toti Globe Theater, Largo Aqua Felix on the Viale Pietro Canonica, Villa Borghese* ☎ 06/0608 ⊕ *www.globetheatreroma.com.*

Museo Nazionale Etrusco di Villa Giulia. The world's most outstanding collection of Etruscan art and artifacts is housed in Villa Giulia, built around 1551 for Pope Julius III (hence its name). Among the team called in to plan and construct the villa were Michelangelo and his fellow Florentine Vasari. Most of the actual work, however, was done by Vignola and Ammannati. The villa's *nymphaeum*—or sunken sculpture garden—is a superb example of a refined late-Renaissance setting for princely pleasures. No one knows precisely where the Etruscans originated. Many scholars maintain they came from Asia Minor, appearing in Italy about 2000 BC, and creating a civilization that was a dazzling prelude to the ancient Romans. Unfortunately, the exhibitions here are as dry as their subject matter—hundreds of glass vitrines stuffed with objects. Even so, you'll find great artistic treasures. Among the most striking pieces are the terra-cotta statues, such as the *Apollo of Veio* and the serenely beautiful *Sarcophagus of the Wedded Couple.* Dating 530–500 BC, this couple, or Sposi, look at the viewer with almond eyes and archaic smiles, suggesting an openness and joie de vivre rare in Roman art. Also look for the cinematic frieze from a later Temple (480 BC) from Pyrgi, looking like a sort of Etruscan Elgin marbles in terra-cotta. Note the fabulous Etruscan jewelry, which makes Bulgari look like your village blacksmith. ⊠ *Piazzale Villa Giulia 9, Villa Borghese* ☎ 06/3226571 ⊕ *www.archeologia.beniculturali.it* 🎟 €4 ☉ *Tues.–Sun.* 8:30–7:30 Ⓜ Tram 19, Bus 3.

Porta Pinciana *(Pincian Gate).* Framed by two squat, circular towers, the gate was constructed in the 6th century. Here you can see just how well the Aurelian walls have been preserved and imagine hordes of Visigoths trying to break through them. Sturdy as the walls look, they couldn't always keep out the barbarians: Rome was sacked three times during the 5th century alone. ⊠ *Piazzale Basile, junction Via Veneto and Corso d'Italia, Villa Borghese.*

> **ROME'S PRETTIEST RESTAURANT**
>
> Ever since it was designed in 1814, the park pavilion restaurant known as the **Casina Valadier** (Piazza Bucarest, Pincio Gardens ☎ 06/6992-2090) has always attracted celebrities like King Farouk of Egypt, Richard Strauss, Gandhi, and Mussolini, all who came to see the lavish Empire-style salons and, of course, be seen. In 2007, the elegant pavilion reopened and now has a new array of eateries. Reviews have been decidedly mixed about the food but the decor is as delicious as it comes.

PIAZZA DEL POPOLO

Very round, very explicitly defined, and very photogenic, the Piazza del Popolo—the People's Square—is one of Rome's biggest. With twin churches (and two adjacent ritzy caffà) at one end and the Porta del Popolo—the city's northern gateway—at the other, this square was laid out in its present form by papal architect Giuseppe Valadier (1762–1839). Part of an earlier urban plan, the three streets to the south radiate straight as spokes to other parts of the city, forming the famed "tridente" that nicknames this neighborhood. The center is marked with a stolen obelisk that rightfully belongs to Egypt—and has since the 13th century BC when it was carved for Ramses II. Today, it is guarded by four water-gushing lions and steps that mark the end of many a sunset passeggiata. The *couleur locale* is strong here, but for real splashes of color head to the northeast corner to find often overlooked Santa Maria del Popolo, snuggled against the 400-year-old Porta del Popolo (Rome's northern city gate), home to great masterpieces by Raphael and Caravaggio.

TOP ATTRACTIONS

♺ **Piazza del Popolo.** With its obelisk and twin churches, this immense square is a famed Rome landmark. It owes its current appearance to architect Giuseppe Valadier, who designed it about 1820, also laying out the terraced approach to the Pincio and the Pincio's gardens. It marks what was for centuries the northern entrance to the city, where all roads from the north converge and where visitors, many of them pilgrims, would get their first impression of the Eternal City. The desire to make this entrance to Rome something special had been a pet project of popes and their architects over three centuries. The piazza takes its name from the 15th-century church of Santa Maria del Popolo, huddled on the right side of the Porta del Popolo, or city gate. In the late 17th century, the twin churches of Santa Maria in Montesanto (on the left as you face them) and Santa Maria dei Miracoli (on the right) were added to the piazza at the point where Via del Babuino, Via del Corso, and Via di Ripetta converge. The piazza has always served as a meeting place, crowded with fashionable carriages and carnival revelers in the past. It's now a pedestrian zone and serves as a magnet for the fashionable young and old at its caffè tables. At election time, it's the scene of huge political rallies, and on New Year's Eve Rome stages a mammoth alfresco party in the piazza. ✉ *Junction of Via del Babuino, Via del Corso, and Via di Ripetta, Piazza del Popolo* Ⓜ *Flaminio.*

NEED A BREAK? Off Piazza del Popolo on Via di Ripetta you'll find places where you can stop for sustenance. For a quick sit-down lunch with a good assortment of hot and cold dishes, including pizza, try **Panefformaggio** (✉ *Via di Ripetta 8a* ☎ *06/3212754*). **PizzaRé** (✉ *Via di Ripetta 14* ☎ *06/3211468*) offers a wide choice of toppings for pizza cooked in a wood-burning oven. **Buccone** (✉ *Via di Ripetta 19* ☎ *06/3612154*) is a wineshop serving light snacks at lunchtime and wine by the glass all day long.

★ **Santa Maria del Popolo.** Standing inconspicuously in a corner of the vast Piazza del Popolo, this church often goes unnoticed, but the treasures inside make it a must for art lovers, as they include an entire chapel designed by Raphael and one adorned with striking Caravaggio masterpieces. Bramante enlarged the apse of the church, which had been rebuilt in the 15th century on the site of a much older place of worship. Inside, in the first chapel on the right, you'll see some frescoes by Pinturicchio from the mid-15th century; the adjacent **Cybo Chapel** is a 17th-century exercise in marble decoration. Heading to the second chapel on the left, you'll see Raphael's famous **Chigi Chapel,** built around 1513 and commissioned by the banker Agostino Chigi (who also had the artist decorate his home across the Tiber, the Villa Farnesina). Raphael provided the cartoons for the vault mosaic—showing God the Father in benediction—and the designs for the statues of Jonah and Elijah in the Chigi Chapel. More than a century later, Bernini added the oval medallions on the tombs and the statues of Daniel and Habakkuk, when, in the mid-17th century another Chigi, Pope Alexander VII, commissioned him to restore and decorate the building.

The organ case of Bernini in the right transept bears the Della Rovere family oak tree, part of the Chigi family's coat of arms. The **choir,** with vault frescoes by Pinturicchio, contains the handsome tombs of Ascanio Sforza and Girolamo delle Rovere, both designed by Andrea Sansovino. The best is for last: The **Cerasi Chapel,** to the left of the high altar on the sidewalls, has two Caravaggios, both key early-baroque works that show how modern 17th-century art can be. Compare their earthy realism and harshly dramatic lighting with the much more restrained and classically "pure" *Assumption of the Virgin* by Caravaggio's contemporary and rival, Annibale Carracci; it hangs over the altar of the chapel. ⊠ *Piazza del Popolo 12, near Porta Pinciana Piazza del Popolo* ☎ *06/3610836* ◷ *Mon.–Sat. 7–noon and 4–7, Sun. 8–1:30 and 4:30–7:30* Ⓜ *Flaminio.*

WORTH NOTING

MAXXI—Museo Nazionale delle Arti del XXI Secolo (National Museum of 21st-Century Arts). Billed as a cultural space for the art of the 21st century, this museum—opened May 2010 and a healthy walk from the Parco della Musica complex—contains 350 works from Warhol to tomorrow's hottest artists. Arguably the most impressive exhibit of all is the now dramatically angular, now swooping building designed by Anglo-Iranian starchitect Zaha Hadid. Get to MAXII by taking Line 2 of the Metro at Flaminia (near Piazza del Popolo) two stops to Appolodoro. ⊠ *Via Guido Reni 4, near Villa Borghese* ☎ *06/3201829* ⊕ *www.maxxi.darc.beniculturali.it* ✉ *Not set at this writing* ◷ *Not set at this writing.*

Santa Maria dei Miracoli. A twin to Santa Maria in Montesanto, this church was built in the 1670s by Carlo Fontana as an elegant frame for the entrance to Via del Corso from Piazza del Popolo. ⊠ *Via del Corso 528, Piazza del Popolo* Ⓜ *Flaminio* ☎ *06/3610250* ◷ *Daily 6–1 and 4–7:30.*

Santa Maria in Montesanto. One of the two bookend churches on the eastern side of Piazza del Popolo, this edifice was built by Carlo Fontana, supervised by his brilliant teacher, Bernini (whose other pupils are responsible for the saints topping the facade). ⊠ *Via del Babuino 197, Piazza del Popolo* ☎ *06/3610594* Ⓜ *Flaminio.*

Trastevere and the Ghetto

ISOLA TIBERINA, SANTA MARIA IN
TRASTAVERE, PORTICO D'OTTAVIA

WORD OF MOUTH

"After we took in Santa Maria in Trastevere's stunning mosaics, we walked back having gelati on the way (of course, one gelato a day!). After dinner we returned to the basilica for a concert featuring a beautiful choir before the stroll back-it was lovely crossing the Tiber with Castel Sant'Angelo in the background."
— AmanteDelLimoncello

GETTING ORIENTED

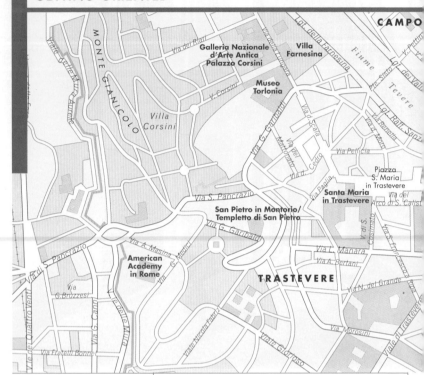

GETTING HERE	TOP 5 REASONS TO GO
From the Vatican or Spanish Steps, expect a 20- to 30-minute walk to reach either the Ghetto or Trastevere.	**Santa Maria in Trastevere:** Tear yourself away from the piazza scene outside to take in the gilded glory of one of the city's oldest and most beautiful churches, fabled for its medieval mosaics.
From Termini, nab the No. 40 Express or the No. 64 bus to Largo Torre Argentina, where you can get off to visit the Ghetto area.	**"Tiber, Father Tiber":** Cross over the river on the Ponte Fabricio—the city's oldest bridge—for a stroll on the paved shores of the adorable Isola Tiberina (and don't forget to detour for the lemon ices at La Gratachecca).
Switch to Tram 8 to get to Trastevere.	**Portico d'Ottavia:** This famed ancient Roman landmark casts a spell over Rome's time-stained Ghetto Ebraico, now getting more gentrified by the minute.
As for ascending the very steep Janiculum Hill, take the No. 41 bus from Ponte Sant'Angelo, then enjoy the stately walk down to the northern reaches of Trastevere.	**I Love the Nightlife:** Trastevere has become one of Rome's hottest nighttime scene-arenas, with hipsterious clubs at nearly every turn.
	Get Middle-Aged: With cobblestone alleyways and medieval houses, the area around Trastevere's Piazza di Piscinula offers a magical dip into Rome's Middle Ages.

BEST TIME-OUTS

Caffè di Marzio (✉ *Piazza Santa Maria in Trastevere 15* ☎ *06/5816095*), in the heart of Trastevere, is the perfect spot to sit and gaze upon the glistening golden facade of Santa Maria in Trastevere church and watch the world go by. The wood-paneled interior is warm and welcoming. Expect a mix of local regulars and tourists.

The **Russian Tea Room** (✉ *Via dei Falegnami 7/9* ☎ *06/6869164*) will provide you with your own pot of tea, a sweet or savory crepe (along with a tempting lineup of cakes to choose from), and a slightly kitsch but welcoming ambience for your sightseeing break.

The specialty is in the name of the **Casa del Tramezzino** (*House of Sandwiches* ✉ *Viale Trastevere 81* ☎ *No phone*), which offers a tantalizing variety of choices, Roman- and mom-style, on white bread with the crusts cut off. Try Roman classics like tuna with artichoke hearts, or spinach with mozzarella. Counter service only.

9

O.K., WHERE DO I START?

Piazza Venezia is the starting point for touring the ancient Ghetto quarter of the city. From the piazza, walk to the base of the Campidoglio, take Via del Teatro Marcello, and turn right across the street onto Via Montanara and enter Piazza Campitelli, with its baroque church and fountain. Take Via dei Funari at the northwest end of the piazza and follow it into Piazza Mattei, where one of Rome's loveliest fountains, the 16th-century Fontana delle Tartarughe (Fountain of the Turtles), is tucked away. A few steps down Via Caetani, off the north side of Piazza Mattei, you'll find a doorway into the courtyard of the venerable Palazzo Mattei—festooned with baroque sculpture busts, it's a stunner. From Piazza Mattei go south on Via della Reginella onto Via Portico d'Ottavia, heart of the Jewish Ghetto and home to the ancient Portico d'Ottavia (not far away is the even older Teatro di Marcello). Cross Ponte Fabricio over the Isola Tiberina (Tiber Island) to Trastevere. Begin with the medieval little streets around picturesque Piazza in Piscinula. Then make for Bernini's San Francesco a Ripa at the Villa Farnesina.

Sightseeing
★★★★★
Nightlife
★★★★
Dining
★★★★
Lodging
★★★
Shopping
★★★

If New York has its Greenwich Village, then Rome has its Trastevere. In Trastevere's case, however, the sense of being a world apart goes back more than two millenia. The inhabitants don't even call themselves Romans but Trasteverini, going on to claim that they, not the citizens north of the river, are the true remaining Romans. No matter: A trip to Trastevere (literally, "across the Tiber") still feels a bit like entering a different time and place. Some call it the world's third-smallest nation (after the Vatican, No. 2). A living chronology, the district remains an enchanting confusion of past and present. With its charming, crumbling streets lined with medieval bell towers and chic *osterie,* this is one big little town where strangers don't remain strangers too long.

Though right in the geographic heart of the city, Trastevere and the Ghetto have always been considered outsiders. Trastevere began as a farming settlement for immigrants from the East; until the 14th century, it wasn't even considered part of Rome. Since then, locals regard them as a breed apart, with their own dialect and traditions. The Ghetto—historically known as the Ghetto Ebraico (Jewish Ghetto)—was established by papal decree in the 16th century. It was by definition a closed community, where Roman Jews lived under lock and key until Italian unification in 1870. In 1943–44, the already small Jewish population there was decimated by deportations.

In a city where the past counts at least as much as the present, this history of exclusion endures, and has shaped the present-day neighborhoods in some unexpected ways. Today, Trastevere and the Ghetto are two of the city's hottest real-estate markets, sought after by Italian lefties and bohemian expats, who value their history as much as their earthy, old-fashioned atmosphere. True Trasteverini are now few and far between, most of the older generation having sold their now valuable family apartments, and most of Rome's Jews live outside the Ghetto. But something of them remains. Trastevere's new residents promote a new kind of outsider identity, embodied variously in yoga centers, social outreach programs, and innumerable funky bars. The Ghetto, while undergoing some of the same changes, remains the spiritual and cultural home of Rome's Jews, and that proud heritage permeates its small commercial area of Judaica shops, kosher bakeries, and restaurants.

The heart of Trastevere is the lovely Piazza Santa Maria, presided over by the gilded and floodlit church of the same name. Nearby are a variety of historic churches, set in alleys and sunny piazzas, but the greatest artistic treasures are to be found a short walk to the north, in Raphael's frescoes at the Villa Farnesina, and the baroque paintings, including a Caravaggio, in the collection at the Palazzo Corsini. The neighborhood's greatest attraction, however, is simply its atmosphere—traditional shops set along crooked streets, peaceful during the day, and alive with throngs of restaurant- and partygoers at night. From here, a steep hike up stairs and the road to the Gianicolo earns you a panoramic view over the whole city.

The turn-of-the-20th-century synagogue, with its museum dedicated to the history of Jewish Rome, is a must for understanding the Ghetto. Tight, teeming alleys lead from there up to Giacomo della Porta's unmistakable Turtle Fountain; nearby is the picture-perfect Palazzo Mattei. Via Portico d'Ottavia is a walk through the olden days: Most businesses in the Ghetto observe the Jewish Sabbath—it's a ghost town on Saturdays. At its east end, the street leads down to a path past the 1st-century Teatro di Marcello. Separating the Ghetto and Trastevere is the Tiber River, but they are connected by one of the world's prettiest "bridges"—the Isola Tiberina (Tiber Island). Cross over the rushing river by using the Ponte Fabricio, the oldest bridge in Rome.

9

TRASTEVERE

Sometimes futilely resisting the tides of change, Rome has several little communities that have staunchly defended their authenticity over the centuries; the Tiber separates two of them—the Ghetto and Trastevere. Just beyond the charming Tiberina Island lies Trastevere, which, despite galloping gentrification, remains about the most tightly knit community in Rome. Perfectly picturesque piazzas, tiny winding medieval alleyways, and time-burnished Romanesque houses all cast a frozen-in-amber spell, while grand art awaits at Santa Maria in Trastevere, San Francesco a Ripa, and the Villa Farnesina. On the northern border of the district looms the Janiculum Hill, Rome's highest, with views to prove it.

TOP ATTRACTIONS

Gianicolo *(Janiculum Hill).* The Gianicolo is famous for offering panoramic views of the city, a noontime cannon, statues of Giuseppe and Anita Garibaldi (Garibaldi was the guiding spirit behind the unification of Italy in the 19th century; Anita was his long-suffering wife), and, as on the Pincio, noseless and bedaubed busts. Note that Rome does not have the most exciting cityscape in the world—the vista here is of endless buildings, although it is hard to pick out the famous church spires and Vittorio Emmanuele monument. At the plaza here there's a daily free puppet show (☉ *Weekdays 4–7, weekends 10:30–1 and 4–7*) in Italian. ✉ *Via Garibaldi and Passeggiata del Gianicolo, Trastevere.*

> **TRASTEVERE STEP-BY-STEP**
>
> This enchanting neighborhood was made for walking, so check out our "Roamin' Holiday" chapter for a complete and fascinating tour of Trastevere and the Isola Tiberina, with many more sights outlined in these especially picturesque districts.

Palazzo Corsini. A brooding example of baroque style, the palace houses part of the 16th- and 17th-century sections of the collection of the Galleria Nazionale d'Arte Antica and is across the road from the Villa Farnesina. Among the most famous paintings in this large, dark collection are Guido Reni's *Beatrice Cenci* and Caravaggio's *St. John the Baptist.* Stop in, if only to climb the 17th-century stone staircase, itself a drama of architectural shadows and sculptural voids. Behind the palazzo is the **Orto Botanico,** Rome's only botanical park containing 3,500 species of plants. There are various greenhouses, around a recently restored stairway/fountain with 11 jets. Or, if you prefer, it's just a peaceful park where kids can run and play. The park is open Monday through Saturday, 9 to 6:30 (5:30 in winter); admission is €4. ✉ *Via della Lungara 10, Trastevere* ☎ *06/68802323, 06/32810 tickets booking* ⊕ *www.galleriaborghese.it* 💷 *€4 (€1 reservations fee)* ☉ *Tues.– Sun. 8:30–7:30.*

Piazza in Piscinula. One of Trastevere's most historic and time-burnished squares, this piazza takes its name from some ancient Roman baths on the site (*piscina* means "pool"). The tiny church of **San Benedetto** on the piazza is the smallest church in the city and, despite its 18th-century facade, dates back to the 4th century AD. Opposite is the medieval **Casa dei Mattei** (Mattei House). Rich and powerful, the Mattei family lived here until the 16th century, when, after a series of murders on the premises, they decided to move out of the district entirely, crossing the river to build their magnificent palace in the Ghetto. ✉ *Via della Lungaretta, Piazza della Gensola, Via in Piscinula, and Via Lungarina, Trastevere.*

☮ **Piazza Santa Maria in Trastevere.** At the very heart of the Trastevere *rione*
★ (district) is this beautiful piazza, with its elegant raised fountain and sidewalk caffè, a sort of outdoor living room, open to all comers. The showpiece is the 12th-century church of Santa Maria in Trastevere. The striking mosaics on the church's facade—which add light and color to the piazza especially at night when they are spotlighted—are believed to represent the Wise and Foolish Virgins. Through innumerable generations, this piazza has seen the comings and goings of tourists and travelers, intellectuals and artists, who lounge on the steps of the fountain or eat lunch at an outdoor table at Sabatini's. Here the paths of Trastevere's residents intersect repeatedly during the day; they pause,

ISOLA TIBERINA

✉ *Tiber Island, accessed by the Ponte Fabricio bridge (Lungotevere dei Pierleoni near Via Ponte Quattro Capi) and the Ponte Cestio bridge (Lungotevere degli Anguillara near Piazza San Bartolomeo all'Isola).*

TIPS

■ Sometimes called the world's most beautiful movie theater, the open-air Cinema d'Isola di Tiberina operates from mid-June to early September as part of Rome's big summer festival called Estate Romana (www.estateromana. comune.roma.it/). The 450-seat Arena Maxischermo unfolds its silver screen against the backdrop of the ancient Ponte Fabricio bridge while the 50-seat CineLab is set against Ponte Garibaldi facing Trastevere. Screenings usually start at 7:30 and admission is around €5.

■ Line up at the kiosk of "La Gratachecca del 1915" (near the Ponte Cestio) for the most yumptious frozen ices in Rome.

Unless you're sick or need to pray, this tiny island in the Tiber is easy to overlook. In terms of history and sheer picturesqueness, however, this most charming of Rome's backwaters gets high marks.

Cross onto the island via Ponte Fabricio, constructed in 62 BC, the oldest bridge in the city; on the north side of the Isola is the romantic ruin of the Ponte Rotto (Broken Bridge), which dates back to 179 BC.

Descend the steps down to the lovely river embankment to see the island's claim to fame—a Roman relief of Aesculapius, the great god of healing. In 291 BC a temple to Aesculapius—whose sign was a snake—was erected on the island, and thereby hangs a tale.

A ship had been sent to Epidaurus in Greece—heart of the cult of Aesculapius—to obtain a statue of the god. As the ship sailed back up the Tiber, a great serpent was seen escaping from it and swimming to the island—a sign that a temple to Aesculapius should be built here.

In imperial times, Romans sheathed the entire island with marble to make it look like Aesculapius's ship, replete with a towering obelisk as a mast.

The ancient sculpted ship's prow amazingly still exists—marvel at it on the downstream end of the embankment.

Today, medicine still reigns here—the island is home to the hospital of Fatebenefratelli (literally, "Do good, brothers"). Nearby is San Bartolomeo, built at the end of the 10th century by the Holy Roman Emperor Otto III and restored in the 18th century.

9

gathering in clusters to talk animatedly in the broad accent of Rome or in a score of foreign languages. At night, it's the center of Trastevere's action, with street festivals, musicians, and gamboling dogs vying for attention from the throngs of people taking the evening air. ✉ *Via della Lungaretta, Via della Paglia, and Via San Cosimato, Trastevere.*

★ **San Francesco a Ripa.** Set near the southern end of Trastevere, this baroque church attached to a 13th-century Franciscan monastery is noted for one of Bernini's last works, a statue of the Blessed Ludovica Albertoni. This is perhaps Bernini's most hallucinatory sculpture, a dramatically lighted figure ecstatic at the prospect of entering heaven as she expires on her deathbed. She clutches her breast as a symbol, art historians have recently deciphered, of the "milk of human kindness" and Christian *caritas* (charity). Gracing the altar is Baciccia's *Madonna and St. Anne.* St. Francis is supposed to have stayed at this monastery when visiting the city; to see his cell, ask the Sacristan. ✉ *Piazza San Francesco d'Assisi 88, Trastevere* ☎ *06/5819020* ☉ *Daily 9–noon and 4–5:30.*

★ **San Pietro in Montorio.** Built in part by command of Ferdinand and Isabella of Spain in 1481 near the spot where, tradition says (evidently mistakenly), St. Peter was crucified, this church is a handsome and dignified edifice. It contains a number of well-known works, including, in the first chapel on the right, the *Flagellation* painted by the Venetian Sebastiano del Piombo from a design by Michelangelo, and *St. Francis in Ecstasy,* in the next-to-last chapel on the left, in which Bernini made one of his earliest experiments with concealed lighting effects.

However, the most famous work here is the circular **Tempietto** (Little Temple) in the monastery cloister next door. This sober little building—though tiny, holding only 10 people, it's actually a church in its own right—marks the spot where (legend has it that) St. Peter's cross once stood. It remains one of the key Renaissance buildings in Rome. Designed by Bramante (the original architect of the new St. Peter's Basilica) in 1502, it represents one of the earliest and most successful attempts to reproduce an entirely classical building with the lessons of ancient Greek and Roman architecture fully evident. The basic design was derived from a circular temple on the grounds of the emperor Hadrian's great villa at Tivoli outside Rome. ✉ *Piazza San Pietro in Montorio 2 (Via Garibaldi); entrance to cloister and Tempietto at portal next to church, Trastevere* ☎ *06/5813940* ⊕ *www. sanpietroinmontorio.it* ☉ *Church daily 8–noon and 3–4, Tempietto daily 8–noon and 3–5:30.*

Santa Cecilia in Trastevere. The aristocratic St. Cecilia, patron saint of music, is commemorated here. One of ancient Rome's most celebrated Early Christian martyrs, she was put to a supernaturally long death by the emperor Diocletian around the year AD 300. After an abortive attempt to suffocate her in the baths of her own house (a favorite means of quietly disposing of aristocrats in Roman days), she was brought before the executioner. But not even three blows of the executioner's sword could dispatch the young girl. She lingered for several days, converting others to the Christian cause, before finally dying. Sculpted by Stefano Maderno, a striking white marble statue of the saint languishing

Dining "al fresco" in Trastevere—now *this* is what you came to Italy for.

in martyrdom, her head half-severed, lies below the main altar. If you time your visit to the church for Tuesday or Thursday morning between 10 and noon, you can enter the cloistered convent to see what remains of Pietro Cavallini's *Last Judgment,* dating from 1293. It's the only major fresco in existence known to have been painted by Cavallini, a forerunner of Giotto. ✉ *Piazza Santa Cecilia in Trastevere 22, Trastevere* ☎ *06/5899289* 🖾 *Church free; frescoes €2.50* ⊙ *Daily 9:30–12:30 and 4–6:30; Frescoes, weekdays 10:15–12:15, weekends 11:15–12:15*

Fodor's Choice ★ **Santa Maria in Trastevere.** Originally built sometime before the 4th century, this is certainly one of the oldest churches in the city, and one of the grandest, too. With a nave framed by a processional of two rows of gigantic columns (22 in total) taken from ancient Roman temples and an altar studded with gilded mosaics, this interior conjures up the splendor of ancient Rome better than any other in the city. Although there are larger Roman naves, none seems so majestic, as it's bathed in a sublime glow from the 12th- and 13th-century mosaics and Domenichino's gilded ceiling (1617). Supposedly Rome's first church dedicated to the Virgin Mary, it was rebuilt in the 12th century by Pope Innocent II (who hailed from Trastevere). The 19th-century portico seems to focus attention on the facade's 800-year-old mosaics, which represent the parable of the Wise and Foolish Virgins. The piazza is enhanced by their aura, especially at night, when the church front and its bell tower are illuminated. Back inside, the semicircular apse is covered with the most important mosaics, Pietro Cavallini's six panels of the *Life of the Virgin* (Their new sense of realism is said to have to have inspired the great Giotto). Note the little building labeled "Taberna Meritoria" just under the figure of the Virgin in the Nativity scene, with a stream of oil flowing from it. It recalls the legend that on the day Christ was born, a stream of pure oil flowed from the earth on the site of the piazza, signifying the coming of the grace of God. Off the north side of the piazza, there's a little street called Via delle Fonte dell'Olio in honor of this miracle. ⊠ *Piazza Santa Maria in Trastevere, Trastevere* ☎ 06/5814802 ☾ *Daily 7:30–9.*

> ### ROMOLO'S
>
> Raphael's model and mistress, the dark-eyed Fornarina (literally, "the baker's daughter"), is believed to have been a Trasteverina. The artist reportedly took time off from painting the district's Villa Farnesina to romance—and perhaps marry—the winsome girl. Her family house, legend states, is Trastevere's landmark restaurant, Romolo (Via di Porta Settimiana 8), replete with enchanting, leafy dining garden, menus embellished by Miró, and the city's best artichoke sauces.

NEED A BREAK? *Pubs, snack bars, beer bars, book bars, pizzeria, restaurants upmarket or down: almost every other building in Trastevere offers just that. However, for good honest Cucina Romana at good honest prices you can't better,* **Trattoria Da Augusto** (⊠ V*Piazza De'Renzi 15, Trastevere* ☎ *06/5803798*), *off to the right before you reach Santa Maria in Trastevere.*

★ **Villa Farnesina.** Money was no object to extravagant host Agostino Chigi, a banker from Siena who financed many a papal project. His munificence is evident in this elegant villa, built for him about 1511. He was especially proud of the delicate fresco decorations in the airy loggias, now glassed in to protect their artistic treasures. When Raphael could steal a little time from his work on the Vatican Stanze, he came over to execute some of the frescoes himself, notably a luminous *Galatea.* In his villa, host Agostino entertained the popes and princes of 16th-century Rome. He delighted in impressing his guests at alfresco suppers held in riverside pavilions by having his servants clear the table by casting the precious silver and gold dinnerware into the Tiber. His extravagance was not quite so boundless as he wished to make it appear, however: he had nets unfurled a foot or two under the water's surface to catch the valuable ware.

In the magnificent **Loggia of Psyche** on the ground floor, Giulio Romano and others worked from Raphael's designs. Raphael's lovely *Galatea* is in the adjacent room. On the floor above you can see the trompe l'oeil effects in the aptly named **Hall of Perspectives** by Peruzzi. Agostino Chigi's bedroom, next door, was frescoed by Il Sodoma with scenes from the life of Alexander the Great, notably the *Wedding of Alexander and Roxanne,* which is considered to be the artist's best work. The palace also houses the **Gabinetto Nazionale delle Stampe,** a treasurehouse of old prints and drawings. When the Tiber embankments were built in 1879, the remains of a classical villa were discovered under the Farnesina gardens, and their decorations are now in the Museo Nazionale Romano's collections in Palazzo Massimo alle Terme. ⊠ *Via della Lungara 230, Trastevere* ☎ *06/68027268* ⊕ *www.lincei.it* 🎫 *€5* ☾ *Mon.–Sat. 9–1.*

THE GHETTO

The downside of spiritual revival can be religious intolerance. With the Counter-Reformation and its new religious orders, also came a papal decree that Trastevere's longstanding Jewish community should be moved north of the river to the so-called Ghetto. A community going back to 180 BC suddenly found itself walled in and subjected to a nightly curfew. With the Italian Unification of 1870 the Ghetto walls were demolished, but less than a century later Vittorio Emmanule III, King of Italy and Emperor of Abyssinia, signed into effect the Race Laws whereby the Jewish community were deprived of the right to education, jobs, and then property. With the coming of the Nazis, worse was to follow as a visit to this district's synagogue will show. More recently, in 1967, Jewish refugees from Libya found a welcome here. The area now abounds with Kosher restaurants—its picturesque atmosphere once more prevailing over the frequent ugliness of history.

TOP ATTRACTIONS

Crypta Balbi. The fourth component of the magnificent collections of the Museo Nazionale Romano and visitable on the same ticket, this museum is unusual in its equitable apportioning of Rome's archaeological cake: a slice of Roman history—the crypt being part of the Balbus Theater complex (13 BC)—but also a slice of the largely vanished medieval Rome that once stood on top. The written explanations accompanying the well-lit exhibits are also excellent, making this museum much visited by teachers and schools. ⊠ *Via delle Botteghe Oscure 31, Largo Argentina* ☎ *06/39967700* ♥ *€7 (with 3-day access to 3 sister museums)* Ⓜ *Buses 64 and 40, and Tram 8 from Trastevere.*

Fontana delle Tartarughe. Set in venerable Piazza Mattei, designed by Giacomo della Porta in 1581 and sculpted by Taddeo Landini, this 16th-century fountain is Rome's most charming. The focus of the fountain is four bronze boys, each grasping a dolphin spouting water into a marble shell. Bronze turtles held in the boys' hands drink from the upper basin. The turtles are thought to have been added in the 17th century by Bernini. ⊠ *Piazza Mattei, Ghetto.*

★ **Portico d'Ottavia.** A landmark of ancient Rome, the Portico d'Ottavia looms over the Ghetto district and comprises one of its most picturesque set pieces, as the time-stained church of Sant'Angelo in Pescheria was built right into its ruins. With a few surviving columns, the Portico d'Ottavia is a huge porticoed enclosure, named by Augustus in honor of his sister Octavia. Originally 390 feet wide and 433 feet long, it encompassed two temples, a meeting hall, and a library, and served as a kind of grandiose entrance foyer for the adjacent Teatro di Marcello. The ruins of the portico became Rome's *pescheria* (fish market) during the Middle Ages. A stone plaque on a pillar, a relic of that time, admonishes in Latin that the head of any fish surpassing the length of the plaque was to be cut off "up to the first fin" and given to the city fathers or else the vendor was to pay a fine of 10 gold florins. The heads were used to make fish soup and were considered a great delicacy. At press time, the church was closed for restoration. ⊠ *Via Tribuna di Campitelli 6, Ghetto* ☎ *06/68801819.*

Stop in at the bakery **Dolceroma** (✉ *Via Portico d'Ottavia 20/b, Ghetto* ☎ *06/6892196*) to indulge in American and Austrian baked treats. **Franco e Cristina** (✉ *Via Portico d'Ottavia 5, Ghetto*) is a stand-up pizza joint with the thinnest, crispiest pizza in town.

Sinagoga. This aluminum-roof synagogue is the city's largest Jewish temple and a Roman landmark since its construction in 1904. At the back the Jewish Museum, with its precious ritual objects and other exhibits, documents the uninterrupted presence of a Jewish community for nearly 22 centuries. Until the 13th century the Jews were esteemed citizens of Rome. Among them were the bankers and physicians to the popes, who had themselves given permission for the construction of synagogues. But later, popes of the Counter-Reformation revoked this tolerance, confining the Jews to the Ghetto and imposing a series of restrictions, some of which were enforced as late as 1870. For security reasons, guided visits are mandatory; entrance to the synagogue is through the museum located in Via Catalana (Largo 16 Ottobre 1943). ✉ *Lungotevere Cenci 15, Ghetto* ☎ *06/68400661* ⊕ *www.museoebraico.roma.it* 🖃 *€7.50* ⊘ *Mid-Sept.–mid-June, Sun.–Thurs. 10–4:15; mid-June–mid-Sept., Sun.–Thurs. 9–1:15.*

Teatro di Marcello. This place was begun by Julius Caesar and completed by the emperor Augustus in AD 13. It was Rome's first permanent building dedicated to theater, and it held 20,000 spectators. Like other Roman monuments, it was transformed into a fortress during the Middle Ages. Later, during the Renaissance, it was converted into a residence by the Savelli, one of the city's noble families. The small archaeological zone is used as a summer venue for open-air classical music and lyrical concerts. ✉ *Via del Teatro di Marcello, Ghetto* ☎ *06/87131590 for concert information* ⊕ *www.tempietto.it.*

WORTH NOTING

Fodor'sChoice
★

Palazzo Mattei di Giove. Astonishingly Roman and opulently baroque, the arcaded, multistory courtyard of this palazzo is a masterpiece of late-16th-century style. Designed by Carlo Maderno, it is a veritable panoply of sculpted busts, heroic statues, sculpted reliefs, and Paleo-Christian epigrams, all collected by Marchese Asdrubale Mattei. Have your Nikon ready as Roman and Renaissance heads cross glances across the ages. Inside are various scholarly institutes, including the Centro Italiano di Studi Americani (Center for American Studies), which also contains a library of American books. Various salons are decorated with frescoes by Cortona, Lanfranco, and Domenichino. ✉ *Via Michelangelo Caetani 32, other entrance in Via dei Funari, Ghetto.*

Aventino

AVENTINE HILL, PIAZZA BOCCA
DELLA VERITA, TESTACCIO

WORD OF MOUTH

"Walk around Monte Testaccio. A triumph of marketing, this is the world's best trash heap. Hiding a pile of ancient wine amphorae, this huge hill has become a hip neighborhood with great nightlife and restaurants—we loved Checchino dal 1870 where you can have any part of the cow you wish."

—AmanteDelLimoncello

GETTING ORIENTED

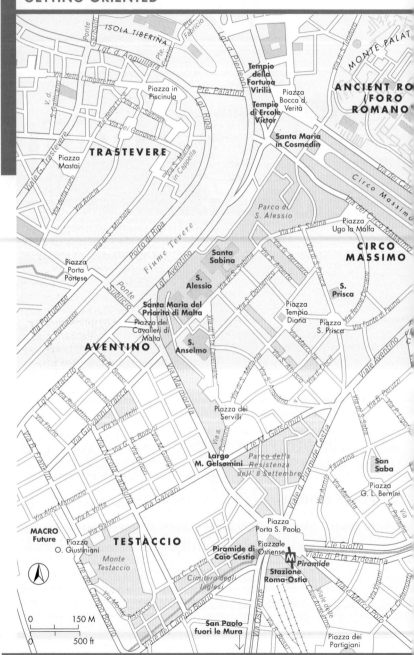

TOP 5 REASONS TO GO

Santa Maria in Cosmedin: Test your truthfulness (or someone else's) at the yawning mouth of the Bocca della Verità.

Cimitero degli Inglesi: Swoon over Keats's body and Shelley's heart in this romantic graveyard.

Piazza Cavalieri di Malta: Peek through the keyhole of the Priorato di Malta for a privileged view—one of Rome's most surprising delights.

Tempting Testaccio: Like New York City's Meatpacking District, this new "It" neighborhood is a sizzling combo of factories and nightclubs.

Roseto Comunale: Overlooking the Circo Massimo (where speeds the ghost of Ben Hur), this rose garden offers a fitting and fragrant vestibule to Rome's most poetic hill.

O.K., WHERE DO I START?

After first exploring the two ancient Roman temples and Santa Maria in Cosmedin on Piazza Bocca della Verità, head up the Aventine Hill by crossing broad Via della Greca and walk along the street, turning into the first street on the right, Clivo dei Publici. This skirts Valle Murcia, the city's rose garden, open in May and June. Where Clivo dei Publici veers off to the left, continue on Via di Santa Sabina. You'll see Santa Sabina ahead, but just before you reach it, you can take a turn around the delightful walled park, known as the Giardino degli Aranci, famous for its orange trees and wonderful view of the Tiber and St. Peter's Basilica. (This park is very quiet, so don't go alone.) On the right side of Via di Santa Sabina are two Aventine main attractions: the Early Christian landmark of Santa Sabina and the famous keyhole on Piazza Cavalieri di Malta. Via di Sant'Anselmo winds through quiet residential streets. Cross busy Viale Aventino at Piazza Albania and climb the so-called Piccolo Aventino on Via di San Saba to the medieval church of San Saba. Or from Piazza Cavalieri, head directly down the hill to hip and happening Testaccio.

GETTING HERE

Reaching the Aventine Hill on foot from either the Roman Forum or the Campidoglio makes for a spectacular 20-minute walk through ancient remains such as Circo Massimo. Happily, the subway stop of the same name sits at the bottom of the Aventino. Coming from the Vatican, hop on the No. 3 tram. Arriving from the Spanish Steps, take Bus No. 160; from Termini, Bus No. 175. For the Testaccio section, use the Piramide (Ostiense) Metro stop. Coming down the Aventine Hill, Fodor's Talk Forum poster tomassocroccante notes: "Not far from the famous Priorato di Malta keyhole, walk down the street to the lovely Parco Savelli (great views), near Santa Sabina. At the park's far end is a stone gate leading to a path that descends to the Lungotavere Aventino, not far from famed Piazza Bocca Della Verità."

BEST TIME-OUTS

A short walk away from the Piramide monument toward the Tiber River, **Divinare di Cavaterra Angelo Enoteca** (✉ *Via Aldo Manuzio 12* ☎ *06/57250432*) is a quiet, sophisticated spot that offers a small sampling of excellent cheeses and salamis to go with its impressive range of wine.

Near the Circo Massimo, tiny **Arte del Gusto** (✉ *Via San Teodoro 88* ☎ *06/6798469*) is easy to miss. Don't. The bakery's pastries, sandwiches, and pizzas are superb.

10

Sightseeing
★★
Nightlife
★★★
Dining
★★
Lodging
★★★
Shopping
★

Rising like a massive headland above the Tiber, the Aventino hill is the one area in Rome where trills of birdsong win out over the din of traffic. That's highly appropriate, as the hill's name derives from the Latin "avis," the swallows here having once featured in the bird-watching contest whereby Romulus and Remus decided the best site on which to build their city. As it happened, the Aventine lost out to the Palatine. Still, to Romans, the Aventino is known as the most "poetic" of the city's seven hills, D'Annunzio and other poets long having sung its praises. Scented here with roses (from the Roseto Comunale), there with orange blossom (from the Giardino dei Aranci), and everywhere with pines, it seems the opposite of urban: Rome's most idyllic oasis of calm.

This is a rarefied district, where some houses still have their own bell towers and private gardens are called "parks," without exaggeration. Like the emperors of old on the Palatine, the fortunate residents here look out over the Circus Maximus and the river, winding its way far below. And today's travelers still enjoy the great views, including the famous one spotted through the peculiar keyhole at the gates to the headquarters of the Knights of Malta, which may be the most peered-through in the world—take a look and see why. It's a lovely district for a walk, all shady streets and quiet gardens, with public gardens affording panoramic vistas over the city and river.

At the foot of the Aventine Hill to the north, the 1st-century temples to Vesta and Hercules are two of the most complete ancient monuments in the city. They remind us that, under the Republic, this area was home to the "plebs," becoming under the Gracchi a populist stronghold. By Imperial times, however, its tradesman and merchants were displaced by patricians seeking fresh air and space, with grandstand views over the Vallis Murcia, the arena-shaped dip dividing this hill from the Palatine. Sumptuous villas and gardens sprang up, giving Alaric, when the Goths visited the city in 410 AD, a ready supply of plunder. The Aventino never quite recovered from such depredations.

South of the Aventine, there's an entirely different flavor. Blue-collar Testaccio is flat and homely but as lively as it gets; ancient Rome's dockyard has, in the modern age, an up-and-coming arts scene with music and dancing clubs that go all night. You'll know you've reached Testaccio when you see its most incongruous landmark, the Pyramide, a large marble pyramid built as a nod to the pharaohs in 12 BC as a tomb for a rich merchant. Behind the monument lie the remains of some of the English poets who put the Rome in Romantic in the 19th century, in the aptly named, and appropriately scenic, Cimitero degli Inglesi (English Cemetery).

AVENTINO

One of the seven hills on which the city was founded, the Aventine Hill enjoys a serenity hard to find elsewhere in Rome. Approach from the Circus Maximus; at the hill's foot, you'll find Piazza Bocca della Verità—the ancient Foro Boario (cattle market)—which is set with two ancient temples and one Romanesque church: three of Rome's most camera-ready landmarks.

TOP ATTRACTIONS

Piazza dei Cavalieri di Malta. Peek through the keyhole of the **Priorato di Malta,** the walled compound of the Knights of Malta, and you'll get a surprising eyeful: a picture-perfect view of the dome of St. Peter's Basilica, far across the city. This priory landmarks the Piazza dei Cavalieri di Malta. Piranesi—18th-century Rome's foremost engraver—is more famous for drawing architecture than creating it, yet the square is his work along with the Priory (1765) within. Stone insignia of the Knights notwithstanding, the square's most famed feature is that initially nondescript keyhole in the dark green door of Number 3. Bend slightly and surprise your eyes with a view that is worth walking miles for. As for the Order of the Knights of Malta, it is the world's oldest and most exclusive order of chivalry, founded in the Holy Land during the Crusades. Though nominally ministering to the sick in those early days, a role that has since become the order's raison d'être, the knights amassed huge tracts of land in the Middle East. From 1530 they were based on the Mediterranean island of Malta but in 1798 Napoléon expelled them and, in 1834, they established themselves in Rome, with headquarters on Via Condotti. The gardens can be viewed only by appointment (for which you need to consult the Knights' headquarters in Via Condotti). ⊠ *Via Santa Sabina and Via Porta Lavernale, Aventino* ☎ *06/67581234 to book group tours* ⊙ *Group tours at 10 and 11* Ⓜ *Circo Massimo. Buses 3, 60, 81, 118, 175, 271, 715.*

Roseto Comunale. As signified by the paths shaped like a Menorah, this was once a Jewish cemetery (a tombstone is still visible on the side of the garden across from Valle Murcia, the name for the swamp that once separated this area from the Palatine.) The garden is laid out to reflect the history of roses from antiquity to the present day. ⊠ *Viale di Valle Murcia, Aventino* ۞ *Daily 9–7:30* Ⓜ *Circo Massimo. Buses 3, 60, 81, 118, 160, 271, 628, 715.*

۞
Fodor's Choice
★

Santa Maria in Cosmedin. Though this is one of Rome's oldest churches, with a haunting, almost exotic interior, it plays second fiddle to the renowned artifact installed in the church portico. The **Bocca della Verità** (Mouth of Truth) is in reality nothing more than an ancient drain cover, unearthed during the Middle Ages. Legend has it, however, that the teeth will clamp down on a liar's hand, and to tell a lie with your hand in the fearsome mouth is to risk losing it. Hordes of tourists line up to take the test every day, with kids especially getting a bang out of it. Few churches, inside or out, are as picturesque as this one. The church was built in the 6th century for the city's burgeoning Greek population. Heavily restored at the end of the 19th century, it has the typical basilica form, and stands across from the **Piazza della Bocca della Verità,** originally the location of the Forum Boarium, ancient Rome's cattle market, and later the site of public executions. ⊠ *Piazza Santa Maria in Cosmedin, Aventino* ☎ *06/6781419* ۞ *Summer, daily 9:30–5:50; winter, 9:30–4:30* Ⓜ *Circo Massimo. Buses 3, 60, 75, 81, 118, 160, 175, 271, 628.*

Santa Sabina. This Early Christian basilica demonstrates the severe simplicity common to churches of its era. Although some of the side chapels were added in the 16th and 17th centuries, the essential form is as Rome's Christians knew it in the 5th century. Once the church was bright with mosaics but the only one that remains is above the entrance door (its gold letters announcing how the church was founded by one Peter of Illyria, "rich for the poor," under Pope Celestine I). Meanwhile the mosaics in the apse have been at least partially reproduced in Taddeo Zuccari's Renaissance fresco of Christ and his Apostles. The beautifully carved and 5th century cedar-wooden doors to the left of the outside entrance are the oldest of their kind in existence. ⊠ *Piazza Pietro d'Illiria 1, Via di Santa Sabina, Aventino* ☎ *06/5743573* ۞ *Daily 6:30–12:45 and 3–6, until 7 May–Sept.* Ⓜ *Circo Massimo. Buses 3, 60, 75, 81, 118, 160, 175, 715.*

Tempio della Fortuna Virilis. A picture-perfect, if dollhouse-size, Roman temple, this rectangular edifice from the 2nd century BC is built in the Greek style, as was the norm in Rome's early years. It owes its fine state of preservation, considering its venerable age, to the fact that it was consecrated and used as a Christian church. ⊠ *Piazza Bocca della Verità, Aventino* Ⓜ *Circo Massimo. Buses 3, 60, 75, 81, 118, 160, 175, 271.*

Tempio di Vesta. Long called the Temple of Vesta because of its similarity in shape to the building of that name in the Roman Forum, it's now recognized as a temple to Hercules Victor. All but one of the 20 Corinthian columns of this evocative ruin remain intact. Like its next-door neighbor, the Tempio della Fortuna Virilis, it was built in the 2nd century BC. ⊠ *Piazza Bocca della Verità, Aventino* Ⓜ *Circo Massimo. Buses 3, 60, 75, 81, 118, 160, 175, 271.*

WORTH NOTING

San Saba. Formerly a monastery founded by monks of the order of San Saba after they had fled from Jerusalem following the Arab invasion, this is a major monument of Romanesque Rome. Inside, an almost rustic interior harbors a famed Cosmatesque mosaic pavement, and a hodgepodge of ancient marble pieces. ⊠ *Piazza Gianlorenzo Bernini 20, Via San Saba, Aventino* ☎ *06/5743352* ◷ *Daily 8–noon and 4–7* Ⓜ *Circo Massimo.*

TESTACCIO

Testaccio is perhaps the world's only district built on broken pots: the hill of the same name was born from discarded pottery used to store oil, wine, and other goods loaded from the nearby Ripa, when Rome had a port and the Tiber was once a mighty river to an empire. Today, the area is now home to one of Rome's best outdoor food markets, and its construction led to the discovery of a new archaeological area below, with ancient storerooms yielding pots galore. Quiet during the day but on Saturday buzzing with the very loud music from rows of discos and clubs— this is sometimes hailed as Rome's new "Left Bank" neighborhood—

> **WORD OF MOUTH**
>
> "In the once proletariat Testaccio neighborhood, we first visited Volpetti (Via Marmorata 47), perhaps Rome's best food store, famed for its hard-to-find, Slow Food–resurrected Roman foodstuffs. Laden with purchases, we turned round the corner to the Piazza del Testaccio market, with fishmongers on the left, butchers at the back, cheesemongers at the front. And at the center is the produce market—the most dynamic and beautiful one we visited in two weeks in Italy."   —wrldpeas

the area is also a must for those seeking authentic and comparatively cheap Roman cuisine. Sights hereabouts are few but choice and include the Protestant cemetery where Keats lies buried.

TOP ATTRACTIONS

★ **Cimitero degli Inglesi** *(Non-Catholic or English Cemetery).* Reminiscent of a country churchyard, this famed cemetery was intended for the interment of non-Catholics. This is where you'll find the tomb of John Keats, who tragically died in Rome after succumbing to consumption at age 25 in 1821. The stone is famously inscribed with "Here lies one whose name was writ in water" (the poet said no dates or name should appear). Nearby is the place where Shelley's heart was buried, as well the tombs of Goethe's son, Italian anarchist Antonio Gramsci, and America's famed beat poet Gregory Corso. It is about a 20-minute walk south from the Arch of Constantine along Via San Gregorio and Viale Aventino but the easiest way to get here is to catch the Metro B line from Termini which deposits you almost directly outside the cemetery. ⊠ *Via Caio Cestio 6, Testaccio* ☎ *06/5741900* ⊕ *www.protestantcemetery. it* ◷ *Mon.–Sat. 9–5, Sun. 9–1; ring bell for cemetery custodian* Ⓜ *Piramide. Buses 3, 23, 30, 60, 75, 95, 118, 715.*

10

CLOSE UP

Testaccio: Rome's New

After taking in the historic peace and quiet of the Aventine Hill, switch lanes and head for the hip-hopping 'hood of Testaccio, especially on Saturday night, when a panoply of clubs and discos rend the air (but is one person's music another's noise pollution?). From the Piazza dei Cavalieri di Malta, take Via di Porta and the Lavernale to Via Marmorata. Testaccio has plain early-1900s housing, a down-to-earth working-class atmosphere, and plenty of good trattorias. And, of course, Monte Testaccio, a grassy knoll about 150 feet high. What makes this otherwise unremarkable-looking hill special is the fact that it's made from pottery shards—pieces of amphorae, large jars used in ancient times to transport oil, wheat, wine, and other goods. Make your way to Piazza Testaccio, dominated by the covered market where you can sample everything from wild strawberries to horsemeat sausage. Move on to the prettier Piazza di Santa Maria Liberatrice. There are some quintessential Roman trattorias along Via Marmorata and near the Mattatoio, the former slaughterhouse. The area sights—Porta San Paolo, one of the ancient city gates in the 3rd-century AD Aurelian walls, the big white Piramide di Caio Cestio, and the Cimiterio degli Inglesi—are found several blocks to the south around Piazziale Ostiense.

🐾 **Piramide di Caio Cestio.** This monumental tomb was designed in 12 BC for the immensely wealthy praetor Gaius Cestius in the form of a 120-foot-tall pyramid. Though little else is known about him, he clearly had a taste for grandeur. The structure was completed in just over a month, an extraordinary feat even for the ancient Romans. On the site of the pyramid is a cat colony run by the famous Roman *gattare* (cat ladies). They look after and try to find homes for some 300 of Rome's thousands of strays. For further details and possible tours consult ⊕ *www.igattidellapiramide.it* or *www.gattidiroma.com*. ⊠ *Piazzale Ostiense, Testaccio* Ⓜ *Pyramide. Buses 3, 30, 60, 75, 95, 118, 130, 175, 719.*

San Paolo fuori le Mura *(St. Paul's Outside the Walls).* For all the dreary location and its dull exterior (19th-century British writer Augustus Hare said the church resembled "a very ugly railway station"), St. Paul's is one of Rome's most historic and important churches. Its size (second only to St. Peter's Basilica) also allows ample space for the 272 roundels depicting every pope from St. Peter to Benedict XVI (found below the ceiling, with 27 more spaces left blank for pontiffs to come). Built in the 4th century AD by Constantine over the site where St. Paul had been buried, St. Paul's was then rebuilt and enlarged. But in July 1823 a fire burned the church to the ground. Although the rebuilt St. Paul's has a sort of monumental grandeur, it's only in the cloisters that you get a real sense of what must have been the magnificence of the original building (for guided tours for a fee of €3, call ☎ *06/69880800*). In the middle of the nave is the famous baldachino created by sculptor Arnolfo di Cambio. ⊠ *Piazzale San Paolo, Via Ostiense 190, Testaccio* ☎ *06/5410341* ⊕ *www.basilicasanpaolo.org* ⊗ *Daily 7–6:30; cloister 9–1 and 3–6* Ⓜ *Piramide.*

Esquilino and Celio

CELIAN HILL, BATHS OF CARACALLA, ESQUILINE HILL, THE CATACOMBS

WORD OF MOUTH

"In the Esquilino area, you get a sense of the real Rome, rather than just following the tourist hoards of the Pantheon/Navona area. The frescoes on the Santa Maria Maggiore front are lit up at night: stunning, to sit across the street in a café and stare, in that quiet neighborhood. Nothing like it."

—girlspytravel

GETTING ORIENTED

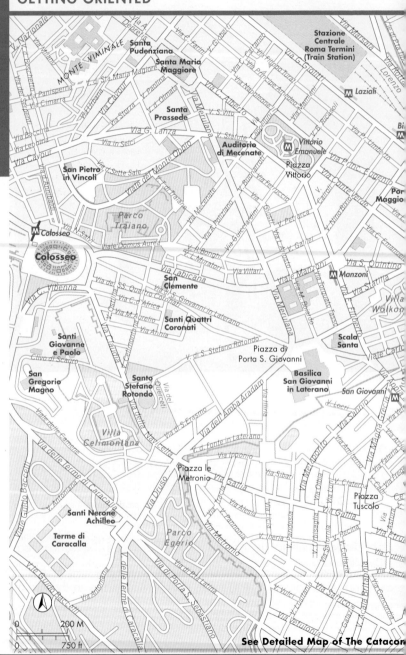

Stazione Centrale Roma Termini (Train Station)

V. Nazionale

MONTE VIMINALE

Santa Pudenziana

Santa Maria Maggiore

Laziali

Via Cavour

Santa Prassede

Via G. Lanza

Auditorio di Mecenate

Vittorio Emanuele

Piazza Vittorio

San Pietro in Vincoli

Parco Traiano

Por Maggio

Colosseo

Colosseo

Via Labicana

San Clemente

Viale Domus Aurea

Manzoni

Villa Walkon

V. C. Vibenna

Santi Quattri Coronati

Scala Santa

Santi Giovanne e Paolo

Santo Stefano Rotondo

Piazza di Porta S. Giovanni

San Gregorio Magno

Basilica San Giovanni in Laterano

San Giovanni

Villa Celimontana

Piazza le Metronio

Piazza Tuscolo

Santi Nerone Achilleo

Terme di Caracalla

Parco Egerio

0   200 M

0   750 ft

See Detailed Map of The Catacon

TOP 5 REASONS TO GO

San Pietro in Vincoli: Hike uphill past Lucrezia Borgia's palace to visit Michelangelo's magisterial *Moses*.

San Clemente: Hurtle back through three eras—ancient Roman, Early Christian, and medieval—by descending through four excavated levels of this venerated church.

Baths of Caracalla: South of the lovely Villa Celimontana parks towers the Terme di Caracalla, ruins of what once was a spectacular bathing complex of ancient Rome.

Magnificent Mosaics: In a neighborhood once home to the first Christians, Santa Pudenziana gleams with a stunning 4th-century mosaic of Christ while Santa Prassede shimmers with Byzantine beauty nearby.

Catacomb Country: Be careful exploring the underground graves of the earliest Christians—one wrong turn and you may only surface days later.

BEST TIME-OUT

Enoteca Il Pentagrappola (✉ *Via Celimontana 21/B* ☎ *06/7096301*), with its exposed-brick arches and soft candlelight, offers an ample spread of cheeses and salamis with sampling from its more than 250 wines. Run by a sommelier-musician, the enoteca (a wineshop and bar) has a piano providing an atmospheric soundtrack in the after-dinner hours.

GETTING HERE

To reach the Celio, take Bus No. 117 from the Corso, the No. 3 tram from Trastevere, or the No. 75 bus from Termini. From the Colosseo subway stop it is about a 10-minute walk.

The Esquilino neighborhood, including Piazza Vittorio Emanuele, can be handily reached with the Piazza Vittorio Emanuele subway stop, about a 10-minute walk from Termini.

O.K., WHERE DO I START?

If you're tackling the Celian Hill area first, head out from the Arch of Constantine—right by the Colosseum—and walk south along the left side of Via di San Gregorio to the Clivo di Scauro. Ascend this magically picturesque lane to Santi Giovanni e Paolo. Follow the wall lining peaceful Villa Celimontana park and turn right on Via Celimontana to Santo Stefano Rotondo (beware its hyper-gory frescoes).

Backtrack to Piazza Celimontana and head uphill Via Capo di Africa to the hauntingly medieval church of Santi Quattro Coronati. On the other side of the hill, in Via San Giovanni in Laterano, waits that time machine of a church, San Clemente.

Head back to the Colosseum area and ascend the Esquiline Hill using the Colosseo metro steps to reach the grandly scenic Largo Agnesi overlook.

Up on the Esquilino hill, to the north side of the Colosseum, you'll find San Pietro in Vincoli, home to Michelangelo's *Moses*. Walk down Salita dei Borgia, passing under the haunted Torre Borgia palace, to Via Cavour.

Turn right and head northeast to gigantic Santa Maria Maggiore; nearby are wonderful mosaics in San Prassede and Santa Pudenziana. ⇨ *For Catacomb Country, see that section below.*

Sightseeing
★★★★
Nightlife
★★
Dining
★★★
Lodging
★★★★
Shopping
★★

Located east of the Termini railway station, Rome's most sprawling hill—the Esquiline—lies at the edge of the tourist maps, another Rome. Even Imperial Rome could not have matched this mini-cosmopolis for sheer internationalism. Here sons of the soil, the so-called "romani romani," mingle with Chinese, Sri Lankans, Sikhs, and a hundred nationalities in-between, and all give Esquilino and the neighboring Celian Hill—together referred to as Monti ("Mounts") by Romans—a kind of bare-knuckled charm. Venture on to the main streets here, especially on the Esquiline, and you'll find them all lotto shops and buzzing Vespas, with nary a wine bar in view. But, as in the rest of central Rome, ancient ruins, historic churches, and Renaissance masterworks are never far—in this sector, however, you won't have to wait in line to see them.

This area takes in some of the city's best sights, including Michelangelo's *Moses*, the Baths of Caracalla, and dazzling Early Christian mosaics at San Clemente and San Pudenziana. Historically speaking, it also took in some of the worst, including the Suburra, Rome's most notorious slum. A dark, warrenlike sector of multistory dwellings populated in part by gladiators from the nearby Colosseum, it lived by its own rules, or lack of them. The empress Messalina would often venture here for illicit pleasures. So mean were the Suburra's streets that it's thought that the great fire of AD 64, which all but destroyed the neighborhood, may have been ordered by Nero as a public-order measure. But elsewhere on the Esquilino and Celio hills Augustus built impressive public markets and the area became the "in" place to be. Palaces of Ancient Rome's Who's Who sprang up with sumptuous gardens to match.

Signs of this remote past are everywhere. The Colosseum's marble-clad walls loom at the end of narrow, shadowy streets with Latin-sounding names: Panisperna, Baccina, Fagutale. Other walls, built for the Caesars, shore up medieval towers. Amid the hints of antiquity, several great churches of the Christian era stand out like islands, connected by broad avenues. The newer streets—laid out by the popes and, later, by city planners at the time of Italy's unification—slice through the meandering byways, providing more direct and navigable routes for pilgrims heading to majestic Santa Maria Maggiore, its interior gleaming with gold from the New World, and San Giovanni in Laterano, with its grand, echoing vastness.

Via Cavour, the main drag of a web of streets, extends through the old Suburra to the rough and ready quarter around Termini, Rome's central train station. Predictably gritty, although not unsafe, this area is undergoing a steady transformation as immigration diversifies the face of the city. North of the station, Ethiopian and Eritrean restaurants abound, while just south of the station, Piazza Vittorio and its surrounding streets are an ethnic kaleidoscope, full of Asian and Middle Eastern shops and restaurants. A highlight is the Nuovo Mercato Esquilino, a covered market hall where goods from the four corners of the earth are sold in a multitude of languages. A walk south on Via Merulana leads to San Giovanni, a working-class neighborhood, of late colonized by trendy students, which surrounds Rome's cathedral, San Giovanni in Laterano.

Farther south lies a lovely contrast to the bustle of the Esquiline and San Giovanni quarters: quiet and green Monte Celio. Like the Aventino, the Celio (or Celian Hill) seems aloof from the bustle of central Rome. On the slopes of the hill, paths and narrow streets wind through a public park and past walled gardens and some of Rome's earliest churches, such as San Clemente and Santi Quattro Coronati, whose medieval poetry is almost palpable.

South of the Celio lies Catacomb Country—the haunts of the fabled underground graves of Rome's earliest Christians, arrayed to either side of the Queen of Roads, the Appian Way. The gateway to this timeless realm is one of the largest relics of ancient Rome, the Baths of Caracalla. Farther on, the church of Domine Quo Vadis announces you are entering sacred turf, as this is the spot where Jesus is said to have appeared to Peter and posed his eternal question. As you venture to the Catacombs, the countryside is dotted with landmarks like the Tomb of Cecilia Metella that make you feel that the days of the Caesars were not that long ago. Look down from your bus window and you will see chariot ruts.

MONTI AND ESQUILINO

The valley between the Esquiline Hill and the Celian Hill underscores the area's nickname—Monti ("Mounts"). The Esquiline stretches down a hurly-burly slide of the city, from the frantic Termini train station to San Giovanni, a neighborhood long known for its working-class vibe. But if you manage to successfully dodge all the scooters and trucks, you'll find a staggering array of historic churches here, from great pilgrimage basilicas to chapels aglitter with Early Christian mosaics.

TOP ATTRACTIONS

Porta Maggiore *(Main Gate)*. The massive 1st-century AD monument is not only a *porta* (city gate) but also part of the Acqua Claudia aqueduct. It gives you an idea of the grand scale of ancient Roman public works. On the Piazzale Labicano side of the portal, to the east, is the curious **Baker's Tomb**, erected in the 1st century BC by a prosperous baker, with stone ovens signaling the deceased's trade. The site is especially accessible given that Rome's first tram depot (going back to 1889) is just nearby. ⊠ *Junction of Via Eleniana, Via di Porta Maggiore, and Via Casilina, Monti and Esquilino* Ⓜ *Trams 3, 19.*

Fodor's Choice   **San Clemente.** One of the most impressive archaeological sites in Rome, ★   San Clemente is an archaeological triple-decker of a church. A 12th-century church was built on top of a 4th-century church, which in turn was built over a 2nd-century pagan temple to the god Mithras. Little of the temple remains, but the 4th-century church is largely intact, perhaps because it wasn't unearthed until the 19th century. (It was discovered by Irish Dominican monks; members of the order still live in the adjacent monastery.)

The upper church, which you enter from street level, holds a beautiful early-12th-century mosaic showing a cross on a gold background, surrounded by swirling green acanthus leaves, teeming with little scenes of everyday life. The marble choir screens, salvaged from the 4th-century church, are decorated with Early Christian symbols: doves, vines, and fish. In the left nave is the Castiglioni chapel, holding frescoes painted around 1400 by the Florentine artist Masolino da Panicale (1383–1440), a key figure in the introduction of realism and one-point perspective into Renaissance painting. Note the large Crucifixion and scenes from the lives of Sts. Catherine, Ambrose, and Christopher, plus an Annunciation (over the entrance). Before you leave the upper church, take a look at the pretty cloister—evening concerts are held here in summer.

To the right of the sacristy (and bookshop) descend the stairs to the 4th-century church, active until 1084, when it was damaged beyond repair during a siege of the area by the Norman prince Robert Guiscard. Still intact, though, are some colorful 11th-century frescoes depicting stories from the life of St. Clement.

Descend an additional set of stairs to the famed Mithraeum, a shrine dedicated to the god Mithras, whose cult spread from Persia and gained a hold in Rome during the 2nd and 3rd centuries AD. Mithras was believed to have been born in a cave and was thus worshipped in underground, cavernous chambers, where initiates into the all-male cult would share a meal while reclining on stone couches, some visible here along with the altar block. Most such pagan shrines in Rome were destroyed by Christians, who often built churches over their remains, as happened here. ⊠ *Via San Giovanni in Laterano 108, Monti and Esquilino* ☎ *06/70451018* ✉ *Archaeological area €5* ⊘ *Mon.–Sat. 9–12:30, 3–6; Sun., noon–6* Ⓜ *Colosseo.*

> **TO MARKET, TO MARKET**
>
> For a piece of the new buzzing Esquiline Hill action, try one of Rome's most distinctive luncheon options: the Piazza Vittorio Emanuele, a historic Roman square and its famed food market nearby on Via Principe Amadeo. The surrounding streets are chockablock with international food stores and offer a glimpse at the emerging immigrant scene in the city.

San Giovanni in Laterano. This is Rome's cathedral; it's here that the pope officiates in his capacity as bishop of Rome. The towering facade dates from 1736 and was modeled on that of St. Peter's Basilica. The 15 colossal statues (Christ, John the Baptist, John the Evangelist, and the 12 Apostles of the church) look out on the sea of dreary suburbs that have spread from Porta San Giovanni to the lower slopes of the Alban Hills. San Giovanni was founded in the 4th century on land donated by the emperor Constantine, who had obtained it from the wealthy patrician family of the Laterani. Vandals, earthquakes, and fire damaged the original and successive constructions. Finally, in 1646, Pope Innocent X commissioned Borromini to rebuild the church, and its Borromini's rather cool, tense nave that you see today.

Under the portico on the left stands an ancient statue of Constantine. Another link with Rome's past is the central portal's ancient bronze doors, brought here from the Curia building in the Forum. Inside, little is left of the early decorations. The fragment of a fresco on the first pillar in the double aisle on the right depicts Pope Boniface VIII proclaiming the first Holy Year in 1300; it's attributed to the 14th-century Florentine painter Giotto. The altar's rich Gothic tabernacle dates from 1367 and, somewhat gruesomely, contains what are believed to be the heads of Sts. Peter and Paul. You shouldn't miss the church **cloister,** with its twin columns encrusted with 13th-century Cosmatesque mosaics by the Vassallettos, a father-and-son team. Enter the cloister from the last chapel at the end of the left aisle. ⊠ *Piazza di Porta San GiovanniMonti and Esquilino* ☎ *06/69886433* ✉ *Church free, cloister €2.50, museum €4* ⊘ *Church Apr.–Sept., daily 7–6:30; Oct.–Mar., daily 7–6. Vassalletto Cloister daily 9–6. Museum Sat. guided tours at 9:15, 10:30, and noon; 1st Sun. of each month 8:45–1. Baptistery daily 9–1* PM *and 5* PM*–1 hr before sunset* Ⓜ *San Giovanni.*

★ **San Pietro in Vincoli.** What has put this church on the map is the monumental statue of Moses carved by Michelangelo in the early 16th century for the never-completed tomb of his patron, Pope Julius II, which was to include dozens of statues and stand nearly 40 feet tall when installed in St. Peter's Basilica. Only three statues—*Moses* and the two that flank it here, *Leah* and *Rachel*—had been completed when Julius died. His successor as pope, from a rival family, had other plans for Michelangelo, and Julius's tomb was abandoned unfinished. The fierce power of this remarkable sculpture dominates its setting. People say that you can see the sculptor's profile in the lock of Moses's beard right under his lip, and that the pope's profile is also there somewhere. But don't let the search distract you from the overall effect of this marvelously energetic work. As for the rest of the church, St. Peter takes second billing to Moses. What are reputed to be the chains *(vincoli)* that bound St. Peter during his imprisonment by the Romans in Jerusalem are in a bronze and crystal urn under the main altar. Other treasures in the church include a 7th-century mosaic of St. Sebastian, in front of the second altar to the left of the main altar, and, by the door, the tomb of the Pollaiuolo brothers, two lesser 15th-century Florentine artists. ✉ *Piazza San Pietro in Vincoli, Monti and Esquilino* ☎ *06/4882865* ☉ *Daily 8–12:30 and 3–6* Ⓜ *Cavour.*

> ### A CALENDAR MIX-UP
>
> Every August 5, a special mass in Santa Maria Maggiore's Cappella Sistina commemorates the miracle that led to the founding of the basilica: the Virgin Mary appeared in a dream to Pope Liberio and ordered him to build a church in her honor on the spot where snow would fall on the night of August 5 (an event about as likely in a Roman August as snow in the Sahara). The Madonna of the Snows is celebrated with a shower of white rose petals from the ceiling.

Santa Maria Maggiore. The exterior of the church, from the broad sweep of steps on Via Cavour to the more elaborate facade on Piazza Santa Maria Maggiore, is that of a gracefully curving 18th-century building, a fine example of the baroque architecture of the period. But in fact Santa Maria Maggiore is one of the oldest churches in Rome, built around 440 by Pope Sixtus III. One of the four great pilgrimage churches of Rome, it's by far the most complete example of an Early Christian basilica in the city—one of the immense, hall-like structures derived from ancient Roman civic buildings and divided into thirds by two great rows of columns marching up the nave. The other six major basilicas in Rome—San Giovanni in Laterano and St. Peter's Basilica are the most famous—have been entirely transformed, or even rebuilt. Paradoxically, the major reason why this church is such a striking example of Early Christian design is that the same man who built the incongruous exteriors about 1740—Ferdinando Fuga—also conscientiously restored the interior, throwing out later additions and, crucially, replacing a number of the great columns.

Precious 5th-century mosaics high on the nave walls and on the triumphal arch in front of the main altar are splendid testimony to the basilica's venerable age. Those along the nave show 36 scenes from the Old Testament (unfortunately, they are hard to see clearly without binoculars), and those on the arch illustrate the Annunciation and the Youth of Christ. The resplendent carved wood ceiling dates from the early 16th century; it's supposed to have been gilded with the first gold brought from the New World. The inlaid marble pavement (called Cosmatesque

11

after the family of master artisans who developed the technique) in the central nave is even older, dating from the 12th century.

The **Cappella Sistina** (Sistine Chapel), which opens onto the right-hand nave, was created by architect Domenico Fontana for Pope Sixtus V in 1585. Elaborately and heavily decorated with precious marbles "liberated" from the monuments of ancient Rome, the chapel includes a lower level museum in which some 13th-century sculptures by Arnolfo da Cambio are all that's left of what was once the incredibly richly endowed chapel of the *presepio* (Christmas crèche), looted during the Sack of Rome in 1527.

Directly opposite, on the other side of the church, stands the **Cappella Paolina** (Pauline Chapel), a rich baroque setting for the tombs of the Borghese popes Paul V—who commissioned the chapel in 1611 with the declared intention of outdoing Sixtus's chapel across the nave—and Clement VIII. The **Cappella Sforza** (Sforza Chapel) next door was designed by Michelangelo and completed by della Porta. Just right of the altar, next to his father, lies Gian Lorenzo Bernini; his monument is an engraved slab, as humble as the tombs of his patrons are grand. Above the loggia, the outside mosaic of Christ raising his hand in blessing, when it is lit up at night, is one of the most beautiful sights of Rome. ✉ *Piazza Santa Maria Maggiore, Monti and Esquilino* ☎ 0669886802 ✆ *Daily 7 AM–7 PM; museum 9–6* 🎟️€4 Ⓜ *Termini.*

Santa Prassede. This small and inconspicuous 9th-century church is known above all for the exquisite little **Cappella di San Zenone,** just to the left of the entrance. It gleams with vivid mosaics that reflect their Byzantine inspiration. Though much less classical and naturalistic than the earlier mosaics of Santa Pudenziana, they are no less splendid, and the composition of four angels hovering on the sky-blue vault is one of the masterstrokes of Byzantine art. Note the square halo over the head of Theodora, mother of St. Pasquale I, the pope who built this church. It indicates that she was still alive when she was depicted by the artist. The chapel also contains one curious relic: a miniature pillar, supposedly part of the column at which Christ was flogged during the Passion. It was brought to Rome in the 13th century. Over the main altar, the magnificent mosaics on the arch and apse are also in rigid Byzantine style; in them Pope Pasquale I wears the square halo of the living and holds a model of his church. ✉ *Via di Santa Prassede 9/a, Monti and Esquilino* ☎ 06/4882456 ✆ *Daily 7:15–12:15 and 4–6:45* Ⓜ *Cavour.*

Fodor's Choice ★ **Santa Pudenziana.** Outside of Ravenna, Rome has some of the most opulent mosaics in Italy and this church has one of the most striking examples. Commissioned during the papacy of Innocent I, its late 4th-century apse mosaic represents "Christ Teaching the Apostles" and sits high on the wall perched above a baroque altarpiece surrounded by a bevy of florid 18th-century paintings. Not only is it the largest Early Christian apse mosaic extant, it is remarkable for its iconography. At the center sits Christ Enthroned, looking a bit like a Roman emperor, presiding over his apostles. Each apostle faces the spectator, literally rubs shoulders with his companion (unlike earlier hieratic styles where each figure is isolated), and bears an individualized expression. Above the figures and a landscape that symbolizes the Heavenly Jerusalem floats the signs of the four evangelists in a blue sky flecked with an orange sunset, all done in thousands of tesserae. This extraordinary composition seems a sort of paleo-Christian forerunner of Raphael's *School of Athens* in the Vatican.

To either side of Christ, Sts. Praxedes and Pudentia hold wreaths over the heads of Sts. Peter and Paul. These two women were actually daughters of the Roman senator Pudens (probably the one mentioned in 2 Tim 4:21), whose family befriended both apostles. During the persecutions of Nero, both sisters collected the blood of many martyrs and then suffered the same fate. Pudentia transformed her house into a church, but this namesake church was constructed over a 2nd-century bathhouse. Beyond the sheer beauty of the mosaic work, the size, rich detail, and number of figures make this both the last gasp of ancient Roman art and one of the first monuments of early Christianity. ⊠ *Via Urbana 160, Monti and Esquilino* ☎ *06/4814622* ☉ *Mon.–Sat. 8:30–noon, 3–6* Ⓜ *Termini.*

Scala Santa. A 16th-century building encloses the Holy Steps, which tradition holds to be the staircase from Pilate's palace in Jerusalem, brought to Rome by St. Helena, mother of the emperor Constantine. Wood protects the 28 marble steps worn smooth by the knees of pilgrims through the centuries. There are two other staircases that you can ascend to see the **Sancta Sanctorum,** the private chapel of the popes. The chapel is richly decorated with well-preserved Cosmatesque mosaics and a famous painting of Jesus, claimed to have been painted by angels. ⊠ *Piazza San Giovanni in Laterano, Monti and Esquilino* ☎ *06/69886433* ☉ *Winter, daily 6:15–noon and 3–6:15; summer, 6:15–noon and 3:30–6:45* Ⓜ *San Giovanni.*

CELIO

As quiet and bucolic as the Esquilino is bustling, the Celian Hill lies across the valley to the south. Celio is like a dip into the Middle Ages. Just off massive Via di S. Gregorio, the most magical gateway to the quarter is the Clivo di Scauro, practically unchanged since medieval times. Picturesquely passing under the Romanesque arches of Santi Giovanni e Paolo, the Clivo was described by author Georgina Masson—in her classic *Companion Guide to Rome*—as one of the few spots in Rome that a medieval pilgrim would easily recognize. And if you continue up the lane to the Villa Celimontana park, you'll find more churches and saintly peace gracing the Celian Hill.

TOP ATTRACTIONS

★ **Case Romane del Celio.** Formerly accessible only through the church of San Giovanni e Paolo, this important ancient Roman excavation was opened in 2002 as a full-fledged museum. An underground honeycomb of rooms, this comprises the lower levels of a so-called "insula," or apartment tower, the heights of which were a wonder to ancient Roman contemporaries. Through the door on the left of the Clivo di Scauro lane a portico leads to the Room of the Genie, where painted figures gracing walls as if untouched by two millennia. Farther on is the Confessio altar of Sts. John and Paul, officials at Constantine's court who were executed under Julian the Apostate. Still lower is the Antiquarium, where state-of-the-art lighting showcase amphorae, pots, and stamped ancient Roman bricks, the stamps so fresh they may've been imprinted yesterday. ⊠ *Clivus Scauri, Celio* ☎ *06/70454544* ⊕ *www.caseromane. it* ⊠ *€6* ☉ *Thurs.–Mon., 10–1 and 3–6* Ⓜ *Colosseo. Buses 60, 75, 81, 117, 118, 175, Tram 3.*

☾ **Terme di Caracalla** *(Baths of Caracalla).* Although not the largest in
★ ancient Rome, these public baths seem to have been by far the most opulent. Begun in AD 206 by the emperor Septimius Severus and completed by his son, Caracalla, they could accommodate 1,600 bathers at a time.

For the Romans, the baths were much more than places to wash. Although providing bathing facilities was their main purpose, there were also recital halls, art galleries, and libraries to improve the mind, and massage and exercise rooms as well as sports grounds to improve the body, in addition to halls and gardens just for talking and strolling. Even the smallest public baths had at least some of these amenities, and in the capital of the Roman Empire, they were provided on a lavish scale. Their functioning depended on the slaves who cared for the clients, checking their robes, rubbing them down, and seeing to their needs. Under the magnificent marble pavement of the stately halls, other slaves toiled in a warren of tiny rooms and passages, stoking the fires that heated the water.

Taking a bath was a long and complex process, which is eminently understandable if you see it as a social activity first and foremost. Remember, too, that for all their sophistication, the Romans didn't have soap. You began in the *sudatoria,* a series of small rooms resembling saunas. Here you sat and sweated. From these you moved to the *calidarium,* a large circular room that was humid rather than simply hot. This was where the actual business of washing went on. You used a *strigil,* or scraper, to get the dirt off; if you were rich, your slave did this for you. Next you moved to the *tepidarium,* a warmish room, the purpose of which was to allow you to begin gradually to cool down. Finally, you splashed around in the *frigidarium,* the only actual "bath" in the place, in essence a shallow swimming pool filled with cold water. The rich might like to complete the process with a brisk rubdown with a scented towel. It was not unusual for a member of the opposite sex to perform this favor for you (the baths were open to men and women, though the times when they could use them were different). There was a nominal admission fee, often waived by officials and emperors wishing to curry favor with the plebeians. In summer, the Baths are a stunning open-air venue for operas and ballet performances of the Teatro dell'Opera di Roma (prices from €25 to €110; reserve through ☎ *0039/0648078400).* ⊠ *Via delle Terme di Caracalla 52, Aventino* ☎ *06/39967700* ⊕ *www.pierreci.it* ⊠ *€6* ☉ *Tues.–Sun. 9–6:30, Mon. 9–1* Ⓜ *Circo Massimo.*

Fodor's Choice
★

Santi Giovanni e Paolo. Perched up the incline of the Clivus di Scauro—a magical time-machine of a street where the dial seems to be stuck somewhere in the 13th century—Santi Giovanni e Paolo is an image that would tempt most landscape painters. Landmarked by one of Rome's finest Romanesque bell towers, it looms over on a poetic piazza. Underneath, however, are other treasures, whose excavations can be seen in the new Case Romane del Celio museum (*see above*). A basilica erected on the spot was, like San Clemente, destroyed in 1084 by attacking Normans. Its half-buried columns, near the current church entrance, are visible through misty glass. The current church has its origins at the start of the 12th century, but the interior dates mostly from the 17th century and later. The lovely, incongruous chandeliers are a hand-me-down from New York's Waldorf-Astoria hotel, a gift arranged by the late Cardinal Francis Spellman of New York, whose titular church this was. Spellman also initiated the excavations here in 1949. ⊠ *Piazza Santi Giovanni e Paolo 13, Celio* ☎ *06/772711* ⊘ *Daily 10–1 and 3–6* Ⓜ *Colosseo.*

Fodor's Choice
★

Santi Quattro Coronati. One of the evocative cul-de-sacs in Rome where history seems to be holding its breath, this church is strongly imbued with the sanctity of the Romanesque era. Marvelously redolent of the Middle Ages, this is one of the most unusual and unexpected corners of Rome, a quiet citadel that has resisted the tide of time and traffic flowing below its ramparts. The church honors the Four Crowned Saints—the four brothers Seveus, Severinus, Carpophorus, and Victorius, all Roman officials who were whipped to death for their faith by Emperor Diocletian (284–305). The original 9th-century church was twice as large as the current one. The abbey was partially destroyed during the Normans' sack of Rome about 1085, but it was reconstructed about 30 years later. This explains the inordinate size of the apse in relation to the small nave. Don't miss the **cloister,** with its well-tended gardens and 12th-century fountain. The entrance is the door in the left nave; ring the bell if it's not open.

There's another medieval gem hidden away off the courtyard at the church entrance: the **Chapel of San Silvestro.** (Enter the door marked MONACHE AGOSTINIANE and ring the bell at the left for the nun; she will press a button to open the chapel door automatically.) The chapel has remained, for the most part, as it was when consecrated in 1246, decorated with marbles and frescoes. These tell the story of the Christian emperor Constantine's recovery from leprosy thanks to Pope Sylvester I. Note, too, the delightful *Last Judgment* fresco above the door, in which the angel on the left neatly rolls up sky and stars like a backdrop, signaling the end of the world. A donation is highly appropriate. ⊠ *Via Santi Quattro Coronati 20, Celio* ☎ *06/70475427* ⊘ *Mon.–Sat., 6:30–12:30 and 3:30–7:30; Sun., 6:45–12:30 and 3–7:30. Cloister and San Silvestro Chapel, 9–10:40 and 4–5:30* Ⓜ *Colosseo.*

Santo Stefano Rotondo. This 5th-century church was inspired perhaps by the design of the church of the Holy Sepulchre in Jerusalem. Its unusual round plan and timbered ceiling set it apart from most other Roman churches. The vast barnlike space has walls aplenty, and most of them are covered with frescoes that lovingly depict the most gory martyrdoms of Catholic saints. You've been warned: these are not for the fainthearted, cataloging, above the names of different emperors, every type of violent death conceivable. ✉ *Via Santo Stefano Rotondo 7, Celio* ☎ *06/421199* ⊙ *Tues.–Sat. 9:30–12:30 and 3–6, Sun. 9:30–noon, Mon. 2–4* Ⓜ *Colosseo.*

WORTH NOTING

San Gregorio Magno. Set amid the greenery of the Celian Hill, this church wears its baroque facade proudly. Dedicated to St. Gregory the Great (who served as pope 590–604), it was built about 750 by Pope Gregory II to commemorate his predecessor and namesake. The church of San Gregorio itself has the appearance of a typical baroque structure, the result of remodeling in the 17th and 18th centuries. But you can still see what's said to be the stone slab on which the pious Gregory the Great slept; it's in the far right-hand chapel. Outside are three chapels. The right chapel is dedicated to Gregory's mother, St. Sylvia, and contains a Guido Reni fresco of the *Concert of Angels*. The chapel in the center, dedicated to St. Andrew, contains two monumental frescoes showing scenes from the saint's life. They were painted at the beginning of the 17th century by Domenichino (*The Flagellation of St. Andrew*) and Guido Reni (*The Execution of St. Andrew*). It's a striking juxtaposition of the sturdy, if sometimes stiff, classicism of Domenichino with the more flamboyant and heroic baroque manner of Guido Reni. Unfortunately, at this writing, the church was deemed unstable and awaits the judgment of Rome's fire brigade before reopening. ✉ *Piazza San Gregorio, Celio* ☎ *06/7008227* ⊙ *Daily 8–12:30 and 1:30–7* Ⓜ *Colosseo.*

THE CATACOMBS AND VIA APPIA ANTICA

Strewn with classical ruins and dotted with grazing sheep, the Via Appia Antica (Appian Way) stirs images of chariots and legionnaires returning from imperial conquests. It was completed in 312 BC by Appius Claudius, who laid it out to connect Rome with settlements in the south, in the direction of Naples. Here Peter is said to have been stopped by Christ, as commemorated by the Domine Quo Vadis church. Though time and vandals have taken their toll on the ancient relics along the road, the Catacombs remain to cast their spirit-warm spell. As Christianity took hold in Rome, Christians buried their dead in group crypts known as catacombs. Persecution of Christians under pagan emperors made martyrs of many, and their remains became objects of veneration in secret meetings for worship underground. Today, the dark, gloomy catacombs contrast strongly with the fresh air, verdant meadows, and evocative classical ruins along the ancient Via Appia Antica, one of Rome's most magical places for a picnic.

The initial stretch of the Via Appia Antica is not pedestrian-friendly—there is fast, heavy traffic and no sidewalk all the way from Porta San Sebastiano to the Catacombe di San Callisto. To reach the catacombs, one route is Bus No. 218 from San Giovanni in Laterano. Alternatively, take Metro line A to Colli Albani and Bus No. 660 to the Tomb of Cecilia Metella. A more expensive option is No. 110 Archaeobus from Piazza Venezia; with an open-top deck the big green buses allow you to

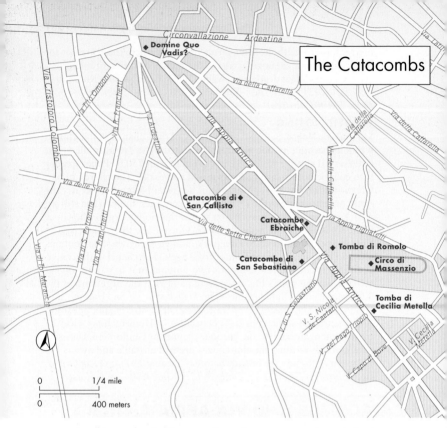

The Catacombs

Domine Quo Vadis?

Catacombe di San Callisto

Catacombe Ebraiche

Catacombe di San Sebastiano

Tomba di Romolo

Circo di Massenzio

Tomba di Cecilia Metella

0   1/4 mile

0   400 meters

hop on and off as you please, but at a price of €13 daily. An attractive and much cheaper alternative is to hire a bike.

TOP ATTRACTIONS

Catacombe di San Callisto *(Catacombs of St. Calixtus).* Burial place of many popes of the 3rd century, this is the oldest and best-preserved underground cemetery. One of the (English-speaking) friars who act as custodians of the catacomb will guide you through its crypts and galleries, some adorned with Early Christian frescoes. Watch out for wrong turns: this is a five-story-high catacomb! ⊠ *Via Appia Antica 110/126, Via Appia Antica* ☎ *06/5310151* ⊕ *www.catacombe.roma.it* ✉ *€6* ☉ *Thurs.–Tues. 9–noon and 2–5. Closed Feb.*

Catacombe di San Sebastiano *(Catacombs of St. Sebastian).* The 4th-century church was named after the saint who was buried in the cata-comb, which burrows underground on four different levels. This was the only Early Christian cemetery to remain accessible during the Middle Ages, and it was from here that the term "catacomb" is derived—it's in a spot where the road dips into a hollow, known to the Romans as *catacumbas* (Greek for "near the hollow"). The Romans used the name to refer to the cemetery that had existed here since the 2nd century BC, and it came to be applied to all the underground cemeteries discovered

Walk in the footsteps of St. Peter along the Via Appia Antica, stretches of which seem barely altered from the days of the Caesars.

in Rome in later centuries. ⊠ *Via Appia Antica 136, Via Appia Antica* ☎ *06/7850350* 🖃 *€6* ⏱ *Mon.–Sat. 9–noon and 2–5.*

Domine Quo Vadis? *(Church of Lord, Where Goest Thou?).* This church was built on the spot where tradition says Christ appeared to St. Peter as the apostle was fleeing Rome and persuaded him to return and face martyrdom. A paving stone in the church bears an imprint said to have been made by the feet of Christ. In 2009, the church was shuttered for renovation work; hopefully, the doors have reopened in 2010. ⊠ *Via Appia Antica at Via Ardeatina, Via Appia Antica* ☎ *06/5120441* ⏱ *Daily 7–6:30.*

Fodor's Choice ★ **Tomba di Cecilia Metella.** For centuries, sightseers have flocked to this famous landmark, one of the most complete surviving tombs of ancient Rome. One of the many round mausoleums that once lined the Appian Way, this tumulus-shape tomb is a smaller version of the Mausoleum of Augustus, but impressive nonetheless. It was the burial place of a Roman noblewoman, wife of the son of Crassus, one of Julius Caesar's rivals and known as the richest man in the Roman empire (infamously entering the English language as "crass"). The original decoration includes a frieze of bulls' skulls near the top. The travertine stone walls were made higher and the medieval-style crenellations added when the tomb was transformed into a fortress by the Caetani family in the 14th century. An adjacent chamber houses a small museum of the area's geological phases. ⊠ *Via Appia Antica 162, Via Appia Antica* ☎ *06/39967700* 🖃 *€6 (also includes entry to Terme di Caracalla and Villa dei Quintili)* ⏱ *Summer, Tues.–Sun. 9–7:30; winter, Tues.–Sun. 9–6:30.*

NEED A BREAK?

Placed strategically at the bus stop, the Appia Antica Caffè (⊠ Via Appia Antica 175 ☎ 3383465440) is a bar rare for its sound of birdsong. It also offers lunch and hires out bikes, which is an economical way of exploring the Catacombs and other monuments to the right, spread as they are over several miles (if you're heading leftward, opt for the bus as those bike routes can be blocked off).

WORTH NOTING

Circo di Massenzio. Of the Circus of Maxentius, built in AD 309, remain the towers at the entrance; the *spina*, the wall that divided it down the center; and the vaults that supported the tiers of seating for the spectators. The obelisk now in Piazza Navona was found here. The adjacent **Mausoleo di Romolo** is a huge tomb built by the emperor for his son Romulus, who died young. The tomb and circus were on the grounds of the emperor's villa, now closed for further excavation/restoration. ⊠ *Via Appia Antica 153, Via Appia Antica* ☎ *06/7801324* ⊙ *Closed at this writing for excavation/restoration.*

Villa dei Quintili. After recent excavation this splendid villa and its 52 rooms about a central exedra—probably a sports hall of sorts—are now visitable, albeit best included in a separate itinerary from the Catacombs, being 5 km (3 mi) away and accessible by a different route. Why Emperor Comodus of "damned memory"—also the villain in *Gladiator*—coveted the Quintili's sumptuous property is still evident. To get hold of it, he accused the family of plotting against him, and had them executed before moving in himself, using, perhaps, the exedra of sports hall for training for his fights with ostriches back in the Colisseum. ⊠ *Via Appia Nuova 1092, Via Appia Antica* ☎ *0639967700* 💰 *€3* ⊙ *Summer, Tues.–Sun. 9–7:15 (last entrance 6:15); winter, Tues.–Sun. 9–4:30 (last entrance 3:30). Closed Mon. and Dec. 25 and Jan. 1* Ⓜ *Bus 664 from Colli Albani Metro A.*

Where to Eat

WORD OF MOUTH

"We loved La Pergola. After looking through the water menu (it took me a few minutes to realize it was water), I asked for the salt menu. They immediately came with a tray of many small hills of different salts. Yes, it was over the top but [the restaurant] is great for a special occasion."

—Elainee

THE SCENE

Updated by
Dana Klitzberg

In Rome, wonderfully simple, traditional cuisine reigns. Most chefs prefer to follow the mantra of freshness over fuss, simplicity of flavor and preparation over complex cooking methods. So when Romans keep on ordering the old standbys, it's easy to understand why.

And we're talking about some very old standbys: some restaurants re-create dishes that come from ancient recipes of Apicius, probably the first "celebrity chef" (to Emperor Tiberius) and cookbook author of the Western world. Today, Rome's cooks excel at what has taken hundreds, sometimes thousands, of years to perfect. This is why the basic trattoria menu is similar wherever you go.

Still, if you're hunting for newer-than-now developments, things are slowly changing. Talented young chefs are exploring new culinary frontiers, with results that tickle the taste buds: potato gnocchi with sea urchin sauce, artichoke strudel, and oysters with red onion foam are just a few recent examples. Of course, there's grumbling about the number of chefs who, in a clumsy effort to be *nuovo*, end up with collision rather than fusion. That noted, Rome is the capital city, and the influx of residents from other regions of the country allows for many variations on the Italian theme. Sicilian, Tuscan, Pugliese, Bolognese, Sardinian, and other Italian regional cuisines from the Alps to the northern reaches of Africa, are all represented. You'll also find a number of good-quality foreign food outposts here, particularly Japanese, Indian, and Ethiopian restaurants.

Most Romans don't care about the fanfare of decor in a city where you can sit outside on a glorious piazza and dine in a virtual baroque painting. Still, Rome has its fair share of both slick interiors, which are slowly starting to catch on, and historic settings that offer amazing views or gorgeous settings. In any case, if you can look beyond the trappings, as Romans do, you can eat like an emperor—or at least a well-fed member of the Roman working class—for very little money.

VATICAN
residential, refined neighborhood favorites

SPAGNA, TREVI & QUIRINALE
celebrity hot spots & shopping-spree respites

BORGHESE & VENETO
former "dolce vita" haunts now overpriced tourist traps

REPUBBLICA & SAN LORENZO
student haunts & innovative regional cuisine

NAVONA
hot young chefs' outposts; traditional pizza joints

PANTHEON
creative assortment of mid-range dining options

MONTI & ESQUILINO
ethnic spots & hip up-and-comers

CAMPO DE' FIORI
trattorias featuring market-fresh ingredients

GHETTO
traditional Roman & Jewish Roman fare among the ruins

TRASTEVERE & GIANICOLO
cheap joints, local favorites

COLOSSEO
local pizzerias & trattorias for tourists & locals alike

AVENTINO & TESTACCIO
old-school Roman eateries meet club/lounge scene

WHERE TO EAT PLANNER

Eating Out Strategy

Where should we eat? With hundreds of eateries competing for your attention, it may seem like a daunting question. But fret not—our expert writers and editors have done most of the legwork. The 90-plus selections here represent the best the city has to offer, from *caffè* and *gelaterias* to formal *alta cucina* restaurants.

Search Best Bets for top recommendations by price, cuisine, and experience. Sample local flavor in the neighborhood features, or find a review quickly in the listings. They're organized alphabetically within each neighborhood. Delve in and enjoy!

With Kids

In restaurants and trattorias you may find a high chair or a cushion for the child to sit on, but there's rarely a children's menu. Order a *mezza porzione* (half portion) of any dish, or ask the waiter for a *porzione da bambino* (child's portion). Generally, kids will feel welcomed at casual establishments such as trattorias, but only very well-behaved children should go to higher-end restaurants.

Restaurant Types

Until relatively recently, there was a distinct hierarchy delineated by the names of Rome's eating places. A *ristorante* was typically elegant and expensive; a *trattoria* served more traditional, home-style fare in a relaxed atmosphere; an *osteria* was even more casual, essentially a wine bar and gathering spot that also served food. The terms still exist but the distinction has blurred considerably. Now, an osteria in the center of town may be pricier than a ristorante across the street.

In a Roman sit-down restaurant, whether a ristorante, trattoria, or osteria, you're expected to order at least a two-course meal. It could be a *primo* (first course) with a *secondo* (second course, which is really a "main course" in English parlance); an *antipasto* (starter) followed by a primo or secondo; or a secondo and a *dolce* (dessert).

In a pizzeria, it's common to order just one dish. The handiest places for a snack between sights are bars, caffè, and *pizza al taglio* (by the slice) shops. Bars are places for a quick coffee and a sandwich, rather than drinking establishments. A *caffè* (café) is a bar but usually with more seating. If you place your order at the counter, ask if you can sit down: some places charge more for table service. Often you'll pay a cashier first, then give your *scontrino* (receipt) to the person at the counter who fills your order.

It was not so long ago that the wine you could get in Rome was strictly local; you didn't have to walk far to find a restaurant where you could buy wine straight from the barrel then sit down to drink and nibble a bit. The tradition continues today, as many Roman wine shops also serve food, and are called *enotecas* (wine bars). Behind the bar you'll find serious wine enthusiasts—maybe even a sommelier—with several bottles open to be tasted by the glass. There are often carefully selected cheeses and cured meats, and a short menu of simple dishes and desserts, making a stop in an enoteca an appealing alternative to a three-course restaurant meal.

What to Wear

We mention dress only when men are required to wear a jacket or a jacket and tie. Keep in mind that Italian men never wear shorts in a restaurant or *enoteca* (wine bar) and infrequently wear sneakers or running shoes, no matter how humble. The same "rules" apply to ladies' casual shorts, running shoes, and flip-flop sandals. Shorts are acceptable in pizzerias and caffé.

Meal Times and Closures

Breakfast (*la colazione*) is usually served from 7 AM to 10:30 AM, lunch (*il pranzo*) from 12:30 PM to 2:30 PM, dinner (*la cena*) from 7:30 PM to 11 PM. Peak times are around 1:30 PM for lunch and 9 PM for dinner.

Enotecas (wine bars) are sometimes open in the morning and late afternoon for snacks. Most pizzerias open at 8 PM and close around midnight–1 AM. Most bars and caffé are open from 7 AM to 8 or 9 PM. Almost all restaurants close one day a week (in most cases Sunday or Monday) and for at least two weeks in August. The city is zoned, however, so that there are always some restaurants in each zone that remain open, to avoid tourists (and residents) getting stuck without any options whatsoever.

Prices

Most restaurants have a "cover" charge, usually listed on the menu as *"pane e coperto."* It should be modest (€1–€2.50 per person) except at the most expensive restaurants. Some restaurants instead charge for bread, which should be brought to you (and paid for) only if you order it. When in doubt, ask about the cover policy before ordering. Note that the price of fish dishes is often given by weight (before cooking); the price on the menu will be for 100 grams, not for the whole fish. An average fish portion is about 350 grams.

WHAT IT COSTS IN EUROS

	¢	$	$$	$$$	$$$$
AT DINNER	under €15	€15–€25	€25–€35	€35–€45	over €45

Prices are for first course (primo), second course (secondo), and dessert (dolce).

In This Chapter

12

Using the Maps

Throughout the chapter, you'll see mapping symbols and coordinates (✛ *4:F4*) after property names or reviews. To locate the property on the map, turn to the Rome Dining and Lodging Atlas at the end of this chapter. The first number after the ✛ symbol indicates the map number. Following that is the property's coordinate on the map grid.

Tipping and Taxes

All prices include tax. Restaurant menu prices include *servizio* (service) unless indicated otherwise. It's customary to leave a small tip (from a euro to 10% of the bill) in appreciation of good service. Tips are always given in cash.

BEST BETS FOR ROME DINING

With thousands of restaurants to choose from, how will you decide where to eat? Fodor's writers and editors have selected their favorite restaurants by price, cuisine, and experience in the Best Bets lists below. In the first column, Fodor's Choice properties represent the "best of the best." You can also search by neighborhood for excellent eats—just peruse the following pages. Or find specific details about a restaurant in the full reviews, listed later in the chapter.

ROMAN

Alle Fratte di Traste-vere, p. 275

Checchino dal 1887, p. 280

Da Sergio, p. 261

Piperno, p. 264

SEAFOOD

Acquolina, p. 267

F.I.S.H., p. 265

Il Sanlorenzo, p. 263

La Rosetta, p. 258

San Teodoro, p. 264

SOUTHERN ITALIAN

La Gensola, p. 278

La Locanda del Pel-legrino, p. 261

Monte Caruso, p. 266

Tram Tram, p. 268

TUSCAN

Dal Toscano, p. 275

Il Ciak, p. 276

Papa Baccus, p. 268

WINE BAR

L'Angolo Divino, p. 261

L'Enoteca Antica di Via della Croce, p. 271

Cavour 313, p. 265

Cul de Sac, p. 257

Roscioli, p. 262

By Experience

CHILD-FRIENDLY

Alle Fratte di Traste-vere, p. 275

'Gusto, p. 270

La Montecarlo, p. 258

Panattoni, p. 278

GOOD FOR GROUPS

Alle Fratte di Traste-vere, p. 275

Dar Poeta, p. 276

'Gusto, p. 270

La Montecarlo, p. 258

Maccheroni, p. 256

Panattoni, p. 278

ReCafe, p. 272

GORGEOUS SETTING

Il Convivio, p. 257

Il Palazzetto, p. 271

Il Simposio di Costan-tini, p. 275

La Pergola, p. 282

La Veranda dell'Hotel Columbus, p. 272

Osteria dell'Ingegno, p. 258

Vecchia Roma, p. 264

OUTDOOR DINING

Boccondivino, p. 259

Dal Bolognese, p. 269

Osteria della Quercia, p. 263

Osteria dell'Ingegno, p. 258

ReCafe, p. 272

San Teodoro, p. 264

Z'Imberto, p. 279

HOT SPOTS

Duke's, p. 269

Etablì, p. 257

Il Sanlorenzo, p. 263

Primo, p. 266

Uno e Bino, p. 268

LATE-NIGHT

Cul de Sac, p. 257

'Gusto, p. 270

Maccheroni, p. 256

Panattoni, p. 278

MOST ROMANTIC

Antico Arco, p. 280

El Toulà, p. 270

Il Bacaro, p. 256

Il Convivio, p. 257

Il Simposio di Costan-tini, p. 275

La Pergola, p. 282

San Teodoro, p. 264

BEST DESSERT

Antico Arco, p. 280

Glass Hostaria, p. 276

La Pergola, p. 282

San Teodoro, p. 264

BUSINESS DINING

Al Ceppo, p. 269

Caffè Romano dell'Hotel Inghilterra, p. 269

Il Convivio, p. 257

Il Palazzetto, p. 271

Papá Baccus, p. 268

Sora Lella, p. 264

LOTS OF LOCALS

Dar Poeta, p. 276

'Gusto - Osteria, p. 271

Panattoni, p. 278

Perilli, p. 281

Primo, p. 266

Tram Tram, p. 268

Trattoria Monti, p. 265

HOTEL DINING

Caffè Romano dell'Hotel Inghilterra, p. 269

La Pergola, p. 282

La Verandah dell'Hotel Columbus, p. 272

PANTHEON, NAVONA, TREVI, AND QUIRINALE

These central areas see as many tourists as they do locals, but the heart of the *centro storico* (historic center) beats here in these narrow *vicolos* (squares) and grand piazzas.

Between the piazzas and cobblestone back streets leading to and from these public gathering spots, you have the widest range of culinary offerings. Here one finds some of Rome's best pizza, in no-frills pizza joints where the waiters scribble the bill on your paper tablecloth. Yet here you also find some of the city's most revered foodie temples, featuring star chefs, inventive cuisine, and decidedly higher bills placed on the finest high-thread-count damask tablecloths. Quite a range, and yet this coexistence of high- and lowbrow is decidedly Roman.

The Troiani brothers at **Il Convivio** (⊠ *Vicolo dei Soldati 31* ☎ *06/6869432*) have been running what is essentially a high altar to *alta cucina* (haute cuisine) for many years, where revering top-notch ingredients is an art form. Pizzas are the thing at the famed **Da Baffetto** (⊠ *Via Governo Vecchio 114* ☎ *06/6861617*), where there's always a line, and **Pizzeria Montecarlo** (⊠ *Vicolo Savelli 13* ☎ *06/6861877* ✛ *4:C3*), which is one of few pizzerias to serve pizza at lunch as well.

ROMAN PIZZA 101

The concept is simple: Naples may lay claim to the invention of pizza, but to many pizza purists, Rome perfected the dish. Roman pizza has a thin crust, which makes it important that the crust has the right ratio of crisp-to-chewy. Toppings are spare and of high quality so as not to weigh down the disc of dough with superfluous stuff. And, of course, the wood-burning ovens that reach extremely high temperatures are of the utmost importance (look for a sign stating they use wood-burning ovens: *forno a legno*). Since they're so hot, they're usually fired up only in the evenings, which is why Roman pizzerias serving pizza *tonda* (whole rounds) are open almost exclusively for dinner.

TASTE OF THE CITY

Angelo Troiani
Chef and co-owner of Il Convivio and Acquolina Ristorante

As a dominant force in the capital city's dining scene for two decades, chef and restaurateur Angelo Troiani speaks to us about his cooking style, his adopted home city, and pleasing even the toughest food lovers.

Q: Can you tell us a bit about your cooking style?
A: My cooking is healthy, above all else. It's not about being organic, which it often is, but that's not the focus. Primary materials are paramount, but it's also about letting the food be what it is, and tweaking it as little as possible.

Q: Why did you decide to set up shop in Rome?
A: Though I grew up in Le Marche, my mother's family is from Rome, so it was like coming home in a way. I opened the restaurant with my two brothers, 20 years ago. Back then, Rome was just a beautiful place, a sleeping giant, with so much history. I felt there was a lot of opportunity and potential, and still do.

Q: What was your impetus for opening a second restaurant in Rome?
A: I wanted to create a different dining experience, and to compete with myself, in a way, as a challenge. Acquolina (✉ *Via Antonio Serra 60* ☎ *06/3337629* ✛ 1:G1)

specializes in seafood, so it's very different from Convivio (✉ *Vicolo dei Soldati 31* ☎ *06/6869432* ✛ 4:D1). Restaurants are like children: having two is more challenging than having one, but it's also more rewarding. As for Rome, the city has "woken up" and so many entities are reinventing in Rome; everyone wants to be here.

Q: Who dines at Convivio and Acquolina?
A: Of course we have an international clientele whose first priority is great food. At the same time, we have a very loyal Roman and Italian customer base that we turn to as a measure of our success. If the Italians, who can be tough critics, are happy, we know we're doing something right.

FOLLOW THE SANPIETRINI . . .

This narrow, medieval street off Piazza Navona is known for its interesting boutiques, although there are just as many charming spots for a predinner aperitivo or an after-dinner cocktail. **Cul de Sac** (✉ *Piazza di Pasquino 73* ☎ *06/68801094* ✛ 4:D3) serves tasty nibbles—from an enormous cheese and salumi selection to baba ghanouj and patés—with its extensive wine list, which is why its deservedly famous all over Rome. Oddly enough there are Irish pubs all over Rome, but the **Abbey Theatre Pub** (✉ *Via Governo Vecchio 51* ☎ *06/6861341* ✛ *4:C3*) is in a great location and screens international sports events (Superbowl, NCAA basketball, etc.) that can be difficult to find elsewhere in the city. **Shaki Wine Bar** (✉ *Via Governo Vecchio 123* ☎ *06/68308796* ✛ *1:H2*), with a sister location near the Spanish Steps, is a great spot for an aperitivo, like the classic Italian negroni or a glass of prosecco.

CAMPO DE' FIORI AND GHETTO

Roman cuisine meets Jewish cuisine at the historical crossroads between Campo de' Fiori and the Ghetto.

The two neighborhoods, located right next to each other, represent the coming-together of a raucous *carnevale-like people parade*, and the reverential preservation of tradition. Campo de' Fiori has always been the secular crossroads of the city: even in ancient Rome, pilgrims would gather here to eat, drink, and be merry. And the Ghetto is home to Europe's oldest Jewish community, and offers staple dishes introduced by Jewish cooks centuries ago that have been enveloped into the Roman culinary canon. What they share (other than Via Arenula) is a real Roman dedication to cooking. The main square in Campo de' Fiori is home to one of the city's biggest open-air produce markets, and the shoppers are not just housewives and tourists; many of the local chefs concoct their menus based on what looks good at the market that day. Restaurants line the piazza of Campo de' Fiori; however, many of them are quite touristy, so don't limit yourself to the main square.

GUANCIALE AND ANCHOVIES

Variations on cured pork, such as *guanciale* (pig's cheek), *prosciutto* (smoked ham), and *pancetta* (bacon), are signature flavorings for Roman dishes, and can be found at butchers like **Viola** (✉ *Campo de' Fiori 43, Campo de' Fiori* ☎ *06/68806114* ✛ *4:C4*) and food shops like **Roscioli** (✉ *Via del Giubbonari 21-22/A, Campo de' Fiori* ☎ *06/6875287*). When Jewish culinary culture started intermingling with Roman, it was discovered that Jewish cooks used *alici* (anchovies) to flavor dishes the way Romans used cured pork: for salt and a deepening of flavor. To find a great can of anchovies, make your way to any Jewish *alimentary* (food shop) in the Ghetto.

IT'S THE LITTLE THINGS

ON THE GO: AT THE FORNO

Sometimes the most satisfying meal you can grab on the go—and on the cheap—is from the *forno*, or bakery.

Il Forno di Campo de' Fiori (⊠ *Campo de' Fiori 22, Campo de' Fiori* ☎ *06/68806662* ⊕ 4:C4) is easily the most popular bakery in the area, and their outstanding pizzas—*bianca* (white) and *rossa* (red)—leave you happily wondering how something so simple can be so flavorful.

If you prefer your baked goods kosher, go to the 100-year-old **Antico Forno del Ghetto** (⊠ *Piazza Costaguti 30, Ghetto* ☎ *06/68803012* ⊕ 4:F5), which also offers tasty bianca and rossa pizzas, as well as a crusty bread that they refer to as *ossi* (bones).

ROMAN VS. JEWISH ARTICHOKES

If there's one vegetable Rome is known for, it's the artichoke, or *carciofo*. The classic *carciofo alla romana* is a large, globe-shaped artichoke that is stuffed with wild mint and garlic and then braised. The *carciofo alla giudia* is deep-fried twice, until crisp and leathery brown in color and tender at the heart.

Roman cuisine is very seasonably based, so when artichokes are "in season"—spring!—they're served everywhere. For a good traditional Romana artichoke, go to **Ar Galletto** (⊠ *Piazza Farnese 102, Campo de' Fiori* ☎ *06/6861714* ⊕ 4:C4) or **Da Sergio** (⊠ *Vicolo delle Grotte 27* ☎ *06/6864293*).

For the best Giudia, you'll have to try out **Da Giggetto** (⊠ *Via Portico d'Ottavia 21A-22, Ghetto* ☎ *06/6861105* ⊕ 4:F5) or **Piperno** (⊠ *Monte Cenci 9, Ghetto* ☎ *06/6833606*) and decide on a winner for yourself, or head to **Sora Margherita** (⊠ *Piazza delle Cinque Scole 30, Ghetto* ☎ *06/6874216* ⊕ 4:E5), a delicious little ghetto hole-in-the-wall, and try them both side by side.

FORNO VS. PASTICCERIA

Forno means "oven" in Italian, but it's also the word for a bakery that specializes in bread and simple baked goods, like biscotti, pound cakes, and pine nut tarts. The *pasticceria*, on the other hand, specializes in more complicated Italian sweets, like fruit tarts, *montebianco* (a piped chestnut-cream creation resembling an alpine mountain), and *millefoglie* (puff pastry layered with pastry cream). Straddling the line between the forno and the pasticceria, on the "main drag" of the Ghetto, **Pasticceria Boccioni** (⊠ *Via del Portico d'Ottavia 1* ☎ *06/6878637* ⊕ 4:F5), commonly known as Forno del Ghetto, is famous across the city for being the only establishment specializing in a handful of Roman Jewish specialties. They make Rome's most delicious ricotta cheesecake, filled with cherries or chocolate, baked in an almondy crust. (Try to get there early on Friday as they sell out before closing for the Sabbath.)

12

MONTI, ESQUILINO, REPUBBLICA, AND SAN LORENZO

These distinctly different neighborhoods encompass the best *mista,* or mix, of traditional Italian and ethnic cuisines in all of Rome.

Monti is a chic, boutique-clad neighborhood with the best offerings of ethnic restaurants in the *centro*—from the Pan-Asian-Mediterranean seafood at **F.I.S.H.** (⊠ *Via dei Serpenti 16* ☎ *06/47824962*) to Punjab Indian at **Maharajah** (⊠ *Via dei Serpenti 124* ☎ *06/4747144* ✛ *2:C5*).

Esquilino is Rome's main ethnic artery, containing many tourist traps, but also some real gems, like the **Italian Bistrò** (⊠ *Via Palestro 40* ☎ *06/44702868* ✛ *2:D3*) and the **Mercato Esquilino** (⊠ *Via Principe Amedeo*), where one can shop alongside locals for bargain-priced Italian meats and produce as well as Asian and African specialties.

You'll find a lot of hotels (and unremarkable food) in Repubblica, just north of Termini station. Head east of the station, to San Lorenzo, to sample Rome's latest hipster 'hood. It's quiet during the day, but is worth an evening trip for the *burrata* (a creamier mozzarella-like cheese) and puff pastry at **Uno e Bino** (⊠ *Via degli Equi 58* ☎ *06/4466702*) and the *orrechiette* (ear-shaped pasta) with clams and broccoli at **Tram Tram** (⊠ *Via dei Reti 44* ☎ *06/490416*).

PERFECT PIZZA

Pizza is sold on practically every block in Rome, and while hardly any of it is bad, you might be wondering: Where's the best stuff? Check out the prevailing pizzerias in this area to find out: **La Gallina Bianca** (⊠ *Via A. Rosmini 5, Esquilino* ☎ *06/4743777* ✛ *2:F1*) for classic thin-crust Roman pizza; **La Soffitta** (⊠ *Via dei Villini 1/e, Esquilino* ☎ *06/4404642* ✛ *2:F1*) for Neapolitan-certified thick, crispy-crust pizza; **Formula Uno** (⊠ *Via degli Equi 13, San Lorenzo* ☎ *06/4453866*) for thin crusts and a feeding frenzy; and **Panella** bakery (⊠ *Via Merulana 54, Esquilino* ☎ *06/4872435* ✛ *2:E5*) for delicious slices to go.

12

LOCAL FAVES 2 WAYS

	SAVE	SPLURGE
Roman Flavor	Roman Pommidoro (✉ Piazza dei Sanniti 44, San Lorenzo ☎ 06/4452692) serves up traditional Roman fare with a focus on grilled meat and fish at fair prices.	One of Rome's most beloved spots, **Agata e Romeo** (✉ Via Carlo Alberto 45, Esquilino ☎ 06/4466115), pleases Roman palates with updated versions of old standards.
Regional Italian	Explore the roasted meats and game of Le Marche region without leaving Rome at **Trattoria Monti** (✉ Via San Vito 13, Monti ☎ 06/4466573).	**Monte Caruso** (✉ Via Farini 12, Esquilino ☎ 06/483549) serves up southern Italian delicacies from Lucania.

TO MARKET, TO MARKET

Long known as the people's market of Rome, the **Mercato Esquilino** (✉ *Via Principe Amedeo* ✛ *2:F5*) has, in recent years, become even more eclectic and egalitarian. This is not a market where you only see the same Italian ingredients (as beautiful and high-quality as they may be) as in other markets. Here, African vegetable vendors sell yams and okra; Asian vendors sell rice noodles and miso paste, vinegars and lemongrass. Halal butchers abut *macellerie* specializing in pig parts. The seafood hall teems with vendors—Bangladeshi, Chinese, Italian—hawking fish for pasta and for sushi; some live, and some already filleted. And yes, Italian vendors still sell their many varieties of tomato, eggplant, zucchini, pizza and bread, and all the wonderful Italian local goods you'd expect to find. A trip to this market is an incredibly energizing experience, allowing shoppers a window onto the daily life of the many hungry and diverse locals that make up the Eternal City.

VINI, FORMAGGI, AND ANTIPASTI

Wine, cheese, and assorted cured meats are the star items on the city's *enoteche* (wineshops) menus. There's no better way to join the Italians than to raise a glass of their country's fine wine and bid them *Salute*. **Enoteca Trimani** (✉ *Via Goito 20, San Lorenzo* ☎ *06/4469661*), the oldest wine shop in Rome, dates back to 1821 and stocks more than 4,000 labels from around the world. The Trimani family also owns the highly regarded **Trimani Il Wine Bar** (✉ *Via Cernia 37B, San Lorenzo* ☎ *06/4469630*) around the corner where you can wine and dine with the best selections in town. Closer to the *centro*, **Cavour 313** (✉ *Via Cavour 313, Monti* ☎ *06/678 5496*) offers more than 25 wines by the glass, plus an array of gourmet cheese and meat plates.

VENETO, BORGHESE, AND SPAGNA

The exclusive neighborhoods of Via Veneto, Villa Borghese, and the Tridente encompass an area of Rome densely populated by deluxe hotels and Rome's upscale shopping district.

The area around Via Veneto, the Villa Borghese Park, and Spagna (from Piazza del Popolo down the length of Via di Ripetta, over to Via del Tritone and up to the Spanish Steps) could be considered Rome's downtown, for its business district. But its feeling is much more uptown, as it's also the city's fashion epicenter.

Workday lunchtime offerings include classic trattorias and chic cafès like **TAD Café** (⊠ *Via del Babuino 53* ☎ *06/36004675* ✢ *1:G1*), where you can get a panino, a salad, or even a bite of sushi. Come sundown, the options increase as modern trattoria-pizzerias like 'Gusto and ReCafé throng with tastemakers and young professionals. Perennially popular hot spots include Nino and Dal Bolognese. And the upscale hotels in the area—the Hassler, Hotel Eden, and Hotel de Russie—offer great aperitivi in their distinguished bars.

EMPIRE OF "TASTE"

When **'Gusto** (⊠ *Piazza Agusto Imperatore 9* ☎ *06/3226273* ✢ *1:G2*) opened in the late '90s, the concept was new to Rome: a sprawling ground-floor pizzeria, a wine bar with nibbles, and an upstairs upscale restaurant, all in one space. It caught on quickly, and they added on a store selling cookware, cookbooks, and a variety of cooking tools. The pizzeria offers a popular buffet-style lunch popular with nearby office workers. Or try the always-packed **Gusto–Osteria** (⊠ *Via della Frezza 16* ☎ *06/32111482* ✢ *1:G2*), around the corner, which offers plenty of snack-size tasting portions, even for pastas and secondi.

CELEB HOT SPOTS

Rome is the city in Italy where the idea of *la bella figura* (the art of looking good) is most often at work—or shall we say, at play. Parioli is considered the neighborhood where many of the posh live, but they work and play in the Spagna, Via Veneto, and Borghese areas. And when celebrities come to town, they frequently reside in the many five-star luxury hotels in the *zona. Below, we break down who goes where and why.*

12

IN VINO VERITAS

Nestled in the Palazzetto, alongside the Spanish Steps, the **Wine Academy of Rome** (✉ *Vicolo del Bottino 8* ☎ *06/6990878* 🌐 *www.wineacademyroma. com*) is a multifaceted institution that opened in October 2002. It is a place where you can learn about wine through various tastings and classes held throughout the year, almost always given in both Italian and English. It's also home to Il Palazzetto restaurant; the Enoteca wine bar, which has a rooftop area boasting an amazing view of the city; and a handful of elegant hotel rooms. In order to attend the tastings or classes (each carry their own cost), you must also sign up for an annual membership fee, but for only €20, this is one of the better epicurean deals in the city. Think of it as an oenological investment.

	WHO'S FREQUENTED	WHY IT'S HOT
Dal Bolognese, Piazza del Popolo 1	Film industry insiders like Martin Scorsese, Gwyneth Paltrow, and Cate Blanchett, along with fashion luminaries like Valentino Garavani.	Hearty food and elegant setting take backseat to ambience. Tables are perfectly spaced for passing head shots and air kisses.
Nino, Via Borgognona 11	Tom Cruise and Katie Holmes hosted their prenuptial feast for friends and guests like Jim Carrey, Posh and Becks, and Brooke Shields.	"Old-school" waiters in tuxedos and perfect location among the offices of fashion houses and print media make it a shoo-in for the business lunch crowd.
Bar Stravinjsky, Hotel de Russie, *Via del Babuino 9*	Cast of Oceans Twelve, including George Clooney, Brad Pitt, Julia Roberts, and Catherine Zeta-Jones and hubby Michael Douglas; and Leo DiCaprio.	Great service, bartenders who mix a mean cocktail, and the beautiful outdoor *giardino dell'arancio* (patio filled with orange trees) makes this a great place to people-watch.

VATICAN, BORGO, AND PRATI

The Vatican is the heart of ecclesiastical Rome, and this part of the city has a more serious, less chaotic feel to it.

The massive and awe-striking St. Peter's Basilica dominates the landscape; the streets are teeming with clergy; and despite herds of tourists, it's somehow less chaotic, better organized, and maybe even a little more civilized than classical Rome.

Outside of the Vatican walls lies the little 'burb of Borgo, a quieter neighborhood buzzing with typical Roman life, and home to some genuinely good restaurants off the usual tourist-radar.

Prati is a little farther up the river, and known as something of a retail shopping heaven for both Romans and foreign visitors—clothes, handbags, shoes, perfume, makeup, and more. Prati is also known—especially among Romans—for its dining scene, so don't omit it from your itinerary, just because you've never heard anything about it.

FOODIE FINDS

Via Cola di Rienzo is home to two of Rome's best specialty shops: **Franchi** (✉ *Via Cola di Rienzo 204, Prati* ☎ *06/6874651*), a gastroshop that sells high-quality cured meats, Italian cheeses, wines, pastas, and fresh truffles, and next door, **Castroni** (✉ *Via Cola di Rienzo 196/198, Prati* ☎ *06/6874383* ✛ *1:D2*), well-known among expats for its imported foreign foods from the U.S., Great Britain, Japan, India, and Mexico, as well as its impressive selection of candies, preserves, olive oils, and balsamic vinegars.

TRADITIONAL FARE WITH FLAIR

Many tourists think the area around the Vatican is rip-off central when it comes to drinking and dining. Despite the overwhelming number of tourist trap-ttorias, the Borgo and Prati are home to many restaurants revered by Romans in the zona and beyond.

Girarrosto (✉ *Via Germanico 56, Prati* ☎ *06/39725717* ✛ *1:C2*): The Tuscan region is known for its generous cuts of quality meat, and this Prati restaurant is renowned for grilling up the best Tuscan beef in Rome. Treat yourself to the *Fiorentina* steak.

Velando (✉ *Borgo Vittorio 26, Borgo* ☎ *06/68809955* ✛ *1:C2*): Departing from the usual Roman fare, the owners of this restaurant serve up traditional dishes from their hometown of Val Camonica in northern Italy. Try the *pizzocheri*, a buckwheat ribbon pasta—you likely won't find it anywhere else in Rome.

Settembrini (✉ *Via Luigi Settembrini 25, Prati* ☎ *06/3232617* ✛ *1:D1*): Chef Mark Poddi uses Moroccan inspiration to give Italian cuisine a new taste. Try his couscous and tajine, his fresh and affordable Friday fish menu, or the plentiful *aperitivo*, snacks served with an early evening cocktail.

THE SECRET'S IN THE SAUCE

What may appear to the naked eye of a non-Italian as plain, old spaghetti with red sauce, is actually pasta *all'amatriciana* or *matriciana*—a more sophisticated dish with a complexity of flavor owing to an important ingredient: *guanciale*. The English translation—fat of cured pig's cheek—is unappetizing, but once you taste a guanciale-flavored sauce, you'll understand why Romans swear by it. You'll find it at virtually every trattoria in Rome, but two of the most savory and delicious versions of it are made in Prati at **Dino & Tony** (✉ *Via Leone IV 60, Prati* ☎ *06/39733284* ✛ *1:B1*) and the 100-year-old **Il Matriciano** (✉ *Via dei Gracci 55, Prati* ☎ *06/3213040* ✛ *1:D2*), whose signature dish is—you guessed it—the classic Matriciana.

ARTIGIANALE

The artisanal food movement, which focuses on craftsmanship and often emphasizes local products, has made its way to Rome, and many Roman specialists are in and around Prati. Pizza expert Gabriele Bonci has breathed new life into the same-old storefront *pizzeria al taglio* (by-the-slice pizza joint) at **Pizzarium** (✉ *3 Via della Meloria* ☎ *06/39745416* ✛ *1:A2*). Bonci collects yeast from centuries-old sourdough starters from southern Italian villages, and has his flour stone ground by a specialist in Piemonte. The dough is thicker than that of traditional Roman slices, but this Roman rebel thinks the proof is in … well, the pizza. **Gelateria dei Gracchi** (✉ *272 Via dei Gracchi* ☎ *06/3216668* ✛ *1:E1*) is a favorite among Roman foodies. Try the pistachio gelato, which uses Sicilian *pistacchi Bronte* from Mt. Etna. Seasonal flavors also abound, like wild strawberry in late spring, when the nearby hillside town of Nemi is awash in berry-red.

TRASTEVERE AND GIANICOLO

The new Trastevere is awash in fantastic foodie haunts. After a long lunch, work off the calories by hiking up Gianicolo hill for the most breathtaking views of the city.

Trastevere is a neighborhood that has always been known for its "otherness," but it has undergone a transformation in recent years, trading in its old-school bohemian roots for something much trendier and more upscale. The maze of cobbled streets on the other side of the Tiber that was once home to working-class people, artists, and foreigners has skyrocketed in price and is now lined with so many trattorias and wine bars that it's starting to feel a bit like a Roman gastro-theme park.

While the explosion of hip new places to wine and dine may have had some negative effects on this old village, Trastevere's gritty charm still prevails. The Gianicolo is more subdued, but some of the restaurants at the top are definitely worth hiking all the way up the hill for (of course, you can also go easy on yourself and take a cab or bus).

PEPPERY PASTA

Cacio e pepe is a simple pasta dish from the *cucina povera*, or rustic cooking, tradition. It's also a favorite Roman primo, usually made with tagliatelle (a long, flat noodle), *tonnarelli* (a narrower squarish noodle), or spaghetti, which is then coated with pecorino cheese and a generous amount of freshly ground black pepper. **Roma Sparita** (⊠ *Piazza Santa Cecilia 24* ☎ *06/5800757* ⊹ *3:C2*), on the quiet side of Trastevere beyond Viale di Trastevere, makes one of the city's best cacio e pepes, and they serve it in an edible bowl of paper-thin, baked cheese. Mamma mia!

12

SMILE AND SAY "FORMAGGIO": THE BEST CHEESES IN ROME

The "trinity" of cheeses most used in *cucina romana* are mozzarella, ricotta, and pecorino romano. Here's why these varieties can make or break a true Roman dish.

MOZZARELLA

True *mozzarella di bufala*, made from water buffalo milk, comes from the Campania area, between Rome and Naples. You'll know it by its distinctive flavor and its soft consistency. Reverential treatment is given to fresh mozzarella in its many forms at Ōbikā (⊠ *Piazza di Firenze at Via dei Prefetti, Pantheon* ☎ *06/6832630*), which is basically a mozzarella bar based on the sushi bar format. Compare and contrast different mozzarella types from different areas paired with delicious accompanying *salumi* (cured meats) and salads.

RICOTTA

This versatile fresh cheese is used in both sweet and savory dishes. As a savory ingredient, it's used as a filling in ravioli and stuffed pastas and as an accompaniment to various vegetable dishes. The taste varies depending upon the kind of milk it's made from. The famed ricotta cheesecake puts Rome's love of ricotta on the dessert table, and the cheese is even sometimes served with little tampering—a touch of golden honey or some fresh Roman *mentuccia,* wild Roman mint.

PECORINO ROMANO

A *pecora* is a sheep, so technically any cheese made from sheep's milk is a pecorino cheese, and most other regions have their own version of a local pecorino. But *pecorino romano*, the hard, aged cheese grated over Roman pasta dishes, is perhaps the most famous of all pecorinos. With a telltale black rind and pale color, it can be found in most food shops in the city. Some say this most Roman of cheeses is much like the Romans themselves: sharp and salty. But it marries beautifully with the gutsy flavors it's often paired with.

BOHEMIAN RHAPSODY

Trastevere has always been a bohemian bastion, densely packed with inexpensive Roman pizzerias, trattorias, and countless bars filled with artists and local characters. **Bar San Calisto** (⊠ *Piazza di San Calisto 3* ☎ *06/5835869* ✛ *3:B1*) is the classic bohemian Trastevere bar. The drinks are cheap, the tables difficult to snag, and the piazza in front, swollen with local pierced and tattooed fringe types. Surprisingly, the hot chocolate and chocolate gelato here are some of the best in the city. The owners of **Freni e Frizioni** (⊠ *Via del Politeama 4* ☎ *06/58334210* ⊕ *www. freniefrizioni.com* ✛ *3:B1*) know how to capture a bohemian crowd. The aperitivo here is abuzz most nights of the week, with free nibbles to accompany the mojitos and negronis. The locale's grit remains despite the shabby-chic interior: the space is a converted auto garage.

COLOSSEO, AVENTINO, AND TESTACCIO

These neighborhoods are considered the archaeological and the working-class centers of the city, where dining among the ruins takes on a whole new meaning.

Perhaps the most iconic image of Rome since ancient times has been the Colosseum. It's most charming, however, not with gladiator-actors posing for photos out front by day, but by night—as a backdrop for drinking and dining in the city. A plate of pasta at **Ai Tre Scalini** (⊠ *Via SS. Quattro Coronati 30* ☎ *06/7096309*), just steps from the Colosseum, or a glass of wine and some nibbles at **Cavour 313** (⊠ *Via Cavour 313* ☎ *06/67855496*), will make you feel unabashedly Roman. For a special Roman evening, head to **San Teodoro** (⊠ *Via dei Fienili 50* ☎ *06/6780933*), where the food is delicious, and descending from the piazza after dinner, one practically stumbles upon the back side of the Roman Forum and Campidoglio.

If you go to the Testaccio neighborhood in the south of the city, dine at **Checchino dal 1887** (⊠ *Via di Monte Testaccio 30* ☎ *06/5746318*). It's an only-in-Rome experience, as the restaurant is carved out of Monte Testaccio, a mountain composed of strata of shards of ancient Roman ceramics.

TAKING HOME A TASTE OF ROME

Volpetti (⊠ *Via Marmorata 153* ☎ *06/5742352* ✛ *3:D4*) is probably Rome's most famous and best-loved *alimentari*, or specialty foods shop. Located on an old passageway between the Tiber River and the Testaccio neighborhood, this shop is a family affair. Its jocular owners are highly knowledgeable about their products. They give samples of everything, and will tell you why Sicilian cow's milk cheese is square (so it didn't roll when being shipped to the mainland), why aged balsamic vinegar is so delicious, and what makes some chocolates better quality than others. They'll even vacuum-pack and wrap everything you purchase.

12

THE ANCIENT QUARTIERE AND ITS CUISINE

Testaccio, the neighborhood at the southernmost tip of the city, is the place to go for old Roman cuisine. You'll need to take a cab to this out-of-the-way spot, which once was a center of ancient trade along the Tiber River. It is considered one of the most authentically Roman *zonas*—the "Romani di Roma" (real Romans) hail from this part of town; to wit, the AS Roma soccer team was founded right in this neighborhood.

Head first to Piazza Testaccio to experience an authentic farmers' market, the Mercato di Testaccio, where Italian housewives haggle over the price of vegetables and butchers cut meat to order. Appropriately enough, this area once was a major butchering center: the old slaughterhouse nearby has been converted and now houses modern art galleries and live music venues.

In keeping with that tradition, Testaccio is the birthplace of some of the most famous—and infamous—dishes in the *cucina romana* repertoire, those of the *quinto quarto*, or "fifth quarter." This is comprised of offal and throwaway parts that remained after the butchers had sold the choice parts to paying customers.

In Testaccio restaurants, you'll find dishes like *coda alla vaccinara*: a sweet-and-sour stew made of oxtail with tomatoes and celery, and seasoned with garlic, pancetta, and a touch of cocoa. The stew is typically cooked a day or two in advance before being served, so the flavors can marry. Another favorite is *rigatoni alla pajata*: pasta with baby lamb or calf intestines that still hold the mother's milk. Cooking the intestines coagulates the milk, creating creamy cheese curds, which are then stewed in tomato sauce, *as in the photo below from Checchino dal 1887*. Other common dishes are *coratella*, a mix of lamb innards including heart, with artichokes; and *trippa alla romana*, tripe stewed in a savory tomato sauce.

Just a note: Most of these dishes are rarely translated properly on English menus, so forewarned is forearmed.

SUSHI SPOTS

The area in and around Testaccio boasts some particularly popular places for dining with chopsticks and here are just a few of our favorites: **Sushisen** (✉ *Via Giuseppe Giuietti 21* ☎ *06/5756945* ✛ *3:D5*) is an authentic Japanese eatery featuring freshly prepared sushi. In the dining room, a conveyor belt carries Asian goodies like tempura shrimp and panko-breaded chicken with a sweet-spicy dipping sauce. **Bishoku Kobo** (✉ *Via Ostiense 110b* ☎ *06/5744190* ✛ *3:D6*) is a local favorite, which means it's always crowded. Be prepared to wait if you haven't made a reservation. Sushi "boats" and noodle dishes are on offer. Trendy **Ketumbar** (✉ *Via Galvani 24* ☎ *06/57305338* ✛ *3:C5*) is many things: bar, restaurant (serving both Italian fare and sushi), and club after dinner hours. Built into Monte Testaccio, the setting is breathtaking.

RESTAURANT REVIEWS

Listed alphabetically within neighborhoods.

PANTHEON, NAVONA, TREVI, AND QUIRINALE

PANTHEON

$ | WINE BAR | ✕**Enoteca Corsi.** Very convenient to the historic center for lunch or an afternoon break, this little hole-in-the-wall looks like it missed the revolution; prices and decor are *come una volta* (like once upon a time) when the shop sold—as the sign says—wine and oil. The genuinely dated feel of the place has its charm: you can still get wine here by the liter, or choose from a good variety of fairly priced alternatives in bottles. The place is packed at lunch, when a few specials—classic pastas and some second dishes like veal roast with peas—are offered. ⊠ *Via del Gesù 88, Pantheon* ☏ *06/6790821* ▭ *AE, DC, MC, V* ⊙ *Closed Sun. No dinner* ✛ *4:F4.*

$$$ | MODERN ITALIAN | ✕**Il Bacaro.** With a handful of choice tables set outside against an ivy-draped wall, this tiny candlelit spot not far from the Pantheon makes for an ideal evening, equally suited for a romantic twosome or close friends and convivial conversation. Pastas—like *orecchiette* (little ear-shaped pasta) with broccoli and sausage, a dish that lip-smacks of Puglia—are star players. As a bonus, the kitchen keeps its clients from picking at each other's plates by offering side dishes of all the pastas ordered among those at the table. The choice main courses are mostly meat—the beef fillet with balsamic vinegar or London broil–style marinated in olive oil and rosemary are winners. ⊠ *Via degli Spagnoli 27, Pantheon* ☏ *06/6872554* ⊕ *www.ilbacaro.com* ◠ *Reservations essential* ▭ *DC, MC, V* ⊙ *Closed Sun. and 1 wk in Aug. No lunch Sat.* ✛ *4:E2.*

$$–$$$ | ROMAN | ✕**Maccheroni.** This boisterous, convivial trattoria north of the Pantheon makes for a fun evening out. The decor is basic: white walls with wooden shelves lined with wine bottles, blocky wooden tables covered in white butcher paper—but there's an "open" kitchen (with even the dishwashers in plain view of the diners) and an airy feel that attracts a young clientele as well as visiting celebrities. The menu sticks to Roman basics such as simple pasta with fresh tomatoes and basil, or rigatoni *alla gricia* (with bacon, sheep's-milk cheese, and black pepper). The specialty pasta, *trofie* (short pasta twists) with a black truffle sauce, inspires you to lick your plate. Probably the best choice on the menu is the *tagliata con rughetta*, a juicy, two-inch-thick steak sliced thinly and served on arugula. ⊠ *Piazza delle Coppelle 44, Pantheon* ☏ *06/68307895* ⊕ *www. ristorantemaccheroni.com* ▭ *AE, MC, V* ✛ *4:E2.*

NAVONA

$ | NORTHERN ITALIAN | ✕**Birreria Peroni.** With its long wooden tables, hard-back booths, and free-flowing beer, this casual restaurant in a palazzo from the 1500s seems to belong more to the genre of Munich beer hall than popular Roman hangout. But let's remember that far to the north of Rome lies a part of Italy in which the people speak as much German as they do Italian, and the simple food seems more *tedesco* than *italiano*. It's from this place that Birreria Peroni draws its inspiration, and the goulash and the many sausage specialties—with sauerkraut and potatoes, of course—certainly provide a nice respite from pasta and tomato sauce. ⊠ *Via di San Marcello 19, Navona* ☎ 06/6795310 ⊕ *www. anticabirreriaperoni.it* ⊟ *AE, DC, MC, V* ⊘ *Closed Sun. and Aug. No lunch Sat.* ✛ *4:G3.*

$ ✕ **Cul de Sac.** This popular wine bar near Piazza Navona is among the city's oldest enoteche and offers a book-length selection of wines from Italy, France, the Americas, and elsewhere. Food is eclectic, ranging from a huge assortment of Italian meats and cheeses (try the delicious *lonza,* cured pork loin, or *speck,* a northern Italian smoked prosciutto) to various Mediterranean dishes, including delicious baba ghanoush, a tasty Greek salad, and a spectacular wild boar pâté. Outside tables get crowded fast, so arrive early, or come late, as they serve until about 1 AM. ⊠ *Piazza Pasquino 73, Piazza Navona* ☎ 06/68801094 ⊟ *AE, MC, V* ⊘ *Closed 2 wks in Aug.* ✛ *4:D3.*

WINE BAR
Fodor's Choice
★

$ ✕ **Da Baffetto.** Down a cobblestone street not far from Piazza Navona, this is Rome's most popular pizzeria and a summer favorite for street-side dining. The plain interior is mostly given over to the ovens, but there's another room with more paper-covered tables. Outdoor tables (enclosed and heated in winter) provide much-needed additional seating. Turnover is fast and lingering is not encouraged. ⊠ *Via del Governo Vecchio 114, Navona* ☎ 06/6861617 ⊟ *No credit cards* ⊘ *Closed Aug. No lunch* ✛ *4:C3.*

PIZZA
Fodor's Choice
★

$$$ ✕ **Etabli.** On a narrow vicolo off beloved Piazza del Fico, this multi-dimensional locale serves as a lounge-bar, and becomes a hot spot by aperitivo hour. Beautifully finished with vaulted wood beam ceilings, wrought-iron touches, plush leather sofas, and chandeliers, it's all modern Italian farmhouse chic. In the restaurant section (the place is sprawling), it's minimalist Provençal hip (*etabli* is French for the regionally typical tables within). And the food is clean and Mediterranean, with touches of Asia in the raw fish appetizers. Pastas are more traditional Italian, and the *secondi* run the gamut from land to sea. Arrive early as the place fills up by dinnertime and it's a popular post-dining spot for sipping and posing. ⊠ *Vicolo delle Vacche 9/a, Navona* ☎ 06/6871499 ⊕ *www.etabli.it* ⊟ *MC, V* ⊘ *Closed Sun. in summer, Mon. in winter* ✛ *4:C2.*

MEDITERRANEAN
Fodor's Choice
★

$$$$ ✕ **Il Convivio.** In a tiny, nondescript vicolo north of Piazza Navona, the three Troiani brothers—Angelo in the kitchen, and brothers Giuseppe and Massimo presiding over the dining room and wine cellar—have quietly been redefining the experience of Italian eclectic *alta cucina* for many years. Antipasti include a "roast beef" of tuna fillet lacquered with chestnut honey, rosemary, red peppercorns, and ginger served with

MODERN ITALIAN
Fodor's Choice
★

12

a green apple salad, while a squid ink risotto with baby cuttlefish, sea asparagus, lemongrass, and basil sates the appetites of those with dreams of *fantasia*. Main courses include a fabulous version of a cold-weather pigeon dish for which Il Convivio is famous. Service is attentive without being overbearing, and the wine list is exceptional. It is definitely a splurge spot. ⊠ *Vicolo dei Soldati 31, Navona* 🕾 *06/6869432* ⌲ *Reservations essential* ⊟ *AE, DC, MC, V* ⊙ *Closed Sun., 1 wk in Jan., and 2 wks in Aug. No lunch* ✛ *4:D1*.

$ ✕ **La Montecarlo.** Run by the niece of the owner of the pizzeria Da Baf-
PIZZA fetto, La Montecarlo has a similar menu and is almost as popular as
ℭ its relative around the corner. Pizzas are super-thin and a little burned around the edges—the sign of a good wood-burning oven. It's one of few pizzerias open for both lunch and dinner. ⊠ *Vicolo Savelli 13, Navona* 🕾 *06/6861877* ⊟ *No credit cards* ⊙ *Closed 2 wks in mid-Aug. and Mon. Nov.–Apr.* ✛ *4:C3*.

$$$$ ✕ **La Rosetta.** Chef-owner Massimo Riccioli took the nets and fishing
SEAFOOD gear off the walls of his parents' trattoria to create what is widely known as *the* place to go in Rome for first-rate seafood. But beware: the staff may be friendly and the fish may be of high quality, but the preparation is generally very simple, and the prices can be numbingly high. Start with the justifiably well-known selection of marinated seafood appetizers, like carpaccios of fresh, translucent fish drizzled with olive oil and perhaps a fresh herb. Pastas tend to mix shellfish, usually with a touch of oil, white wine, and lemon. Simple dishes such as the classic *zuppa di pesce* (fish soup) deserve star billing under the title of secondi—and command star prices. ⊠ *Via della Rosetta 9, Navona* 🕾 *06/6861002* ⊕ *www.larosetta.com* ⌲ *Reservations essential* ⊟ *AE, DC, MC, V* ⊙ *Closed Sun. and 3 wks in Aug.* ✛ *4:E2*.

$$$ ✕ **Ōbikā.** If you've ever wanted to take in a "mozzarella bar," here's
ITALIAN your chance. Mozzarella is featured here much like sushi bars show-case fresh fish—even the decor is modern Japanese minimalism–meets–ancient Roman grandeur. The cheese, in all its varieties, is the focus of the dishes: there's the familiar cow's milk, the delectable water buffalo milk varieties from the Campania region, and the sinfully rich *burrata* from Puglia (a fresh cow's milk mozzarella encasing a creamy center of unspun mozzarella curds and fresh cream). They're all served with various accompanying cured meats, vegetables, sauces, and breads. An outdoor deck is a great spot for dining alfresco. Also visit the new, super-central smaller location in Campo de'Fiori. The concept has been such a success that other locations recently opened in Florence and midtown Manhattan. ⊠ *Piazza di Firenze 26, Navona* ⊕ *www.obika.it* 🕾 *06/6832630* ⊟ *AE, DC, MC, V* ✛ *4:E1*.

$$$ ✕ **Osteria dell'Ingegno.** This casual, yet trendy place is a great spot to
MODERN ITALIAN enjoy a glass of wine or a gourmet meal in the city center. The cheery,
Fodor's Choice modern interior decor—walls made vibrant with modern paintings by
★ local artists and lots of colorful glass bottles—and hip young waiters will bring you back to the present day. So, too, will the simple but innovative menu, including dishes like the panzanella salad, the beef tagliata with red wine reduction and potato tortino, and the perfectly cooked duck breast with a seasonal fruit sauce. If ever there was a

place to linger outdoors over limoncello, this is it. ✉ *Piazza di Pietra 45, Pantheon* ☎ *06/6780662* ▭ *AE, DC, MC, V* ☉ *Closed Sun. and 2 wks in Aug.* ✥ *4:F2.*

QUIRINALE

$$$–$$$$

TUSCAN

✕ **Tullio.** Just off Piazza Barberini sits this Tuscan-accented upscale trattoria. The decor is basic wood paneling and white linens, with the requisite older—and often grumpy—waiters. The menu is heavy on Tuscan classics such as white beans and the famed *bistecca alla fiorentina*, a carnivore's dream. Meat dishes other than beef, such as lamb and veal, are also dependably good. The homemade pappardelle *al cinghiale* (wide, flat noodles in a tomato and wild boar sauce) are delectable. A few key Roman dishes and greens are offered, like *brocoletti*, sautéed to perfection with garlic and olive oil. The wine list favors robust Tuscan reds and thick wallets. ✉ *Via San Nicola da Tolentino, near Piazza Barberini, Quirinale* ☎ *06/4745560* ⊕ *www.tullioristorante.it* ▭ *AE, DC, MC, V* ☉ *Closed Sun. and Aug.* ✥ *2:C3.*

CAMPO DE' FIORE AND GHETTO

CAMPO DE' FIORI

$$

PIZZA

✕ **Acchiappafantasmi.** This popular pizzeria near Campo de' Fiori offers pizza—and much more. In addition to the traditional margherita and capricciosa, you'll find a spicy pizza with chili peppers and hot salami, and their prizewinning version with buffalo mozzarella and cherry tomatoes, shaped like a ghost (a theme throughout, hence the name, which means "Ghostbusters"). Appetizers are just as delicious—as well as the traditional fried goodies. The menu includes a variety of items not standard to pizzerias, such as a version of eggplant parmesan with prosciutto and egg, and tongue-tingling spicy specialties. And true to the owners' Calabrian roots, they offer spicy homemade *'nduja*, a spreadable sausage comprised of pork and chili pepper at a ratio of 50-50—not for the weak of constitution! ✉ *Via dei Cappellari 66, Campo de' Fiori* ☎ *06/6873462* ⊕ *www.acchiappafantasmi.it* ▭ *AE, DC, MC, V* ☉ *Closed Mon. and 1 wk in Aug.* ✥ *4:C3.*

$$$–$$$$

MODERN ITALIAN

✕ **Boccondivino.** The four pillars around which the structure is built are ancient Roman, but when you walk through the 16th-century door, it's clear that Boccondivino ("divine mouthful") is all about the here-and-now, with the animal-print chairs and glass-fronted dining room. The outdoor seating in the intimate piazzetta out front is a great summer spot. This is also the perfect place for a dinner date. Start, perhaps, with a citrus-marinated salmon served with peppery Roman arugula, then move on to (or split) the delicious angler fish ravioli made elegant by a *salsa di fiori di zucca* (pumpkin flower sauce). Then go for a secondo—like a turbot with cherry tomatoes and potatoes. ✉ *Piazza Campo Marzio 6, Campo de' Fiori* ☎ *06/68308626* ⊕ *www.boccondivino.it* ▭ *AE, DC, MC, V* ☉ *Closed Sun. and 3 wks in Aug.* ✥ *4:E2.*

$$

ITALIAN

✕ **Brasia.** This spacious trattoria on a back street off the Campo de' Fiori is a welcome, inexpensive addition to an area filled with tourist-riddled pizzerias and overpriced restaurants. The place itself is a huge

Gelaterie

For many travelers, the first taste of *gelato*—Italian ice cream—is one of the most memorable moments of their Italian trip. Almost a cross between regular American ice cream and soft serve, gelato's texture is lighter and fluffier than hard ice cream because of the process by which it's whipped when freezing. Along with the listings here, you can find a number of gelaterias in Via di Tor Millina, a street off the west side of Piazza Navona, where there are also a couple of good places for frozen yogurt and delicious *frullati*—shakes made with milk, crushed ice, and fruit of your choosing.

Il Gelato di San Crispino (⊠ *Via della Panetteria 54, Piazza di Trevi* ☎ *06/6793924* ⊗ *Closed Tues.* ✛ *4:H2*) makes perhaps the most celebrated gelato in all of Italy, without artificial colors or flavors. It's worth crossing town for—nobody else creates flavors this pure. To preserve the "integrity" of the flavor, the ice cream is only served in paper cups. For years **Giolitti** (⊠ *Via degli Uffici del Vicario 40, Pantheon* ☎ *06/6991243* ✛ *4:F2*) was considered the best gelateria in Rome, and it's still worth a stop if you're near the Pantheon. **Della Palma** (⊠ *Via della Maddalena 20/23, Pantheon* ☎ *06/68806752* ✛ *4:E2*) is close to the Pantheon on a street just north of the Piazza della Rotonda. It serves 100 flavors of gelato, and

for sheer gaudy display and range of choice it's a must. Immediately beside the Pantheon is **Cremeria Monteforte** (⊠ *Via della Rotonda 22, Pantheon* ☎ *06/6867720* ✛ *4:E2*), which has won several awards for its flavors. Also worth trying is its chocolate sorbetto—it's an icier version of the gelato without the dairy. **Fiocco di Neve** (⊠ *Via del Pantheon 51, Pantheon* ☎ *No phone* ✛ *4:F2*) has excellent *granita di caffè* (coffee ice slush) as well as gelato. The chocolate chip and After Eight (mint chocolate chip) flavors are delicious. **Gelateria alla Scala** (⊠ *Via della Scala 51, Trastevere* ☎ *06/5813174* ⊗ *Closed Dec. and Jan.* ✛ *3:B1*) is a tiny place, but don't let the size fool you. It does a good business offering artisanal gelato prepared in small batches, so when one flavor runs out on any given day, it's finished. **Cremeria Ottaviani** (⊠ *Via Leone IV 83/85, Vatican* ☎ *06/37514774* ⊗ *Closed Wed.* ✛ *1:C2*) is an old-fashioned gelateria with an excellent granita di caffè. On Prati's main shopping street, **Pellacchia** (⊠ *Via Cola di Rienzo 3–5, Prati* ☎ *06/3210807* ⊗ *Closed Mon.* ✛ *1:E2*) is a classic *artigianale* (homemade) ice-cream parlor that has been going since the 1920s. **Al Settimo Gelo** (⊠ *Via Vodice 21/a, Prati* ☎ *06/3725567* ✛ *1:A1*), in Prati, has been getting rave reviews for both classic flavors and newfangled inventions such as cardamom and chestnut.

space, but remains cozy because of brick walls and arched ceilings (the space actually harks back to the 17th century, and the name of the street it's on means "street of caves"). There's a wood-burning oven for homemade pizzas, and grilled meats are the other house specialty; here less expensive than in most spots. All typical Roman menu staples are found here as well: bruschette, mixed salumi and antipasti, and a variety of pasta standards. ⊠ *Vicolo delle Grotte 17, Campo de' Fiori* ☎ *06/97277119* ✛ *4:D5*.

12

$$–$$$
ROMAN

✗ **Da Sergio.** Every neighborhood has at least one "old-school" Roman trattoria and, for the Campo de' Fiori area, Da Sergio is it. Once you're seated (there's usually a wait), the red-and-white-check paper table-covering, bright lights, '50s kitsch, and the stuffed boar's head on the wall remind you that you're smack in the middle of the genuine article. Go for the delicious version of pasta *all'amatriciana*, or the generous helping of gnocchi with a tomato sauce and lots of Parmesan cheese, served, as tradition dictates, on Thursday. ⊠ *Vicolo delle Grotte 27* ☎ *06/6864293* ▭ *DC, MC, V* ⊘ *Closed Sun. and 2 wks in Aug.* ✛ *4:D5.*

$$$
ITALIAN

✗ **Ditirambo.** Don't let the country-kitchen ambience fool you. At this little spot off Campo de' Fiori, the constantly changing selection of offbeat takes on Italian classics is a step beyond ordinary Roman fare. The place is usually packed with diners who appreciate the adventuresome kitchen, though you may overhear complaints about the brusque service. Antipasti can be delicious and unexpected, like Gorgonzola-pear soufflé drizzled with aged balsamic vinegar, or a mille-feuille of eggplant, wild fennel, and anchovies. But people really love this place for rustic dishes like osso buco, Calabrian eggplant "meatballs," and hearty pasta with rabbit ragù. Vegetarians will adore the cheesy potato gratin with truffle shavings. Desserts can be skipped in favor of a *digestivo.* ⊠ *Piazza della Cancelleria 74, Campo de' Fiori* ☎ *06/6871626* ⊕ *www.ristoranteditirambo.it* ▭ *AE, MC, V* ⊘ *Closed Aug. No lunch Mon.* ✛ *4:D4.*

¢
ITALIAN
Fodor's Choice
★

✗ **Dar Filettaro a Santa Barbara (Filetti di Baccalà).** For years, Filetti di Baccalà has been serving just that—battered, deep-fried fillets of salt cod—and not much else. You'll find no-frills starters such as *bruschette al pomodoro* (garlic-rubbed toast topped with fresh tomatoes and olive oil), sautéed zucchini, and, in winter months, the cod is served alongside *puntarelle*, chicory stems topped with a delicious anchovy-garlic-lemon vinaigrette. The location, down the street from Campo de' Fiori in a little piazza in front of the beautiful Santa Barbara church, begs you to eat at one of the outdoor tables, weather permitting. Long operating hours allow those still on U.S. time to eat as early (how gauche!) as 6 PM. ⊠ *Largo dei Librari 88, Campo de' Fiori* ☎ *06/6864018* ▭ *No credit cards* ⊘ *Closed Sun. and Aug. No lunch* ✛ *4:D5.*

$$
SOUTHERN
ITALIAN

✗ **La Locanda del Pellegrino.** This sunny trattoria on a main artery leading into Campo de' Fiori is a welcome, affordable spot with some unusual offerings. The traditional Roman pasta dishes are there to satisfy local traditionalists, but the owner's Calabrian roots come through in the many dishes featuring 'nduja, a spicy spreadable sausage. Calabrian prosciutto, cheeses, honeys, and a variety of *piatti piccanti* (spicy dishes) reflect the importance of the Southern Italian region's love for pepperoncino, while the gelato from Pizzo Calabro—considered by some to be Italy's ice cream mecca—cools down the palate. ⊠ *Via del Pellegrino 107, Campo de' Fiori* ☎ *06/6872776* ⊘ *Closed Mon.* ✛ *4:C3.*

$
WINE BAR

✗ **L'Angolo Divino.** There's something about this cozy wine bar that feels as if it's in a small university town instead of a bustling metropolis. Serene blue-green walls lined with wood shelves of wines from around the Italian peninsula add to the warm atmosphere. Smoked fish, cured meats, cheeses, and salads make a nice lunch or light dinner, and the kitchen stays open until the wee hours. Ask about tasting evenings dedicated to single grape varieties or regions. ⊠ *Via dei Balestrari 12, Campo de' Fiori* ☎ *06/6864413* ▬ *MC, V* ☺ *Closed 1 wk in Aug. No dinner Mon.* ⊹ *4:C5.*

$$$
SEAFOOD
✕ **Monserrato.** In a high-rent area dense with design stores, antiques shops, and jewelers, this simple spot is just a few steps from elegant Piazza Farnese and yet happily devoid of throngs of tourists. Monserrato's signature dishes are its fish specials: carpaccio *di pesce* (fresh fish carpaccio, served with lemon and arugula), *insalatina di seppie* (cuttlefish salad), *bigoli con gamberi e asparagi* (homemade pasta with shrimp and asparagus), and grilled fish that are simple but very satisfying. There's also a nice antipasto assortment so you can eat your share of veggies as well. Select a nice white from the Italo-centric wine list and when the weather heats up, you can enjoy it all with a breeze at umbrella-covered tables on the small, adjacent piazza. ⊠ *Via di Monserrato 96, Campo de' Fiori* ☎ *06/6873386* ▬ *AE, DC, MC, V* ☺ *Closed Mon., 1 wk at Christmas* ⊹ *4:C4.*

$$$–$$$$
WINE BAR
✕ **Roscioli.** This food shop and wine bar is dark and decadent, more like a Caravaggio painting than a place of business. The shop in front beckons with top-quality comestibles: wild Alaskan smoked salmon, more than 300 cheeses, and a dizzying array of wines. Venture farther inside to be seated in a wine cavelike room where you'll be served artisanal cheeses and salumi, as well as an extensive selection of unusual menu choices and interesting takes on classics. Try the caprese salad with DOC buffalo milk mozzarella, fresh and roasted tomatoes with bread crumbs and pistachios, or go for pasta with *bottarga* (dried mullet roe). The menu is further divided among meats, seafood (including a nice selection of tartars and other *crudi* (raw fish preparations), and vegetarian-friendly items. ■TIP➔ Book ahead to reserve a table in the cozy wine cellar beneath the dining room. And afterward head around the corner to their bakery for rightfully famous breads and sweets. ⊠ *Via dei Giubbonari 21/22, Campo de' Fiori* ☎ *06/6875287* ⊕ ▬ *AE, DC, MC, V* ☺ *Closed Sun.* ⊹ *4:D4.*

$$
ITALIAN
✕ **Trattoria Moderna.** The space is as the name implies—modern, with high ceilings, and done in shades of beige and gray—and an oversize chalkboard displays daily specials, such as a delicious chickpea and *baccalà* (salt cod) soup. The food runs toward the traditional but with a twist, like a pasta *all'amatriciana* with kosher beef instead of the requisite *guanciale* (cured pork jowl). Main courses are more creative, as well as more hit-or-miss. The jumbo shrimp in a cognac sauce with couscous was tasty, but the scant four shrimp a drawback. The trattoria gets an "A" for effort, with its friendly serving staff and very reasonable prices, and an extra bonus is the outdoor seating—a few tables surrounded by greenery, off the lovely cobblestone street. ⊠ *Vicolo dei Chiodaroli 16, Campo de' Fiori* ☎ *06/68803423* ▬ *AE, DC, MC, V* ⊹ *4:E4.*

GHETTO

$$$$
ROMAN
✕ **Al Pompiere.** The entrance on a narrow side street leads you up a charming staircase and into the main dining room of this neighborhood favorite. Its Roman Jewish dishes, such as fried zucchini flowers,

battered salt cod, and gnocchi, are all consistently good and served without fanfare on white dishes with a simple border. There are also some nice, historic touches like a beef-and-citron stew that comes from an ancient Roman recipe of Apicius. And if you come across the traditional Roman *porchetta* (roasted suckling pig) special, make sure to order it before it runs out—

12

it is truly divine. In 2004, there was a terrible fire in a shop below the restaurant, but the kitchen was soon back in business, though the irony here is as thick as the chef's tomato sauce: *Al Pompiere* means "the fireman." ⊠ *Via Santa Maria dei Calderari 38, Ghetto* ☎ *06/6868377* ⊟ *AE, MC, V* ⊗ *Closed Sun. and Aug.* ✛ *4:E5.*

$$$
JEWISH
✕ **Ba' Ghetto.** This new hot spot is a welcome addition to the main drag in the Jewish ghetto. The kitchen is kosher (many places featuring Roman Jewish fare are not), and not only do they feature an assortment of Roman Jewish dishes, they also offer a variety of Mediterranean-middle eastern Jewish fare. Enjoy starters like phyllo "cigars" stuffed with ground meat and spices, or the brik—egg and tomato wrapped in phyllo traiangles and briefly fried. There's a nice assortment of pasta dishes, but we advise going for main plates like the assortment of couscous dishes (the spicy seafood is delicious), or baccalà with raisins and pinenuts. Interesting sides like chicory with *bottarga* (cured mullet roe) round out the meal. Kosher wines are on offer as well. Beware the strictly adhered-to hours: Saturday night, the restaurant posts post-Sabbath/sundown opening times to the minute on a blackboard out front. ⊠ *Via del Portico d'Ottavia 57, Ghetto* ☎ *06/68892868* ⊕ *www.kosherinrome.com* ⊟ *AE, MC, V* ⊗ *No dinner Fri. No lunch Sat.* ✛ *4:F5.*

$$$$
SEAFOOD
Fodor's Choice
★
✕ **Il Sanlorenzo.** This revamped, gorgeous space—think chandeliers and soaring original brickwork ceilings—houses one of the better seafood spots in the eternal city. Tempting tasting menus are on offer, as well as à la carte items like a wonderful series of small plates in their *crudo* (raw fish) appetizer, which can include a perfectly seasoned fish tartare trio, sweet *scampi* (local langoustines), and a wispy-thin carpaccio of red shrimp. The restaurant's version of spaghetti with lobster is an exquisite example of how this dish should look and taste (the secret is cooking the pasta in a lobster stock!). Try a main course of a freshly caught seasonal fish prepared to order. Menu items often change based on the chef's whim and the catch of the day. A subterranean lounge and wine room offer refuge for those who seek private dining. ⊠ *Via dei Chiavari 4/5, Campo de' Fiori* ☎ *06/6865097* ⊕ *www.ilsanlorenzo. it* ⊟ *AE, DC, MC, V* ⊗ *No lunch Sat.–Mon.* ✛ *4:D4.*

$$
ITALIAN
✕ **Osteria della Quercia.** The beautiful Piazza della Quercia, was once devoid of any restaurants up until this casual trattoria opened its doors. Now diners can sit under the gorgeous looming oak tree that lends the square its name. Its menu is simple—the usual suspects include fried starters like stuffed zucchini flowers and baccalà, as well as Roman

pasta dishes like spaghetti carbonara and *amatriciana*. Main dishes include baby lamb chops, *involtini* (thinly sliced beef stuffed with herbs and bread crumbs, that is rolled and baked), and meatballs in tomato sauce. The ubiquitous Roman sautéed *cicoria* (chicory) with olive oil and chili pepper is a good choice for a green side. Service is friendly and allows for lingering on balmy Roman afternoons and evenings—so close, and yet so seemingly far from the chaos of nearby Campo de'Fiori. ⊠ *Piazza dela Quercia 23, Campo de'Fiori* ☎ *06/68300932* ▭ *AE, DC, MC, V* ✚ *4:C4.*

$$$$ ✗ **Piperno.** *The* place to go for Rome's extraordinary *carciofi alla giudia*
ROMAN   (fried whole artichokes), Piperno has been in business for more than a century. The location, up a tiny hill in a piazza tucked away behind the palazzi of the Jewish Ghetto, lends the restaurant a rarefied air. It's a popular location for Sunday brunch. Try the exquisite prosciutto and mozzarella di bufala plate, the *fiori di zucca ripieni e fritti* (fried stuffed zucchini flowers), and *filetti di baccalà* (fillet of cod) to start. The display of fresh local fish is enticing enough to lure diners to try offerings from sea instead of land. Service is in the old school style of dignified formality. ⊠ *Monte dei Cenci 9, Ghetto* ☎ *06/68806629* ⊕ *www.ristorantepiperno.it* ▭ *DC, MC, V* ☾ *Closed Mon. and Aug. No dinner Sun.* ✚ *4:E5.*

$$$$ ✗ **San Teodoro.** The atmosphere: far removed from the madding crowds.
SEAFOOD   The setting: a pair of enclosed piazzas, walls covered in ivy, nestled by the Roman Forum and the Campidoglio. The specialty: refined Roman cuisine, featuring tastes of Roman Jewish fare and specializing in seafood. In spring and summer there's a lovely outdoor dining deck, and in cooler months, the bright rooms decorated with contemporary art offer pleasant surroundings. The menu includes classic fried artichokes (among the best in the city), homemade ravioli *con cipolla di Tropea* (filled with red onion and tossed in balsamic vinegar), and favorite local fish turbot, barely adorned with perfectly roasted potatoes and extra-virgin olive oil. Everything down to the last bite (make your dessert choice the chocolate medley) is a pleasure, even if it doesn't come cheaply. ⊠ *Via dei Fienili 50-51, Ghetto* ☎ *06/6780933* ▭ *AE, DC, MC, V* ☾ *Closed Sun.* ✚ *3:E1.*

$$$ ✗ **Sora Lella.** It may not be the most original spot in town, but Sora
ROMAN   Lella can boast that it's the only restaurant that is open year-round on Isola Tiburina, a rocky island in the middle of the Tiber river between the Jewish ghetto and Trastevere. The dining rooms on two floors are elegant, and service is discreet. As for the food, try the delicious prosciutto and mozzarella to start, and move on to classics like pasta *all'amatriciana*, meatballs in tomato sauce, or Roman baby lamb chops. The stuffed calamari in white wine sauce is worthy of *facendo una scarpetta*—taking a piece of bread to sop up the savory sauce. The family owners have now ventured to American soil: their latest outpost is in New York City. ⊠ *Via di Ponte Quattro Capi 16, Ghetto* ☎ *06/6861601* ⊕ *www.soralella.com* ▭ *AE, MC, V* ☾ *Closed Sun., Tues. lunch, 3 weeks Aug.* ✚ *3:D1.*

$$$–$$$$ ✗ **Vecchia Roma.** Though the frescoed dining rooms are lovely, the choice
SEAFOOD   place to dine is outside, under the big white umbrellas. Here, you can

select from interesting appetizers—we recommend the seafood selection, which may include an assortment of fresh anchovies in vinegary goodness, seafood salad, baby shrimp, and whatever else is fresh and seasonal. Portions are generally large, so select one of their wonderful pasta dishes or skip straight to their *secondi*.

Though there are meat and veggie dishes on offer, seafood is a house specialty, and simple southern Italian preparations, such as fresh white flaky fish in a potato crust with cherry tomatoes, are excellent no-fail choices. Sample the house-made fruit desserts for a light(ish) finish to the meal. ⊠ *Piazza Campitelli 18, Ghetto* ☎ *06/6864604* ⊕ *www.ristorantevecchiaroma.com* ▭ *AE, DC, MC, V* ⊗ *Closed Wed.* ✢ *4:F5.*

MONTI, ESQUILINO, REPUBBLICA, AND SAN LORENZO

MONTI

$
WINE BAR
✕ **Cavour 313.** Wine bars are popping up all over the city, but Cavour 313 has been around much longer than most. With a tight seating area in the front, your best bet is to head to the large space in the rear, which is divided into sections with booths that give this bar a rustic feel, halfway to a beer hall. Open for lunch and dinner, it serves an excellent variety of cured meats, cheeses, and salads, with a focus on DOP, organic, and artisanal products. Choose from about 25 wines by the glass or uncork a bottle (there are more than 1,200) and stay a while. ⊠ *Via Cavour 313, Monti* ☎ *06/6785496* ⊕ *www.cavour313.it* ▭ *AE, DC, MC, V* ⊗ *Closed Aug. No lunch weekends. No dinner Sun., June 15–Sept.* ✢ *2:B5.*

$$$–$$$$
SEAFOOD
✕ **F.I.S.H.** The name stands for Fine International Seafood House, which sums up the kitchen's approach. This is fresh, *fresh* fish cooked by capable and creative hands—from Italian fish-based pastas to a Thai mollusk soup with lemongrass and coconut milk that awakens the senses. The menu is divided into three sections: sushi, Asian, and Mediterranean. Seating is divided into the front aqua lounge, the middle sushi bar, and the back dining room, but it is limited, so book ahead. ⊠ *Via dei Serpenti 16, Monti* ☎ *06/47824962* ⬧ *Reservations essential* ⊕ *www.f-i-s-h.it* ▭ *AE, D, MC, V* ⊗ *Closed Mon. and 2 wks in Aug.* ✢ *2:C5.*

$$
CENTRAL ITALIAN
Fodor's Choice
★
✕ **Trattoria Monti.** Not far from Santa Maria Maggiore, Monti is one of the most dependable, moderately priced trattorias in the city, featuring the cuisine of the Marches, an area to the northeast of Rome. There are surprisingly few places specializing in this humble fare considering there are more people hailing from Le Marche in Rome than in the whole region of Le Marche. The fare served up by the Camerucci family is hearty and simple, represented by various roasted meats and game, and a selection of generally vegetarian timbales and soufflés that change seasonally. The region's rabbit dishes are much loved, and here

the *timballo di coniglio con patate* (rabbit casserole with potatoes) is no exception. ✉ *Via di San Vito 13, Monti* ☎ *06/4466573* ▭ *AE, DC, MC, V* ☺ *Closed Aug., 2 wks at Easter, and 10 days at Christmas* ✛ *2:E5.*

ESQUILINO

$$ ✕ **La Gallina Bianca.** This pizzeria's location right down the road from
PIZZA Termini station makes it a perfect place for a welcome-to-Rome meal. A bright, noisy locale, La Gallina Bianca attracts a young crowd and serves classic thin-crust pizzas. Try the "full-moon" specialty, perfect for cheese lovers, with ricotta, Parmesan, mozzarella, ham, and tomato. There are other menu items available from the trattoria menu for those who may be trying to stick to a less carb-loaded diet. ✉ *Via A. Rosmini 5, Esquilino* ☎ *06/4743777* ▭ *AE, MC, V* ☺ *Closed Aug.* ✛ *2:4D.*

$$$ ✕ **Monte Caruso.** The regional delicacies of certain areas of Italy are
SOUTHERN grossly underrepresented in Rome. Monte Caruso is truly a standout,
ITALIAN as its menu focuses on food from Lucania, an area of Italy divided between the southern regions of Basilicata and Calabria. Homemade pastas have strange-sounding names, such as *cautarogni* (large cavatelli with Sicilian broccoli) and *cauzuni* (enormous ricotta-stuffed ravioli), but the dishes are generally simple and hearty. ✉ *Via Farini 12, Esquilino* ☎ *06/483549* ⊕ *www.montecaruso.com* ▭ *AE, DC, MC, V* ☺ *Closed Sun. and Aug. No lunch Mon.* ✛ *2:D4.*

$$–$$$ ✕ **Primo.** Primo is a modern Italian restaurant highlighting local ingre-
ITALIAN dients and simplified cooking techniques. The young and hip sip from a selection of 250 wines, and nibble on hand-cut prosciutto, anchovy-and-broccoli gratin, and salads with goat cheese and radicchio. Pastas on offer include gnocchi with seafood, lemon, and thyme, and long pasta with artichokes and dried mullet roe. Seafood mains, like scorpionfish with seafood reduction and fried polenta, or grilled calamari, are also good choices. Those more carnivorous sink their teeth into meat dishes like the duck breast, sliced beefsteak, or braised rabbit with wild fennel and "sour" tomatoes. Desserts are tasty if fairly standard, so we recommend instead lingering over *digestivi*: the name "*Primo*" references the primary ingredients that are the focus of the menu, but it could just as easily refer to the *prime* people-watching spot the restaurant enjoys on the 'hood's main drag. ✉ *Via del Pigneto 46, Pigneto* ☎ *06/7013827* ⊕ *www.primoalpigneto.it* ▭ *AE, MC, V* ☺ *Closed Mon.* ✛ *2:H6.*

REPUBBLICA

$$–$$$ ✕ **Trimani Il Winebar.** Trimani operates nonstop from 11 AM to 12:30 AM
WINE BAR and serves hot food at lunch and dinner. Decor is minimalist, and the second floor provides a subdued, candlelit space to sip wine. There's always a choice of a soup and pasta plates, as well as second courses and *torte salate* (savory tarts). Around the corner is a wineshop, one of the oldest in Rome, of the same name. Call about wine tastings and classes (in Italian). ✉ *Via Cernaia 37/b, Repubblica* ☎ *06/4469630* ▭ *AE, DC, MC, V* ☺ *Closed Sun. and 2 wks in Aug.* ✛ *2:D2.*

SAN LORENZO

$$$$
SEAFOOD

✗ **Acquolina.** Famed chef Angelo Troiani, chef-proprietor of Il Convivio, has branched out, heading out of the city center to the Flaminio area, while narrowing his culinary scope to concentrate on high-quality seafood. The results are delicious and understated: some dishes on the menu reflect the time-honored Italian tradition of letting great seafood speak for itself, and other dishes get spiffed-up treatments. The aquatic version of *olive ascolane* are battered and fried as tradition dictates, but are stuffed with salt cod instead of the usual ground meat. And the seafood lasagna is more of a composed pasta Napoleon, with paper-thin pasta, delicate white fish, sea urchin, and deliciously light saucing. The owners are concerned about sustainability, and as such, don't serve certain endangered sea creatures, so don't expect to find bluefin tuna carpaccio on the menu. Desserts are surprisingly sophisticated. Service is helpful and thorough, though this barely makes up for the slowness of the kitchen. ⊠ *Via Antonio Serra 60, San Lorenzo* ☎ *06/3337192* ▭ *AE, MC, V* ⊗ *Closed Sun. No lunch* ✛ *1:G1.*

$
ETHIOPIAN

✗ **Africa.** Ethiopia was the closest thing Italy ever had to a "colony" at one point. As a result, what Indian food is to London, Ethiopian/Eritrean food is to Rome. Interesting offerings include braised meat main courses, yogurt-based breakfasts, and vegetarian-friendly stews—all under the category of utensil-free dining. ⊠ *Via Gaeta 26, Termini* ☎ *06/4941077* ▭ *No credit cards* ⊗ *Closed Mon.* ✛ *2:E2.*

$$$$
MODERN ITALIAN
Fodor'sChoice
★

✗ **Agata e Romeo.** For the perfect marriage of fine dining, creative cuisine, and rustic Roman tradition, the husband-and-wife team of Agata Parisella and Romeo Caraccio is the top. Romeo presides over the dining room and delights in the selection of wine-food pairings. And Chef Agata was perhaps the first in the capital city to put a gourmet spin on Roman ingredients and preparations, elevating dishes of the common folk to new levels, wherein familiar staples like *cacao e pepe* are transformed with the addition of even richer Sicilian aged cheese and saffron. From antipasti (try the seafood crudo tasting: it's so artfully presented, it's actually served on a glass plate resembling a painter's palette) to desserts, many dishes are the best versions of classics you can get. The prices here are steep, but for those who appreciate extremely high-quality ingredients, an incredible wine cellar, and warm service, dining here is a real treat. ⊠ *Via Carlo Alberto 45, Termini* ☎ *06/4466115* ▭ *AE, DC, MC, V* ⊗ *Closed weekends, 2 wks in July, and 2 wks in Aug.* ✛ *2:E5.*

¢–$
PIZZA

✗ **Formula 1.** Posters of Formula 1 cars and drivers past and present attest to the owner's love for auto racing. The atmosphere is casual and friendly and draws students from the nearby university as well as pizza lovers from all over the city. Its location in the trendy San Lorenzo neighborhood makes it a convenient stop for dinner before checking out some of the area's bars. ⊠ *Via degli Equi 13, San Lorenzo* ☎ *06/4453866* ▭ *No credit cards* ⊗ *Closed Sun. and Aug. No lunch* ✛ *2:G5.*

$$$ ✕ **Tram Tram.** This bustling trattoria is usually snugly packed with hun-
SOUTHERN gry Romans. The name refers to its proximity to the tram tracks, but
ITALIAN could also describe its size, as it's narrow-narrow and often stuffed to
Fodor'sChoice the rafters-rafters. In warmer weather, there's a "side car" of tables
★ enclosed along the sidewalk. The cuisine is derived from cook's home-
town region of Puglia. You'll find an emphasis on seafood and vegeta-
bles—maybe prawns with saffron-kissed sautéed vegetables—as well
as pastas of very particular shapes. Try the homemade *orecchiette*, ear-
shaped pasta, made here with clams and broccoli. ⊠ *Via dei Reti 44/46,
San Lorenzo* ☏ *06/490416* ⊟ *AE, DC, MC, V* ⊘ *Closed Mon. and 1
wk in mid-Aug.* ✛ *2:H4.*

$$$$ ✕ **Uno e Bino.** The setting is simple: wooden tables and chairs on a stone
MODERN ITALIAN floor with little more than a few shelves of wine bottles lining the walls
Fodor'sChoice for decor. Giampaolo Gravina's restaurant in this artsy corner of the
★ San Lorenzo neighborhood is popular with foodies and locals alike, as
the kitchen turns out inventive cuisine inspired by the family's Umbrian
and Sicilian roots. Dishes like octopus salad with asparagus and carrots,
and spaghetti with swordfish, tomatoes, and capers are specialties. The
Parmesan soufflé is a study in light, silky, salty, and absolute perfection.
Delicious and simple, yet upscale, desserts cap off the dinner, making
this small establishment one of the top dining deals—and pleasurable
meals—in Rome. ⊠ *Via degli Equi 58, San Lorenzo* ☏ *06/4460702*
⊟ *MC, V* ⊘ *Closed Mon. and Aug. No lunch* ✛ *2:G5.*

VENETO, BORGHESE, AND SPAGNA

VENETO

$$$ ✕ **Moma.** Almost a sister in spirit to the Hotel Aleph, a new favorite of
ITALIAN the design *trendoisie* across the street, Moma is modern, moody, and
very "concept." The menu has hits and misses, and attempts to raise
the nouvelle bar in Rome—foie gras *millefoglie* with apple slices and
cider vinegar geleé, anyone? Seared scallops, plump and sweet, were a
find, and the rigatoni *all'amatriciana* was tasty. The main dish of Argen-
tinian rib eye with balsamic vinegar was delicious. There are several
basic desserts, of which the molten chocolate cake is probably the best,
served with pear sorbetto and chocolate sauce. ⊠ *Via San Basilio 42/43,
Veneto* ☏ *06/42011798* ⊕ *www.momaristorante.com* ⊟ *AE, DC, MC,
V* ⊘ *Closed Sun. and 2 wks in Aug.* ✛ *2:C2.*

$$$$ ✕ **Papá Baccus.** Italo Cipriani takes his meat as seriously as any Tus-
TUSCAN can, using real Chianina beef for the house specialty, the *bistecca alla
fiorentina*, a thick grilled steak served on the bone and rare in the center.
Cipriani brings many ingredients from his hometown on the border of
Emilia-Romagna and Tuscany. Try the sweet and delicate prosciutto
from Pratomagno or the *ribollita*, a traditional bread-based minestrone
soup. Tuscans are nicknamed "the bean eaters," and after a taste of the
fagioli zolfini (tender white beans), you'll understand why. The welcome
is warm, the service excellent, and the glass of prosecco (gratis) starts
the meal on the right foot. ⊠ *Via Toscana 36, Veneto* ☏ *06/42742808*
⊕ *www.papabaccus.com* ⊟ *AE, DC, MC, V* ⊘ *Closed Sun. and 2 wks
in Aug. No lunch Sat.* ✛ *4:B3.*

12

BORGHESE

$$$$ ✕ **Al Ceppo.** The well-heeled, the business-minded, and those of more
ITALIAN refined palate frequent this outpost of tranquillity. Its owners hail from
Le Marche, the region north of Rome that borders the Adriatic, and they
dote on their customers as you'd wish a sophisticated Italian *mamma*
would. There's always a selection of dishes from their native region,
such as *olive ascolane* (green olives stuffed with ground meat, breaded,
and fried), various fresh pasta dishes, and succulent roast lamb. Other
temptations include a beautiful display of seafood and a wide selection
of meats ready to be grilled in the fireplace in the front room. ⊠ *Via
Panama 2, Parioli* ☎ *06/8419696* ⊕ *www.ristorantealceppo.it* ⊟ *AE,
DC, MC, V* ☯ *Closed Mon. and 2 wks in Aug.* ✛ *2:C1.*

$$$ ✕ **Duke's.** It dubs itself a California-style restaurant and bar, although
AMERICAN the California rolls have tuna and carrot in them and they've added
mint leaves to the Caesar salad. But the truth is, once you look at Duke's
menu after a stretch of Italian-only bingeing, you may actually want it
all. Perhaps a nice, juicy beef fillet, and the finishing touch of the warm
apple pie served with gelato. The decor is Malibu–beach house–mini-
malist. The outdoor patio in the back is consummately SoCal chic. And
up front, opening out onto the street, all the beautiful people from the
neighborhood (read: plenty of unnatural blondes) are huddled around
the bar, sipping frozen cocktails, the whir of blenders and music blar-
ing in the background. ⊠ *Viale Parioli 200, Borghese* ☎ *06/80662455*
⊕ *www.dukes.it* ⊟ *AE, MC, V* ☯ *Closed Sat.; June–Sept. closed Sat.
and Sun., and 1 wk in Aug.* ✛ *2:C1.*

$ ✕ **La Maremma.** This pizza place has been one of the biggest draws in
PIZZA Parioli for years, and its popularity has spawned a second outpost,
closer to Via Veneto. Pizzas are available Roman style with a thin crust,
or Neapolitan style, thicker and more filling. Outside tables can be had
year-round, thanks to heaters that warm the terrace in winter. ⊠ *Viale
Parioli 93/c, Parioli* ☎ *06/8086002* ⊠ *Via Alessandria 119/d, Veneto*
☎ *06/8554002* ⊟ *MC, V* ☯ *Closed Mon. and Aug. No lunch* ✛ *2:C1.*

SPAGNA

$$$$ ✕ **Caffè Romano dell'Hotel d'Inghilterra.** One of Rome's most soigné hotels,
ECLECTIC the d'Inghliterra houses this standard-issue symphony in beige marbles,
beechwood walls, and Tuscan columns. You can tell that jet-setters like
this spot—it's got an *orario continuato,* or nonstop opening hours, from
10 AM on, so snacking or having a late lunch is a possibility here. Best
bets include authentic northern Italian meat preparations and south-
ern Italian pasta and seafood dishes. Try interesting selections like the
glazed boar with polenta, the guinea hen with stewed chestnuts and
bacon, or the seafood soup, as well as a variety of pasta choices. Tables
are close together, so you might have eavesdropping neighbors. ⊠ *Via
Borgongna 4M, Spagna* ☎ *06/69981500* ⊟ *AE, DC, MC, V* ✛ *1:H2.*

$$$$ ✕ **Dal Bolognese.** The darling of the media, film, and fashion communities,
EMILIAN this classic restaurant on Piazza del Popolo is not only an "in-crowd"
dinner destination but makes a convenient shopping-spree lunch spot.
As the name promises, the cooking adheres to the hearty tradition of
Bologna. Start with a plate of sweet *San Daniele* prosciutto with melon,

then move on to the traditional egg pastas of Emilia-Romagna. Second plates include the famous Bolognese *bollito misto,* a steaming tray of an assortment of boiled meats (some recognizable, some indecipherable) served with its classic accompaniment, a tangy, herby *salsa verde* (green sauce). ⊠ *Piazza del Popolo 1, Spagna* ☎ *06/3222799* ⊟ *AE, DC, MC, V* ⊘ *Closed Mon. and 3 wks in Aug.* ✣ *1:G1.*

$$$$ ✕ **El Toulà.** One of Rome's more celebrated outposts of luxe, El Toulà has
ITALIAN   the warm, welcoming comforts of a 19th-century country house: white walls, antique furniture in dark wood, framed prints, vaulted ceilings, and Venetian-style lamp shades. Along with the usual suspects of high-roller choices (caviar and blini), the chef offers a menu of contemporary interpretations of Italian classics, as well as those special El Toulà dishes with a Venetian slant (the mother restaurant is in Treviso): delicious, expertly prepared risottos, and a nod to the various sea creatures of the Adriatic coast and Venetian lagoon. Note that jacket and tie are required November through February. ⊠ *Via della Lupa 29/b, Spagna* ☎ *06/6873750* ⊕ *www.toula.it* ⌁ *Reservations essential* ⊟ *AE, DC, MC, V* ⊘ *Closed Sun. and Aug. No lunch Mon. and Sat.* ✣ *4:E1.*

$–$$ ✕ **GiNa.** "Homey minimalism" isn't a contradiction at this whitewashed
ITALIAN   caffè with a modern edge. The block seats and sleek booths, the single flowers in Mason jars, white chandeliers, and multiplicity of mirrors, make this small but multilevel space a tiny gem tucked away on the street leading from Piazza di Spagna up to Villa Borghese. With a menu ranging from various bruschette to interesting mixed salads, sandwiches, and pastas, this is the perfect spot for a light lunch, an aperitivo, or a light dinner that won't break the bank in this high-end neighborhood. Also available are fully stocked gourmet picnic baskets, complete with checked tablecloth, to pick up on the way to the Villa Borghese. ⊠ *Via San Sebastianello 7A, Spagna* ☎ *06/6780251* ⊕ *www. ginaroma.com* ⊟ *AE, MC, V* ⊘ *Closed Sun. and Aug.; open only for lunch and aperitivi (until 8* PM*) in summer* ✣ *1:H2.*

$$$–$$$$ ✕ **'Gusto.** There's an urban-loft feel to this trendy two-story space, a bit
ITALIAN   like Pottery Barn exploded in Piazza Agusto Imperatore (the name of
🜂   the restaurant is a play on this location and the Italian word for taste/flavor). The ground floor contains a buzzing pizzeria-trattoria, while upstairs is the more upscale restaurant. We prefer the casual-but-hopping vibe of the ground-floor wine bar in the back, where a rotating selection of wines by the glass and bottle are served up alongside a vast array of cheeses, salami, and bread products. And for the kitchen enthusiast, the 'Gusto "complex" includes a store, selling everything from cookware to cookwear. ⊠ *Piazza Augusto Imperatore 9, Spagna* ☎ *06/3226273* ⊟ *AE, DC, MC, V* ✣ *1:G2.*

$$–$$$ ✕ **'Gusto al 28.** This offshoot of the 'Gusto Empire focuses specifically
ITALIAN   on fish and vegetable dishes, and is a light, modern version—both architecturally and culinarily—of its earlier siblings. A sardine appetizer with fried zucchini is a sophisticated Italian version of fish-and-chips. The zuppa di pesce (fish stew) is as packed with flavor as one would hope, and an interesting collection of other fish and vegetable dishes are prettily presented and live up to the visuals with great taste all around. Service can be a bit slow, but hey, the waiters show a "bella

figura"—meaning they look good, which is so important in Rome, even among the waitstaff. ⊠ *Piazza Augusto Imperatore 28, Piazza di Spagna* ☎ *06/68134221* ⊕ *www.gusto.it* ▬ *AE, DC, MC, V* ✢ *1:G2.*

$$–$$$ ✕ **'Gusto–Osteria.** You can get regular osteria fare and service at this
ITALIAN member of the 'Gusto restaurant empire, but why would you? The beauty of this spot is what makes it *different*: its adaptation of the idea of *cichetti*, a sort of Italian tapas that originated in the venerable bars of Venice. Head to the bar area here (the only place this service is available) and, for between €2 and €4, sample pretty much anything on the regular menu in a snack-size portion. Many will want to begin by choosing from the incredible selection of 400 cheeses in the basement cellar, then from the various *fritti* (fried items), moving onto pastas such as sheep's milk and pepper spaghetti. Even enjoy mini desserts: the portions make you feel as if you're behaving! ⊠ *Via della Frezza 16, Spagna* ☎ *06/32111482* ⊕ *www.gusto.it* ▬ *AE, DC, MC, V* ✢ *1:G2.*

$$$ ✕ **Il Brillo Parlante.** Il Brillo Parlante's location near Piazza del Popolo
WINE BAR makes it convenient for lunch or dinner after a bit of shopping in the Via del Corso area. Choose from 20 wines by the glass at the bar or eat downstairs in one of several wood-panel rooms. The menu is extensive for a wine bar; choose from cured meats, *crostini* (toasted bread with various toppings such as pâté or prosciutto), pastas, grilled meats, and even pizzas. ⊠ *Via della Fontanella 15, Spagna* ☎ *06/3243334* ⊕ *www.ilbrilloparlante.com* ▬ *AE, DC, MC, V* ☺ *Closed Mon. and 1 wk in mid-Aug.* ✢ *1:G1.*

$ ✕ **Il Leoncino.** Lines out the door on weekends attest to the popularity
PIZZA of this fluorescent-lighted pizzeria in the otherwise big-ticket neighborhood around Piazza di Spagna. This is one of the few pizzerias open for lunch as well as dinner. ⊠ *Via del Leoncino 28, Spagna* ☎ *06/6876642* ▬ *AE, MC, V* ☺ *Closed Sun. and Aug.* ✢ *1:G3.*

$$$–$$$$ ✕ **Il Palazzetto.** This small restaurant near the Piazza di Spagna is part of
MODERN ITALIAN the International Wine Academy of Rome. Chef Antonio Martucci creates seasonal menus using traditional Roman ingredients, which he gives a unique "twist" to in preparation and flavor pairings. Stuffed calamari on an eggplant puree with sautéed baby peppers is a study in contrasting flavor and texture; homemade ricotta-filled gnocchi with sausage and asparagus hits all the right notes. It's wise to call in advance, both for reservations and to find out about regular prix-fixe dinners, sometimes with guest chefs, focusing on wine-food pairings. ⊠ *Vicolo del Bottino 8, Spagna* ☎ *06/6993400* ▬ *AE, DC, MC, V* ✢ *1:H2.*

$–$$ ✕ **L'Enoteca Antica di Via della Croce.** This wine bar is always crowded,
WINE BAR and for good reason. It's long on personality: colorful ceramic-tile tables are always filled with locals and foreigners, as is the half moon–shaped bar where you can order from the large selection of salumi and cheeses on offer. Peruse the chalkboard highlighting the special wines by-the-glass for that day to accompany your nibbles. There's waiter service at the tables in back and out front on the bustling Via della Croce, where people-watching is in high gear. ⊠ *Via della Croce 76/b, Spagna* ☎ *06/6790896* ▬ *AE, DC, MC, V* ☺ *Closed 2 wks in Aug.* ✢ *1:G2.*

$$–$$$ ✕ **Margutta Vegetariano.** Parallel to posh Via del Babuino, Via Margutta
VEGETARIAN has long been known as *the* street where artists have their studios in

Rome. How fitting, then, that the rare Italian vegetarian restaurant, with changing displays of modern art, sits on the far end of this gallery-lined street closest to Piazza del Popolo. Here it takes on a chic and cosmopolitan air, where you'll find meat-free versions of classic Mediterranean dishes as well as more daring tofu concoctions. Lunch is essentially a pasta/salad bar to which you help yourself, while dinner offers à la carte and prix-fixe options. ⊠ *Via Margutta 118, Spagna* ☎ *06/32650577* ⊟ *AE, DC, MC, V* ✚ *1:G1.*

$$$ ✕ **Nino.** Tom Cruise and Katie Holmes had their celeb-studded rehearsal
ITALIAN   dinner here, a testament that this dressed-up trattoria has been a favorite among international journalists and the rich and famous for decades. Nino sticks to the classics, in food and decor, as well as in its waiters. Much of what you find on the menu here are Roman staples with a Tuscan slant. To start, try a selection from the fine antipasto spread, or go for the cured meats or warm *crostini* (toasts) spread with liver pâté. Move on to pappardelle *al lepre* (a rich hare sauce) or the juicy grilled beef. One warning: if you're not Italian, or a regular, or a celebrity, the chance of brusque service multiplies—so insist on good service and you'll win the waiters' respect (and probably their attention). ⊠ *Via Borgognona 11, Spagna* ☎ *06/6786752* ⊟ *AE, DC, MC, V* ☉ *Closed Sun. and Aug.* ✚ *1:H3.*

$$$ ✕ **ReCafé.** Here in a soaring space in the center of the city, we have
ITALIAN   another nod to perhaps the greatest Neapolitan contribution to Italian cuisine (at least on a popularity scale): pizza. There's an upstairs space, cathedral-like in proportion, and a downstairs room with the look of a sleek sound studio where diners relax at tables piled high with fried starters, pizzas, and salads. There's also a vast outside piazza set with tables plus the alfresco zone up front. On the menu, there are a series of Neapolitan starters—often fried or from the sea (stewed octopus with black olives), and local mozzarella is highlighted as well. But the real reason to come here is the pizza. It's fresh, well-made, and thicker than the typical Roman pizza. ⊠ *Piazza Augusto Imperatore 36, Spagna* ☎ *06/68134730* ⊕ *www.recafe.it* ⊟ *AE, DC, MC, V* ☉ *Closed 2 wks in Aug.* ✚ *1:G2.*

VATICAN, BORGO, AND PRATI

BORGO

$$$–$$$$ ✕ **La Veranda dell'Hotel Columbus.** Deciding where to sit at La Veranda is
ROMAN   not easy, since both the shady courtyard, torch-lit at night, and the frescoed dining room are among Rome's most spectacular settings. While La Veranda has classic Roman cuisine on tap, the kitchen offers nice, refreshing twists on the familiar with an innovative use of flavor combinations. Try the unusual duck leg confit starter, stuffed with raisins and pinenuts with an onion compote and plum sorbet. Or go for the grilled tuna bites with anchovy-caper dumplings and an eggplant torta. Even the pastas are unexpected: saffron fettucine with cuttlefish and zucchini flowers is subtle and elegant—much like the surroundings. Call ahead, especially on Saturday, because the hotel often hosts weddings, which close the restaurant, and you don't want to miss passing a few

Refueling the Roman Way

CLOSE UP

Staggering under the weight of a succession of three-course meals, you may ask yourself, how do the Romans eat so much, twice a day, every day? The answer is, they don't.

If you want to do as the Romans do, try lunch at a *tavola calda* (literally, hot table), a cross between a caffè and a cafeteria where you'll find fresh food in manageable portions.

There's usually a selection of freshly prepared pastas, cooked vegetables such as *bietola all'agro* (cooked beet greens with lemon), roasted potatoes, and grilled or roasted meat or fish.

Go to the counter to order an assortment and quantity that suits your appetite, and pay by the plate, usually about €5 plus drinks. Tavole calde

aren't hard to find, particularly in the city center, often marked with "tavola calda" or "self-service" signs.

The other ubiquitous options for a light lunch or between-meal snack are pizza *al taglio* (by the slice) shops, bars, and enoteche (wine bars). At bars throughout Italy, coffee is the primary beverage served (drinking establishments are commonly known as pubs or American bars); at them you can curb your appetite with a panino (a simple sandwich) or tramezzino (sandwich on untoasted white bread, usually heavy on the mayonnaise).

Wine bars vary widely in the sophistication and variety of food available. You can count on cheese and cured meats at the very least.

---

hours of your Roman Holiday in these environs. ⊠ *Borgo Santo Spirito 73, Borgo* ☎ *06/6872973* ⊕ *www.hotelcolumbus.net* ⊸ *Reservations essential* ▤ *AE, DC, MC, V* ✛ *1:D3*.

$$$
MODERN ITALIAN
Fodor'sChoice
★

✗ **Taverna Angelica.** The area surrounding St. Peter's Basilica isn't known for culinary excellence, but Taverna Angelica is an exception. Its tiny size allows the chef to concentrate on each individual dish, and the menu is creative without being pretentious. Dishes such as warm octopus salad on a bed of mashed potatoes with a basil-parsley pesto drizzle are more about taste than presentation. The lentil soup with pigeon breast brought hunter's cuisine to a new level. And the breast of duck in balsamic vinegar was exquisitely executed. It may be difficult to find, on a section of the street that's set back and almost subterranean, but it's worth searching out. ⊠ *Piazza A. Capponi 6, Borgo* ☎ *06/6874514* ⊕ *www.tavernaangelica.it* ⊸ *Reservations essential* ▤ *AE, V* ✛ *1:D3*.

PRATI

$$$
ITALIAN

✗ **Cesare.** An old standby in the residential area near the Vatican known as Prati, Cesare is a willing slave to tradition. The refrigerated display of fresh fish of the day is a tip-off of what's on offer. Classic fish dishes, such as fresh marinated anchovies and sardines, and mixed seafood salad dressed in a lemon citronette, quell those seafood cravings. Homemade pasta with meat sauce is the primo to get, and *saltimbocca* (thinly sliced veal with prosciutto and sage) or the thick Florentine steaks are the ultimate meat-lover's dishes. As with any other traditional Roman restaurant, gnocchi are served on Thursday and pasta with chickpeas on

12

Friday. Also try the €38 "menu toscano"—a great, multicourse value. The look of the place is quite clubby, and the menu's tendency toward stick-to-the-ribs comfort food make it a great place to go in the autumn and winter, when the cooler weather ushers in dishes featuring truffles, game, and heartier fare. ✉ *Via Crescenzio 13, Prati* ☎ *06/6861227* ⊕ *www.ristorantecesare.com* ☰ *AE, DC, MC, V* ✆ *Closed Sun., Aug., and Easter wk* ✦ *1:E2.*

$$$

TUSCAN

✕ **Dal Toscano.** An open wood-fired grill and classic dishes such as *ribollita* (a thick bread and vegetable soup) and *pici* (fresh, thick pasta with wild hare sauce) are the draw at this great family-run Tuscan trattoria near the Vatican. The cuts of beef visible at the entrance tell you right away that the house special is the prized *bistecca alla fiorentina*—a thick grilled steak left rare in the middle and seared on the outside, with its rub of gutsy Tuscan olive oil and sea salt forming a delicious crust to keep in the natural juices of the beef. Seating outside on the sidewalk in warm weather is a nice touch. ✉ *Via Germanico 58/60, Prati* ☎ *06/39723373* ⊕ *www.ristorantedaltoscano.it* ☰ *AE, DC, MC, V* ✆ *Closed Mon., 3 wks in Aug., and 1 wk in Jan.* ✦ *1:C2.*

$$$$

WINE BAR

✕ **Il Simposio di Costantini.** At the most upscale wine bar in town, decorated with wrought-iron vines, wood paneling, and velvet, you come for the wine, but return for the food. Everything here is appropriately *raffinato* (refined): marinated and smoked fish, composed salads, top-quality salami and other cured meats and pâtés. There are plenty of dishes with classic Roman leanings, like the artichoke dish prepared three ways. Main courses favor carnivores, as roast lamb, a fillet with foie gras, or game (like pigeon, in season) complement the vast offering of top-notch red wines. The restaurant boasts 80 assorted cheeses to savor with your dessert wine. ✉ *Piazza Cavour 16, Prati* ☎ *06/32111131* ⊕ *www.pierocostantini.it* ☰ *AE, DC, MC, V* ✆ *Closed Sun. and last 2 wks of Aug. No lunch Sat.* ✦ *1:E2.*

$

PIZZA

✕ **L'Isola della Pizza.** Right near the Vatican Metro stop, the "Island of Pizza" is also known for its copious antipasti. Simply ask for the house appetizers, and a waiter will swoop down with numerous plates of salad, seafood, bruschetta, prosciutto, and crispy pizza Bianca. Though it's all too easy to fill up on these fun starters, the pizza is dependably good, and meat-lovers can get a decent steak. ✉ *Via degli Scipioni 47, Prati* ☎ *06/39733483* ⊕ *www.lisoladellapizza.com* ☰ *AE, MC, V* ✆ *Closed Sun., Aug., and Christmas wk. No lunch* ✦ *1:C2.*

TRASTEVERE AND GIANICOLO

TRASTEVERE

$$

ROMAN

☺

Fodor's Choice

★

✕ **Alle Fratte di Trastevere.** Here you can find staple Roman trattoria fare as well as dishes with a southern slant. This means that *spaghetti alla carbonara* (with pancetta, eggs, and cheese) shares the menu with the likes of penne *alla Sorrentina* (with tomato, basil, and fresh mozzarella). For starters, the bruschette here are exemplary, as is the pressed octopus carpaccio on a bed of arugula. As for secondi, you can again look south and to the sea for a mixed seafood pasta or a grilled sea bass with oven-roasted potatoes, or go for the meat with a fillet *al pepe* *verde* (green peppercorns in a brandy cream sauce). Service is always with a smile, as the owners and their trusted waitstaff make you feel at home. ✉ *Via delle Fratte di Trastevere 49/50* ☎ *06/5835775* ⊕ *www. allefratteditrastevere.com* ▭ *AE, DC, MC, V* ☺ *Closed Wed. and 2 wks in Aug.* ✛ *3:B2.*

$ ✕ **Dar Poeta.** Romans drive across town for great pizza from this neigh-

PIZZA   borhood institution on a small street in Trastevere. Maybe it's the dough—it's made from a secret blend of flours that's reputed to be easier to digest than the competition. They offer both thin-crust pizza and a thick-crust (*"alta"*) Neapolitan-style pizza with any of the given toppings. For dessert, there's a ridiculously good calzone with Nutella chocolate-hazelnut spread and ricotta cheese, so save some room. Service from the owners and friendly waitstaff is smile-inducing. ✉ *Vicolo del Bologna 45, Trastevere* ☎ *06/5880516* ▭ *AE, MC, V* ✛ *4:B6.*

$$$–$$$$ ✕ **Ferrara.** What used to be a well-stocked enoteca with a few nibbles

ITALIAN   has become what locals now know as the "Ferrara block": the enoteca has expanded to become a restaurant, wine bar, and a gastronomic boutique taking over a good section of one of the area's most famous streets. The renovations have resulted in an airy, modernist destination. Service can be iffy to slow, and, in the end, the results coming out of the kitchen are inconsistent. A fine starter is the ricotta and herb-stuffed zucchini flowers sprinkled with crispy pancetta. Secondi range from seared tuna in a sesame seed crust to roast pork with prunes. But true to its enoteca roots, it's the wine selection that impresses here. ✉ *Piazza Trilussa 41, Trastevere* ☎ *06/58333920* ⊕ *www.enotecaferrara.it* ▭ *AE, DC, MC, V* ✛ *4:C6.*

$$$–$$$$ ✕ **Glass Hostaria.** After 14 years in Austin, Texas, Glass chef Cristina

MODERN ITALIAN   Bowerman returned to Rome to reconnect with her Italian roots. Her cooking is as innovative as the building she works in—which has received numerous recognitions for its architecture and design since opening in May 2004—but Bowerman still abides by some cardinal Italian kitchen rules, such as the use of fresh, local, and seasonal ingredients. With an impassioned sense for detail, taste, and presentation, she serves a delicious pumpkin gnocchi with fontina fondue, black truffle, and toasted almonds. Another favorite dish is the pistachio crusted scallops with crunchy pancetta and lemongrass sauce. And for dessert: a white truffle crème brûlée. Need help pairing your wine? Glass offers more than 600 labels for the interested oenophiles. ✉ *Vicolo del Cinque 58, Trastevere* ☎ *06/58335903* ⊕ *www.glass-hostaria.com* ▭ *AE, DC, MC, V* ☺ *Closed Mon. No lunch* ✛ *4:C6.*

$$$ ✕ **Il Ciak.** This Tuscan staple in Trastevere is a carnivore's delight. Spe-

TUSCAN   cializing in the Tuscan *chianina* beef as well as the many game and pork dishes of the region (Wild boar sausage, anyone? Or perhaps pasta with wild hare sauce?), Il Ciak prepares reliably tasty fare. It's probably best appreciated during the autumn and winter months, when hunter's dishes get accompaniments like porcini mushrooms and truffles with polenta. Be prepared to share the pleasure of your oversize fiorentina steak—prepared *al sangue* (rare), of course. ✉ *Vicolo del Cinque, Trastevere* ☎ *06/5890774* ▭ *MC, V* ☺ *Closed Sun.* ✛ *4:C6.*

CLOSE UP

Caffè

Although Rome may not boast the grand caffè of Paris or Vienna, it does have hundreds of small places on pleasant side streets and piazzas to while away the time. Many cafés have tons of personality and are quite friendly to lingering patrons. The coffee is routinely of high quality. Locals usually stop in for a quickie at the bar, where prices are much lower than for the same drink taken at the table.

Pricey **Antico Caffè Greco** (✉ *Via dei Condotti 86, Piazza di Spagna* ☎ *06/6791700* ✛ *1:H2*) is a national landmark; its red-velvet chairs and marble tables have hosted the likes of Byron, Shelley, Keats, Goethe, and Casanova. Located in the middle of shopping madness on the upscale Via Condotti, this place is indeed filled with tourists, but there are some locals who love to breathe the air of history within these dark-wood walls. Coming at off-hours is your best bet to glimpse authenticity.

Caffè Sant'Eustachio (✉ *P. Sant'Eustachio 82, Pantheon* ☎ *06/68802048* ✛ *4:E3*), traditionally frequented by Rome's literati, has what is generally considered Rome's best cup of coffee. Servers are hidden behind a huge espresso machine, vigorously mixing the sugar and coffee to protect their "secret method" for the perfectly prepared cup. (If you want your *caffè* without sugar here, ask for it *amaro.*

Tazza d'Oro (✉ *Via degli Orfani, Pantheon* ☎ *06/6789792* ✛ *4:E2*) has many admirers who contend it serves the city's best cup of coffee. The hot chocolate in winter, all thick and gooey goodness, is a treat. And in warm weather, the coffee granita is the perfect cooling alternative to a regular espresso.

You can sit yourself down and watch the world go by at **Rosati** (✉ *Piazza del Popolo 5, Spagna* ☎ *06/3225859* ✛ *1:G1*), where tourists and locals have met for decades to sip and be seen. This is one of the closest "institution"-like places that Rome has in its caffè culture.

With its sidewalk tables taking in Santa Maria della Pace's adorable piazza, **Caffè della Pace** (✉ *Via della Pace 3, Navona* ☎ *06/6861216* ✛ *4:C2*) has long been the haunt of Rome's *beau monde.* Set on a quiet street near Piazza Navona, it also has two rooms filled with old-world personality.

Caffè Teichner (✉ *Piazza San Lorenzo in Lucina 15–18, Spagna* ☎ *06/6871449* ✛ *1:G3*), just off the Corso, is a relatively pricey establishment on a lively piazza. It offers all the basic nibbles (tramezzini, panini) of most bars, but with the patronage of true Roman residents.

As you walk toward Viale di Trastevere, you'll discover the small and wonderfully down-at-the-heels **Bar San Calisto** (✉ *Piazza San Calisto 4, Trastevere* ☎ *06/5895678* ✛ *3:B1*), immensely popular with the old local community and expat crowd, but largely unfrequented by tourists. The drinks are cheap, cheap, cheap.

Caffè della Scala (✉ *Via della Scala 4, Trastevere* ☎ *06/5803610* ✛ *4:B6*) is a mellow locale with old photos of jazz artists lining the walls. The decor is French-Moroccan-brothel-meets-Louisiana-piano-bar, but the clientele is mixed Roman and expat. As is so often the case, the outdoor tables are the ones to snag.

12

$$ ✕ **Jaipur.** Named after the pink city in India, this restaurant meets the
INDIAN standards of the most discerning Londoners, who know a thing or two
about their curries. Here, in this large space just off the main Viale di
Trastevere, you'll find a vast, high-ceilinged dining room decked in
retina-burning yellow with festive Indian decorations on the huge walls
(there's also dining outside when the weather calls for it). Portions are
small but made for sharing, so go ahead and get a variety of dishes to
"divide and conquer." ✉ *Via di San Francesco a Ripa 56, Trastevere*
☎ *06/5803992* ▭ *MC, V* ⊙ *Closed Mon.* ✛ *3:C2.*

$$–$$$ ✕ **La Gensola.** For Italian "mainlanders," going out for Sicilian fare is
SICILIAN like international dining: it's a culinary adventure involving out-of-the-
ordinary tastes and flavor combinations, many thanks to the island's
interesting mix of Arab, African, and Mediterranean influences. La
Gensola, tucked away on a back street on the "quiet side" of Viale
Trastevere, offers a respite from the Roman standards, and a welcome
alternative it is. Start with antipasto, perhaps the fresh tuna "meatballs"
or gratinéed scallops with squid ink. Pastas, like a homemade taglia-
telle with sun-dried tomatoes, baby calamari, and spicy peperoncino,
are zippy on the palate. Since Sicily is a Mediterranean island, its cui-
sine leans heavily on the bounty of the sea, so a fresh fish like turbot
with tomatoes, red onion, and capers is a wonderful choice. Allow
the knowledgeable servers to guide you through the selective wine list
featuring some lesser-known southern Italian labels. And for dessert,
don't pass up an opportunity to try a cannoli or a piece of cassata cake.
Mmm, buono! ✉ *Piazza della Gensola 15, Trastevere* ☎ *06/5816312*
⊕ *www.osterialagensola.it* ▭ *AE, MC, V* ✛ *3:C1.*

$ ✕ **Ombre Rosse.** Set on lovely Piazza Sant'Egidio in the heart of Traste-
ITALIAN vere, this open-day-and-night spot is a great place to pass the time. You
can have a morning cappuccino and read one of their international
newspapers; have a light lunch (soups and salads are fresh and deli-
cious) while taking in some sun; enjoy an aperitivo and nibbles at an
outdoor table; or finish off an evening with friends at the bar. Ombre
Rosse bustles with regulars and expats who know the value of a well-
made cocktail and an ever-lively atmosphere. ✉ *Piazza Sant'Egidio 12,
Trastevere* ☎ *06/5884155* ▭ *AE, MC, V* ⊙ *No lunch Sun.* ✛ *3:B1.*

¢ ✕ **Panattoni.** Nicknamed "the mortuary" for its marble-slab tables,
PIZZA Panattoni is actually about as lively as you can get. Packed every night,
☺ it serves crisp pizzas that come out of the wood-burning ovens at top
speed. The fried starters here, like a nice *baccalà*, are light and tasty.
Panattoni stays open past midnight, convenient for a late meal after the
theater or a late movie nearby. ✉ *Viale Trastevere 53–57, Trastevere*
☎ *06/5800919* ▭ *No credit cards* ⊙ *Closed Wed. and 3 wks in mid-
Aug. No lunch* ✛ *3:C2.*

$$$ ✕ **Rivadestra.** The name is a reference to the right bank of the river—
ITALIAN which in Rome encompasses Trastevere, a neighborhood similar in
spirit to Paris's historic left bank of bohemians and intellectuals. Here,
Rivadestra stands out among the old-school Roman eateries and amber-
lit bars; walking through the heavy doors of the entrance is like walking
into an oasis. The backlit bar and candelabras create a warm glow, and
the service is quite welcoming. The streamlined menu offers starters like

12

a pumpkin flan or eggplant stewed with olive oil and herbs, but better to head straight for well-executed *primi*, like the *gramigna* pasta with a sea bass and zucchini ragù with shrimp. Main dishes included a delicate sea bass in a potato crust, and seared tuna steak with a pepper compote. Finish off with a molten chocolate cake or a cheese plate paired with their extensive list of digestivi. You won't leave overly stuffed, but you will leave happily content. ☒ *Via della Penitenza 7, Trastevere* ☎ *06/68307053* ⊕ *www.rivadestra.com* ▬ *AE, MC, V* ☙ *Closed Sun. (summer), Mon. (winter).* ✛ *4:A5.*

$$$
ROMAN

✕ **Romolo.** The setting is a cozy corner in Trastevere, right by the arch of Porta Settimiana. The menu is a familiar mélange of Roman staples that have been perfected throughout the years. And though belly-warming winter meals can be enjoyed in this ancient palazzo, it's the outdoor garden seating that makes this a coveted dining spot in the summer months. Who can resist classic spaghetti alla carbonara or pasta all'amatriciana in these surroundings? Service is equally warm and the wine list as local as the staff. ☒ *Via di Porta Settimiana 8, Trastevere* ☎ *06/5818284* ▬ *AE, DC, MC, V* ☙ *Closed Mon.* ✛ *4:B6*

$$$$
ITALIAN

✕ **Spirito di Vino.** At this restaurant on the less-traveled side of Viale Trastevere, diners can enjoy an evening of historic and culinary interest. The restaurant itself was rebuilt on the site of a 12th-century Jewish synagogue, and as such, the spot is rich with history—several ancient sculptures, now in the Vatican and Capitoline museums, were unearthed in the basement. The food ranges from inventive (mini-meatballs seasoned with coriander) to traditional (spaghetti with pecorino cheese and pepper), to historical (braised pork shoulder with apples and leeks, following an ancient Roman recipe). The proud owner is happy to explain every dish on the menu, and he even offers a postdinner tour of the wine cellar—and that basement. ☒ *Via dei Genovesi 31, Trastevere* ☎ *06/5896689* ⊕ *www.spiritodivino.com* ▬ *AE, MC, V* ☙ *Closed Sun. and 2 wks in Aug.* ✛ *3:C1.*

$$$
SEAFOOD

✕ **Z'Imberto.** Under a brightly lit awning covering a lively Trastevere piazza, you find the kind of casual trattoria one expects to stumble upon in every Italian seaside village: locals waiting for tables, a bustling casual setting, and ebullient servers pushing heaping plates of fresh seafood and pasta. Here, waiters serve with a smile and a wink, joking with clients while dishing out large portions of the house specialty: local seafood. Of course, traditional Roman meat staples are present on the menu, but really, with itsy-bitsy baby calamari the size of a fingertip fried up so perfectly, why stick to the standards? Pastas with all varieties of sea creatures abound, as do main plates of swordfish and grilled calamari. But we think the best plan is to order up the mixed house seafood antipasto for the table, order some salads and a couple of pastas to share, and close the meal with samplings from frosty bottles of *digestivi* planted firmly on your table. *This* is what they meant when they coined the term "*la dolce vita.*" ☒ *Piazza San Giovanni della Malva, Trastevere* ☎ *06/5816646* ▬ *MC, V* ☙ *Closed Mon.* ✛ *3:B1*

GIANICOLO

$$$$ ✕ **Antico Arco.** Founded by three
MODERN ITALIAN friends with a passion for wine
and fine food, Antico Arco attracts
foodies from Rome and beyond
with its culinary inventiveness and
high style. The location up on top
of the Janiculum hill provides for
a charming setting and a homey
ambience difficult to come by elsewhere in the city. Seating upstairs
is cozy, particularly in winter. The
menu changes with the season, but
you may find delights such as *flan di
taleggio con salsa di funghi* (taleggio
cheese flan with mushroom sauce),
or a *carré d'agnello* (rack of lamb)
with foie gras sauce and pears in
port wine. The chocolate soufflé
with a molten chocolate center, is
justly famous among chocoholics
all over the city. ✉ *Piazzale Aurelio 7, Gianicolo* ☎ *06/5815274* ⊕ *www.
anticoarco.it* ⟐ *Reservations essential* ▬ *AE, DC, MC, V* ⊘ *Closed Sun.
and 2 wks in Aug. No lunch* ✛ *3:A1.*

COLOSSEO, AVENTINO, AND TESTACCIO

COLOSSEO

$$$ ✕ **Ai Tre Scalini.** A traditional restaurant by the Colosseum, Ai Tre Scalini
ROMAN is old-school Roman with touches of the Sicilian. The seating outside
in warm weather is pleasant, and some dishes highlight the chef's
playfulness, like the unusual radicchio and cheese-stuffed *zagnolotti*
(small ravioli) in a lobster sauce. A wide variety of second courses,
from gilthead bream topped with paper-thin potato rounds, to simple
beef with rosemary, are indeed what they seem, served by waiters who
have clearly been around for quite some time. ✉ *Via SS. Quattro 30,
Colosseo* ☎ *06/7096309* ▬ *AE, DC, MC, V* ⊘ *Closed Mon. and 10
days in Sept.* ✛ *3:G1.*

TESTACCIO

$ ✕ **Acqua e Farina.** Not quite a pizzeria, trendy Acqua e Farina sticks close
PIZZA to its name, which translates as "water and flour." The menu offers
takeoffs on pizza, such as *strufolini*, cylinders of pizza dough stuffed
with mozzarella, anchovies, and zucchini flowers, or smoked provolone,
mushrooms, and prosciutto. Try other shapes and fillings to create a
fun meal. ✉ *Piazza O. Giustiniani 2, Testaccio* ☎ *06/5741382* ▬ *AE,
MC, V* ⊘ *No lunch* ✛ *3:C5.*

$$$$ ✕ **Checchino dal 1887.** Literally carved out of a hill of ancient shards
ROMAN of amphorae, Checchino remains an example of a classic, family-run
Roman restaurant, with one of the best wine cellars in the region.
Though the slaughterhouses of Testaccio are long gone, an echo of

12

their past existence lives on in the restaurant's soul food—mostly offal and other less–appealing cuts like *trippa* (tripe), *pajata* (intestine with the mother's milk still inside), and *coratella* (sweetbreads and heart of beef) are all still on the menu for die-hard Roman purists. For the less adventuresome, house specialties include braised milk-fed lamb with seasonal vegetables. Head here for a taste of old Rome, but note that Checchino is really beginning to show its age. ⊠ *Via di Monte Testaccio 30* ☎ *06/5746318* ⊟ *AE, DC, MC, V* ☉ *Closed Sun., Mon., Aug, and 1 wk at Christmas* ✢ *3:C5.*

$ ✗ **Da Oio a Casa Mia.** This classic Roman trattoria has all the usual
ROMAN suspects, including locals straight out of central casting and gruff but good-natured service. The Roman classic pastas here are good bets, with delicious versions of carbonara, *amatriciana,* and rigatoni with a *coda alla vaccinara* (stewed oxtail) tomato sauce. Secondi like meatballs, *straccetti* (strips of beef in wine sauce over a bed of arugula), chicken hunter's style, and stewed tripe (for those who enjoy it) are all excellent options. Outdoor seating in warm months is a relaxing option. ⊠ *Via Galvani 43–45, San Lorenzo* ☎ *06/5782680* ⊟ *AE, DC, MC, V* ☉ *Closed Sun.* ✢ *3:C4.*

$$$ ✗ **Perilli.** In this restaurant dating from 1911, the old Testaccio remains,
ITALIAN and it has the decor to prove it. A seasonal antipasto table starts things off, offering Roman specialties like stewed Roman artichokes and *puntarelle* (curled chicory stems in a garlicky vinaigrette based on lots of lemon and anchovy). The waiters wear crooked bow ties and are just a little bit too hurried—until, that is, you order classics like pasta all'amatriciana and carbonara, which they relish tossing in a big bowl tableside. This is also the place to try rigatoni *con pajata* (with calves' intestines)—if you're into that sort of thing. Secondi plates are for carnivores only, and the house wine is a golden enamel-remover from the Castelli Romani. ⊠ *Via Marmorata 39, Testaccio* ☎ *06/5742415* ⊟ *AE, DC, MC, V* ☉ *Closed Wed.* ✢ *3:D4.*

$ ✗ **Remo.** Expect a wait at this perennial favorite in Testaccio frequented
PIZZA by students and locals. You won't find tablecloths or other nonessentials, just classic Roman pizza and boisterous conversation. ⊠ *Piazza Santa Maria Liberatrice 44, Testaccio* ☎ *06/5746270* ⊟ *No credit cards* ☉ *Closed Sun., Aug., and Christmas wk. No lunch* ✢ *3:C4.*

BEYOND THE CITY CENTER

$$$ ✗ **L'Archeologia.** In this farmhouse just beyond the catacombs, you dine
ITALIAN indoors beside the fireplace in cool weather or in the garden under age-old vines in summer. The atmosphere is friendly and intimate. Specialties include fettuccine *al finocchio salvatico* (with wild fennel), *abbacchio alla scottadito,* and fresh seafood. But remember that the food here is secondary: you're paying for the view and the setting more than any culinary adventure or excellence with the classics. ⊠ *Via Appia Antica 139, Via Appia, south side of Rome* ☎ *06/7880494* ⊕ *www.larcheologia.it* ⊟ *AE, MC, V* ☉ *Closed Tues.* ✢ *2:E6.*

$$$$

MODERN ITALIAN

Fodor's Choice

★

✕ **La Pergola.** La Pergola's rooftop location offers a commanding view of the city, and as you're seated in your plush chair, you know you're in for a three–Michelin star experience. First, your waiter will present you with menus—food, wine, and water (you read correctly). Then you must choose between the German Wunder-chef Heinz Beck's *alta cucina* specialties, though most everything will prove to be the best version of the dish you've ever tasted. Lobster is oh-so-lightly poached, and melt-in-your-mouth lamb in a veggie-accented jus is deceptively simple but earthy and perfect. Each course comes with a flourish of sauces or extra touches that makes it an event in its own right, while the cheese cart is well-explained by knowledgeable servers. The dessert course is extravagant, including tiny petits fours and treats tucked away in small drawers that make up the serving "cabinet." The wine list is as thrilling as one might expect with the financial backing of the Hilton and their investment in one of the top wine cellars in Italy. ✉ *Cavalieri Hilton, Via Cadlolo 101, Monte Mario, Northwest Rome* ☎ *06/3509221* ⊕ *www. romecavalieri.com/lapergola.php* ⟐ *Reservations essential. Jacket and tie* ⊟ *AE, DC, MC, V* ⊗ *Closed Sun. and Mon., and 2 wks in Dec. No lunch* ⟐ *1:A1.*

Rome Dining and Lodging Atlas

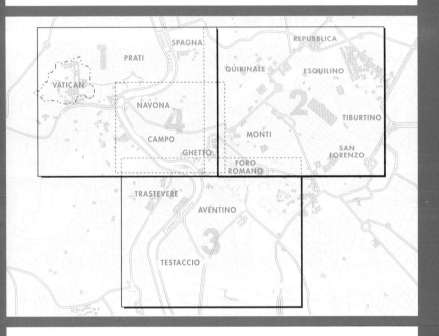

SPAGNA

PRATI

VATICAN

NAVONA

CAMPO

GHETTO

REPUBBLICA

QUIRINALE

ESQUILINO

MONTI

FORO
ROMANO

TIBURTINO

SAN
LORENZO

TRASTEVERE

AVENTINO

TESTACCIO

KEY	
☐	Hotels
■	Restaurants
■	Restaurant in Hotel

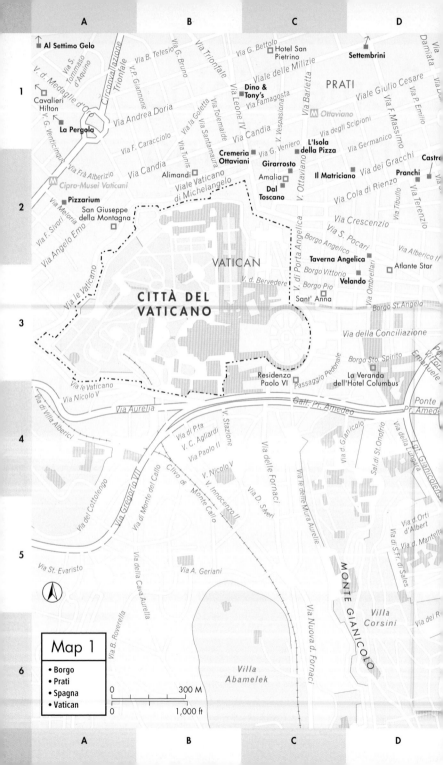

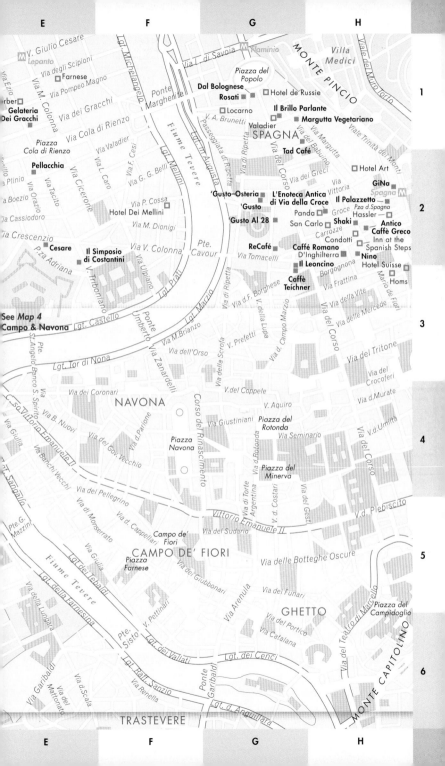

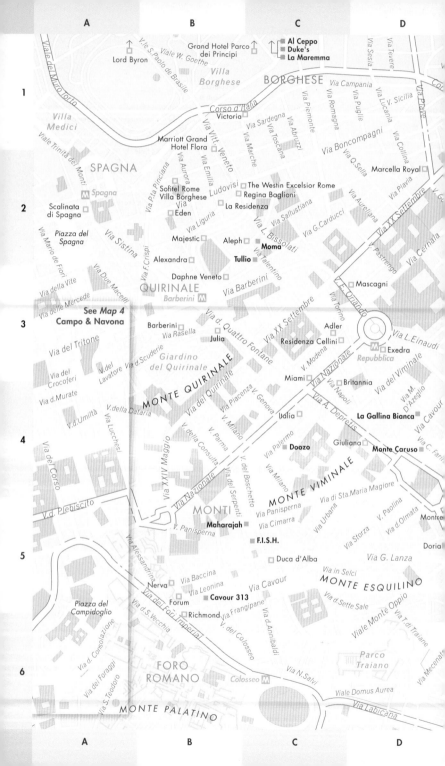

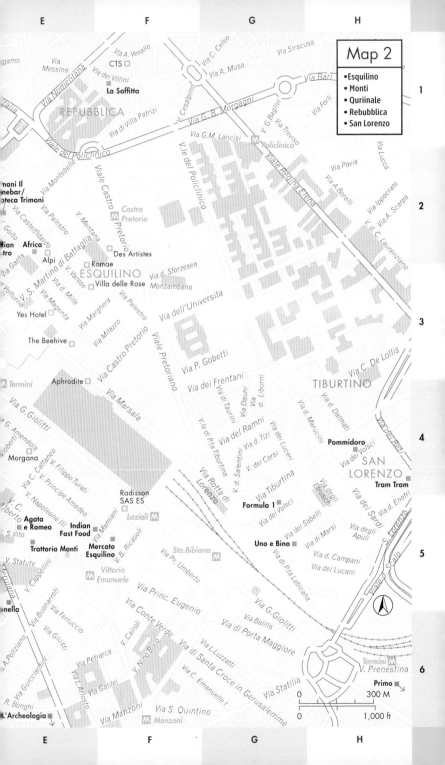

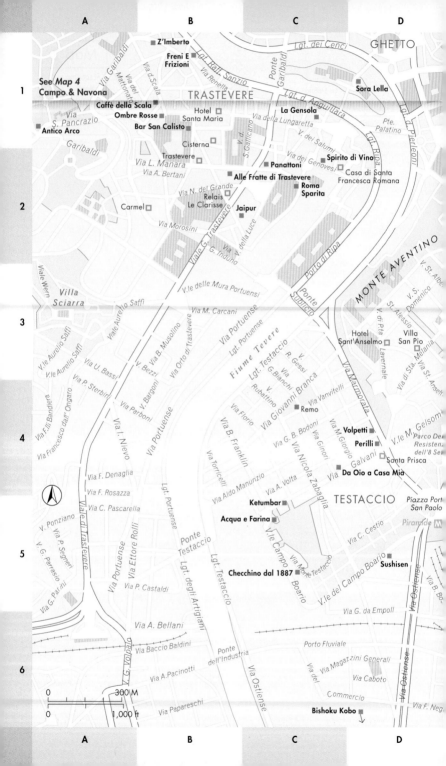

A

See Map 4
Campo & Navona

Via S. Pancrazio

■ Antico Arco

Garibaldi

Via Garibaldi

Via d. Scala

Via del Mattonato

Via d'Scala

Caffè della Scala ■
Ombre Rosse ■
Bar San Calisto ■

Cisterna

Trastevere

Via L. Manara

Via A. Bertani

Carmel ■

Via Morosini

*Villa
Sciarra*

Viale Wern

V.le Aurelio Saffi

V.le Aurelio Saffi

Viale Aurelio Saffi

Via U. Bassi

Via P. Sterbini

Via F.lli Bandiera

Via Francesco dall' Ongaro

V. Ponziano

V. P. Segneri

V. G. Parrasio

Via G. Parini

B

■ Z'Imberto

**Freni E
Frizioni** ■

Via Renella

Lgt. Rall. Sanzio

TRASTEVERE

Hotel
Santa Maria □

Trastevere □

Via N. del Grande

Alle Fratte di Trastevere ■

**Relais
Le Clarisse** □

Jaipur ■

Viale G. Trastevere

Via G. Induno

Via della Luce

V.le delle Mura Portuensi

Via M. Carcani

Via B. Musolino

Via B. Bezzi

V. Orto di Trastevere

Via Portuense

Via V. Bargoni

Via I. Nievo

Via F. Denaglia

Via F. Rosazza

Via C. Pascarella

Viale di Trastevere

Via Portuense

Via Ettore Rolli

Via P. Castaldi

Via G. Baccio Baldini

Via A. Bellani

Via A. Pacinotti

Via Papareschi

C

Lgt. dei Cenci

Ponte
Garibaldi

Lgt. d. Anguillara

La Gensola ■

Via della Lungaretta

V. dei Salumi

Via dei Genovesi

Panattoni ■

**Roma
Sparita** ■

S. Gallicano

V. d. S. Gallicano

Porto di Ripa

Ponte
Sublicio

Via Portuense

Lgt. Portuense

Fiume Tevere

Lgt. Testaccio

V. R. Gessi

Via G. Bianchi Branca

Via Rubattino

Via Vanvitelli

Remo ■

Via Florio

Via Giovanni Branca

Via B. Franklin

Via G. B. Bodoni

Via Ginori

Via Nicola Zabaglia

Via Torricelli

Via Aldo Manunzio

Via A. Volta

Via M. Giorgio

Galvani

Ketumbar ■

Acqua e Farina ■

V.le Campo Boario

Via M. le Testaccio

Checchino dal 1887 ■

Lgt. Testaccio

Lgt. degli Artigiani

Ponte
Testaccio

V.le del Campo Boario

Ponte
dell'Industria

Via Ostiense

Porto Fluviale

Via del Commercio

D

GHETTO

■ Sora Lella

Lgt. d. Pierleoni

Lgt. d. Ripa

Pte.
Palatino

Spirito di Vino ■

Casa di Santa
Francesca Romana

MONTE AVENTINO

V. St. Albe

V. S. Domenico

St. Alessio

Via di Pta.
Lavernale

Via di Sta. Melania

V. St. Ansel

Hotel
Sant'Anselmo □

Villa
San Pio

Via Marmorata

Volpetti ■

Perilli ■

V.le M. Gelsom

*Parco De
Resisten.
dell'8 Se*

Santa Prisca □

Da Oio a Casa Mia ■

TESTACCIO

Piazza Port
San Paolo

Piramide Ⓜ

Via C. Cestio

Sushisen ■

Via G. da Empoli

Via Magazzini Generali

Via Caboto

Via Ostiense

Via F. Neg

Bishoku Kobo ■

0 —————— 300 M
0 —————— 1,000 ft

| A | B | C | D |

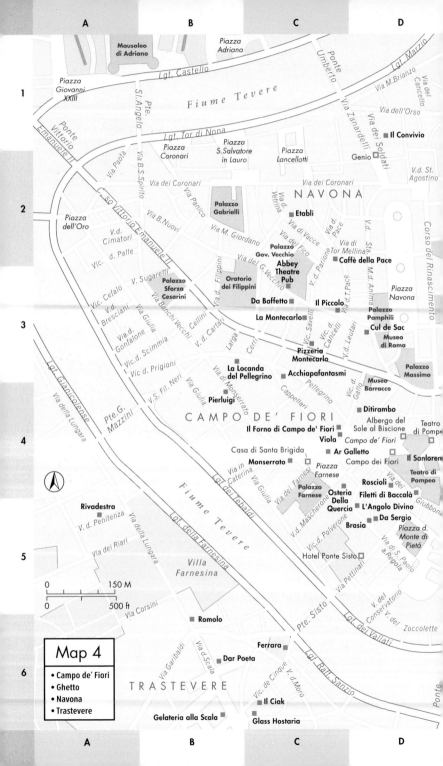

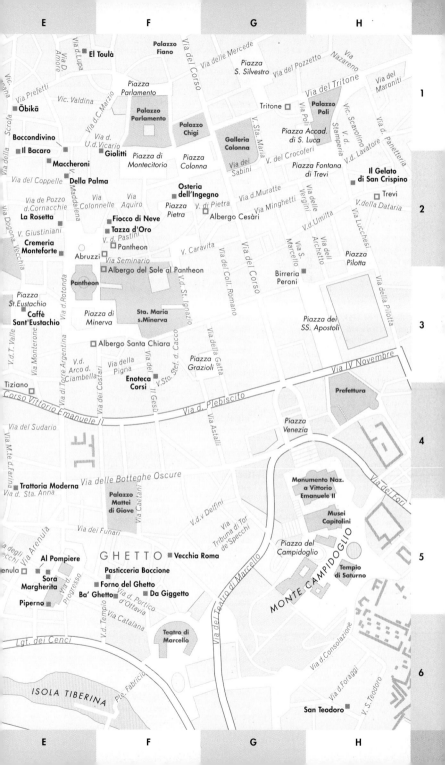

Dining

Abbey Theatre Pub, 4:C3
Acchiappafantasmi, 4:C3
Acqua e Farina, 3:C5
Acquolina, 1:G1
Africa, 2:E2
Agata e Romeo, 2:E5
Ai Tre Scalini, 3:G1
Al Ceppo, 2:C1
Al Pompiere, 4:E5
Al Settimo Gelo, 1:A1
Alle Fratte di Trastevre, 3:B2
Antico Arco, 3:A1
Antico Caffè Greco, 1:H2
Antico Forno del Ghetto, 4:F5
Ar Galletto, 4:C4
Ba' Ghetto, 4:F5
Bar San Calisto, 3:B1
Birreria Peroni, 4:G3
Bishoku Kobo, 3:D6
Boccondivino, 4:E2
Brasia, 4:D5
Caffè della Pace, 4:C2
Caffè della Scala, 4:B6
Caffé Romano dell'Hotel d'Inghilterra, 1:H2
Caffè Sant'Eustachio, 4:E3
Caffè Teichner, 1:G3
Castroni, 1:D2
Cavour 313, 2:B5
Cesare, 1:E2
Checchino dal 1887, 3:C5
Cremeria Monteforte, 4:E2
Cremeria Ottaviani, 1:C2
Cul de Sac, 4:D3
Da Baffetto, 4:C3
Da Giggetto, 4:F5
Da Oio a Casa Mia, 3:C4
Da Sergio, 4:D5
Dal Bolognese, 1:G1
Dal Toscano, 1:C2
Dar Poeta, 4:B6
Della Palma, 4:E2
Dino & Tony's, 1:B1
Ditirambo, 4:D4
Duke's, 2:C1
El Toulà, 4:E1
Enoteca Corsi, 4:F4
Etablì, 4:C2
F.I.S.H., 2:C5
Ferrara, 4:C6
Filetti di Baccalà, 4:D5
Fiocco di Neve, 4:F2
Formula 1, 2:G5
Freni E Frizioni, 3:B1

Gelateria alla Scala, 3:B1
Gelateria dei Gracchi, 1:E1
GiNa, 1:H2
Giolitti, 4:F2
Girarrosto, 1:C2
Glass Hostaria, 4:C6
'Gusto, 1:G2
'Gusto al 28, 1:G2
'Gusto - Osteria, 1:G2
Il Bacaro, 4:E2
Il Brillo Parlante, 1:G1
Il Ciak, 4:C6
Il Convivio, 4:D1
Il Forno di Campo de' Fiori, 4:C4
Il Gelato di San Crispino, 4:H2
Il Leoncino, 1:G3
Il Matriciano, 1:D2
Il Palazzetto, 1:H2
Il Sanlorenzo, 4:D4
Il Simposio di Costantini, 1:E2
Italian Bistro, 2:D3
Jaipur, 3:C2
Ketumbar, 3:C5
La Gallina Bianca, 2:4D
La Gensola, 3:C5
La Locanda del Pellegrino, 4:C3
La Maremma, 2:C1
La Montecarlo, 4:C3
La Pergola, 1:A1
La Rosetta, 4:E2
La Soffitta, 2:F1
La Veranda dell'Hotel Columbus, 1:D3
L'Angolo Divino, 4:C5
L'Archeologia, 2:E6
L'Enoteca Antica di Via della Croce, 1:G2
L'Isola della Pizza, 1:C2
Maccheroni, 4:E2
Maharajah, 2:C5
Margutta Vegetariano, 1:G1
Mercato Eesquilino 2: F5
Moma, 2:C2
Monserrato, 4:C4
Monte Caruso, 2:D4
Nino, 1:H3
Ōbikä, 4:E1
Ombre Rosee, 3:B1
Osteria della Quercia, 4:C4
Osteria dell'Ingegno, 4:F2
Panattoni, 3:C2
Panella, 2:E5
Papá Baccus, 4:B3

Pasticceria Boccioni, 4:F5
Pellacchia, 1:E2
Perilli, 3:D4
Piperno, 4:E5
Pizzarium, 1:A2
Pizzeria Montecarlo, 4:C3
Primo, 2:H6
ReCafé, 1:G2
Remo, 3:C4
Rivadestra, 4:A5
Roma Sparita, 3:C2
Romolo, 4:B6
Rosati, 1:G1
Roscioli, 4:D4
San Teodoro, 3:E1
Settembrini, 1:D1
Shaki Wine Bar, 1:H2
Sora Lella, 3:D1
Sora Margherita, 4:E5
Spirito di Vino, 3:C1
Sushisen, 3:D5
Tad Café, 1:G1
Taverna Angelica, 1:D3
Tazza d'Oro, 4:E2
Tram Tram, 2:H4
Trattoria Moderna, 4:E4
Trattoria Monti, 2:E5
Trimani Il Winebar, 2:D2
Tullio, 2:C3
Uno e Bino, 2:G5
Vecchia Roma, 4:F5
Velando, 1:C2
Vioila, 4:C4
Volpetti, 3:D4
Z'Imberto 3:B1

Lodging

Abruzzi, 4:F3
Adler, 2:C3
Albergo Cesàri, 4:G2
Albergo del Sole al Biscione, 4:D4
Albergo del Sole al Pantheon, 4:F3
Albergo Santa Chiara, 4:E3
Aleph, 2:C2
Alexandra, 2:C2
Alimandi, 1:B2
Alpi, 2:E2
Amalia, 1:C2
Aphrodite, 2:E3
Arenula, 4:E5
Atlante Star, 1:D3
Barberini, 2:B3
Britannia, 2:C4
Capo d'Africa, 4:C6
Carmel, 3:B2

Casa di Santa Brigida, 4:C4
Casa di Santa Francesca Romana, 3:C2
Cavalieri Hilton, 1:A!
Celio, 3:G1
Cisterna, 3:B2
Condotti, 1:H2
Daphne Veneto, 2:B3
Dei Borgognoni, 1:H3
Des Artistes, 2:F2
D'Inghilterra, 1:H3
Domus Aventina, 3: E3
Doria, 2:E5
Duca d'Alba, 2:C5
Eden, 2:B2
Exedra, 2:D3
Genio, 4:D2
Gerber, 1:E1
Giuliana, 2:D4
Grand Hotel de la Minerve, 4:F3
Grand Hotel Parco dei Principi, 2:C1
Hassler, 1:H2
Hotel Art, 1:H2
Hotel Campo de'Fiori, 4: D4
Hotel de Russie, 1:G1
Hotel Dei Mellini, 1:F2
Hotel Forum, 2:C5
Hotel Homs, 1:H3
Hotel Lancelot, 2:H2
Hotel Ponte Sisto, 4:D5
Hotel San Anselmo, 3:D3
Hotel San Pietrino, 1:B1
Hotel Santa Maria, 3:B1
Hotel Suisse, 1:H3
Hotel Trastevere, 3:B2
Inn at the Spanish Steps, 1:H2
Italia, 2:C4
Julia, 2:B3
La Residenza, 2:B2
Locarno, 1:G1
Lord Byron, 2:A1
Majestic, 2:B2
Marcella Royal, 2:D4
Marriott Grand Hotel Flora, 2:B1
Mascagni, 2:D3
Mecenate Palace Hotel, 2:D5
Miami, 2:C4
Montreal, 2:D5
Morgana, 2:E4
Nerva, 2:B5
Panda, 1:H2
Pantheon, 4:F2
Radisson SAS Es, 2:F5
Regina Baglioni, 2:B2

Relais Le Clarisse, 3:B2
Residenza Cellini, 2:C3
Residenza Paolo VI, 1:C4
Richmond, 2:B6
Romae, 2:E3
San Carlo, 1:H2
San Giuseppe della Montagna, 1:A2
Santa Prisca, 3:D4
Sant'Anna, 1:C3
Scalinata di Spagna, 2:A2
Sofitel, 2:B2
Teatro di Pompeo, 4:D4
The Beehive, 2:E3
Tiziano, 4:E4
Trevi, 1:H2
Tritone, 4:G1
Valadier, 1:G1
Victoria, 2:C1
Villa San Pio, 3:D3
Westin Excelsior, 2:C2
Yes Hotel, 2:E3

Where to Stay

WORD OF MOUTH

"Trastevere was WONDERFUL!!!! I would totally tell anyone who was going to Rome to stay there. The food was cheap and fantastic, wow! Overall, as someone who's been to Rome many, many times, Trastevere put a new spin on it and gets an A++ in my book. Can't say enough good things about it!"

—GiuliaPiraino

THE SCENE

Updated
by Nicole
Arriaga

It's the click of your heels on inlaid marble, the whisper of 600-count Frette sheets, the murmured "buongiorno" of a coat-tailed porter bowing low as you pass. It's a wrought-iron balcony for your morning cappuccino, a white umbrella on a roof terrace, a 400-year-old palazzo with Casanova's name in the guest book. Whatever your Roman holiday hotel fantasy, Audrey Hepburn couldn't have had it better. Dolce Vita, here you come.

There are more luxury lodgings, bed-and-breakfasts, and designer "boutique" hotels in Rome than ever before, but if you prefer more modest accommodations (because really, who comes to Rome to hang out in the hotel room?), you still have plenty of options. There are many mid-range and budget hotels and *pensioni* (small, family-run lodgings) available. You may also consider staying at a monastery or convent, a hostel, or an apartment.

If fancy is what you're looking for, you're bound to find it on the Via Veneto and the Spanish Steps area. On the flip side, many of the city's cheapest and modest accommodations are scattered near the Stazione Termini. But for the most authentic Roman experience, stay in or near the *centro storico* (the historic center).

Breakfast is an increasingly popular trend in new millennium Rome. High-end places generally serve a full American-style breakfast including eggs and bacon, cereals, and cold-cuts. However, most still consist of a lighter more traditional Italian breakfast: a Continental-style buffet of pastries, cereal, cold cuts, juice, and cappuccino. Proprietors are also becoming more conscientious about hotel appearance, opting for updated—or at least, tastefully simple—decor.

WHERE SHOULD I STAY?

	NEIGHBORHOOD VIBE	PROS	CONS
Pantheon, Navona, Trevi, and Quirinale	In the heart of the city center, you're surrounded by history, mazes of cobbled streets, and many of Rome's main attractions.	Everything is within walking distance: from fine restaurants and cheap eats to couture shopping and Rome's most famed museums and monuments.	Hotels may set you back a pretty penny and, depending on where your hotel is positioned, street noise may also be an issue. Beware of tourist traps as well.
Campo de' Fiori and Ghetto	The Campo is famous for its outdoor farmer's and flower market and its nightly revelry in the main square. The Ghetto, or Jewish quarter, is much quieter.	Many restaurants, bars, boutiques, and specialty stores. Fresh fruits and veggies at the market. Plenty of Jewish-style fried artichokes.	At night, Campo is chaotic, noisy, and full of drunken American college students. No public transportation inside the Ghetto. Tons of tourist traps.
Monti, Esquilino, Repubblica, and San Lorenzo	Where shabby chic meets the sketchy parts of Rome. It's also become the city's most diverse immigrant neighborhood (with great ethnic food).	Hotels are generally cheaper. Tons of cool bars, restaurants, and boutiques. Close to the major transportation hub, Termini train station.	When it comes to shacking up, you may get what you pay for. The area around Termini and even Monti can be sketchy at night. San Lorenzo has limited transportation.
Veneto, Borghese, and Spagna	Luxury hotels, renovated palazzos, and five-star dining that revolve around the Borghese Gardens.	Historically caters to royalty, movie stars, or anyone willing to dish out some major dough.	Off the beaten paths at night. Far from the typical centro hot spots. Everything is expensive.
Vatican, Borgo, and Prati	Holy! More clergy than you've ever seen in one place. Safe, quiet, and residential area. Prati is full of chic shopping and trendy caffè and restaurants.	If you're Catholic, this is a heavenly place to be. The neighborhoods are tranquil when you get away from St. Peter's. Great shopping and eating.	Inflated prices. Massive crowds on Catholic holidays. Situated away from the other tourist attractions. Traveling will require you to take the bus or metro.
Trastevere and Gianicolo	The heart of old, picturesque Rome. Tiny, winding alleyways. Dining mecca with hip watering holes.	Great mom-and-pop trattorias and pizzerias. A buzzing nightlife that goes on into the wee hours of the night.	Trastevere is crowded and noisy, especially on the weekends. Beware pickpockets in the main piazza.
Aventino, Testaccio, and Palatino	Quiet, leafy, residential streets (and spacious hotels) in Aventino. Testaccio is the heart of Rome's nightlife.	Tranquillity and amazing views on the Aventino. See and be seen in Rome's most nocturnal neighborhood.	Not much public transportation on the Aventine hill. Testaccio is insanely crowded on weekend nights.
Colosseo Area	Ancient Rome meets Christian Rome with an array of parks and residential neighborhoods.	Quieter than most of the centro storico. Sightseeing at the Colosseum, the Basilica di San Giovanni in Laterano.	Limited accommodations get booked up with tourist groups in spring and summer. You'll pay for views of the Colosseum.

13

WHERE TO STAY PLANNER

Lodging Strategy

Where should we stay? With hundreds of hotels to choose from in Rome, it may seem like a daunting question. But fret not—our expert writers and editors have done most of the legwork. The 90-plus selections here represent the best lodging this city has to offer—from spartan convents to opulent palaces. Scan Best Bets on the following pages for top recommendations by price and experience. Or locate a specific review in the listings. They're organized alphabetically within each neighborhood. Happy hunting!

Reservations

It's always wise to book in advance, even if only a few days ahead, especially in May and June and around major Catholic holidays like Easter and Christmas. There's never a period when the city's hotels are predictably empty, though July and August and late January to February are relatively slow months. Always inquire about special rates.

Be as specific as possible about the accommodations you desire. Request the room size (single, double, or triple), type (standard, deluxe, or suite), and whether you want air-conditioning, a no-smoking room, a private bathroom with a shower or tub (or both), a terrace or balcony, or a view of the city (and ask whether there are extra costs associated with any of these). You may be required to leave a deposit; get a statement from the hotel about its refund policy before releasing your credit card number or mailing a money order. Insist on a written confirmation from the hotel stating the duration of your stay, room rate, any extras, location, room size, and type.

With Kids

Italians love kids, and most hotels allow children to stay in their parents' room at no charge. However, hotel rooms and beds are often undersized by American standards, so inquire about triples, connecting rooms or suites, or consider taking a short-term apartment rental or residence hotel for the duration of your stay.

Checking In

The Roman approach to life is a leisurely one, and that's reflected in the fact that there's no real standard for check-in times. If you arrive early in the morning (as is often the case with North American flights), you may find that your room is more than likely not ready yet. In which case, most hotels will store your luggage and encourage you to go out sightseeing. If you think you'll arrive later in the day or evening, it's best to mention this upon reserving or confirming. This is because some of the smaller hotels may not have a 24-hour reception staff and you could find yourself locked out for the night. Check-out times are a little stricter, between 10 AM and noon. If you need more time than that, the hotel may try to charge you for an extra night. However, if you just want to store your luggage for a few hours on your last day, most hotels will accommodate this request.

Meal Plans

At the end of each review, a set of initials indicates the meal plan that is included with the room rate. European Plan, indicated by EP, means no meals are included; Breakfast Plan, BP, indicates that a full, hot breakfast is included; Continental Plan, CP, means a continental breakfast is included; Full American Plan, FAP, means all meals are included; Modified American Plan, MAP, means breakfast and dinner are included; and All-Inclusive, AI, indicates that all meals and most activities are included.

Facilities

The most expensive hotels have all the amenities you would expect at top levels and rates, with full services, spacious lounges, bars, restaurants, and some fitness facilities. Mid-range hotels may have refrigerators, in-room safes, and double-glazed windows to keep out street noise. Budget hotels will have in-room direct-dial telephone and TV, and most will have air-conditioning. In less expensive places, you may have to pay extra for air-conditioning, and the shower may be the drain-in-the-floor type that hovers over the toilet and drenches the whole bathroom.

Unless stated in the review, hotels are equipped with elevators, and all guest rooms have air-conditioning, TV, and telephones. The number of rooms listed at the end of each review reflects those with private bathrooms (which means they have a shower or a tub, but not necessarily both).

Prices

In the off-season months of late January, February, July, and August, prices can be considerably discounted (sometimes up to half off the regular rate). Inquire about specials and weekend deals, and you may be able to get a better rate per night if you are staying a week or longer. Rates are inclusive of service, but it's customary to tip porters, waiters, maids, and concierges.

WHAT IT COSTS IN EUROS

	¢	$	$$	$$$	$$$$
FOR TWO PEOPLE	under €75	€75–€150	€151–€225	€226–€300	over €300

Prices are for a standard double room in high season.

In This Chapter

Spotlight On

Internet

Note that we use "Wi-Fi" when wireless access is available, and "Internet" when any other type of Internet access is available, aside from Wi-Fi.

Using the Maps

Throughout the chapter, you'll see mapping symbols and coordinates (✠ 3:F2) after property names or reviews. To locate the property on a map, turn to the Rome Dining and Lodging Atlas at the end of the Where to Eat chapter. The first number after the ✠ symbol indicates the map number. Following that is the property's coordinate on the map grid.

13

BEST BETS FOR ROME LODGING

Fodor's offers a selective listing of quality lodging experiences at every price range, from the city's best budget motel to its most sophisticated luxury hotel. Here, we've compiled our top recommendations by price and experience. The very best properties—in other words, those that provide a particularly remarkable experience in their price range—are designated in the listings with the Fodor's Choice logo.

HOTEL REVIEWS

Listed alphabetically within neighborhoods.

PANTHEON, NAVONA, TREVI, AND QUIRINALE

Encompassing the area around and between spectacular Piazza Navona and the Pantheon and Trevi Fountain to the east, this is an upscale and picturesque area. There's a range of places to stay here, from frayed-at-the-edges *pensioni* to top-of-the line historic hotels, all housed in the 17th- and 18th-century buildings that make up this part of Rome. Much of the area is pedestrian-only, with a lively mix of restaurants and nightlife.

13

PANTHEON

$$ **Abruzzi.** Rarely do magnificent views of world-famous ancient monuments come with such a relatively gentle price tag. From the windows of this old-fashioned little establishment, the Pantheon is literally in your face. The decor is nothing to brag about but the beds are comfortable and the location is key. **Pros:** views of the Pantheon; sizeable bathrooms; the piazza is a hot spot. **Cons:** the smell of cigarette smoke is ever-present; some staff seem to want to avoid running credit cards (though the hotel accepts them); breakfast is not served in the hotel but at a bar in the piazza. ⊠ *Piazza della Rotonda 69, Pantheon* ☎ *06/6792021* ⊕ *www.hotelabruzzi.it* 🛏 *22 rooms* ⚭ *In-room: safe, refrigerator. In-hotel: laundry service, no-smoking rooms* ═ *MC, V* ⦶*CP* ✛ *4:F3*.

$$$ **Albergo Cesàri.** The exterior of this intimate hotel on a traffic-free street is as it was when Stendhal stayed here in the 1800s. Inside, the hotel has been renovated and there's no patina left from the days when Garibaldi and Gregorovius were guests, yet most rooms are sweetly embellished with old prints of Rome and soft-green drapes and bedspreads, creating an air of comfort and serenity. Furniture is new, yet traditionally styled. Bathrooms are done in smart two-tone blue marble. At the rooftop bar, guests can marvel over the views during breakfast, or in the evening over cocktails. **Pros:** prime location and soundproofed from the street noise; computer with Internet access available; friendly staff that provides good service. **Cons:** inside the hotel, the walls seem to be paper-thin (and you can hear your neighbors); a/c is not especially strong. ⊠ *Via di Pietra 89a, Pantheon* ☎ *06/6749701* ⊕ *www.albergocesari.it* 🛏 *47 rooms* ⚭ *In-room: safe, refrigerator, Wi-Fi. In-hotel: room service, bar, laundry service, public Wi-Fi, parking (paid), some pets allowed, no-smoking rooms* ═ *AE, DC, MC, V* ⦶*CP* ✛ *4:G2*.

$$$–$$$$ **Albergo del Sole al Pantheon.** Grandly situated directly opposite the immortal portico of the Pantheon, this place is in the running as a candidate for the world's oldest hotel. Welcoming the great ever since it opened in 1467, the Albergo del Sole al Pantheon has hosted Frederick III, Ariosto, Cagliostro, and Pietro Mascagni (who came here to celebrate the opening night of his opera, *Cavalleria Rusticana*). Needless to say, the hotel has been renovated many times over and most vestiges of the distant past are long gone. The good news is that the refurbishment has been done in high style: artfully placed columns, Rococo windows, renaissance-style beds, high ceilings, and terra-cotta floors all lend a certain authenticity to your stay. Obviously, specify if you want a room with a view over the Pantheon; with it, you'll also get the din of the piazza's gorgeous caffè scene, but double-glaze windows work their magic. **Pros:** real Roman atmosphere and character; all rooms have Jacuzzi tubs. **Cons:** next to McDonald's; old hotel with an old feel; rooms are not particularly luxurious. ✉ *Piazza della Rotonda 63, Pantheon* ☎ *06/6780441* 🌐 *www.hotelsolealpantheon.com* *33 rooms* *In-room: safe, refrigerator, Wi-Fi. In-hotel: room service, bar, laundry service, Internet terminal* ▭ *AE, DC, MC, V* *CP* ✥ *4:D4.*

$$$ Fodor's Choice ★ **Albergo Santa Chiara.** The Santa Chiara, which has been in the family for some 200 years, is situated just behind the Pantheon and near Michelangelo's obelisk in Piazza della Minerva. The hotel lobby is *alla Romana*—an all white affair, elegantly accented with a Venetian chandelier, a stucco statue, a gilded Baroque mirror, and a walnut concierge desk. Upstairs, the pricier rooms are slightly more swanky with stylish, yet comfortable furniture. Each room has built-in oak headboards, a marble-top desk, and a travertine bath. Double-glaze windows keep out the noise, especially for those rooms facing the piazza. There are also three apartments, for two to five people, with full kitchens. **Pros:** great location in the historical center behind the Pantheon; most of the rooms are spacious; the staff is both polite and helpful. **Cons:** layout is mazelike (you must take two elevators to some of the rooms); rooms don't get a lot of light. ✉ *Via Santa Chiara 21, Pantheon* ☎ *06/6872979* 🌐 *www.albergosantachiara.com* *96 rooms, 3 suites, 3 apartments* *In-room: safe, kitchen (some), refrigerator. In-hotel: room service, bar, Wi-Fi, laundry service* ▭ *AE, DC, MC, V* *CP* ✥ *4:E3.*

$$$$ **Grand Hotel de la Minerve.** The Minerve is the stylish reincarnation of the hostelry that occupied this 17th-century palazzo for hundreds of years, hosting literati from Stendhal to Sartre and de Beauvoir along with a bevy of crowned heads. It sports one of Rome's to-die-for locations: on the famous piazza with Bernini's elephant obelisk, and just a few feet from the Pantheon and the church of Santa Maria sopra Minerva. Inside, an extensive renovation nearly gutted the building. What emerged was a vast and sleek lobby (complete with 19th-century statues and some rather gaudy stained glass), big banquet facilities, the lush La Cesta restaurant, and guest rooms aswim in Italian modern furnishings. Guests love the staff here, and no one can resist the lavish roof terrace. **Pros:** about 50 yards from the Pantheon on quiet Piazza della Minerva; some rooms have terraces; the staff is both friendly and helpful. **Cons:** the property is a little worn around the edges; some say it seems expensive for what you get; at the time of writing, the all-American breakfast buffet costs €31 and a simple continental breakfast costs €22. ✉ *Piazza della Minerva 69, Pantheon* ☎ *06/695201* 🌐 *grandhoteldelaminerve.it*

119 rooms, 16 suites ⌂ In-room: safe, refrigerator, Internet. In-hotel: restaurant, room service, bar, gym, laundry service, Internet terminal, public Wi-Fi, parking (paid), no-smoking rooms ⌸ AE, DC, MC, V ⎢OⒾ EP ✚ 4:F3.

$$$ ⌸ **Pantheon.** The Pantheon is a superb place to stay right next door to the grand monument of the same name. The lobby is the very epitome of a Roman hotel lobby—a warm, cozy, yet opulent setting that comes replete with stained glass, sumptuous wood paneling, a Renaissance beamed ceiling, and a massive and glorious chandelier. A print of one of Rome's obelisks on the door welcomes you to your room, where you'll find antique walnut furniture, fresh flowers, and more wood-beam ceilings. **Pros:** proximity to the Pantheon; big, clean bathrooms; friendly staff. **Cons:** rooms are in need of some upgrading; the lighting is low and the carpets are worn; the breakfast lacks variety. ⊠ *Via dei Pastini 131, Pantheon* ☎ *06/6787746* ⊕ *www.hotelpantheon.com* *13 rooms, 1 suite ⌂ In-room: safe, refrigerator, Wi-Fi. In-hotel: room service, bar, laundry service, public Wi-Fi, no-smoking rooms ⌸ AE, DC, MC, V* ⎢OⒾ *CP* ✚ *4:F2.*

NAVONA

$–$$ ⌸ **Genio.** If this hotel were any closer to Piazza Navona, you'd actually be in the fountain. This medium-size hotel offers top-floor rooms with terraces and citywide views. There's also a roof terrace for all, where you can eat your breakfast. Modeled along classic Roman lines, the lobby and public areas are cozy. Rooms are decorated in warm colors and have parquet floors and a harmonious mix of modern and antique reproduction furnishings. **Pros:** you can sip wine on the rooftop and take in the view; rooms are a decent size for a Roman hotel; the bathrooms have been designed especially well. **Cons:** Genio is on a busy street so there is often traffic noise; you might hear your neighbors through the walls; both the decor and the carpet have seen better days. ⊠ *Via G. Zanardelli 28, Navona* ☎ *06/6832191* ⊕ *www.hotelgeniroma.it* *60 rooms ⌂ In-room: refrigerator. In-hotel: room service, bar, laundry service, Wi-Fi (paid), Internet terminal (paid), parking (paid), safe ⌸ AE, DC, MC, V* ⎢OⒾ *CP* ✚ *4:D2.*

TREVI

$$ ⌸ **Trevi.** Location, location, location: this delightful place is tucked away down one of Old Rome's quaintest alleys near the Trevi Fountain. The smallish rooms are bright and clean, and a few of the larger ones have antique furniture and wooden ceilings with massive beams. There's also an arborlike roof-garden restaurant where you can eat marvelous pasta as you peer out at the city below. **Pros:** pass the Trevi Fountain each day as you come and go; comfortable rooms; roof-garden restaurant. **Cons:** breakfast room is cramped; staff is brusque. ⊠ *Vicolo del Babbuccio 20/21, Piazza di Trevi* ☎ *06/6789563* ⊕ *www.hoteltrevirome.com* *29 rooms ⌂ In-room: safe, refrigerator, Internet. In-hotel: restaurant, room service, laundry service, parking (paid), no-smoking rooms, pets allowed (some) ⌸ AE, DC, MC, V* ⎢OⒾ *CP* ✚ *4:H2.*

$$–$$$ ⌸ **Tritone.** Toss your coin in the Trevi fountain and then quickly toss your bags into your room. That's how close you are to the famous

CLOSE UP

Renting an Apartment in Rome

For parties of more than two, Roman hotel rooms can be a little too cramped for comfort. If you're traveling in a group or with your family, the best solution may be a short-term apartment rental. Apartments are generally rented out the old-fashioned way by their owners, though in some cases a realtor or management company is involved. There is usually a minimum of a three-night stay. Prices will vary, but expect them to be higher in the historic city center, the Vaticano/Borgo, the Campo de' Fiori, and Trastevere areas. ■ TIP➜ Keep in mind that there's sometimes an extra charge involved for final cleaning, utilities, and Internet access when renting an apartment. When seeking a holiday home in Rome, start your research online. Rome's official tourism Web site (⊕ en.turismoroma.it or ⊕ www.060608.it/en) offer a search function for a number of different housing options.

Wanted in Rome (⊕ www.wantedinrome.com) is a popular English language "expat" magazine that features a classifieds section on their Web site. The Bed & Breakfast Association of Rome (⊕ www.b-b.rm.it) offers an online apartment rental search in addition to their B&B search. They personally inspect all properties on their site. Cross-Pollinate (⊕ www.cross-pollinate.com), an accommodation service owned by the people who run the Beehive Hotel, gives visitors the autonomy to find something a little different. They personally screen all properties. San Francisco–based Craigslist hosts classifieds for 450 cities worldwide, including Rome. CraigsList Rome lists postings for apartments, houses, swaps, sublets, and other vacation rentals at ⊕ rome.en.craigslist.it/.

HOTELS WITH APARTMENTS
More and more hotels in Rome now offer a selection of apartments (either located on the grounds or just nearby), in addition to rooms and suites to their prospective guests. **Albergo Santa Chiara** (⊠ Via Santa Chiara 21, Pantheon ☎ 06/6872979 ⊕ www.albergosantachiara.com)3 apartments. **Hotel Campo de' Fiori** (⊠ Via del Biscione 6, Campo de' Fiori ☎ 06/68806865 ⊕ www.hotelcampodefiori.it) 13 apartments. **Italia** (⊠ Via Venezia 18, Termini ☎ 06/4828355 ⊕ www.hotelitaliaroma.com) 1 apartment. **Julia** (⊠ Via Rasella 29, Via Veneto ☎ 06/4881637 ⊕ www.hoteljulia.it) 2 apartments. **Mecenate Palace Hotel** (⊠ Via Carlo Alberto 3, Termini ☎ 06/44702024 ⊕ www.mecenatepalace.com ✛ 2:D5) 2 apartments. **Trastevere** (⊠ Via Luciano Manara 24–25, Trastevere ☎ 06/5814713 ⊕ www.hoteltrastevere.net) 3 apartments.

RESIDENCE HOTELS
Residence hotels also specialize in short-let vacation rentals. They usually have fully equipped kitchens and offer linens, laundry, and cleaning services. Most are available for weekly or monthly rentals. Costs for an apartment for two range from about €1,300 for a week to €2,600 per month. **Residence Aldrovandi** (⊠ Via Ulisse Aldrovandi 11, Parioli ☎ 06/3221430 ⊕ www.aldrovandiresidence.it). **Residence Ripetta** (⊠ Via di Ripetta 231, Piazza di Spagna ☎ 06/3231144 ⊕ www.ripetta.it). **Palazzo al Velabro** (⊠ Via del Velabro 16, Ghetto ☎ 06/6792758 ⊕ www.velabro.it). **Mecenate Palace Hotel** (⊠ Via Carlo Alberto 3, Termini ☎ 06/44702024 ⊕ www.mecenatepalace.com) 10 executive "residence" rooms.

fountain, as well as several other important sights in the historic city center. The flip side is that you're on one of Rome's busiest thoroughfares, so noise can be an issue, though high-quality soundproofing helps keep the din down. Rooms have modern decor with wall-to-wall carpeting, plasma-screen satellite TV, and spacious travertine bathrooms. A buffet breakfast can be taken in the roof garden, with panoramic views of the city. **Pros:** walking distance to major attractions; modern decor with flat-screen TVs; friendly staff. **Cons:** cramped reception area; most rooms have twin beds; despite soundproofing, street-side rooms can be noisy. ✉ *Via del Tritone 210, Piazza di Trevi* ☎ *06/69922575* ⊕ *www.tritonehotel.com* ⊅ *43 rooms* ♿ *In-room: safe, refrigerator, DVD (some), Internet. In-hotel: room service, bar, laundry service, Internet terminal, public Wi-Fi, parking (paid), no-smoking rooms* ▭ *AE, DC, MC, V* ⏏*BP* ✣ *4:G1.*

CAMPO DE' FIORI AND GHETTO

You're in the heart of gorgeously beautiful *Vecchia Roma* (Old Rome) here—a neighborhood that spreads out from two of the most colorful squares in town, Campo de' Fiori and Piazza Farnese, and not far from the city's most elegant residential address, Via Giulia. That noted, many hotels here are refurbished (or not) medieval tenements, with small rooms and precipitous stairs, so it's probably not the place to come looking for sybaritic luxury.

A little to the south in the Ghetto, the impossibly narrow alleyways and deep quiet of most of this small quarter make it easy to imagine its bohemian-chic condos as the teeming tenements they once were.

CAMPO DE' FIORI

$–$$ **Albergo del Sole al Biscione.** Built on the ruins of the ancient Theater of Pompey, in the very heart of the timeless Campo de' Fiori area, this little gem has one of the quaintest multilevel terraces in old Rome; stunning views are guaranteed, with center stage taken by the great dome of Santa Andrea della Valle. Don't be put off by the hotel's neon-ish sign out front—the atmosphere inside is cozy, with open-beam ceilings and old-fashioned furnishings. Modern comforts include an elevator. Rooms are set out in simple pensione style, featuring early-20th-century wardrobes and veneer bed frames. Don't confuse this with the famous Albergo del Sole al Pantheon hotel. If you ask ahead of time, the hotel will make special arrangements for breakfast at the bar down the street. **Pros:** some truly spacious rooms for this area (but beware, some rooms are also quite small); parking garage in the hotel; roof garden with views of the neighborhood and local cupolas. **Cons:** some rooms are small and lack a/c; there is no elevator on the first floor; it can be noisy both inside and out. ✉ *Via del Biscione 76, Campo de' Fiori* ☎ *06/68806873* ⊕ *www.solealbiscione.it* ⊅ *59 rooms* ♿ *In-room: no a/c (some), refrigerator (some), Wi-Fi. In-hotel: parking (paid), no-smoking rooms* ▭ *No credit cards* ⏏*EP* ✣ *4:D4.*

$$ **Casa di Santa Brigida.** One of the nicest convents to stay in is run by
Fodor's Choice the friendly sisters of Santa Brigida. The convent overlooks the Piazza
★   Farnese (where one of Michelangelo's buildings surveys all), and a most

Hassler

Scalinata di Spagna

Eden

Relais Le Clarisse

Daphne Veneto

Yes Hotel

enviable location in the heart of Old Baroque Rome. It's also conveniently close to Campo de' Fiori. But you have to remember this is part of the Convent of St. Bridget, so guest rooms are simple (and serene—no TV), the nuns don't bend over backward to get you ice for your soda (presumably they have more important things on their minds), and the breakfast is served after they've finished their prayers. Still, the atmosphere is redolent. There's a lovely roof terrace overlooking the Palazzo Farnese, as well as a fine chapel and library. The Brigidine sisters wear a distinctive habit and veil with a caplike headband and they are known for their gentle manner. Sometimes, the sisters also offer their guests insider tickets to the papal audience. It's hard to book a room here, so try to reserve well in advance. If you're interested in eating at the Casa, inquire about meal plans when you book. Note that the address is that of the church of Santa Brigida, but the guesthouse entrance is around the corner at Via Monserrato 54. **Pros:** no curfew in this historic convent; insider papal tickets; location in the Piazza Farnese. **Cons:** weak a/c; no TVs in the rooms (though there is a common TV room); mediocre breakfast. ⊠ *Piazza Farnese 96, Campo de' Fiori* ☎ *06/68892497* ⊕ *www.brigidine.org* ⤳ *2 rooms* ⟁ *In-room: no TV, Internet. In-hotel: no-smoking rooms* ⊟ *AE, DC, MC, V* ⦿ *CP* ⊹ *4:C4.*

$$ ⛼ **Hotel Campo de' Fiori.** Frescoes, exposed brickwork, and picturesque effects throughout this little hotel could well be the work of a set designer, but a recent renovation attributes the charming ambience to interior designer Dario di Blasi. Each room is entirely unique in its colors, furniture, and refined feel. The hotel underwent a complete renovation in 2006, retaining its old-world charm, but modernizing with soundproofing, air-conditioning, flat-screen TVs, DSL, and Wi-Fi in all the rooms. There is also a marvelous view from the roof terrace. If you desire more extensive accommodations, Hotel Campo de' Fiori offers an additional selection of 14 different apartments in the area that can accommodate two to five guests. **Pros:** newly renovated; superb location; modern amenities that many Roman hotels haven't caught up with yet; rooftop terrace. **Cons:** some of the rooms are very small; breakfast works on a voucher system with a nearby caffè; the staff can be a bit rude and don't necessarily go out of their way to help you settle in. ⊠ *Via del Biscione 6, Campo de' Fiori* ☎ *06/68806865* ⊕ *www. hotelcampodefiori.it* ⤳ *23 rooms* ⟁ *In-room: safe, refrigerator, Internet, Wi-Fi. In-hotel: no-smoking rooms* ⊟ *MC, V* ⦿ *CP* ⊹ *4:D4.*

$$$$ ⛼ **Hotel Ponte Sisto.** With one of the prettiest patio-courtyards in Rome, this hotel offers its own blissful definition of *Pax Romana*. Peace, indeed, will be yours sitting in this enchanting spot, shadowed by palm trees, set with tables, and adorned with pink and white flowers, all surrounded by the ochre walls of the hotel, which was renovated in 2001 from a palazzo built by the noble Venetian Palottini family. Some rooms overlook the garden of the historic Palazzo Spada. Inside, the sleek decor, replete with cherry wood accents, recessed lighting, and luminous marble floors also gives a calming effect. Guest rooms are refined—suites come with Jacuzzis and furnished balconies or terraces, bathrooms can be lavishly modern, and there's also a bar and restaurant. The location is an award-winner—just off the Ponte Sisto, the pedestrian bridge that

connects the Campo de' Fiori area with Trastevere (whose trattorias and bars are thus just a quick jaunt away), and a second from Via Giulia, Rome's prettiest street. **Pros:** staff is friendly; rooms with views (and some with balconies and terraces); luxury bathrooms; beautiful court-yard garden. **Cons:** street-side rooms can be a bit noisy; some rooms are on the small side; restaurant doesn't serve lunch or dinner. ⊠ *Via dei Pettinari 64, Campo de' Fiori* ☎ *06/686310* ⊕ *www.hotelpontesisto.it* ⤳ *103 rooms, 4 suites* ⌂ *In-room: safe, refrigerator, Internet. In-hotel: restaurant, room service, bar, laundry service, Internet terminal, park-ing (paid), some pets allowed, no-smoking rooms* ⊟ *AE, DC, MC, V* ��◎ǀ *BP* ✛ *4:D5.*

$$ ⊞ **Teatro di Pompeo.** Where else can you breakfast under the ancient stone vaults of Pompey's Theater, the historic site of Julius Caesar's assassination? At this intimate and refined little hotel in the heart of Old Rome you are part of that history. At night, you sleep under restored beamed ceilings that date from the days of Michelangelo. Rooms are simple but tasteful, with terra-cotta floors, comfortable old-fashioned beds, and attractive antique furniture. The staff is also sincere and helpful. Hotel Teatro di Pompeo is the kind of place that really makes you feel like you're living among the true Romans. Do yourself a favor, and book well in advance. **Pros:** location is central to the Campo but not right on the market square; helpful staff; affordable with an old-school Roman feel. **Cons:** it can be noisy on both the street side and the interior courtyard; rooms are small. ⊠ *Largo del Pallaro 8, Campo de' Fiori* ☎ *06/68300170* ⊕ *www.hotelteatrodipompeo.it* ⤳ *12 rooms* ⌂ *In-room: safe, refrigerator, Wi-Fi (some). In-hotel: room service, bar, laundry service, Wi-Fi, Internet terminal* ⊟ *AE, DC, MC, V* ◎ǀ *CP* ✛ *4:D4.*

$$–$$$ ⊞ **Tiziano.** Smack-dab in the middle of everything, this former 18th-cen-tury palace—the grand Palazzo Pacelli—allows you to enjoy the buzz of modern-day Rome from a comfortable distance. Outside, the Corso Vittorio Emanuele is teeming with shoppers and tourists; inside, the cool, quiet marble lobby is a haven of calm. On the second floor—the old *piano nobile*—you'll find guest rooms with some of the loftiest ceil-ings in Rome, all extrovertedly done with Roman cornices, bold color schemes, French windows, parquet floors, and "modern" furnishings. Some rooms have balconies, set over church cupolas. No question—this is an ideal base for sampling the historic Campo de' Fiori and Piazza Navona districts. **Pros:** a very "European" feel; excellent value and location; computer terminal with Internet access at the reception for guests to use. **Cons:** the Corso is a busy thoroughfare, so some rooms are noisy; loud hallways, especially when hosting student university groups; small lobby. ⊠ *Corso Vittorio Emanuele II 110, Campo de' Fiori* ☎ *06/6865019* ⊕ *www.tizianohotel.it* ⤳ *51 rooms* ⌂ *In-room: safe, refrigerator, Wi-Fi. In-hotel: restaurant, room service, bar, laundry service, public Wi-Fi, Internet terminal, parking (paid), no-smoking rooms* ⊟ *AE, DC, MC, V* ◎ǀ *BP* ✛ *4:E4.*

GHETTO

$ 🖼 **Arenula.** Standing on an age-worn byway off central Via Arenula, this hotel is a superb bargain by Rome standards. With an imposingly elegant stone exterior, this hotel welcomes you with a luminous and cheerful all-white interior. Guest rooms are simple in decor but have pale-wood furnishings and gleaming bathrooms, as well as double-glaze windows and air-conditioning (in summer only; ask when you reserve). Two of the rooms accommodate four beds. Of course, you can't have everything, so that the graceful oval staircase of white marble and wrought iron in the lobby cues you that there is no elevator. Those guests with rooms on the fourth floor had better be in good shape! **Pros:** it's a real bargain; conveniently located in the Ghetto (close to Campo de' Fiori and Trastevere), and it's spotless. **Cons:** totally no-frills accommodations; four floors and no elevator; traffic and tram noise can be heard throughout the night despite the double-glazing. ⊠ *Via Santa Maria dei Calderari 47, off Via Arenula, Ghetto* ☎ *06/6879454* ⊕ *www.hotelarenula.com* ⤳ *50 rooms* ⅙ *In-room: Wi-Fi. In-hotel: public Wi-Fi, Internet terminal* ⊟ *AE, DC, MC, V* ⦿ *CP* ✛ *4:E5.*

13

MONTI, ESQUILINO, REPUBBLICA, AND SAN LORENZO

The wide, busy streets around Rome's central train station feel much more urban than the rest of the city center. Traffic is heavier, 19th-century buildings are taller, and the overall feeling is gray and commercial—not the Rome of travel brochure fantasies. But the hotel density here is the highest in the city, and you're assured of finding a room in a pinch. Although most travelers choose this neighborhood because it's cheap, there are a surprising number of top-end hotels here as well, and if you're looking for a luxurious room, the price-quality ratio here is better than in swankier parts of town.

MONTI

¢ 🖼 **Italia.** It looks and feels like a classic pensione: low-budget with a lot of heart. A block off the very trafficky Via Nazionale, this friendly, family-run hotel offers inexpensive rooms with big windows, desks, parquet floors, and baths with faux-marble tiles, but the rooms aren't really the point. The price is, and it's made all the more tempting by a generous buffet breakfast and thoughtful touches like an ice machine and free wireless Internet access. Ask for even lower midsummer rates. **Pros:** free Wi-Fi and Internet access in the rooms and lobby; great price; individual attention and personal care. **Cons:** it's sometimes noisy; a/c is an extra €10. ⊠ *Via Venezia 18, Monti* ☎ *06/4828355* ⊕ *www.hotelitaliaroma. com* ⤳ *31 rooms, 1 apartment* ⅙ *In-room: safe, Wi-Fi. In-hotel: bar, Internet terminal, public Wi-Fi, parking (paid), no-smoking rooms* ⊟ *AE, DC, MC, V* ⦿ *CP* ✛ *2:C4.*

$ 🖼 **Montreal.** A good choice for budget travelers, this hotel is on a central avenue across the square from Santa Maria Maggiore, three blocks from Stazione Termini, Rome's main transportation hub. The modest Montreal occupies three floors of an older building and has been totally renovated and offers bright, fresh-looking, though small, rooms. The owner-managers are pleasant and helpful, and the neighborhood has plenty of reasonably priced restaurants. **Pros:** informative staff provides maps and good recommendations; bathrooms are spacious; hotel has a cozy feel. **Cons:** location can be noisy at night; it's either a bus, metro, or long walk to most historic sights. ⊠ *Via Carlo Alberto 4, Monti* ☎ *06/4457797* ⊕ *www.hotelmontrealroma.com* ↻ *27 rooms* ⚬ *In-room: safe, refrigerator. In-hotel: room service, bar, Internet terminal, parking (paid), no-smoking rooms* ▭ *AE, DC, MC, V* ⍐⍐ *CP* ✛ *2:D5.*

$$ ⌕ **Richmond.** Right at the beginning of Via Cavour, this charming little hotel is ideally situated for visits to the Forum, the Colosseum, and all the major sites of ancient Rome. Enjoy breakfast at one of the caffè downstairs, or head up to the attractive rooftop terrace and take in the panoramic views. The decor is highlighted with tasteful, classical touches, and the modern rooms feature hand-painted frescoes. The staff is helpful and multilingual. **Pros:** in the heart of ancient Rome with impressive views of the Forum; friendly and courteous staff; modern bathrooms. **Cons:** rooms are small; expect to see some signs of wear; some rooms lack private bathrooms. ⊠ *Largo Corrado Ricci 36, Monti* ☎ *06/69941256* ⊕ *www.hotelrichmond.it* ↻ *13 rooms* ⚬ *In-room: safe, refrigerator, Wi-Fi. In-hotel: bar, laundry service, public Wi-Fi, parking (paid), some pets allowed, no-smoking rooms* ▭ *AE, D, DC, MC, V* ⍐⍐ *BP* ✛ *2:B6.*

ESQUILINO

$ ⌕ **Adler.** This tiny pensione, run by the same family for more than three decades, provides a comfortable stay on a quiet street near the main station for a very good price. Ideal for families, Adler has six spacious rooms that sleep three, four, or five, as well as a single and a double. Rooms are basic, but impeccably clean. Worn but cozy chairs line the lobby, and in summer, breakfast can be taken on the leafy courtyard balcony. **Pros:** breakfast on the terrace; free Internet point in the lobby; strong a/c. **Cons:** some rooms are dark; showers are tiny; no safes in the rooms. ⊠ *Via Modena 5, Esquilino* ☎ *06/484466* ⊕ *www. hoteladler-roma.com* ↻ *8 rooms* ⚬ *In-room: refrigerator. In-hotel: room service, bar, Internet terminal, parking (paid)* ▭ *AE, DC, MC, V* ⍐⍐ *CP* ✛ *2:C3.*

$$–$$$ ⌕ **Britannia.** Set in a very regal white villa, smartly fitted out with black shutters (and a not so smart neon sign), the Britannia is a very enticing option. The attention to detail is evident in every corner, from the frescoed halls to the breakfast room. Downstairs, public rooms have somewhat crass allusions to Empire 19th-century style. But upstairs, the individual layout of the guest rooms makes you feel like you're in a private home, furnished with luxury fabrics and original artwork, as well as handsome marble bathrooms. One has a wall lined with photos, another has a bed with a tondo painting of a rose hovering above it. Others cosset with sweet 19th-century style moldings. The caring management provides amenities such as English-language dailies and local weather reports delivered to your room each morning. A light-filled rooftop suite opens onto a private terrace. **Pros:** spacious; comfortable rooms with big, marble bathrooms; some pets are allowed; good service. **Cons:** light sleepers may find the walls a little thin; neighborhood traffic can be noisy; not very close to the city's main attractions. ⊠ *Via Napoli*

64, Esquilino ☎ 06/4883153 ⊕ www.hotelbritannia.it ⬐ 33 rooms, 1 suite ⟐ In-room: safe, refrigerator, Wi-Fi. In-hotel: bar, laundry service, Internet terminal, public Wi-Fi, parking (paid), some pets allowed, no-smoking rooms ⊟ AE, DC, MC, V ⫟ CP ⊹ 2:C4.

$$ ⊡ **Doria.** A convenient location and reasonable rates are the advantages of this small hotel. Space is ingeniously exploited, from the minuscule elevator to the nicely furnished though smallish rooms. The rooms all feature soundproof windows. One of the hotel's most attractive assets is the roof garden—again, not very large, but fine for enjoying an alfresco breakfast and a pleasant view. The Doria has a clone, the Hotel Amalfi, across the street, with the same amenities and some larger rooms with three beds. **Pros:** smart use of space; breakfast on the rooftop terrace; good daily maid service. **Cons:** minuscule elevator; small reception area; despite soundproofing there's still some traffic noise. ⊠ *Via Merulana 4, Esquilino ☎ 06/4465888 ⊕ www.doriahotel.it ⬐ 20 rooms ⟐ In-room: safe (some), refrigerator, Internet. In-hotel: bar, public Wi-Fi, parking (paid) ⊟ AE, DC, MC, V ⫟ CP ⊹ 2:E5.*

$-$$ ⊡ **Giuliana.** A friendly family operates this small, cozy residence with pride. The decor is unprepossessing, with 1960s modern furniture but guest rooms are large (if sparely furnished) and the tiled baths are shiny clean. Make sure to specify bath or shower when you make your reservation; it's one or the other. If you need to check your e-mail while you're on vacation, there is wireless Internet access in the lobby, though it's limited to daytime hours. The hotel doesn't provide laundry service, but you can drop your clothes at the laundry service right next door (and there are several coin-operated laundries in the neighborhood if you need them). **Pros:** spacious, clean rooms; staff is warm and welcoming; with only 11 rooms, it's an intimate experience. **Cons:** you may hear noise from the local market; air-conditioning is an extra €10 charge. ⊠ *Via Agostino Depretis 70, Esquilino ☎ 06/4880795 ⊕ www. hotelgiuliana.com ⬐ 11 rooms ⟐ In-room: no a/c (some), safe, refrigerator. In-hotel: room service, Wi-Fi, bar, parking (paid), no-smoking rooms ⊟ MC, V ⫟ CP ⊹ 2:D4.*

$$ ⊡ **Morgana.** Step into the richly marbled lobby and lounges done up in tartan wallpapers, antiquarian mezzotints, and framed landscape paintings and thus experience an elegance rare at this price level. Among Rome's lower-price hotels, the Morgana is relatively large, with 121 rooms. What that means here is a wide choice of amenities—four different categories of rooms (with corresponding prices) offer a chance to mix and match: modern or antique furniture, Jacuzzi tub or data port, or both. Ask and you shall receive—but no matter which guest room you land, you'll have few complaints about the decor, which is chic and charming in most instances. You would never use those adjectives to describe the immediate neighborhood—just a block removed from Stazione Termini—but you can't have everything. **Pros:** with direct bookings, Morgana offers special packages with free airport transfer or a free guided tour; they also offer cable TV with CNN and free in-house movies. **Cons:** neighborhood is run-down; removed from most sightseeing (though you can take buses or the metro). ⊠ *Via Filippo Turati 33/37, Esquilino ☎ 06/4467230 ⊕ www.hotelmorgana.com ⬐ 121*

13

rooms, 2 suites ⬧ In-room: safe, refrigerator, Wi-Fi. In-hotel: room service, bar, laundry service, Wi-Fi, parking (paid), no-smoking rooms, pets allowed (some) ▭ AE, DC, MC, V ⊙ CP ✛ 2:E4.

$$ ▦ **Radisson SAS Es.** In this hotel, the rooms themselves are an experience. The minimalist and ultra-contemporary design is in complete contrast to most of what you will find throughout the city. Imagine taking a room at a big-city modern art museum, and you'll start to get the picture. There are colorful accents throughout the hotel that contrast with an overarching minimalist theme of white or muted tones. Even the windows light up in color at night. The rooms are spacious with funky fixtures. The beds are smack in the middle of each guest room. The bathroom walls are glass, which may be a little too open for the more private traveler. There's also a swimming pool and sundeck on the roof, a health and fitness room with spa, a bar, and two restaurants, plus free hi-speed Internet and Wi-Fi everywhere. **Pros:** distinctive design; convenient, transportation-wise, as it's so close to Termini; friendly and helpful staff, plus a lot of extras (like free Wi-Fi). **Cons:** Termini can be a bit unsavory at night; some may find the über-design off-putting; you don't get much privacy with a glass bathroom. ⊠ *Via Filippo Turati 171, Esquilino* ☎ *06/444841* ⊕ *www.rome.radissonsas.com* ⤳ *232 rooms, 27 suites* ⬧ *In-room: safe, refrigerator, Internet, Wi-Fi. In-hotel: 2 restaurants, room service, bar, pool, gym, spa, laundry service, Internet terminal, public Wi-Fi, parking (paid), no-smoking rooms* ▭ *AE, DC, MC, V* ⊙ *CP* ✛ *2:F5.*

REPUBBLICA

$–$$ ▦ **Alpi.** The sweeping marble entrance here is cool and welcoming; it sets the tone for the rest of this reasonably priced hotel. What sets it apart is the feeling of space—high ceilings with elegant chandeliers, white walls, and marble or parquet floors give it an elegance that is unusual for the price. Some of the bedrooms have antique furniture, and all are tastefully decorated, although the beds are old-fashioned. Fresh flowers are decadently displayed throughout the hotel, and on the terrace. There are slightly formal lounges and a cozier bar downstairs, as well as a restaurant that serves traditional Mediterranean cuisine. **Pros:** clean and comfortable; hard-working concierge; numerous common spaces to lounge in. **Cons:** not all rooms are created equal; slow elevator; you'll probably want to take a bus/metro to most major sights. ⊠ *Via Castelfidardo 84, Repubblica* ☎ *06/4441235* ⊕ *www.hotelalpi.com* ⤳ *48 rooms* ⬧ *In-room: safe, refrigerator, Internet. In-hotel: restaurant, room service, bar, laundry service, public Wi-Fi, parking (paid), some pets allowed, no-smoking rooms* ▭ *AE, DC, MC, V* ⊙ *CP* ✛ *2:E2.*

$ ▦ **The Beehive.** You won't feel like you're in Rome once you step foot

Fodor's Choice
★

into this hip alternative budget hotel. Rather, one might mistake it for a cross between a holistic center and a place that holds yoga classes. Started by a Los Angeles couple following their dream in 1999, the Beehive might be the most unique budget hotel in Rome in that it also offers hostel accommodations, a vegetarian caffè, a yoga space and art gallery with a garden, a reading lounge, and a few off-site apartments. It offers a respite from Rome's chaos, but is conveniently located only a few blocks from Termini. All of the rooms come with shared bathrooms

13

(where, along with the facilities, you'll find handmade vegetable-based soaps and recycled toilet paper). There is a lovely little garden with fruit trees, herbs, and flowers. The Beehive offers complimentary Wi-Fi, but no TVs or air-conditioning (though rooms do have ceiling fans). If you would prefer your own self-catering apartment (with a kitchen and private bathroom) for your group or family, or if you'd just like an individual room in an apartment, the Beehive also has three apartments in the neighborhood that can be rented. **Pros:** yoga, massage, and other therapies offered on-site; no set price for meals served at the vegetarian caffè—it's left entirely up to the guest to decide how much he/she thinks the meal is worth. **Cons:** no TV, a/c, baggage storage, or private bathroom; breakfast is not included in the room rate. ⊠ *Via Margherita 8, Repubblica* ☎ *06/44704553* ⊕ *www.the-beehive.com* ⤵ *8 rooms, 1 dormitory, 3 apartments* ♨ *In-room: no a/c, kitchen (some), no TV, Wi-Fi. In-hotel: public Wi-Fi, no-smoking rooms* ▭ *MC, V* ⍥*EP* ✛ *2:E3.*

$$$$ ⬚ **Exedra.** If Rome's semi-stodgy hotel scene has an It-Girl, it's the Exedra. High-rollers love to host splashy parties here and magazines love to rave about them; this luxury hotel is indeed, hard to top. Unlike its naughty younger brother the Aleph, the Exedra is a model of neo-classical respectability, all gilt-framed mirrors and fresh flowers, but there's a glint of cutting edge in the paparazzi-inspired (and inspiring) Tazio brasserie. Rooms are predictably luscious in an uptown way, with silky linens and handsome nouveau-colonial bedsteads, and many face the spectacular fountain in the piazza outside. Why stay here, rather than at the umpteen other expensively elegant hotels in central Rome? You can think about it while you lounge by the rooftop swimming pool. **Pros:** spacious and attractive rooms; great spa and food; terrace with cocktail service; close to Termini station. **Cons:** food and beverages are expensive; beyond the immediate vicinity; parts of the neighborhood seem unsavory. ⊠ *Piazza della Repubblica 47, Repubblica* ☎ *06/489381* ⊕ *www.boscolohotels.com* ⤵ *240 rooms, 18 suites* ♨ *In-room: safe, refrigerator, Wi-Fi. In-hotel: 3 restaurants, room service, bars, pool, gym, spa, laundry service, Internet terminal, public Wi-Fi, parking (paid), some pets allowed, no-smoking rooms* ▭ *AE, DC, MC, V* ⍥*CP* ✛ *2:D3.*

$$–$$$ ⬚ **Marcella Royal.** A midsize hotel with the feel of a smaller, more intimate establishment, the Marcella is 10 minutes from Via Veneto and Termini Station. Here you can do your sightseeing from the roof terrace, taking in the view while you breakfast. Marcella Royal also offers a light dinner service for guests who prefer to relax at the hotel in the evening. Many rooms also have good views, and they are all furnished with flair, using tasteful color schemes, floral prints, and mirrored walls, echoing the elegant winter-garden decor of the lounges and bar. The spacious suites are ideal for families. **Pros:** start the day with breakfast in the roof garden; aperitivo at the piano bar; light dinner offered; staff goes the extra mile to help guests with all of their needs. **Cons:** small rooms; small showers; distant from most major attractions. ⊠ *Via Flavia 106, Repubblica* ☎ *06/42014591* ⊕ *www.marcellaroyalhotel.com* ⤵ *85 rooms, 2 suites* ♨ *In-room: safe, Wi-Fi. In-hotel: bar, Wi-Fi, parking (paid)* ▭ *AE, DC, MC, V* ⍥*BP* ✛ *2:D4.*

$$$–$$$$ ⊞ **Mascagni.** Situated on one of Rome's busiest streets and close to one
ⓒ   of Rome's most impressive piazzas (*Piazza della Repubblica*), sits the
          hotel Mascagni. The public spaces of the hotel have been cleverly styled
          with contemporary art pieces, and the bedrooms feature black and
          white photographs of Rome. The intimate lounges and charming bar—
          very cozy and attractive with its floral fabric and wood bar—follow the
          same decorating scheme, as does the breakfast room, where a gener-
          ous buffet is laid in the morning, complete with free newspapers. The
          friendly, creative management is always coming up with new offers,
          including the "Family Perfect" room, which includes a PlayStation, a
          DVD player with Disney movies, and wooden blocks for small children
          to play with. **Pros:** staff is friendly and attentive with good advice; eve-
          ning lounge that serves up cold cuts or light pasta dishes; bathrooms
          are spacious and they come with nice toiletries; great for families with
          kids. **Cons:** small lobby; weak a/c; slow Internet. ⊠ *Via Vittorio Emanu-
          ele Orlando 90, Repubblica* ☎ *06/48904040* ⊕ *www.hotelmascagni.
          com* ⤳ *40 rooms* ⌂ *In-room: safe, refrigerator, DVD (some), Internet.
          In-hotel: bar, laundry service, Internet terminal, parking (paid), no-
          smoking rooms* ▭ *AE, DC, MC, V* ⅋⊙⎮ *BP* ✛ *2:D3.*

$$ ⊞ **Miami.** Rooms at this low-key hotel, in a dignified 19th-century build-
          ing on Rome's busy Via Nazionale, are soundproof and tastefully styled
          with coordinated curtains, bedspreads, and wallpaper. The location,
          on main bus lines and near Termini Station and the Metro, is very
          central for sightseeing and shopping, although it's not ideal for eating
          out. Winter rates from November through February are a good bar-
          gain. And remember, rooms on the courtyard are quieter. **Pros:** pleasant
          staff; soundproof windows; strong a/c. **Cons:** Wi-Fi not available in all
          of the rooms; no alarm clock; small breakfast room. ⊠ *Via Nazionale
          230, Repubblica* ☎ *06/4817180* ⊕ *www.hotelmiami.com* ⤳ *42 rooms,
          4 suites, 1 apartment* ⌂ *In-room: safe, refrigerator, Internet. In-hotel:
          room service, Wi-Fi, bar, bicycles, laundry service, parking (paid), no-
          smoking rooms* ▭ *AE, D, DC, MC, V* ⅋⊙⎮ *BP* ✛ *2:C4.*

$$–$$$ ⊞ **Residenza Cellini.** Fresh flowers in the foyer help make this small,
          family-run residence feel like a gracious home. The lobby's glossy par-
          quet floors, elegant door moldings, and handsome wood Empire-style
          desk and chairs make a sweet impression. Traditionally furnished guest
          rooms have king-size beds with hypoallergenic orthopedic mattresses,
          padded headboards, and Persian-style rugs. There are only six rooms,
          so you're guaranteed personal attention from the eager-to-please staff.
          This is yet another hotel that is somewhat distant from the city's main
          historic attractions, but the Stazione Termini is very close and has all
          the transportation links you could want. **Pros:** it feels like you're visiting
          Rome in another era; Jacuzzi bathtubs and Hydrojet showers; person-
          alized care from the staff. **Cons:** not close to the main attractions; the
          orthopedic mattresses may be too firm for some; breakfast is the stan-
          dard Continental fare. ⊠ *Via Modena 5, Repubblica* ☎ *06/47825204*
          ⊕ *www.residenzacellini.it* ⤳ *6 rooms* ⌂ *In-room: safe, refrigerator,
          Wi-Fi. In-hotel: room service, laundry service, Internet terminal, pub-
          lic Wi-Fi, parking (paid), no-smoking rooms* ▭ *AE, D, DC, MC, V*
          ⅋⊙⎮ *CP* ✛ *2:C3.*

$–$$ ⊡ **Romae.** In the better part of the Termini Station neighborhood, the Romae has the advantages of a strategic location—it's within walking distance of many sites, and handy to bus and metro lines. The pictures of Rome in the small lobby and breakfast room, the luminous white walls and light-wood furniture in the rooms, and the bright little baths all have a fresh look. Amenities such as satellite TV, in-room safe, and hair dryer are unusual for a hotel of this price. There are special rates and services for families. Some of the cheapest rooms in Rome can be found in the Romae's adjacent B&B facility—a pretty good deal at a €100 room rate. **Pros:** well-appointed, spacious rooms with ample wardrobes; complimentary beverages offered throughout the day; international newspapers available; reasonable rates; located on the nicer side of Termini. **Cons:** breakfast is served at the bar across the street; not much action in the neighborhood at night; the elevator can be temperamental. ✉ *Via Palestro 49, Repubblica* ☎ *06/4463554* ⊕ *www.hotelromae.com* ☎ *40 rooms* ♿ *In-room: no a/c (some), safe, refrigerator, Internet. In-hotel: Internet terminal, public Wi-Fi, parking (paid), no-smoking rooms* ▭ *AE, DC, MC, V* ⊗ *CP* ✢ *2:E3.*

$–$$ ⊡ **Villa delle Rose.** Although just two blocks away from the hustle and bustle of Termini Station, this is a comfortable retreat. The entrance is grand, set within a 19th-century palazzo with a rusticated base. Guest rooms here are a little old-fashioned, with simple furnishings dressed up by table lamps and faux-Persian rugs over the wall-to-wall carpeting, but the lobby is elegant. Have breakfast or tea in the small garden, blooming with bougainvillea, roses, and jasmine. **Pros:** gorgeous garden; free parking; some special family-size rooms. **Cons:** no Internet in the rooms; some of the rooms are small (ask for a larger one); the elevator is also small. ✉ *Via Vicenza 5, Repubblica* ☎ *06/4451795* ⊕ *www.villadellerose.it* ☎ *37 rooms* ♿ *In-room: safe, refrigerator (some). In-hotel: room service, bar, laundry service, Internet terminal, parking (free), some pets allowed* ▭ *AE, DC, MC, V* ⊗ *CP* ✢ *2:E3.*

SAN LORENZO

$ ⊡ **Aphrodite.** Given a recent design makeover, this hotel offers plenty of panache for the money. The mod, minimalist reception area strikes an elegant note (a little off-key since the immediate area here is right next door to Termini Station). Guest rooms are clean and friendly, adorned with colorful prints. Some rooms are on the spartan side, but the overall feel is fresh and modern. White walls and curtains lend a peaceful, almost monastic quality to the place. You can't beat it for the value. **Pros:** panache for a low price; big bathrooms; quiet. **Cons:** not much in the way of amenities; Wi-Fi not available in all of the rooms; small rooms. ✉ *Via Marsala 90, San Lorenzo* ☎ *06/491096* ⊕ *www.accommodationinrome.com* ☎ *50 rooms* ♿ *In-room: safe, refrigerator, Wi-Fi (some). In-hotel: bar* ▭ *AE, DC, MC, V* ⊗ *CP* ✢ *2:E3.*

$–$$ ⊡ **Des Artistes.** The three personable Riccioni brothers have transformed their hotel into the best in the neighborhood in its price range. It's bedecked with paintings and handsome furnishings in mahogany, and rooms are decorated in attractive fabrics. Marble baths are smallish but luxurious for this price, and they're stocked with hair dryers and towel warmers. Des Artistes hasn't forgotten its roots, though: there's also a "hostel" floor with 11 simpler rooms for travelers on a budget. Book well ahead. As for location, this is somewhat on the fringe, being several blocks (in the wrong direction) from Stazione Termini. **Pros:** good value; decent-size rooms; relaxing roof garden. **Cons:** breakfast area is overcrowded; reception is on the fifth floor. ⊠ *Via Villafranca 20, San Lorenzo* ☎ *06/4454365* ⊕ *www.hoteldesartistes.com* ☏ *40 rooms, 27 with bath* ⎈ *In-room: no a/c (some), safe, refrigerator, Wi-Fi. In-hotel: bar, parking (paid), public Wi-Fi, no-smoking rooms* ☐ *AE, DC, MC, V* ⎛❂⎠ *BP* ✛ *2:F2.*

$ ⚏ **Yes Hotel.** Don't let the contemporary coolness of this hotel fool you.
Fodor's Choice It is a budget hotel. A new comer to the scene, the Yes was opened in
★ April 2007 by the owners of the Hotel Des Artistes. It's situated just near Stazione Termini, which is key for moving around, and also has plenty of dining options in the area from which to choose. Yes also offers the kind of amenities that are usually found in more expensive hotels, including mahogany furniture, decorative art, electronic safes, flat-screen TVs, and air-conditioning. Wireless Internet access is available in the rooms and throughout the hotel for an extra free. **Pros:** flat-screen TVs with satellite TV; it doesn't feel like a budget hotel, but it is; discount if you pay cash; great value. **Cons:** rooms are small; no individual climate control or refrigerators in the rooms. ⊠ *Via Magenta 15, San Lorenzo* ☎ *06/44363836* ⊕ *www.yeshotelrome.com* ☏ *29 rooms, 1 suite* ⎈ *In-room: safe, Wi-Fi (paid). In-hotel: parking (paid) Wi-Fi (paid), no-smoking rooms* ☐ *MC, V* ⎛❂⎠ *CP* ✛ *2:E3.*

VENETO, BORGHESE, AND SPAGNA

Central Rome's most fashionable neighborhoods are packed with hotels, mostly suiting the style and budget of patrons of the local shops—Gucci, Prada, Fendi—although there are a few less-expensive choices that book up far in advance. Absolutely central for shopping, caffè-ing, and eating out, it's the best location for enjoying Rome's luxurious and leisurely pleasures.

If you're looking for Fellini's glamorous boulevard, packed with movie stars and the paparazzi who stalk them, you're about 40 years too late. While the glitz and the glamour of Via Veneto has fizzled a bit, it still retains a stately elegance, and a wide choice of large luxury hotels, that make it the clear choice for many business travelers. The American Embassy is here, and it's convenient to Villa Borghese, the Spanish Steps, and Rome's metro—Barberini station is at the bottom of the uphill-winding (and rather steep) street.

VENETO

$$$$ ⚏ **Aleph.** Wondering where the beautiful people are? Look no farther
Fodor's Choice than the Aleph, the most unfalteringly fashionable of Rome's design
★ hotels. The just-this-side-of-kitsch theme here is Dante's Divine Comedy, and you can walk the line between heaven and hell through the Angelo bar, the red-red-red Sin restaurant, and Paradise spa. The shiny blood-red-and-black color scheme looks great, but guest rooms are thankfully less threatening, in subdued neutral tones with wood furniture, made galleryesque by giant black-and-white photos of Rome. As many will

guess, this hotel was über-designed by Adam Tihany (who also did the honors at Rome's Exedra). His relentless, in-your-face decors throw everything into the mix, from Shogun suits to his signature red twigs to shirred silk lamps. Fortunately, he likes to poke fun at himself (clothes hooks shaped like devil's horns; tiny TVs set in the bathroom floors in front of your toilet), and earnestly cool staff notwithstanding, the Aleph doesn't take itself as seriously as might be feared. When old Rome feels, well, old—this is something new. **Pros:** award-winning design; the invitation to test the temptations of heaven and hell; the sauna, Turkish bath, and thermal swimming pool at Paradise spa. **Cons:** rooms are too petite for the price; cocktails are expensive; Internet is costly, too. ⊠ *Via San Basilio 15, Veneto* ☎ *06/422901* ⊕ *www.boscolohotels.com* ↝ *96 rooms, 6 suites* ⌂ *In-room: safe, refrigerator, Internet (paid). In-hotel: restaurant, room service, bars, gym, spa, laundry service, Wi-Fi (paid), Internet terminal, parking (paid), no-smoking rooms* ⊟ *AE, DC, MC, V* ⋈ *EP* ✛ *2:C2.*

$$–$$$ 🏨 **Alexandra.** An old-fashioned hotel that recalls a time of yester-year, the Alexandra has been run by the same family for nearly a century. The modest poise of this hotel is a bit of an anomaly compared to its flashier big brothers and sisters on the Via Veneto. In fact, it seems its antique-flair appears as if its remained untouched since King Vittorio Emanuele II's time. But one thing you can count on is that the rooms are neat and clean. Breakfast is served in a sunny conservatory. All in all, it's a great bargain for the pricey Via Veneto district. **Pros:** great location near Piazza Barberini for sightseeing, restaurants, and transportation; especially good value for the location; decorated with authentic antiques. **Cons:** mostly tiny rooms and tinier bathrooms; some of the rooms don't get much natural light; breakfast is just the standard fare (and no cappuccino). ⊠ *Via Veneto 18, Veneto* ☎ *06/4881943* ⊕ *www.hotelalexandraroma.com* ↝ *60 rooms* ⌂ *In-room: refrigerator, Internet. In-hotel: restaurant, room service, laundry service, Internet terminal, public Wi-Fi, parking (paid), no-smoking rooms* ⊟ *AE, DC, MC, V* ⋈ *CP* ✛ *2:C2.*

$$$$ 🏨 **Barberini.** Here you can find about all you could ask for in a Roman hotel: charm, taste, and the good fortune to look out onto one of the best museums in town, Palazzo Barberini. The marble-floor lobby is light and welcoming, and upstairs each room is furnished with fixtures designed exclusively for the hotel. The breakfast buffet (not included and not cheap either) on the rooftop is in a league of its own: fresh, delicious, and copious. The creative management often has special deals to offer for dinners, theater tickets, and other events, so make sure to ask. **Pros:** beautiful view from the terrace; located on a quiet side street (but not far from attractions); facilities for the disabled; spa facilities. **Cons:** breakfast buffet costs €30 extra; some rooms are on the small side; not all rooms have bathtubs; room service is limited. ⊠ *Via Rasella 3, Veneto* ☎ *06/4814993* ⊕ *www.hotelbarberini.com* ↝ *35 rooms, 4 suites* ⌂ *In-room: safe, refrigerator, Internet. In-hotel: room service, bars, laundry service, public Wi-Fi, Internet terminal, parking (paid), no-smoking rooms* ⊟ *AE, DC, MC, V* ⋈ *BP* ✛ *2:B3.*

13

$$ 🔲 **Daphne Veneto.** Inspired by baroque artist Gianlorenzo Bernini's
Fodor's Choice   exquisite Apollo and Daphne sculpture at the Borghese Gallery, the
★   Daphne Inn at Via Veneto is an "urban B&B" run by people who love
Rome and who will do their best to make sure you love it, too. This
boutique hotel offers an intimate lodging experience, elegantly designed
rooms, comfortable beds, fresh fruit and pastries with your coffee each
morning, and a small staff of people who promise to give you the oppor-
tunity to see Rome "like an insider." A cell phone is even provided for
you to use during your stay in Rome (though, you have to pay for the
calls). They will help you map out your destinations, schedule itinerar-
ies, plan day trips, book tours, choose restaurants, and organize your
transportation. It's like having your own personal travel planner. **Pros:**
if rooms at Daphne Veneto are booked, inquire about its sister hotel,
Daphne Trevi; you get a priceless introduction to Rome by lovers of
Rome; the beds have Simmons mattresses and fluffy comforters. **Cons:**
no TVs; some bathrooms are shared; Daphne only accepts Visa or Mas-
terCard to hold bookings (though you can actually pay with an AmEx).
⊠ *Via di San Basilio 55, Veneto* ☎ *06/87450087* ⊕ *www.daphne-rome.
com* ↘ *7 rooms, 2 suites* ⚐ *In-room: safe, refrigerator, no TV, Wi-Fi. In-
hotel: bicycles, laundry service, Internet terminal, public Wi-Fi, parking
(paid), no-smoking rooms* ⊟ *AE, MC, V* ⵏ◯ⵏ *CP* ⊹ *2:B3.*

$$$$ 🔲 **Eden.** Once the preferred haunt of Hemingway, Ingrid Bergman, and
Fodor's Choice   Fellini, this superlative hotel combines dashing elegance and stunning
★   vistas of Rome with the warmth of Italian hospitality. Set atop an oh-
my-weary-feet hill near the Villa Borghese (and a bit out of the his-
toric center for serious sightseers), this hotel was opened in the late
19th century and quickly became famous for its balcony views and
Roman splendor. After an extensive restoration in the 1990s by Lord
Forte, you'll now dive deep here into the whoooooossh of luxury, with
antiques, sumptuous Italian fabrics, linen sheets, and marble baths com-
peting for your attention. Even the most basic room here is elegantly
designed (which is as it should be if your basic double room goes for
some €700). Banquette window seats, rich mahogany furniture, soaring
ceilings, Napoléon-Trois sofas are just some of the allurements here.
Pros: gorgeous panoramic view from roof terrace; you could be rubbing
elbows with the stars; 24-hour room service. **Cons:** expensive (unless
money is no object for you); no Wi-Fi in the rooms; some say the staff
can be hit-or-miss. ⊠ *Via Ludovisi 49, Veneto* ☎ *06/478121* ⊕ *www.
lemeridien.com/eden* ↘ *121 rooms, 13 suites* ⚐ *In-room: safe, refrig-
erator, DVD (some), Internet. In-hotel: restaurant, room service, bars,
gym, Wi-Fi, laundry service, Internet terminal, parking (paid), some
pets allowed, no-smoking rooms* ⊟ *AE, DC, MC, V* ⵏ◯ⵏ *EP* ⊹ *2:B2.*

$$ 🔲 **Hotel Suisse.** Long known (and beloved) as the Pensione Suisse, this
old standby of the budgeteer set recently got a makeover into hotel sta-
tus (all rooms now enjoy their own bath). The biggest plus about this
place is its address: Via Gregoriana, the picturesque and fabled street
that debouches into the top of the Spanish Steps (the painter Ingres
and the author Hans Christian Andersen used to live a few doors up
the block). Set in a somewhat unprepossessing apartment building, the
hotel itself is sweet and serviceable, with rooms on an array of floors. If

possible, opt for the ones facing the back—blissfully quiet even though you're in the thick of things. **Pros:** good value for reasonable price; the rooms are obviously cared for; great location. **Cons:** breakfast is taken in your room; you will need to be buzzed in during certain hours; there are a few stairs to climb before you reach the elevator. ⊠ *Via Gregoriana 54, Veneto* ☎ *06/6783649* ⊕ *www.hotelsuisserome.com* ⤴ *12 rooms* ⚖ *In-room: no a/c (some), safe, refrigerator (some). In-hotel: room service, bar, laundry service, Wi-Fi, Internet terminal, no-smoking rooms* ⊟ *MC, V* ⦿| *CP* ✛ *1:H3.*

13

$-$$ ⊡ **Julia.** Tucked away behind Piazza Barberini down a sinuous cobbled lane, this small establishment welcomes you with a reception area that is surprisingly modern and straightforward. The guest rooms are more traditional, and though they're short on character, they're marvelously spacious and clean. Guests also have access to free, wireless, high-speed Internet. **Pros:** safe neighborhood; convenient to sights and transportation; quiet (since it's just off Piazza Barberini on a small side street). **Cons:** no frills; very basic accommodations; some of the rooms are dark. ⊠ *Via Rasella 29, Veneto* ☎ *06/4881637* ⊕ *www.hoteljulia. it* ⤴ *33 rooms, 30 with bath, 2 suites, 3 apartments* ⚖ *In-room: safe, Internet. In-hotel: bar, laundry service, Internet terminal, public Wi-Fi, no-smoking rooms* ⊟ *AE, DC, MC, V* ⦿| *CP* ✛ *2:B3.*

$$-$$$ ⊡ **La Residenza.** Mainly Americans frequent this cozy hotel in a converted town house near Via Veneto. Rooms are basic, comfortable, and tasteful (although single rooms are windowless), but the real charm of the hotel is found in its bar, terrace, and lounges, which are adorned with stylish wallpaper and love seats that invite you to make yourself at home. Rates include a generous American-style buffet breakfast and an in-house movie every night. **Pros:** big American breakfast; spacious; quiet rooms with balconies; friendly staff; cocktail parties. **Cons:** the building's exterior doesn't compare to its interior; located on a street with some "gentleman's" clubs; if you're in Rome for the Vatican, it's a long walk (or a metro ride) from here. ⊠ *Via Emilia 22, Veneto* ☎ *06/4880789* ⊕ *www.thegiannettihotelsgroup.com* ⤴ *29 rooms* ⚖ *In-room: safe, refrigerator, Internet. In-hotel: room service, bar, laundry service, parking (paid), some pets allowed* ⊟ *AE, MC, V* ⦿| *BP* ✛ *2:B2.*

$$$$ ⊡ **Majestic.** Back in the days of the *dolce vita*, this luxury hotel was a favorite among Rome's royalty and social climbers. The Majestic was the first luxury hotel built on the Via Veneto in 1889 and continues to be a major contender among world-class hotels. It's interior is lined with luxurious furnishings, spacious, light-filled rooms, up-to-date accessories, and white marble bathrooms. There are authentic antiques in the public rooms, and the excellent restaurant looks like a Victorian conservatory. If that's not enough *dolce vita* for you (a scene from the famed Fellini film was set outside the hotel), some suites have whirlpool baths. The grill-caffè on street level is a good spot for people watching. **Pros:** old-world elegance; silk and linen bedding on queen- or king-size beds; flat-screen TVs; some rooms even have their own balconies that overlook the Via Veneto. **Cons:** pricey; breakfast is especially expensive; not all of the rooms are spacious. ⊠ *Via Veneto*

50, Veneto ☎ *06/421441* ⊕ *www.hotelmajestic.com* ➵ *85 rooms, 13 suites* ✍ *In-room: safe, refrigerator, Internet. In-hotel: 2 restaurants, bar, laundry service, parking (paid), no-smoking rooms* ▭ *AE, DC, MC, V* ⧖ *EP* ✛ *2:B2.*

\$\$\$ 🖼 **Marriott Grand Hotel Flora.** This handsome hotel at the top of Via Veneto next to the Villa Borghese park is something of a beacon on the Rome landscape. The Grand Hotel Flora's standard of excellence is among the highest in the city. No expense has been spared in decorating the rooms and suites. Each one is unique, and carefully chosen antiques grace them all; the bathrooms are the last word in ablution chic. There's a lovely roof-garden restaurant on the seventh floor and a large conference hall. **Pros:** convenient location and pleasant staff; spectacular view of the Borghese Gardens and the Roman skyline from the breakfast terrace; free Internet. **Cons:** rooms are small; breakfast goes fast; sometimes the noise from Via Veneto drifts in. ⊠ *Via Veneto 191, Veneto* ☎ *06/489929* ⊕ *www.mariotthotels.com* ➵ *156 rooms, 24 suites* ✍ *In-room: safe, refrigerator, Internet. In-hotel: 2 restaurants, bar, gym, laundry service, Internet terminal, parking (free), no-smoking rooms* ▭ *AE, DC, MC, V* ⧖ *CP* ✛ *2:B1.*

\$\$\$\$ 🖼 **Regina Baglioni.** A former playground of kings and poets, the Regina Baglioni resembles somewhat of a neo-classical ballroom when you first enter the building. Though it enjoys a prime spot on the Via Veneto, convenient for the street's dolce vita caffè and the Villa Borghese; its noisy neighbor, the Hard Rock Cafe is also too close for comfort. The lobby is royal in its elegance, replete with chandeliers, grand staircases, red carpets, and gigantic statues. The guest rooms continue the palatial theme in their appointments, with Oriental carpets, luxury brocades, wall silks, and period antiques. Le Grazie restaurant is notable for its fine cuisine and equally fine table settings. The seventh-floor suites enjoy superb views of the Eternal City. **Pros:** over-the-top decor; refurbished rooms; new Brunello Lounge and Restaurant. **Cons:** not all the rooms have been refurbished; staff is hit-or-miss; the Internet connection doesn't always work. ⊠ *Via Veneto 72, Veneto* ☎ *06/421111* ⊕ *www. reginabaglioni.com* ➵ *136 rooms, 7 suites* ✍ *In-room: safe, refrigerator, Internet (some), Wi-Fi (some). In-hotel: restaurant, room service, bar, laundry service, parking (paid), some pets allowed, no-smoking rooms* ▭ *AE, DC, MC, V* ⧖ *EP* ✛ *2:B2.*

\$\$\$–\$\$\$\$ 🖼 **Sofitel Rome Villa Borghese.** Luxury seekers and business travelers alike are drawn to the Sofitel. Set in a refurbished 1902 Victorian palace, the hotel exudes old-world elegance, albeit with a modern design sensibility. Located on a quiet street between the hot spots of Via Veneto and the Spanish Steps, Sofitel Roma offers its own bar and restaurant, the Antico Boston, which serves both international and Italian cuisine. Rooms are decorated in rich tones and whimsical patterns of stripes and floral prints. You'll return each evening to find fresh linen sheets and turndown service with the classic chocolate-on-your-pillow touch. **Pros:** luxury lodging, off the main drag (but not too far from it); first-rate concierge and porter. **Cons:** luxury chain hotel with business clientele that could make it a bit stuffy at times; some say the a/c could be stronger; the showers are a bit leaky. ⊠ *Via Lombardia 47, Veneto*

06/478021 ⊕ *www.sofitel.com* ↝ *113 rooms, 4 suites* ♿ *In-room: safe, refrigerator, Internet. In-hotel: restaurant, room service, bar, laundry service, public Wi-Fi, parking (paid), no-smoking rooms* ▭ *AE, DC, MC, V* �“◎” *BP* ✛ *2:B2.*

$$$ ▣ **Victoria.** Oriental rugs, oil paintings, and fresh flowers are scattered throughout the lobbies and guest rooms. This is a hotel that is heavy on traditional-style wallpapers and well furnished with armchairs and other amenities. American businesspeople who prize the hotel's personalized service, restful atmosphere, and elegantly designed restaurant and bar, are frequent guests. Some upper rooms and the roof terrace overlook the majestic pines of the Villa Borghese. **Pros:** view of the Borghese Gardens; quiet and comfortable; rooftop bar and restaurant. **Cons:** it's a long walk to most sights; service is inconsistent; rooms are small. ✉ *Via Campania 41, Veneto* 06/473931 ⊕ *www.hotelvictoriaroma. com* ↝ *110 rooms* ♿ *In-room: safe, refrigerator, Internet. In-hotel: restaurant, room service, bar, laundry service, Internet terminal, no-smoking rooms* ▭ *AE, DC, MC, V* �“◎” *EP* ✛ *2:C1.*

$$$$ ▣ **The Westin Excelsior, Rome.** Ablaze with lights at night, this seven-layer-
♻ cake hotel is topped off by its famous corner cupola, a landmark nearly as famous as the American Embassy palazzo sitting next door. Once a herding pen for princes and maharajahs, the Excelsior today is the hotel of choice for visiting diplomats, celebrities, and, well, American business conferences. Every corner is lavished with mirrors, moldings, Oriental rugs, crystal chandeliers, and huge, baroque floral arrangements. Guest rooms have elegant drapery, marble baths, top-quality linens, and big, firm beds. While traditional, refined, and luxurious, the cheaper rooms here don't really offer a lot of bang for the buck, so spring for the better ones, or settle elsewhere. The hotel has an array of restaurants and bars, none more famous than Doney's—once the epicenter of Fellini's paparazzi. Recently renovated, Doney's now features a patisserie, an American bar, and fine dining. **Pros:** elegant period furnishings and decor; potential for star-sightings; health club and indoor pool. **Cons:** not all rooms are created equal; some say the Excelsior's age is starting to show; extras are extra-expensive. ✉ *Via Veneto 125, Veneto* 06/47081 ⊕ *www.westin.com* ↝ *319 rooms, 32 suites* ♿ *In-room: safe, kitchen (some), refrigerator, Internet, Wi-Fi. In-hotel: restaurant, bars, pool, gym, spa, children's programs (ages toddler–12), laundry service, Internet terminal, public Wi-Fi, parking (paid), some pets allowed, no-smoking rooms* ▭ *AE, DC, MC, V* ⊚“◎” *EP* ✛ *2:C2.*

BORGHESE

$$$$ ▣ **Grand Hotel Parco dei Principi.** The 1960s-era facade of this large, seven-story hotel contrasts with the turn-of-the-20th-century Italian court decor, and the extensive botanical garden, right on the border of the exclusive Parioli district and the Villa Borghese park. The result is a combination of traditional elegance and contemporary pleasure: picture windows in every room with views over an ocean of green, surmounted by St. Peter's dome; a wonderful free-form swimming pool; a piano bar with stained glass and carved walnut appointments; and chamber music in the garden. **Pros:** quiet location on the Borghese Gardens; nice pool; outstanding service. **Cons:** beyond the city center; extras are expensive;

a bit of a walk to caffè and restaurants. ✉ *Via G. Frescobaldi 5, Borghese* ☎ *06/854421* ⊕ *www.parcodeiprincipi.com* ↘ *160 rooms, 20 suites* ⚘ *In-room: Internet, Wi-Fi. In-hotel: 3 restaurants, room service, bar, pool, gym, laundry service, Internet terminal, parking (paid)* ▭ *AE, DC, MC, V* ⦿*BP* ✛ *2:C1.*

SPAGNA

$$$ ▦ **Condotti.** As its name suggests, this small hotel is two blocks from Rome's premier shopping street, Via Condotti (that is, not on it), and one block from the Spanish Steps. The emphasis here is on peace and comfort, created by surprisingly elegant period furnishings and a relatively quiet location. All rooms are soundproof, and many enjoy views of the rooftops of Rome. Walnut furniture and gilt-edge mirrors raise the rent, and rich fabrics used for the curtains and bedspreads. Each room has its own temperature control, a rarity in Rome. **Pros:** soundproof rooms with terraces; individual climate control; friendly and helpful staff. **Cons:** small rooms; Wi-Fi is only available in some of the rooms; you might have to send your bags up in the elevator and follow them separately—that's how tiny it is. ✉ *Via Mario de' Fiori 37, Spagna* ☎ *06/6794661* ⊕ *www.hotelcondotti.com* ↘ *16 rooms, 2 suites* ⚘ *In-room: safe, refrigerator, Wi-Fi (some). In-hotel: room service, bar, bicycles, laundry service* ▭ *AE, DC, MC, V* ⦿*CP* ✛ *1:H2.*

$$$ ▦ **Dei Borgognoni.** This quietly chic hotel is on a byway in the heart of the smart shopping district near Piazza San Silvestro and features a small private art collection that is on view throughout the hotel. The centuries-old palazzo building has been remodeled to provide spacious lounges, a glassed-in garden courtyard, and stylishly furnished rooms that are cleverly arranged to create an illusion of space, though they are actually petite. Some rooms have balconies or terraces on the interior court, and the hotel offers free bicycles for guests to putter around the city. **Pros:** reasonably priced but still very central; some rooms have private balconies or terraces. **Cons:** some of the rooms are surprisingly small for their price; the breakfast lacks variety; some say the staff is stuffy. ✉ *Via del Bufalo 126, Spagna* ☎ *06/69941505* ⊕ *www. hotelborgognoni.it* ↘ *51 rooms* ⚘ *In-room: safe, refrigerator, Internet. In-hotel: restaurant, room service, bar, bicycles, laundry service, public Wi-Fi, Internet terminal, parking (paid), no-smoking rooms* ▭ *AE, D, DC, MC, V* ⦿*BP* ✛ *1:H3.*

$$$$ ▦ **D'Inghilterra.** From monarchs and movie moguls to some of the greatest writers of all time (John Keats, Mark Twain, and Hemingway), the D'Inghilterra has welcomed Rome's most discerning tourists since it opened its doors in 1845. The hotel's name pays tribute to the Brits who once colonized the Spanish Steps district back in the Grand Tour era. Set on a potted-palm cobblestone stretch of posh Via Bocca di Leone, this "albergo" is like an old sepia-toned photograph come to life. With a marvelous residential feel and a staff that is as warm as the surroundings are velvety, this hotel has lots going for it. The lobby is a jewel—tiny, unassuming, like a sentry box against the hustle and bustle outside the front door. In fact, you're in the heart of the shopping district here, so traffic noises can intrude even the double-pane windows (the best rooms here overlook a quiet, plant-covered terrace).

Upstairs, some guest rooms include wall-to-wall carpeting or wood floors with Chinese tapestry and Baroque mirrors. But what guests really adore about the hotel is its public salons on the first floor, including the Bar, which is James Bond–suave. The hotel's restaurant Cafè Romano is another favorite, especially among Rome's ladies that lunch who stop in for a light snack or *aperitivo* in between their shopping. **Pros:** distinct character and opulence; turndown service (with chocolates!); a genuinely friendly and attentive staff. **Cons:** the elevator is both small and slow; bathrooms are surprisingly petite; the location—despite soundproofing—is still noisy. ✉ *Via Bocca di Leone 14, Spagna* ☎ *06/699811* ⊕ *www.hoteldinghilterraroma.it* ⤶ *97 rooms, 11 suites* ⚙ *In-room: safe, refrigerator, Internet. In-hotel: restaurant, room service, bar, laundry service, Internet terminal, parking (paid), no-smoking rooms* ▤ *AE, DC, MC, V* ⊙ *EP* ✛ *1:H3.*

> **WORD OF MOUTH**
>
> "Take a deep breath and go to the Hassler—worth every blessed penny. We had a marvelous room overlooking the Spanish Steps with a small balcony, gorgeous, comfy bed, and huge bathroom. While it's a very lively spot the noise was never an issue up on the 6th floor. Service was extremely good. Public spaces are lovely. Just do it. You'll love it."
> —laurela

13

$$$$
Fodor's Choice
★

🛏 **Hassler.** When it comes to million-dollar views, this exclusive hotel has the best seats in the house. Which is why movie stars, money shakers, and the *nouveau riche* are all willing to pay top dollar (or top euro, shall we say) to stay at the best address in Rome, just atop the Spanish Steps. The hotel is owned by the Wirth family, a famous dynasty of Swiss hoteliers that also owns Il Palazzetto—a small yet stylish boutique hotel—and The International Wine Academy (also nearby), which offers wine tastings and wine appreciation courses. The exterior of the Hassler is rather bland, but the guest rooms are certainly among the world's most extravagant and lavishly decorated. You can get more standard rooms at the back of the hotel, which will spare you and your wallet of the V.I.P. prices. Of course, even the lowest prices at the Hassler can't compare with what you could find somewhere else. The recently renovated penthouse boasts the largest terrace in Rome. The Rooftop Restaurant, the Imagò (which guests use for the breakfast buffet), is world-famous for its view, if not for its food; and the Palm Court Garden, which becomes the hotel bar in summer, is overflowing with flowers. **Pros:** charming old-world feel; prime location and panoramic views at the top of the Spanish Steps; just "steps" away from some of the best shopping in the world. **Cons:** VIP prices; many think the staff is too standoffish; some say the cuisine at the rooftop restaurant isn't worth the gourmet price tag. ✉ *Piazza Trinità dei Monti 6, Spagna* ☎ *06/699340* ⊕ *www.lhw.com* ⤶ *85 rooms, 13 suites* ⚙ *In-room: safe, refrigerator, Internet. In-hotel: restaurant, room service, bar, gym, spa, laundry service, public Wi-Fi, parking (paid), no-smoking rooms* ▤ *AE, DC, MC, V* ⊙ *EP* ✛ *1:H2.*

$$$–$$$$
🛏 **Hotel Art.** It's *Alta Roma Moda* meets a chic contemporary art gallery at this hotel that sits cleverly on Via Margutta, "the street of painters."

As you glide your way through the stylish lobby, the smart furnishings and fixtures in the public spaces of the hotel will build up your urge to bid on an item as if you were at an auction at Christie's. The real gem is the Crystal Bar, set in an old chapel, with gilded panels in Raphaelesque style and topped off with a glittering chandelier. Guest rooms—color-coordinated, inexplicably, with hallways—are a more standard upper-middle contemporary style, with sleek wood headboards, puffy white comforters, bathrobes, and hi-speed Internet connection. **Pros:** feels like you've checked into an ultra-hip art gallery; helpful and pleasant staff; close to two metro stops; comfortable beds. **Cons:** the glass floors are noisy at night; the courtyard bar crowd may keep you awake; the a/c is sometimes temperamental. ⊠ *Via Margutta 56, Spagna* ☎ *06/328711* ⊕ *www.hotelart.it* ⤴ *44 rooms, 2 suites* ⟳ *In-room: safe, refrigerator, Internet. In-hotel: restaurant, room service, bar, gym, spa, public Wi-Fi, no-smoking rooms* ⊟ *AE, DC, MC, V* ⟦⦾⟧ *CP* ✛ *1:H2.*

$$$$ ⌂ **Hotel de Russie.** A ritzy retreat for government big wigs and Hol-
 ⟳   lywood high-rollers, de Russie raises the bar on lavish lodging. The hotel lies just steps away from the famed Piazza del Popolo and is set in a 19th-century historic hotel which once boasted a clientele that included royalty. Famed hotelier Sir Rocco Forte decided to give de Russie a major makeover in 2002 and transformed it into one of the swankiest hotels in Eternal City. The furnishings are Donghia-style, the colors scream gloomy glamour, and the bathrooms have Roman mosaic motifs. The hotel's most prized possession is the spectacular glimpse of the garden courtyard from many (but not all) of the rooms and its sharp Le Jardin de Russie restaurant. When not lounging outside on their plushy terrace, VIPs can be found at the world-class spa facil-ity or sipping on a *prosecco* poolside. **Pros:** big potential for celebrity sightings; special activities for children; extensive gardens (including a butterfly reserve); first-rate luxury spa. **Cons:** hotel is a bit worn around the edges; decor is a little generic; breakfast is nothing special. ⊠ *Via del Babuino 9, Spagna* ☎ *06/328881* ⊕ *www.rfhotels.com* ⤴ *122 rooms, 33 suites* ⟳ *In-room: safe, refrigerator, Internet. In-hotel: res-taurant, room service, bar, pool, gym, spa, children's programs (ages toddler–12), public Wi-Fi, parking (paid), no-smoking rooms* ⊟ *AE, DC, MC, V* ⟦⦾⟧ *BP* ✛ *1:G1.*

$$–$$$ ⌂ **Hotel Homs.** At this midsize hotel, on a quiet street in the heart of the historic center, two rooftop terraces provide fine views of the whole area; the larger terrace is suitable for breakfast year-round. Although room furnishings are a bit plain overall, beautiful antiques accent stra-tegic spots for an air that's a cut above average. Rome's most complete English-language bookshop, the Anglo-American, is directly across the street. **Pros:** walking distance to Piazza di Spagna; steps away from a big bus hub; recently renovated; helpful staff. **Cons:** no breakfast included in the room rate; small rooms; fee for Wi-Fi. ⊠ *Via della Vite 71–72, Spagna* ☎ *06/6792976* ⊕ *www.hotelhoms.it* ⤴ *53 rooms, 5 suites, 1 apartment* ⟳ *In-room: safe, refrigerator, Internet. In-hotel: room service, bar, laundry service, public Wi-Fi, parking (paid), some pets allowed, no-smoking rooms* ⊟ *AE, DC, MC, V* ⟦⦾⟧ *EP* ✛ *1:H3.*

$$$–$$$$ 🏨 **Inn at the Spanish Steps.** After a hard day of shopping on Rome's Rodeo Drive, Via dei Condotti, you'll be pleased to see that this quaint yet cushy hotel fits right in with its neighbors. The plush hotel occupies the upper floors of a centuries-old town house it shares with Casanova's old haunt, Antico Caffè Greco. The inn wins a gold star for its smart design and sharp decor. All junior suites are handsomely decorated with damask fabrics, antiques, and a great sense of style. The simpler rooms glow with ochre walls and framed paintings, while the grander ones are jewel boxes complete with frescoed ceilings and elegantly striped walls. **Pros:** some of the world's best shopping at your doorstep; rooms with superb views of the Spanish Steps; afternoon snacks and outstanding breakfast buffets. **Cons:** interior rooms are claustrophobic; the crowd on the Spanish Steps is often noisy; not all rooms are graced with the stunning Steps view. ✉ *Via Condotti 85, Spagna* ☎ *06/69925657* ⊕ *www.atspanishsteps.com* ⇨ *22 suites* ♿ *In-room: safe, refrigerator, Internet. In-hotel: room service, bar, laundry service, Internet terminal, some pets allowed, no-smoking rooms* ⊟ *AE, DC, MC, V* ¶◯ *BP* ✢ *1:H2.*

13

$$–$$$ 🏨 **Locarno.** The sort of place that inspired a movie (Bernard Weber's 1978 *Hotel Locarno,* to be exact), this has been a longtime choice for art aficionados and people in the cinema. But everyone will appreciate this hotel's fin de siècle charm, intimate feel, and central location off Piazza del Popolo. Exquisite wallpaper and fabric prints are coordinated in the rooms, and some rooms are decorated with antiques—the grandest room looks like an art director's take on a Medici bedroom. Everything is lovingly supervised by the owners, a mother-daughter duo. The buffet breakfast is ample, there's bar service on the panoramic roof garden, and complimentary bicycles are available if you feel like braving the traffic. A newly renovated annex is done in Art Deco style. **Pros:** luxurious feel (it may even seem like you're in a movie); spacious rooms (even by American standards); free bicycles for exploring Rome. **Cons:** some of the rooms are dark; the annex doesn't compare to the main hotel; the regular staff probably won't go out of their way to help you. ✉ *Via della Penna 22, Spagna* ☎ *06/3610841* ⊕ *www.hotellocarno.com* ⇨ *64 rooms, 2 suites* ♿ *In-room: safe, refrigerator, Wi-Fi. In-hotel: restaurant, bar, bicycles, laundry service, Internet terminal, public Wi-Fi, no-smoking rooms* ⊟ *AE, DC, MC, V* ¶◯ *BP* ✢ *1:G1.*

$ 🏨 **Panda.** You couldn't possibly find a better deal in Rome than here at the Panda, especially given its key location just behind the Spanish Steps. The small hotel is situated on one of the poshest shopping streets in the centro, Via della Croce. Guest rooms are outfitted in terra-cotta, wrought iron, and very simple furnishings; they're on the small-side, spotlessly clean, and quiet, thanks to double-glaze windows. Pay even less by sharing a bath—in low season, you may have it to yourself anyway. **Pros:** discount if you pay cash; free Wi-Fi; located on a quiet street, but still close to the Spanish Steps. **Cons:** some say the Wi-Fi signal is weak; not all rooms have private bathrooms; no elevator; no TVs in the rooms. ✉ *Via della Croce 35, Spagna* ☎ *06/6780179* ⊕ *www.hotelpanda.it* ⇨ *20 rooms, 14 with bath* ♿ *In-room: no a/c (some), no TV, Wi-Fi. In-hotel: laundry service, public Wi-Fi* ⊟ *AE, DC, MC, V* ¶◯ *CP* ✢ *1:H2.*

$$ ⊞ **San Carlo.** Marble accents are everywhere at this renovated 17th-century mansion, and there's an overall effect that's refined and decidedly classical. Rooms are bright and comfortable; some have their own terraces with rooftop views. A top-floor terrace is ideal for having breakfast or taking in the sun throughout the day. The rooms also feature flat-screen TVs and free Wi-Fi. **Pros:** rooms with terraces and views of historic Rome; rooftop garden; attentive staff. **Cons:** there are a lot of stairs and no elevator; breakfast is basic Italian fare (great coffee but otherwise just cornetti, cereal, and yogurt); the rooms can be noisy. ⊠ *Via delle Carrozze 92–93, Spagna* ☎ *06/6784548* ⊕ *www.hotelsancarloroma.com* ⤳ *50 rooms, 2 suites* ♿ *In-room: refrigerator, Wi-Fi. In-hotel: bar, laundry service, public Wi-Fi, no-smoking rooms* ⊟ *AE, DC, MC, V* ⦿| *CP* ✛ *1:H2.*

$$$ ⊞ **Scalinata di Spagna.** A long-time favorite of hopeless romantics, it's
Fodor's Choice often hard to snag a room at this tiny hotel as it's often booked up for
★ months, even years at a time. And it's not hard to guess why. For starters, its prime location at the top of the Spanish Steps, inconspicuous little entrance, and quiet, sunny charm all add to the character that guests fall in love with over and over again. Rooms were renovated in a stylish manner, focusing on accentuated floral fabrics and Empire-style sofas. Rooms that overlook the Spanish Steps are the first to go. But don't fret it you don't snatch up the room of your choice. You can always escape to the hotel's extravagant rooftop garden and gaze over ancient Rome as you nibble on your *cornetto* and sip on your *cappuccino*. Amenities, such as breakfast service until noon and in-room Internet access, are a nice touch. **Pros:** friendly and helpful concierge; fresh fruit in the rooms; free Wi-Fi throughout the Scalinata. **Cons:** it's a hike up the hill to the hotel; no porter and no elevator; service can be hit-or-miss. ⊠ *Piazza Trinità dei Monti 17, Spagna* ☎ *06/6793006* ⊕ *www.hotelscalinata.com* ⤳ *16 rooms* ♿ *In-room: safe, refrigerator, Wi-Fi. In-hotel: room service, laundry service, Internet terminal, public Wi-Fi, parking (paid), no-smoking rooms* ⊟ *AE, D, MC, V* ⦿| *BP* ✛ *2:A2.*

$$$–$$$$ ⊞ **Valadier.** Oh, if these walls could talk. Once a convent, later a house of ill repute, this palazzo has seen it all. Not a trace remains of either incarnation, and today it's a hotel known for comfortable rooms with marble and travertine bathrooms and a fine location that's just off Piazza del Popolo and a few minutes' walk from the Spanish Steps. As for decor, it's traditional hotel luxe, with a lot of polished surfaces, mirrors, and shiny lights, so don't expect any time-burnished patina. However, the view from the rooftop terrace restaurant, complete with a panorama of domes and cupolas, is enchanting. **Pros:** excellent American-style breakfast buffet; piano bar; flat-screen TVs; good water pressure and cool a/c. **Cons:** cocktails are a pretty penny (or, rather, a pretty centesimo); rooms are smaller than you'd expect for a luxury hotel; some rooms don't have closets. ⊠ *Via della Fontanella 15, Spagna* ☎ *06/3611998* ⊕ *www.hotelvaladier.com* ⤳ *60 rooms* ♿ *In-room: safe, refrigerator, Wi-Fi. In-hotel: 3 restaurants, room service, bars, bicycles, laundry service, Internet terminal, public Wi-Fi, no-smoking rooms* ⊟ *AE, DC, MC, V* ⦿| *BP* ✛ *1:G1.*

VATICAN, BORGO, AND PRATI

Although you won't be able to stay in Vatican City itself, the neighborhoods to the east of the city-state host a wide range of hotels, from pilgrim-simple to cardinal-luxe. The Borgo, directly outside the Vatican walls, has medieval charm, but can be overrun by tourists. A 10-minute walk to the north lie the residential streets of Prati and many of the hotels listed below.

VATICAN

13

$$ 🏨 **Alimandi.** Just behind the Vatican Museums, this family-run hotel is a real bargain considering the location and service. A spiffy lobby, spacious lounges, a tavern, terraces, and roof gardens are some of the perks, as is a recreation room with a billiard and an exercise room equipped with step machines and a treadmill. Rooms are spacious and well-furnished; many can accommodate extra beds. Needless to say, the location here is quite far away from Rome's historic center. However, a few stops on the metro (there's a stop nearby) and you're there. If requested, the hotel will also arrange for a shuttle to pick you up from the airport at an extra cost of €5 per person for all flights that arrive before 2 PM. **Pros:** nice family-owned hotel with a friendly staff, a terrace, a gym and reasonably priced restaurants and shops in the area. **Cons:** breakfast is a good spread but it goes quickly; rooms are small; not close to much of interest other than the Vatican. ✉ *Via Tunisi 8, Vatican* ☎ *06/39723948* ⊕ *www.alimandi.it* ⟲ *35 rooms* △ *In-room: safe, refrigerator (some), Wi-Fi. In-hotel: bar, gym, Wi-Fi, Internet terminal, parking (paid), no-smoking rooms* ▭ *AE, DC, MC, V* ❍❘ *BP* ✛ *1:B2.*

$$–$$$ 🏨 **Residenza Paolo VI.** Set in a former monastery that is still an extraterritorial part of the Vatican and magnificently abutting Bernini's colonnade of St. Peter's Square, the Paolo VI (pronounced Paolo Sesto, Italian for Pope Paul VI) is unbeatably close to St. Peter's. Replete with a stone terrace that directly overlooks Bernini's 17th-century porticoes, this hotel enjoys one of the most spectacular perches in Rome. As for the decor, guest rooms are luxurious and comfortable and amazingly quiet. Within breathing distance of the residence of Benedict XVI, it's not surprising that the management here is devoutly Catholic, as you may gather from the framed portraits of the pope on the front desk and the daily prayer slipped under your door in lieu of a newspaper. But heaven can wait once you settle into your breakfast buffet on the wonderful roof terrace and drink in the view of Michelangelo's great dome. **Pros:** unparalleled views of St. Peter's from the roof terrace; a sound sleep is assured in these quiet rooms; the breakfast spread is huge. **Cons:** the small rooms are really small; bathrooms are small. ✉ *Via Paolo VI 29, Vatican* ☎ *06/68134108* ⊕ *www.residenzapaolovi.com* ⟲ *29 rooms* △ *In-room: safe, refrigerator, Wi-Fi. In-hotel: bar, laundry service, Internet terminal parking (paid), no-smoking rooms* ▭ *AE, D, MC, V* ❍❘ *BP* ✛ *1:C4.*

BORGO

$$–$$$ 🏨 **Atlante Star.** The lush rooftop-terrace garden caffè with probably the best views of St. Peter's Basilica and the rest of Rome is one of the prime reasons why guests book their stay here. Other reasons include close proximity to the Vatican, top-notch service, and superb shopping all at your fingertips. In a distinguished 19th-century building, the guest rooms are attractively decorated with striped silks and prints for an old-world atmosphere; many bathrooms have hot tubs. The friendly family management is attentive to guests' needs and they take pride in offering extra-virgin olive oil from their own trees in the country. A sister hotel, the **Atlante Garden,** just around the corner, has larger rooms at slightly lower rates. If requested, the Atlante Star will pick you up at Fiumicino airport for free. **Pros:** close to St. Peter's; impressive view from the restaurant and some of the rooms. **Cons:** some rooms are nicer than others (and some aren't as pretty as the ones on the Web site); the area can be overrun with tourists; it's not close to Rome's other attractions. ✉ *Via Vitelleschi 34, Borgo* ☎ *06/6873233* 🌐 *www.atlantehotels.com* ⮎ *65 rooms, 10 suites* ♿ *In-room: safe, refrigerator, Internet. In-hotel: restaurant, room service, bar, laundry service, Internet terminal, public Wi-Fi, parking (paid), no-smoking rooms* ▭ *AE, DC, MC, V* 🍴 *BP* ✥ *1:D3.*

$–$$ **Sant'Anna.** In the picturesque old Borgo neighborhood in the shadow of St. Peter's, this fashionable small hotel has exceedingly stylish ample bedrooms with new wood-beam ceilings, designer fabrics, and comfy beds. The frescoes in the vaulted breakfast room and fountain in the courtyard add an individual touch. The marvelously decorated and spacious attic rooms also have tiny terraces. **Pros:** Borgo Pio is a pedestrian-only zone during the day; beds are comfy; staff is eager-to-please. **Cons:** street-side rooms are noisy; not many amenities; no bar or restaurant in the hotel. ✉ *Borgo Pio 133, Borgo* ☎ *06/68801602* 🌐 *www.hotelsantanna.com* ⮎ *20 rooms* ♿ *In-room: safe, refrigerator. In-hotel: parking (paid)* ▭ *AE, DC, MC, V* 🍴 *BP* ✥ *1:C3.*

PRATI

$–$$ **Amalia.** Convenient to St. Peter's, the Vatican, and Prati's Cola di Rienzo shopping district, this small hotel appears crisp and smart with striped bedspreads and freshly painted walls. The hotel furnishings are simple and nothing to brag about but the rooms are spacious and clean. The Ottaviano stop of Metro line A is a block away, which is convenient for getting into the historic center. **Pros:** good location for visiting the Vatican and for shopping; 24-hour turnaround on laundry services; large beds. **Cons:** breakfast is more sweet than savory; sometimes hot water in bathrooms runs out quickly; no restaurant in the hotel. ✉ *Via Germanico 66, Prati* ☎ *06/39723356* 🌐 *www.hotelamalia.com* ⮎ *33 rooms, 26 with bath, 1 suite* ♿ *In-room: safe, refrigerator, Wi-Fi (paid). In-hotel: bar, laundry service, parking (paid), no-smoking rooms, Wi-Fi (paid)* ▭ *AE, DC, MC, V* 🍴 *CP* ✥ *1:C2.*

$ **Gerber.** On a quiet side street eight blocks from the Vatican and across the river from Piazza del Popolo, this intimate, unpretentious hotel offers genuinely friendly service. The facilities are immaculately maintained throughout, and feature a garden and sun terrace for breakfast or a relaxed moment. The simple rooms have pleasant, neutral-tone, modern furnishings. **Pros:** good value for your money; great service; comfortable beds and big bathrooms. **Cons:** elevator is tiny; some of the rooms are quite small; you'll probably need to take a taxi, bus, or metro to the other sights around town. ✉ *Via degli Scipioni 241, Prati* ☎*06/3221001* ⊕ *www.hotelgerber.it* ⤳*27 rooms* ⚬ *In-room: safe, refrigerator, Wi-Fi. In-hotel: bar, laundry service, public Wi-Fi, Internet terminal (paid), parking (paid), no-smoking rooms* ☰*AE, DC, MC, V* ⏐⚬⏐ *CP* ✛ *1:E1.*

$$$ 🏨**Hotel Dei Mellini.** On the west bank of the Tiber between the Spanish Steps and St. Peter's Basilica (a three-minute stroll from Piazza del Popolo), this place has style to match its setting. The luxurious reception rooms are a welcome haven for weary sightseers, as antique prints and fresh flowers give warmth to the light-filled rooms. Guest rooms are sleek and sumptuous; grand drapes, wood-grain headboards, marble-top sinks, elegant chairs, and framed photos all make for a luxurious stay. Marble bathrooms complete the pampered feel. There is also a bar, cafeteria, roof garden, and solarium. Free parking is available nearby. **Pros:** spacious and spotless rooms; turndown service; the neighborhood is quiet, so you'll get a good night's rest. **Cons:** if you want to be near the action, this is not the place for you; not a lot of dining options in the immediate vicinity; restaurant in the hotel is used primarily for breakfast and serves light sandwiches upon request. ✉ *Via Muzio Clementi 81, Prati* ☎ *06/324771* ⊕ *www.hotelmellini.com* ⤳ *80 rooms* ⚬ *In-room: safe, refrigerator, Wi-Fi (paid). In-hotel: restaurant, room service, bar, laundry service, Internet terminal (paid), Wi-Fi (paid), parking (paid), no-smoking rooms* ☰*AE, DC, MC, V* ⏐⚬⏐ *CP* ✛ *1:F2.*

¢ 🏨**Hotel San Pietrino.** How this simple, but cute hotel within close proximity to the Vatican manages to keep its bargain prices is definitely a mystery. It's located on the third floor of a 19th-century palazzo that's only a five-minute walk to St. Peter's Square. In addition to clean, simple rooms, San Pietrino offers air-conditioning, TVs with DVD players, and high-speed Internet to guests. There is no breakfast included and no bar in the hotel, but not to worry—with all the local caffè and bars, you won't have any trouble finding yourself a *cornetto* and cappuccino in the morning or a prosecco for aperitivo in the evening. **Pros:** heavenly prices near the Vatican; TVs with DVD players; high-speed Internet; close to Rome's famous farmers' market, Mercato Trionfale. **Cons:** a couple of metro stops away from the center of Rome; no breakfast; no bar. ✉ *Via Giovanni Bettolo 43, Prati* ☎ *06/3700132* ⊕ *www.sanpietrino.it* ⤳ *12 rooms* ⚬ *In-room: DVD (some), Internet, Wi-Fi. In-hotel: Internet terminal, public Wi-Fi* ☰*MC, V* ⏐⚬⏐ *EP* ✛ *1:B1.*

Fodor'sChoice
★

¢ 🏨**San Giuseppe della Montagna.** Guests looking to add a little spirituality to their trip might try staying at this convent just outside the Vatican walls, near the entrance to the Vatican Museums. Some of the guest rooms have three beds, and all have private bathrooms. As opposed to most convents and monasteries, San Giuseppe della Montagna not only doesn't have a curfew but they also give their guests keys, which makes their stay even more convenient. There are also two parking spaces that guests may use if they're available. **Pros:** near the Vatican; no curfew; keys are provided. **Cons:** no credit cards; hardly any amenities; no refrigerator in the rooms (but there is one in the convent that may be used by guests). ✉ *Viale Vaticano 87, Vatican* ☎ *06/39723807* ⤳ *15*

13

rooms & *In-room: no a/c, safe, no TV. In-hotel: no-smoking rooms* ⊟ *No credit cards* †⊙| *CP* ✛ *1:A2.*

TRASTEVERE AND GIANICOLO

Once Raphael's Rome, this has been transformed from artist's haven to working-class ghetto to, currently, the home base of many of Rome's expats and exchange students. Hotels, squeezed into the neighborhood's former denizens' very modest buildings, tend toward the budget pension, although a few mid-range hotels set in stylishly converted convents have sprung up in the last few years.

TRASTEVERE

$ 🖵 **Carmel.** Rome's only kosher hotel sits across the Tiber from the main synagogue. Although its room furnishings are sparse, the staff is very friendly and there's a charming vine-covered terrace. There are two kitchens for use by guests keeping kosher, and prepared kosher meals can be arranged. Breakfast is not included in the price and is served in the snack bar next door. Not all rooms have a private bath, so make sure to inquire before booking. **Pros:** good budget choice; kosher-friendly; short walk to Jewish Ghetto. **Cons:** pay in cash upon check-in; no breakfast served on Sundays; no-frills accommodations; reception is closed after 8 PM. ⊠ *Via Goffredo Mameli 11, Trastevere* 🕾 *06/5809921* ⊕ *www.hotelcarmel.it* ↰ *10 rooms, 8 with bath, 1 suite* & *In-room: safe, kitchen (some), refrigerator. In-hotel: parking (paid), no-smoking rooms, pets allowed (some)* ⊟ *No credit cards* †⊙| *CP* ✛ *3:B2.*

$ 🖵 **Casa di Santa Francesca Romana.** In the heart of Trastevere but tucked away from all of the hustle and bustle that goes with the medieval *quartiere,* lies this former monastery built to honor the 15th-century St. Francesca Romana. A large complex, the hotel is centered on an impressive ochre-colored courtyard, lined with potted trees and tables. There isn't much on the amenities front aside from a TV-room and a private reading room, available to all guests. Guest rooms are standard-issue and the cool white walls, tile floors, and simple desks won't win any design-awards, but for the money, this is a fabulous location and spectacular buy, made even more attractive if you want to opt for the half- or full-board options available. **Pros:** the price can't be beat; excellent restaurants nearby; breakfast is delicious; quiet and excellent location; away from rowdy side of Trastevere. **Cons:** not many amenities; thin walls; no Internet access. ⊠ *Via dei Vasceillari 61, Trastevere* 🕾 *06/5812125* ⊕ *www.sfromana.it* ↰ *36 rooms, 1 suite* & *In-room: TV. In-hotel: no-smoking rooms* ⊟ *AE, DC, MC, V* †⊙| *CP* ✛ *3:C2.*

$ 🖵 **Cisterna.** On a quiet street in the very heart of medieval Trastevere, this basic but comfortable hotel is ideally located for getting to know Rome's most authentic neighborhood, a favorite of artists and bohemians for decades. Beamed ceilings add a rustic touch, and there's a marble terrace-garden with a classical fountain. One room, No. 40, has its own private terrace. **Pros:** simple accommodations for budget travelers; friendly staff; good location in trendy Trastevere. **Cons:** hotel decor does not match the trendiness of the neighborhood; street-side rooms are noisy; the block is popular for just hanging out. ⊠ *Via della*

Cisterna 7–8–9, Trastevere ☎ *06/5817212* ⊕ *www.cisternahotel.it* ↘ *20 rooms* ⚓ *In-room: Wi-Fi* ⚓ *In-hotel: room service, Wi-Fi, bar, Internet terminal, no-smoking rooms* ▭ *AE, DC, MC, V* ⧎ *CP* ✛ *2:B2.*

$$ **Hotel Santa Maria.** A Trastevere treasure, this hotel has a pedigree going back four centuries. This ivy-covered, mansard-roofed, rosy-brick-red, erstwhile Renaissance-era convent has been transformed by Paolo and Valentina Vetere into a true charmer. Surrounded by towering tenements, the complex is centered on a monastic porticoed courtyard, lined with orange trees—a lovely place for breakfast. The guest rooms are sweet and simple: a mix of brick walls, "cotto" tile floors, modern oak furniture, and stylishly floral bedspreads and curtains. Best of all, the location is *buonissimo*—just a few blocks from the Tiber and its *isola*. **Pros:** a quaint and pretty oasis in a chaotic city; relaxing courtyard; stocked wine bar. **Cons:** it might be tricky to find; some of the showers drain slowly; it's not always easy finding a cab in Trastevere. ✉ *Vicolo del Piede 2, Trastevere* ☎ *06/5894626* ⊕ *www.htlsantamaria. com* ↘ *18 rooms, 2 suites* ⚓ *In-room: safe, refrigerator. In-hotel: bar, bicycles, laundry service, Internet terminal, no-smoking rooms* ▭ *AE, DC, MC, V* ⧎ *BP* ✛ *3:B1.*

$ **Hotel Trastevere.** This tiny hotel captures the villagelike charm of the Trastevere district. The entrance hall features a mural of the famous Piazza di Santa Maria, a few blocks away, and hand-painted Art Nouveau wall designs add a touch of graciousness throughout. Open medieval brickwork and a few antiques here and there complete the mood. Most rooms face Piazza San Cosimato, where there's an outdoor food market every morning except Sunday. **Pros:** cheap with a good location; convenient to transportation; friendly staff. **Cons:** no frills; few amenities. ✉ *Via Luciano Manara 24–25, Trastevere* ☎ *06/5814713* ⊕ *www. hoteltrastevere.net* ↘ *20 rooms, 3 apartments* ⚓ *In-room: safe (some), Wi-Fi. In-hotel: no-smoking rooms* ▭ *AE, DC, MC, V* ⧎ *CP* ✛ *3:B2.*

$$ **Relais Le Clarisse.** In one of Rome's most popular neighborhoods, this charming little oasis features five simple, but classically styled accommodations (two doubles and three suites) with terra-cotta-tiled floors, wrought-iron bed frames, and oak furnishings. Each room opens up onto a bright courtyard surrounded by a Mediterranean garden of grapevines and olive and lemon trees. Though Le Clarisse is set on the former cloister grounds of the Santa Chiara order, its rooms are equipped with the most modern technologies, including individual climate control, flat-screen TVs, air-conditioning, high-speed Internet and Wi-Fi, as well as Jacuzzi showers and tubs. Travelers feel more like personal guests at a friend's villa rather than at a hotel, thanks to the comfortable size of the accommodations and the personal touches and service extended by the staff. Le Clarisse is also located across the street from the Alcazar movie theater, which shows original language films (as opposed to versions that have been dubbed into Italian) on Monday nights. **Pros:** spacious rooms with comfy beds; high-tech showers/tubs with good water pressure; staff is multilingual, friendly, and at your service. **Cons:** this part of Trastevere can be noisy at night; the rooms here fill up quickly; they only serve American coffee. ✉ *Via Cardinale Merry del Val 20, Trastevere* ☎ *06/58334437* ⊕ *www.leclarisse.com*

Fodor's Choice
★

13

↘ *5 rooms, 3 suites* ♿ *In-room: safe, refrigerator, Internet. In-hotel: room service, laundry service, Internet terminal, public Wi-Fi, parking (paid), no-smoking rooms* 🖃 *AE, MC, V* ❙◯❙ *CP* ✛ *3:B2.*

AVENTINO, TESTACCIO, AND PALATINO

Leafy residential streets, quiet nights, and fresh hilltop breezes are some of the perks of staying in this well-heeled (and relatively unhistoric) neighborhood. Hotels take full advantage of the extra space and the sylvan setting, most with gardens or courtyards where you can enjoy alfresco R & R far from the madding crowds. Bear in mind that public transportation is somewhat limited up here, and allow a half hour by foot to major sights.

AVENTINO

$$ 🏨 **Domus Aventina.** The best part of this quaint, friendly hotel is that it's situated between two of Rome's loveliest gardens: a municipal rose garden and Rome's famous Orange Garden, where you can often catch a glimpse of brides and grooms taking their wedding pictures. The Domus Aventina is located in the *cuore* of the historic Aventine district not far from the Temple to Mithras and the House of Aquila and Priscilla (where St. Peter touched down). The 17th-century facade has been restored so it almost looks modern—ditto for the inside, where guest rooms have standard modern decor. Half of the rooms also have balconies. **Pros:** quiet location; walking distance to tourist attractions; complimentary Wi-Fi in rooms and public spaces. **Cons:** no elevator in the hotel; small showers; no tubs. ✉ *Via di Santa Prisca 11/b, Aventino* ☎ *06/5746135* ⊕ *www.domus-aventina.com* ↘ *26 rooms* ♿ *In-room: safe, refrigerator, Wi-Fi. In-hotel: bar, laundry service, public Wi-Fi, parking (paid)* 🖃 *AE, DC, MC, V* ❙◯❙ *CP* ✛ *3:E3.*

$$ 🏨 **Hotel San Anselmo.** Birdsongs add to the mood and charm of this already romantic retreat. The Hotel San Anselmo is far from the bustle of the city center, perched on top of the Aventine Hill in a residential neighborhood. This full-scale 19th-century villa was completely refurbished in 2006 and given a sleek metropolitan feel. The new look blends bits of baroque antique-flair such as the chandelier from the 800s mixed with contemporary pieces such as the sharp stainless steel fireplace in the public spaces. Others will find the best features here are the verdant garden and terrace bar. Guest rooms are each carefully designed to follow a particular theme. Among the favorites are: "Room of Poems" which feature poems beautifully scrawled onto the walls and the "Room of Kisses" which has a big canopy bed with romantic and suggestive drapes. All in all, the San Anselmo is *molto* charming. **Pros:** historic building with artful decor; great showers with jets; a garden where you can enjoy your breakfast. **Cons:** some consider it a bit of a hike to sights; limited public transportation; the wireless is pricey. ✉ *Piazza San Anselmo 2, Aventino* ☎ *06/570057* ⊕ *www.aventinohotels.com* ↘ *45 rooms* ♿ *In-room: safe, refrigerator, Internet. In-hotel: room service, bar, laundry service, public Wi-Fi (paid), parking (paid), no-smoking rooms* 🖃 *AE, DC, MC, V* ❙◯❙ *BP* ✛ *3:D3.*

TESTACCIO

$ ⊞ **Santa Prisca.** The interior design of this hotel is definitely nothing to brag about. However, if a clean room and a trusty place to stay at low prices is what you're looking for, then you've come to the right hotel. Rooms are spacious, and those on the third floor have French windows; some have small balconies. There's also an ample terrace. The extensive grounds offer plenty of parking, and though it's up the hill, the hotel borders on the area of Testaccio, known for its pizzerias, lounges, and nightclub scene. Another plus is a nearby park where, if you're lucky, can catch one of the free concerts that goes on during the weekends in summer months. **Pros:** near public transportation (trams and metro); complimentary Wi-Fi in the lounge; outside terrace with chairs and tables for relaxing. **Cons:** small rooms (it was a convent); some say the breakfast is mediocre; the school next door can be a little noisy on weekdays. ⊠ *Largo M. Gelsomini 25, Testaccio* ☎ *06/5741917* ⊕ *www.hotelsantaprisca.it* ⌁ *49 rooms, 2 suites* ⌂ *In-hotel: restaurant, bar, laundry service, public Wi-Fi, parking (paid), no-smoking rooms* ⊟ *AE, DC, MC, V* ⎮⦿⎮ *BP* ✛ *3:D4.*

13

COLOSSEO AREA

When Nero fiddled, this neighborhood burned—the lowlands around the Colosseum and the Forum were the Suburra, the Imperial City's most notorious slum. There's nary a trace of evildoing now, and narrow alleys are quaint rather than sinister. This is a fine base for the sights of the ancient city, but area eating and drinking establishments can have a touch of the tourist trap. Waking up to views of the Forum, maybe you won't mind.

$$$$ ⊞ **Capo d'Africa.** Many find the modern look and feel of Capo d'Africa—not to mention its plush beds and deep bathtubs—refreshing after a long day's journey through ancient Rome. Each room is decorated in warm, muted color tones with sleek furniture, stylish accents, and contemporary art. The hotel features a nonsmoking floor, fitness center, and solarium. It sits on a quiet street near the Colosseum, Palatine, and Forum, and it's not far from the metro. A delicious breakfast is served on the rooftop terrace, where you can also enjoy an *aperitivo* overlooking Rome at the end of your day. And if you're not too tuckered out, you can take a spin at the gym before bed. **Pros:** quiet, comfortable rooms; fitness center. **Cons:** despite proximity to Colosseum, there isn't a great view of it from the hotel; far from the other Roman sites and the rest of the city scene; not a lot of restaurants in the immediate neighborhood. ⊠ *Via Capo d'Africa 54, Colosseo* ☎ *06/772801* ⊕ *www. hotelcapodafrica.com* ⌁ *64 rooms, 1 suite* ⌂ *In-room: safe, refrigerator, DVD (some), Wi-Fi. In-hotel: room service, bar, gym, Wi-Fi, parking (paid), no-smoking rooms* ⊟ *AE, DC, MC, V* ⎮⦿⎮ *CP* ✛ *4:C6.*

$$–$$$ ⊞ **Celio.** There's much more to brag about than the Colosseum when it comes to the location of this chic boutique hotel in the romantic Celian Hill setting. Consider them to be hidden treasures that are often overlooked by the masses looking to cross off everything from their Must-See list: the haunting Santi Quattro Coronati church, the time-

capsuled Piazza Santi Giovanni e Paolo, and the verdant slopes of the Villa Celimontana park, are just a stroll away. Not far is Nero's Golden House, but lest you lose track of modern times, this hotel offers free Wi-Fi access and a rooftop gym. A cute historical note is the decor of the guest rooms, all small but sumptuously frescoed with "faux" paintings in styles ranging from Pompeiian to Renaissance. French windows and elegant marble bathrooms (some with Jacuzzis) are also nice touches. But the hidden-corner-of-Rome locale may be the trump card. **Pros:** rooftop garden and gym; mosaic floors and over-the-top decor; comfortable beds. **Cons:** some say they wish the management picked the staff as thoughtfully as the antiques; very small bathrooms; breakfast is nothing to write home about. ⊠ *Via dei Santissimi Quattro 35/c, Colosseo* ☎ *06/70495333* ⊕ *www.hotelcelio.com* ⇆ *20 rooms, 2 suites* ⚲ *In-room: safe, refrigerator, Wi-Fi. In-hotel: restaurant, room service, bar, gym, laundry service, public Wi-Fi, Internet terminal, parking (paid), no-smoking rooms* ⊟ *AE, DC, MC, V* �◯ *CP* ✛ *3:G1.*

$$–$$$ ▥ **Duca d'Alba.** First impressions are important, and as soon as you walk into this little boutique hotel near the Colosseum, you know you've hit a winner. Between the marble decor and reproductions of antiquated paintings, the Duca d'Alba definitely gives the traveler the impression that their stay will be a clean and comfortable one. The tasteful neoclassical-style decor includes custom-designed furnishings and marble bathrooms. Recently, some of the rooms underwent a facelift and now feature a modern motif feel with its striped walls, flat-screen TVs, and hardwood floors. The presence of fresh flowers around the hotel and in the rooms is also a nice touch. Breakfast consists of an ample buffet. With its attentive staff and reasonable rates, Duca d'Alba is a good value. **Pros:** proximity to ancient Rome; great cappuccinos for your morning pick-me-up; a fitness center with a treadmill and weights; near the metro. **Cons:** rooms are a bit cramped; despite soundproofing, you may need earplugs to drown out the late-night noise from the Irish bar across the street. ⊠ *Via Leonina 14, Colosseo* ☎ *06/484471* ⊕ *www. hotelducadalba.com* ⇆ *27 rooms, 1 suite* ⚲ *In-room: safe, kitchen (some), refrigerator, Wi-Fi. In-hotel: room service, bar, Wi-Fi, Internet terminal, gym, laundry service, no-smoking rooms* ⊟ *AE, DC, MC, V* ◯ *BP* ✛ *2:C5.*

$$$–$$$$ ▥ **Hotel Forum.** A longtime favorite, this converted 18th-century convent remains a fine lodging choice. The setting is truly unique, on one side of the Fori Imperiali, with a cinematic view of ancient Rome across the avenue (remember, you can also drink all this in at the rooftop bar). The hotel itself is considerably less exciting. The decor is traditional in the extreme, with the requisite gold wall sconces, walnut paneling, red-velvet armchairs, and Asian carpets painting the usual lobby picture. Upstairs, the guest rooms are similarly low-key, although comfortable; suites offer velvety fabrics and some antiques. Bathrooms have been restyled using antique tiles. Little on the restaurant menu can compete with the view—if you get the view (many tables are not ringside, so to speak). **Pros:** bird's-eye view of ancient Rome; award-winning restaurant; "American" bar on the rooftop terrace. **Cons:** small rooms; noisy pub-crawlers congregate in the street below; food and drinks are

expensive. ⊠ *Via Tor de' Conti 25–30, Colosseo* ☎ *06/6792446* ⊕ *www.
hotelforumrome.com* ↩ *80 rooms* ⌂ *In-room: safe, refrigerator, Wi-Fi.
In-hotel: restaurant, room service, bars, laundry service, public Wi-Fi,
parking (paid), no-smoking rooms* ═ *AE, DC, MC, V* ⦿ *BP* ✛ *2:C5.*

$$ 🛏 **Hotel Lancelot.** This home away from home close to the Colosseum
⟳ has been run by the same family since 1970 and is quite popular thanks
to its carefully and courteously attentive staff who go the extra mile for
their guests. Located in a quiet residential area, rooms at Hotel Lancelot
tend to have big windows, so they're bright and airy, and some have
terraces or balconies as well. Over the years, the hotel has undergone
a number of renovations. They most recently updated the rooms with
air-conditioning, en-suite bathrooms, TVs, and Wi-Fi. In the restaurant,
where hearty breakfasts and dinners are served, guests sit at Lancelot's
"round tables"—partly a play on the knight's tale and partly an effort
to encourage communal dining among guests from around the world.
And these round tables seem to be a big hit, since Hotel Lancelot boasts
that most of their guests are either return visitors or new guests rec-
ommended by others who've spent vacations here. **Pros:** hospitable
staff; secluded and quiet; very family-friendly. **Cons:** some of the bath-
rooms are on the small side; no refrigerators in the rooms; room walls
are a bit thin which means you can sometimes hear your neighbors
next door. ⊠ *Via Capo d'Africa 47, Colosseo* ☎ *06/70450615* ⊕ *www.
lancelothotel.com* ↩ *60 rooms* ⌂ *In-room: safe, Wi-Fi. In-hotel: restau-
rant, room service, bar, laundry service, Internet terminal, public Wi-Fi,
parking (paid), no-smoking rooms* ═ *AE, DC, MC, V* ⦿ *CP* ✛ *2:H2.*

$$ 🛏 **Nerva.** Step out of this hotel and you'll feel like you're literally in the
middle of an ancient imperial stomping ground. This charming hotel,
strategically located a stone's throw from the Forum, is surrounded by
the breathtaking splendor of ancient ruins and relics. The hotel itself
is clean and well-run, and rooms are soundproofed, air-conditioned,
and feature orthopedic beds. Guest rooms are on the small side, but
some of them still have original wooden ceiling beams overhead. If
you pay in cash, the hotel will sometimes give you a discount. **Pros:**
a stone's throw from the Forum; friendly staff; orthopedic beds; and
a great pizzeria (*La Base*) that's open into the wee-hours of the night
nearby. **Cons:** showers are tiny; a wall blocks what would otherwise
be a fantastic view of Rome's ancient Forum. ⊠ *Via Tor de' Conti 3/4,
Colosseo* ☎ *06/6781835* ⊕ *www.hotelnerva.com* ↩ *19 rooms* ⌂ *In-
room: safe, refrigerator. In-hotel: restaurant, room service, bar, Wi-Fi,
laundry service, parking (paid), no-smoking rooms* ═ *AE, DC, MC, V*
⦿ *CP* ✛ *2:B5.*

BEYOND THE CITY CENTER

$$$–$$$$ 🛏 **Cavalieri Hilton.** Though the Cavalieri is outside the city center, dis-
tance has its advantages, one of them being the magnificent view over
Rome (ask for a room facing the city), and another, that elusive element
of more central Roman hotels: space. Occupying a vast area atop mod-
ern Rome's highest hill, this oasis of good taste often feels more like a
resort than a city hotel. Central to its appeal, particularly in summer, is
a terraced garden that spreads out from an Olympic-size pool and smart

poolside restaurant and caffè; legions of white-clothed cushioned lounge chairs are scattered throughout the greenery, so there's always a place to sun yourself. Inside, spacious rooms, often with large balconies, are done up in striped damask, puffy armchairs, and Hiltonesque amenities, such as a "pillow menu." If you can tear yourself away, the city center is just a 15-minute complimentary shuttle bus ride away. The strawberry on top: La Pergola restaurant is renowned as one of Rome's very best. **Pros:** beautiful bird's-eye view of Rome; shuttle to the city center; three-Michelin-star dining. **Cons:** you definitely pay for the luxury of staying here—everything is expensive; outside the city center; not all rooms have the view. ⊠ *Via Cadlolo 101, Monte Mario* ☎ *06/35091* ⊕ *www.cavalieri-hilton.com* ↘ *357 rooms, 17 suites* ♿ *In-room: safe, refrigerator, DVD (some), Internet. In-hotel: 2 restaurants, bars, tennis court, pools, gym, spa, laundry service, Internet terminal, no-smoking rooms* ⊟ *AE, DC, MC, V* ⫱◯⫮ *CP* ✛ *1:A1.*

$$$$ ⊞ **Lord Byron.** In the '90s this was favorite among Rome's elite who loved to wine and dine: money movers and shakers, top businesspeople and yacht-brokers all loved to stay here. Today the Art Deco retreat upholds its chicness while serving up a presidential clientele. When this villa first opened (with a rather over-restored exterior), it was Rome's first boutique hotel and still retains much of that jewel-like charm inside. Inside the design is marble meets modern. The downstairs bar—a magnificent piece of cabinetry—is a conversation piece. Upstairs, modern and antique styles combine to create highly polished opulence in the guest rooms. Surrounded by the twittering of birds in the posh and pricey Parioli district, the Lord Byron feels like a small country hotel, or better, a small country manor where you are the lord. **Pros:** luxury bathrobes and slippers; friendly and helpful staff; free shuttle to some of the major tourist attractions. **Cons:** too far to walk to sights; not many caffè and shops in the area; cabs to and from the hotel and *centro* are expensive; a/c is weaker on the upper floors. ⊠ *Via Giuseppe de Notaris 5, Parioli* ☎ *06/3220404* ⊕ *www.lordbyronhotel.com* ↘ *23 rooms, 9 suites* ♿ *In-room: safe, refrigerator, Wi-Fi. In-hotel: restaurant, room service, bar, laundry service, public Wi-Fi, parking (paid), no-smoking rooms* ⊟ *AE, DC, MC, V* ⫱◯⫮ *BP.*

Nightlife and the Arts

WORD OF MOUTH

"Take advantage of the Italian tradition of the Passeggiata (evening stroll). Visit the sites in the historical center, particularly Piazza Navona. There you'll see world-famous fountains, and the people-watching can't be beat. And in summer, outdoor concerts spring up everywhere."

—Vicki

NIGHTLIFE AND THE ARTS PLANNER

Information Please

Rome is finally au courant with advance publication and promotion of cultural events. Leading off is the city's official Web site ⊕ www.comune.roma.it. Events listings can also be found in the *Cronaca* and *Cultura* section of Italian newspapers, as well as in *Metro* (the free newspaper). The most comprehensive listings are in the weekly *roma c'è* booklet, which comes out every Wednesday. Flip to the back for the brief yet very detailed English-language section.

On the Web, check out ⊕ *inromenow.com*, an events site written exclusively for the English-speaking community, as well as the monthly updated *Time Out: Rome* (⊕ *www.timeout.com/travel/rome*) and *The American* (⊕ *www.theamericanmag.com*). The monthly English-language periodical (with accompanying Web site), *Wanted in Rome* (⊕ *www.wantedinrome.com*), is available at many newsstands and has good coverage of arts events. Visit Rome's top cultural, news, and events Web site: *06blog* (⊕ *www.06blog.it*) and *RomaToday* (⊕ *www.romatoday.it*), with postings practically hourly. Events and concert listings can also be found in both English and Italian at ⊕ *www.musicguide.it*.

When to Go

Discoteche opens about 10:30 PM, but the most fun to be had happens later, so never arrive before midnight.

At *enoteche*, aperitivi hour, is from 6:30 to 9 PM—this is when the majority of Italians and foreigners mix together for wine tasting and cocktails.

Fees and Tickets

Most clubs charge a cover charge, between €10 and €20, which often includes the first drink.

Depending on the venue, most concert tickets cost between €7 and €50, and as much as several hundred euro for an exclusive, sold-out event.

Often, you can find seating that is non-reserved (identified in Italian as *posti non numerati*), or even last-minute tickets. Inquire about this when you buy the tickets; you may have to arrive early to get a good seat.

Procure opera and concert tickets in advance at the box office, or just before the performance.

Tickets for major events can be bought online at **Ticket One** (⊕ *www.ticketone.it*).

Tickets for larger musical performances as well as many cultural events can usually be found at **Hello Ticket** (⊕ *www.helloticket.it*) or **Ticketeria** (⊕ *www.ticketeria.it*), which list all cultural events and the many *punta di vendita*, ticket sellers, in Rome.

Go in person to **Orbis** (✉ Piazza dell'Esquilino 37, Repubblica ☎ 06/4744776) for a wide array of tickets.

Mondadori (✉ Via del Corso 472, Spagna ☎ 06/684401), has a tickets desk in its huge and central store that sells music, DVDs, books, and concert tickets.

By Erica Firpo

14

As the famous Italian film director Federico Fellini showed us over and over again, Roman nightlife has been setting trends since time immemorial—and being a native son, he would know. *Fellini Satyricon* focused on those Lucullan all-night banquets (and some more naughty entertainments) of the days of the emperors; *La Dolce Vita* immortalized the nightclubs and *paparazzi* of the city's Hollywood-on-the-Tiber era. And as the director lovingly showed in *Fellini Roma*, the city streets sometimes offered the best place for parties and al fresco dinners. Many visitors would agree with Fellini: Rome, the city, is entertainment enough.

The city's piazzas, fountains, and delicately colored palazzi make impressive backdrops for Rome's living theater, with a *fortissimo* of motor vehicles. It has learned to make the most of its spectacular cityscape, transforming its most beautiful places into settings for the performing arts, outdoors in summer and in splendid palaces and churches in winter. When performances are held at such locations as Villa Celimontana, Piazza Trinità dei Monti, the Baths of Caracalla, or the church of Sant'Ignazio, the venue often steals the show.

Of all the performing arts, music is what Rome does best to entertain people, whether it be opera or jazz or disco. The cinema is also a big draw, particularly for Italian-language speakers, and there's a fantastic array of other options. Toast the sunset with Camparis while overlooking a 1st-century temple. Listen to authors read excerpts in the Roman Forum and actors recite Shakespeare in the recreation of the Globe theater in the Villa Borghese park. Or get down at Rome's many bars and *discoteches,* where celeb-spotting remains a favorite sport (recently spotted were Owen Wilson grabbing drinks in Piazza Navona and George Clooney enjoying a table at the glam Hotel de Russie). When all else fails, there's always late-night caffè-sitting, watching the colorful crowds parade by on a gorgeous piazza—it's great fun, even if you don't speak the language. Little wonder Rome inspired Fellini to make people-watching into an art form in his famous films.

THE ARTS

Since the start of the new millennium, Rome has been experiencing a cultural renaissance. In the past, Rome based its value on its vast historical buildings and Renaissance and baroque art, but with the help of international architecture competitions, contemporary art initiatives, and the Internet, the city is embracing the future. Enhanced by new buildings, such as the Auditorium, the MAXXI, and Ara Pacis, Rome has never before looked so good, juxtaposing the classic with the contemporary.

DANCE

Rome is well known for the strength of its visual arts, when it comes to classical and modern dance, the city plays understudy to Milan, Bologna, Florence, and even Cremona. This is changing: more dance performances have been added to the calendar at the Auditorium, many of which showcase international performers, and lately, the avant-garde RomaEuropa Festival has focused more on dance than on visual arts.

The **Rome Opera Ballet** performs throughout the year at **Teatro dell'Opera** (⊠ *Piazza Beniamino Gigli 8, Repubblica* ☏ *06/481601, 06/48160255 tickets* ⊕ *www.operaroma.it*). Ex–prima ballerina Carla Fracci is the director of the Corps de Ballet, and performances include many of the classics, often with leading international guest stars. During the summer season, the Rome Opera Ballet stages ballets alfresco at the Baths of Caracalla, mixing contemporary set design with the classic structure.

Teatro Olimpico (⊠ *Piazza Gentile da Fabriano 17, Flaminio* ☏ *06/3265991* ⊕ *www.teatroolimpico.it*) is the venue for contemporary dance companies, visiting international ballet companies, and touring Broadway shows like *Stomp*. The **Teatro Greco** (⊠ *Via Leoncavallo 10, Roma Nord* ☏ *06/8607513* ⊕ *www.teatrogreco.it*) also showcases international contemporary dance and often hosts the fall's Festa della Danza. From June to August, the gardens of the **Museo Nazionale degli Strumenti Musicali** (⊠ *Piazza di Santa Croce in Gerusalemme 9/a, San Giovanni* ☏ *06/7014796* ⊕ *www.museostrumentimusicali.it*) are the stage for a festival of classical and contemporary dance.

FILM

Andiamo al cinema! Rome has dozens of movie houses, where you'll find both blockbuster and art house films. All films, unless noted "V.O." in the listing, which means *versione originale* (original version or original language), are shown in Italian.

For show times, see the entertainment pages of daily newspapers, *roma c'è*, or Rome's English-language publications. Check out ⊕ *www. inromenow.com* for the most up-to-date reviews of all English-language films or visit ⊕ *www.mymovies.it* or ⊕ *www.cinemadelsilenzio.it* for a list of current features and theatres. Tickets range in price from €4.50 for matinees and some weekdays, up to €8 for weekend evenings.

★ The **Alcazar** (✉ *Via Merry del Val 14, Trastevere* ☎ *06/5880099*) has V.O. movies (sometimes with Italian subtitles) on Monday. Rule of thumb: check in advance that the film has in fact arrived in its original version. For the film buff, the **Casa del Cinema** (✉ *Largo Marcello Mastroianni 1* ☎ *06/423601* ⊕ *www.casadelcinema.it*) shows many new and retro films, and often showcases the original language films from the fall's Venice Film Festival

and Roma Cinema Fest (⊕ *www.romacinemafest.it*). The **Metropolitan** (✉ *Via del Corso 7, Spagna* ☎ *06/32600500*) is Rome's most popular cinema with the English-speaking community. Recently refurbished and with four small screens, the Metropolitan always hosts one screen for English-language films. The **Nuovo Olimpia** (✉ *Via in Lucina 16/b, Navona* ☎ *06/6861068*) is just off Via del Corso, and features classic and current films, often in their original languages. Wednesday night tickets are half-price. **Warner Village Moderno** (✉ *Piazza della Repubblica 45–46, Repubblica* ☎ *06/47779202*) is perhaps the most "American" of all Rome's theaters (hint: great concessions; comfortable, couchlike chairs; and stadium seating). Easy to find, the Moderno is located in the porticoes of Piazza Repubblica, next to the classic Exedra Hotel. The cinema has five screens, one of which is dedicated to English-language and V.O. films.

GALLERIES

Cappuccinos and Carvaggio, and bellinis and Bernini may be what come to mind when you dream of Rome—provocative contemporary art? Not so much. But remember, Rome is never predictable, and right now, the city is setting ground as the center for contemporary art in southern Europe, with Rome's churches, palazzos, and ancient sites making unique backdrops for contemporary art exhibitions. The city's traditional exhibition spaces have joined in and are hosting modern exhibits as well as classical, renaissance, and baroque shows. Up-to-date exhibition lists can best be found at ⊕ *www.exibart.com*.

The stately **Scuderie del Quirinale** (✉ *Via E. de Nicola 78, Quirinale* ☎ *06/696270* ⊕ *www.scuderiequirinale.it*) has showcased everything from the ancient to the avant-garde. Giotto, Renoir, Gaugin, Picasso, and Chagall have all made appearances at the **Vittoriano** (✉ *Via Di San Pietro In Carcere, Venezia* ☎ *06/6780363*). And the expansive walls of **Palazzo Venezia** (✉ *Via del Plebiscito 118, Venezia* ☎ *06/699941* ⊕ *www.galleriaborghese.it*) has showcased the paintings of Sebastiano del Piombo and Julian Schnabel.

The City of Eternal Festivals

The City of Eternal Festivals, Rome has gone from "provincial" to "provocative" thanks in large part to its bevy of internationally recognized festivals. In the fall and spring especially, you'll see the best of local and international talent in some of the most beautiful venues in the city.

ART AND DESIGN

The last week in February, look out for the **RomaContemporary** (⊕ *www.romacontemporary.it*), a contemporary art fair designed to put Rome on the circuit with Basel, Miami, and London. In mid-October, **RomaEuropa** (⊕ *www.romaeuropa.net*), a multivenue avant-garde performing and visual arts program, run shows from international artists, including installations, film, and performance

FILM

During the first two weeks of September, several of Rome's movie theaters take part in the **Da Venezia a Roma Festival** (⊕ *www.agisanec.lazio.it*), showing films just days after their debut at the Venice Film Festival.

Both widely distributed films and art house specials like *Mr. Nobody*, make fleeting screen appearances months before international release in Italy. Check out the local press or the Web site for more details.

Never content to be outshined by any other Italian city, Rome has begun hosting its very own film festival in mid-October, the **Cinema Festival di Roma** (⊕ *www.romacinemafest.org*). Designed to compete with Venice, London, Cannes, and New York, the festival features international films, and honors silver-screen icons like Sophia Loren and Al Pacino, as well as presents lectures from *The Actors Studio*.

The festival is headquartered Casa del Cinema (⊠ *Largo Marcello Mastroianni 1, Villa Borghese,* ☎ *06/423601* ⊕ *www.casadelcinema.it*), Rome's new projection house and film library in Villa Borghese. This fabulous new asset has a library, a caffè, and a DVD library with 24 laptops available for private viewings. It screens both new and vintage films, sometimes in English, throughout the year.

MUSIC

In spring and in some summer months, Rome stages fill with internationally recognized musicians of all genres.

Estate Romana (⊕ *www.estateromana.comune.roma.it*) (Roman Summer) is Rome's most celebrated summer concert series.

Starting out as a bunch of low-budget concerts during June and July, Estate Romana now extends through September and draws an audience from all over the peninsula to see music acts and cultural events from around the world. Most venues are outdoors, in and around the city, and are often free. Events include cinema, theater, book fairs, and guided tours of some of Rome's monuments by night.

Big-name acts like Genesis, Billy Joel, Elton John, and Simon & Garfunkel headline free concerts that fill the area from Piazza Venezia, down Via dei Fori Imperiali, to the stage directly in front of the Colosseum.

Fiesta! (✉ *Ippodromo delle Capannelle, Via Appia Nuova 1245, Appia* ☎ *06/7182139* ⊕ *www.fiesta.it*) is 90,000 square meters of world music and culture with a dominant Latin American component, and is very popular among young Italians.

The event includes more than 4,000 hours of live Latin and Caribbean music, as well as jazz and blues stars of international stature every summer, along with exhibits related to Latin American culture, dozens of shops and stands selling food and goods from all over the world, and four outdoor dance floors. Events run in the evenings from mid-June through August.

For more than 10 years, Villa Doria Pamphilj has been organizing **I Concerti nel Parco** (✉ *Piazza Porta di San Pancrazio, Monteverde* ⊕ *www. iconcertinelparco.it*), a concert series under the stars and amid the greenery of Rome's largest park on the Janiculum Hill. Running from June through August, the concerts take place at sunset and last late into the evening.

The location also doubles as the home to Rock in Roma summer concert (✉ *Ippodromo delle Capannelle, Via Appia Nuova 1245, Appia* ☎ *06/45496350* ⊕ *www.rockinroma. com*), which has hosted international acts like the Killers, Subsonica, Motorhead, and Franz Ferdinand.

Roma Incontra il Mondo (✉ *Laghetto di Villa Ada, Via di Ponte Salario, Villa Ada [Roma Nord]* ⊕ *www.villaada.*

org) has grown in a few short years to become one of Europe's most impressive world-music festivals. Live music most evenings from late June to early August starts at 10 PM, followed by dancing until 2 AM. Stands sell handmade goods and ethnic cuisine from around the world.

RomaEstate al Foro Italico (✉ *Viale delle Olimpiadi, Stadio Olimpico* ☎ *06/8073026* ⊕ *www.romaestate. net*) is one of Rome's many summer fairs dedicated solely to entertainment. Every day, from June through August, the former Olympic Stadium holds live concerts, dining, dancing, and fitness activities. Food stands, vendors, and playgrounds line the stadium grounds. Admission is €6, though some concerts—Chemical Brothers, for example—cost considerably more. Concerts usually start at 9 PM.

Villa Celimontana Jazz Festival (✉ *Villa Celimontana, Piazza della Navicella, San Giovanni* ☎ *06/5897807* ⊕ *www. villacelimontanajazz.com*) is the longest-running jazz festival in Europe.

From mid-June to early September it brings a program of everything from contemporary electronic and acid jazz to earlier, more classic styles, to the lawns of the restored baroque Villa Celimontana, on the Caelium Hill adjacent to the Colosseum. Admission is approximately €8.

At the beginning of the summer, the **Teatro di Marcello** (✉ *Via Teatro di Marcello, Ghetto* ☎ *06/87131590* ⊕ *www.tempietto.it*) lights up in the evening as a spectacular backdrop to a summer classical-music concert series.

14

The quiet **Chiostro del Bramante** (✉ *Via della Pace 5, Navona* ☎ *06/68809036* ⊕ *www.chiostrodelbramante.it*) is a charming former cloister that now serves as art venue/cultural center; it's attached to the evocative church of Santa Maria della Pace. The Bramante-designed Chiostro hosts smaller shows of modern and contemporary artists like Warhol, Balla, and Basquiat but has expanded its shows to include classical works, as well. Testaccio, the gentrified warehouse neighborhood, is home to late-night **MACRO Future** (✉ *Piazza Orazio Giustiniani 4, Testaccio* ⊕ *www.macro.roma.museum*), at the ex-Mattatoio ("slaughterhouse"), a multispace venue for visual and performance art. Meanwhile, across town is its sister gallery **MACRO** (✉ *Via Reggio Emilia 54, Nomentana* ☎ *06/671070400* ⊕ *www.macro.roma.museum*), a redesigned city-owned gallery in a former brewery, known for its contemporary shows. **Galleria Nazionale di Arte Moderna** (✉ *Viale Belle Arti, 131, Flaminio* ☎ *06/32298221* ⊕ *www.gnam.beniculturali.it*) has added stronger shows lately, including a Cy Twombly retrospective; its permanent collection includes modern Italian masters from the noted Macchaioli and Futurists like Severini and Balla to Transavantguardia, Arte Povera, and contemporary with Fontana, Manzoni, Chia, and Clemente. Stepping up the level of game and glam is **Gagosian Gallery** (✉ *Via Francesco Crispi 16, Barberini* ☎ *06/42746429* ⊕ *www.gagosian.com*), owned by the art world's top gallerist Larry Gagosian (whose gallery locations include New York, Los Angeles, and London). Located in a 19th-century former bank, the gorgeous oval exhibition hall has seen shows by Cindy Sherman, Cy Twombly, and Anselm Kiefer.

Fodor's Choice ★ The **MAXXI** (*Museo di Arte del XXI Secolo, or Museum of 21st-Century Art* ✉ *Via Guido Reni 2f, Flaminio* ☎ *06/3210181* ⊕ *www.darc. beniculturali.it/MAXXI*) is scheduled to open in the new Zaha Hadid building at the beginning of 2010. While awaiting the MAXXI's opening, the museum hosts temporary and site specific shows at the adjacent (temporary) building, as well as all over Italy. Peruse the Web site's "Another Places" link for "outside-the-MAXXI" exhibitions. The **Museo Carlo Bilotti** (✉ *Viale Fiorello La Guardia, Villa Borghese* ☎ *06/82059127* ⊕ *www.museocarlobilotti.it*) is a tiny modern-art collection with contemporary exhibitions of international icons like Willem de Kooning, Damien Hirst, and Jenny Saville, along with Bilotti's bequeathed and permanent collection of Di Chirico and friends. The **Palazzo delle Esposizioni** (✉ *Via Nazionale 194, Repubblica* ☎ *06/39967500* ⊕ *www.palazzoesposizioni. it*) has finally reopened, with blockbuster exhibitions of Rothko, Darwin, Bulgari, and Calder.

Completing the modern and contemporary art scene are the cultural branches of international embassies that have actively been promoting their country's artists with monthly and seasonal shows. The **American Academy** (✉ *Via Angelo Masina 5, on the Janiculum Hill, Monteverde* ☎ *06/58461* ⊕ *www.aarome.org*) has shows and lectures by internationally renowned artists, architects, writers, and photographers, as well as scholars in residence. The **British School** (✉ *Via Gramsci 61, Parioli* ☎ *06/3264939* ⊕ *www.bsr.ac.uk*) often hosts special exhibitions and free lectures by visiting professors. **Istituto Giapponese di Cultura** (✉ *Via Gramsci 74, Parioli* ☎ *06/3224794* ⊕ *www.jfroma.it*) has exhibits and a traditional Japanese garden. **Istituto Svizzero di Roma** (✉ *Via Ludovisi 48, Via Veneto* ☎ *06/48904071* ⊕ *www.istitutosvizzero.it*) has ultra-innovative art shows. Likewise, France's **Villa Medici** (✉ *Viale Trinitá dei Monti 1, Spagna* ☎ *06/67611* ⊕ *www.villamedici.it*) has a revolving door of avant-garde French artists, and a lovely evening music and film series on its terrace.

MUSIC

CLASSICAL

Fodor'sChoice ★ Designed by famous architect Renzo Piano, the **Auditorium–Parco della Musica** (✉ *Viale Pietro de Coubertin 30, Flaminio* ☎ *06/80241, 06/68801044 information and tickets* ⊕ *www.auditorium.com*) is *the* place to perform in Rome. The amazing space features three halls with nearly perfect acoustics, and a large courtyard for outdoor classical, jazz, and pop concerts. In addition, it hosts dance troupes and cultural festivals. The venue is a 10-minute tram ride north of Piazza del Popolo. ⇨ *See the special Spotlight page on the Parco in this chapter.*

14

The **Accademia Filarmonica Romana** concerts are performed at the **Teatro Olimpico**(✉ *Piazza Gentile da Fabriano 17, Flaminio* ☎ *06/3265991; 06/3201752* ⊕ *www.teatroolimpico.it.* The internationally respected **Oratorio del Gonfalone** (✉ *Via del Gonfalone 32/a, Campo* ☎ *06/6875952* ⊕ *www.oratoriogonfalone.it*) series focuses on baroque music in an exquisite setting. A major concert series is organized year-round by the **Accademia di Santa Cecilia** (*Concert hall and box office* ✉ *Via Pietro de Coubertin 34, Flaminio* ☎ *06/8082058* ⊕ *www.santacecilia.it*), featuring Rome's Orchestra dell'Accademia di Santa Cecilia and frequent guest soloists. The **Teatro Eliseo** (✉ *Via Nazionale 183, Repubblica* ☎ *06/4882114* ⊕ *www.teatroeliseo.it*) collaborates with Santa Cecilia, and its modern theater has classical concerts throughout the year.

★ **Il Tempietto** (✉ *Area Archeologica del Palatino, Cortile di San Teodoro, Via di San Teodoro 7, Circo Massimo* ☎ *06/87131590* ⊕ *www.tempietto.it*) organizes music festivals and concerts throughout the year in otherwise inaccessible sites. Depending on the venue, tickets run from about €10 to €30. The Renaissance-era **Chiostro del Bramante** (✉ *Vicolo della Pace 2, Navona* ☎ *06/68809098*) has a summer concert series. The **Orto Botanico** (✉ *Largo Cristina di Svezia 23/a, Trastevere* ☎ *06/6868441*), off Via della Lungara in Trastevere, has a summer concert series with a beautiful, verdant backdrop.

HALLOWED SOUNDS

Throughout the year, churches like Sant'Ivo alla Sapienza, San Francesco a Ripa, and San Paolo entro le Mura usually have afternoon and evening performances. Look for posters outside churches announcing free concerts, particularly at **Sant'Ignazio** (✉ *Piazza Sant'Ignazio, Pantheon* ☎ *06/6794560*), which often hosts concerts in a spectacularly frescoed setting. You could also sit in the shadow of the **Theatre of Marcello** (✉ *Via del Teatro Marcello, Ghetto* ☎ *06/488991*) for its summertime concert series.

AUDITORIUM–PARCO DELLA MUSICA

✉ *Viale Pietro de Coubertin 30, Flaminio* ☎ *06/80241, 06/6880144 information and tickets* ⊕ *www.auditorium. com.*

Tips

■ To get to the Auditorium from Rome's Termini train station, take Bus No. 910, which stops directly in front of the complex at Viale Pietro de Coubertin. If you're coming from the city center, walk to Piazzale Flaminio (the other side of Piazza del Popolo) and hop on the Tram #2 for six stops. Using the Metro, take Line A to Flaminio, and above ground to Tram #2, again six stops. Access the Auditorium's underground parking using Viale Maresciallo Pilsudski and Via Giulio Gaudini.

■ To book guided tours, e-mail: visiteguidate@musicaperroma.it

Once a performing arts backwater, Rome grabbed a front-row seat on the world music scene in 2002 thanks to the spectacular Auditorium—Parco della Musica, a complex of three enormous pod-shaped concert halls designed by famed architect Renzo Piano.

Everyone from Luciano Pavarotti and Philip Glass to Tracy Chapman and Burt Bacharach have performed at this "City of Music," which attracts culture-seeking Romans with its excellent caffè and restaurants, bookstore, outdoor amphitheater (which becomes a skating rink is in winter), archaeological site, and children's playground—indeed, Piano's dream of the space as a "cultural factory" seems realized.

The Auditorium is in the Flaminio/Villaggio Olimpico neighborhood, 10 minutes outside the city center.

The futuristic concert halls have been likened to anything from beetles to computer "mice," and most weeks they are jammed with people: the Sala Santa Cecilia is a massive hall for grand orchestra and choral concerts; the Sala Sinopoli is more intimately scaled for smaller troupes; while the Sala Petrassi was designed for alternative events. All three are arrayed around the "Cavea," the vast Greco-Roman-style amphitheater. On any given day you might chance on hearing the Orchestra dell'Accademia di Santa Cecilia in the big hall, the Parco della Musica Jazz Orchestra in Sinopoli, and Peter Gabriel giving a rock "chamber event" in Petrassi. But the calendar here is not just confined to music: Rome's hot new film festival (www.romacinemafest.org) is held during the second half of October, while other festivals—Math, Science and even Philosophy highlight the spring.

CLOSE UP

Opera Alfresco

What could epitomize a Roman evening more than a moonlight serenade? Following the outdoor exodus of the city's pubs, restaurants, and discos, opera heads outside for its summer season. Rome's many opera companies commandeer church courtyards, ancient villas, and soccer *campi* (fields) with performances that range from mom-and-poperas to full-scale, large-budget extravaganzas. Quality is generally quite high, even for smaller,

low-budget productions. Tickets cost €15 to €40. To find these productions, listen closely or look for the old-fashioned posters advertising classic operas like *Tosca* and *La Traviata*. The weekly *roma c'e*, the monthly *Wanted in Rome*, and the Web site ⊕ *www.inromenow.com* also have complete lists of performances.

OPERA

Fodor's Choice
★

Although Rome is not considered part of the circuit done by opera afficionados, its company does command an audience during its mid-November to May season at **Teatro dell'Opera** (⊠ *Piazza Beniamino Gigli 8, Repubblica* ☎ *06/481601, 06/48160255 tickets* ⊕ *www.operaroma.it*). Tickets go on sale at the start of the season; the box office (⊠ *Piazza Beniamino Gigli 1*) is open 9–5 Tuesday to Saturday and 9–1:30 Sunday. Prices range from €20 to €100 for performances. Special events, such as an opening night or the appearance of an internationally acclaimed guest singer, can cost much more. In the hot summer months, the company moves to the **Terme di Caracalla** (⊠ *Via Antoniniana 14, Caracalla* ⊕ *www.operaroma.it*), a 3rd-century AD bath complex at the edge of the ancient city. The preferred performance is Aida for its spectacle, which includes real elephants. The company has taken a new direction, using projections atop the ancient ruins to create cutting-edge sets.

THEATER

★

Rome's official theater, the **Teatro Argentina** (⊠ *Largo Argentina, Campo* ☎ *06/684000345* ⊕ *www.teatrodiroma.net*), with its turn-of-the-century opulence—burgundy velvet upholstery and large crystal chandeliers—is Belle Epoque glamour. Most productions are in Italian; however, it occasionally showcases some dance performances, which don't require subtitles. The **Teatro India** (⊠ *Via Pierantoni 6, Lungotevere dei Papareschi, Testaccio* ☎ *06/55300894* ⊕ *www.teatrodiroma.net*) has productions in English as well as Italian. The space in a former soap factory is funky but does not have the most comfortable seating.

Original English-language plays are performed weekly by the **English Theatre of Rome** (⊠ *Teatro l'Arciliuto, Piazza Montevecchio 5 107, Navona* ☎ *06/687941* ⊕ *www.rometheatre.com*). For a bit of comedy with a Monty Python slant, check out the **Miracle Players** (⊕ *www.miracleplayers.org*), an English-speaking comedy troupe performing original plays. During the summer, they perform in the Roman Forum.

NIGHTLIFE

E mo'facciamo un giro—And now let's take a spin . . . To enjoy a night out in Rome, all you have to do is hop on your *motorino* (or take a walk), and you will always bump into an *enoteca*—those classic wine bars, which abound in all parts of the city and rarely disappoint. But finding great nightlife is not quite not as easy as a walk around the block. Although Rome offers a cornucopia of evening bacchanalia, from ultrachic to super cheap, all that glitters is not gold. Insiders and visitors alike understand that finding "the scene" in Rome is the proverbial needle in the haystack: It requires patience and pursuit. Word-of-mouth may be the best source, but also look to the entertainment guides like *roma c'è and ⊕ www.roma.tonight.eu. Trovaroma* provides up-to-date listings of bars and clubs. Most visitors prefer to head out to one of three locations: between Piazza Navona and the Pantheon; the Campo de' Fiori and Trastevere; or Testaccio. (The Spanish Steps area is a ghost town by 9 PM.) Remember, Romans love an after-party—after dinner, of course—so plenty of nightlife doesn't start until midnight.

14

BARS

Leading off the bar scene is the *enoteca*, found (often with outdoor seating) in just about every piazza and on side streets throughout the city. These establishments are mostly small, and offer a smattering of antipasti to accompany a variety of wines and bubblies.

If you're looking for a beer and some telly, peppered around the city are stereotypical English and Irish pubs, complete with a steady stream of Guinness, darts, and footie and rugby on their satellite, flat-screen televisions. Lately, these pubs show American football, baseball, and basketball—ideal for those who don't want to miss a playoff game.

Last on the list but perhaps the most impressive is the swanky lounge or hotel bar, preferably outdoors and perched on rooftops. These expensive bars have modern designs and creative cocktail lists that would compete with the posh bars of any major metropolis, and everyone dresses to impress.

CAFFÈS, ENOTECHE, AND WINE BARS

Ai Tre Scalini (⊠ *Via Panisperna 251, Monti* ☎ *06/48907495* ⊕ *www.aitrescalini.org*) is a rustic local hangout with a wooden bar in Monti, Rome's boho 'hood. It serves delicious antipasti and light entrées.

★ The wood-panel walls of **L'Angolo Divino** (⊠ *Via dei Balestrari 12, Campo* ☎ *06/6864413*) are racked with more than 700 of bottles of wine. A quiet enoteca in a back alley behind Campo, L'Angolo Divino allows you to sidestep the crowds while enjoying homemade pastas with a vintage bottle.

Antica Enoteca (⊠ *Via della Croce 76/b, Spagna* ☎ *06/6790896* ⊕ *www.anticaenoteca.com*) is Piazza di Spagna's most celebrated wine bar, occupying a prime people-watching corner just below the piazza. In addition to a vast selection of wine (also available for take-away), Antica Enoteca has delectable antipasti, perfect for a snack or a light lunch.

★ Celebrities and literati hang out at the coveted outdoor tables of **Antico Caffè della Pace** (⊠ *Via della Pace 5, Navona* ☎ *06/6861216*), a turn-of-the-20th-century-style caffè nestled in the side streets behind Piazza Navona. Known also as Bar della Pace, the caffè's atmosphere ranges from peaceful to percolating. La Pace's location is equally enchanting, situated in the *piazzatina* (tiny piazza) of Santa Maria della Pace, by baroque architect Pietro da Cortona. The only drawbacks: overpriced table service and distracted waiters.

The wood-panel walls and fireplace provide a cozy mood at **Artù** (⊠ *Largo F. Biondi 5, off Piazza Santa Maria, Trastevere* ☎ *06/5880398*), a popular hangout with an ample selection of beer, wine, and tasty snacks and bar food.

Once a modest neighborhood coffee bar, **Bar del Fico** (⊠ *Piazza del Fico 27, Navona* ☎ *06/6865205*) is a favorite meeting spot for locals and artists who prefer the earthy to the intellectual. The place attracts huge crowds on weekend and summer nights.

Fluid (⊠ *Via del Governo Vecchio 46/47, Navona* ☎ *06/6832361* ⊕ *www.fluideventi.com*), with its slick design and zen waterfall, is all about the scene, especially with its looking-glass front window where pretty young things primp on ice cube–shaped chairs. For the cocktail crowd, Fluid's many variations on the traditional martini are quite laudable.

★ Rome's latest artsy hangout is **Freni e Frizioni** (⊠ *Via del Politeama 4, Trastevere* ☎ *06/58334210* ⊕ *www.freniefrizioni.com*). Here hipsters meet up for coffees, teas, aperitivi, and late-night hanging out. In warmer weather, Freni e Frizioni opens up its large terrazzo, which overlooks the Tiber.

★ For the wine connoisseur, **Il Goccetto** (⊠ *Via dei Banchi Vecchi 14, Campo* ☎ *06/6864268*) is *the* stop. Specializing in wines from smaller vineyards from Sicily to Venice, Il Gocetto also offers a small but carefully chosen selection of Italian delicacies (meats and cheeses) from up and down the peninsula. Though primarily an indoor venue, Il Gocetto is a popular meeting point where patrons often overflow into the street.

Fodor's Choice
★ **Shaki** (⊠ *Via Mario de Fiori 29a, Spagna* ☎ *06/6791694*), Piazza di Spagna's mod wine bar and restaurant (think Los Angeles meets Rome) is perfect for aperitivi, after-dinner drinks, and simply being seen.

Fodor's Choice
★ **Stardust** (⊠ *Via dell'Anima 52, Navona*) is a Piazza Navona favorite for locals and ex-pats. Slightly more upscale than its previous Trastevere incarnation, Stardust stills possesses a bohemian vibe.

With the help of the never-ending cantina of the Trimani wineshop, the elegant, bi-level **Trimani Il Winebar** (⊠ *Via Cernaia 37/b, Repubblica* ☎ *06/4469630* ⊕ *www.trimani.com*) is the enoteca to hit for wine tasting. Sommeliers frequent Trimani daily to stock up their restaurants.

Fodor's Choice
★ **Vinoteca Novecento** (⊠ *Piazza Delle Coppelle 47, Navona* ☎ *06/6833078*) is a small enoteca with a vast selection of wines, proseccos, vin santos, and grappas. Inside is a stand-up wine bar, with salami- and cheese-tasting menus. In good weather, sit outside on one of the oak barriques.

CLOSE UP

Hollywood-on-the-Tiber

Famous Italian film director Federico Fellini's *La Dolce Vita* focuses on the nightclubs and paparazzi of the city's Hollywood-on-the-Tiber era. The 1960s that Fellini put on film is long gone, but Rome's film industry is experiencing a renaissance.

Home to Cinecittà—one of the world's largest film studios in one of the most delightful climates—Rome is often the choice location for international film productions, such as Wes Anderson's *Life Aquatic*, JJ Abrams' *Mission Impossible III*, Steven Soderbergh's *Ocean's Twelve*, and Martin Scorsese's *Gangs of New York*, not to mention the HBO/BBC Production's series *Rome*. What's more, the presence of so many actors in the city has also reinvigorated the city's theater productions.

14

Vineria Reggio (⊠ *Campo de' Fiori 15, Campo* ☎ *06/68803268*), or "Vineria" as those in-the-know call it, is the quintessential local Roma wine bar where the crowd ranges from grandfathers to glitterati.

CLASSIC BARS AND PUBS

★ **Antica Birreria Peroni** (⊠ *Via di San Marcello 19, Corso* ☎ *06/6795310* ⊕ *www.anticabirreriaperoni.net*) is a Stil Liberty (Art Nouveau)–era beer hall near Piazza Venezia. Expect filling canteen-style meals and big steins of German beer. Need a hot dog fix? Best place for hot dogs in Rome.

Fiddler's Elbow (⊠ *Via dell'Olmata 43, Esquilino* ☎ *06/4872110* ⊕ *www. thefiddlerselbow.com*) is the oldest Irish pub in Rome, and its scruffy authenticity shows up the fancier usurpers that have opened all over town. Singing is encouraged.

Victoria House (⊠ *Via Gesù e Maria 18, Spagna* ☎ *06/3201698*), off Via del Corso and a stone's throw from Piazza del Popolo, is Rome's very first English pub. Still considered one of the best for its beer selection and English menu, it has an authentic, worn-in feel—like an old shoe.

ROOFTOP TERRACES AND UPSCALE BARS

Crudo (⊠ *Via Degli Specchi 6, Campo* ☎ *06/6838989* ⊕ *www. crudoroma.it*) is a spacious, modern, New York–style lounge serving well-made cocktails and *crudo* (raw) nibbles such as sushi and carpaccio. With a large lounge decked out in mod design and hued in gray, white, and red, Crudo also doubles as art space with videos projected on one large wall throughout the evening and paintings displayed throughout the interior.

The street-side **h club> doney at the Westin Excelsior** (⊠ *Via Vittorio Veneto 145, Veneto* ☎ *06/47082805* ⊕ *www.starwoodhotels.com*) is Rome's grand dame of outdoor caffè. Sharply dressed businesspeople mingle with laughing tourists, all sipping aperitifs made with fresh berries and other fruits while reclining in wicker chairs. During the rainy season and colder months, the party moves inside, where opulent reds and luscious velvets create a cozy, sexy interior.

For a dip into La Dolce Vita, the **Jardin de Hotel de Russie** (⌧ *Via del Babuino 9, Popolo* ☎ *06/328881* ⊕ *www.hotelderussie.it*) is the location for every Hollywood VIP, as well as up-and-coming starlets. Mixed drinks are well above par, as are the prices.

Fodor's Choice
★ For a sneak peak at the Pantheon's dome, **Roof Garden Bar at Grand Hotel della Minerve** (⌧ *Piazza della Minerve 69, Pantheon* ☎ *06/695201* ⊕ *www.grandhoteldelaminerve.com*) has the best view. Sunset is the ideal time to come—especially if you want to make a surprise proposal. Note that in the later evening hours, you can hum along to 1970s favorites played live by a singer/keyboardist.

Roof Top Lounge Bar at the St. George Hotel (⌧ *Via Giulia 62, Campo* ☎ *06/686611* ⊕ *www.stgeorgehotel.it*) is the latest front-runner in Rome's ever-growing list of rooftop sweet spots. With a delicious oyster selection headlining its seafood-based menu, the Roof Top's dizzying drink selection includes cocktails, beer, and many rosés—from pink champagnes to Italian *rosati*. Note, *the Rooftop is only open in the summer season.*

Sitting in front of a 2nd-century temple, **Salotto 42** (⌧ *Piazza di Pietra 42, Pantheon* ☎ *06/6785804* ⊕ *www.salotto42.it*) holds court from morning until late in the evening. The cozy-sleek room (high-backed velvet chairs, zebra-print rugs, chandeliers) is a smorgasbord of the owners' Roman–New York–Swedish pedigree. The den, complete with art books, local sophisticates, and models moonlighting as waitresses, is the fashionista's favorite choice for late-night drinks. It's the perfect watering hole in the fall and winter months.

★ **Tazio** (⌧ *Hotel Exedra, Piazza della Repubblica 47, Repubblica* ☎ *06/489381* ⊕ *www.boscolohotels.it*), named after the original Italian *paparazzo* (celebrity photographer), is an Adam Tihany–designed champagne bar. The red, black, and white lacquered interior, with crystal chandeliers, has a distinct '80s feel (think Robert Palmer, *Addicted to Love*). The favorite pastime here is sipping champagne while watching the people parade through the colonnade. In summer, the hotel's rooftop bar **Sensus** is the place to be, with its infinity pool and terrace view overlooking downtown.

Terrace Bar of the Hotel Raphael (⌧ *Largo Febo 2, Navona* ☎ *06/682831* ⊕ *www.raphaelhotel.com*) is noted for its bird's-eye view of the campaniles and palazzi of the Piazza Navona. High up in the moonlit sky, the Terrace Bar tends to be the choice place for a romantic evening.

DISCOS AND NIGHTCLUBS

When it comes to clubs, discos, and DJs in Rome, you have two choices: clubland Testaccio, considered the turntable epicenter—or everywhere else, as *discoteche* are in every nook and cranny of Rome. On average, drinks are range between €10 and €15, and one is often included with the entrance (€10–€20). In June, July, and August, many clubs relocate to the beach or the Tiber, so call ahead to confirm location and hours.

l'Alibi (✉ *Via di Monte Testaccio 40* ☎ *06/5743448* ⊕ *www.lalibi.com*), with its weekly Gloss Party, is one of the most famous gay discos in town. Though a bit lackluster lately, the large space has an open terrace for summer dancing. **Circolo Mario Mieli** (☎ *06/5413985* ⊕ *www. mariomieli.org*) is a gay advocacy group that promotes events at other venues like **Alphaeus**(✉ *Via del Commercio 36, Testaccio* ☎ *06/5747826* ⊕ *www.alpheus.it*) and **Muccassassina** (✉ *Via di Portonaccio 212, San Lorenzo* ☎ *06/5413985* ⊕ *www.muccassassina.com*).

Gilda (✉ *Via Mario de' Fiori 97, Spagna* ☎ *06/6784838* ⊕ *www.gildabar. it*), once a late-night spot for Italian actors and politicians, now is host to B-actors, politniks, and soccer players; it reinvents itself every few years with a different crowd. This nightspot near the Spanish Steps has a piano bar as well as a restaurant and dance floors with live and disco music.

Hulala (✉ *Via dei Conciatori 7, Testaccio* ☎ *06/57300429* ⊕ *www. desamis.it*) is home to Rome's fashionistas. Mod films are projected on the walls, and champagne is drunk through straws.

Via Galvani is Rome's Sunset Strip, spawning most of the city's schizophrenic restaurant-clubs (combinations of chill restaurants and large, booming clubs).

Reigning as King and Queen of the strip are **Joia** (✉ *Via Galvani 20, Testaccio* ☎ *06/5740802* ⊕ *www.joiacafe.it*) and **Ketum Bar** (✉ *Via Galvani 24, Testaccio* ☎ *06/57305338* ⊕ *www.ketumbar.it*). For people-watchers, evenings here are a delight, with crowds ranging from romantic twosomes to post-teens to personable pickup artists of all ages.

★ Housed in a medieval palazzo is **La Cabala** (✉ *Via dei Soldati 23, Navona* ☎ *06/68301192* ⊕ *www.hdo.it*), Rome's version of a supper club. This three-level space has a piano bar, restaurant, and club, and often has a very dressy crowd vying to get past the velvet rope.

★ Lounge fever is all over Rome, with **La Maison** (✉ *Vicolo dei Granari 4, Navona* ☎ *06/6833312* ⊕ *www.lamaisonroma.it*) as one of the best. Bedecked in purple velvet and crystal chandeliers, the club has two distinct spaces, a VIP area and a dance floor, with a DJ dishing up the latest dance tunes. Head straight to the back room and grab a couch.

★ **Micca Club** (✉ *Via P. Micca 7, Terminia* ☎ *06/87440079* ⊕ *www. miccaclub.com*) is in a multilevel former warehouse. DJs spin different styles of music in each of the rooms and some spaces have live music.

★ **Supperclub** (✉ *Via dei Nari 14, Pantheon* ☎ *06/68807207* ⊕ *www. supperclub.com*) is not only a place for dinner-in-recline, but also a trendy club where DJs and live entertainment draw a sexy crowd to the various rooms, most lined with big white beds and fluffy pillows (no shoes, please), complete with roaming masseurs. Monday nights feature a laidback hip-hop party organized by a former L.A. club promoter.

★ **Testaccio** (✉ *Via di Monte Testaccio* ☎ *06/57288333*) is a DJ Disneyworld with thematic clubs lining Via Galvani and Via Monte di Testaccio; it truly undulates until the wee hours of the morning. Some old favorites have been around for what feels like forever, while others have rocked only a season or two in Rome. No matter what, Testaccio is a sure thing for late night dancing.

> **IT TAKES A VILLAGE**
>
> At the end of May, Roman residents look forward to the cleverly publicized Gay Village (⊕ *www.gayvillage.it*), an outdoor megaparty held in a different location each summer from June through August. Along with bars and clubs, the highly sponsored event has international guest stars including DJs and performance artists.

MUSIC CLUBS

Palalottamattica (✉ *Palazzo dello Sport, EUR* ☎ *199/128800* ⊕ *www.forumnet.it*) hosts some heavy hitters in the Italian and international music scene, like Michael Bublé and Zucchero. The futuristic ex-sports hall is in the EUR neighborhood (i.e., Rome's outer limits).

★ **Alexanderplatz** (✉ *Via Ostia 9, Vatican* ☎ *06/39742171* ⊕ *www.alexanderplatz.it*), Rome's most important live jazz and blues club, consistently books the best of Italian and international performers. It has both a bar and a restaurant. Reservations are a good idea.

★ **Big Mama** (✉ *Vicolo San Francesco a Ripa 18, Trastevere* ☎ *06/5812551* ⊕ *www.bigmama.it*), a Roman institution for live music, including jazz, blues, rhythm and blues, African, and rock, has finally reopened, freshly renovated and with a plethora of new music listings.

Fodor's Choice
★
Holed up in Monti is **Charity Café** (✉ *Via Panisperna 68, Monti* ☎ *06/47825881* ⊕ *www.charitycafe.it*), a small and romantic jazz club in Rome's boho neighborhood.

Near Castel Sant'Angelo, **Fonclea** (✉ *Via Crescenzio 82/a, Prati* ☎ *06/6896302* ⊕ *www.fonclea.it*) is a cellar with a publike atmosphere, and live music every night of the week—from jazz to Latin American to rhythm and blues. The kitchen serves Italian and Mexican food.

Latin rhythms are the specialty at **No Stress Brasil** (✉ *Via degli Stradivari 35, Trastevere* ☎ *06/5813249*), which has live music with a Brazilian orchestra from Tuesday to Saturday. Monday is karaoke night, and Sunday is dinner only.

The Place (✉ *Via Alberico II 27–29, Vatican* ☎ *06/68307137* ⊕ *www.theplace.it*), a low-key music venue, offers an excellent mixture of live funk, Latin, and jazz sounds accompanied by excellent fusion cuisine.

★ **Rialtosantambrogio** (✉ *Via S. Ambrogio 4, Ghetto* ☎ *06/68133640* ⊕ *www.rialtosantambrogio.org*) is Rome's experimental haven for DJs and artists. Rialto's "projects" are bimonthly and announced by word of mouth, or through the Web site.

Shopping

WORD OF MOUTH

"Ooh, romance! Perhaps you could buy your sweetheart an Italian handbag (Furla maybe, or if you are really flush, Fendi or D&G) and then fill it with surprises for that evening—tickets to the Rome opera or a corkscrew, for the bottle of wine you will purchase to drink on the Spanish Steps after dinner (don't forget plastic cups!)."

—nnolen

SHOPPING PLANNER

Opening Hours

Store hours vary according to the type of goods sold and the whims of shopkeepers, so it's best to remain flexible. In general, retailers in the heart of the city open their doors between 9 and 9:30 AM, breaking for lunch at 1 PM. Shops reopen at 4 PM and stay open until 7:30 or 8 PM. Most clothing stores adhere to the general operating hours listed above but close Sunday and Monday mornings. Family-owned food shops may be closed all day Sunday and also Thursday afternoon (except during the summer when they are closed on Saturday afternoon and Sunday). Summer travelers should be aware that most small shops close for two to three weeks just before or after August's Ferragosto holiday.

Sizing It Up

Italian sizes are not uniform, so always try on or measure items. Children's sizes are all over the place, and though they usually go by age, sizes are calibrated to Italian children. (Average size-per-age standards vary from country to country.) Check washing instruction labels on all garments (often in English as well as Italian); many are not washable, and those that are may not be preshrunk. Glove sizes are universal.

Counterfeits

The Prada, Gucci, Fendi, and Vuitton bags sold by side-walk vendors are fakes. An underground network organizes the illegal manufacture, distribution, and sale of these seemingly perfect counterfeits of stylish status symbols. Reliable stores sell at the prices indicated by the manufac-turers—so any enormous discount is suspect.

Duty-Free Shopping

Value-added tax (IVA) is 20% on clothing and luxury goods, but it's already included in the amount on the price tag of consumer goods. If you're not a resident of the European Union, you may be eligible, under certain conditions, for a refund of this tax on goods purchased here—Tax-Free for Tourists V.A.T. tax refunds are available at most large stores for purchases of more than €155.

Sales

Saldi (end-of-season sales) can mean real bargains in clothing and accessories. The main sale periods are January 6 through February and late July to mid-September. Most stores adopt a no-exchange, no-return policy for sale goods. At other times of year, a *liquidazione* sign indicates a close-out sale, but take a hard look at the goods; they may be bottom-of-the-barrel.

Bargaining

If you're a bargain shopper, know that the notice PREZZI FISSI (fixed prices) means just that: in shops displaying this sign it's a waste of time to bargain unless you're buying a sizable quantity of goods or a particularly costly object. Always bargain, however, at outdoor markets (except food markets) and when buying from street vendors. Remember that Italian stores generally will *not* give refunds and often cannot exchange goods because of limited stock.

By Lynda Albertson

Veni, Vidi, Vici. I came, I saw, I conquered.

This was Julius Caesar's triumphant statement, scribbled with a flourish to Rome's senators following his victory at the Battle of Zela. And just as they had with their previous successes in Gaul and Egypt, Rome's legions returned bringing riches from the lands they had conquered. With the world's most luxurious silks, linens, and wools at their disposal, the city's civilized patricians became the empire's arbiters of chic.

Centuries later, Romans still have an insatiable appetite for drawing upon the best of the world's finery and modifying it into something uniquely Roman. From the cornucopia of haute couture fresh off Milan's trendy catwalks to the breezy avant-garde styles of the city's next generation of designers, this dazzling metropolis continues to make its own personalized statement about what's "in." Visitors with a sumptuous sense of *bella figura* and a strong constitution for heart-stopping price tags will enjoy beginning their Roman shopping adventures by paying homage to fashion's heavy hitters. The best of Italy's design ateliers are clumped tightly together along the city's three primary fashion arteries: Via dei Condotti, Via Borgognona, and Via Frattina.

Whether you are looking for that special pair of Prada shoes, a Pollini handbag, or some other chichi fashions, you are bound to find what you are looking for here. How about a special bottle of wine for your wedding anniversary or a pair of one-of-a-kind earrings for your daughter's upcoming graduation? From Piazza di Spagna to Piazza Navona and on to Campo de' Fiori, shoppers will find an explosive array of shops within walking distance of one another. A shop for fine handmade Amalfi paper looks out upon the Pantheon, while slick boutiques anchor the corners of 18th-century Piazza di Spagna. In Monti, a second-generation mosaic-maker creates Italian masterpieces on a street named for a pope who died before America was even discovered. Even in Trastevere, one can find one of Rome's rising shoe designers creating next-century *nuovo chic* shoes nestled on a side street beside one of Rome's oldest churches.

In the immortal words of Mrs. Julius Caesar, when she returned from the forum: "Vini, Vidi, Visa." I came, I saw, I charged it.

15

PIAZZA DI SPAGNA

To shop or not to shop in Rome? For people who put Bulgari and Fendi right up there with the Forum and the Colosseum there has never been any doubt. In the fashion golden triangle that fans down from the Spanish Steps, they ricochet from Versace to Valentino with less effort than it takes to whip out platinum cards.

Rome has been setting fashion trends since the days of the Caesars, so it's little wonder that this is the city that gave us the Gucci "moccasin" loafer, the Fendi bag, and the Valentino dress Jackie O wore when she became Mrs. Onassis. While the famous double-Gs can now be found in boutiques around the world, the mother store is right here on Via Condotti, a "shopping mall" lined with Bulgari diamonds and Pratesi linens where people, not cars, have the right of way (although every now and then an Alfa Romeo roars by to an operatic chorus of oaths). Here and on Via Borgognona, you'll find the top names from Armani to Zegna.

BEST TIME TO GO

Tuesday through Friday afternoons if you want to be rubbing elbows with Rome's gran signoras—the ladies who lunch and buy a little something at Valentino for dessert. But for the liveliest see-and-be-scene vibe, the evening passeggiata can transform Via Condotti into one gigantic catwalk.

BEST FIND FOR MERMAIDS

The "Chanel" of bathing suits, Marisan Padovan (Via delle Carrozze 81) has been creating one-of-a-kind bikinis and monokinis ever since Audrey Hepburn and Claudia Cardinale discovered her. Rhinestones often gild the lilies here.

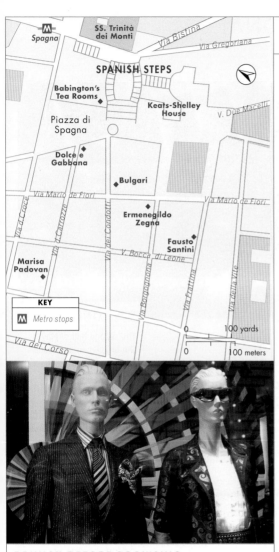

SPANISH STEPS

Spagna M
SS. Trinità dei Monti
Via Bistina
Via Gregoriana
Babington's Tea Rooms
Piazza di Spagna
Keats-Shelley House
V. Due Macelli
Dolce e Gabbana
Bulgari
Via Mario de Fiori
Via Mario de Fiori
Ermenegildo Zegna
Via di Croce
Via Carrozze
Via dei Condotti
Fausto Santini
V. Bocca di Leone
Marisa Padovan
Via Bogognona
Via Frattina
Via della Vite
Via del Corso

KEY
M Metro stops

0   100 yards
0   100 meters

BRUNCH BEFORE BROWSING

With sumptuous shopping, one needs sumptuous dining, and Casa Bleve (⊠ *Via del Teatro Valle 48, Spagna* ☎ *06/6865970*), frequented by politicians, gastronomes, and connoisseurs, is a great place to stop for a Saturday luncheon. Located where the ancient bath complex of Agrippa once stood, this eatery is set in a 16th-century palazzo. Wine is artfully displayed and dozens of dining tables have plenty of elbow room—to show off all those shopping bags.

TROPPO ELEGANTE

STRIKE A POSE
Long favored by Madonna, *glamazons,* and super-models everywhere, Dolce & Gabbana has a High Baroque look, just like Rome itself. Brocade jeans, jeweled Sicilian bustiers, tassels and taffeta—Armani coolsters should look elsewhere.

SAVE YOUR SOLES
Born and bred in Rome, Fausto Santini makes some of the city's most stylish shoes—he is known for the softest hides, his subtle designs, and those must-haves, like his '70s platform showstoppers.

BECAUSE YOU'RE WORTH IT
If Holly Golightly got the Mean Reds in Rome, she'd have to hurry over to Rome's "Tiffany's"—Bulgari, where the cabochons are world-famous and the prices made even Eliza-beth Taylor blanch. If you want super Roman style, it doesn't get haute-er than this.

MARK OF ZEGNA
Ermenegildo Zegna did for bespoke men's couture what prêt-à-porter did for Dior and the ladies—he took Rome's great legacy of custom-made men's wear and brought it to the masses. The vibe is styl-ish, as proved by Zegna's poster-boy Adrian Brody.

15

PIAZZA NAVONA

In Rome, shopping and sightseeing are often hard to separate from one another. This is especially fortissimo in the Baroque quarter around Piazza Navona, queen of Roman squares. Here, you can buy an antique or an artisan creation in a shop that is sometimes an historic monument in its own right.

Want to purchase an 18th-century engraving of the Piazza Navona fountain from a print shop located just a few feet away from its splashing waters? Head to Nardecchia, whose windows overlook Bernini's sculpted masterpiece. Or buy a porcelain centerpiece in a china store set in the 16th-century Palazzo Drago? Bowl yourself over at IN.OR. Italian handicraft traditions are still very much alive in this area, where the largest concentrations of craftspeople and workshops are around the Pantheon (a few blocks south of Piazza Navona) and Campo de Fiori. Silversmiths, antique furniture restorers, decorators, and jewelers work away at their craft and many are pleased to explain their techniques.

BEST TIME TO GO

The second half of May is the time when an antiques fair takes over Via dei Coronari, which runs off the northern end of Piazza Navona. Many elegant and gorgeous antiques stores line the ancient street and stay open during the evening during the fair.

BEST GIFT OF ALL?

At Ai Monasteri, established in 1894 and specializing in the unique products handcrafted in Italy's abbeys, you can buy a flacon of the shop's Elixir of Happiness, a bargain—if it works—at €14.50.

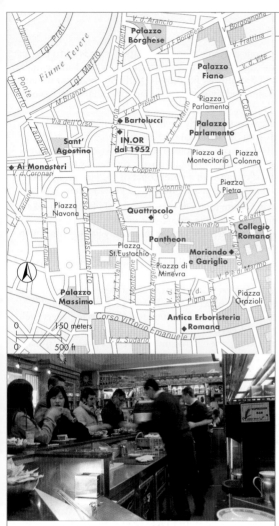

ONLY IN ROME

ROMA THERAPY

Set in a shop dating to 1783, the Antica Erboristeria Romana offers plenty of fragrance products, venerated herbal remedies, and a spectacularly evocative decor that is right out of the 18th century.

DOLL YOURSELF UP

Bartolucci, not far from the Pantheon, is a store that is devoted to Pinocchio. Hundreds of his figures, puppets to dolls, are fashioned by an artisan family from the Marche region—a store Gepetto himself would love.

BEAUTIFUL BITS

Quattrocolo, housed in historic quarters that date to 1938, is famous for their antique mirco-mosaic jewelry—an art form that was born and perfected in Rome during the 18th-century Neoclassical period. Or opt for a 19th-century cameo.

WILLY WONKA ALLA ROMANA

Moriondo e Gariglio was once the favorite chocolatier of the royal House of Savoy. Now, its *caleidoscopio* of gift-boxed candies are available to all.

CRYSTAL CLEAR

For the most *selezionatissima* array of crystal, silver, and china, Roman brides always go to IN.OR. dal 1952.

15

NEIGHBORHOOD NIBBLES

Need an early-morning nibble or an afternoon pick-me-up? Sant'Eustachio il Caffè in Rome is something of a legend. This legendary coffee house located in Piazza Sant'Eustachio, where you where find yourself rubbing shoulders with an Italian politician or two. Or opt for Tazzo d'Oro, on Via degli Orfani on the east side of Piazza del Pantheon, which may have Rome's best cup of espresso. Head to Moriondo e Gariglio, at Via Piè di Marmo 21, for handmade chocolates. For a top gelateria, it's Giolitti right by the Pantheon—savor your granita knowing that the ancient Romans also enjoyed sweet ices.

SHOPPING DISTRICTS

CAMPO

Campo de' Fiori is one of Rome's most captivating piazzas and a perfect starting point for exploring the heart of the city. By the 16th century, this neighborhood was already bustling—a gathering place for the citizens of Rome dominated by number of majestic Renaissance palaces and churches.

The piazza takes center stage early in the morning as an extraordinary spectacle unfolds with the arrival of the *bancarellari* (the moveable cart vendors) just before sunrise. Imbuing the square with a village atmosphere, these hard-working merchants ply their wares six days a week, tables filled to overflowing with a cornucopia of such goods as freshly picked chicory, blood oranges, artichokes, and lavender honey.

Under the billowing white umbrellas, visitors should be sure to take a moment to hunt for an Italian espresso pot or to snap a photo of the pyramids of dried spice where the vendors cheerfully boast—often with exaggerated comedy—the quality of their goods.

Don't forget to explore the labyrinth of narrow streets named for the merchants that once populated the area: Via del Giubbonari (Street of the Jacket Makers), *Via dei Cappellari* (Street of the Hat Makers), and Via degli Specchi (Street of Mirrors). These meandering side streets have an abundance of shops and boutiques sure to please everyone's budget. Getting here is easy, as many buses pass through Torre Argentina (a short walk away), though the most direct are buses 44, 63, 81, and 95.

MONTI

Getting lost is a good way for inveterate shoppers to explore Rome, and Monti is the perfect place to re-"charge" yourself. Here you will find a plethora of treasures tucked in a maze of streets between the Viminal and Esquiline hills. Originally home to prosperous patricians, the *rione* (city ward) is one of the city's oldest. It became one of the most densely populated and impoverished parts of the city at the height of the Roman Empire, a zone known for its local color and its courtesans.

From an ancient and checkered past to today's urban renewal, Monti has developed a boho-chic feel that is becoming an integral part of the neighborhood's cultural identity. Take a walk along its cobbled streets and enjoy sleek teashops and sassy boutiques that feature up-and-coming avant-garde designers, as well as a peppering of workshops from some of the finest old-world artisans and ateliers, including noted tailor Mimmo Siviglia.

Whether you fancy a pair of tango shoes or simply to enjoy the wealth of window-shopping opportunities, Monti's shops will prove to be one-of-a-kind jewels. Be sure to stop and rest your feet in the picturesque piazza Modanna dei Monti, where you can catch your breath before the next round of shopping and sightseeing. To get here, take Metro B to the Cavour metro stop.

BARBERINI

For reasons that elude most of us, Romans seem to make impeccable fashion sense look like a walk in the park. The city is studded with great places to shop; just keep in mind that a stroll along the winding tree-lined Via Veneto is no place for your casual Fridays blue jeans. One of the chicest streets in Rome, there is perhaps no other street that captures the essence of *la dolce vita*. Around the corner at Piazza Barberini, expect to encounter a parade of über-stylish locals and fashionable tourists shopping at one of Italy's most prestigious tailors and purveyors of classy men's ready-to-wear. Can't afford to indulge? Head up Via del Tritone for posh without the dosh (as Brits refer to money) and a great selection of shops offering mid-price clothing, shoes, and leather apparel. To get to the area take the Metro (Line A) to Piazza Barberini, or any of a number of buses, including the 116.

VIA DEL CORSO

Running right through the heart of Rome, this crowded and bustling thoroughfare attracts droves of both locals and visitors who overflow from the district's narrow sidewalks onto the streets, dodging taxis and buses. Crowds are elbow-to-elbow in front of display windows full of clothing and accessories. In a city of walkers and strollers, Piazza Venezia and Piazza del Popolo mark the beginning and end points of a shopping-inspired afternoon stroll the Romans call a *passeggiata*, in which window-shopping and chatting are more the point than exercise.

Young Romans come here for jeans and inexpensive, trendy wear, some of which is sold in the 17th- and 18th-century mansions that line the street. At the Piazza Venezia end of things, for example, Stefanel has a sales outlet in the former Bonaparte palace. In the chic area tucked next to Piazza San Lorenzo in Lucina, smart and expensive specialty shops, such as the Profumeria Materozzoli, cater to the people who live in the palaces nearby. Piazza della Fontanella Borghese, flanking the palace once inhabited by the uninhibited Pauline Borghese (she posed nude for Canova), has a picturesque street market of permanent stalls selling prints and old books.

Here you will also find the palatial pink-marble Galleria Alberto Sordi at Piazza Colonna, Rome's most elegant shopping mall. Recently restored, and a good place to take a coffee break and enjoy a bit of people-watching under the soaring Stil Liberty (Art Nouveau) glass roof. The gallery's Art Nouveau corridors are filled with fun stores, including Zara, Jam, Tacchini, Coccinelle, Imagination, and C'art. And, if you have a sweet tooth, there is even a Lindt chocolate shop. Via del Corso is the dividing line between the designer-centric fancy shops of the Spagna district and the more reasonably priced emporia near the Pantheon. If you don't feel like walking—though this area is very central—take Bus 62, 63, 117, 199, or 492.

TRASTEVERE

Just across the Tiber from the city center, Trastevere is a tangle of atmosphere-soaked medieval streets known as *er core de Roma*—the heart of Rome. Although you won't find as many cultural sights situated in this right-bank enclave, the rione is a guaranteed hit for teenagers and college students who flock to this buzzing, colorful neighborhood for its creative and funky shops. From Piazza Trilussa northward, the streets are crammed with young people chatting, shopping, and dining. Sunday's Porta Portese flea market is a bargain-hunters paradise. Foodies, too, will find plenty in the way of excitement and can select from both open-air markets and old-world food and wine shops, complete with a stool-perched owner scribbling daily accounts in an old-fashioned ledger book. Be sure to look up Dermit O'Connell, owner of the Almost Corner Bookshop in Via del Moro 45, who will be happy to chat and give you a resident's insight into life in Rome. If you don't feel like walking across the Ponte Sisto bridge to get here, take Tram 8 from Largo Argentina three stops.

SAN LORENZO

Rome has passed through many incarnations since its founding, and the slightly worn-around-the-edges neighborhood of San Lorenzo has followed in its same transformational footsteps. A working class ghetto in the 1880s that housed the city's railway workers, the area was also a casualty of allied bombs during the World War II.

Haphazardly rebuilt, the area's narrow streets and graffiti-tagged palazzi complement once-condemned factories that have been converted into hip lofts, giving the quarter a Felliniesque finesse. Shabby-chic theater spaces and bookstores abound, along with colorful boutiques and cafés, all making this one of the city's hottest destinations—especially among Rome's free thinkers and students.

For a fashion fix, visit buzzing L'Anatra all'Arancia, with its captivating prêt-à-porter window displays. Just across Via Tiburtina is a recently launched menswear shop, 130 Uomo. For aficionados of contemporary art, the boundary-pushing artist studios in the old Cerere pasta factory on Via degli Ausoni won't disappoint—don't miss Maurizio Savini's flamboyant lifelike bubblegum sculptures.

San Lorenzo's raw earthiness has a certain Italian sophistication that can be lost on those used to the city's elegant monuments and statuary. Take the time to delve beneath the neighborhood's scruffy surface, and visitors will find the quartieri a perfect canvas to express Rome's flamboyant lyricism. The district is a 10-minute walk or a Bus 71 ride away from Termini Station.

DEPARTMENT STORES

Rome has few department stores. The classiest are the two Rinascente stores and the three main Coin stores. These outposts have welcome desks, multilingual guides, and tax-free refund desks. They're open daily, including Sunday.

Rome's handiest central shopping mall is the **Il Forum Termini** (⊠ *Stazione Temini, Repubblica* ⊕ *www.grandistazioni.it*), a cluster of shops that stay open until 10 PM (even on Sunday), conveniently located directly inside Rome's biggest train station, Stazione Termini. In a city not known for its convenient shopping hours, this "shop before you hop/ buy before you fly" hub is a good spot for last-minute goodies or a book for your train or airplane ride. There are more than 50 shops, including the ever-popular United Colors of Benetton, Intimissimi for sassy undergarments, Sephora, and Optimissimo, which has more than 3,000 super-stylish glasses and sunglasses by top Italian designers.

Coin (✉ *Via Cola di Rienzo 173, Vatican* ☎ *06/36004298* ✉ *Piazzale Appio 7, San Giovanni* ☎ *06/7080020* ⊕ *www.coin.it*) is a perfect place for upscale merchandise in a comfortable, discount-department store atmosphere. With convenient locations in the center of Rome, customers can select from trendy merchandise, including clothing separates, lingerie, and sportswear for men, women, and children. Searching for a pressure-driven espresso machine, a simpler stove-top Bialetti model, or a mezzaluna? You can find these and other high-quality, stylish cookware items that are difficult to find back home.

La Rinascente (✉ *Piazza Colonna, Piazza di Spagna* ☎ *06/6797691* ✉ *Piazza Fiume* ☎ *06/8841231* ⊕ *www.rinascente.it*) is Italy's best-known department store and where Italian fashion mogul Giorgio Armani got his start as a window dresser. Rome's flagship store, located in the early-1900s building at Piazza Colonna, provides five delectable floors of upscale clothing and accessories. Ground-floor shoppers will find a phalanx of perfumes and cosmetics alongside blockbuster handbags, costume jewelry, hats, and beautiful silk scarves. Upstairs, wallet-friendly sportswear and big-ticket designers share ample retail turf geared toward businesspeople on lunch breaks and the ubiquitous tourist. Their Piazza Fiume location has more floor space and a wider range of goods, including a housewares department.

15

BUDGET

Both the Oviesse and Upim department store chains are good places for families to shop for bargain sportswear, bathing suits, underwear, and scarves—where quality doesn't break the bank. Both no-frills franchises have multiple locations throughout Rome where you can also pick up toiletries, makeup, and hair-care supplies. Some even have invaluable while-you-wait shoe-repair counters. There's a large central Upim store in Stazione Termini and another on Piazza Santa Maria Maggiore. Oviesse has a store on Viale Trastevere 62/64.

MARKETS

FLEA MARKETS

Treasure-seekers and bargain-hunters alike will appreciate Rome's open-air markets. Well-supplied and oh-so-Roman, these markets both large and small are great spots to get an insight into the shopping spirit of the capital. Just don't get there too late, or you'll find all the good things have been snapped up. Usually a mecca for discount clothing and shoes, the stalls often attract a young clientele. Watch out for pickpockets and tricksters inviting you to play their card games: they *always* win the bets!

Rome's biggest flea market is at **Porta Portese** (✉ *Via Portuense and adjacent streets between Porta Portese and Via Ettore Rolli, Trastevere*), which welcomes 100,000 visitors every Sunday. Like one vast yard sale, this market disgorges mountains of new and secondhand clothing, furniture, pictures, old records, and antiques—all at rock-bottom prices (especially if you're adept at haggling). There is a jovial atmosphere, with an aroma of foods wafting in the air and people crowding around the stalls, hoping to pick up a 1960s Beatles album or a rare Art Deco figurine. Just make sure you bring cash, as stallholders don't accept credit cards and the nearest available cash machine is a hike. Though not strictly a flea market, the *mercato* **Via Sannio** (⊠ *Near La Basilica di San Giovanni in Laterano, San Giovanni*) is entirely without pretension and open weekdays 8–2 and Saturday 8–5. Here you can find military surplus, leather jackets, cosmetics, and many other bargains. Also expect great deals on shoes—you can buy good-quality name-brand shoes that have served their time only as shop-window displays.

There are a number of monthly or weekly markets selling bric-a-brac, arts and crafts, rare books and old comics, and secondhand laces and linen. Dates vary, so you should check first. One of the most picturesque is the **Ponte Milvio Antiques Market** (⊠ *On banks of Tiber between Ponte Milvio and Ponte Duca d'Aosta, Flaminia* ☎ 06/9077312), an antiques and collector's market, with stands set up on the riverbank beside the old stone bridge marking the spot where the Roman emperor Constantine won the battle that subsequently heralded in the Christian era. Cycling paths along the embankment can turn this into a pleasant day's outing. This is held on the first weekend of every month. **Soffitta Sotto i Portici** (⊠ *Piazza Augusto Imperatore, Piazza di Spagna* ☎ 06/36005345) has more than 100 stands. This market is held every first and third Sunday of the month from 9 AM until sunset. **Mercatino Piazza Verdi** (⊠ *Piazza Verdi, Parioli* ☎ 06/8552773), in Rome's upper-crust neighborhood, has quality crafts, rare old books, collectors' pieces, bric-a-brac, and food items. Look for it every fourth Sunday of the month from 9 AM until sundown.

FOOD MARKETS

★ Still shadowed by the massive 16th-century Orsini palazzo and a statue of the famed philosopher Giordano Bruno, who was burned at the stake here on accusations of heresy in 1600, the **Campo de' Fiori** (near Piazza Navona) is Rome's oldest food market, situated just south of Rome's Renaissance/baroque quarter and the Piazza Farnese. Too congested to be called picturesque, the market is nevertheless a favorite photo-op, due to the *ombrelloni* (canvas umbrellas) food stands, which proffer everything from cheese to fish to every spice imaginable. The Terrina fountain that was once served as water bowl to cattle and now keeps the vendors' flowers fresh, is inscribed with the words FA DEL BEN A LASSA DIRE—"Do well and let them talk"—a suitable phrase for the chatty crowd that works the marketplace.

Two other big and colorful food markets are **Mercato Andrea Doria** (on Via Andrea Doria in the Prati neighborhood, north of the Vatican) and **Nuovo Mercato Esquilino** (in a former barracks with its main entrance on Via Filippo Turati, between Via Mamiani and Via G. Pepe), the latter strongly influenced by the ethnic diversity of the Esquiline area not far from the station. There are also smaller daily outdoor markets peppering just about every neighborhood, and most of which are open Monday to Saturday from early morning until about 2; some markets (among them Trionfale and Piazza dell'Unita, on Via Cola di Rienzo) stay open all day.

SPECIALTY SHOPS

ANTIQUES AND PRINTS

Rome is one of Italy's happiest hunting grounds for antiques and bric-a-brac. Here you'll find streets lined with shops groaning with gilded Rococo tables, charming Grand Tour memorabilia, fetching 17th-century *veduti* (view) engravings, and curios, perhaps even Lord Byron's snuff spoon. Via dei Coronari is Rome's traditional center of antiques but other top prestigious dealers are concentrated around Via del Babuino. The street's focal point is the time-weathered statue of the "baboon" (actually a satyr) that gave it its name. Right next to the baboon is the charmingly picturesque Museum Atelier Canova-Tadolini, where the great 18th-century Neoclassical sculptor worked. Inside the museum, there's also a coffee bar and restaurant. What better place to stop and have lunch?

15

Antichitá Tanca (⊠ *Salita dei Crescenzi 12, Navona* ☎ *06/6875272* ⊕ *www.antichitatanca.it*) is a fourth-generation Rome dealer in 20th-century table ornaments, lamps, candlesticks, and first-edition prints. You can hunt through piles and boxes in one of the three rather cluttered rooms; in another are vitrines full of Art Nouveau jewelry, old silver, and objets d'art.

Fratelli Alinari (⊠ *Via Alibert 16/a, Piazza di Spagna* ☎ *06/6792923* ⊕ *www.alinari.it*) is the gallery store of the world's oldest photography firm, founded by brothers Leopoldo, Giuseppe, and Romualdo Alinari in 1852. Patrons can browse through a vast archive of prints, books, rare collotypes, and finely detailed reproductions of historical images, drawings, and paintings. Several of the more interesting subjects re-created using this technique are Dante's *Divine Comedy* and both the *Plan de Paris* and *The Origin of New York*, detailed reproductions of the first recorded maps of these two cities.

Ex Libris (⊠ *Via dell'Umilta 77à, Corso* ☎ *06/6791540* ⊕ *www. exlibrisroma.it*) was founded in the early 1900s and is one of the oldest antiquarian bookshops in Rome. In addition to modern authors, browsers will also find a selection of rare editions, prints, and maps from the 16th to 20th centuries that will make bookworms drool. The shop is lined from floor-to-ceiling wooden bookshelves that are filled to overflowing.

Galleria Benucci (⊠ *Via del Babuino 150/C, Piazza di Spagna* ☎ *06/36002190* ⊕ *www.galleriebenucci.it*) is a treasure trove, with carved and gilded late baroque and Empire period furniture and paintings culled from the noble houses of Italy's past. An establishment favored by professionals from Europe and abroad, this elegant gallery has a astonishing selection of objects in a hushed atmosphere where connoisseurs will find the proprietors only too happy to discuss their latest finds.

Galleria Biagiarelli (⊠ *Piazza Capranica 97, Navona* ☎ *06/6784987* ⊕ *www.biagiarelli.it*) occupies a superb setting in the former chapel of the Pre-Renaissance Palazzo Capranica, where the windows still have the cardinal's coat of arms. Rome's leading antiques dealer of 18th- and 19th-century Russian icons, Carlo Maria Biagiarelli also has amassed a collection of Eastern European antique china figurines as well as some unsigned *antique watercolors.*

Nardecchia (⊠ *Piazza Navona 25, Navona* ☎ *06/6869318* ⊕ *www.nardecchia.it*) knows that there are three major considerations when it comes to antique prints and reproductions: value, aesthetics, and rarity. In the heart of Piazza Navona, this shop showcases some of its large selection of beautiful 19th-century prints of the city in its display window in front of the famous Bernini Fountain of the Four Rivers. The view, combined with its attentive and knowledgeable staff, makes a visit to this famous store an especially pleasant experience. Be sure to take a look at the 18th-century etchings by Giovanni Battista Piranesi.

Gherardo Noce Begnigni Olivieri (⊠ *Via della Scrofa 20, Navona* ☎ *06/6861837*) enjoys Christmas morning *every* morning in his shop that specializes in handmade 18th- and 19th-century Neapolitan crèche figures. Rococo Baby Jesus figurines, carved wooden camels, and historic blackamoor figurines are all superbly represented and are of the craftsmanship prized by obsessive collectors.

Quattrocolo (⊠ *Via della Scrofa 54, Navona* ☎ *06/68801367* ⊕ *www.quattrocolo.com*) is a historic shop dating to 1938 that showcases exquisite antique micro-mosaic jewelry painstakingly crafted in the style perfected by the masters at the Vatican mosaic studio. You'll also find 18th- and 19th-century cameos and beautiful engraved stones. Small works beloved by cosmopolitan clientele of the Grand Tour age, these pieces offer modern-day shoppers a taste of yesteryear's grandeur.

BOOKSTORES

English-language books are widely available in Rome; many of the larger booksellers dedicate at least a few shelves of books for English-speaking patrons. In the city center, many newsstands carry English-language newspapers—one located on Via Veneto and one adjacent to Piazza di Spagna cater specifically to foreigners, with larger selections of international dailies as well as hard to find magazines like the *New Yorker*. The following shops are the best in the city for English-language publications.

Almost Corner Bookstore (⊠ *Via del Moro 45, Trastevere* ☎ *06/5836942*) is a well-loved meeting point for English-speaking residents and visitors to the lively Trastevere district. Owner Dermot O'Connell, from Kilkenny, Ireland, stocks an inviting selection ranging from translated Italian classics to today's latest bestsellers. With a reputation for being able to find anything a customer requests, the shop is a good place to special order books; it has a wonderful selection of obscura if you've got the time to poke through the large selection.

Via Condotti Shopping

Castroni is a foodie favorite for most Romans and just the place to pick up the fixings for a gourmand's picnic.

Anglo-American Book Co. (✉ *Via della Vite 102, Piazza di Spagna* ☎ *06/6795222* ⊕ *www.aab.it*) is a large and friendly English-language bookstore with more than 45,000 books. It's been a mecca for English language reading material in Rome for more than 25 years. Whether you are a study-abroad student in need of textbooks or a visitor searching for a little light reading for the train, there is something for everyone here. Among shelves stuffed from floor to ceiling and sometimes several rows deep, book lovers can easily spend hours just browsing, though its bilingual staff are excellent at offering recommendations for those wanting some direction.

La Feltrinelli (✉ *Galleria Alberto Sordi 33, Piazza Colonna, Piazza di Spagna* ☎ *06/69755001* ⊕ *www.lafeltrinelli.it* ✉ *Via V.E. Orlando 84/86, Repubblica* ☎ *06/4827878* ✉ *Largo Torre Argentina, Campo* ☎ *06/68663001*) is Rome's biggest bookstore chain with 12 stores peppered throughout the city. The Piazza Colonna flagship dominates the elegant 19th-century Galleria Alberto Sordi and fills three floors with books, music, postcards, holiday items, and small gifts. You can rest your feet while having a snack in the caffè. The Torre Argentina shop also has a ticketing office for music and cultural events.

Mel Bookstore (✉ *Via Nazionale 254–255, Repubblica* ☎ *06/4885433* ⊕ *www.melbookstore.it*) is the place to come if you like discounts on remainder stock and secondhand books. Browse through the large basement and find a treasure trove of marked-down merchandise as well as a modest selection of English-language paperbacks. Upstairs, shop for books in Italian on a variety of subjects or pick up a DVD of *Roman*

Holiday. Afterward, relax with your purchases while you treat yourself to a coffee and dessert in the spacious art deco–style caffè.

Mondadori (✉ *Via San Vincenzo 10, Corso* ☎ *06/6976501* ⊕ *www. mondadori.it*) is conveniently located close to the Trevi Fountain. Air-conditioned, it is an enjoyable reprieve from the heat and crowds. There is a small English-language department on the ground floor near the caffè. The top floor has a generous selection of computer software and accessories, printers, mobile phones, and digital cameras. Mondadori remains one of the most prestigious Italian publishers and carries books of every genre for all readers.

The **Lion Bookshop** (✉ *Via dei Greci 33/36, Piazza di Spagna* ☎ *06/32654007* ⊕ *www.thelionbookshop.com*) is Italy's oldest English-language bookstore. For 50 years the shop, with its children's reading corner and small caffè with American cookies and bagels, has been a welcoming haven for moms in search of that special children's book. In addition to books for kids, they also have a broad assortment of contemporary and classic fiction and nonfiction titles, as well as books on Rome and Italy in general, plus art, architecture, cooking.

CERAMICS AND DECORATIVE ARTS

Italy has always been beloved for its wonderful craftsmanship and decorative arts. In Rome, where museums are sometimes overwhelming, sometimes the best treasures are found not in its galleries but in artisan shops along twisty alleyways where works of art are within everyone's budget.

Arte del Vetro Natolli Murano (✉ *Corso Rinascimento 53/55, Navona* ☎ *06/68301170*) specializes in handmade blown Venetian art glass pieces, including Murano glass jewelry (necklaces and pendants), tableware, glass vases, and extravagant chandeliers. Every individual piece is hand-crafted from the furnaces of Natolli's master glassmakers using ancient techniques kept alive by the island's artisans since 1291. Some limited-edition designs show not only the craftsman's mastery of the art form but the artisan's love for the vibrant aesthetic of the glassmaking tradition.

Arte Italiana (✉ *Via della Conciliazione 4f, Vatican* ☎ *06/68806373*) stands out among the religious souvenir shops that line the avenue leading to St. Peter's Basilica. Whether you're looking for a unique First Holy Communion gift or something meaningful to bestow on your parish back home, the multilingual staff will help you find what you are looking for. The store stocks a wide variety of detailed crèche statuettes, alabasters sculptures, tapestries, saints medals, and rosaries. The pieces aren't cheap, but they are of the highest quality and make great mementos to personalize your Vatican experience.

Fratelli Samperi (✉ *Via Marmorata 143/147, Testaccio* ☎ *06/5758741*) is a magnificent old-fashioned shop that sells paints, brushes, canvases, and artists' supplies. Whether you want watercolors, jewelry-making tools, or ceramics supplies, the Samperi brothers are happy to lend a hand in selecting the right materials. They also teach courses in a variety of subjects.

15

Il Giardino di Domenico Persiani (⊠ *Via Torino 92, Repubblica* ☎ *06/4883886*) is a refreshing open-air terra-cotta shop nestled in a cool courtyard garden under the shade of an expansive oak tree. Whether you're looking for a chubby cherub, a replica of Bacchus, or your very own Bocca della Verità, this is your chance to bring a little piece of Rome home to your garden. With a large selection of handmade Roman masks, busts, flower pots, and vases there is something here for anyone with a green thumb.

★ **IN.OR. dal 1952** (⊠ *Via della Stelletta 23, Navona* ☎ *06/6878579*) is a grand silver and china store occupying the *piano nobile* of an 18th-century palazzo in the characteristic Campo Marzo area. For more than 50 years, Romans have registered their bridal china and gifts under the store's frescoed ceilings in hopes of receiving something elegant. The shop specializes in work handcrafted by the silversmiths of Pampaloni in Florence and Bellotto of Padua.

Le IV Stagioni (⊠ *Via dell' Umiltà 30/b, Corso* ☎ *06/69941029*) stocks a colorful selection of traditional Italian pottery from well-known manufacturers like Capodimonte, Vietri, Deruta, Caltagirone, and Faenza. If you're looking for something *alla Romana,* opt for the brown glazed pots with a lacy white border and charming flower basket wall ornaments, made in the Rome area.

Le Terre di AT (⊠ *Via degli Ausoni 13, San Lorenzo* ☎ *06/491748*) is a modern potters' workshop nestled in the belly of San Lorenzo, Rome's burgeoning university district. Working on the premises, artist Angela Torcivia creates vases, cups, ceramic jewelry, and necklaces. Her pieces have an otherworldly style, combining ancient shapes with fiery contrasting colors, and are modern while still paying homage to the rich history of Roman clay pottery.

Musa (⊠ *Via Campo Marzo 29, Spagna* ☎ *06750082* ⊕ *www. ceramichemusa.it*) is the place to shop if you're looking for decorative ceramic accents. Be sure to pop up to the second floor, where you can find a fine array of hand-painted ceramic tiles from Vietri, a region renowned for the quality of its clays and artisanal ceramic tradition. Shipping can be arranged whether you're planning to tile an entire bathroom or just pick up a few pieces to use in your kitchen as hotplates.

Polveri del Tempo (⊠ *Via del Moro 59, Trestevere* ☎ *06/05880704*) is the place to go if you are looking for decorative timepieces. Here you will find sundials and handcrafted hourglasses—including a giant 18-hour model that is quite memorable. The owner, architect and craftsman Adrian Rodriguez, will tell you how monks once used marked candles, like those on sale here, to note the passage of time. Also on offer is a selection of ancient gizmos that would make any child happy.

Savelli Arte e Tradizione (⊠ *Via Paolo VI, 27–29, Vatican* ☎ *06/68307017* ⊕ *www.savellireligious.com*) offers the widest selection of artwork and sacred objects available in Rome and has been a Roman landmark since 1878. The Savelli name belongs to an old Roman family with four popes among its ancestors: Benedict II, Gregory II, Honorius III, and Honorius IV. The shop is famous for its collection of 18th- and

19th-century–style micromosaics; it's a great spot for watching artists demonstrating this ancient craft.

CLOTHING

CHILDREN'S CLOTHING — Although consumers may be cutting back on luxury purchases, visitors still can't help but indulge when it comes to the little ones. Note that sizes are completely different from U.S. children's sizes, so be sure to take measurements before you leave home and bring along your tape measure, or get a good size-conversion chart.

Bonpoint (⊠ *Piazza San Lorenzo in Lucina 25, Corso* ☎ *06/6871548*) brings a little of Paris to Rome in fine French children's wear. The crème de la crème when it comes to styling, refinement, and price, Bonpoint's casual and classic children's clothing are both picture-perfect and fashion-forward. Well-heeled mums will appreciate their soft, cuddly onesies, and hand-stitched party dresses.

★ **I Vippini** (⊠ *Via Fontanella di Borghese 65, Corso* ☎ *06/68803754*) is not a place to shop for everyday wear—it lives up to its name ("Little V.I.P.s"). This is haute couture for kids, perfect for special occasions or for everyday if your youngster is on par with the likes of Tinseltown tots Suri Cruise and Zuma Stefani.

La Cicogna (⊠ *Via Frattina 138, Piazza di Spagna* ☎ *06/6791912* ⊕ *www.lacicognaabbigliamento.it* ⊠ *Via Cola di Rienzo 268, Vatican* ☎ *06/6896557*) is a well-known designer children's clothier found throughout Italy. With clothing for little ones from birth to age 14, this is one-stop, name-brand shopping for antsy kids and tired parents. The stores carry clothes, shoes, baby carriages, and nursery supplies as well as child-size versions of designer names like Armani, Burberry, Guru, Timberland, Replay, Blumarine, and DKNY.

Pinco Pallino (⊠ *Via del Babuino 115, Spagna* ☎ *06/69190549*) is a must-stop-shop for mini-trend-setters who know no boundaries. This Italian designwear—as hot in Russia and Japan as it is on its home turf—is known for its luxurious children's clothes. Be sure to check out their super-stylish woven fedoras and Harry Potter Hogwarts–wear.

Pùre (⊠ *Via Frattina 111, Piazza di Spagna* ☎ *06/6794555*) is the mothership for fashionistas in the making; designer brands include Dolce & Gabbana, Cavalli Angel's, E. Scervino, and Dondup. The store has plush carpet to crawl on, and children's clothes for newborns to age 12.

Rachele (⊠ *Vicolo del Bollo 6–7, Campo* ☎ *06/6864975*) is a small, charming shop tucked down an alley not far from the Campo de' Fiori piazza. The clothes are handmade by Rachele herself. Choose from whimsical crocheted hats and a cute selection of pants, skirts, and rainbow-colored tops for tykes up to age 7.

HIGH-FASHION BOUTIQUES — **Dolce & Gabbana** (⊠ *Piazza di Spagna 94, Piazza di Spagna* ☎ *06/6782990* ⊕ *www.dolcegabbana.com*) remains one of the crowning jewels of fashion in Piazza di Spagna. With an aesthetic that is anything but coy, Dolce & Gabbana has always been about excess. Launching their first collection in 1986, the dynamic duo create clothing that Fellini would approve of—richly colored fabrics, underwear as outerwear, and provocative youthful styling that embodies young Italian trends. The Rome store is the obvious choice for *glamazons* who want to push the envelope, mixing old-world glam fabrics (think velvet, corduroy, jacquard, silk, and boiled wool) with a sexy attitude.

★ **Fendi** (✉ *Largo Carlo Goldoni 419–421, Piazza di Spagna* ☎ 06/696661 ⊕ *www.fendi.com* ✉ *Via Borgognona 39, Piazza di Spagna* ☎ *06/69940808*) has been a fixture of the Roman fashion landscape since "Mamma" Fendi first opened shop with her husband in 1925. With a good eye for genius, she hired Karl Lagerfeld, who began working with the group at the start of his career. His furs and runway antics have made him one of the world's most influential designers of the 20th century and brought international acclaim to Fendi along the way. The atelier is now owned by the Louis Vuitton group and continues to symbolize Italian glamour at its finest. Their latest designs can be experienced at "Palazzo Fendi," inside the 19th-century Neoclassical Palazzo Boncompagni located on the square connecting two of Rome's most important fashion avenues, Via del Corso and Via Condotti.

Giorgio Armani (✉ *Via Condotti 77, Piazza di Spagna* ☎ 06/6991460 ⊕ *www.giorgioarmani.com*) remains one of the world's hottest designers in Italian haute couture, with slim silhouettes, gorgeous gowns, and stylish pantsuits. Despite Giorgio's sometimes abrasive comments towards other Italian fashion leaders, his collections are generally snapped up immediately by loyal couture customers. With three of his famous five lines represented within footsteps of each other near the Spanish Steps—look for Emporio Armani and Armani Jeans—there is a style and price point to please every shopper. Famous for his ultra-expensive haute couture line, Armani Collezioni, the source of many gowns worn by Hollywood starlets on Oscar night, his plunging necklines and breezy simple styling are light and elegant. Armani's sportswear line can be found at Emporio Armani and combines casual Italian elegance with just the right touch of sexiness. His super popular jeans are perfect for those who want to be both active and stylish. Want to live *La Bella Vita* the Armani way? The brand is also selling luxury apartments in Rome, complete with his personalized interiors.

Krizia (✉ *Piazza di Spagna 87* ☎ 06/6793772) is the name designer Mariuccia Mandelli chose to market her designs by, borrowing the name from the title of Plato's unfinished dialogue on women's vanity. Born in 1933, she began designing dresses for her dolls at age 8. The designer's collections have gone through many top stylists and have recently returned to its originating stylized roots. The current prêt-à-porter line emphasizes the use of black and dove grey, mixed with animal prints; it's dramatic, yet classy: Wearing Krizia will get you noticed.

★ **Laura Biagiotti** (✉ *Via Borgognona 43/44, Piazza di Spagna* ☎ 06/6791205 ⊕ *www.laurabiagiotti.it*) is considered the Queen of Cashmere for introducing it in her first collection and for continuing to promote its sophistication in her comfortable styles. She has a fascinating approach to men's clothing. For the scent of success, check out her line of his-and-her perfumes.

Missoni (✉ *Piazza di Spagna 78* ☎ 06/6792555 ⊕ *www.missoni.it*) is the place for quintessential style in ready-to-wear knit classics. Like other designers, the Missoni label has been thinking hard about its roots, which started as a family-run affair with just four knitting machines. The brand's now-legendary patterned knits of zigzags, waves, and stripes (some of which are influenced by folk art) began in 1948 when founders Rosita and Tai met in London. Daughter Angela took over designing in 1996, and sons and grandchildren now oversee the operations of the business. The label, which has been worn by Demi Moore, Cameron Diaz, and Nicole Richie, is never afraid of rocking the fashion boat.

Fodor's Choice **Patrizia Pepe** (⊠ *Via Frattina 44, Piazza di Spagna* ☎ *06/6781851*
★ ⊕ *www.patriziapepe.com*) is one of Florence's best-kept secrets for up-and-coming fashions. Emerging on the scene in 1993, Pepe's designs are both minimalist and bold, combining classic styles with low-slung jeans and jackets with oversize lapels that are bound to draw attention. Her line of shoes are hot-hot-hot for those who can walk in stilts. It's still not huge on the fashion scene as a stand-alone brand, but take a look at this shop before the line becomes the next fast-tracked craze.

★ **Prada** (⊠ *Via Condotti 92/95, Piazza di Spagna* ☎ *06/6790897* ⊕ *www. prada.com*) is not just worn by the devil, but also by serious shoppers season after season, especially those willing to sell their souls for one of their ubiquitous handbags. If you are looking for that blend of old-world luxury with a touch of fashion forward finesse, this is where you will hit pay dirt. Designs emphasize neutral coloring with an unusual use of materials, fabrics, and deconstructed shapes. You'll find the Rome store more service-focused than the New York City branches—a roomy elevator delivers you to a series of thickly carpeted rooms where a flock of discreet assistants will help you pick out dresses, shoes, lingerie, and fashion accessories.

Trussardi (⊠ *Via Condotti 49/50, Piazza di Spagna* ☎ *06/6780280* ⊕ *www.trussardi.com*) is a classic design house moving in a youthful direction. Since 1973 the brand has been symbolized by its greyhound logo. Today, with Gaia Trussardi at the helm and following in her father and brother's footsteps, the line is making use of leather accent pieces like suede tunics and wider belts. Tru Trussardi (in Galleria Alberto Sordi) addresses a modern woman's need for both luxury and comfort in upscale daily wear.

Fodor's Choice **Valentino** (⊠ *Via Condotti 13, Piazza di Spagna* ☎ *06/6795862* ⊕ *www. valentino.com* ⊠ *Via del Babuino 61* ☎ *06/36001906*) remains the epitome of ultra-elegant luxury despite the designers official retirement. In the 1960s, Valentino put Rome on the fashion map, knocking Dior and Balenciaga off their elevated Parisian pedestals in the process. Under the new helm of Pier Paolo Piccioli and Maria Grazi Chiuri, Valentino is still the darling of the château and luxury yacht haute couture set and continues to win the hearts of new generations of fashion divas. At their principal Via Condotti store, plush red carpet leads to gilded salons filled with glamorous but restrained evening gowns and flirty cocktail dresses where off-duty celebs like Nicole Kidman and Gwyneth Paltrow have been known to shop while dreaming of their next Oscar nomination.

15

Versace (⊠ *Via Bocca di Leone 23, 26–27, Piazza di Spagna* ⊕ *www.versace.com* ⊠ *Via Vittorio Veneto 104* ☎ *06/69925574* ☎ *06/42012876*) occupies the ground floor of a noble palazzo with wrought-iron gratings on the windows and mosaic pavement. The store is as formal and staid as this collection is imaginative. Here shoppers will find sandals, handbags, and sunglasses to complement the dresses, shirts, skirts, and pants in outrageous colors and improbable patterns. The designs are as flamboyant as Donatella herself. Adding to the label is a new collection by Gianni's niece (Donatella's daughter) showcased under her debut Francesca V label. Be sure to check out the new contemporary Via Veneto location.

KNITWEAR **Taro** (⊠ *Via della Scrofa 50, Navona* ☎ *06/6896476*) produces chic handmade knitwear in unusual yarns and striking colors. Designed by owners Marisa Pignataro and Enrico Natoli, the pieces are handmade in Rome. Selections from their casual, easy-to-wear line include luxuriously textured tunics, loose sleeveless jackets, and shawls and pants.

LEATHER CLOTHING Leather clothing for men and women is a good buy in Rome, where savvy shoppers can choose from a wide range of well-tailored jackets, boots, bags, belts, shirts, hats, and pants for men and women. You can also find small workshops where delicious jackets, coats, and handbags can be made to measure.

Renard (⊠ *Via dei Due Macelli 53, Piazza di Spagna* ☎ *06/6797004*) is a leather boutique displaying a selection of styles made exclusively in Italy. Their classic leather blazers and trench styles are sporty and sophisticated and come in unexpected pale shades as well as traditional tones. Be sure to eye their supple leather pencil skirts, as they are sure to become a wardrobe staple and will look fantastic with both pumps and high boots. Shoppers will also find racy motorcycle styles perfect for all their windswept and gutsy motorino rides.

Viroel (⊠ *Via del Tritone 76, Corso* ☎ *06/42014643*) occupies an entire corner of the busy intersection with Via Francesco Crispi. Whatever your budget, there's something made of leather to suit you. Blazers, car coats, bombers, and racing jackets are just a few of the many styles in men's and women's apparel—all available at reasonable prices. Salespeople are friendly and definitely have their sales pitch down pat.

MEN'S CLOTHING FodorsChoice ★ **Brioni** (⊠ *Via Barberini 79, Barberini* ☎ *06/4620161* ⊕ *www.brioni.it* ⊠ *Via Condotti 21/A, Piazza di Spagna* ☎ *06/485855*) is often hailed as the best of all men's tailors in Italy, a distinction it's held for more than 50 years. This legendary shop creates impeccable custom-made and ready-to-wear business suits, overcoats, and sumptuous jackets. Customers have more than 5,000 different fabrics to select from. Unlike its big rival Zegna, Brioni has refused to move any of its manufacturing out of Italy to cheaper locales like Mexico: Its flawlessly executed garments are all made in Italy by master tailors, trained by the company's own four-year school in Abruzzo. On average, each garment takes a minimum of 18 hours to stitch. Past and present clients include Clark Gable, Nelson Mandela, and Donald Trump.

Eddy Monetti (✉ *Via Borgognona, 35, Piazza di Spagna* ☎ *06/6794389* ⊕ *www.eddymonetti.com*) is a conservative but upscale men's store featuring jackets, sweaters, slacks, and ties made out of wool, cotton, and cashmere. Sophisticated and pricey, the store carries a range of stylish British- and Italian-made pieces. The women's store is at Via Borgognona 35.

Ermenegildo Zegna (✉ *Via Borgognona 7/e, Piazza di Spagna* ☎ *06/6789143* ⊕ *www.zegna.com*), of the unpronounceable name, is a powerhouse manufacturer of men's clothing, controlling 30 percent of the luxury menswear market it Italy with fans like actors Jude Law and Diego Luna. The classic ready-to-wear line is made of the firm's premier fabrics (the family has been legendary for their fabrics for more than a century) and require two individual measurements. Most Zegna suits cost in the €1,500–€2,000 range, with the top of the line, known as "Couture," costing considerably more.

15

Grima' S (✉ *Via del Gambero 11/a, Piazza di Spagna* ☎ *06/6784423*) is a store that has an old-world charm, with its retro wooden counter and display shelves. Styles are classic: smart as well as casual (and prices are reasonable). The man who prefers *La Dolce Vita* styling will feel at home here.

Mimmo Siviglia (✉ *Via Urbana 14a, Monti* ☎ *06/48903310* ⊕ *www.mimmosiviglia.com*) is shirtmaking at its apex; it has been one of Rome's best-kept secrets for more than 50 years. The fabrics used by this atelier are incredible, as is the whole experience of fitting and selection of collars and cuffs, all of which will be interspersed with interesting discussions about the merits of high-end fabrics such as Riva. Aficionados of fine tailoring will be impressed by the amount of attention each customer is given as well as the precision dedicated to each order. Once Mimmo has your size in the computer, future orders can be shipped anywhere in the world.

Schostal (✉ *Via del Corso 158, Piazza di Spagna* ☎ *06/6791240* ⊕ *www.schostalroma.com*) is one of the few family-run clothiers in the area that has managed to survive Piazza di Spagna's sky-high rents—It just celebrated 139 years! Serving the gentlemen of Rome since 1870, the shop still preserves that genteel ambience. Fine-quality shirts come with spare collars and cuffs. Ultraclassic underwear, handkerchiefs, and pure wool sweaters are also available at affordable prices.

MEN'S AND WOMEN'S CLOTHING **Davide Cenci** (✉ *Via Campo Marzio 1–7, Navona* ☎ *06/6990681* ⊕ *www.davidecenci.com*) is a Roman classic for high-quality clothing and accessories for every occasion, from a sailboat party to a formal wedding. Trench coats, cashmere sweaters, and beautifully tailored ready-to-wear, are Cenci specialties. Their know-how translates into a comfortable dress code with a perfect fit and inspiring color combinations in the finest materials. Alterations can also be done quickly, with purchases delivered directly to your hotel.

★ **Il Cuoio Cucito a Mano** (✉ *Via di S. Ignazio 38, Navona* ☎ *06/6795119*) actually translates as "leather sewn by hand." This little boutique tucked away in a side street produces an amazing variety of handcrafted clothes and accessories. Antonio Ferretti makes his exclusive bags from top-quality leather tanned in Tuscany, while Maria Rita Tegolini designs knitted tops, dresses, and two-piece outfits in bold and striking colors. For men, there are waistcoats, ties, and sweaters. They will also make to order.

Fodor's Choice
★
L'Anatra all'Arancia (✉ *Via Tiburtina 105, San Lorenzo* ☎ *06/4456293*) has the locals in this bustling working-class district agog at its window displays of flowing innovative designer clothes from Marina Spadafora, Marithé + François Girbaud, Sonia Speciale, and Donatella Baroni (the store's owner and buyer). The men's shop is across the road at No. 130, where style-conscious hipsters can find pure linen shirts and trousers in unusual colors. The clientele includes university students and Italian TV and stage personalities who live in this boho neighborhood.

TEENS'
CLOTHING
Fiorucci (✉ *Via Nazionale 236/A, Repubblica* ☎ *06/4883175* ⊕ *www. fiorucci.it*) displays its signature angels on T-shirts, which tend to delight adolescents (and some aggressively youthful women). Downstairs are feminine dresses, skirts, and blouses by Fiorucci, Kenzo, Gaultier Soleil, Kookai, and D&G. Upstairs are kitschy shoes, gadgets, and T-shirts by Indian Rose and Miss Sixty. Clothes are for the young at heart and mostly affordable.

Hydra (✉ *Via Urbana 139, Monti* ☎ *06/48907773*) is an avant-garde clothing shop for older teens and twentysomethings who believe clothing should make a statement. Styles range from voluptuous Betty Boop retro dresses, to Indie underground to in-your-face T-shirts that would make your grandmother blush.

Replay (✉ *Via della Rotonda 25, Navona* ☎ *06/6833073* ⊕ *www.replay. it*), is a typical example of young Italians' passion for American trends. Jeans and T-shirts with American sports teams emblazoned on them have that little extra kiss of Italian styling that transforms sloppy hip into fashionable casual chic. Styles range from punk to hip-hop. Clothes are rugged and moderately priced.

VINTAGE
CLOTHING
In Rome, fashion archaeology is all about mystery—and of course the flaunting of a one-of-a-kind vintage look that provokes an envious "Where'd you get that?" With several shops showcased around Piazza Navona, Monti, and San Lorenzo, it can be easy to dig up a 1970s Armani or a suede fringe jacket worthy of Janis Joplin.

★ **Le Gallinelle** (✉ *Via del Boschetto 76, Monti* ☎ *06/4881017*) is a tiny boutique in a former butcher's shop—hence the large metal hooks. Owner Wilma Silvestri transforms vintage, ethnic, and contemporary fabrics into retro-inspired clothing with a modern edge without smelling like mothballs from your great aunt Suzie's closet.

Mado (✉ *Via del Governo Vecchio 89/a, Navona* ☎ *06/6875028*) has been vintage cool in Rome since 1969 and is still a leader in nostalgia styling. The shop is funky, glamorous, and often over-the-top wacky. Whether you are looking for a robin's-egg-blue empire-waist dress or a '50s gown evocative of a lindy-hop, Mado understands the challenges of incorporating vintage pieces into a modern wardrobe.

La vita è bella, non? Add shopping to the passeggiata evening stroll and who knows what will happen!

Pifebo (⊠ *Via dei Volsci 101, San Lorenzo* ☎ *No phone*) is a sensational San Lorenzo vintage-clothing emporium packed with thousands of items. The boutique has a loyal following of university students, offbeat musicians, and even the occasional costume designer. Specializing in '80s and '90s clothes and shoes, the prices are great.

Vestiti Usati Cinzia (⊠ *Via del Governo Vecchio 45, Navona* ☎ *06/6832945*) has mainly 1960s and '70s styles—there's a fun, unique, and diverse inventory of vintage apparel beloved by private clients, costume designers, and fashion designers and stylists alike. You'll find lots of flower power and psychedelic clothing here, along with trippy boots and dishy shoes that Twiggy would have loved.

WOMEN'S
CLOTHING
★

Antiprima (⊠ *Via Quattro Fontane, 38/41, Monti* ☎ *06/4828445*) is filled with revolutionary ready-to-wear separates that make a bold statement. Carrying a large selection of day and evening wear constructed with lustrous fabrics, the style here is offbeat. A deliberate contradiction of colors make the clothing dazzlingly original. Friendly and helpful staff have a unique eye for putting together accessories and shoes from their ever-changing collection.

Arsenale (⊠ *Via del Governo Vecchio 64, Navona* ☎ *06/6861380*) has a sleek layout and a low-key elegance that stands out, even in Rome. Rest your feet awhile in an overstuffed chair before sifting through the racks. Whether you are looking for a wedding dress or a seductive bustier, you are bound to find something unconventional here. Designer and owner Patriza Pieroni creates many of the pieces on display, all cleverly cut and decidedly captivating.

Elena Mirò (✉ *Via Frattina 11–12, Piazza di Spagna* ☎ 06/6784367 ⊕ *www. elenamiro.com* ✉ *Via Nazionale 197, Repubblica* ☎ 06/4823881) is a friendly and attentive shop from an up-and-coming atelier making Italian vogue history designing clothes for those of us who don't have the dimensions of Kate Moss. The label's mission is to make European-styled women's clothing for size 46 (U.S. size 12, U.K. size 14) and up. Using strong, contrasting colors and strikingly posh fabrics, the line of day and evening wear is trendy and sexy, a celebration of what curves are all about.

Galassia (✉ *Via Frattina 21, Piazza di Spagna* ☎ 06/6797896) has ingenious and extravagant women's styles by Gaultier, Westwood, and Yamamoto. If you are the type who dares to be different, you will love their funky hats, feather boas, and flashy costume jewelry, strikingly in contrast with the shop's austere gray walls and black floor.

Save the Queen (✉ *Via del Babuino 49, Spagna* ☎ 06/36003039 ⊕ *www. savethequeen.com*) is a hot Florentine design house with exotic and creative pieces for women and girls with artistic and renaissance frills, cut-outs, and textures. The dresses, shirts, and skirts are ultrafeminine and not the least bit discreet. Pieces radiate charm, and the silhouette is youthful chic.

Le Tartarughe (✉ *Via Piè di Marmo 17, Navona* ☎ 06/6792240) can be found at two locations close to the Pantheon. Up-and-coming design star Susanna Liso, a Rome native, adds elements of oriental styling to her haute couture and ready-to-wear lines. Here you can select a decorative obi-sashed skirt made with natural fibers and touches of raw silk or a billowy kimono-sleeved blouse that is unlike anything you will find back home.

★ **Maga Morgana** (✉ *Via del Governo Vecchio 27, Navona* ☎ 06/6879995) is a family-run business where everyone's nimble fingers contribute to producing the highly original clothes and accessories. From hippie chick to bridal chic, designer Luciana Iannace creates lavishly ornate clothes that are as inventive as they are distinguishing. Her son Marco makes natural-dyed knitwear and tops, while his twin brother Fabio fashions the original sculptures you can see in both shops.

Mariella Burani (✉ *Via Bocca di Leone 28, Piazza di Spagna* ☎ 06/6790630 ⊕ *www.mariellaburana.com*) has classy yet sensual ready-to-wear that borrows judiciously from several of the company's other principal lines. The clothes are highly wearable and never boring. Recently they have begun adding jewelry and accessories to complete their fashion portfolio.

Red Frame Shop (✉ *Via degli Equi, 70, San Lorenzo* ☎ 06/4955795) is a small and somewhat hard-to-find boutique that is identified only by its red-brick framed door. Open odd hours, the shop is filled with original sweaters and skirts, each handmade with attention to detail. If you don't find what you want in your size, let the owner know and they can make it for you.

★ **Victory** (✉ *Via S. Francesco a Ripa 19, Trastevere* ☎ 06/5812437) spotlights youthful, lighthearted styles that are a hit with the college crowd.

Created by stylists such as Rose D, Nina, Alessandrini, and Marithé et François Girbaud, victory's clothing is made for flaunting.

COSMETICS AND PERFUME

Antica Erboristeria Romana (⊠ *Via Torre Argentina 15, Navona* 🕾 *06/6879493* ⊕ *www.anticaerboristeriaromana.it*) has maintained its old-world apothecary feel, complete with hand-labeled wooden drawers holding its more than 200 varieties of herbs, flowers, and tinctures including aper, licorice, hellbane. The shop stocks an impressive array of herbal teas and infusions, more than 700 essential oils, bud derivatives, and powdered extracts.

Castelli (⊠ *Via Frattina 54, Piazza di Spagna* 🕾 *06/6790339; 06/6780066 beauty salon* ⊕ *www.profumeriecastelli.com* ⊠ *Via Condotti 22, Piazza di Spagna* 🕾 *06/6790998* ⊠ *Via Oslavia 5, Vatican* 🕾 *06/3728312*) is a perfumed paradise offering everything imaginable in the way of beauty aids, cosmetics, and hair accessories, plus a dazzling selection of high-quality costume jewelry. Writer James Joyce started his masterpiece *Ulysses* in what is now the Castelli beauty salon at Via Frattina 52, where Rome's high-society ladies still go for treatments and pampering.

★ **Ai Monasteri** (⊠ *Corso del Rinascimento 72, Navona* 🕾 *06/68802783* ⊕ *www.monasteri.it*) has dark-wood paneling, choirlike alcoves, and painted angels. Here you'll find traditional products made by Italy's diligent friars and monks. The herbal decoctions, liqueurs, beauty aids, and toiletries are all explained in English, as well as Italian. The recipe for its Elixir dell'Amore (love potion) is centuries old, or opt for a bottle of its always popular Elixir of Happiness. There are myriad products, ranging from bath oils specially formulated to protect your suntan, colognes for children, quince-apple jams, Royal Jelly honeys, Barolo grappas, and a wide array of skin treatments.

Fodor's Choice **Profumeria Materozzoli** (⊠ *Piazza San Lorenzo in Lucina 5, Piazza di* ★ *Spagna* 🕾 *06/68892686*) is the place to go if you are searching for hard-to-find perfumes and old-world shaving supplies. Located on the ground floor of the aristocratic Palazzo Fiano on the site where workmen discovered Augustus's Altar of Peace, the Ara Pacis, in 1568, this La Belle Epoque perfumeria is a mixture of spicy scents and European attention to detail. Founded as an herbalist shop in 1870, their pomades and perfumes were a favorite with the aristocracy and those in service to it. With an expansive line of Italian, English, and French perfumes, the shop continues to attract those with a sense of tradition and refinement. Not sure what scent befits the guy or gal in your life? Ask their knowledgeable staff to introduce you to the magical Florentine perfumes created by Lorenzo Villoresi, whose clients included the late Jackie Onassis and Madonna.

PRO FVMUM Durante (⊠ *Via Ripetta 10, Spagna* 🕾 *06/3200306*) lives by the family's motto that a scent can be more memorable than a photograph. Started in 1996 by the grandchildren of Celestino Durante, this perfume label is fast on its way to becoming a new cult classic in Italian fragrance design. Each of the 20 scents is designed to be unisex and comes complete with a poem that describes the intention of the artisans. Pricey but worth it, some of their top-selling perfumes are Acqua e Zucchero, Fiore d'Ambra, Thvndra, Vola Az 686 (named after a direct flight from Rome to the Caribbean), and Ichnvsa.

FOOD, WINE, AND DELICACIES

La Bottega del Cioccolata (⌧ *Via Leonina 82, Monti* ☎ *06/4821473*) is the first shop you'll smell when walking down this picturesque street. Master chocolate maker Maurizio Proietti and his father before him have been making chocolates as mouth-watering and beautiful as those seen in the famous film *Chocolat*.

Buccone (⌧ *Via di Ripetta 19, Piazza del Popolo* ☎ *06/3612154* ⊕ *www. enotecabuccone.com*) is a landmark wine shop inside the former coach house of the Marquesse Cavalcabo. Its 10 layers of shelves are packed with quality wines and spirits ranging in price from a few euros to several hundred for rare vintages. The old ambience has been preserved with the original wood-beamed ceiling and an antique till. You can also buy sweets, biscuits, and packaged candy perfect for inexpensive gifts. Lunch is available daily and dinner is served Friday and Saturday (reservations essential). Book a week in advance, and they can also give you a guided wine tasting, highlighting vintages from many of Italy's important wine-producing regions.

Castroni (⌧ *Via Cola di Rienzo 196, Vatican* ☎ *06/6874383* ⌧ *Via Nazionale 71, Nazionale* ☎ *06/48947474*) has a broad and aromatic range of food products from all over the world. This is where expatriates and study-abroad students come to find specialties from home like pumpkin pie spices, maple syrup, and British tea biscuits. You'll also find plenty of Italian goodies and several roasts of Italian coffee that are some of the best in the city and their new Via Nazionale superstore will leave foodies smiling for a long time.

Enoteca al Parlamento (⌧ *Via dei Prefetti 15, Navona* ☎ *06/6873446* ⊕ *www.enotecaalparlamento.it*) is filled with gastronomic treasures. The tantalizing smell of truffles from the snack counter, where a sommelier waits to organize your wine-tasting session, is enough alone to lure you in. This is another of the city's traditional enoteca wine shops and its proximity to Montecitorio, the Italian Parliament building, makes it a favorite with journalists and politicos who often stop in for a glass of wine after work. Ask to take a look at the enoteca's most prized possessions: bottles of the Brunello di Montalcino vintages 1891 and 1925, strictly not for sale.

Moriondo e Gariglio (⌧ *Via Piè di Marmo 21, Navona* ☎ *06/6990856*) is the Willy Wonka of Roman chocolate factories. Opening its doors in 1850, the shop uses the finest cocoa beans and adheres strictly to family recipes passed down from generation to generation. Known for rich, gourmet chocolates, they soon were the favored chocolatier to the House of Savoy. In 2009, the shop partnered with Bvlgari and placed 300 pieces of jewelry in their Easter eggs to benefit cancer research. While you may not find diamonds in your bonbons, marrons glacés, or dark-chocolate truffles, you'll still delight in choosing from more than 80 delicacies.

Trimani Vinai a Roma dal 1821 (✉ *Via Goito 20, Repubblica* ☎ 06/4469661 🖥 *www.trimani.com*) is one of Rome's best-known enotecas. For more than 180 years, this shop has been the place for French and Italian wines, spumante, and liqueurs. With a selection of more than 1,000 bottles from all regions of Italy managed by knowledgeable wine stewards, Trimani will give you the opportunity to explore the country's diverse wine regions without leaving the city.

Fodor's Choice ★ **Volpetti** (✉ *Via Marmorata 47, Testaccio* ☎ 06/5742352), a Roman institution, sells excellent, if pricey, cured meats and salami. You'll also find a vast selection of cheeses, genuine buffalo-milk mozzarella (much tastier that the more common cow's milk version), balsamic vinegars, olive oils, and pastas made with tomatoes, spinach, or squid ink.

Urbana47 (✉ *Via Urbana 47, Monti* ☎ 06/47884006) is both bohemian café and food vendor. The place is furnished with gently used couches and chairs from Zoc, a retro store in nearby Via delle Zoccolette, which is owned by the same people. Artisanal cured meets and cheeses are purchased fresh from local Lazio producers as part of the zero-kilometer food movement—perfect for a picnic!

HANDBAGS AND LUGGAGE

Really good bags—the classic kind that you can carry for years—are not inexpensive. Almost all the leading fashion houses have their own line of bags, but there are also hundreds of small, lesser-known companies producing bags of good quality that are gentler on the pocketbook.

A. Testoni (✉ *Via Condotti 80, Piazza di Spagna* ☎ 06/6788944) is known for its handmade leather bags, wallets, and shoes. Their soft, calfskin sneakers, and matching messenger bags all carry the fire-embossed "T" insignia. Their limited-edition "Turtle bag," with interlaced strips of leather, is perfect for fashionably carrying just about anything and is certain to become a collector's item.

★ **Bracciolini** (✉ *Via Mario De' Fiori 73, Piazza di Spagna* ☎ 06/6785750) is an innovative Florentine stylist. The bags are authentic works of art, with eccentric shapes, like little gold taxis or Santa Fe stagecoaches. The delightfully quirky beach bags have picture postcard scenes of Italian resorts made of brightly colored appliquéd leather: expensive, but to treasure.

Furla (✉ *Piazza di Spagna 22* ☎ 06/69200363) has 15 franchises in Rome alone. Its flagship store, to the left of the Spanish Steps, sells bags like hot cakes. Be prepared to fight your way through crowds of passionate handbag lovers, all anxious to possess one of the delectable bags, wallets, or watch straps in ice-cream colors.

Gherardini (✉ *Via Belsiana 48/b, Piazza di Spagna* ☎ 06/6795501) has taken over a deconsecrated church and slickly transformed it into a showplace for their label, which is known for its retro handbags and logo-stamped synthetic materials. In business since 1885, Gherardini's leather totes, colorful bags, and soft luggage are truly classic and worth the investment.

★ **Gucci** (✉ *Via Condotti 8, Piazza di Spagna* ☎ 06/6790405) began back in 1906, when Guccio Gucci (hence the double-G trademark) began

15

creating saddles and luggage for the very rich. During the 1920s and '30s, the shop's reputation grew, but it took serendipity to make Gucci a household word. During World War II leather was scarce, so Gucci developed a line of luggage in sturdy canvas, printed with the double-G design and trimmed with woven red-and-green webbing. With that fashion history was made. Purchased by virtually every A-list celebrity, Gucci designs are sensual and lush and sometimes scandalous—think urban and trendy with a little rock star thrown in for spice. Although prices should be lower in Italy, there's no such thing as a Gucci bargain. Gucci means expensive the world over.

Mandarina Duck (⊠ *Via dei Due Macelli 59/F, Piazza di Spagna* ☎ *06/ 6786414*) appeared on the Italian design scene in 1997. The design team of Paolo Trento and Piero Mannato makes snappy, colored soft bags and luggage in durable synthetic fabrics, with the Mandarina Duck logo trim. With numerous zippered pockets, they are eminently practical in form and design and can be folded up and slipped easily into a suitcase. An added bonus, many of their bags are washable, a boon to travelers.

★ **Serafini Ferruccio Pelletteria** (⊠ *Via Caio Mario 14, Vatican* ☎ *06/3211719*) is one of Rome's last remaining saddlers. Fifty years ago, there were more than 200 workshops in Rome making handmade leather handbags and shoes, but today only a handful of these artisans remain. In this subterranean emporium, both Bobby and Jack Kennedy once ordered loafers and Marlon Brando fancied the maker's doeskin moccasins. Today, at 75, Serafini still works the leather just as he has since beginning his career in the 1940s. Discerning clients adore him for his lavish retro-styled handbags. For those who love a provocative and sexy look that challenges the traditional, take a look at the collection of Era Balestrieri, Serafini's precocious apprentice. Her edgy designs emphasize supple sensuality in a contemporary approach that accentuates both the choice of leather and dramatic contrast coloring. Choose from premade stock or, if you have time, select your own style and accompanying leathers. Custom work takes 3–10 days.

HATS, GLOVES, AND TIES

Borsalino Boutique (⊠ *Piazza del Popolo 20, Corso* ☎ *06/32650838* ⊕ *www.borsalino.it*) may be expensive, but there is a reason for the exorbitant prices. Considered by many to be the Cadillac of fedoras, the Borsolino has been a staple of the fashionable Italian man since 1857. Today, few hats are made with such exacting care and attention; the company's milliners still use machines that are more than 100 years old.

La Coppola Storta (⊠ *Via delle Croce 81/a, Pantheon* ☎ *06/6785824* ⊕ *www.lacoppolastorta.com*) describes a type of Sicilian beret and the jaunty way it was worn by Mafiosi. They say the more the hat was twisted to the side, the more connected the wearer was to organized crime. In defiance of Mafia influence across Sicily, activist Guido Agnello helped to open a factory in San Giuseppe specializing in the manufacture of these colorful caps, giving jobs to local sewers, many of whom were previously unemployed or connected to the black market.

With the help of some of Italy's best designers, they have created a line of dapper Coppola for adults, children, and even puppies, which have become a sought-after fashion accessory and an unexpected ambassador for the anti-mafia struggle all over the world. With every color and fabric imaginable, hat prices start at €55.

Di Cori (✉ *Piazza di Spagna 53* ☎ *06/6784439*) packs a lot of gloves into a tiny space, offering a rainbow of color choices. Made of the softest lambskin, and lined with silk, cashmere, rabbit fur, or wool, a pair of these gloves will ensure warm and fashionable hands. They also carry a smaller selection of unlined, washable versions.

Roxy (✉ *Via Frattina 115, Piazza di Spagna* ☎ *06/6796691* ✉ *Via Barberini 112, Barberini* ☎ *06/4883931*) is filled with rows of silk ties in every color and pattern. Their selection is bewilderingly large and moderately priced, and the store is usually packed with customers.

Sermoneta (✉ *Piazza di Spagna 61* ☎ *06/6791960*) allures with its stacks of nappa leather, deerskin, and pigskin gloves in all colors. They carry an internationally known, diverse selection of hand-stitched gloves (lined or unlined) for men and women. You can even find opera-length gloves for those special evenings or you can have your purchases personalized with initials, logos, and other designs.

JEWELRY

Agua (✉ *Via della Vite 57, Piazza di Spagna* ☎ *06/69380699*) is the brainchild of a group of four young Roman designers, who make striking chunky jewelry, mostly in silver with semiprecious stones, amber, and pearls. Their enormous rings will never go unnoticed.

Art Privé (✉ *Via Leonina 8, Monti* ☎ *06/47826347*) is a small, brightly lighted little shop, where Tiziana Salzano designs charming jewelry sets and individual pieces inspired by nature—flowers and butterflies are favorite themes.

Buccellati (✉ *Via Condotti 31, Piazza di Spagna* ☎ *06/6790329* ⊕ *www.buccellati.com*) is a tradition-rich gold and silversmith established in 1919. Inspired by the jewelry of Italian Renaissance, its patriarch, Mario Buccellati, opened his original store near the La Scala opera house in Milan. With a sharp eye for luxurious stones and meticulous skill, Mario created distinctive collections that were sought after by European royalty, princes, and the famous Italian poet Gabriele D'Annunzio. Since then, three generations of family designers have continued to uphold his creative commitment, designing fine handmade Italian jewelry that is as much art as heirloom. Pieces are often elaborately worked in the serginato style and some collections currently reflect Greek as well as Renaissance Italian influences. If you are looking for a piece of jewelry you will want to pass down from generation to generation, this is the place to find it.

Bulgari (✉ *Via Condotti 10, Piazza di Spagna* ☎ *06/6793876* ✉ *Via Condotti 61, Piazza di Spagna*) is to Rome what Tiffany's is to New York and Cartier is to Paris. Every capital city has its famous jeweler and Bulgari allures star customers ranging from Queen Juliana of the Netherlands to Nicole Kidman. In the middle of the 19th century, the great-grandfather of the current Bulgari brothers began working with silver in his native Greece. He later moved to Rome, where, with his son, he started perfecting a style that used Byzantine-style gold and cabochon precious stones. Bulgari's current must-have is their line of women's serpent watches. These retro pieces sparkle with diamonds or semi-precious stones and will look glamorous on any princess.

Creazioni D'Arte Diego Percossi Papi (⊠ *Via Sant'Eustachio 16, Navona* ☎ *06/68801466* ⊕ *www.percossipapi.com*) has his tiny atelier in the former mews of the ancient Sant'Eustachio church. This Roman master jeweler has a client list that includes Hollywood starlets and royalty. Specializing in Renaissance-influenced pieces, he creates stunning, one-of-a-kind pieces featuring emeralds, rubies, pearls, and semiprecious stones.

Fodor's Choice **Gioielli in Movimento** (⊠ *Via della Stelletta 22/b, Navona* ☎ *06/6867431*)
★ draws famous customers who, like us, are hooked on Carlo Cardena's ingenious designs. Carlo's "Twice as Nice" earrings, which can be transformed from fan-shaped clips into elegant drops, were Uno Erre's best-selling earrings between 1990 and 1998; his "Up and Down" pendant and earrings, from his recent collection, are bound to be his next hits.

Orologi e Design (⊠ *Via Urbana 123, Navona* ☎ *06/4742284*) specializes in nostalgic mechanical watches and chronographs from the 1900s through the 1970s. Whether you are looking for a solid gold dress watch or a vintage World War II military pilot's chronograph, chances are you'll find the piece you are looking for here. Have an heirloom piece that has stopped working or that needs a little tuning? Two expert watchmakers have the parts and skilled precision to clean, regulate, and repair your grandfather's vintage timepiece and get it tick-tocking again in no time.

LINGERIE AND LINENS

Brighenti (⊠ *Via Frattina 7–10, Piazza di Spagna* ☎ *06/6791484*) looks like what it is—a traditional Roman shop from a gentler era, replete with a marble floor and a huge crystal chandelier suspended overhead. Sensual silk nightgowns and exquisite peignoirs that have a vintage silver screen feel are displayed downstairs. Upstairs are swimsuits and underwear crafted with wonderful attention to detail.

★ **Cesari** (⊠ *Via del Babuino 195, Piazza di Spagna* ☎ *06/3613456*) is where Italian brides traditionally buy their trousseaux. The frilly, seductive lingerie, high-quality household linens, and sumptuous decorator fabrics are a dream for old-fashioned girls of all ages.

Frette (⊠ *Piazza di Spagna 11* ☎ *06/6790673* ⊠ *Via Nazionale 80, Repubblica* ☎ *06/4882641*) has been a leader in luxurious linens and towels for homes and hotels since 1860. Their sophisticated bed linens in cotton satine, percale, and silk are just what the doctor ordered for a great night's sleep. You'll find lower prices here than you will at their American outposts.

La Perla (⊠ *Via Condotti 78/79, Piazza di Spagna* ☎ *06/69941934* ⊕ *www.laperla.com*) has glamorous lingerie and lacy underwear for that special night, your bridal trousseau, or to just spoil yourself on your Roman Holiday. If you like decadent finery that is both stylish and romantic, you will find something here for sure will make you feel like a princess.

Marisa Padovan (✉ *Via delle Carrozze 81, Piazza di Spagna* ☎ 06/6793946) is the place to go for exclusive, made-to-order lingerie and bathing suits. The shop has been sewing for Hollywood starlets like Audrey Hepburn and the well-heeled women of Rome for more than 40 years. Whether you want to purchase a ready-made style trimmed with Swarovski crystals and polished turquoise stones or to design your own bikini or one-piece, their made-to-measure precision is unbeatable.

Tebro (✉ *Via dei Prefetti 46–54, Navona* ☎ 06/6873441 ⊕ *www.tebro.it*), which first opened its doors in 1867, is listed with the Associazione Negozi Storici di Roma (Associaction of Historic Shops of Rome). A classic Roman department store that epitomizes quality, Tebro specializes in household linens and sleepwear. You can even find those 100-percent cotton, Italian waffle-weave bath sheets that are synonymous with Italian hotels.

15

Venier e Colombo (✉ *Via Frattina 79, Piazza di Spagna* ☎ 06/6787705) is one of Rome's most historic shops. For the coquette that favors retro classicism and has a penchant for all things Victorian, the shop offers a breathtaking selection of lace-trimmed lingerie and linens, as well as exquisite christening robes for babies and hand-embroidered lavender bags.

Yamamay (✉ *Piazza di Spagna 33, Piazza di Spagna* ☎ 06/69190953 ⊕ *www.yamamay.it*) is the place to get intimate with celebrity lines in Rome. With anything from Jennifer Lopez's new JLO swimwear and lingerie collection to Yamamay's own line, there are plenty of elegant pieces here, in a range of hues, from bottle-green to a dark winter's grey. There are branches of the store located throughout the city.

MUSIC AND FILMS

Most video stores have a section with English and American movies in the original language, sometimes with Italian subtitles.

Disfunzioni Musicali (✉ *Via Estruschi 4–5, San Lorenzo* ☎ 06/45436094) is a San Lorenzo landmark for both new and used underground records. Tightly packed and with music always blaring, the store has an extensive selection of new and used CDs and vinyl records of all genres.

Messaggerie Musicali (✉ *Via del Corso 472, Piazza di Spagna* ☎ 06/684401) has central Rome's largest selections of music, DVDs, and concert tickets. Owned by Mondadori, the store also has a book section.

Remix (✉ *Via del Fiume 8/9, Corso* ☎ 06/3216514 ⊕ *www.re-mix.it*) is an underground favorite for famous producers and distributors of legendary Roman vinyl labels like Sounds Never Seen, ACV, and many others. Specializing in techno, the shop also has a great back catalogue—all at prices new collectors will smile about.

SHOES

Roman women have long had a fascination for fabulous footwear, cramming their closets full of impractical but delicious high-heeled concoctions. Not surprisingly, Rome's shoe stores seem to be as numerous as the *motorini* (mopeds) buzzing around downtown. Most Italian shoes are made to a single, average width; if you need a narrower shoe, you may have to try on many before you find the right fit. Valleverde and Melluso brands make wider, softer shoes for men and women.

AVC (⊠ *Via Frattina 141, Piazza di Spagna* ☎ 06/6790891) represents the initials of designer Adriana V. Campanile, whose glamorous creations and eye-catching, supple boots make her a favorite with young Italians. If you are looking for something with a little more style for the kids, check out their children's selection upstairs. The men's shop is inside the Galleria Colonna.

Bruno Magli (⊠ *Via Condotti 6, Piazza di Spagna* ☎ 06/69292121 ⊕ *www.brunomagli.it*) has high-end, well-crafted, classically styled shoes for both men and women. Magli and his siblings Marino and Maria learned the art of shoemaking from their father and grandfather. From its humble family origins to the corporate design powerhouse it has become today, Bruno Magli footwear always has kept the focus on craftsmanship: It's not uncommon for 30 people to touch each shoe during the course of its manufacture.

Fausto Santini (⊠ *Via Frattina 120, Piazza di Spagna* ☎ 06/6784114 ⊕ *www.faustosantini.it*) gives a hint of extravagance in minimally decorated, all-white show windows displaying surprising shoes that fashion mavens love. For almost 20 years, Santini has successfully attracted an avant-garde clientele of both men and women who flock to his preppy-hipster/nerdy-chic shoes which are bright and colorful, and sport unusual forms.

Salvatore Ferragamo (⊠ *Via Condotti 64, Piazza di Spagna* ☎ 06/6781130 ⊕ *www.salvatoreferragamo.it* ⊠ *Via Condotti 73/74, Piazza di Spagna* ☎ 06/6791565) is one of the top-10 most-wanted men's footwear brands. Ferragamo fans will think they have died and followed the white light when they enter this store, which for years has been providing Hollywood glitterati and discerning clients with unique handmade designs. The Florentine design house also specializes in handbags, small leather goods, men's and women's ready-to-wear, and scarves and ties. Men's styles are found at Via Condotti 64, women's at 73/74.

Fratelli Rossetti (⊠ *Via Borgognona 5/a, Piazza di Spagna* ☎ 06/6782676 ⊕ *www.rossetti.it*) *is* an old-world company with modern attention to customer satisfaction. Well known to shoe hounds, their men's loafers and women's heels aren't the most fashion forward, but there is something to be said for a classically designed shoe with an emphasis on quality and craftsmanship.

★ **Joseph DeBach** (⊠ Vicolo del Cinque 19, *Trastevere* ☎ 06/5562756) is the best kept shoe secret in Rome. Open only in the evenings, when Trastevere diners begin to strut their stuff, Debach's creations are more art than foot covering. Entirely handmade from wood and leather in a small and chaotic studio, his shoes are an obsession among the fashion elite in London, New York, and Tokyo. Styles are capricious and sometimes finished with hand-painted strings, odd bits of comic books, newspapers, or other unexpected bits and baubles.

Superga (⊠ *Via della Maddalena 30/a, Navona* ☎ *06/6868737* ⊕ *www. superga-usa.com*) sells those timeless sneakers that every Italian wears at some point, in classic white or—yum—in a rainbow of colors. If you are a sneakerhead who has been stuck on Converse, be sure to give these Italian brethren a look.

Fodor'sChoice **Tod's** (⊠ *Via Fontanella di Borghese 56a/c, Piazza di Spagna* ☎ *06/*
★ *68210066* ⊕ *www.tods.com*) has gathered a cult following among style mavens worldwide, due in large part to owner Diego Della Valle's ownership of Florence's soccer team. The brand's trademark is its simple, understated designs that are casually classy. Tod's occupies the ground floor in the celebrated 16th-century Palazzo Ruspoli.

STATIONERY

★ **Cartoleria Pantheon dal 1910** (⊠ *Via dei Crociferi 17, Pantheon* ☎ *06/* *69920537* ⊕ *www.pantheon-roma.it*) is the place to go if a blank page inspires you. Whether you're looking for a unique leather journal or fine paper for writing a special note or letter, this extraordinary shop has it all. Hand-bound leather journals in a beautiful array of colors and sizes are the specialty here. Writers and artists can choose from simple, refillable blank journals to fancier journals with thick, handmade sheets of Amalfi paper.

Il Papiro (⊠ *Via del Pantheon 50, Navona* ☎ *06/6795597* ⊕ *www. ilpapirofirenze.it*) sells hand-decorated paper items for those who love being creative when writing, journaling, sketching, or scrapbooking. Famous for their "à la cuve" marbleized paper created using a technique developed in the 17th century, this stationery shop is a must for unique lithography, engraving, and watermarked paper.

Fodor'sChoice **Pineider** (⊠ *Via di Fontanella Borghese 22, Piazza di Spagna* ☎ *06/*
★ *6878369* ⊕ *www.pineider.com*) has been making exclusive stationery in Italy since 1774; this is where Rome's aristocratic families have their wedding invitations engraved and their stationery personalized. For stationery and desk accessories, hand-tooled in the best Florentine leather, it has no equal.

TOYS

Al Sogno (⊠ *Piazza Navona 53* ☎ *06/6864198* ⊕ *www.alsogno.com*) greets you with a life-size stuffed bear in the doorway. Run by the same family for three generations, the shop has a large collection of fanciful puppets as well as collectible dolls, masks, stuffed animals, and an assortment of curios. If you are a fan of *Pinocchio* by Carlo Lorenzini of Collodi, this is where you can buy the original (non-Disney) version of this classic tale. If a teddy bear is too prosaic, how about an almost-life-size giraffe? Just be sure your little one's room has 18-foot ceilings.

★ **Bartolucci** (⊠ *Via dei Pastini 98, Navona* ☎ *06/69190894*) attracts shoppers with a life-size Pinocchio pedaling furiously on a wooden bike. Inside is a shop that would have warmed Gepetto's heart. For more than 60 years and three generations, this family has been making whimsical,

15

handmade curiosities out of pine, including clocks, bookends, bedside lamps, and wall hangings. You can even buy a child-size vintage car entirely made of wood, including the wheels.

Bertè (✉ *Piazza Navona 107–111* ☎ *06/6875011*) is one of the oldest toy shops in Rome and carries a large selection of stuffed animals, dolls, Legos, and other collectibles. It specializes in dolls, both the crying, eating, and talking types, as well as the ribbon-bedecked old-fashioned beauties.

La Città del Sole (✉ *Via della Scrofa 65, Navona* ☎ *06/68803805*) is the progressive parent's ideal store, chock-full of educational toys arranged by age. This Rome branch has shelves and floor are crammed with puzzles, gadgets, books, and toys in safe plastics and wood sure to light up your child's eyes.

Side Trips from Rome

WORD OF MOUTH

"With sufficient time to visit the Villa d'Este gardens, you can have a coffee in the small restaurant there, see some of Tivoli (and enjoy lunch in town if you wish), and then make your way on to Villa Adriana using a bus that stops a short distance from Villa d'Este."

—Julia1

Updated by
Margaret
Stenhouse

All roads may lead to Rome, but today's sightseers should take a cue from imperial emperors and Renaissance popes and head fuori porta—"beyond the gates." In one such locale, the province known as Lazio, those privileged people built spectacular palaces and patrician villas in hopes of exchanging the overheated air of the capitol for a breath of refreshing country air. So why not follow their lead and head to the hills for a change of scenery?

The province surrounding Rome is called Lazio and it remains one of Italy's most fascinating but least known regions. Befitting the former playground of popes, princes, and prelates, it offers a spectacular harvest of sights. At Tivoli, Hadrian's Villa reveals the scale of individual imperial Roman egos—an emperor's dream come true, it was the personal creation of the scholarly ruler, who, with all the resources of the known world at his command, filled his vast retreat with structures inspired by ancient monuments that had impressed him during his world travels. Moving on to Tivoli's Villa d'Este, you can see how a worldly cardinal diverted a river so that he could create a garden stunningly set with hundreds of fountains, demonstrating that the arrival of the Renaissance did not diminish the bent of the ruling classes for self-aggrandizement. To the east lies Ostia Antica, called the "Pompeii" of Rome; to the south, the enchanting Castelli Romani villages, dotted with great castles and lovely lakes. Obviously, if Lazio weren't so obscured by the glare and fame of nearby Rome, it would be one of Italy's star attractions.

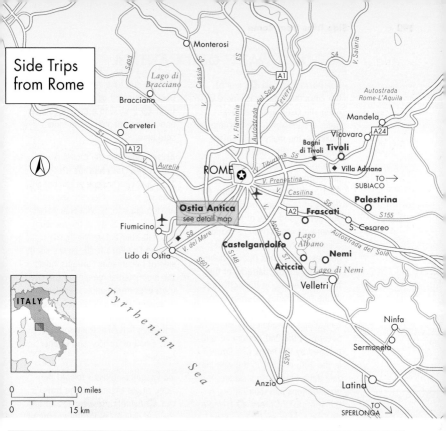

OSTIA ANTICA

26 km (16 mi) west of Rome.

GETTING HERE

The best way to get to Ostia Antica is by train. The Ostia Lido train leaves every half hour from the station adjacent to Rome's Piramide Metro B subway station, stopping off at Ostia Antica en route. The trip takes 35 minutes. By car, take the Via del Mare that leads off from Rome's EUR district. Be prepared for heavy traffic, especially at peak hours, on weekends, and in summer.

EXPLORING

Founded around the 4th century BC, Ostia served as Rome's port city for several centuries until the Tiber changed course, leaving the town high and dry. What has been excavated here is a remarkably intact Roman town in a pretty, parklike setting. Fair weather and good walking shoes are essential. On hot days, be here when the gates open or go late in the afternoon. A visit to the excavations takes two to three hours, including 20 minutes for the museum. Inside the site, there's a snack bar and a bookshop. Ostia Antica is 30 km (19 mi) southwest of Rome.

A GOOD WALK: OSTIA ANTICA

The **Porta Romana** ❷, one of the city's three gates, is where you enter the Ostia Antica excavations. It opens onto the Decumanus Maximus, the main thoroughfare crossing the city from end to end. To your right, a staircase leads to a platform—the remains of the upper floor of the **Terme di Nettuno** ❸ (Baths of Neptune)—from which you get a good view of the mosaic pavements representing a marine scene with Neptune and the sea goddess Amphitrite. Directly behind the baths are the barracks of the fire department. On the north side of the Decumanus Maximus is the beautiful **Teatro** ❹ (Theater), built by Agrippa, remodeled by Septimius Severus in the 2nd century AD, and restored by the Rome City Council in the 20th century. In the vast Piazzale delle Corporazioni, where trade organizations had their offices, is the **Tempio di Cerere** ❺ (Temple of Ceres)—only appropriate for a town dealing in grain imports, Ceres being the goddess of agriculture. From there you can visit the **Domus di Apuleio** ❻ (House of Apuleius), built in Pompeian style, lower to the ground and with fewer windows than was characteristic of Ostia. Next door, the **Mithraeum** ❼ has balconies and a hall decorated with symbols of the cult of Mithras, a male-only religion imported from Persia.

On Via Semita dei Cippi, just off Via dei Molini, the **Domus della Fortuna Annonaria** ❽ (House of Fortuna Annonaria) is the richly decorated residence of a wealthy Ostian; one of the rooms opens onto a secluded garden. On Via dei Molini you can see a **molino** ❾ (mill), where grain was ground with stones that are still here. Along Via di Diana you come upon a **thermopolium** ❿ (bar) with a marble counter and a fresco depicting the foods sold here.

At the end of Via dei Dipinti is the **Museo Ostiense** ⓫ (Ostia Museum), which displays sarcophagi, massive marble columns, and statuary too large to be shown anywhere else. (The last entry to the museum is a half hour before the Scavi closes.) The **Forum** ⓬, on the south side of Decumanus Maximus, holds the monumental remains of the city's most important temple, dedicated to Jupiter, Juno, and Minerva. It's also the site of other ruins of baths, a basilica (which in Roman times was a hall of justice), and smaller temples.

Via Epagathiana leads toward the Tiber, where there are large **horrea** ⓮ (warehouses) erected during the 2nd century AD for the enormous amounts of grain imported into Rome during the height of the Empire. West of Via Epagathiana, the **Domus di Amore e Psiche** ⓭ (House of Cupid and Psyche), a residence, was named for a statue found here (now on display in the museum); the house's enclosed garden is decorated with marble and mosaic motifs and has the remains of a large pool. The **Casa di Serapide** ⓯ (House of Serapis) on Via della Foce is a 2nd-century multilevel dwelling. Nearby, the **Termi dei Sette Sapienti** ⓰ (Baths of the Seven Wise Men) are named for a group of bawdy frescoes. The **Porta Marina** ⓱ leads to what used to be the seashore and the ancient sinagoga ⓲, from the 4th century AD.

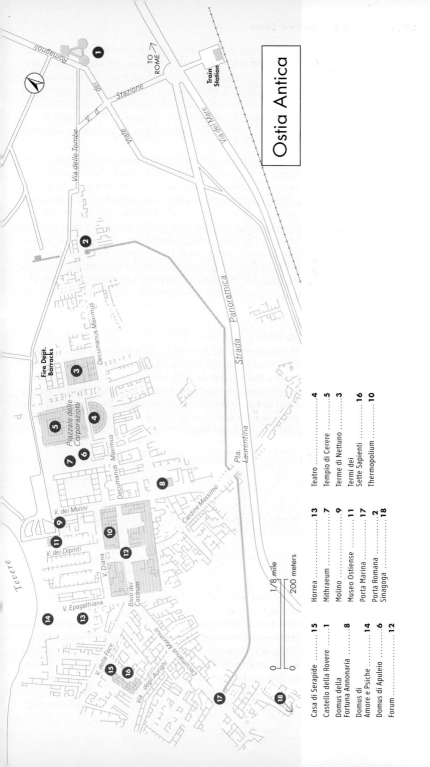

Ostia Antica

To ROME

Train Station

Romagnoli
V. del
Viale
Stazione
Via delle Tombe
Via del Mare
Decumanus Maximus
Strada Panoramica
Fire Dept. Barracks
Piazzale delle Corporazioni
Decumanus Maximus
Pta. Laurentina
Cardine Massimo
V. dei Molini
V. dei Dipinti
V. Diana
Bivio del Castrum
V. Epagathiana
Decumanus Maximus
V. della Foce
V. degli Aurighi
Tevere

1/8 mile
200 meters

Before exploring Ostia Antica's ruins, it's worthwhile to take a tour through the medieval *borgo* (town). The distinctive **Castello della Rovere**, easily spotted as you come off the footbridge from the train station, was built by Pope Julius II when he was the cardinal bishop of Ostia in 1483. Its triangular form is unusual for military architecture. Inside are (badly faded) frescoes by Baldassare Peruzzi. ⊠ *Piazza della Rocca* 📞 *06/56358024* 🎟 *Free* ☉ *Tues.–Sun. tours at 10 and noon; Tues. and Thurs. additional tour at 3.*

Tidal mud and windblown sand covered the ancient port town, which lay buried until the beginning of the 20th century when it was exten-

Fodor's Choice
★

sively excavated. The **Scavi di Ostia Antica** *(Ostia Antica excavations)* continue to be well maintained today. A cosmopolitan population of rich businessmen, wily merchants, sailors, slaves, and their respective families once populated the city. The great warehouses were built in the 2nd century AD to handle huge shipments of grain from Africa; the *insulae* (forerunners of the modern apartment building) provided housing for the city's growing population. Under the combined assaults of the barbarians and the malaria-carrying mosquito, and after the Tiber changed course, the port was eventually abandoned. ⊠ *Viale dei Romagnoli 717* 📞 *06/56350215* 🌐 *www.ostiantica.it* 🎟 *€6.50 includes Museo Ostiense* ☉ *Tues.–Sun. 8:30–1 hr before sunset.*

WHERE TO EAT

$ ✕ **Cipriani.** Tucked away in the little medieval town under the shadow of
ITALIAN   the castle, this cozy trattoria is decorated with reproductions of fresco fragments from a Roman palace. The kitchen offers a varied menu of Roman specialties and seasonal fare. Owner Fabrizio Cipriani speaks English and will be happy to guide you in your choice of dishes and wine from his comprehensive wine list. ⊠ *Via del Forno 11* 📞 *06/56359560* 💳 *AE, DC, MC, V* ☉ *Closed Wed.*

TIVOLI

36 km (22 mi) northeast of Rome.

In ancient times, just about anybody who was anybody had a villa in Tivoli, including Crassius, Trajan, Hadrian, Horace, and Catullus. Tivoli fell into obscurity in the medieval era until the Renaissance, when popes and cardinals came back to the town and built villas showy enough to rival those of their extravagant predecessors. Nowadays Tivoli is small but vibrant, with winding streets and views over the surrounding countryside, including the deep Aniene river gorge, which runs right through the center of town, and comes replete with a romantically sited bridge, cascading waterfalls, and two jewels of ancient Roman architecture that crown its cliffs—the round Temple of Vesta and the ruins of the rectangular Sanctuary of the Sibyl, probably built earlier. These can be picturesquely viewed across the gorge from the park of the Villa Gregoriana park, named for Pope Gregory XVI, who saved Tivoli from chronic river damage by diverting the river through a tunnel, weakening its flow. An unexpected (but not unappreciated) side effect was the creation of the Grande Cascata (Grand Cascade), which shoots a huge jet of water into the valley below. The Villa Gregoriana is at Largo Sant'Angelo (from the Largo Garibaldi bus stop, follow V. Pacifici—it changes name six times—and veer left on V. Roma to the Largo). There's a small admission charge to the park, which affords a sweaty, steep hike down to the river, so you may prefer to repair to the Antico Ristorante Sibilla, set right by the Temple of Vesta. From its dining terrace, you can drink in one of the most memorably romantic landscape views in Italy, one especially prized by 19th-century painters.

GETTING HERE

Unless you have nerves of steel, it's best not to drive to Tivoli. Hundreds of industries line the Via Tiburtina from Rome and bottleneck traffic is nearly constant. You can avoid some, but not all, of the congestion by taking the Roma–L'Aquila toll road. Luckily, there is abundant public transport. Buses leave every 15 minutes from the Ponte Mammolo stop on the Metro A line. The ride takes an hour. Regional Trenitalia trains connect from both Termini and Tiburtina stations and will have you there in under an hour. Villa d'Este is in the town center, and a frequent bus service from Tivoli's main square goes to Hadrian's Villa.

VISITOR INFORMATION

Tivoli tourism office (⊠ *Piazzale Nazioni Unite* ☎ *0774/313536* ⊕ *www. comune.tivoli.rm.it*).

16

EXPLORING

★ The astonishingly grand 2nd-century **Villa Adriana** *(Hadrian's Villa)*, 6 km (4 mi) south of Tivoli, was an emperor's theme park, an exclusive retreat below the ancient settlement of Tibur where the marvels of the classical world were reproduced for a ruler's pleasure. Hadrian, who succeeded Trajan as emperor in AD 117, was a man of genius and intellectual curiosity, fascinated by the accomplishments of the Hellenistic world. From AD 125 to 134, architects, laborers, and artists worked on the villa, periodically spurred on by the emperor himself when he returned from another voyage full of ideas for even more daring constructions (he also gets credit for Rome's Pantheon). After his death in AD 138 the fortunes of his villa declined. It was sacked by barbarians and Romans alike; many of his statues and decorations ended up in the Vatican Museums, but the expansive ruins are nonetheless compelling. It's not the single elements but the delightful effect of the whole that makes Hadrian's Villa a treat. Oleanders, pines, and cypresses growing among the ruins heighten the visual impact. To help you get your bearings, maps are issued free with the audio guides (€4). A visit here takes about two hours, more if you like to savor antiquity slowly. In summer visit early to take advantage of cool mornings. ⊠ *Bivio di Villa Adriana off Via Tiburtina 6 km (4 mi) southwest of Tivoli* ☎ *0774/382733 reservations* 🎟️ *€6.50* ☽ *Daily 9–one hr before sunset.*

★ In the center of Tivoli, **Villa d'Este**, created by Cardinal Ippolito d'Este in the 16th century, was the most amazing pleasure garden of its day and still stuns visitors with its beauty. Inspired by the recent excavation of Villa Adriana and a devotee of the Renaissance celebration of human ingenuity over nature, Este (1509–72) paid architect Pirro Ligorrio an astronomical sum to create a mythical garden with water as its artistic centerpiece. To console himself for his seesawing fortunes in the political intrigues of his time (he happened to be cousin to Pope Alexander VI), he had his builders tear down part of a Franciscan monastery to clear the site, then divert the Aniene River to water the garden and feed the fountains—and what fountains: big, small, noisy, quiet, rushing, running, and combining to create a late-Renaissance, proto–Busby Berkeley masterpiece in which sunlight, shade, water, gardens, and carved stone create an unforgettable experience. To this day, several hundred fountains cascade, shoot skyward, imitate birdsongs, and simulate rain. The musical **Fontana dell'Organo** and the animated **Fontana della Civetta** have been restored to working order: the organ plays a watery tune every two hours from 10:30 to 6:30 (until 2:30 in winter), and the mechanical *civetta* (owl) chases warbling sparrow figures out of the bath every two hours from 10 to 6 (10–2 in winter). Romantics will love the night tour of the gardens and floodlit fountains, available on Friday and Saturday from June until September. Allow at least an hour for the visit, and bear in mind that there are a lot of stairs to climb. There's also a caffè on the upper terrace leading from the palace entrance, where you can sit and admire the view. ⊠ *Piazza Trento 1* ☎ *0774/312070* ⊕ *www.villadestetivoli.info* 🖅 *€6.50* ⊗ *Tues.–Sun. 8:30–one hr before sunset.*

WHERE TO EAT AND STAY

$$$$
ITALIAN
Fodor's Choice
★

✕ **Antico Ristorante Sibilla.** This famed restaurant should be included among the most beautiful sights of Tivoli. Built in 1730 beside the circular Roman Temple of Vesta and the Sanctuary of the Sibyl, the terrace garden has a spectacular view over the deep gorge of the Aniene River, with the thundering waters of the waterfall in the background. Marble plaques on the walls list the royals who have come here to dine over 2½ centuries. In decades gone by, the tour buses arrived and the food suffered. Today, however, food, wine, and service standards are high, as befits the sublime setting. ⊠ *Via della Sibilla 50* ☎ *0774/335281* ⊕ *www.ristorantesibilla.com* 🖃 *AE, DC, MC, V* ⊗ *Closed Mon.*

$$
⛉ **Adriano.** At the entrance to Hadrian's Villa, this small inn is a handy place to have lunch before or after your trip around the ruins. The à la carte restaurant offers delicacies such as risotto *ai fiori di zucchine* (with zucchini flowers) or grilled porcini mushrooms in season, while the coffee shop offers a set lunch menu at a very reasonable price (€14 all inclusive). There is a garden for outdoor dining in summer. In a converted 19th-century mansion, the rooms have old-fashioned furnishings that can't quite qualify as antiques. The dowdy decor would benefit from a makeover. **Pros:** wonderfully location; peaceful garden; attentive service. **Cons:** busloads of tourists disembark under the windows; restaurant can be crowded. ⊠ *Via di Villa Adriana 194* ☎ *0774/382235* ⊕ *www.hoteladriano.it* ➲ *10 rooms* ⚲ *In-room: safe, refrigerator. In-hotel: restaurant, bar, tennis court* 🖃 *DC, MC, V* ⊗ *No dinner Sun. Nov.–Mar.* ⛋ *BP.*

$$
⛉ **Hotel Torre Sant'Angelo.** This deluxe hotel 1 km (½ mi) outside Tivoli has a magnificent view of the old town, the Aniene Falls, and the Temple of the Sybil. For many centuries the building housed a monastery, which became the summer residence of the princes Massimo in 1700.

Reconstructed as a hotel in 1994, its rooms come with Jacuzzi, minibar, air-conditioning, safe, and satellite TV. The elegant restaurant serves Italian and international cuisine. The garden has a swimming pool, and there's a golf course nearby. ⊠ *Via Quintilio Varo* ☎ *0774/332533* ⊕ *www.hoteltorresangelo.it* ⤳ *25 rooms, 10 suites* ⊟ *AE, DC, MC, V* ⊚ *BP.*

THE CASTELLI ROMANI

The "castelli" aren't really castles, as their name would seem to imply. They're little towns that are scattered on the slopes of the Alban Hills near Rome. And the Alban Hills aren't really hills, but extinct volcanoes. There were castles here in the Middle Ages, however, when each of these towns, fiefs of rival Roman lords, had its own fortress to defend it. Some centuries later, the area became given over to villas and retreats, notably the pope's summer residence at Castelgandolfo, and the 17th- and 18th-century villas that transformed Frascati into the Beverly Hills of Rome. Arrayed around the rim of an extinct volcano that encloses two crater lakes, the string of picturesque towns of the Castelli Romani are today surrounded by vineyards, olive groves, and chestnut woods— no wonder overheated Romans have always loved to escape here.

Ever since Roman times, the Castelli towns have been renowned for their wine. In the narrow, medieval alleyways of the oldest parts, you can still find old-fashioned hostelries where the locals sit on wooden benches, quaffing the golden nectar straight from the barrel. Following the mapped-out **Castelli Wine Route** (⊕ *www.stradadeivinideicastelliromani. it*) around the numerous vineyards and wine cellars is a more-sophisticated alternative. Exclusive local gastronomic specialties include the bread of Genzano, baked in traditional wood-fire ovens, the *porchetta* (roast suckling pig) of Ariccia, and the *pupi* biscuits of Frascati, shaped like women or mermaids with three or more breasts (an allusion to ancient fertility goddesses). Each town has its own feasts and saints' days, celebrated with costumed processions and colorful events. Some are quite spectacular, like Marino's annual Wine Festival in October, where the town's fountains flow with wine, or the Flower Festival of Genzano in June, when an entire street is carpeted with millions of flower petals, arranged in elaborate patterns.

FRASCATI

20 km (12 mi) south of Rome.

GETTING HERE
An hourly train service along a single-track line through vineyards and olive groves takes you to Frascati from Termini station. The trip takes 45 minutes. By car, take the Via Tuscolano, which branches off the Appia Nuova road just after St. John Lateran in Rome, and drive straight up.

VISITOR INFORMATION
Frascati Point (tourism office) (⊠ *Piazza G. Marconi 5* ☎ *06/94015378* ⊕ *www.aptprovroma.it*).

EXPLORING

It's worth taking a stroll through Frascati's lively old center. Via Battisti, leading from the Belvedere, takes you into Piazza San Pietro with the imposing gray-and-white cathedral. Inside is the cenotaph of Prince Charles Edward, last of the Scottish Stuart dynasty, who tried unsuccessfully to regain the British Crown, and died an exile in Rome in 1788. A little arcade beside the monumental fountain at the back of the piazza leads into Market Square, where the smell of fresh baking will entice you into the Purificato family bakery to see the traditional pupi biscuits, modeled on old pagan fertility symbols.

Take your pick from the caffè and trattorias fronting the central Piazzale Marconi, or do as the locals do—buy fruit from the market gallery at Piazza del Mercato, then get a huge slice of porchetta from one of the stalls, a hunk of *casareccio* bread, and a few *ciambelline frascatane* (ring-shaped cookies made with wine), and take your picnic to any one of the numerous *cantine* (homey wine bars), and settle in for some sips of tasty, inexpensive vino.

Frascati was the chosen sylvan retreat of prelates and princes, who built magnificent villas on the sun-drenched slopes overlooking the Roman plain. The most spectacular of these is **Villa Aldobrandini,** which dominates Frascati's main square from the top of its steeply sloped park.

Built in the late 16th century and adorned with frescoes by the Zuccari brothers and the Cavalier d'Arpino, the hulking villa is still privately owned by the Princes Aldobrandini. However, its park is a marvel of baroque fountains and majestic box-shaded avenues and you can go and see the magnificent Water Theater that Cardinal Pietro Aldobrandini, Pope Clement VIII's favorite nephew, built to impress his guests, thinking nothing of diverting the water supply that served the entire area in order to make his fountains play. The gigantic central figure of Atlas holding up the world is believed to represent the pope. You can also see another Water Theater in the grounds of nearby Villa Torlonia, which is now a public park. Visitors to the Villa Aldobrandini must apply for a permit from the Frascati Tourist Information office first, located at Piazza Marconi 5. ⊠ *Via Cardinale Massaia* ☎ *06/94015378* 🖃 *Free* ☺ *Weekdays 9–1 and 3–5.*

Villa Aldobrandini looks across Piazza Marconi to the Belvedere terrace, a sort of outdoor parlor for the town. This is a favorite gathering place for young and old alike, especially on summer evenings when the lights of Rome can be seen twinkling in the distance. It's worth taking a stroll through Frascati's lively old center. Via Battisti, leading from the Belvedere, takes you into Piazza San Pietro with the imposing gray-and-white **Cathedral.** Inside is the cenotaph of Prince Charles Edward, last of the Scottish Stuart dynasty, who tried unsuccessfully to regain the British Crown, and died an exile in Rome in 1788. A little arcade beside the monumental fountain at the back of the piazza leads into Market Square, where the smell of fresh baking will entice you into the Purificato family bakery to see the traditional *pupi* biscuits, modeled on old pagan fertility symbols.

Take your pick from the caffè and trattorias fronting the central Piazzale Marconi, or do as the locals do—buy fruit from the market gallery at Piazza del Mercato, then get a huge slice of *porchetta* (roast suckling pig) from one of the stalls, a hunk of *casareccio* bread, and a few *ciambelline frascatane* (ring-shape cookies made with wine), and take your picnic to any one of the numerous local *cantine* (homey wine bars), and settle in for some sips of tasty, inexpensive vino. ⊠ *Via Cardinale Massaia* ☎ *06/9420331 tourist office* ☑ *Free* ☉ *Weekdays 9–1 and 3–6.*

WHERE TO EAT AND STAY

$$$

CENTRAL ITALIAN

★

✕ **Al Fico Vecchio.** This historic coaching inn, dating to the 16th century, is on an old Roman road a couple of miles outside Frascati. It has a charming garden shaded by the old fig tree that gave the place its name. The dining room has been tastefully renovated, preserving many of the characteristic antique features. The menu offers a wide choice of local dishes, such as gnocchi with cheese and truffles. ⊠ *Via Anagnini 257* ☎ *06/9459261* ⊟ *AE, DC, MC, V.*

$$$

★

🏨 **Park Hotel Villa Grazioli.** One of the region's most famous residences, this elegant patrician villa halfway between Frascati and Grottaferrata is now a first-class hotel. Modeled after Rome's Villa Farnesina, the 1580 house was owned over the centuries by the regal Borghese and Odelscalchi families, and was nearly destroyed by bombs in World War II. Happily, the vast reception rooms on the main floor—covered with frescoes of landscapes, mythological figures, and garden scenes by eminent 17th-century painters—survived mostly unscathed. The showpiece remains the South Gallery, frescoed by Giovanni Paolo Pannini in a swirl of trompe-l'oeil scenes, a masterpiece of baroque decorative art. The drama ends when you get to the guest rooms, which are standard-issue salons with white walls and traditional furniture; rooms found in the adjacent rustic-style lodge have lovely wood-beam ceilings. The cherry on top is the luxurious Acquaviva restaurant, where you can enjoy half- or full-board plans. **Pros:** wonderful views of the countryside; elegant atmosphere; professional staff. **Cons:** difficult to find. ⊠ *Via Umberto Pavoni 19, Grottaferrata* ☎ *06/9454001* ⊕ *www.villagrazioli.com* ⇗ *56 rooms, 2 suites* ⌂ *In-room: refrigerator. In-hotel: restaurant, bar, pool* ⊟ *AE, DC, MC, V* �ⓞ *BP.*

16

CASTELGANDOLFO

8 km (5 mi) southwest of Frascati, 25 km (15 mi) south of Rome.

GETTING HERE

There is an hourly train service for Castelgandolfo from Termini station (Rome–Albano line). Otherwise, buses leave frequently from the Anagnina terminal of the Metro A subway. The trip takes about 30 minutes. By car, take the Appian Way from San Giovanni in Rome and follow it straight to Albano, where you branch off for Castelgandolfo (about an hour, depending on traffic).

EXPLORING

This little town is well known as the pope's summer retreat. It was the Barberini pope Urban VIII who first headed here, eager to escape the malarial miasmas that afflicted summertime Rome; before long, the city's princely families also set up country estates around here.

The 17th-century **Villa Pontificia** has a superb position overlooking Lake Albano and is set in one of the most gorgeous gardens in Italy; unfortunately, neither the house nor the park are open to the public (although crowds are admitted into the inner courtyard for papal audiences). On the little square in front of the palace there's a fountain by Bernini, who also designed the nearby Church of San Tommaso da Villanova, which has works by Pietro da Cortona.

The village has a number of interesting craft workshops and food purveyors, in addition to the souvenir shops on the square. On the horizon, the silver astronomical dome belonging to the Specola Vaticana observatory—one of the first in Europe—where the scientific Pope Gregory XIII indulged his interest in stargazing, is visible for miles around.

⟳ The **lakeside lido** is lined with restaurants, ice-cream parlors, and caffè and is a favorite spot with Roman families. No motorized craft are allowed on the lake, but you can rent paddleboats and kayaks. The waters are full of seafowl, such as swans and herons, and nature trails are mapped out along both ends of the shore. All along the central part there are bathing establishments where you can rent deck chairs, or stop to eat a plate of freshly prepared pasta or a gigantic Roman sandwich at one of the little snack bars under the oak and alder trees. There's also a small, permanent fairground for children.

WHERE TO EAT

$$$

CENTRAL ITALIAN

★

✕ **Antico Ristorante Pagnanelli.** One of most refined restaurants in the Castelli Romani, this has been in the same family since 1882. The present generation—Aurelio Pagnanelli, his Australian wife Jane, and their four sons—have lovingly restored this old railway inn perched high above Lake Albano. The dining room windows open onto a breathtaking view across the lake to the conical peak of Monte Cavo. In winter a log fire blazes in a corner; in summer dine out on the flower-filled terrace. Many of the dishes are prepared with produce from the family's own farm. The wine cellar, carved out of the living tufa rock, boasts more than 3,000 labels. ✉ *Via Gramsci 4* ☎ *06/9360004* 🖃 *AE, DC, MC, V.*

ARICCIA

8 km (5 mi) southwest of Castelgandolfo, 26 km (17 mi) south of Rome.

GETTING HERE

For Ariccia, take the COTRAL bus from the Anagnina terminal of the Metro A underground line. All buses on the Albano–Genzano–Velletri line go through Ariccia. If you take a train to Albano, you can proceed by bus to Ariccia or go on foot (it's just under 3 km [2 mi]). If you are driving, follow the Appian road to Albano and carry on to Ariccia.

EXPLORING

Ariccia is a gem of baroque town planning. When millionaire banker Agostino Chigi became Pope Alexander VII, he commissioned Gian Lorenzo Bernini to redesign his country estate to make it worthy of his new station. Bernini consequently restructured not only the existing 16th-century palace, but also the town gates, the main square with its loggias and graceful twin fountains, and the round church of **Santa Maria dell'Assunzione** (the dome is said to be modeled on the Pantheon). The rest of the village coiled around the apse of the church down into the valley below.

Strangely, Ariccia's splendid heritage has been largely forgotten in the 20th century, and yet it was once one of the highlights of every artist's and writer's Grand Tour. Corot, Ibsen, Turner, Longfellow, and Hans Christian Andersen all came to stay here.

★ **Palazzo Chigi** is a rare example of a baroque residence whose original furniture, paintings, drapes, and decorations are still mostly intact. Italian film director Lucchino Visconti used the villa for most of the interior scenes in the film *The Leopard*. The rooms contain intricately carved pieces of 17th-century furniture, as well as textiles and costumes from the 16th to the 20th century. See the Room of Beauties, lined with paintings of the loveliest ladies of the day, and the Nuns' Room, with portraits of 10 Chigi sisters, all of whom took the veil. The park stretching behind the palace is a wild wood, the last remnant of the ancient Latium forest, where herds of deer still graze under the trees. Book ahead for tours in English. ⊠ *Piazza di Corte 14* ☎ *06/9330053* ⊕ *www.palazzochigiariccia.it* ⊠ *€7* ⊗ *Tues.–Fri. at 11, 4, and 5:30; weekends every hr 10:30–6:30.*

WHERE TO EAT

$ ✕ **L'Aricciarola.** Tucked in a corner among the string of informal eateries you find clustered under the Galloro bridge (on the right-hand side of Palazzo Chigi), this is a great place for people-watching while you enjoy the local *porchetta* (whole roast pig stuffed with herbs), washed down with a carafe of local Castelli wine. ⊠ *Via Borgo S. Rocco 9* ☎ *06/9334103* ⊟ *No credit cards* ⊗ *Closed Mon.*

CENTRAL ITALIAN

16

NEMI

8 km (5 mi) west of Ariccia, 34 km (21 mi) south of Rome.

GETTING HERE

Nemi is a bit difficult to get to unless you come by car. Buses from the Anagnina Metro A station go to the town of Genzano, where a local bus travels to Nemi every two hours. If the times aren't convenient, you can take a taxi or walk the 5 km (3 mi) around Lake Nemi. By car, take the panoramic route known as the Via dei Laghi (Road of the Lakes). Follow the Appia Nuova from St. John Lateran and branch off on the well-signposted route after Ciampino airport. Follow the Via dei Laghi toward Velletri until you see signs for Nemi.

EXPLORING

Nemi is the smallest and prettiest village of the Castelli Romani. Perched on a spur of rock 600 feet above the small crater lake of the same name, it has an eagle's-nest view over the rolling Roman countryside as far as the coast some 18 km (11 mi) away. The one main street, Corso Vittorio Emanuele, takes you to the (now privately owned) baronial Castello Ruspoli, with its 11th-century watchtower, and the quaint little Piazza Umberto 1, lined with outdoor caffè serving the tiny wood-strawberries harvested from the crater bowl.

If you continue on through the arch that joins the castle to the former stables, you come to the entrance of the dramatically landscaped public gardens, which curve steeply down to the panoramic **Belvedere** terrace. If you enjoy walking, you can follow the road past the garden entrance and go all the way down to the bottom of the crater.

Nemi may be small, but it has a long and fascinating history. In Roman times it was an important sanctuary dedicated to the goddess Diana that drew thousands of pilgrims from all over the Roman Empire. In the 1930s, the Italian government drained the lake in order to recover two magnificent ceremonial ships, loaded with sculptures, bronzes, and art treasures, that were submerged for 2,000 years. Unfortunately, the ships were burned during World War II. The state-of-the-art **Museo delle Navi Romani** *(Roman Ship Museum)* on the lakeshore, which was built to house them, has scale models and photographs of the complex recovery operation, as well as some finds from the sanctuary. ⊠ *Via del Tempio di Diana 9* ☎ *06/9398040* 🖃 *€2* ☉ *Daily 9–7.*

WHERE TO EAT

$$
ITALIAN

✕ **Specchio di Diana.** Halfway down the main street is the town's most historic inn—Byron reputedly stayed here when visiting the area. A wine bar and caffè are on street level, while the restaurant proper on the second floor offers marvelous views, especially at sunset. Pizzas are popular, but don't neglect Nemi's regional specialties: *fettucine al sugo di lepre* (fettucine with hare sauce), roasted *porcini* mushrooms, and the little wood-strawberries with whipped cream. ⊠ *Corso Vittorio Emanuele 13* ☎ *06/9368805* 🖃 *AE, DC, MC, V.*

ITALIAN
VOCABULARY

ITALIAN VOCABULARY

	ENGLISH	ITALIAN	PRONOUNCIATION
BASICS			
	Yes/no	Sí/No	see/no
	Please	Per favore	pear fa-**vo**-ray
	Yes, please	Sí grazie	see **grah**-tsee-ay
	Thank you	Grazie	**grah**-tsee-ay
	You're welcome	Prego	**pray**-go
	Excuse me, sorry	Scusi	**skoo**-zee
	Sorry!	Mi dispiace!	mee dis-spee-**ah**-chay
	Good morning/ afternoon	Buongiorno	bwohn-**jor**-no
	Good evening	Buona sera	**bwoh**-na **say**-ra
	Good-bye	Arrivederci	a-ree-vah-**dare**-chee
	Mr. (Sir)	Signore	see-**nyo**-ray
	Mrs. (Ma'am)	Signora	see-**nyo**-ra
	Miss	Signorina	see-nyo-**ree**-na
	Pleased to meet you	Piacere	pee-ah-**chair**-ray
	How are you?	Come sta?	**ko**-may **stah**
	Very well, thanks	Bene, grazie	**ben**-ay **grah**-tsee-ay
	Hello (phone)	Pronto?	**proan**-to
NUMBERS			
	one	uno	**oo**-no
	two	due	**doo**-ay
	three	tre	tray
	four	quattro	**kwah**-tro
	five	cinque	**cheen**-kway
	six	sei	say
	seven	sette	**set**-ay
	eight	otto	**oh**-to
	nine	nove	**no**-vay
	ten	dieci	dee-**eh**-chee
	twenty	venti	**vain**-tee

ENGLISH	ITALIAN	PRONOUNCIATION
thirty	trenta	**train**-ta
forty	quaranta	kwa-**rahn**-ta
fifty	cinquanta	cheen-**kwahn**-ta
sixty	sessanta	seh-**sahn**-ta
seventy	settanta	seh-**tahn**-ta
eighty	ottanta	o-**tahn**-ta
ninety	novanta	no-**vahn**-ta
one hundred	cento	**chen**-to
one thousand	mille	**mee**-lay
ten thousand	diecimila	dee-eh-chee-**mee**-la

USEFUL PHRASES

Do you speak English?	Parla inglese?	**par**-la een-**glay**-zay
I don't speak Italian	Non parlo italiano	non **par**-lo ee-tal-**yah**-no
I don't understand	Non capisco	non ka-**peess**-ko
Can you please repeat?	Può ripetere?	pwo ree-**pet**-ay-ray
Slowly!	Lentamente!	**len**-ta-men-tay
I don't know	Non lo so	non lo **so**
I'm American	Sono americano(a)	**so**-no a-may-ree-**kah**-no(a)
I'm British	Sono inglese	so-no een-**glay**-zay
What's your name?	Come si chiama?	**ko**-may see kee-**ah**-ma
My name is . . .	Mi chiamo . . .	mee kee-**ah**-mo
What time is it?	Che ore sono?	kay **o**-ray **so**-no
How?	Come?	**ko**-may
When?	Quando?	**kwan**-doe
Yesterday/today/tomorrow	Ieri/oggi/domani	**yer**-ee/**o**-jee/do-**mah**-nee
This morning/	Stamattina/Oggi	sta-ma-**tee**-na/**o**-jee
afternoon	pomeriggio	po-mer-**ee**-jo

ENGLISH	ITALIAN	PRONOUNCIATION
Tonight	Stasera	sta-**ser**-a
What?	Che cosa?	kay **ko**-za
Why?	Perché?	pear-**kay**
Who?	Chi?	kee
Where is . . .	Dov'è . . .	doe-**veh**
the bus stop?	la fermata dell'autobus?	la fer-**mah**-ta del ow-toe-**booss**
the train station?	la stazione?	la sta-tsee-**oh**-nay
the subway	la metropolitana?	la may-tro-po-lee-**tah**-na
the terminal?	il terminale?	eel ter-mee-**nah**-lay
the post office?	l'ufficio postale?	loo-**fee**-cho po-**stah**-lay
the bank?	la banca?	la **bahn**-ka
the . . . hotel?	l'hotel . . .?	lo-**tel**
the store?	il negozio?	eel nay-**go**-tsee-o
the cashier?	la cassa?	la **kah**-sa
the . . . museum?	il museo . . .?	eel moo-**zay**-o
the hospital?	l'ospedale?	lo-spay-**dah**-lay
the elevator?	l'ascensore?	la-shen-**so**-ray
the restrooms?	Dov'è il bagno?	do-**vay** eel **bahn**-yo
Here/there	Qui/là	kwee/la
Left/right	A sinistra/a destra	a see-**neess**-tra/a **des**-tra
Straight ahead	Avanti dritto	a-**vahn**-tee **dree**-to
Is it near/far?	È vicino/lontano?	ay vee-**chee**-no/lon-**tah**-no
I'd like . . .	Vorrei . . .	vo-**ray**
a room	una camera	**oo**-na **kah**-may-ra
the key	la chiave	la kee-**ah**-vay
a newspaper	un giornale	oon jor-**nah**-lay
a stamp	un francobollo	oon frahn-ko-**bo**-lo
I'd like to buy . . .	Vorrei comprare . . .	vo-**ray** kom-**prah**-ray

ENGLISH	ITALIAN	PRONOUNCIATION
How much is it?	Quanto costa?	**kwahn**-toe **coast**-a
It's expensive/ cheap	È caro/economico	ay **car**-o/ay-ko-**no**-mee-ko
A little/a lot	Poco/tanto	**po**-ko/**tahn**-to
More/less	Più/meno	pee-**oo**/**may**-no
Enough/too (much)	Abbastanza/troppo	a-bas-**tahn**-sa/tro-po
I am sick	Sto male	sto **mah**-lay
Call a doctor	Chiama un dottore	kee-**ah**-mah oondoe-**toe**-ray
Help!	Aiuto!	a-**yoo**-toe
Stop!	Alt!	ahlt
Fire!	Al fuoco!	ahl **fwo**-ko
Caution/Look out!	Attenzione!	a-ten-**syon**-ay

DINING OUT

A bottle of . . .	Una bottiglia di . . .	**oo**-na bo-**tee**-lee-ahdee
A cup of . . .	Una tazza di . . .	**oo**-na **tah**-tsa dee
A glass of . . .	Un bicchiere di . . .	oon bee-key-**air**-ay dee
Bill/check	Il conto	eel **cone**-toe
Bread	Il pane	eel **pah**-nay
Breakfast	La prima colazione	la **pree**-ma ko-la-**tsee**-oh-nay
Cocktail/aperitif	L'aperitivo	la-pay-ree-**tee**-vo
Dinner	La cena	la **chen**-a
Fixed price menu	Menù a prezzo	may-**noo** a **pret**-so **fee**-so
Fork	La forchetta	la for-**ket**-a
I am diabetic	Ho il diabete	o eel dee-a-**bay**-tay
I am vegetarian	Sono vegetariano/a	**so**-no vay-jay-ta-ree-**ah**-no/a
I'd like . . .	Vorrei . . .	vo-**ray**
I'd like to order	Vorrei ordinare	vo-**ray** or-dee-**nah**-ray
Is service included?	Il servizio è incluso?	eel ser-**vee**-tzee-o ay een-**kloo**-zo

ENGLISH	ITALIAN	PRONOUNCIATION
It's good/bad	È buono/cattivo	ay **bwo**-no/ka-**tee**-vo
It's hot/cold	È caldo/freddo	ay **kahl**-doe/**fred**-o
Knife	Il coltello	eel kol-**tel**-o
Lunch	Il pranzo	eel **prahnt**-so
Menu	Il menù	eel may-**noo**
Napkin	Il tovagliolo	eel toe-va-lee-**oh**-lo
Please give me . . .	Mi dia . . .	mee **dee**-a
Salt	Il sale	eel **sah**-lay
Spoon	Il cucchiaio	eel koo-kee-**ah**-yo
Sugar	Lo zucchero	lo **tsoo**-ker-o
Waiter/Waitress	Cameriere/ cameriera	ka-mare-**yer**-ay/ ka-mare-**yer**-a
Wine list	La lista dei vini	la **lee**-sta **day**-ee **vee**-nee

Travel Smart
Rome

GETTING HERE AND AROUND

Almost all of the main attractions in the *centro storico* can be covered on foot, or by bus or metro (subway).

The first thing you should know, especially when moving around the historic city center, is that most street names are posted on ceramiclike plaques on the side of buildings, which can be hard to see. Addresses are fairly straightforward: the street is followed by the street number. It's worth noting that the streets of Rome, even in the newer outskirts, are numbered erratically. Numbers are usually even on one side of the street and odd on the other, but sometimes numbers are in ascending consecutive order on one side of the street and descending order on the other side.

▮ AIR TRAVEL

Flying time to Rome is 7.5–8.5 hours from New York, 10–11 hours from Chicago, 12–13 hours from Los Angeles, and 2.5 hours from London.

Although the trend on international flights is to drop reconfirmation requirements, many airlines still ask you to reconfirm each leg of your international itinerary. Failure to do so may result in your reservations being canceled. When flying out of Italian airports, always check with the airport or tourist agency about upcoming strikes, which are frequent in Italy and often affect air travel.

Smoking policies vary from carrier to carrier. Many airlines prohibit smoking on all of their flights; others allow smoking only on certain routes or certain departures. Ask your carrier about its policy.

Airlines and Airports Airline and Airport Links.com (⊕ *www.airlineandairportlinks.com*) has links to many of the world's airlines and airports.

Airline Security Issues Transportation Security Administration (⊕ *www.tsa.gov*) has answers for almost every question that might come up.

AIRPORTS

The principal airport for flights to Rome is Leonardo da Vinci Airport, commonly known by the name of its location, Fiumicino (FCO). It's 30 km (19 mi) southwest of the city, on the coast. It has been enlarged and equipped with computerized baggage handling and has a direct train link with downtown Rome. Rome's other airport is Ciampino (CIA), on Via Appia Nuova, 15 km (9 mi) south of downtown. Ciampino is a civil and military airport now used by most low-cost airlines that fly both nationally and internationally. There are no trains linking the Ciampino airport to downtown Rome.

Airport Information Ciampino
(☎ *06/794941* ⊕ *www.adr.it*).

Leonardo da Vinci Airport/Fiumicino
(☎ *06/65951* ⊕ *www.adr.it*).

TRANSFERS BETWEEN FIUMICINO AND DOWNTOWN

When approaching by car, follow the signs for Rome and the GRA (the ring road that circles Rome). The direction you take on the GRA depends on where your hotel is located. If it's in the Via Veneto area, for instance, you would take the GRA in the direction of the Via Aurelia, turn off the GRA onto the Via Aurelia, and follow it into Rome. Get a map and directions from the car-rental desk at the airport.

A new law implemented by the Comune di Roma requires all Rome taxi drivers to charge a fixed fare of €40, including luggage handling, if your destination is within the Aurelian walls (this covers the centro storico, Trastevere, the Vatican area, and parts of San Giovanni). To make sure your hotel falls within the Aurelian walls, ask when you book your room. If your hotel is outside of the walls, the cab ride will run you about €60 plus *supplementi* (extra charges) for luggage. (Of course, this also depends on traffic.) The ride from the airport to the city center takes about 30–45 minutes. Private limousines can be booked at booths in the Arrivals hall; they charge a little more than taxis but can carry more passengers. The Comune di Roma now has a representative in place outside the International Arrivals hall (Terminal B), where the taxi stand is located to help assist tourists get into a taxi cab safely (hopefully without getting ripped off). Use only licensed white or older yellow taxis. When in doubt, always ask for a receipt and write the cab company and taxi's license number down (it's written on a metal plate on the inside of the passenger door). Avoid drivers who may approach you in the Arrivals hall; they charge exorbitant, unmetered rates and are most often unauthorized taxi drivers.

Airport Shuttle has shuttles that cost €25 (for one person) and €6 for each additional passenger. This fee also includes two bags per person. Airport Connection Services charges €35 (for one person) and €39 (for two people). The fee includes bags and all taxes.

Two trains link downtown Rome with Fiumicino. Inquire at the APT tourist information counter in the International Arrivals hall (Terminal B) or train information counter near the tracks to determine which takes you closest to your destination in Rome. The 30-minute nonstop Airport-Termini express (called the Leonardo Express) goes directly to Track 25 at Termini Station, Rome's main train station, which is well served by taxis and is a hub of Metro and bus lines. The ride to Termini takes about 30 minutes; departures are every half hour beginning at 6:36 AM from the airport, with a final departure at 11:36 PM. Trains depart Termini to the airport starting at 5:52 AM and the last train leaves at 10:52 PM. Tickets cost €11.

FM1, the other airport train, leaves from the same tracks and runs to Rome and beyond, serving commuters as well as air travelers. The main stops in Rome are at Trastevere (27 minutes), Ostiense (30 minutes), and Tiburtina (45 minutes); at each you can find taxis and bus and/or Metro

NAVIGATING ROME

At the center of a huge city, the historic districts of Rome are quite large. Streets can be quaint and adorable but there are zillions of them, so pace yourself accordingly; as much as visitors feel they can proudly stride across the city in one glorious day, this would leave them in bad need of a week's rest. Happily, if all roads no longer lead to Rome, many streets in the city lead to the Termini, or Stazione Centrale, Rome's main train station and the city's main transportation hub.

Make sure the bus you're waiting for actually runs during that part of the day or on that particular day of the week. For example, *notturno* buses (late-night buses), which can be distinguished by the "N" sign just above the bus number, don't run until after midnight. Oftentimes, tourists get confused while waiting at the bus stop, since the notturno bus schedules are listed side by side with the regular day bus schedules.

Also, be aware that *deviata* buses run on bus lines that have been re-routed due to road construction or public demonstrations. And *festivi* buses are ones that only run on Sunday and holidays. Both notturno buses and festivi buses don't run as often as other buses do on weekdays and Saturdays.

Regular buses will either say *feriali,* which means "daily," or won't have any special distinction.

The Metro A line will take you to a chunk of the main attractions in Rome: Piazza di Spagna, Piazza del Popolo, St. Peter's Square, and the Vatican Museums. The B line will take you to the Colosseum, Circus Maximus, and also lead you to the heart of Testaccio, Rome's nightlife district.

connections to other parts of Rome. FM1 trains run from Fiumicino between 5:57 AM and 11:27 PM, with departures every 30 minutes; the schedule is similar going to the airport. Tickets cost €5.50. For either train, buy your ticket at a vending machine or at ticket counters at the airport and at some stations (Termini Track 25, Trastevere, Tiburtina). At the airport, stamp the ticket at the gate. Remember when using the train at other stations to stamp the ticket in the little yellow or red machine near the track before you board. If you fail to stamp your ticket before you board, you could receive a hefty fine, as much as €100.

At night, take COTRAL buses from the airport to Tiburtina Station in Rome (45 minutes); they depart from in front of the International Arrivals hall at 1:15, 2:15, 3:30, 5, 10:55 AM, noon, and 3:30 PM. Buses leave Tiburtina Station for the airport at 12:30, 1:15, 2:30, 3:45, 9:30, 10:30 AM, 12:35 PM, and 5:30 PM. Tickets either way cost €4.50 or €7 if bought on board. The two stations are connected by Bus 40N.

TRANSFERS BETWEEN CIAMPINO AND DOWNTOWN

By car, go north on the Via Appia Nuova into downtown Rome.

The new taxi fare law implemented by the Comune di Roma that affects Fiumicino applies to this airport, too. All taxi drivers are supposed to charge a fixed fare of €30, including luggage handling, if your destination is within the Aurelian walls (this covers the centro storico, Trastevere, the Vatican area, and parts of San Giovanni). If your hotel is outside of the walls, the cab ride will run you about €60, plus *supplementi* (extra charges) for luggage. The ride takes about 20 minutes. Take only official cabs with the TAXI sign on top; unofficial cabs often overcharge disoriented travelers.

Airport Connection Services has shuttles that cost €37 for one person and €44 for two people. Airport Shuttle charges €25 for the first person, and €6 for each additional passenger.

A COTRAL bus connects the airport with the Anagnina Station of Metro Line A or Ciampino railway station, which takes you into the center of the city. Buses depart from in front of the airport terminal around 25 times a day between 6 AM and 11:40 PM. The fare is €1.20 and tickets can be bought on the bus.

TRANSFERS BETWEEN AIRPORTS

It's not easy to move from one airport to another in Rome—the airports aren't connected by a railway system or by the metro. The only way to make the transfer is by car, taxi, or a combination of bus, metro, and train. The latter option is not advisable because it would take you at least two to three hours to get from one airport to the other.

A taxi ride from Fiumicino Leonardo Da Vinci Airport to Ciampino Airport will take approximately 45 minutes and could cost roughly €60–€70, plus *supplementi* (extra charges) for luggage.

Contacts **Airport Connection Services** (☎ 06/3383221 ⊕ www.airportconnection. it). **Airport Shuttle** (☎ 06/42013469 or 06/4740451 ⊕ www.airportshuttle.it).

FLIGHTS

When flying internationally, you must usually choose between a domestic carrier, the national flag carrier of the country you're visiting, and a foreign carrier from a third country. You may, for example, choose to fly Alitalia to Rome. National flag carriers have the greatest number of nonstops. Domestic carriers may have better connections to your hometown and serve a greater number of gateway cities. Third-party carriers may have a price advantage.

For travel within Italy and around Europe, a number of low-cost airlines can get you where you need to go, often at cheaper rates than by train. Because there are too many of these carriers to name, the best advice is to check out a useful Web site called Sky Scanner (⊕ *www.skyscanner. net*) that will scan all of the major airlines and most of the low-cost airlines for you and give you the dates and companies with the most affordable rates. Keep in mind that low-cost airlines offer no-frills service. Any extras, such as meals, fast check-ins and boarding, extra luggage, and even slightly overweight luggage will cost you. Make sure to read all of the fine print when booking a flight with a low-cost airline, especially the rules pertaining to boarding and luggage.

The least expensive airfares to Rome are priced for round-trip travel and must usually be purchased in advance. Airlines generally allow you to change your return date for a fee; most low-fare tickets, however, are nonrefundable.

Airline Contacts Alitalia (☎ *800/223–5730, 0870/544–8259 in U.K., 06/65631 or 06/2222 in Rome* ⊕ *www.alitalia.it*). **American Airlines** (☎ *800/433–7300, 06/66053169 in Rome* ⊕ *www.aa.com*). **British Airways** (☎ *0845/773–3377 in U.K., 199/712266 within Italy* ⊕ *www.britishairways.com*). **Delta Airlines** (☎ *800/221–1212 for U.S. reservations, 800/241–4141 for international reservations, 848/780376 within Italy* ⊕ *www.delta.com*). **easyJet** (☎ *899/656505* ⊕ *www.easyjet.com*). **United Airlines** (☎ *800/864–8331 for U.S. reservations, 800/538–2929 for international reservations, 02/69633707 within Italy* ⊕ *www.united.com*). **US Airways** (☎ *800/428–4322 for U.S. and Canada reservations, 800/622–1015 for international reservations, 848/813177 within Italy* ⊕ *www.usairways.com*).

Low-Cost Airlines Blu Express (☎ *899/199034 within Italy, 06/60214577 from abroad* ⊕ *www.blu-express.com*). **Eurofly** (☎ *199/411109 within Italy, 0789/52640 from abroad* ⊕ *www.eurofly.it*). **Meridiana** (☎ *892/928 Call Center, 0789/52682 from U.S.* ⊕ *www.meridiana.it*). **Ryanair** (☎ *0871/246–000, 899/678910 within Italy* ⊕ *ryanair.com*). **Wind Jet** (☎ *899/656505* ⊕ *www.volawindjet.it*).

∎ BUS TRAVEL

An extensive network of bus lines that covers all of the Lazio region is operated by COTRAL (Consorzio Trasporti Lazio).

There are several main bus stations. Long-distance and suburban COTRAL bus routes terminate either near Tiburtina Station or at outlying Metro stops, such as Rebibbia and Ponte Mammolo (Line B) and Anagnina (Line A).

Fares are reasonable, especially with the BIRG (Bigletto Integrale Regionale Giornali), which allows you to travel on all of the lines (and some railroad lines) up to midnight on the day of the ticket's first validation. The cost of a BIRG depends upon the distance to your destination and how many "zones" you travel through. Because of the extent and complexity of the system, it's a good idea to consult with your hotel concierge or to telephone COTRAL's central office when planning a trip. COTRAL buses and other similar bus companies such as SENA are good options for taking short day trips from Rome. There are several buses that leave daily from Rome's Ponte Mammolo (Line B) metro station for the town of Tivoli, where Hadrian's Villa and Villa D'Este are located. SENA buses leave from Rome's Tiburtina metro and train station (Line B) and will take you to Siena and other towns in Tuscany.

While the bus may be an affordable way of moving around, keep in mind that it's also affordable for locals trying to get to and from work. This means certain buses experience heavy commuter traffic and are often very crowded. Just because you've managed to purchase a ticket doesn't mean you're guaranteed a seat. If you don't manage to get a seat, you might have to stand for the entire ride. Hence, what may be more affordable isn't exactly more comfortable.

Bus Information COTRAL (☎ *800/150008* ⊕ *www.cotralspa.it*). **SENA** (☎ *800/930960* ⊕ *www.sena.it*).

∎ CAR TRAVEL

The main access routes from the north are A1 (Autostrada del Sole) from Milan and Florence and the A12–E80 highway from Genoa. The principal route to or from points south, including Naples, is the A2. All highways connect with the Grande Raccordo Anulare Ring Road (GRA), which channels traffic into the city center. Markings on the GRA are confusing: take time to study the route you need. Be extremely careful of pedestrians and scooters when driving: Romans are casual jaywalkers and pop out frequently from between parked cars. People on scooters tend to be the worst and most careless drivers, as they tend to weave in and out of traffic.

For driving directions, check out ⊕ *www.tuttocitta.it.*

GASOLINE
Only a few gas stations are open on Sunday, and most close for a couple of hours at lunchtime and at 7 PM for the night. Many, however, have self-service pumps that accept both currency and credit cards and are operational 24 hours a day. Most service stations have attendants that pump the gas for you, though self-service pumps are also available. After-hours at self-service stations, it is not uncommon to find someone who will pump your gas for you. While they're not official employees of the gas station, a small tip is usually expected (about €0.30–€0.40 is acceptable). Gas stations on autostrade are open 24 hours. Gas costs about €1.32 per liter. Diesel costs about €1.20 per liter.

PARKING
Be warned: parking in Rome can be a nightmare. The situation is greatly compounded by the fact that private cars are not allowed access to the entire historic center during the day (weekdays 8–6; Saturday 2 PM–6 PM), except for those belonging to residents with resident permits. If you dare enter these restricted areas, also called ZTL zones, without a special permit, you will receive a hefty fine. Space is at a premium, and your car may be towed away if it's illegally parked. When you book your hotel, inquire about parking facilities.

There's limited free parking space in the city. Spaces with white lines are free

parking, while spaces with yellow lines are for the handicapped only. Make sure to check with your hotel regarding appropriate places to park nearby. Spaces with blue lines are paid parking. All other color-coded spaces are usually reserved for residents, disabled drivers, or carpooling and require special permits. If you park in one of these spaces without a permit, your car could be ticketed or towed. Meter parking costs €1–€1.20 per hour (depending on what area you're in) with limited stopping time allowed in many areas. However, if you pay for four consecutive hours, you will get eight hours of meter time for just €4. Parking facilities near the historic sights exist at the Villa Borghese underground car park (entrance at Viale del Muro Torto) and the Vatican (entrance from Piazza della Rovere).

ROAD CONDITIONS
Italians drive fast and are impatient with those who don't, a tendency that can make driving on the congested streets of Rome a hair-raising experience. Traffic is heaviest during morning and late-afternoon commuter hours, and on weekends. Watch out for mopeds.

ROADSIDE EMERGENCIES
There are phone boxes on highways to report breakdowns. Major rental agencies often provide roadside assistance, so check your rental agreement if a problem arises. Also, ACI (Auto Club of Italy) Service offers 24-hour road service. Dial 803–116 from any phone, 24 hours a day, to reach the nearest ACI service station. When speaking to ACI, ask and you will be transferred to an English-speaking operator. Be prepared to tell the operator which road you're on, the direction you're going, for example, "*verso* (in the direction of) Pizzo," and the *targa* (license plate number) of your car.

Auto Club of Italy (*ACI* ☎ *803–116*).

RULES OF THE ROAD
Driving is on the right. Regulations are largely similar to those in Britain and the U.S., except that the police have the

power to levy on-the-spot fines. Although honking abounds, the use of horns is forbidden in many areas; a large sign, ZONA DI SILENZIO, indicates where. Speed limits are 50 KPH (31 MPH) in Rome, 130 KPH (80 MPH) on autostrade, and 110 KPH (70 MPH) on state and provincial roads, unless otherwise marked. Talking on a cell phone while driving is strictly prohibited, and if caught, the driver will be issued a fine. Not wearing a seat belt is also against the law. The blood-alcohol content limit for driving is 0.5 gr/l with fines up to €5,000 and the possibility of six months' imprisonment for surpassing the limit. Fines for speeding are uniformly stiff: 10 KPH (6 MPH) over the speed limit can warrant a fine of up to €500; over 10 KPH, and your license could be taken away from you.

Whenever the city decides to implement an "Ecological Day" in order to reduce smog levels, commuters are prohibited from driving their cars during certain hours of the day and in certain areas of the city. These are usually organized and announced ahead of time. However, if you're planning to rent a car during your trip, make sure to ask the rental company and your hotel if there are any planned, because the traffic police won't cut you any breaks, even if you say you're a tourist.

CAR RENTAL

When you reserve a car, ask about cancellation penalties, taxes, drop-off charges (if you're planning to pick up the car in one city and leave it in another), and surcharges (for being under or over a certain age, for additional drivers, or for driving across state or country borders or beyond a specific distance from your point of rental). All these things can add substantially to your costs. Request car seats and extras such as GPS when you book. Make sure to ask the rental car company if they require you to obtain an International Driver's Permit beforehand (most do).These can generally be obtained for a fee through AAA in the U.S. Rates are sometimes—but not always—better if you book in advance or reserve through a rental agency's Web site. There are other reasons to book ahead, though: for popular destinations, during busy times of the year, or to ensure that you get certain types of cars (vans, SUVs, exotic sports cars).

■ TIP→ Make sure that a confirmed reservation guarantees you a car. Agencies sometimes overbook, particularly for busy weekends and holiday periods.

Rates in Rome begin at around $75 a day for an economy car with air-conditioning, a manual transmission, and unlimited mileage. This includes the 20% tax on car rentals. Note that Italian legislation now permits certain rental wholesalers, such as Auto Europe, to drop the value-added tax (V.A.T.). All international car rental agencies in Rome have a number of locations.

It's usually cheaper to rent a car in advance through your local agency than to rent on location in Italy. Or book ahead online— you can save as much as $10 per day on your car rental. Within Italy, local rental agencies and international ones offer similar rates. Whether you're going with a local or international agency, note that most cars are manual; automatics are hard to find, so inquire about those well in advance.

In Italy your own driver's license is acceptable. An International Driver's Permit is a good idea; it's available from the American or Canadian Automobile Association and, in the United Kingdom, from the Automobile Association or Royal Automobile Club. These international permits are universally recognized, and having one in your wallet may save you a problem with the local authorities.

In Italy you must be 21 years of age to rent an economy or subcompact car, and most companies require customers under the age of 23 to pay by credit card. Upon rental, all companies require credit cards as a warranty; to rent bigger cars (2,000 cc or more), you must often show two credit cards. Debit or check cards are not accepted. Call local agents for details. There are no special restrictions on senior-citizen drivers.

Car-Rental Resources

AUTOMOBILE ASSOCIATIONS		
U.S.: American Automobile Association (AAA)	315/797–5000	www.aaa.com; most contact with the organization is through state and regional members.
National Automobile Club	650/294–7000	www.thenac.com; membership is open to California residents only.
Automobile Association (AA)	0870/600–0371	www.theaa.co.uk
Royal Automobile Club	0800/731–1104	www.rac.co.uk
LOCAL AGENCIES		
Europcar	06/79340387	www.europcar.it
MAJOR AGENCIES		
Alamo	800/462–5266	www.alamo.com
Avis	800/331–1084	www.avis.com
Budget	800/472–3325	www.budget.com
Hertz	800/654–3001	www.hertz.com
National Car Rental	800/227–7368	www.nationalcar.com
WHOLESALERS		
Auto Europe	888/223–5555	www.autoeurope.com
Europe by Car	212/581–3040 in New York, 800/223–1516	www.europebycar.com
Eurovacations	877/471–3876	www.eurovacations.com
Kemwel	877/820–0668	www.kemwel.com

Car seats are required for children under 3 and must be booked in advance. The rental cost is €5 upward, depending on the type of car.

The cost for an additional driver is about €5–€7 per day.

CAR INSURANCE

Everyone who rents a car wonders whether the insurance that the rental companies offer is worth the expense. No one—including us—has a simple answer. It all depends on how much regular insurance you have, how comfortable you are with risk, and whether or not money is an issue.

If you own a car, your personal auto insurance may cover a rental to some degree, though not all policies protect you abroad; always read your policy's fine print. If you don't have auto insurance, then seriously consider buying the collision- or loss-damage waiver (CDW or LDW) from the car-rental company, which eliminates your liability for damage to the car. If you choose not to purchase the CDW coverage, you could be liable for the first €500 worth of damage. Some credit cards offer CDW coverage, but it's usually supplemental to your own insurance and rarely covers SUVs, minivans, luxury models, and the like. If your coverage is secondary, you may still be liable for loss-of-use costs from the car-rental company. But no credit-card insurance is valid unless you use that card for *all* transactions, from reserving to paying the final bill. All companies exclude car rental in some countries, so be sure to find out about the destination to which you are traveling.

Some rental agencies require you to purchase CDW coverage; many will even include it in quoted rates. All will strongly encourage you to buy CDW—possibly implying that it's required—so be sure to ask about such things before renting. In most cases it's cheaper to add a supplemental CDW plan to your comprehensive travel-insurance policy than to purchase it from a rental company. That said, you don't want to pay for a supplement if you're required to buy insurance from the rental company.

∎ MOPED TRAVEL

As bikes are to Beijing, so mopeds are to Rome; that means they are everywhere. Riders are required to wear helmets, and traffic police are tough in enforcing this law. Producing your country's driver's license should be enough to convince most rental firms that they're not dealing with a complete beginner; but if you're unsure of exactly how to ride a moped, think twice, and at least ask the assistant for a detailed demonstration.

If you don't feel up to braving the Roman traffic on a moped, you can hire an electric car to scoot around the city. The MELEX is a four-seater, golf-cart-style car, with battery power lasting up to eight hours. To rent the MELEX, you need a valid driver's license. Cost: €18 per hour.

Rental Agencies Free Rome (MELEX cars) (✉ *Via Ludovisi 60, Via Veneto* ☎ *06/42013110*). **Scoot-a-Long** (✉ *Via Cavour 302, Termini* ☎ *06/6780206*). **St. Peter Moto** (✉ *Via di Porta Castello 43, San Pietro* ☎ *06/6875714*). **Treno e Scooter** (✉ *Piazza dei Cinquecento, in the parking lot in front of the train station, Termini* ☎ *06/48905823*).

∎ PUBLIC TRANSPORTATION: BUS, TRAM, AND METROPOLITANA

Although most of Rome's sights are in a relatively circumscribed area, the city is too large to be seen solely on foot. Try to avoid rush hours when taking the Metro (subway) or a bus, as public transport can be extremely crowded. Mid-morning or the middle of the day up until early afternoon tend to be less busy. Otherwise, it's best to take a taxi to the area you plan to visit if it is across town. But you should always expect to do a lot of walking in Rome (especially considering how limited the subway stops are) and so plan on wearing a pair of comfortable, sturdy shoes to cushion the impact of the *sampietrini* (cobblestones). Get away from the noise and polluted air of heavily trafficked streets by taking parallel streets whenever possible. You can get free city and transportation-route maps at municipal information booths.

Rome's integrated transportation system includes buses and trams (ATAC), Metropolitana (subway, often nicknamed the Metro), and suburban trains and buses (COTRAL), and some other suburban trains (Trenitalia) run by the state railways. A ticket (BIT) valid for 75 minutes on any combination of buses and trams and one entrance to the Metro costs €1. However, once you exit the Metro station even if you get off the wrong stop by mistake, you will be required to purchase and validate another ticket.

Tickets are sold at tobacconists, newsstands, some coffee bars, automatic ticket machines in Metro stations, some bus stops, and ATAC and COTRAL ticket booths (in some Metro stations and at a few main bus stops). You can buy them singly or in quantity; it's always a good idea to have a few tickets handy so you don't have to hunt for a vendor when you need one. Time-stamp your ticket when boarding the first vehicle, and stamp it again when boarding for the last time within 75 minutes. You stamp the ticket at Metro sliding electronic doors, and in the little yellow machines on buses and trams. If you fail to validate your ticket, you could receive a fine of €51 if you pay the ticket controllers on the spot; otherwise, it'll cost you €101 to pay it later.

A BIG ticket—or *Biglietto integrato giornaliero* (integrated daily ticket)—is valid for one day (only for the day it is stamped, not 24 hours) on all public transport and costs €4. A three-day pass (BTI)—or *Biglietto turistico integrato*—costs €11. A weekly ticket (*settimanale*, also known as CIS) costs €16 and gives unlimited travel on ATAC buses, COTRAL urban bus services, trains for the Lido and Viterbo, and subway (Metro). There's an ATAC kiosk at the bus terminal in front of Termini station.

If you're going farther afield, or planning to spend more than a week in Rome, think about getting a BIRG regional ticket or a CIRS (regional weekly ticket) from the railway station. These give you unlimited travel on all state transport throughout the region of Lazio. This can take you as far as the Etruscan city of Tarquinia or medieval Viterbo.

The Metropolitana (or Metro) is the easiest and fastest way to get around Rome (see our Metro map on the inside back cover of this edition). There are stops near most of the main tourist attractions (street entrances are marked with red "M" signs). The Metro has two lines—A and B—which intersect at Termini Station. Line A runs from the eastern part of the city, with stops, among others, at San Giovanni in Laterano, Piazza Barberini, Piazza di Spagna, Piazzale Flaminio (Piazza del Popolo), and Ottaviano/San Pietro, near the Basilica di San Pietro and the Musei Vaticani. Line B has stops near the Colosseum, the Circus Maximus, the Pyramid (Ostiense Station and trains for Ostia Antica), and the Basilica di San Paolo Fuori le Mura. The Metro opens at 5:30 AM, and the last trains leave the last station at either end at 11:30 PM (on Friday and Saturday nights the last train leaves at 1:30 AM).

Although not as fast as the Metropolitana, bus travel is more scenic. With reserved bus lanes and numerous tram lines, surface transportation is surprisingly efficient, given the volume of Roman traffic. At peak times, however, buses can be very crowded.

If the distance you have to travel is not too great, walking can be a more comfortable alternative. ATAC city buses are orange, gray-and-red, or blue-and-orange; trams are orange or green. Remember to board at the rear and to exit at the middle; you must buy your ticket before boarding, and stamp it in a machine as soon as you enter. If you find the bus too crowded to get to the ticket machine, manually cancel the ticket by writing on it the date and time you got on. The ticket is good for a transfer within the next 75 minutes. Buses and trams run from 5:30 AM to midnight, plus there's an extensive network of night buses throughout the city.

The bus system is a bit complicated to navigate due to the number of lines, but ATAC has a Web site (⊕ *www.atac.roma.it*) that will help you calculate the number of stops and bus route needed, and even give you a map directing you to the appropriate stops. To navigate the site, look at the middle of the page where it says "Calcola il percorso"; click on word "vai," and this will take you to a page that will allow you to change the site into English. Look for the small British flag in the upper right-hand corner.

TICKET/PASS	PRICE
Single Fare	€1
Weekly Pass	€16
Monthly Unlimited Pass	€30

ZONE	PRICE
A	€1
B	€2
C	€3

Information **ATAC urban buses** (☎ *06/57003, 800/431784 Freephone 8–8 except Sun.* ⊕ *www.atac.roma.it*). COTRAL (☎ *800/150008* ⊕ *www.cotralspa.it*). Trenitalia suburban trains (⊕ *www.trenitalia.it*).

▌ TAXI TRAVEL

Taxis in Rome do not cruise, but if free they will stop if you flag them down. They wait at stands but can also be called by phone, in which case you're charged a supplement. The various taxi services are considered interchangeable and are referred to by their phone numbers rather than names. Taxicabs can be reserved the night before if you're traveling to and from the airport or the train station. Only some taxis are equipped to take credit cards. Inquire when you phone to make the booking.

The meter starts at €2.80 during the day, €5.80 after 10 PM, and €4 on Sunday and holidays. There's a supplement of €1 for each piece of baggage. There's even a €2 supplement for rides originating from Termini train station. Unfortunately, these charges do not appear on the meter, causing countless misunderstandings. If you take a taxi at night and/or on a Sunday, or if you have baggage or have called the cab by phone, the fare will legitimately be more than the figure shown on the meter. When in doubt, always ask for a receipt (*ricevuta*). This will encourage the taxicab driver to be honest and charge you the correct amount. After 9 PM, women traveling alone in a taxi are entitled to a *"sconta rosa"*—a special 10% discount for women implemented by the city of Rome. Unfortunately, taxi drivers won't always apply the discount to the fare. You'll have to make sure to ask for it. Use only licensed, metered white or yellow cabs, identified by a numbered shield on the side, an illuminated taxi sign on the roof, and a plaque next to the license plate reading SERVIZIO PUBBLICO. Avoid unmarked, unauthorized, unmetered gypsy cabs (numerous at Rome airports and train stations), whose drivers actively solicit your trade and may demand astronomical fares.

Taxi Companies Cab (☎ 06/6645, 06/3570, 06/4994, 06/5551, or 06/4157).

▌ TRAIN TRAVEL

State-owned Trenitalia trains are part of the Metrebus system and also serve some destinations on side trips outside Rome. The main Trenitalia stations in Rome are Termini, Tiburtina, Ostiense, and Trastevere. Suburban trains use all of these stations. The Ferrovie COTRAL line departs from a terminal in Piazzale Flaminio, connecting Rome with Viterbo.

Trenitalia trains do not have first and second classes. Local trains can be crowded early morning and evening as many people commute to and from the city, so try to avoid these times. Be ready to stand if you plan to take one of these trains and don't arrive early enough to secure a seat. On long-distance routes (to Florence and Venice, for instance), you can either travel by the cheap (but slow) *diretto* trains, or the fast, but more expensive *Intercity,* or the *Eurostar.* Seat reservations are obligatory on both Intercity and Eurostar trains. This can be done directly at the station when you buy your ticket, online, or through a travel agent.

For destinations within 200 km (124 mi) of Rome, you can buy a *kilometrico* ticket. Like bus tickets, they can be purchased at some newsstands and in ticketing machines, as well as at Trenitalia ticket windows. Buy them in advance so you won't waste time in line at station ticket booths. Like all train tickets, they must be date-stamped in the little yellow or red machines near the track before you board. Within a range of 200 km (124 mi) they're valid for six hours from the time they're stamped, and you can get on and off at will at stops in between for the duration of the ticket's validity.

The state railways' excellent and user-friendly site at ⊕ *www.trenitalia.it* will help you plan any rail trips in the country.

Information Trenitalia (☎ 892/2021 or 199/892021 within Italy, 06/68475475 from abroad ⊕ www.trenitalia.it).

ESSENTIALS

■ COMMUNICATIONS

INTERNET

Getting online in Rome isn't difficult: public Internet stations and Internet caffè are common. Prices differ from place to place, so spend some time to find the best deal. This isn't always readily apparent: a place might have higher rates, but because it belongs to a chain you won't be charged an initial flat fee again when you go to a different location of the same chain. Some hotels have in-room modem lines, but, as with phones, using the hotel's line is relatively expensive. Always check modem rates before plugging in. You may need an adapter for your computer for the European-style plugs. As always, if you're traveling with a laptop, carry a spare battery and an adapter. Never plug your computer into any socket before asking about surge protection. IBM sells a pea-size modem tester that plugs into a telephone jack to check whether the line is safe to use.

There are several Wi-Fi hot spots around Rome. In fact, many bars and caffè around the city will let you connect to their wireless network for free if you purchase something to eat or drink.

Internet Cafés Call Net (✉ Galleria Stazione Termini ☎ 06/87406008). **Cybercafes** (⊕ www.cybercafes.com) lists more than 4,000 Internet cafés worldwide. **Internet Café** (✉ Via Cavour 208 ☎ 06/4740068). **Pantheon Internet Point** (✉ Via di Santa Caterina da Siena ☎ 06/69200501). **Tourist Friend** (✉ Via Crescenzio 41 ☎ 06/68210410). **TreviNet Place** (✉ Via in Arcione 103 ☎ 06/69922320).

Cafés with Wi-Fi Friends Café (✉ Piazza Trilussa 34, Trastevere ☎ 06/5816111). **The Library** (✉ Vicolo della Cancelleria 7, Piazza Navona ☎ 333/3517581 ⊕ www.thelibrary.it). **Wine Time** (✉ Piazza Pasquali Paoli 15, Castel Sant'Angelo ☎ 06/875706 ⊕ www.winetime.it).

PHONES

The good news is that you can now make a direct-dial telephone call from virtually any point on earth. The bad news? You can't always do so cheaply. Calling from a hotel is almost always the most expensive option; hotels usually add huge surcharges to all calls, particularly international ones. In some countries you can phone from call centers or even the post office. Calling cards usually keep costs to a minimum, but only if you purchase them locally. And then there are mobile phones (⇨ below)— as expensive as mobile phone calls can be, they are still usually a much cheaper option than calling from your hotel.

The country code for Italy is 39. The area code for Rome is 06. When dialing an Italian number from abroad, do not drop the initial 0 from the local area code.

The country code is 1 for the United States, 61 for Australia, 1 for Canada, 64 for New Zealand, and 44 for the United Kingdom.

CALLING WITHIN ITALY

For general information in English, dial 176. To place international telephone calls via operator-assisted service (or for information), dial 170 or long-distance access numbers (⇨ Long Distance Services).

Phone numbers in Rome, and throughout Italy, don't have a set number of digits. All calls (except for cell phones) in Rome are preceded by the city code 06, with the exception of three-digit numbers (113 is for general emergencies). Emergency numbers can be called for free from pay phones.

Throughout Italy, long-distance calls are dialed in the same manner as local calls: the city code plus the number. Rates vary, depending on the time of day, with the lowest late at night and early in the morning.

LOCAL DO'S AND TABOOS

GREETINGS

Italians greet friends with a kiss, usually first on the right cheek, and then on the left. When you meet a new person, shake hands.

SIGHTSEEING

Italy is teeming with churches, many with significant works of art in them. Because they are places of worship, care should be taken with appropriate dress. Shorts, cropped tops, miniskirts, and bare midriffs are taboo at St. Peter's in Rome, and in many other churches throughout Italy. So, too, are short shorts anywhere. When touring churches—especially in summer when it's hot and no sleeves are desirable—it's wise to carry a sweater, or scarf, to wrap around your shoulders before entering the church. Do not enter a church with food, and do not drink from your water bottle while inside. Do not go in if a service is in progress. And if you have a cellular phone, turn it off before entering.

OUT ON THE TOWN

In Italy, almost nothing starts on time except for maybe a theater, opera, or movie showing. Italians even joke about a "15-minute window" before actually being late somewhere.

LANGUAGE

You can always find someone who speaks at least a little English in Rome, albeit with a heavy accent. Remember that the Italian language is pronounced exactly as it's written—many Italians try to speak English as it's written, with bewildering results.

You may run into a language barrier in the countryside, but a phrase book and close attention to the Italians' astonishing use of pantomime and expressive gestures will go a long way.

Try to master a few phrases for daily use, and familiarize yourself with the terms you'll need to decipher signs and museum labels. Some museums have exhibits labeled in both English and Italian, but this is the exception rather than the rule.

Most exhibitions have multilanguage headphones you can rent and English-language guidebooks are generally available at museum shops.

Many newsstands and bookstores stock a useful guide called *Rome, Past & Present*. It has photos of the most famous ancient monuments, together with drawings of what they originally looked like, and is particularly useful to get children interested in what seems (to them) just heaps of old stones.

A phrase book and language-tape set can help get you started.

Fodor's *Italian for Travelers* (available at bookstores everywhere) is excellent.

Private language schools and U.S.- and U.K.-affiliated educational institutions offer a host of Italian language study programs in Rome.

Language Schools American University of Rome (⊠ *Via Pietro Rosselli 4* ☎ *06/58330919* ⊕ *www.aur.edu*). Arco di Druso (⊠ *Via Tunisi 4* ☎ *06/39750984* ⊕ *www.arcodidruso.com*). Berlitz (⊠ *Via Torre Argentina 21* ☎ *06/6834000* ⊕ *www.berlitz.com*). Centro Linguistico Italiano Dante Alighieri (⊠ *Piazza Bologna 1* ☎ *06/44231490*). Ciao Italia (⊠ *Via delle Frasche 5* ☎ *06/4814084* ⊕ *www.ciao-italia.it*). Dilit International House (⊠ *Via Marghera 22* ☎ *06/4462592* ⊕ *www.dilit.it*). Scuola Leonardo da Vinci (⊠ *Piazza dell'Orologio 7* ☎ *06/68892513* ⊕ *www.scuolaleonardo.com*).

CALLING OUTSIDE ITALY

Hotels tend to overcharge, sometimes exorbitantly, for long-distance and international calls. Use your AT&T, MCI, or Sprint card or buy an international phone card, which supplies a local number to call and gives a low rate. Or make your calls from Telefoni offices, designated TELECOM, where operators will assign you a booth, sell you an international telephone card, and help you place your call. You can make collect calls from any phone by dialing ☎ 800/172444, which will get you an English-speaking AT&T operator. Rates to the United States are lowest round the clock on Sunday and 10 PM–8 AM, Italian time, on weekdays.

The country code for the United States is 1.

Access Codes AT&T Direct (☎ *800/172–444*). **MCI WorldPhone** (☎ *800/172–905825*). **Sprint International Access** (☎ *800/172–405*). From cell phones call 892–176.

CALLING CARDS

Few pay phones now accept coins only. Most require *schede telefoniche* (phone cards). You buy the card (values vary—€2.50, €5, and so on) at post offices, newsstands (called *edicole*), and tobacconists. Tear off the corner of the card and insert it in the slot. When you dial, its value appears in the window. After you hang up, the card is returned so you can use it until its value runs out. The best cards for calling North America or Europe is the €5 or €10 Eurocity, Eurotel, and Editel cards, which give you a local number to dial and a pin number, and roughly 180 minutes and 360 minutes, respectively, of calling time.

MOBILE PHONES

If you have a multiband phone (some countries use different frequencies from those used in the United States) and your service provider uses the world-standard GSM network (as do T-Mobile, AT&T, and Verizon), you can probably use your phone abroad. Roaming fees can be steep, however: 99¢ a minute is considered reasonable. And overseas you normally pay the toll charges for incoming calls. It's almost always cheaper to send a text message than to make a call, since text messages have a very low set fee (often less than 10¢).

If you just want to make local calls, consider buying a new SIM card (note that your provider may have to unlock your phone for you to use a different SIM card) and a prepaid service plan in the destination. You'll then have a local number and can make local calls at local rates. If your trip is extensive, you could also simply buy a new cell phone in your destination, as the initial cost will be offset over time.

Renting phones may seem like an inexpensive way to go, but in the end it could cost you more than using your own cell phone from home. The per-minute rates tend to be higher, and a lot of times there are hidden costs. Usually, companies ask you to leave a credit card number when renting the phone, which can be iffy, as hidden costs sneak up onto your bill at the end of the month.

Contacts Cellular Abroad (☎ *800/287–5072* ⊕ *www.cellularabroad.com*) rents and sells GMS phones and sells SIM cards that work in many countries. **Mobal** (☎ *888/888–9162* ⊕ *www.mobalrental.com*) rents mobiles and sells GSM phones (starting at $49) that will operate in 140 countries. Per-call rates vary throughout the world. **Planet Fone** (☎ *888/988–4777* ⊕ *www.planetfone.com*) rents cell phones, but the per-minute rates are expensive.

❚ CUSTOMS AND DUTIES

You're always allowed to bring goods of a certain value back home without having to pay any duty or import tax. But there's a limit on the amount of tobacco and liquor you can bring back duty-free, and some countries have separate limits for perfumes; for exact figures, check with your customs department. The values of so-called "duty-free" goods are included in these amounts. When you shop abroad, save all your receipts, as customs inspectors may ask to see them as well as the items you purchased. If the total value of your goods is more than the duty-free limit, you'll have to pay a tax (most often a flat percentage) on the value of everything beyond that limit.

Of goods obtained anywhere outside the EU or goods purchased in a duty-free shop within an EU country, the allowances are as follows: (1) 200 cigarettes or 100 cigarillos or 50 cigars or 250 grams of tobacco; (2) 2 liters of still table wine or 1 liter of spirits over 22% volume or 2 liters of spirits under 22% volume or 2 liters of fortified and sparkling wines; and (3) 50 ml of perfume and 250 ml of toilet water.

Of goods obtained (duty and tax paid) within another EU country, the allowances are (1) 800 cigarettes or 400 cigarillos (under 3 grams) or 200 cigars or 1 kilogram of tobacco; (2) 90 liters of still table wine or 10 liters of spirits over 22% volume or 20 liters of spirits under 22% volume or 110 liters of beer.

Information in Rome Italian Customs, Fumicino Airport (✉ *Circoscrizione Doganale Roma 2* ☎ *06/6595434*).

U.S. Information U.S. Customs and Border Protection (⊕ *www.cbp.gov*).

▌ ELECTRICITY

The electrical current in Italy is 220 volts, 50 cycles alternating current (AC); wall outlets take Continental-type plugs, with two or three round prongs.

Consider making a small investment in a universal adapter, which has several types of plugs in one lightweight, compact unit. Most laptops and mobile phone chargers are dual voltage (i.e., they operate equally well on 110 and 220 volts), so require only an adapter. These days the same is true of small appliances such as hair dryers. Always check labels and manufacturer instructions to be sure. Don't use 110-volt

outlets marked FOR SHAVERS ONLY for high-wattage appliances such as hairdryers.

Note that straightening irons from the U.S. don't heat up very well and tend to blow a fuse even with correct adapters—as do American hair dryers.

Contacts Steve Kropla's Help for World Traveler's (⊕ *www.kropla.com*) has information on electrical and telephone plugs around the world. **Walkabout Travel Gear** (⊕ *www.walkabouttravelgear.com*) has a good coverage of electricity under "adapters."

▌ EMERGENCIES

No matter where you are in Italy, dial 113 for all emergencies, or find somebody (your concierge, a passerby) who will call for you, as not all 113 operators speak English; the Italian word to use to draw people's attention in an emergency is *Aiuto!* (Help!, pronounced ah-*you*-toh). *Pronto soccorso* means "first aid." When confronted with a health emergency, head straight for the Pronto Soccorso department of the nearest hospital or dial 118. To call a Red Cross ambulance *(ambulanza)* dial 06/5510. If you just need a doctor, you should ask for *un medico*; most hotels will be able to refer you to a local doctor *(medico)*. Don't forget to ask the doctor for *una ricevuta* (an invoice) to show to your insurance company to get a reimbursement. Alternatively, the city of Rome has recently opened a medical clinic dedicated to tourists suffering from symptoms (flu, fever, minor aches and pains, etc.) that would probably have them waiting into the wee hours of the night at the emergency room. The Nuovo Regina Margherita Hospital offers a 24-hour tourist medical service and is staffed by one medical doctor and two nurses. The tourist medical service is free of charge every night 8–8 and on weekends. On weekdays (8–8), there is a charge of €20.66. Patients under 6 years old or over 65 years old are always free. The tourist service is located at the Nuovo Regina Margherita Hospital on *Via Morosini 30* (Trastevere); the phone number is ☎ *06/58441.*

Other useful Italian words to use are *Al fuoco!* (Fire!, pronounced ahl fuh-*woe*-co) and *Al ladro!* (Follow the thief!, pronounced ahl *lah*-droh).

Italy has a national police force (*carabinieri*) as well as local police (*polizia*). Both are armed and have the power to arrest and investigate crimes. Always report any theft or the loss of your passport to either the carabinieri or the police, as well as to your embassy. Local traffic officers are known as *vigili* (though their official name is *polizia municipale*)—they are responsible for, among other things, giving out parking tickets and clamping cars, so before you even consider parking the Italian way, make sure you are at least able to spot their white (in summer) or black uniforms (many are women). Should you find yourself involved in a minor car accident, you should contact the vigili. Call the countrywide toll-free number 113 if you need the police.

Most pharmacies are open Monday–Saturday 8:30–1 and 4–8; some are open all night. A schedule posted outside each pharmacy indicates the nearest pharmacy open during off-hours (afternoons, through the night, and Sunday). Farmacia Internazionale Capranica, Farmacia Internazionale Barberini (open 24 hours), and Farmacia Cola di Rienzo are pharmacies that have some English-speaking staff. The hospitals listed below have English-speaking doctors. Rome American Hospital is about 30 minutes by cab from the center of town.

For a full listing of doctors and dentists in Rome who speak English, consult the English Yellow Pages at ⊕ *www.englishyellowpages.it* or pick up a copy at any English-language bookstore. Your embassy will also have a recommended list of medical professionals.

Doctors and Dentists **Aventino Medical Group** (✉ *Via della Fonte Fauno 22* ☎ *06/5780738 or 06/57288329* ⊕ *www.*

aventinomedicalgroup.com). **Pro Dent Medica** (✉ *Via Bisagno 5* ☎ *06/8605056 or 339/3602158*). **Roma Medica (weekends, house calls)** (☎ *338/6224832 24-hour service*). **SDOP Seta (weekends, house calls)** (☎ *06/7005252 24-hour service*).

General Emergency Contacts **Emergencies** (☎ *113*). **Police** (☎ *113*). **Ambulance** (☎ *118*).

Hospitals and Clinics **Rome American Hospital** (✉ *Via Emilio Longoni 69, Via Prenestina* ☎ *06/22551* ⊕ *www.rah.it*). **Salvator Mundi International Hospital** (✉ *Viale delle Mura Gianicolensi 66, Trastevere* ☎ *06/588961* ⊕ *www.ministerosalute.it*).

Hotlines **Highway Police** (☎ *06/22101*). **Road Breakdown** (☎ *116*). **Women's Rights and Abuse Prevention** (☎ *06/37511362 or 800/001122*).

Pharmacies **Farmacia Cola di Rienzo** (✉ *Via Cola di Rienzo 213/215, San Pietro* ☎ *06/3243130 or 06/3244476*). **Farmacia Internazionale Barberini** (✉ *Piazza Barberini 49, Via Veneto* ☎ *06/4825456 or 064871195*). **Farmacia Internazionale Capranica** (✉ *Piazza Capranica 96, Pantheon* ☎ *06/6794680*).

▌ HEALTH

From March 2005, smoking has been banned in Italy in all public places. This includes trains, buses, offices, and waiting rooms, as well as restaurants, pubs, and discotheques (unless the latter have separate smoking rooms). If you're an unrepentant smoker, you would be advised to check with restaurants before making a booking, as very few can offer smokers' facilities. Fines for breaking the law are so stiff that they have succeeded (for the moment) in curbing the Italians' propensity to light up everywhere. Outside dining is exempt from the rule, so if smoking annoys you, you may find it better to eat indoors even in warm weather. Many restaurants are now equipped with air-conditioning. There are no smoking cars on any FS (Italian state railway) trains.

It's always best to travel with your own tried and true medicines. The regulations regarding what medicines require a prescription are not likely to be exactly the same in Italy and in your home country—all the more reason to bring what you need with you. Aspirin (*l'aspirina*) can be purchased at any pharmacy, but Tylenol and Advil are nearly unavailable. Note that over-the-counter remedies, including cough syrup, antiseptic creams, and headache pills are only sold in pharmacies.

■ HOURS OF OPERATION

Banks are typically open weekdays 8:30–1:30 and 2:45–3:45 or 3–4. Exchange offices are open all day, usually 8:30–8.

Post offices are open Monday–Saturday 8–2; central and main district post offices stay open until 8 or 9 PM on weekdays for some operations. You can buy stamps *(francobolli)* at tobacconists.

Only a few gas stations are open on Sunday, and most close during weekday lunch hours and at 7 PM for the night. Many, however, have self-service pumps that are operational 24 hours a day, and gas stations on autostrade are open 24 hours.

Museum hours vary and may change with the seasons. Many important national museums are closed one day a week, often on Monday. The Roman Forum, other sites, and some museums may be open until late in the evening during the summer. Always check locally.

Most churches are open from early morning until noon or 12:30, when they close for two hours or more; they open again in the afternoon, generally around 4 PM, closing about 7 PM or later. Major cathedrals and basilicas, such as the Basilica di San Pietro, are open all day. Note that sightseeing in churches during religious rites is usually discouraged. Be sure to have some coins handy for the *luce* (light) machines that illuminate the works of art in the perpetual dusk of ecclesiastical interiors. A pair of binoculars will help you get a good look at painted ceilings and domes. Many churches do not allow you to take pictures inside. When permitted, use of flash is prohibited.

A tip for pilgrims and tourists keen to get a glimpse of the pope: avoid the weekly general audience on Wednesday morning in Piazza di San Pietro, and go to his Sunday angelus instead. This midday prayer service tends to be far less crowded (unless beatifications or canonizations are taking place) and is also mercifully shorter, which makes a difference when you're standing.

Most pharmacies are open Monday–Saturday 8:30–1 and 4–8; some are open all night. A schedule posted outside each pharmacy indicates the nearest pharmacy open during off-hours (afternoons, through the night, and Sunday).

Shop hours vary. Many shops in downtown Rome are open all day during the week and also on Sunday, as are some department stores and supermarkets. Alternating city neighborhoods also have general once-a-month Sunday opening days. Otherwise, most shops throughout the city are closed on Sunday. Shops that take a lengthy lunch break are open 9:30–1 and 3:30 or 4–7:30 or 8. Many shops close for one half day during the week: Monday morning in winter and Saturday afternoon in summer.

Food shops are open 8–2 and 5–7:30, some until 8, and most are closed on Sunday. They also close for one half day during the week, usually Thursday afternoon from September to June and Saturday afternoon in July and August.

Termini Station has a large, modern shopping mall with more than a hundred stores, many of which are open late in the evening. Pharmacies, bookstores, and boutiques, as well as caffè, bathrooms, ATMs, and money-exchange services, a first-aid station, and an art gallery and exhibition center can all be found here. The Drug Store here is open every day between 6 AM and midnight. It sells sandwiches, fresh fruit, gourmet snacks, toiletries, gifts, and things like cameras, electric razors, and bouquets of fresh flowers (useful if you get an unexpected invitation to someone's home).

Traditionally the worst days to arrive in Rome, or do anything that hasn't been preplanned, are Easter Sunday, May 1 (Labor Day), Christmas Day, and New Year's Day. Expect to find many shops and businesses closed, and only a skeleton transport system working. Ferragosto (the middle weekend of August) will also be challenging.

HOLIDAYS

If you can avoid it, don't travel at all in Italy in August, when much of the population is on the move, especially around *Ferragosto*, the August 15 national holiday, when cities such as Rome are deserted and many restaurants and shops are closed.

National holidays are New Year's Day; January 6 (Epiphany); Easter Sunday and Monday; April 25 (Liberation Day); May 1 (Labor Day or May Day); June 29 (Sts. Peter and Paul, Rome's patron saints); August 15 (Assumption of Mary, also known as Ferragosto); November 1 (All Saints' Day); December 8 (Immaculate Conception); Christmas Day and the feast of Saint Stephen (December 25 and 26).

∎ MAIL

The Italian mail system has improved tremendously with the introduction of a two-tier postal system. A *posta prioritaria* stamp (first-class stamp) costs €0.85 and usually guarantees delivery to EEC destinations within three days. A posta prioritaria stamp within Italy costs €0.60. When you mail letters, pay attention to the mail slot on the mailbox. The red mailboxes have two slots: the slot on the left is for Rome mail, and the slot on the right is for all other destinations, including abroad. Blue mailboxes are for foreign (*estero*) mail only.

The Vatican postal service has a reputation for efficiency and many foreigners prefer to send their mail from there, with Vatican stamps. You can buy these in the post offices on either side of Piazza di San Pietro, one next to the information office and the other under the colonnade opposite. During peak tourist seasons a Vatican Post Office mobile unit is set up in Piazza di San Pietro. All letters with Vatican stamps can only be mailed from the Vatican Post Office or Vatican mailboxes located near San Pietro.

Letters and postcards to the United States and Canada cost €0.85 for up to 20 grams and automatically go airmail. Letters and postcards to the United Kingdom cost €0.65. You can buy stamps at tobacconists.

American Express also has a general-delivery service. There's no charge for cardholders, holders of American Express traveler's checks, or anyone who booked a vacation with American Express.

If you can avoid it, try not to have packages sent to you while you're in Rome or in Italy. Packages sent from abroad are notorious for being stopped by the Italian Customs Office or "Ufficio Dogonale." If your package gets stuck in customs, not only will you likely have to pay hefty customs fees but it could also take weeks for you to receive it. Sending medicine and even vitamins through the mail is highly unadvisable and if discovered, it will definitely be held up in customs for inspection.

Main Branches Main Rome post office (✉ *Piazza San Silvestro 19* ☎ *06/69737213*).

∎ MONEY

Rome's prices are comparable to those in other major capitals, such as Paris and London. Unless you dine in the swankiest places, you'll still find Rome one of the cheapest European capitals in which to eat. Clothes and leather goods are also generally less expensive than in northern Europe. Public transport is relatively cheap.

A Rome 2-km (1-mi) taxi ride costs €6. An inexpensive hotel room for two, including breakfast, is about €100; an inexpensive dinner for two is €45. A simple pasta item on the menu is about €8, and a ½-liter carafe of house wine €3.50. A McDonald's Big Mac is about €4. A pint of beer in a pub is around €4.

Admission to the Musei Vaticani is €14. The cheapest seat at Rome's Opera House runs €17; a movie ticket is €7. A daily English-language newspaper is €2.50.

Though more and more places are starting to accept credit cards as method of payment, cash is still king in Rome. This holds especially true for street markets and small mom-and-pop stores and restaurants.

ITEM	AVERAGE COST
Cup of Coffee	€0.80–€1
Glass of Wine	€3–€5
Glass of Beer	€4
Sandwich	€2.50–€4
One-Mile Taxi Ride	€6–€8
Museum Admission	€8–€12

Prices throughout this guide are given for adults. Substantially reduced fees are almost always available for children, students, and senior citizens when it comes to entrances to monuments and museums.

■ TIP➡ Banks never have every foreign currency on hand, and it may take as long as a week to order. If you're planning to exchange funds before leaving home, don't wait until the last minute.

ATMS AND BANKS

Your own bank will probably charge a fee for using ATMs abroad; the foreign bank you use may also charge a fee. Some banks, such as Citibank, which has a branch in Rome (near Via Veneto), don't charge extra fees to customers who use the Citibank ATM. Other banks may have similar agreements with Italian or foreign banks in Rome where customers won't get charged a transaction fee. Check with your bank to see if they have any

agreements before your trip. Nevertheless, you'll usually get a better rate of exchange at an ATM than you will at a currency-exchange office or even when changing money in a bank. And extracting funds as you need them is a safer option than carrying around a large amount of cash.

■ TIP➡ PIN numbers with more than four digits are not recognized at ATMs in many countries. If yours has five or more, remember to change it before you leave.

ATMs are common in Rome and are the easiest way to get euros. The word for ATM in Italian is *bancomat*, for PIN, *codice segreto*. Four-digit PINs are the standard, though in some machines longer numbers will work. When using an ATM or *bancomat*, always use extra caution when punching in your PIN and collecting your money.

CREDIT CARDS

Throughout this guide, the following abbreviations are used: **AE**, American Express; **DC**, Diners Club; **MC**, MasterCard; and **V**, Visa.

Always make your credit card company and bank aware that you'll be traveling or spending some time abroad, especially if don't travel internationally very often. Otherwise, the credit-card company might put a hold on your card owing to unusual activity—not a good thing halfway through your trip. Record all your credit-card numbers—as well as the phone numbers to call if your cards are lost or stolen—in a safe place, so you're prepared should something go wrong. Both MasterCard and Visa have general numbers you can call (collect if you're abroad) if your card is lost, but you're better off calling the number of your issuing bank, since MasterCard and Visa usually just transfer you to your bank; your bank's number is usually printed on your card.

If you plan to use your credit card for cash advances, you'll need to apply for a PIN at least two weeks before your trip. Although it's usually cheaper (and safer) to use a credit card abroad for large purchases (so you can cancel payments or be reimbursed if there's a problem), note that some credit-card companies *and* the banks that issue them add substantial percentages to all foreign transactions, whether they're in a foreign currency or not. Check on these fees before leaving home, so there won't be any surprises when you get the bill.

Although increasingly common, credit cards aren't accepted at all establishments, and some require a minimum expenditure. If you want to pay with a card in a small hotel, store, or restaurant, it's a good idea to ask before conducting your business. Visa and MasterCard are preferred to American Express, but in tourist areas American Express is usually accepted. Acceptance of Diners Club is rare.

Some credit card companies require that you obtain a police report if your credit card was lost or stolen. In this case, you should go to the police station at Termini train station or at Rome's central police station on Via San Vitale 15.

Reporting Lost Cards American Express (☎ 800/528–4800 in U.S., 336/393–1111 collect from abroad ⊕ www.americanexpress. com). **Diners Club** (☎ 800/234–6377 in U.S., 303/799–1504 collect from abroad, 800/393939 toll-free in Italy ⊕ www. dinersclub.com). **MasterCard** (☎ 800/627–8372 in U.S., 636/722–7111 collect from abroad, 800/870866 toll-free in Italy ⊕ www. mastercard.com). **Visa** (☎ 800/847–2911 in U.S., 410/581–9994 collect from abroad, 800/819014 toll-free in Italy ⊕ www.visa.com).

CURRENCY AND EXCHANGE

The euro is the main unit of currency in Italy, as well as in 12 other European countries. Under the euro system, there are eight coins: 1, 2, 5, 10, 20, and 50 *centesimi* (at 100 centesimi to the euro), and 1 and 2 euros. Note: The 1 and 2 euro coins look very similar. Therefore, pay close attention when using these so that you don't overpay. There are seven notes: 5, 10, 20, 50, 100, 200, and 500 euros.

At this writing, the exchange rate was about €0.69 to the U.S. dollar; €0.63 to the Canadian dollar; €1.09 to the pound sterling; €0.62 to the Australian dollar; and €0.50 to the New Zealand dollar.

■**TIP**➔ Even if a currency-exchange booth has a sign promising no commission, rest assured that there's some kind of huge, hidden fee. (Oh . . .that's right. The sign didn't say no *fee*.) And as for rates, you're almost always better off getting foreign currency at an ATM or exchanging money at a bank.

Currency Conversion Google (⊕ www. google.com) does currency conversion. Just type in the amount you want to convert and an explanation of how you want it converted (e.g., "14 Euro"), and then voilà. **Oanda.com** (⊕ www.oanda.com) also allows you to print out a handy table with the current day's conversion rates. **XE.com** (⊕ www.xe.com) is a good currency conversion Web site.

■ PACKING

Plan your wardrobe in layers, no matter what the season. Rome generally has mild winters and hot, sticky summers. Heavy rain showers are common in spring and late fall, so bring some fashionable rain boots. Take a medium-weight coat for winter; a lightweight all-weather coat for spring and fall; and a lightweight jacket or sweater for summer evenings, which may be cool. Brief summer thunderstorms are common, so take a folding umbrella, and keep in mind that anything more than light cotton clothes is unbearable in the humid heat. Few public buildings in Rome, including museums, restaurants, and shops, are air-conditioned. Interiors can be cold and sometimes damp in the cooler months, so take woolens or flannels.

Dress codes are strict for visits to the Basilica di San Pietro, the Musei Vaticani, and some churches: for both men and women, shorts, scanty tops, bare midriffs, and sometimes even flip-flops are taboo. Shoulders must be covered. Women should carry a scarf or shawl to cover bare arms if the custodians insist. Those who do not comply with the dress code are refused admittance. Although there are no specific dress rules for the huge outdoor papal audiences, you'll be turned away if you're in shorts or a revealing outfit. The Vatican Information Office in Piazza di San Pietro will tell you the dress requirements for smaller audiences.

Most public and private bathrooms are often short on toilet paper. Therefore, it's best to always carry a small packet of tissues with you.

■ PASSPORTS AND VISAS

All U.S., Canadian, U.K., Australian, and New Zealand citizens, even infants, need a valid passport to enter Italy for stays of up to 90 days. Visas are not required for stays under 90 days.

■ **TIP→** Before your trip, make two copies of your passport's data page (one for someone at home and another for you to carry separately). Or scan the page and e-mail it to someone at home and/or yourself.

U.S. Passport Information U.S. Department of State (☎ 877/487–2778 ⊕ travel.state.gov/passport).

U.S. Passport and Visa Expediters A. Briggs Passport & Visa Expeditors (☎ 800/806–0581 or 202/338–0111 ⊕ www.abriggs.com). **American Passport Express** (☎ 800/455–5166 or 800/841–6778 ⊕ www.americanpassport.com). **Passport Express** (☎ 800/362–8196 ⊕ www.passportexpress.com). **Travel Document Systems** (☎ 800/874–5100 or 202/638–3800 ⊕ www.traveldocs.com). **Travel the World Visas** (☎ 866/886–8472 or 301/495–7700 ⊕ www.world-visa.com).

■ RESTROOMS

Public restrooms are a rare commodity in Rome. Although there are public toilets in Piazza di San Pietro, Piazza San Silvestro, Piazza di Spagna, at the Roman Forum, and in a few other strategic locations (all with a charge of €0.50–€0.70), the locals seem to make do primarily with well-timed pit stops and rely on the local bar. Most bars will allow you to use the restroom if you ask politely, though it's courteous to buy a little something—such as a bottle of water or espresso—in exchange for access to the facilities. Standards of cleanliness and comfort vary greatly. Restaurants, hotels, department stores like La Rinascente and Coin, and McDonald's restaurants tend to have the cleanest restrooms. Pubs and bars rank among the worst. It's a good idea to carry a packet of tissues with you as you can't rely on most places having any toilet paper at all. There are bathrooms in all airports, train stations, and in most subway stations. In major train stations you'll also find well-kept pay toilets for €0.70 and in most museums. Carry a selection of coins as some turnstiles do not give change. There are also free facilities at highway rest stops and gas stations: a small tip to the cleaning person is always appreciated. There are no bathrooms in churches, post offices, and public beaches.

■ SAFETY

Wear a bag or camera slung across your body bandolier style, and don't rest your bag or camera on a table or underneath your chair at a sidewalk caffè or restaurant. If you have to bring a purse, make sure to keep it within sight by wearing it toward the front. Women should avoid wearing purses that don't have a zipper or that don't snap shut. Men should always keep their wallet in one of their front pockets with their hand in the same pocket. In Rome, beware of pickpockets on buses, especially Line 64 (Termini–St. Peter's train station); the Line 40 Express, which takes a faster route, and Bus 46 which takes you closer to the basilica; and subways—and when making your way through the corridors of crowded trains. Pickpockets often work in teams and zero in on tourists who look distracted or are in large groups. Pickpockets may be active wherever tourists gather, including the Roman Forum, the Spanish Steps, Piazza Navona, and Piazza di San Pietro. Purse snatchers work in teams on a single motor scooter or motorcycle: one drives and the other grabs.

Groups of gypsy children and young women (often with babies in arms and a scarf or a shawl wrapped around their shoulders) are present around sights popular with tourists and on buses and are adept pickpockets. One well-tried method is to approach a tourist and proffer a piece of cardboard with writing on it. While the unsuspecting victim attempts to read the message *on* it, the children's hands are busy *under* it, trying to make off with wallets and valuables. If you see such a group, do not even allow them near you—they are quick and know more tricks than you do. The phrases *Vai via!* (Go away!) and *Chiamo la polizia* (I'll call the police) usually keep them at bay. The colorful characters dressed as Roman legionaries, who hover around the Colosseum and other monuments, expect a tip if you photograph them. The amount of €5 is quite sufficient.

The difficulties encountered by women traveling alone in Italy are often overstated. Younger women have to put up with much male attention, but it's rarely dangerous or hostile. Ignoring whistling and questions is the best way to get rid of unwanted attention. Do be careful of gropers on the Metro and on Buses 64 and 46 (Vatican buses) and 218 and 660 (Catacombs). They're known to take advantage of the cramped space. React like the locals: forcefully and loudly.

■ TIP➔ Distribute your cash, credit cards, IDs, and other valuables between a deep front pocket, an inside jacket or vest pocket, and a hidden money pouch. Don't reach for the money pouch once you're in public.

Safety Transportation Security Administration (*TSA* ⊕ *www.tsa.gov*).

▌ TAXES

The service charge and IVA, or value-added tax (V.A.T.), are included in the rate except in five-star deluxe hotels, where the IVA (15% on luxury hotels) may be a separate item added to the bill at departure.

Many, but not all, Rome restaurants have eliminated extra charges for service and for *pane e coperto* (a cover charge that includes bread, whether you eat it or not). If it is an extra, the service charge may be 12%–15%. Only part, if any, of this amount goes to the waiter, so an additional tip is customary (⇨ *Tipping*).

Always ask for an itemized bill and a *scontrino*, or receipt. Officially you have to keep this receipt with you for 600 feet from the restaurant or store and be able to produce it if asked by the tax police. Sound absurd? It's something of a desperate measure for the country with the highest taxes in Europe and the highest levels of tax evasion/avoidance, and there have been cases of unwitting customers falling foul of the law, even though this practice is meant to catch noncompliant restaurants.

Value-added tax (IVA in Italy, V.A.T. to English-speakers) is 20% on luxury goods, clothing, and wine. On most consumer goods, it's already included in the amount shown on the price tag; on services, such as car rentals, it's an extra item. If a store you shop in has a EURO TAX FREE sign outside and you make a purchase above €155 (before tax), present your passport and request a "Tax Free Shopping Check" when paying, or at least an invoice itemizing the article(s), price(s), and the amount of tax.

To get an IVA refund when you're leaving Italy, take the goods and the invoice to the customs office at the airport or other point of departure and have the invoice stamped. (If you return to the United States or Canada directly from Italy, go through the procedure at Italian customs; if your return is, say, via Britain, take the

Italian goods and invoice to British customs.) Once back home—and within 90 days of the date of purchase—mail the stamped invoice to the store, which will forward the IVA rebate to you.

V.A.T. Refunds Global Refund (📠 *800/566-9828* ⊕ *www.globalrefund.com*).

▍TIME

Rome is one hour ahead of London, six ahead of New York, seven ahead of Chicago, and nine ahead of Los Angeles. Rome is nine hours behind Sydney and 11 behind Auckland. Like the rest of Europe, Italy uses the 24-hour (or "military") clock, which means that after 12 noon you continue counting forward: 13:00 is 1 PM, 23:30 is 11:30 PM.

Time Zones Timeanddate.com (⊕ *www.timeanddate.com/worldclock*) can help you figure out the correct time anywhere.

▍TIPPING

Many Rome restaurants have done away with the service charge of about 12%–15% that used to appear as a separate item on your check—now service is almost always included in the menu prices. It's customary to leave an additional 5% tip, or a couple of euros, for the waiter, depending on the quality of service. Tip checkroom attendants €1 per person, restroom attendants €0.50. In both cases tip more in expensive hotels and restaurants. Tip €0.05–€0.10 for whatever you drink standing up at a coffee bar, €0.25 or more for table service in a caffè. At a hotel bar tip €1 and up for a round or two of cocktails, more in the grander hotels.

For tipping taxi drivers, it is acceptable if you round up to the nearest euro. Railway and airport porters charge a fixed rate per bag. Tip an additional €0.50, more if the porter is very helpful. Not all theater ushers expect a tip; if they do, tip €0.25 per person, more for very expensive seats. Give a barber €1–€1.50 and a hairdresser's assistant €1.50–€4 for a shampoo or cut, depending on the type of establishment and the final bill; 5%–10% is a fair guideline.

On sightseeing tours, tip guides about €1.50 per person for a half-day group tour, more if they're very good. In museums and other places of interest where admission is free, a contribution is expected; give anything from €0.50 to €1 for one or two people, more if the guardian has been especially helpful. Service station attendants are tipped only for special services.

In hotels, give the *portiere* (concierge) about 15% of his bill for services, or €2.50–€5 if he has been generally helpful. For two people in a double room, leave the chambermaid about €1 per day, or about €4–€6 a week, in a moderately priced hotel; tip a minimum of €1 for valet or room service. Increase these amounts by one half in an expensive hotel, and double them in a very expensive hotel. In very expensive hotels, tip doormen €0.50 for calling a cab and €1 for carrying bags to the check-in desk, bellhops €1.50–€2.50 for carrying your bags to the room, and €2–€2.50 for room service.

▍TOURS AND GUIDES

ORIENTATION TOURS

Some might consider them campy and kitschy, but guided bus tours can prove a blissfully easy way to enjoy a quick introduction to the city's top sights—especially if you can't or don't want to hoof it throughout the day. Sitting in a bus, with friendly tour guide commentary (and even friendlier fellow sightseers, many of whom will be from every country under the sun), can make for a delightful and fun experience—so give one a whirl *even* if you're an old Rome hand. Of course, you'll want to savor these incredible sights at your own leisure later on.

Appian Line, Carrani, Vastours (in collaboration with American Express), and other operators offer half-day and full-day tours in air-conditioned buses with

English-speaking guides. The four main itineraries are: "Ancient Rome," "Classic Rome," "Christian Rome," and "The Vatican Museums and Sistine Chapel." Half-day tours cost around €35 and full-day tours (including lunch and entrance fees) are between €98 and €135. The Musei Vaticani tour costs €56, but offers the advantage of not having to queue (sometimes for an hour or more) at the museum doors, awaiting your turn for admission. All the companies pick you up at centrally located hotels.

All operators can provide a luxury car for up to three people, a limousine for up to seven, or a minibus for up to nine, all with an English-speaking driver, but guide service is extra. Almost all operators offer "Rome by Night" tours, with or without dinner and entertainment. You can book tours through travel agents.

Various sightseeing buses following a continuous circle route through the center of town operate daily. Stop-'n'-Go has eight daily departures and makes 14 scheduled stops at important sites, where you can get on and off at will. Check with the Rome tourist information kiosks or inquire at your hotel for prices and further information.

The least expensive organized sightseeing tour of Rome is that run by ATAC, the municipal bus company. Double-decker bus 110 leaves from Piazza dei Cinquecento, in front of Termini Station, but you can pick it up at any of its 10 stopover points. A day ticket costs about €14 and allows you to stop off and get on as often as you like. The price includes an audio guide system in six languages. The total tour takes about two hours and covers the Colosseum, Piazza Navona, St. Peter's, the Trevi Fountain, and Via Veneto. Tickets can be bought on board. Two-day and three-day tickets are also available. Tours leave from Termini Station every 20 minutes between 9 AM and 8:30 PM.

The Archeobus, which takes you to the Old Appian Way, the Catacombs, and the new Park of the Aqueducts in the open countryside, also operates with the stop 'n' go formula. Little 15-seater buses leave from Piazza della Cinquecento every hour between 10 AM and 4 PM. Tickets cost €8 and are valid all day. A combined 110 and Archeobus ticket costs €20 and is valid for one day.

Of course, you get a real bargain if you do your sightseeing "tours" of Rome by public transport. Many buses and trams pass major sights. With a single €1 ticket you can get in 75 minutes of sightseeing (or an entire day, with a €4 *giornaliero* ticket). Time your ride to avoid rush hours. The little electric Bus 116 scoots through the heart of Old Rome, with stops near the Pantheon, the Spanish Steps, and Piazza del Popolo, among others. The route of Bus 117 takes in San Giovanni in Laterano, the Colosseum, and the Spanish Steps.

Since certain parts of the historic center are open to pedestrians only, some walking is involved in most escorted bus tours of the city. Don't forget to dress appropriately for visits to churches *(see the Local Dos and Taboos section)*. Tour operators can also organize minibus tours for small parties.

Bus Line ATAC (✆ *800/431784 toll-free* ⊕ *www.atac.roma.it*).

Tour Operators **American Express** (✆ *06/67641*). **Appian Line** (✆ *06/48786601* ⊕ *www.appianline.it*). **Carrani** (✆ *06/4742501* ⊕ *www.carrani.com*). **Ciao Roma Trolley Tour** (✆ *06/48976161*). **Vastours** (✆ *06/4814309* ⊕ *www.vastours.it*). **Stop-'n'-go City Tours** (✆ *06/48905729*).

SPECIAL-INTEREST TOURS

You can make your own arrangements (at no cost) to attend a public papal audience at the Vatican or at the pope's summer residence at Castel Gandolfo. You can also book through a travel agency for a package that includes coach transportation to the Vatican for the audience and some sightseeing along the way, returning you to your hotel, for about €35. The excursion outside Rome to Castel Gandolfo on summer Sundays for the pope's blessing costs about €45. Agencies that arrange these tours include Appian Line and Carrani.

Tourvisa Italia organizes lunch and dinner boat trips on the Tiber, departing and returning to Ponte Sant'Angelo. Boats leave four times daily for a cruise that covers all of the main historical bridges of Rome and other important sights. Tickets cost €35 for lunch and €55 for dinner. The company also does combined bus and boat tours lasting 2½ hours.

A ride in a horse-drawn carriage is the Rome equivalent of a gondola ride in Venice. Coachmen can be contacted directly at popular sights like St. Peter's Square and the Colosseum. An hour's ride for four passengers to view the fountains of Rome will cost around €150, depending on your bargaining skills.

Centro Studi Cassia organizes courses in Italian cooking, art, music, and current events in simple Italian. This is an enjoyable way to learn to speak some of the language and, at the same time, find out more about the culture and traditions of the country.

Tour Operators Appian Line (☎ 06/487861 ✉ appian@appianline.it ⊕ www.appianline. it). **Carrani** (☎ 06/4742501 ✉ carrani. viaggi@tiscalinet.it ⊕ www.carrani.com). **Centro Studi Cassia** (☎ 06/33253852 ⊕ www.centrostudicassia.it). **Tourvisa Italia** (☎ 06/6789361).

WALKING TOURS

In Rome, there are tours and there are *tours*. Why pay to be led around by someone who just memorizes some lines and gives you the run-of-the-mill tour, when you can learn firsthand from the experts? Context Rome is an organization formed by a group of architects, archaeologists, art historians, sommeliers, and professors that give specialized walking seminars to small intimate groups (no more than six people) in and around Rome. Every day of the week offers five or six theme walks, which might include Imperial Rome: Architecture and History of the Archaeological Center; Underground Rome: The Hidden City; Baroque Rome: The Age of Bernini; Vatican Collections, and even Rome Shopping. Prices range from €55–€75 per person. If you want to get a "summa cum laude" as a serious Rome tourist and aficionado, the walking tours of Context Rome—with 26 PhDs and 25 Masters docents in its ranks—can't be beat.

All About Rome, Enjoy Rome, Through Eternity, and Argiletum Tour also offer some fascinating walking tours of the city and its sights. Argiletum and the cultural association Genti e Paesi offer regular walking tours and museum visits in English, including private tours of the Sistine Chapel before all the hordes arrive. Book at least one day in advance. If you have a reasonable knowledge of Italian, you can take advantage of the free guided visits and walking tours organized by Rome's cultural associations and the city council for museums and monuments. These usually take place on weekends. Programs are announced in the daily papers and in the weekly magazine *roma c'è*.

Those who want to see everything during their trip to Rome without eliminating their daily run or workout might consider hiring a guide from Sight Jogging Tours. The company consists of highly experienced trainers that give tours of Rome based on the level of difficulty chosen by the client. Routes may take in Villa Borghese, Imperial Forum and Colosseum, St. Peter's Basilica, and many other sights. Trainers meet tourists at their hotel and take them back after the run is over. Most tours take 45–60 minutes and cost about €85 per person per hour.

Tour Operators All About Rome (☎ 06/7100823 ⊕ www.allaboutromewalks. netfirms.com). **Argiletum Tour** (✉ Via Madonna dei Monti 49 ☎ 06/45438906 ⊕ www.argiletumtour.com). **Context Rome** (✉ Via Baccina 40 ☎ 06/4820911 ⊕ www. contextrome.com). **Enjoy Rome** (✉ Via

Marghera 8A, Termini ☎ *06/4451843).* **Genti e Paesi** (✉ *Via Adda 111* ☎ *06/85301758* ⊕ *www.romeguide.it).* **Sightjogging** (☎ *39/347/3353185* ⊕ *www.sightjogging.it).* **Through Eternity** (☎ *06/7009336* ⊕ *www. througheternity.com).*

EXCURSIONS

Most operators offer half-day excursions to Tivoli to see the fountains and gardens of Villa D'Este. Appian Line's afternoon tour to Tivoli includes a visit to Hadrian's Villa, with its impressive ancient ruins, as well as the many-fountained Villa D'Este. Most operators also have full-day excursions to Assisi, to Pompeii and/or Capri, and to Florence.

Tour Operator Appian Line (☎ *06/48786601* ⊕ *www.appianline.it).*

PERSONAL GUIDES

You can arrange for a personal guide through the main APT (Azienda Per Turismo) Tourist Information Office.

Tour Operator APT (✉ *Via Parigi 11* ☎ *06/488991).*

∎ TRIP INSURANCE

Comprehensive trip insurance is valuable if you're booking a very expensive or complicated trip (particularly to an isolated region) or if you're booking far in advance. Comprehensive policies typically cover trip-cancellation and interruption, letting you cancel or cut your trip short because of illness, or, in some cases, acts of terrorism in your destination. Such policies might also cover evacuation and medical care. Some also cover you for trip delays because of bad weather or mechanical problems as well as for lost or delayed luggage.

Another type of coverage to consider is financial default—that is, when your trip is disrupted because a tour operator, airline, or cruise line goes out of business. Generally you must buy this when you book your trip or shortly thereafter, and

it's available to you only if your operator isn't on a list of excluded companies.

Always read the fine print of your policy to make sure that you're covered for the risks that most concern you. Compare several policies to be sure you're getting the best price and range of coverage available.

Insurance Comparison Info Insure My Trip (☎ *800/487–4722* ⊕ *www.insuremytrip.com).* **Square Mouth** (☎ *800/240–0369* ⊕ *www. squaremouth.com).*

Comprehensive Insurers Access America (☎ *800/284–8300* ⊕ *www.accessamerica.com).* **AIG Travel Guard** (☎ *800/826–4919* ⊕ *www. travelguard.com).* **CSA Travel Protection** (☎ *800/873–9855* ⊕ *www.csatravelprotection. com).* **Travelex Insurance** (☎ *888/228–9792* ⊕ *www.travelex-insurance.com).* **Travel Insured International** (☎ *800/243–3174* ⊕ *www.travelinsured.com).*

∎ VISITOR INFORMATION

Rome has an APT (Azienda Per Turismo) Tourist Information Office in the city center. Green APT information kiosks with multilingual personnel are near the most important sights and squares, as well as at Termini Station and Leonardo da Vinci and Ciampino Airports. They're open 9–1 and 3–7:30 and provide information about cultural events, museums, opening hours, city transportation, and so on. You can also pick up free tourist maps and brochures.

In Rome APT Tourist Information Office (✉ *Via Parigi 5–11, Termini* ☎ *06/488991* ⊕ *www.turismoroma.it).* **Call Center–Comune di Roma Ufficio Turismo** (☎ *06/0608).* **ENIT** (*Italian Government Tourist Board* ✉ *Via*

Marghera 2–6, Termini ☎ *06/49711* ⊕ *www. italiantourism.com).*

ONLINE RESOURCES

The APT (Rome tourist board) Web site is ⊕ *www.turismoroma.it* and is packed with information about events and places to visit. For more information specifically on Italy, visit ⊕ *www.italiantourism. com,* ⊕ *www.initaly.com,* and ⊕ *www. wel.it.* Other particularly useful sites are ⊕ *www.romeguide.it* and ⊕ *www. unospitearoma.it,* both of which have English versions. You may also like to consult ⊕ *www.italyhotel.com.* Particularly provocative, fascinating, and up-to-date are the monthly Web issues of *The American,* a popular English magazine based in Rome; their Web site is ⊕ *www. theamericanmag.com.* A fine Web site on all things Roman is ⊕ *www.romecity.it.* Magnificent is the only word to describe this passionate writer's ode to the city's treasures of art and architecture, replete with hundreds of photos and little-known facts: ⊕ *www.romeartlover.it.* An official Web site for many of Rome's most famous sights, and a place to make ticket reservations, is ⊕ *www.pierreci.it.* One example of a top Web site devoted to one sight in Rome is ⊕ *www.capitolium.org.* A dynamic organization offering unusual tours and news about what's happening in Rome is ⊕ *www.nerone.cc,* and ⊕ *www. museionline.it* has invaluable links to almost all the city's many museums and galleries together with news of the latest exhibitions, opening hours, and prices. A handy guide to the bus lines threading Rome and its surrounding areas is ⊕ *www.cotralspa.it.* For special events in and around Rome check out ⊕ *www. whatsonwhen.com.*

INDEX

Photo Credits: 1, *Corbis.* 2, *Paul D'Innocenzo.* 5, *Luciano Romano/Scala/Art Resource, NY.* Chapter 1: Experience Rome: 8-9, *SIME s.a.s/eStock Photo.* 10-11 (all), *Angelo Campus.* 12, *Paul D'Innocenzo.* 13 (both), *Angelo Campus.* 14 and 15 (right), *Paul D'Innocenzo.* 15 (left) and 16, *Angelo Campus.* 17 (both), *Paul D'Innocenzo.* 20 (left), *Angelo Campus.* 20 (top center), *Paul D'Innocenzo.* 20 (top right and bottom right), *Angelo Campus.* 21 (top left), *Paul D'Innocenzo.* 21 (bottom left), *Angelo Campus.* 21 (right), *Paul D'Innocenzo.* 22 (left), *Angelo Campus.* 22 (right), *Paul D'Innocenzo.* 24 (left), *Paul D'Innocenzo.* 24 (right) and 25, *Angelo Campus.* 26, *Paul D'Innocenzo.* 27 (both), *Angelo Campus.* 28-29 (all), *Angelo Campus.* 31 (left), *Paul D'Innocenzo.* 31 (right), *Angelo Campus.* 32-34, *Paul D'Innocenzo.* Chapter 2: Roamin' Holiday: 35, *Angelo Campus.* 36, *Paul D'Innocenzo.* 40, *Anthony Majanlahti.* 43, *Angelo Campus.* 46-47, *Angelo Campus.* 50, *SIME s. a.s/eStock Photo.* 55, *Corbis.* Chapter 3: Ancient Rome: 57, *Frank/Mauritius Images/age fotostock.* 59-62, *Paul D'Innocenzo.* 64, *Angelo Campus.* 73, *Paul D'Innocenzo.* 74, *Amy Nichole Harris/Shutterstock.* 75, *Javarman/Shutterstock.* 76-77, *Altair4 Multimedia Roma, www.altair4. com.* 78-79, *Angelo Campus.* 80 (top and bottom left), *Paul D'Innocenzo.* 80 (center), *Amy Nichole Harris/Shutterstock.* 80 (bottom right), *Interfoto Pressebildagentur/Alamy.* 81 (top left), *Angelo Campus.* 81 (top right), *PhotoBliss/Alamy.* 81 (bottom), *Eugene Mogilnikov/Shutterstock.* 82, *Angelo Campus.* 83 (top left), *Marek Slusarczyk/Shutterstock.* 83 (top right), *Eugene Mogilnikov/Shutterstock.* 83 (center), *Paul D'Innocenzo.* 84, *Paul D'Innocenzo.* 85 (left), *Howard Hudson.* 85 (right), *Alvaro Leiva/age fotostock.* 90, *Paul D'Innocenzo.* Chapter 4: The Vatican: 93, *Doco Dalfiano/age fotostock.* 95, *Angelo Campus.* 96, *iStockphoto.* 100 and 106, *Paul D'Innocenzo.* 108-109 (top), *SuperStock.* 110, *Russell Mountford/age fotostock.* 112-115, *Dave Drapak.* 117, *Gianni Giansanti/Sygma/Corbis.* 124-25, *Paul D'Innocenzo.* Chapter 5: Navona & Campo: 129, *Ping Amranand/SuperStock.* 131, *Angelo Campus.* 132, *Paul D'Innocenzo.* 137, *SIME s.a.s/eStock Photo.* 144 and 145 (top), *Paul D'Innocenzo.* 145 (center), *Nataliya Peregudova/Shutterstock.* 145 (bottom), *Paul D'Innocenzo.* 146 (top left), *Kathy deWitt/Alamy.* 146 (top right and center), *Paul D'Innocenzo.* 146 (bottom), *Thomas Ernsting/Bilderberg/Aurora Photos.* 147 (top left), *Interfoto Pressebildagentur/Alamy.* 147 (top right), *Paul D'Innocenzo.* 147 (bottom left), *Russell Mountford/age fotostock.* 147 (bottom right), *Caro/Alamy.* 148, *Paul D'Innocenzo.* 149, *Zute Lightfoot/Alamy.* Chapter 6: Corso & Spagna: 153, *Alvaro Leiva/age fotostock.* 155, *Angelo Campus.* 156, *M. Borchi/DEA/age fotostock.* 161, *Paul D'Innocenzo.* 165, *Cosmo Condina/Alamy.* Chapter 7: Repubblica & Quirinale: 167, *SuperStock/age fotostock.* 170, *Daniele Caporale/age fotostock.* 173, *Adam Eastland/Alamy.* 177, *Scala/Art Resource.* 178, *Franck Guiziou/age fotostock.* 179, *Achim Bednorz/age fotostock.* 180 (center), *Xavier Florensa/age fotostock.* 180 (bottom), *SuperStock.* 181 (bottom), *Achim Bednorz/age fotostock.* 182, *SIME s.a.s/eStock Photo.* 183 (top left), *Achim Bednorz/age fotostock.* 183 (top center), *Wojtek Buss/age fotostock.* 183 (bottom center), *Rough Guides/Alamy.* Chapter 8: Villa Borghese & Piazza del Popolo: 187, *Alvaro Leiva/age fotostock.* 190, *Adam Eastland/Alamy.* Chapter 9: Trastevere & the Ghetto: 199, *Robert Harding Picture Library Ltd/ Alamy.* 201, *Angelo Campus.* 202 and 205, *Paul D'Innocenzo.* 207, *Russell Mountford/age fotostock.* Chapter 10: Aventino: 211 and 213, *Angelo Campus.* 214, *Paul D'Innocenzo.* Chapter 11: Esquilino & Celio: 219, *Xavier Florensa/age fotostock.* 221, *SIME s.a.s/eStock Photo.* 222, *Sylvain Grandadam/age fotostock.* 233, *Angelo Campus.* Chapter 12: Where to Eat: 235, *Art Kowalsky/Alamy.* 236, *SIME s.a.s/eStock Photo.* 240, *Jono Pandolfi.* 241, *The Rocco Forte Collection.* 242, *Jono Pandolfi.* 243 (top), *Jono Pandolfi.* 243 (bottom), *Gaia Giordano.* 244 and 245 (bottom), *Angelo Campus.* 245 (top), *Jono Pandolfi.* 246, *Clive Sawyer/Alamy.* 247 (top and bottom), *Jono Pandolfi.* 248, *SIME s.a.s/eStock Photo.* 249 (top), *Jono Pandolfi.* 249 (bottom), *The Rocco Forte Collection.* 250, *Jono Pandolfi.* 251 (top), *NemesisINC/Shutterstock.* 251 (bottom), *Jono Pandolfi.* 252, *Angelo Campus.* 253 (bottom), *Riccardo Spila/eStock Photo.* 253 (top), *Jono Pandolfi.* 254, *Adam Eastland/Alamy.* 255 (top), *Angelo Campus.* 255 (bottom), *John Ferro Sims/Alamy.* 273, *Angelo Campus.* Chapter 13: Where to Stay: 293, *Alvaro Leiva/age fotostock.* 294, *Hotel Majestic.* 304 (top left), *Hassler Roma.* 304 (top right), *Hotel Scalinata.* 304 (center left), *Hotel Eden.* 304 (center right), *Relais Le Clarisse.* 304 (bottom left), *Dominique Bollinger.* 304 (bottom right), *Yes Hotel.* Chapter 14: Nightlife & the Arts: 335, *Angelo Campus.* 337, *Daniele*

NOTES

NOTES

NOTES

NOTES

ABOUT OUR WRITERS

Lynda Albertson is a perpetual traveler, adventurer, and general-mischief-and-glamor-seeker hailing from Miami. A writer, editor, and founding member of the Café.Blue list-serve, she is now based in Rome. There she happily writes articles on food, wine (a major passion), living, and traveling as well as foundation grants for conservation groups such as the American Institute for Roman Culture. Her articles can be seen most frequently in *The American* magazine where she serves as a monthly columnist and associate editor. Her upcoming book, *The Misadventures of an American Girl in Italy*, will be published in the U.K. in 2010. For this edition, she updated our Shopping chapter, which she originally wrote for our last edition.

After her first Italian coffee and her first Italian *bacio* in 1999, **Nicole Arriaga** just knew she'd have to find a way to make it back to Rome and moved to the Eternal City in 2003 to earn her Master's Degree in Political Science. There Nicole freelances for several publications including *Venere.com* and *The American*. When not pouring her heart and soul into her first novel about finding love in Italy, Nicole works as a programs coordinator for an American Study Abroad organization based in Rome. For this edition, she updated our Experience Rome chapter, which she originally wrote for our last edition, and also updated our Where to Stay chapter and Travel Smart section.

Martin Wilmot Bennett lives within waking distance of the bells of Santa Maria Maggiore, just down from Rome's Termini train station. Happy not to have a car, he spends much of his time walking around, an ideal activity which has paid off royally in the new "Roamin' Holiday" chapter he wrote for this edition. After graduating from Cambridge University, he's been working as a translator and teacher at Rome's University of Tor Vergata. His vast background in Italian art and civilization led to his writing our special photo-features on Michelangelo's Sistine Ceiling and the Bernini/Borromini rivalry—and his knowledge of all things Roman also greatly enriched our neighborhood Exploring chapters, all of which he updated for this edition.

A University of Pennsylvania grad, **Erica Firpo** moved to Rome full time in 2003 and now writes for an array of publications including *National Geographic Traveler*. In addition, she has penned a series of restaurant guide books starting with *Rome Little Black Book*. She also covers social life issues in her monthly column "Lei Morde" for *The American* magazine and in her biweekly blog, moscerina.com. For this edition, she updated our Nightlife/Arts chapter and wrote our photo-feature on the Campo de' Fiori.

Dana Klitzberg is a chef and culinary expert from New York City. After studying and traveling all over Italy for a decade, she moved to Rome in 2000 after completing culinary school in Manhattan and cooking in top Italian eatery San Domenico NY. Ms. Klitzberg served as top toque in various Roman restaurants, and today continues working in several areas of the food industry through her company *blu aubergine* (www.bluaubergine.com)—catering, offering private chef services, consulting for restaurants, teaching cooking classes, and leading culinary tours around Rome. A food and travel writer, this University of Virginia literature grad updated our Where to Eat chapter, which she originally penned years back.

An award-winning travel writer, **Margaret Stenhouse** has written for *The Herald* and the *International Herald Tribune's* "Italy Daily" supplement, is author of *The Goddess of the Lake: Legends and Mysteries of Nemi*, and updated our Side Trips from Rome chapter.